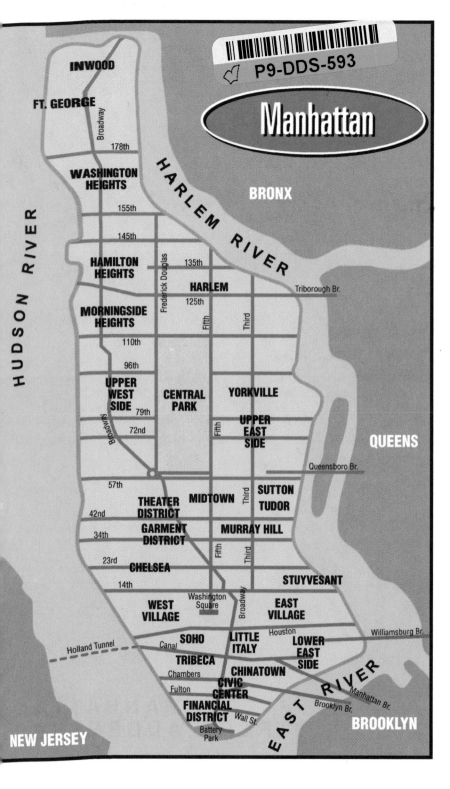

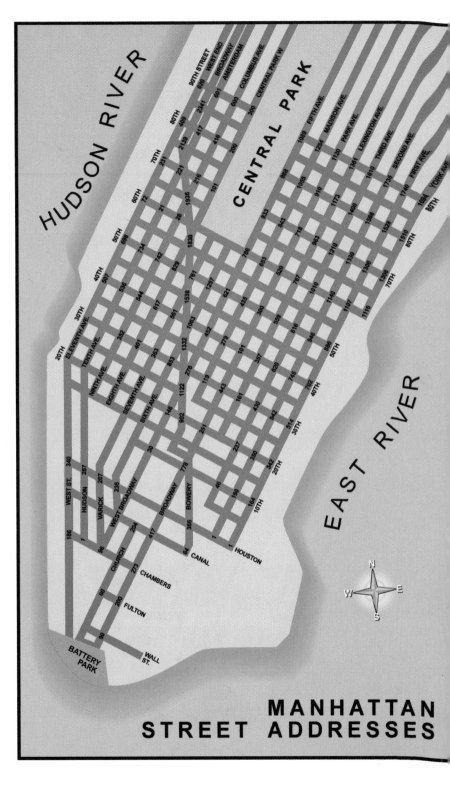

GERRY FRANK'S

Where To Find It, Buy It, Eat It In New York

GERRY FRANK'S

Where To Find It, Buy It, Eat It In New York

For additional copies (special quantity prices available), write or call:

Gerry's Frankly Speaking

P.O. Box 2225
Salem, OR 97308
503/585-8411
800/NYC-BOOK (800/692-2665)
Fax: 503/585-1076
E-Mail: gerry@teleport.com

To Readers:

No fees were paid or services rendered in exchange for inclusion in this book.

Although every effort was made to ensure that all information was accurate and up-to-date at the time of publication, neither the publisher nor the author can be held responsible for any errors, omissions, or adverse consequences resulting from the use of such information. It is recommended that you call ahead to verify information of individual business listings.

Contents

III. WHERE TO FIND IT: MUSEUMS, TOURS, AND OTHER EXPERIENCES

IV. WHERE TO FIND IT: NEW YORK'S BEST FOOD SHOPS

V. WHERE TO FIND IT: NEW YORK'S BEST SERVICES

VI. WHERE TO BUY IT: NEW YORK'S BEST STORES

VII. WHERE TO "EXTRAS"

From the Author . . .

Dear Readers,

I've been coming to New York every several weeks for more than half a century, and I've always kept notes on where to eat, shop, stay, and explore. More than two decades ago, after years of sharing my notes with friends, I decided to organize them into a book. The result was the first edition of *Where to Buy It, Find It, Eat It in New York*, published back in 1981.

Twelve editions have come and gone since then, as have lots of restaurants, stores, galleries, and other places. Neighborhoods have changed, whole areas have been torn down and rebuilt. Indeed, the city itself has changed dramatically over the years. New York today is safer, cleaner, less formal, and immeasurably more welcoming to visitors than ever before. It is also, in the wake of the September 11, 2001 attack on the World Trade Center, a sadder, more sober city.

Despite all those changes, New York remains the most interesting, exciting, challenging, and diverse city in the world. It has an energy and vitality unmatched anywhere. And it has something for everyone: world-class museums, high fashion, foreign films, fine dining, innovative chefs, cutting-edge design, and every kind of music and theater. You name it, New York has it. This book is about finding *your* New York.

While it has become better organized and more professional over the years, this book remains at heart a collection of personal notes and opinions. Nobody tells me what to include or omit, and nobody pays for a listing. I grew up in a retailing family, have traveled extensively, and have eaten in more restaurants than I can count (including nearly 2,500 in Manhattan alone!). I get lots of input from readers, friends, and the wonderfully opinionated people of New York, but in the end I am the final judge.

All that said, this book would not be possible without the help of several people. I am particularly indebted to my researcher (and children's store expert), Carrie Klein; my superb editor, Parke Puterbaugh; my fact-checker, Cathy Shea; my extremely able book assistant, Cheryl Johnson; my incredibly organized executive assistant, Linda Wooters; and my dependable part-time helper, Linda Chase. Tim Prock, a talented graphic artist, created the cover, and the unfailingly patient Tom and Carole Stinski tackled the typesetting. Finally, personal thanks to Esther Benovitz and Bryan Miller.

This book would also not be possible without people like you, and I hope you'll give me your feedback. Whether you're planning your first visit to New York or have lived here all your life, I think you'll find some magic in these pages. I love New York, and I hope you do, too!

Gerry Frank.

Gerry Frank

I. In and Around the World's Greatest City

GETTING TO NEW YORK

So you're headed for New York! Whether you're traveling 90 miles from Philadelphia or 9,000 miles from Singapore, you're in for a wonderful treat. But first you'll need to get here.

AIRPORTS—New York City is served by three major airports, and more than 90 million people pass through them every year. LaGuardia is the most frequently used for domestic flights, while John F. Kennedy has flights to and from just about every nation. Both airports are in the borough of Queens. Newark Airport, across the Hudson River in New Jersey, handles an increasingly large volume of domestic and international flights. The most common ways of traveling between Manhattan and these airports are by taxicab, shuttle bus, and private car or limousine.

Taxi lines form in front of most terminals at all three airports, and the exits to them are usually well marked. These lines are legitimate and generally move quickly. Under no circumstances should you go with someone either inside or immediately outside the terminal who asks if you want a taxi (and be forewarned that the crowd offering taxis and limousines can be quite daunting). It may seem tempting if the airport is crowded, but you'll end up paying far more than you should and will have no recourse. Assuming you don't run into bad traffic, the trip between **LaGuardia** and midtown will take about half an hour and cost roughly $25, plus bridge toll and tip. The trip between **Kennedy** (also called JFK) and anywhere in Manhattan can take as long as an hour and costs a flat fee of $35, plus bridge or tunnel toll and tip. A trip between **Newark** and Manhattan can also take as long as an hour and costs as much as $50 (the metered fare plus a $10 surcharge), plus tolls and a $1 surcharge for each piece of luggage over 24 inches. If you have a preference for which route to take into or out of Manhattan, tell the driver in advance. And be forewarned: although they are required by law to do so, cab drivers in Manhattan often don't like taking people to the airports because it's sometimes hard to get quick fares back. In fact, New York cabbies aren't even allowed to pick up passengers at Newark.

Group Ride from LaGuardia

If you're with a group arriving at LaGuardia and want to take a cab into Manhattan, you can "share" the fare. For a ride to any location on the east side of Fifth Avenue between 23rd and 96th streets, the charge is $7.50 per person. The charge is $8.50 per person west of Fifth Avenue, and $9.50 per person south of 23rd Street.

If taxi fares seem a little steep, there are less expensive alternatives. Several companies run **shuttle buses** and **vans** between Manhattan and the airports. If you're alone and going to a major hotel in midtown, you can really save money by taking a shuttle bus. But it may not be worth it if there are others in your party to share a cab, if you're in a hurry, or if you're headed to a friend's apartment or an out-of-the-way hotel. Shuttle-bus tickets and schedules are available at the ground transportation desks at all three airports. Shuttle-bus options to and from LaGuardia and Kennedy airports include **Super Shuttle** (800/258-3826), **Gray Line** (212/315-3006) and **New York Airport Service** (718/875-8200). Gray Line and Super Shuttle also take passengers to and from Newark, as does **Olympia Airport Express** (212/964-6233). Most of the shuttle buses serving Kennedy and Newark are slightly more expensive than the ones serving LaGuardia, but all of them are under $20. For a complete list of options and prices, call the Port Authority's **Air-Ride** recording (800/247-7433).

AirTrain is an option only to and from Newark, but it is a terrific option. For less than the cost of most shuttle buses, you can take an AirTrain Link to the Newark Rail Link Station and then catch a New Jersey Transit or Amtrak train into Penn Station at the heart of midtown Manhattan. Call 800/626-7433 for more information.

If you really want to save money and are in absolutely no hurry, **public transportation** is also an option. For $3, you can take the M60 bus from LaGuardia to the corner of Lexington Avenue and 125th Street or Broadway and 116th Street and then any one of a half dozen subway lines into midtown and other parts of Manhattan. The same $3 will get you to Kennedy via subway (the E and F lines) and bus (the Green Line Q-10), but it takes almost two hours. (If you're interested in these options, call 718/330-1234 for detailed information.)

A fourth option is calling a private **car service** or **limousine** ahead of time. A driver will meet you at the gate or in the baggage claim area, holding up a sign with your last name on it. Depending on your personality, this will make you feel important, embarrassed, or a little bit of both. Be forewarned that a car or limo service can get pretty pricy, particularly if the driver has to wait because your flight is delayed. (They charge for waiting time.) Costs to and from LaGuardia run anywhere from $25 plus tip, if you just want a sedan and everything goes smoothly, to well over $100, if there are delays or you request a limousine. Prices are higher to and from Kennedy and Newark. You can secure a sedan or limousine after you've arrived as well by going to the ground transportation desks at any of the three airports.

Finally, if you're coming or going from LaGuardia, you can take the **Delta Water Shuttle**. It ferries passengers between LaGuardia's Marine Terminal and Pier 11 near Wall Street, the East 34th street heliport, and a pier at the end of East 62nd street on the East River. You don't need to be a Delta Airlines passenger, and the shuttle often takes less time than a taxi, but it runs only during business hours on weekdays. Tickets cost $15 one-way, $25 round-trip. Call New York Waterways at 800/933-5935 for more information.

TRAINS—Dozens of Amtrak trains come in and out of New York City everyday. The service is concentrated in the Northeast Corridor, between Washington and Boston, but you can catch a train between New York and Florida, Chicago, or even Seattle and many cities in Canada. Trains arrive and depart Pennsylvania Station (commonly referred to as **Penn Station**), underneath

Madison Square Garden between 31st and 33rd streets and Seventh and Eighth avenues. Penn Station is a major subway hub. You also can find a legitimate and well-organized taxicab line immediately outside the station on Seventh Avenue. (Under no circumstances should you go with someone who comes up to you inside or outside Penn Station asking if you need a taxi or help with your bags.)

You can choose between the Acela Express, sleeping cars, and other kinds of Amtrak service. Multi-day excursion passes are also available. Although the station is much improved from its dilapidated state a decade ago and actually includes an enclosed waiting area for ticketed Amtrak passengers in the middle of the main concourse, it's still not a place you will want to spend much time. (Call Amtrak at 800/872-7245 for fare and schedule information.) Train service to and from Connecticut and suburban New York is run by **MetroNorth** (800/METRO-IN) through the wonderfully reborn Grand Central Station.

DRIVING—If you can avoid driving to or in New York, by all means do so. Otherwise, you will end up paying exorbitant prices for tolls and parking (and your mental health will inevitably suffer, too). The fact that most New Yorkers don't own cars ought to tell you something! Traffic in and around the metropolitan area is horrendous and drivers are extraordinarily aggressive. Once you're in New York, the only time you may possibly need a car is if you want to leave for a day or two—and then you can rent one, as many New Yorkers do. The public transportation system in New York is extremely efficient, inexpensive, and used frequently by just about everyone.

If you still aren't convinced or have no alternative, get a map before setting out and study it carefully. The three major approaches to the city involve the New England Thruway (I-95), the New York State Thruway (I-87), and the New Jersey Turnpike (I-95). Expect long waits during rush hour at the bridges and tunnels leading in and out of Manhattan. Turn to AM radio stations 770, 880, or 1010 for area traffic reports if you're trying to decide which approach to take. Expect to pay a hefty toll for whichever bridge or tunnel you choose.

If you need to keep your car in Manhattan, here are some of the cheapest parking spots:
- **Mayor Parking** (Houston St at West St)
- **Chelsea Piers** (23rd St at West Side Highway)
- **5060 Auto Service** (Tenth Ave at 215th St)

Early-bird specials—which require that you check in between 6 a.m. and 9 a.m. and check out before 8 p.m.—are available at many garages throughout the city.

GETTING TO KNOW NEW YORK

In case you haven't already figured it out, this book isn't really about New York. It isn't even about New York City. It's about Manhattan. Most people (including me) use New York, New York City, "the city," and Manhattan synonymously. But New York is one of the Northeast's largest states, and New York City actually comprises five separate boroughs: Manhattan, Staten Island, the Bronx, Queens, and Brooklyn. Of those five boroughs, only the

Bronx is attached to the mainland. Manhattan and the other three are all islands.

A LITTLE HISTORY—Now that you know we're talking only about the island of Manhattan, a little history may help make sense of how the city is laid out. Native Americans were the first known residents of this area. Italian explorer Giovanni da Verrazano (for whom the Verrazano Narrows Bridge, linking Brooklyn and Staten Island, is named) sailed into New York Harbor in 1524 and "discovered" Manhattan for his French patron, King Francis I. In 1609, a trader for the Dutch East India Company named Henry Hudson sailed into the harbor and up the river that now bears his name. The first permanent European settlement in Manhattan, a Dutch trading post called Nieuw Amsterdam, was established in 1625 at the very southern tip of the island, where Battery Park is today. The story you've probably heard since childhood is true, at least to the extent that the various parties understood each other's intentions and expectations: rights to the island were "bought" by the Dutch West India Company a year later from local Indians with inexpensive beads, cloth, and other goods. It was renamed New York in 1664 after the British— in the person of Charles II's brother, the Duke of York—gained control of the still-tiny settlement.

It's hard to imagine today, but such areas as midtown and even Greenwich Village were way out in the country for another 150 years. Indeed, Wall Street is so named because a wall of logs was erected there in the mid-17th century to protect the farms in lower Manhattan from the wilderness beyond. New York's population—which numbered only 60,000 as late as 1800—remained concentrated on the southern tip of the island, while most of Manhattan was used for country estates and farmland or just left as forests and wilderness. When a commission headed by engineer John Randall, Jr., laid out a grid system for the largely undeveloped area from Houston Street north to 155th Street in 1807, most residents thought it entirely unnecessary.

THE RANDALL PLAN—For those trying to find their way around Manhattan, the so-called Randall Plan is a godsend. The streets below Houston (pronounced *House*-ton), particularly those below Canal Street, meander like the Dutch farm trails they once were. Even the relatively straight ones were not built for 21st-century traffic. World-famous Wall Street, for example, is narrower than the typical suburban driveway. Truth be told, not much about the city's layout makes sense south of 14th Street. If you're ever at the corner of West 4th Street and West 10th Street in Greenwich Village, you'll know what I mean!

Thanks to the Randall Plan, however, everything north of 14th Street is just about as simple as a major city can be. With the exception of Broadway— originally a well-worn footpath and now one of the country's longest streets, extending from the southern tip of Manhattan to the capital city of Albany — and some of the streets in northern Manhattan, the streets and avenues are laid out in a north-south, east-west grid. All of the east-west streets are numbered, as are many of the north-south avenues. In general, most avenues are one-way and are alternately northbound and southbound. Most streets are one-way as well: the even-numbered ones tend to be eastbound, and the odd-numbered ones westbound. Two-way exceptions include such major east-west thoroughfares as Canal, Houston, 14th, 23rd, 34th, 42nd, 57th, 72nd, 79th, 86th, 96th, 110th, and 125th streets. (See the "Key to Addresses" section if you need help finding a specific address.)

EAST SIDE, WEST SIDE—Starting just north of Washington Square Park at about 8th Street in Greenwich Village, Fifth Avenue divides the city into East and West sides. Broadway acts as the east-west dividing line south of Washington Square, although it runs a little east of where Fifth Avenue would be. That east-west distinction is important, as most addresses in New York reflect it. For example, 125 East 52nd Street and 125 West 52nd Street are two distinct locations several blocks apart.

Let's start with the East Side of the city. Moving east from Fifth Avenue toward the East River, you'll cross Madison Avenue, Park Avenue (called Park Avenue South below 34th Street and Fourth Avenue below that), Lexington Avenue (called Irving Place between 14th and 20th streets), Third Avenue, Second Avenue, and First Avenue. Madison Avenue doesn't start until 23rd Street, while Lexington Avenue begins as Irving Place at 14th Street. Sutton Place starts at 51st Street between First Avenue and the river, turns into York Avenue at 60th Street, and stops at 92nd Street. East End Avenue runs between York Avenue and the river from 79th Street to 90th Street. All of these avenues run north-south, parallel to Fifth Avenue. FDR Drive ("The FDR" to locals) hugs the river along the east side of the island.

The West Side of Manhattan is a bit more confusing. Moving west from Fifth Avenue toward the Hudson River, you'll find Avenue of the Americas (or Sixth Avenue, as everyone still calls it, despite the official name change in the 1950s), Seventh Avenue, Eighth Avenue (known as Central Park West north of 59th Street), Ninth Avenue (Columbus Avenue north of 59th Street), Tenth Avenue (Amsterdam Avenue north of 59th Street), and Eleventh Avenue (West End Avenue between 59th Street and its end at 107th Street). You'll also find Broadway meandering about the West Side above 23rd Street. Avenue of the Americas and Seventh Avenue both stop at the south end of Central Park. Riverside Drive runs parallel to West End Avenue near the Hudson River north of 72nd Street. All of these avenues run north-south and parallel to Fifth Avenue (except Broadway, which meanders diagonally before more or less straightening out around 79th Street). The Henry Hudson Parkway (also known as the West Side Highway and sometimes called Twelfth Avenue around midtown) runs along the entire West Side of the city.

Central Park occupies land between 59th and 110th streets, further dividing Manhattan's East and West sides. Fifth Avenue runs along the East Side of the park, and everything east of it is known as the Upper East Side. Central Park West runs along the West Side of the park, and everything west of it is known as the Upper West Side. Both the Upper East Side and the Upper West Side are largely residential, although most of the north-south avenues have plenty of shops and stores.

NORTHERN MANHATTAN—The avenues on the East Side remain fairly consistent as they move north of Central Park into the area known as East (or Spanish) Harlem. Lenox Avenue (which soon becomes Malcolm X Boulevard) picks up where Avenue of the Americas left off below the park. Adam Clayton Powell, Jr. Boulevard picks up where Seventh Avenue left off. Central Park West becomes Frederick Douglass Boulevard. Amsterdam Avenue, Broadway, and Riverside Drive all extend into Northern Manhattan, while such major roads as Convent Avenue, St. Nicholas Avenue, Edgecombe Avenue, and Fort Washington Avenue are exclusive to Harlem and the northern tip of Manhattan.

Key to Addresses

So how do you find an address in Manhattan? Just recently, Manhattan phone directories and other publications have begun including cross-street information as part of most address listings. If you have an address without a cross street, however, here's a reliable system for figuring it out:

AVENUES—If you know a numerical address on one of the north-south avenues, you can determine the approximate cross street by dropping the last number, dividing the remainder by two, and adding or subtracting the number indicated.

Avenue A, B, C, or D .... Add 3
First Avenue .... Add 3
Second Avenue .... Add 3
Third Avenue .... Add 10
Lexington Avenue .... Add 22
Fourth Avenue/Park Avenue South ..... Add 8
Park Avenue .... Add 35
Madison Avenue .... Add 26
Fifth Avenue
• addresses up to 200 .... Add 13
• between 201 and 400 .... Add 16
• between 401 and 600 .... Add 18
• between 601 and 774 .... Add 20
• between 775 and 1286 .... Subtract 18
• between 1289 and 1500 .... Add 45
• addresses up to 2000 .... Add 24
Avenue of the Americas/Sixth Avenue .. Subtract 12
Lenox Avenue/Malcolm X Boulevard .. Add 110
Seventh Avenue .... Add 12
Adam Clayton Powell, Jr. Boulevard ... Add 20
Broadway
• addresses up to 754 are below 8th Street
• between 754 and 858 .... Subtract 29
• between 859 and 958 .... Subtract 25
• addresses above 1000 .... Subtract 30
Eighth Avenue .... Add 10
Ninth Avenue .... Add 13
Columbus Avenue .... Add 60
Tenth Avenue .... Add 14
Amsterdam Avenue .... Add 60
Eleventh Avenue .... Add 15
West End Avenue .... Add 60
Convent Avenue .... Add 127
St. Nicholas Avenue .... Add 110
Manhattan Avenue .... Add 100
Edgecombe Avenue .... Add 134
Fort Washington Avenue .... Add 158

Central Park West and Riverside Drive have formulas of their own. To find the cross street for a building on Central Park West, divide the address by 10 and add 60. To find the cross street for a building on Riverside Drive up to 165th Street, divide the address by 10 and add 72.

A word of caution: because certain addresses—particularly those on Fifth, Madison, and Park avenues—are thought to be particularly prestigious, many buildings use them even if their entrances are actually on a side street. This is most common in midtown and along Fifth Avenue on the Upper East Side. If you can't find an address, look around the corner.

CROSS STREETS—Numbered cross streets run east-west. Addresses on them are easy to find. Allow for a little variation below 23rd Street (because Madison, Eleventh, and Twelfth avenues have yet to begin) and throughout the city whenever Broadway is involved.

EAST SIDE

1 to 49	between Fifth Avenue and Madison Avenue
50 to 99	between Madison Avenue and Park Avenue
100 to 149	between Park Avenue and Lexington Avenue
150 to 199	between Lexington Avenue and Third Avenue
200 to 299	between Third Avenue and Second Avenue
300 to 399	between Second Avenue and First Avenue
400 to 499	between First Avenue and York Avenue

WEST SIDE BELOW 59th STREET

1 to 99	between Fifth Avenue and Avenue of the Americas
100 to 199	between Avenue of the Americas and Seventh Avenue
200 to 299	between Seventh Avenue and Eighth Avenue
300 to 399	between Eighth Avenue and Ninth Avenue
400 to 499	between Ninth Avenue and Tenth Avenue
500 to 599	between Tenth Avenue and Eleventh Avenue
600 and up	between Eleventh Avenue and Twelfth Avenue

WEST SIDE ABOVE 59th STREET

1 to 99	between Central Park West and Columbus Avenue
100 to 199	between Columbus Avenue and Amsterdam Avenue
200 to 299	between Amsterdam Avenue and West End Avenue
Above 300	between West End Avenue and Riverside Drive

Odd-numbered addresses on east-west streets are on the north (uptown) side, while even-numbered ones are on the south (downtown) side.

Five area codes and 11 digits!
The proliferation of pagers, cell phones, fax machines, and modems has meant that three new area codes—917, 347, and 646—have been added to 212 (Manhattan) and 718 (New York's other four boroughs). Whether you're calling across the street or out to Staten Island, all calls now require dialing 11 digits: the numeral 1, plus the area code and phone number.

Neighborhoods

It may be hard for visitors to think of a city of millions in this fashion, but New York is really a collection of small neighborhoods. Some are more famous than others, and their borders may ebb and flow over the years, but each has a history and flavor all its own. To get a full sense of this wonderful city, I encourage you to visit as many neighborhoods as possible. From north to south, they include:

INWOOD AND WASHINGTON HEIGHTS—Home to General George Washington's forces during the Revolutionary War, these neighborhoods cover all of Manhattan north of about 151st Street. Racially and ethnically mixed, they have been home to generations of immigrants and now include both middle-class and poor areas. Several large and remarkably unspoiled parks, Yeshiva University, the Dyckman Farmhouse, The Cloisters, Columbia-Presbyterian Hospital, and Audubon Terrace are all in this area, as is the entrance to the George Washington Bridge. As the name implies, Washington Heights contains some surprisingly steep sections.

HARLEM—There are actually two Harlems: East Harlem (also called Spanish Harlem) and Harlem proper. East Harlem begins at about 96th Street and runs along the east side of the island to its northern tip. The population of this area is predominantly Latino, and Spanish is spoken more frequently than English here. El Museo del Barrio is on the southwestern edge of East Harlem.

Harlem itself occupies a small corridor in the middle of the island at the top of Central Park (at 110th Street) and then extends north and west of the famous and always busy 125th Street. That thoroughfare has again become a major shopping and entertainment hub in recent years, thanks in large part to the leadership of former NBA star Magic Johnson. The population of Harlem is almost entirely African-American, and the historic neighborhood is known around the world as a center of African-American music, politics, and culture. Harlem includes both middle-class and poor areas. Here you'll find the Schomburg Center for Research in Black Culture, the Apollo Theatre, Abyssinian Baptist Church, and the Studio Museum of Harlem, as well as the office of former President Bill Clinton.

MORNINGSIDE HEIGHTS—This relatively small but vibrant area runs between Morningside Drive and the Hudson River from 110th Street to 124th Street. The stretch of Broadway between those streets is the neighborhood's economic heart. The area is dominated by three large and well-known institutions: Columbia University, Riverside Church, and the Cathedral Church of St. John the Divine. Grant's Tomb is across from Riverside Church, at 122nd Street in Riverside Park. The neighborhood is full of students and professors from all over the world.

UPPER WEST SIDE—A primarily residential area extending west of Central Park to the Hudson River from 59th Street all the way north to 110th Street, the Upper West Side is home to such famous apartment buildings as the Dakota and the Ansonia. The neighborhood is racially and ethnically mixed, and its residents pride themselves for being politically progressive and tending toward the bohemian (although by downtown standards, Upper West Siders are decidedly conventional).

Like a lot of Manhattan neighborhoods in the last decade, the Upper West Side is brimming with children and families. Thanks in large part to entrepreneur Donald Trump, even the once grim Columbus Circle, at the southwest corner of Central Park, is being reborn. A little further north, the ABC studio (where its talk shows and soap operas are taped) and Lincoln Center dominate the low and high ends of cultural life, respectively. The fabulous food stores Fairway and Zabar's are landmarks a bit further north. So are the American Museum of Natural History and the New-York Historical Society. Barnes & Noble at Broadway and 82nd Street has become a major force in the neighborhood as well. Columbus Avenue, Amsterdam Avenue, and

Broadway are lined with stores, while Central Park West, West End Avenue, and Riverside Drive are almost exclusively residential. The most elegant living areas of the Upper West Side are on Central Park West and the cross streets in the high 60s, the 70s, and the low 80s. Although even many longtime New Yorkers may suppose there's little worth doing between 96th Street and Harlem, that area—particularly on Broadway—is alive with good restaurants, neighborhood shopping, and great jazz clubs.

These Boots Are Made for Walking
New York is a wonderful place for walking. Simply watching the never-ending parade of people is a great pastime, as is gawking at some of the really amazing buildings that soar from the streets here. One of the most spectacular is in midtown: the **Hugo Boss** store at the corner of Fifth Avenue and 56th Street. This fashionable clothing store is particularly dramatic in the evening, when its fabulous light system makes it a standout on this avenue of standouts.

UPPER EAST SIDE—Best known for art museums, galleries, and upscale boutiques, the Upper East Side is also the city's prestigious, old-money residential neighborhood. It covers the area east of Central Park from Fifth Avenue to the East River between 59th Street and 96th Street. Fifth Avenue (also known as Museum Mile) is dominated by such famous institutions as the Metropolitan, Guggenheim, and Cooper-Hewitt museums. It is also home to a large number of expensive apartment buildings, former mansions, and foreign consulates, as well as many of Manhattan's elite private schools. On Madison Avenue you'll find the Whitney Museum and lots of galleries, all sorts of chic international designers and retailers in the 60s and lower 70s, and upscale boutiques and shops in the upper 70s and lower 80s. Park Avenue and most of the cross streets are home to residential buildings and such institutions as the Asia Society and the Americas Society. From Lexington Avenue east to the river above 75th Street (an area known as Yorkville), rents go down a bit. You'll find Gracie Mansion, the mayor's residence in Carl Schurz Park, overlooking the river at about 88th Street. Bloomingdale's has long been a major retail force at the southern end of the Upper East Side.

MIDTOWN—Squarely in the middle of the island south of 59th Street, midtown Manhattan is one of the busiest places on Earth on weekdays and is almost deserted, except for tourists, on Sundays. (During Christmas season, tourists and natives alike flock to midtown.) The area extends from 42nd to 59th streets between about Third and Seventh avenues. Fifth Avenue, home to the most expensive rental real estate in the world, is the heart of midtown and one of the world's most famous shopping areas. The flagship stores of Tiffany's, F.A.O. Schwarz, Saks Fifth Avenue, and Bergdorf Goodman are all here, as are such pop-culture icons as Niketown and the Gap. Many stately mansions once lined this part of Fifth Avenue, but only a few remain and none still serves as a residence.

St. Patrick's Cathedral and several other famous churches are also on Fifth Avenue in midtown. St. Bartholomew's is on Park Avenue, and the stately Central Synagogue is on Lexington Avenue. Landmark buildings like the Citicorp Center, Trump Tower, Rockefeller Center, and the Chrysler Building dominate the skyline. Carnegie Hall, the Ed Sullivan Theater, and Radio City Music Hall occupy the western edge of midtown. The once-elegant 57th Street, on the north edge of midtown, is definitely a little less exclusive these days, as stores like Swatch, Sunglass Hut, and Victoria's Secret sit side-by-side with Chanel, Prada, and Louis Vuitton. Grand Central Station, the New York Public Library, and Bryant Park mark midtown's southern edge.

Believe it or not, part of the old Hell's Kitchen (the gentrified name is now Clinton) has morphed into a wonderful neighborhood for restaurants, international food stores, and great bakeries. Look on Ninth Avenue between the high 30s and low 50s.

CLINTON—Home to the Hell's Kitchen Gang a century ago, this neighborhood was once among the most violent and dangerous in the nation. It stretches south from 59th Street to 34th Street between Eighth Avenue and the Hudson River. Led by the startling transformation of the Times Square area into a family-friendly tourist mecca, much of Clinton has been gentrified. The always crowded and still a bit scruffy Port Authority Bus Terminal is on Eighth Avenue in the southern part of this neighborhood. Ninth Avenue, particularly in the high 30s and low 40s, is home to a lot of ethnic grocers, bakers, and butchers. The west end of 42nd Street boasts some very good off-Broadway theaters. The Jacob K. Javits Convention Center and most of the city's passenger ship terminals are located here along the Hudson River. Long considered one of the few "affordable" neighborhoods in New York, this area has seen lots of high-rise construction in recent years. There's even talk of a new stadium for the New York Jets.

MURRAY HILL—Covering the East Side from 42nd Street south to 34th Street, Murray Hill begins at Park Avenue and runs to the East River. This area is almost entirely residential, and the nicest part can be found around Park Avenue in the upper 30s. The only real visitor attractions are the Morgan Library and the incredible Science, Industry, and Business Library in the old B. Altman building at Madison Avenue and 34th Street.

CHELSEA—As it has been, this area remains one of Manhattan's hottest. Still a largely residential neighborhood despite its hot gallery image, it extends from 34th Street down to 14th Street between Avenue of the Americas and the Hudson River. Madison Square Garden and Penn Station are in the northeast corner of Chelsea, but it's the southern part of the neighborhood that has really taken off. Surprisingly quiet and relatively clean, the southwestern part of Chelsea has lots of turn-of-the-century townhouses and small apartment buildings. It's also home to the lovely grounds of the General Theological Seminary and the Chelsea Piers development. What's really got the city's attention, however, are the almost two hundred galleries that have migrated to the western edge of Chelsea, between 20th and 26th streets, particularly around the Dia Center for the Arts. Meanwhile, the southeastern edge of Chelsea, particularly where Chelsea and the Flatiron District overlap along Avenue of the Americas in the high teens and low 20s, has become what it was a century ago: a retailing hub. Such superstores as Bed Bath & Beyond, Barnes & Noble, and Burlington Coat Factory occupy buildings that once housed famous department stores.

FLATIRON DISTRICT—Named for the historic Flatiron Building, an architectural curiosity at the intersection of Broadway and Fifth Avenue at

23rd Street, this area was known as Ladies' Mile in the late 19th century for its elegant department stores. (A famous jingle at the time: "From 8th Street down, the men are earning it; from 8th Street up, the women are spending it.") Those department stores went out of business a century ago, but the buildings and the neighborhood are again alive and well, thanks in large part to an influx of "superstores." The Flatiron District runs between Park Avenue South and Avenue of the Americas from 23rd Street to 14th Street. Avenue of the Americas is really thriving now, and parts of Fifth Avenue in this area also have undergone a resurgence. The Church of the Transfiguration (affectionately known as "the Little Church Around the Corner"), the Marble Collegiate Church, and the Empire State Building are all just north of here.

Only in New York!
The newsstand at the corner of Broadway and 32nd Street, an area close to the Diamond District and known for its sizable Korean business population, may be the only one in the world that sells newspapers in Hebrew, Korean, and English.

GRAMERCY PARK—This aging but still pleasant neighborhood was once the city's most elegant residential area. It covers the area from Park Avenue South to Second Avenue between 34th Street and 14th Street. The nicest part is Gramercy Park itself. The city's only remaining private park, it is bounded by Park Avenue South, Third Avenue, and 20th and 21st streets. A stroll down Irving Place, which runs from the park south to East 14th Street, can be very pleasant indeed. The Flatiron District and the Gramercy Park area meet at Union Square, a lively area that is home to the city's largest and most popular Greenmarket. The New York Police Academy and Theodore Roosevelt's birthplace are on the western edge of Gramercy Park, and Stuyvesant Square Park occupies both sides of Second Avenue between 15th and 17th streets. Two huge planned residential areas, Stuyvesant Town and Peter Cooper Village, abut the East River, as does Bellevue Hospital.

MEATPACKING DISTRICT—This is one of the city's most bizarre and fascinating neighborhoods. I'm not suggesting that the average tourist would want to wander around here. However, the neighborhood west of Ninth Avenue (from 15th Street south to Gansevoort Street, between Chelsea and the West Village) is being shaped by a collision of interesting forces. Traditionally this dirty, architecturally uninteresting area has been the home of New York's meatpacking industry, as well as a great deal of prostitution. But the number of meat businesses has dropped precipitously in recent years and community action has forced much of the prostitution elsewhere. Meanwhile, artists, bar owners, ultra-trendy boutiques and fashion designers, and even young families are attracted by the neighborhood's relatively cheap rents. The result is a weird mix of trendy bars, fashionable boutiques, wholesale meatpacking plants, studios, transvestites, and families with small children. Only in New York!

EAST VILLAGE—About 150 years ago the Astors, the Vanderbilts, and others of the city's elite lived here, but today the East Village is among the city's funkiest and surprisingly most livable neighborhoods. It lies between Avenue B and Broadway from 14th Street down to Houston Street. Alphabet

City (the avenues in the eastern part of the East Village that have letters for names) and Tompkins Square are much tamer than they were a decade ago, and many parts have become gentrified to the point of being family-friendly, but they're still home to some offbeat and colorful nightclubs, shops, and people. The area along 6th Street between First and Second avenues is a thriving ethnic enclave known as Little India. The area around 7th Street and Third Avenue is home to a great many Ukrainian immigrants, and Stuyvesant Street is a gathering spot for young people from Japan. The Ukrainian Museum, St. Mark's in the Bowery, and Grace Church are all in the northern part of the East Village. Old Merchant's House, the last remnant of the East Village of yesteryear, is on the neighborhood's western edge.

Just as the relative status of various neighborhoods rises and falls over the years, certain streets suddenly become "hot"—and just as suddenly, they're not. At the moment, New York's hot streets include:

Clinton Street: The new Restaurant Row of the Lower East Side, this once dreary and even dangerous street is now home to more than a dozen upscale cafes and restaurants with the sorts of unusual menus and daring chefs that bring limousines and long wait lists night after night.

Smith Street: Over the Brooklyn Bridge in Brooklyn, this is one of the few inducements for New York trendsetters to leave Manhattan. At the intersection of several old Brooklyn neighborhoods, the stretch of Smith Street between Butler and Union streets is bristling with hipness. Cafes and restaurants braved the way here, but now they're joined by bars, clothing boutiques, and home furnishing stores.

West 14th Street (near Tenth Avenue): The cobblestoned heart of the Meatpacking District, West 14th and adjacent Washington Street are home to the trendiest clothing and designer boutiques.

GREENWICH VILLAGE—Although Greenwich Village is best known today for the beatniks and jazz clubs of the 1950s, it's also true that Edgar Allan Poe, Walt Whitman, Edna St. Vincent Millay, Frederic Church, and Edward Hopper all lived here at one time or another. In fact, this area has been among the city's most vibrant centers of culture (and *counter*culture) since relatively affluent New Yorkers began moving here in the early part of the 19th century to avoid the epidemics of the increasingly crowded city to the south. Greenwich Village covers most of the area from Broadway west to the Hudson River between 14th Street and Houston Street. The section from Seventh Avenue to the river is known to locals as the West Village, and the part above Ninth Avenue is the Meatpacking District. The beautiful Jefferson Market Library, the Forbes Magazine Galleries, New York University, and lots of interesting shops and nightclubs are located here, as is the always lively Washington Square Park and its famed arch. If you're going to spend time walking around here, relax and enjoy the Village without worrying about exactly what street you're on. The streets down here are confusing at best, but the area is small and you can't really get lost.

SOHO—Short for *So*uth of *Ho*uston, Soho went from being the center of New York in the middle of the 19th century to an almost entirely abandoned wasteland in the middle of the 20th century. Discovered by artists looking for inexpensive space in the 1960s and by upscale boutiques and retailers in the

1990s, it's now so trendy—that is to say, crowded and overrun with designer boutiques and tourists—that many artists, galleries, and now even the same high-end retailers who flocked to the area just a few years ago have moved to other parts of town. That said, it's still an energetic and dynamic neighborhood. Soho begins several blocks south of Washington Square Park on Houston Street and runs south to Canal Street between Broadway and Avenue of the Americas. The neighborhood comes alive on weekends and in the evening. Almost everything down here stays open later than similar establishments in the rest of the city. Many of the neighborhood's commercial galleries are concentrated on and around West Broadway (a separate street four blocks west of Broadway) between Houston and Broome streets.

TRIBECA—Shorthand for *Tri*angle *Be*low *Ca*nal, Tribeca used to be a rather dull and dirty commercial district but is becoming both residential and every bit as chic as Soho. It covers the area from Canal Street south to Chambers Street between Broadway and the Hudson River. Although it doesn't look as upscale as you might expect and can be very confusing for outsiders wandering around, Tribeca is home to emerging and established artists, commercial galleries, converted loft apartments, movie stars (Robert DeNiro's Tribeca Film Center has become a fixture down here), some good restaurants, and a growing number of boutiques.

CHINATOWN—This neighborhood's 150,000 residents, who occupy roughly 40 square blocks, make up the largest concentration of Chinese outside of Asia. Because it is always growing and increasingly overlaps such neighborhoods as Little Italy and the Lower East Side, Chinatown has boundaries nobody can quite agree how to define. Roughly speaking, it runs from Grand Street south to Worth Street, between Broadway and Allen Street. Its busiest streets are Canal, Mott, and Pell. If you've ever been to Hong Kong or southern China, you'll be overwhelmed by the similarities between those places and this neighborhood. Look for all sorts of wonderful food stores, as well as the Museum of Chinese in the Americas and the marvelous Chinese New Year parade and celebration.

NOLITA—Short for *No*rth of *L*ittle *Ita*ly, Nolita is a tiny neighborhood packed with vibrant restaurants, galleries, and boutiques. The entire neighborhood lies between Houston and Kenmare streets on Mulberry, Lafayette, Mott, and Elizabeth streets.

LITTLE ITALY—No longer home to many Italian immigrants and seemingly shrinking every year as Chinatown and the newer Nolita expand, this area nonetheless remains the emotional heart of the entire region's Italian-American population, many of whom return for weddings, funerals, holidays, and other special occasions. Mulberry Street (better known as Via San Gennaro) around Grand Street forms the heart of Little Italy and is known for its restaurants and festivals.

LOWER EAST SIDE—Many people use the Lower East Side as a geographic umbrella for Chinatown, Little Italy, and the Bowery, but I know it as a distinct neighborhood where generations of Eastern European and other immigrants first settled in overcrowded tenements and worked in sweatshops so their children could have better lives. (Many newer immigrants still live and work here in conditions that are not as much improved as you might think, although the immigrants and longtime retailers are being pushed out by yuppies looking for "affordable" housing and the increasing rents that follow them.) I also know it as what has historically been the best place in Manhattan to shop for high-quality clothing, household goods, and accessories at a discount. Because some of the area's businesses still are run by religiously observant Jews, they are closed on Friday afternoon and Saturday. Sunday is the shopping day here. Canal and Orchard streets are the area's heart, but it extends broadly from Houston to Canal streets and from the Sara D. Roosevelt Parkway east to Ludlow Street. The area still looks pretty run-down and many of the old stores are really struggling these days, but some of the old-timers are becoming more retail savvy as their shops are increasingly interspersed with hip clubs, chic boutiques, art galleries, and new restaurants. Make sure to stop by the Lower East Side Tenement Museum and the Eldridge Street Synagogue to get a sense of the area's rich history.

DOWNTOWN—This area is a little hard to define except to say that it's centered around City Hall. Very roughly speaking, it runs from Chambers Street south to Fulton Street and from West Broadway east to Pearl Street. Many mom-and-pop stores and major chains are sited here, and its streets are always busy. St. Paul's Chapel, the Woolworth Building, the entrance to the Brooklyn Bridge pedestrian walkway, and the beautifully restored City Hall Park are all reasons to spend a little time here. Despite lots of improvements recently, this area always seems dirtier than the rest of the city. The South Street Seaport is located just east of downtown, and it's an easy walk south to Wall Street and Battery Park.

While most of the dozens of distinct shopping districts that once defined New York are gone or in precipitous decline, a few "only in New York" areas—shopping and otherwise—are worth noting:

- **Diamond District**—concentrated on West 47th Street between Fifth Avenue and Avenue of the Americas
- **Financial District** (a.k.a. "Wall Street")—between Broadway and Water Street from Maiden Lane to Exchange Place
- **Museum Mile**—along Fifth Avenue from 70th to 106th streets
- **Theater District**—between Broadway and Eighth Avenue from 44th to 48th streets and on 42nd Street between Ninth and Tenth avenues
- **Crystal District**—A new district that has sprouted up in recent years, the five-block stretch of Madison Avenue between 58th and 63rd streets is home to Steuben, Swarovski, Baccarat, Daum, and Lalique. Wow!

LOWER MANHATTAN—Extending from Wall Street and other parts of the Financial District south to Battery Park, this is the oldest part of New York City and was home to the World Trade Center. The hardest hit by the lingering aftermath of the terrorist attacks of September 11, 2001, it remains a very sober place. Things are very compact and vertical down here: the streets are as narrow as the buildings are tall. The boat to the Statue of Liberty and Ellis Island leaves from near Castle Clinton National Monument in Battery Park, and the Staten Island Ferry's terminal is just east of the park. Look for the exceptional Museum of the American Indian, Trinity Church, the Federal Hall National Memorial, Fraunces Tavern Museum, the Museum of

American Financial History, New York Unearthed, the new home of the New York City Police Museum, and the New York Stock Exchange in Lower Manhattan.

BATTERY PARK CITY—A planned residential area built entirely on the landfill created when the original World Trade Center site was excavated in the 1970s, this collection of high-rise apartment buildings sits on the western side of Manhattan's southern tip, starting a bit north of Battery Park itself. The World Financial Center, where a lot of its residents work, is planted squarely in the middle of this neighborhood, and the Museum of Jewish Heritage is at its southern tip. Of course it's important to note that the World Trade Center sat on this neighborhood's eastern edge, and its absence creates a devastating hole, both physically and emotionally.

GETTING AROUND NEW YORK

Because it is an island and cannot sprawl outward, New York is compact and easier to navigate than most of the world's other large cities. You have a range of choices for how to get around, listed here in order of personal preference.

WALKING—Without question, this is my favorite way to get around New York. It may seem a little overwhelming at first (particularly in midtown at rush hour) and you'll stick out like a sore thumb if you wait on the curb for the "walk" signs, but walking is definitely the best way to see the city and get a sense of its neighborhoods. Often, especially in midtown on a weekday, walking is also the fastest way to travel ten or more blocks. Walking north-south (uptown or downtown), 20 blocks are equivalent to one mile. Most east-west (crosstown) blocks, particularly those between Fifth and Seventh avenues, are much longer. Unless you have small children in tow or are trying to get from Columbia University (at 116th Street) to New York University (at 4th Street), walking is the least expensive and most interesting way to travel. Just be very aware of traffic and wear comfortable walking shoes!

SUBWAY—Some visitors and natives love to ride the subway, while others will do anything to avoid it. The roughly 7 million people who ride subways every weekday know that it's usually the fastest and most efficient way to travel in the city. As those numbers suggest, the subway can get very crowded. If you get claustrophobic, stay away from the subway around rush hour. And whatever time you travel, hold on tightly to the hands of any children who are with you. Thanks to an ongoing anti-grafitti campaign, a beefed-up police presence, an increasingly well-enforced ban on panhandling, and lots of renovations in recent years, the experience also has become significantly more pleasant.

Riding in Style

Next time you're feeling a little claustrophobic on a subway car, think of August Belmont, Jr., who financed construction of the IRT—the city's first subway line—between City Hall and 145th Street. He loved using the subway system but not with everyone else. Belmont had his very own subway car, complete with a rolltop desk, Tiffany glass, and a galley. It even had a name: the *Mineola*.

The subway system is the result of a merger of private lines like the BMT and the IRT that sprang up a hundred years ago. Some of the stations and cars are quite old, so don't expect the relative luxury of BART in San Francisco or the Metro in Washington, D.C. Its 685 miles of track and 468 stations connect every borough except Staten Island. In Manhattan, the system is concentrated south of 110th Street (particularly below 59th Street). Maps of the system are available at station booths and are posted in most subway cars and stations. If you need to study a map, I suggest doing so in your hotel room or some other private place so as not to advertise that you don't know where you're going. You'll also find a detailed map of the subway system in the front section of the Manhattan Yellow Pages.

But Can I Still Get a Subway Token?

For a hundred years, few New Yorkers would go out without subway tokens in their pocket. However, the introduction in recent years of the MetroCard has rendered those small metal tokens obsolete. MetroCards have lots of features that make them appealing: they're renewable, you can buy them with credit and debit cards, subway-to-bus transfers are built in, and all sorts of discounts and deals are available. But if you really want a token, you'll need to go to the New York Transit Museum.

The stairs leading down to most subway stations are marked by signs with a big "M" or "MTA." It's important to know that some are closed on weekends and others are marked for "uptown" or "downtown" access only. Unlike those in some of the other boroughs, Manhattan's subway stations are underground. (This should be noted by anyone who has trouble climbing stairs, as there are lots of steep ones in the subway system and few elevators.) You'll typically find the station booths at the bottom of the stairs. Inside the station, signs point to the appropriate platform for uptown (sometimes "Bronx-bound") or downtown (sometimes "Brooklyn-bound") trains. Keep an eye out for express trains—they're great time-savers if you want to go where they're going, but they make a limited number of stops. Some trains, such as the F line, run "express" in Queens but become "local" in Manhattan. The line number or letter, "local" or "express," and the name of the last stop are written on the side of each subway car, but maps are the best source of such information.

If you pay per ride, the subway costs $2 ($1 for senior citizens with identification and free for up to three children under 44 inches tall with a fare-paying adult). Thanks to the **MetroCard** system, you can buy an unlimited seven-day pass for $21 or a 30-day pass for $70. You can also buy a one-day Fun Pass for $7, but it's available only from MetroCard vending machines, certain MetroCard merchants, and major visitor centers. A $10 card will get you 6 rides for the price of 5, while a $20 card will get you 12 for the price of 10.

While MetroCards can be purchased for cash only at station booths, major credit cards and debit cards can be used in the automated, multilingual vending machines inside the stations. (Be sure to press the "start" button or you'll stand there wondering why the machine won't work!) MetroCards are also available at Rite Aid stores, Associated and D'Agostino supermarkets, Hudson News branches, and other locations throughout the city.

For all its great features, the MetroCard has one not-so-great feature that is worth mentioning: to discourage misuse of unlimited-ride cards, you cannot use the Fun Pass or any multiday, unlimited-ride pass again within 18 minutes of entering or leaving a given subway station. That can be frustrating if you get off at the wrong stop or are just running a quick errand.

Attention Older Visitors!

If you have trouble climbing long flights of stairs, avoid the subway! Most stations have steep stairways and few have elevators. Buses, on the other hand, can kneel to ease access from the curb, and the newest ones have ramps instead of stairs. Thanks to a recently enacted law, taxi drivers are required to help disabled passengers and cannot start the meter until their passengers are safely settled.

Some general subway rules: Once you've passed through the turnstiles and are inside the station, you can transfer between lines or ride for as long as you like. And if you're using a MetroCard, you can even transfer for free onto a bus within two hours with the same card—or anytime you want if you're using an unlimited-ride card! Station names are written on the walls of the stations and are announced inside subway cars, but the former are sometimes obscured and the latter are often garbled, so stay on your toes. (If you miss your stop, you can get off and go back.) Some lines stop running for a couple hours in the early morning, and many have less frequent or different service at night and on weekends, but all stations in the system are served by some train on a regular basis 24 hours a day, seven days a week. If you have questions or a problem, call the Metropolitan Transit Authority at 718/330-1234. (Non-English speakers can call 718/330-4847.)

Up and Running

Among the disastrous consequences of the September 11, 2001, terrorist attacks on the World Trade Center was the destruction of the subway tunnel that connected the 1 and 9 lines to the South Ferry station at the southern tip of Manhattan. Thanks to a tremendously talented and dedicated team of engineers and workers, the tunnel was reconstructed and trains were running again only a year later.

"For me," project superintendent Jan Szumanski told the *New York Times,* "this is my repayment to America for taking me in 20 years ago from Poland, a nobody."

It is to him and everyone else involved in the project we all owe a debt.

Two subway strategies are worth mentioning. One is taking an express to the stop closest to your destination and then waiting for a local to take you the rest of the way. You can always get on one line and then switch trains to get to your destination. This works particularly well on the 4, 5, and 6 lines on the East Side, for example, as only the 6 makes local stops in midtown while the 4 and 5 go all the way down to Bowling Green. So, for instance, you can board the 6 in midtown and switch to a 4 or 5 at 42nd Street, 34th Street, or wherever else the lines meet. A second trick is simply waiting for the next train if one is packed. Chances are there's a less crowded train right behind the first one. Your ride could be significantly more pleasant if you just wait a minute or two. (This is also true for buses.)

Finally, a word about safety. The Metropolitan Transit Authority has worked hard to clean up stations and the sometimes wonderful graffiti art in them, as well as significantly reduce the number of system breakdowns. Still, subway stations and the cars themselves are sometimes dirty, and all sorts of strange people wander through them. Statistically, however, the system is no more dangerous than any other mode of transportation. Indeed, like crime in New York generally, crime in the subway has fallen sharply. But do use common sense. *Don't* ride late at night or very early in the morning, particularly if you're alone. *Don't* enter deserted stations. *Don't* ride in an otherwise empty car. *Don't* wear flashy jewelry. *Don't* wander around aimlessly. *Don't* stand too close to the tracks. *Don't* use the bathroom inside any station. *Do* stick close to the designated off-hours waiting area if you're riding at an off-peak hour so that an attendant can keep an eye on you. And *do* watch your wallet or purse, particularly when riding in crowded cars.

TAXIS—All officially licensed medallion taxicabs in New York are yellow, have the words "NYC Taxi" and fare information written on their side doors, and post their medallion number in a box on the roof. Inside you'll see a meter and the driver's license (with his or her picture) and medallion number displayed on the dashboard, usually on the passenger's side. The city, particularly outside midtown, is full of unregulated "cars for hire" (a.k.a. "gypsy cabs") that are not legally allowed to pick up people south of 96th Street. Still, they sometimes try to do just that. I strongly encourage you to stick with medallion cabs. The cost of a ride in a medallion cab is calculated per trip rather than per person, which means that a short trip for four adults in a cab can actually be cheaper than a bus or subway ride. That said, however, fares can add up quickly, particularly if you're stuck in heavy traffic. The charge begins at $2 the moment you get in and costs 30 cents for every one-fifth of a mile driven and for every 90 seconds the cab sits in traffic. In general, the meter should "click" every four blocks when you're going north-south and every block when you're going east-west (20 cents for every minute of waiting time). You pay for any tolls, and there's a 50 cent surcharge for rides made between 8 p.m. and 6 a.m. The meter in the front keeps a running total of the fare, and the driver is required to give you a receipt if you request one. A tip of between 15% and 20% of the fare is expected, and payment is generally expected in cash. Drivers often cannot make change for bills larger than $20 (and are not required to).

Drivers *are* required to take you anywhere within the five boroughs of New York City, to Westchester and Nassau counties, and to Newark Airport. That's the law, but the reality is that many cab drivers will make a fuss if you want to go to one of the airports, out to one of those suburban counties, or even to lower-income neighborhoods in Manhattan. Moreover, be forewarned that drivers can charge you double the metered fare once they leave the city limits, plus tolls. If you have a problem, jot down the driver's name and medallion number and write or call the New York City Taxi and Limousine Commission (221 West 41st Street, New York, NY 10036; 212/221-8294) to complain. These folks take their oversight responsibilities seriously.

So how do you go about hailing a cab? Stand on or just off a curb and stick your arm up and out. If the number (but not the "off-duty" sign) is lit in the rectangular box on a cab's roof, it's empty and looking for business. Finding a cab in a snowstorm, in midtown, on a rainy Friday afternoon or any day around 5 p.m. is difficult, but you usually won't have trouble finding one in most parts of the city at most times of day. If you do have trouble, go to a major hotel or join the cab line at Penn Station, Grand Central Station, or Port Authority Bus Terminal. If you want the driver to take a particular route (it's a good idea to know exactly where you're going), say so when you get in. Assuming it isn't raining, I also suggest giving the driver the closest intersection rather than a street address as your destination. This will save both time and money. Passengers ride in the back seat, although the driver will usually let one person ride up front if there are four in your party. A final note: A new law requires drivers to help disabled passengers and prohibits them from starting the meter until such passengers are safely settled.

Be Forewarned: Don't Try to Get a Cab at 5 p.m.!

As ridiculous as it sounds, the hardest time of day to catch a cab is late afternoon—right around quitting time and just before dinner. Why? Because cab drivers typically work a 12-hour shift, and 4:30 or 5 p.m. is the end of the day shift. If you're making dinner reservations or planning to get somewhere in late afternoon, plan accordingly!

BUSES—In the earliest editions of this book, I wrote that the only reasons to take a city bus are if you have a lot of time and are afraid of the alternatives. A friend who rode the bus every day objected strongly. First of all, she pointed out, the city's blue and white buses are wheelchair-accessible (which the subway decidedly is not) and "elderly friendly" in that the driver can lower the stairs at the entrance for anyone who has trouble climbing high steps. Some of the city's newest buses are even "low-floor" models with loading ramps instead of stairs. Buses are also "stroller friendly," insofar as the doors don't close automatically and there are only a few steps to climb and descend. Precisely because the people who take the bus aren't in a hurry, they tend to be friendlier than subway riders and often will give an older person or a harried parent their seat. Buses are very safe and usually don't attract the strange people who still sometimes habituate subway cars and stations. Because there is a driver, you can ask questions or get directions. And because the bus stops frequently and you can always see where you're going, it's a good and relatively cheap way to get a flavor of the city. I still find the system frustratingly slow (the average speed of the M96, a bus traversing the length of 96th Street, has been clocked at 4.3 miles per hour at midday), but buses do have some redeeming features, and their popularity has increased so dramatically in recent years that there are now some double-length ("articulated") buses traveling busier routes.

Buses run up and down most avenues and on most major cross streets. Uptown buses stop every two or three blocks, and crosstown buses stop on every block—assuming someone is waiting at a bus stop or a bus rider has pushed the tape to alert the driver that a stop is requested. Many bus lines have a "limited stop" version that stops every ten blocks or so at major intersections; an orange "limited" sign is clearly visible in their front windshields. At a minimum, you can spot a bus stop by its blue sign and route numbers. The city has renovated and added more "Guide-a-Ride" signs and route maps, making the entire system much more user-friendly. Many stops are used by more than one route, so check the screen on the front or side of each bus for its route number or simply ask the driver. Your fare entitles you to one bus transfer, and you should request the transfer ticket from the driver when you board (unless you're paying with a Metrocard, in which case you can transfer automatically within two hours). The transfer is good only for a continuous trip, which means that you cannot get off and then board another bus on the same route. If you're using a MetroCard, you can transfer onto a subway within two hours.

If you pay per ride, the bus costs $2 ($1 for senior citizens with identification and free for up to three children under 44 inches tall with a fare-paying adult). Thanks to the **MetroCard** system, you can buy unlimited ride passes or multiple-ride ones. For more information, see the previous section on the subway, or go to any subway station.

You can get a map of Manhattan bus routes on most buses (ask the driver or look for boxes by the front and back doors) and at most subway token booths. You will also find a detailed map of the bus system in the Manhattan Yellow Pages. The map details where buses run, frequency of service, and which bus to take to major museums and other attractions. If you have questions about how to get from one place to another on the bus, call the Metropolitan Transit Authority between 6 a.m. and 9 p.m. at 718/330-1234.

CAR SERVICES—If you're wondering about the large number of Lincoln Town Cars and other black sedans in midtown and the Financial District, they are car services. Unlike taxicabs, which cruise the streets looking for business, car services are available only by reservation and often are exclusively for corporate clients. If you're in New York on business, your company may arrange to have you picked up from the airport and shuttled around town by one of these services. Chances are you will be given an account number and pay with a voucher provided by either your company or the driver. A client's name and car number will typically be posted in the window of the car, and you'll be told in advance what to look for.

Some car services and limousine companies take reservations from individuals. **Carey Limousine NY** (212/599-1122 or 800/336-4646) is among the larger and more reputable companies. You can have a car meet you at the airport, be shuttled around town for a day, or simply arrive and depart from the opera in style. The cost is calculated by the hour or the trip rather than by mileage, so make sure you agree on a price before making a commitment. Reservations are required. Make them at least a day in advance and call to confirm several hours before you expect to leave. If you want a specific kind of car or limousine, say so when you're making reservations. These car services are on the high end of the business. You'll find lots of gypsy cabs and low-end car services in the outer boroughs and outside midtown, but I suggest avoiding them. Just so you know, licensed limousines are required to post a diamond-shaped decal on the right side of their windshield. On it will be an eight-digit number bookended by "T" and "C."

DRIVING—If you read my comments earlier in this chapter, you already know that I *strongly* recommend against driving in New York. Leave the hassles and headaches to cab and bus drivers. The parking regulations alone ought to discourage you. There are alternate-side-of-the-street rules, special rules for several dozen official holidays, and weekend rules. And that's assuming you can find a space. (The average rental cost of a parking space in an underground lot in midtown is more than $500 a month!) Illegal parking can cost upwards of $200—and that's *after* you've paid for the towing and impoundment of your vehicle. If you can't find a space on the street or want the security of a garage, you're going to pay big bucks. Forty dollars a day is not uncommon.

If that's not bad enough, consider that 750,000 cars come into Manhattan every day and 80,000 more congest midtown during the Christmas season! It's little wonder that the average speed of traffic going uptown or downtown is less than 10 mph . . . and the average crosstown speed is half that! Moreover, it's illegal for anyone under 18 to drive in New York City. If you must drive, I recommend becoming a member of AAA or some other major automobile club and getting all the information they have about traffic laws and driving in the city. Whatever else you do, make sure you know where you're going and be prepared for a lot of honking. Drivers in New York are not very patient.

My Best Advice

- Everybody is in a hurry. You don't need to be. Slow down and take it in.
- Give yourself permission to wander without an agenda in a neighborhood like the West Village or the Upper East Side.
- The subway is by far the most efficient, fastest way to get around the city, but do not use it if you have trouble climbing stairs.

II. Where to Eat It:
Manhattan a la Carte

If you're like most readers, this is the section of the book you'll turn to first and return to most often. New York is a culinary paradise with literally thousands of restaurants and hundreds of good ones. The best of the best in every price category appear in this chapter.

Since the terrorist attacks of September 11, 2001, the New York restaurant scene has changed in subtle ways. More people are eating out, anxious to be around their friends and neighbors. Strangers in restaurants happily talk and exchange stories. Prices at the more expensive places have generally come down, and really good meals can be found for a reasonable tab in scores of places. Portions tend to be smaller, and some rooms specialize in bite-sized offerings. A crammed, overflowing plate is out of style, and dress codes are definitely on the casual side (with a few noted exceptions).

One of the biggest changes in the restaurant business recently has been the emphasis on bar meetings, rather than dinner table conversations. Food could follow later, with the tab considerably less than on full three-course meals. Many restaurants have sizably increased their bar space, plus offering snacks and other menu items in that area. In two words, the emphasis now is on the "cocktail generation."

Everything I have to say about the restaurants in this chapter is my opinion. I am *not* a professional food critic, nor am I a wine expert (which is why I have not commented on wine in the following pages). However, I have eaten in thousands of New York restaurants over the years. I also own a restaurant and gourmet cake shop in Oregon and have decades of experience in the food service industry. So I feel confident in passing judgment and voicing opinions. Speaking of which, everyone has a list of things that bother them about a restaurant. Here's mine:

- Being greeted with disinterest or not greeted at all.
- Being forced to wait at the bar when tables are available.
- Overly chatty waiters who provide their life histories.
- Sloppy, unkempt wait staff.
- Being offered pepper with every course you order.
- Greasy, dirty menus.
- Being asked repeatedly, "Is everything all right?"
- Waiters who scrape food off plates in front of diners.
- Having to ask more than once for the check.
- Unclean restrooms.

With those biases in mind, you will get an idea of the incredible range of the New York dining scene in the following pages. I've devised several categories for the hundreds of restaurants included in the following pages.

- **Quick Reference Guide**—All restaurants are listed by neighborhood. I've provided the address of each restaurant, the type of food served, whether it's open on Sunday, and the page number of the full review.
- **Exclusive List**—Compiled and updated over many years, my list details the best places in New York for hundreds of food items.
- **Restaurants Lists by Food and Atmosphere**—Everything from hamburger joints to solo dining, from kosher restaurants to pet-friendly places.
- **Full Restaurant Reviews**

I have categorized restaurants by the *cost of the meal* (excluding drinks and tax):
- **Inexpensive**: $15 and under per person
- **Moderate**: $16 to $34 per person
- **Moderately expensive**: $35 to $45 per person
- **Expensive**: $46 and up per person

Reservations are essential at most New York restaurants, particularly for dinner. I encourage you to make them well in advance and then confirm them on the day of the reservation. You should not have to give a credit card number (although you may be asked). Ask if there is a dress code and dress appropriately. Also inquire whether or not the restaurant takes credit cards, if that's how you plan to pay. Arrive on time.

If you cannot get reservations for dinner at the restaurant you want, eat at the bar or go there for lunch instead. If you want to get a table, avoid the trendiest restaurants, don't dine out on holidays, and plan to dine when a restaurant might logically be less crowded. (A restaurant in the Theater District, for example, may have more tables available after 8 p.m.) Speaking of reservations, popular restaurants may tell you they don't have anything available for weeks or until after 10 p.m. Often, however, you can just show up and they'll find space for you. Still, that strategy can be risky.

A general rule for tipping is to double the restaurant sales tax (which is 8.25%). Tipping between 15% and 20% of the pre-tax bill is customary for good service. I would consider leaving up to 25% for service that was truly extraordinary.

The New York restaurant scene changes by the day. Chefs and owners come and go. Restaurants change formats overnight. A restaurant is hot one week and out the next. Because I publish this book myself and therefore have a relatively short time between research and publication, my information is more current than guidebooks put out by large publishing houses.

Even so, bear in mind that the occasional listing may become outdated. If you have a particularly good or bad dining experience at one of the restaurants I've recommended—or at one I may not yet know about—please let me know.

Bon appetit!

Quick Reference Guide

CENTRAL PARK AREA

Alain Ducasse (Essex House, a Westin Hotel, 155 W 58th St): French . 86
Atelier (Ritz-Carlton New York, 50 Central Park S): Continental, Sunday . 89
Cafe Atlas (40 Central Park S): Continental, Sunday 99
Cafe Botanica (Essex House, a Westin Hotel, 160 Central Park S): American,
      Sunday 99
Manhattan Ocean Club (57 W 58th St): Seafood, Sunday 137
One C.P.S. (Plaza Hotel, 1 Central Park S): French Brasserie, Sunday .144
Plaza Hotel Palm Court (768 Fifth Ave): Continental, Sunday 152
Tavern on the Green (Central Park W at 67th St): Continental, Sunday .168

CHELSEA

Chelsea Bistro & Bar (358 W 23rd St): French, Sunday 104
Da Umberto (107 W 17th St): Italian 109
F&B Güdtfood (269 W 23rd St): European street food, Sunday 113
Gascogne (158 Eighth Ave): French, Sunday .116
La Lunchonette (130 Tenth Ave): French, Sunday 131
Moran's Chelsea (146 Tenth Ave): American, Sunday 141
Raymond's Cafe (88 Seventh Ave): Continental, Sunday 155

CHINATOWN

Golden Unicorn (18 East Broadway): Chinese, Sunday 118

EAST HARLEM

Rao's (455 E 114th St): Italian 155

EAST SIDE/UPPER EAST SIDE

Annie's (1381 Third Ave): American, Sunday 87
Arabelle (Hotel Plaza Athenee, 37 E 64th St): Continental, Sunday 88
A Tavola (1095 Lexington Ave): Italian, Sunday 89
Aureole (34 E 61st St): New American 89
Bravo Gianni (230 E 63rd St): Italian, Sunday 97
Cafe Boulud (Surrey Suites Hotel, 20 E 76th St): French, Sunday 99
Daniel (60 E 65th St): French 108
Elio's (1621 Second Ave): Italian, Sunday 112
Etats-Unis (242 E 81st St): American, Sunday 113
Gino (780 Lexington Ave): Italian, Sunday 117
Il Riccio (152 E 79th St): Italian, Sunday 125
Il Vagabondo (351 E 62nd St): Italian, Sunday 125
Jackson Hole Burgers (various locations): Burgers, Sunday 125
Jacques (204 E 85th St): French, Sunday 126
King's Carriage House (251 E 82nd St): Continental, Sunday 129
Le Refuge (166 E 82nd St): French, Sunday .134
Manhattan Grille (1161 First Ave): Continental, Sunday 136
Mark's Restaurant (The Mark Hotel, 25 E 77th St): French, Sunday . .138
Nicola's (146 E 84th St): Italian, Sunday 142
92 (Wales Hotel, 45 E 92nd St): American, Sunday 142
Our Place (1444 Third Ave): Chinese, Sunday 147
Pamir (1437 Second Ave): Afghan, Sunday 147

EAST VILLAGE

FLATIRON DISTRICT/GRAMERCY PARK/LOWER BROADWAY/UNION SQUARE

GREENWICH VILLAGE/WEST VILLAGE

LINCOLN CENTER

LOWER EAST SIDE

MEAT DISTRICT

MIDTOWN EAST

MIDTOWN WEST

SOHO/LITTLE ITALY

THEATER DISTRICT/TIMES SQUARE

TRIBECA/DOWNTOWN/FINANCIAL DISTRICT

WEST SIDE/UPPER WEST SIDE

OUTSIDE MANHATTAN

An Exclusive List: Hundreds of the Best Taste Treats in New York City (Eat In and Takeout)

Antipasto bar: **Da Umberto** (107 W 17th St) and **Trattoria dell'Arte** (900 Seventh Ave)

Appetizers, gourmet: **Russ & Daughters** (179 E Houston St)

Apple fritters with caramel ice cream: **Craftbar** (47 E 19th St)

Apple ring: **Lafayette** (26 Greenwich Ave)

Artichoke: **La Lunchonette** (130 Tenth Ave)

Babka: **Gertel's Bake Shop** (53 Hester St)

Bacon: **The Kitchenette** (80 West Broadway)

Baguettes: **Amy's Bread** (75 Ninth Ave and 672 Ninth Ave), **La Baguette Shop** (106 University Pl), and **Tribakery** (186 Franklin St)

Bakery goods, kosher: **Crumbs Bake Shop** (321½ Amsterdam Ave)

Banana split: **Blue Ribbon Bakery** (33 Downing St)

Baskets, gift and corporate: **Basketfull** (276 Fifth Ave, Suite 201),

Manhattan Fruitier (105 E 29th St), and **Petrossian Cafe & Boutique** (911 Seventh Ave)
Bean curd: **Fong Inn Too** (46 Mott St)
Beef, braised (when available): **Danube** (30 Hudson St)
Beef, fillet of (when available): **King's Carriage House** (251 E 82nd St)
Beef (affordable): **Florence Meat Market** (5 Jones St)
Beef and veal (premium): **Lobel's Prime Meats** (1096 Madison Ave)
Beef cheeks (when available): **Fleur de Sel** (5 E 20th St)
Beef Wellington: **One If By Land, Two If By Sea** (17 Barrow St)
Belgian nut squares: **Duane Park Patisserie** (179 Duane St)
Bialys: **Kossar's Bialys** (367 Grand St)
Bigoli (Venetian pasta): **Remi** (145 W 53rd St)
Biscuits, blueberry-peach: **Taylor's Prepared Foods** (523 Hudson St, 228 W 18th St, and 175 Second Ave)
Biscuits, pepper: **Vesuvio Bakery** (160 Prince St)
Blintzes: **Cafe Edison** (228 W 47th St)
Boeuf Bourguignon (menu special): **Country Cafe** (69 Thompson St)
Bomboloncini (fried doughnuts with fillings): **Osteria del Circo** (120 W 55th St)
Bouillabaisse: **Gotham Bar and Grill** (12 E 12th St), **Payard Patisserie** (1032 Lexington Ave), and **Pearl Oyster Bar** (18 Cornelia St)
Bratwurst: **Schaller & Weber** (1654 Second Ave)
Bread, banana: **O Mai** (158 Ninth Ave)
Bread, chocolate: **Amy's Bread** (75 Ninth Ave and 672 Ninth Ave)
Bread, fruit: **Anglers & Writers** (420 Hudson St)
Bread, Indian: **Dawat** (210 E 58th St)
Bread, Irish soda: **Zabar's** (2245 Broadway)
Bread, just baked: **Pasha** (70 W 71st St)
Bread, Semolina raisin fennel: **Amy's Bread** (75 Ninth Ave and 672 Ninth Ave)
Bread, spoon: **Kloe** (243 W 14th St)
Bread, whole wheat: **Dean & Deluca** (560 Broadway)
Bread pudding: **Le Cirque 2000** (455 Madison Ave)
Brioche: **Chez Laurence Patisserie** (245 Madison Ave) and **Lipstick Cafe** (885 Third Ave)
Brisket: **Citarella** (1313 Third Ave and 2135 Broadway)
Brownies, best: **Charles and Laurel Desserts** (537 Greenwich St), **Fat Witch Bakery** (75 Ninth Ave), and **Sarabeth's Kitchen** (1295 Madison Ave, 423 Amsterdam Ave, and 945 Madison Ave, at Whitney Museum)
B'stilla: **Lotfi's Moroccan Restaurant** (358 W 46th St)
Buns, sticky: **William Greenberg Jr. Desserts** (1100 Madison Ave) and **Sarabeth's Kitchen** (423 Amsterdam Ave)
Burrito, breakfast: **Kitchen/Market** (218 Eighth Ave)
Burritos: **Burritoville** (1487 Second Ave and other locations), **Harry's Burrito Junction** (241 Columbus Ave and other locations), **Nacho Mama's Burritos** (2893 Broadway), **Samalita's Tortilla Factory** (1429 Third Ave), and **Taqueria de Mexico** (93 Greenwich Ave)
Burritos (to go): **Benny's Burritos** (113 Greenwich Ave and 93 Ave A)
Butcher: **Balducci's** (155-A W 66th St)
Butcher, Eastern European: **Kurowycky Meat** (124 First Ave)
Butcher, French: **Les Halles** (411 Park Ave S)

Cabbage, pickled with pork and noodles: **Ollie's Noodle Shop and Grill** (200 W 44th St)

Cacik: **Turkish Kitchen** (386 Third Ave)

Cake: **E.A.T.** (1064 Madison Ave), **Edgar's Cafe** (255 W 84th St), and **Ferrara** (195 Grand St)

Cake, Belgian chocolate: **King's Carriage House** (251 E 82nd St)

Cake, blackout: **Gertel's Bake Shop** (53 Hester St) and **Serendipity 3** (225 E 60th St)

Cake, Bohemian: **Cupcake Cafe** (522 Ninth Ave)

Cake, buttercream and chocolate: **Moishe's Bakery** (115 Second Ave)

Cake, carrot: **Carrot Top Pastries** (3931 Broadway and 5025 Broadway)

Cake, chocolate: **Hard Rock Cafe** (221 W 57th St), **Second Avenue Kosher Delicatessen and Restaurant** (156 Second Ave), and **Soutine Bakery** (104 W 70th St)

Cake, chocolate meringue with chocolate mousse: **Soutine Bakery** (104 W 70th St)

Cake, chocolate mousse: **City Bakery** (3 W 18th St)

Cake, chocolate mud: **Umanoff & Parsons** (467 Greenwich St)

Cake, chocolate raspberry: **Caffe Roma** (385 Broome St)

Cake, chocolate soufflé: **Taylor's Prepared Foods** (523 Hudson St, 228 W 18th St, 175 Second Ave, and 156 Chambers St)

Cake, fruit, Milanese Italian: **Pasticceria Bruno** (245 Bleecker St)

Cake, white coconut and marshmallow meringue: **Magnolia Bakery** (401 Bleecker St)

Calamari: **Turkish Kitchen** (386 Third Ave)

Calzone: **Little Italy Gourmet Pizza** (1 E 43rd St)

Candy, Asian: **Aji Ichiban** (167 Hester St)

Candy (bonbons): **Teusher Chocolates** (620 Fifth Ave and 25 E 61st St)

Candy (butter crunch): **Mondel Chocolates** (2913 Broadway)

Candy (caramels): **Fifth Avenue Chocolatiere** (510 Madison Ave)

Candy (fruit jellies): **La Maison du Chocolat** (1018 Madison Ave)

Candy (jelly beans): **Myzel Chocolates** (140 W 55th St)

Cannelle: **Payard Patisserie** (1032 Lexington Ave)

Cannelloni: **Giambelli** (46 E 50th St) and **Piemonte Homemade Ravioli Company** (190 Grand St)

Cannoli: **Caffe Vivaldi** (32 Jones St) and **De Robertis Pastry Shop and Caffe** (176 First Ave)

Caramel bombe, frozen: **Town** (15 W 56th St)

Carpaccio: **Downtown** (376 West Broadway)

Cassoulet: **L'Absinthe** (227 E 67th St)

Caviar: **Caviar Russe** (538 Madison Ave), **Caviarteria** (Trump Building, 502 Park Ave), **Firebird** (365 W 46th St), **Petrossian Cafe & Boutique** (911 Seventh Ave), **Petrossian Restaurant** (182 W 58th St), and **Sable's** (1489 Second Ave)

Caviar (best prices): **Russ & Daughters** (179 E Houston St) and **Zabar's** (2245 Broadway)

Caviar, Urbani: **Cucina & Co.** (Macy's, 151 W 34th St, cellar)

Ceviche (marinated seafood): **Patria** (250 Park Ave S) and **Rosa Mexicano** (1063 First Ave and 61 Columbus Ave)

Champagne: **Flute** (40 E 20th St and 205 W 54th St), **Garnet Liquor** (929 Lexington Ave), and **Gotham Liquors** (2517 Broadway)

Cheese, mozzarella: **DiPalo Fine Food** (200 Grand St)

Cheese, ricotta: **Alleva Dairy** (188 Grand St)

Cheese selection: **Grace's Marketplace** (1237 Third Ave), **Zabar's** (2245 Broadway), and **Murray's Cheese Shop** (257 Bleecker St)

Cheesecake: **Mitchel London Foods** (22A E 65th St and 458 Ninth Ave) and **S&S Cheesecake** (222 W 238th St, Bronx)

Cheesecake, apple mascarpone: **Remi to Go** (145 W 53rd St)

Cheesecake, combination fruit: **Eileen's Special Cheese Cake** (17 Cleveland Pl)

Cheesecake, ricotta: **Primavera** (1578 First Ave)

Chicken, beggar's: **Shun Lee Palace** (155 E 55th St; order in advance) and **Shun Lee West** (43 W 65th St)

Chicken, Dijon: **Zabar's** (2245 Broadway)

Chicken dishes: **International Poultry** (983 First Ave)

Chicken, fried: **Beppe** (45 E 22nd St), **Charles' Southern Style Kitchen** (2839 Frederick Douglass Blvd), **Jezebel** (630 Ninth Ave), **Lola** (30 W 22nd St), and **M&G Diner** (383 W 125th St)

Chicken, grilled: **Da Nico** (164 Mulberry St)

Chicken hash: **21 Club** (21 W 52nd St)

Chicken-in-a-pot: **Fine & Schapiro** (138 W 72nd St)

Chicken, Murray's free-roaming: sold in top-quality meat markets all over the city

Chicken, parmesan: **Il Mulino** (86 W 3rd St)

Chicken, roasted: **Mitchell London Foods** (22A E 65th St and 458 Ninth Ave) and **Montrachet** (239 West Broadway)

Chicken salad: **China Grill** (60 W 53rd St) and **Michael's** (24 W 55th St)

Chicken salad, curry or walnut: **Petak's** (1246 Madison Ave)

Chicken, tandoori: **Curry in a Hurry** (119 Lexington Ave)

Chili: **Manhattan Chili Company** (1500 Broadway)

Chinese vegetables: **Kam Man** (200 Canal St)

Chocolate Bruno: **Blue Ribbon** (97 Sullivan St)

Chocolate desserts: **Four Seasons Hotel** (57 E 57th St)

Chocolate eclairs: **Patisserie Claude** (187 W 4th St)

Chocolate, gratin of (seasonal): **Daniel** (60 E 65th St)

Chocolate tasting: **Payard Patisserie** (1032 Lexington Ave)

Chocolate tasting plate: **Gramercy Tavern** (42 E 20th St)

Chocolate truffles: **La Maison du Chocolat** (1018 Madison Ave)

Cholent: **Second Avenue Kosher Delicatessen and Restaurant** (156 Second Ave)

Chops, mutton: **Keens Steakhouse** (72 W 36th St)

Choucroute garnie: **Maureen's Passion** (1200 Lexington Ave)

Clambake: **Clambakes by Jim Sanford** (205 W 95th St; call 212/865-8976)

Clam chowder: **Aquagrill** (210 Spring St)

Clam chowder, Manhattan: **Rosedale Fish and Oyster Market** (1129 Lexington Ave)

Clam chowder, New England: **Pearl Oyster Bar** (18 Cornelia St) and **Wild Tuna** (1081 Third Ave)

Clams: **Umberto's Clam House** (178 Mulberry St)

Clams, baked: **Frank's Trattoria** (371 First Ave)

Cobbler, apple: **Yura** (1645 Third Ave and 1292 Madison Ave)

Cobbler, strawberry rhubarb (seasonal): **Gramercy Tavern** (42 E 20th St)

Cod, roast: **Gramercy Tavern** (42 E 20th St)

Coffee beans: **Porto Rico Importing Company** (201 Bleecker St, 107 Thompson St, and 40½ St. Marks Pl) and **Zabar's** (2245 Broadway)

Coffee, iced: **Oren's Daily Roast** (several locations)

Coffeecake: **Sticky Fingers** (121 First Ave)

Cookies, butter: **CBK of New York** (226 E 83rd St, 212/794-3383; by appointment only)

Cookies, chocolate chip: **Taylor's Prepared Foods** (523 Hudson St, 228 W 18th St, 175 Second Ave, and 156 Chambers St)

Cookies, chocolate chubbie: **Sarabeth's Kitchen** (423 Amsterdam Ave, 1295 Madison Ave, and 945 Madison Ave, at Whitney Museum) and **Sarabeth's Bakery** (75 Ninth Ave)

Cookies, chocolate hazelnut meringue: **De Robertis** (176 First Ave)

Cookies, chocolate turtles: **Yura** (1645 Third Ave and 1292 Madison Ave)

Cookies, fortune (themed): **Gifted Ones** (150 W 10th St)

Cornbread: **Moishe's Bakery** (115 Second Ave) and 107 West (2787 Broadway)

Corn on the cob, cheese-smeared: **Cafe Habana** (17 Prince St)

Corned beef: **Katz's Delicatessen** (205 E Houston St)

Corned beef hash: **Broadway Diner** (590 Lexington Ave) and **Carnegie Delicatessen and Restaurant** (854 Seventh Ave)

Cotton candy: **Four Seasons** (99 E 52nd St)

Couscous (Sunday only): **Provence** (38 MacDougal St)

Crab: **Pisacane Midtown** (940 First Ave)

Crab cakes: **Acme Bar & Grill** (9 Great Jones St) and **Tropica** (MetLife Building, 200 Park Ave)

Crab claws, stone: **Shelly's New York** (104 W 57th St)

Crab, soft shell (seasonal): **New York Noodle Town** (28 Bowery)

Crab spring rolls: **Vong** (200 E 54th St)

Crème brûlée: **Barbetta** (321 W 46th St), **La Métairie** (189 W 10th St), **Le Cirque 2000** (455 Madison Ave), **Lumi** (963 Lexington Ave) and **Tribeca Grill** (375 Greenwich St)

Crepes: **Palacinka** (28 Grand St)

Croissants: **City Bakery** (22 E 17th St), **Fauchon** (442 Park Ave, 1000 Madison Ave, and 1383 Third Ave), **Le Pain Quotidien** (100 Grand St and 1131 Madison Ave), and **Paris Croissant** (1776 Broadway and other locations)

Croissants, almond: **Butterfield Market** (1114 Lexington Ave) and **Marquet Patisserie** (15 E 12th St)

Cupcakes: **Cupcake Cafe** (522 Ninth Ave), **Magnolia Bakery** (401 Bleecker St), **Mitchel London** (22 E 65th St and 458 Ninth Ave), and **Out of the Kitchen** (456 Hudson St)

Curry: **Baluchis** (193 Spring St), **Brick Lane Curry House** (342 E 6th St), and **Tabla** (11 Madison Ave)

Custard, frozen: **Custard Beach** (225 Liberty St, Grand Central Station, lower food court, and 2 World Financial Center)

Danishes: **Chez le Chef** (127 Lexington Ave)

Dates, piggyback: **Pipa** (ABC Carpet & Home, 38 E 19th St)

Delicatessen assortment: **Dean & Deluca** (560 Broadway)

Dessert, all-natural frozen: **PAX Gourmet Deli** (109 E 59th St)

Dessert, chocolatey caramelized brioche cubes with whipped cream (occasional): **Alain Ducasse** (155 W 58th St)

Dessert, frozen low-calorie: **Tasti D-Lite** (1115 Lexington Ave and other locations)

Doughnuts: **Fisher & Levy** (875 Third Ave), **Krispy Kreme** (six locations), and **Rebecca's Bakery** (127 Ave C)

Doughnuts, filled brioche: **Circo Take Out** (120 W 55th St)
Doughnuts, Sally Darr's: **Mitchel London** (22 E 65th St and 458 Ninth Ave)
Doughnuts, whole wheat: **Cupcake Cafe** (522 Ninth Ave)
Duck: **Apple Restaurant** (17 Waverly Pl)
Duck, Beijing: **Shun Lee Palace** (155 E 55th St)
Duck, braised: **Quatorze Bis** (323 E 79th St) and **Tang Pavilion** (65 W 55th St; order in advance)
Duck, Peking: **Home's Kitchen** (22 E 21st St), **Our Place** (1444 Third Ave), **Peking Duck House Restaurant** (28 Mott St), **Shun Lee Palace** (155 E 55th St), and **Shun Lee West** (43 W 65th St)
Duck, roasted: **Four Seasons** (99 E 52nd St)
Dumplings: **Chef Ho Dumpling House** (148 W 49th St), **Chin Chin** (216 E 49th St), **Excellent Dumpling House** (111 Lafayette St), **Joe's Shanghai** (9 Pell St), and **Peking Duck House Restaurant** (28 Mott St)
Dumplings, chicken: **Chiam** (160 E 48th St)
Egg cream: **Carnegie Delicatessen and Restaurant** (854 Seventh Ave), **EJ's Luncheonette** (447 Amsterdam Ave and 1271 Third Ave), and **Tom's Restaurant** (782 Washington Ave, Brooklyn)
Eggs, fresh Jersey: stand at 72 E 7th St (Thurs only: 7 a.m. 5:30 p.m.)
Eggs, Jersey (extra large): stand at 1750 Second Ave
Eggs, Scotch: **Myers of Keswick** (634 Hudson St)
Eggs, soft-boiled: **Le Pain Quotidien** (100 Grand St and 1131 Madison Ave)
Empanadas: **Ruben's** (64 Fulton St, 15 Bridge St, and 505 Broome St)
Escargots: **Avenue** (520 Columbus Ave), **Artisanal** (2 Park Ave), and **Town** (15 W 56th St)
Espresso: **Caffe Dante** (7981 MacDougal St), **Caffe Reggio** (119 McDougal St), and **Chez Laurence Patisserie** (245 Madison Ave)
Fajitas: **Zarela** (953 Second Ave)
Falafel: **Alfanoose** (150 Fulton St), **Moishe's Street Cart** (46th St at Ave of the Americas), **Sahara East** (184 First Ave), and **Pita Cuisine of Soho** (535 Laguardia Pl)
Fish, Chilean sea bass: **Cellini** (65 E 54th St)
Fish, cod (battered): **A Salt and Battery** (112 Greenwich Ave)
Fish, fresh: **Central Fish Company** (527 Ninth Ave) and **Citarella** (1313 Third Ave and 2135 Broadway)
Fish, gefilte: **Citarella** (1313 Third Ave and 2135 Broadway)
Fish, grilled: **Estiatorio Milos** 125 W 55th St)
Fish, grilled mahi-mahi: **American Park** (Battery Park at State St)
Fish (pickled herring): **Sable's Smoked Fish** (1489 Second Ave)
Fish, smoked: **Russ & Daughters** (179 E Houston St) and **Barney Greengrass** (541 Amsterdam Ave)
Fish, sturgeon: **Barney Greengrass** (541 Amsterdam Ave) and **Sable's Smoked Fish** (1489 Second Ave)
Fish, tuna steak: **Gotham Bar & Grill** (12 E 12th St), **Omen** (113 Thompson St) and **Union Square Cafe** (21 E 16th St)
Fish, tuna tartare: **Le Cirque 2000** (455 Madison Ave) and **Tropica** (MetLife Building, 200 Park Ave)
Fish, turbot (seasonal): **Jean Georges** (1 Central Park W) and **Montrachet** (239 West Broadway)
Flatbreads: **Kalustyan's** (123 Lexington Ave)
Foie gras: **Balthazar** (80 Spring St), **Daniel** (60 E 65th St), **Dining Room** (154 E 79th St), **Gascogne** (158 Eighth Ave), **Gramercy Tavern** (42 E 20th St), **La Caravelle** (33 W 55th St), **Le Bernardin** (155 W 51st St),

Le Périgord (405 E 52nd St), **Park Avenue Cafe** (100 E 63rd St), and **Veritas** (43 E 20th St)

Fondue: **La Bonne Soupe** (48 W 55th St)

Food and kitchen equipment (best all-around store in the world): **Zabar's** (2245 Broadway)

"Forbidden Broadway" (awesome sundae!): **Serendipity 3** (225 E 60th St)

French fries: **Atomic Wings** (528 Ninth Ave), **Cafe de Bruxelles** (118 Greenwich Ave), **Cafe de Paris** (924 Second Ave), **Grand Saloon** (158 E 23rd St), **The Harrison** (355 Greenwich St), **Michael's** (24 W 55th St), **Petite Abeille** (466 Hudson St), **Pfiff** (35 Grand St), and **Steak Frites** (9 E 16th St)

Fries, Belgian: **B. Frites** (1657 Broadway) and **Le Frite Kot** (148 W 4th St)

Fries, steak: **Balthazar** (80 Spring St) and **Montparnasse** (230 E 51st St)

Fries, Tuscan: **Coco Pazzo** (Paramount Hotel, 23 E 74th St)

Frites (French fries with mayonnaise): **B. Frites** (1657 Broadway), **Le Frite Kot** (148 W 4th St), and **Pommes Frites** (123 Second Ave)

Fruits and grains: **Nature's Gifts** (1297 Lexington Ave and 320 E 86th St)

Fruits and vegetables: **Fairway** (2127 Broadway) and **Balducci's** (155-A W 66th St)

Fruit dessert plate: **Primavera** (1578 First Ave)

Game: **Ottomanelli's Meat Market** (285 Bleecker St) and **Da Umberto** (107 W 17th St)

Gateau Charlene Blanche: **Patisserie J. Lanciani** (414 W 14th St)

Gelati: **Caffe Dante** (81 MacDougal St)

Gelato, homemade: **Fiamma Osteria** (206 Spring St)

Gingerbread house (one week notice): **Chez le Chef** (127 Lexington Ave)

Goat, roast baby: **Primavera** (1578 First Ave)

Goulash: **Mocca Hungarian** (1588 Second Ave)

Gourmet food: **Citarella** (1313 Third Ave and 2135 Broadway) and **Grace's Marketplace** (1237 Third Ave)

Groceries, discount: **Gourmet Garage** (453 Broome St, 301 E 64th St, 2567 Broadway, and 117 Seventh Ave S)

Guacamole: **Manhattan Chili Company** (1500 Broadway) and **Rosa Mexicano** (1063 First Ave)

Haggis (Scottish for sheep innards): **St. Andrews** (120 W 44th St)

Halibut, steamed: **Le Bernardin** (155 W 51st St)

Hamburgers: **Corner Bistro** (331 W 4th St), **Hamburger Harry's** (145 W 45th St), **Jackson Hole Burgers** (232 E 64th St , 1270 Madison Ave, 1611 Second Ave, 517 Columbia Ave, and 521 Third Ave), and **Tabla** (11 Madison Ave; occasional)

Hamburgers, roquefort: **Burger Heaven** (9 E 53rd St)

Hen, Cornish: **Lorenzo and Maria's Kitchen** (1418 Third Ave)

Herbs and spices: **Adriana's Caravan** (Grand Central Station)

Heros: **Hero Boy** (492 Ninth Ave) and **Italian Food Center** (186 Grand St)

Heros, sausage: **Manganaro Grosseria Italiana** (488 Ninth Ave)

Hot chocolate: **City Bakery** (22 E 17th St) and **Lunettes et Chocolat** (25 Prince St)

Hot dogs: **Brooklyn Diner USA** (212 W 57th St), **Crif Dogs** (113 St. Marks Pl), **Dawgs on Park** (178 E 7th St), **F&B** (269 W 23rd St), **Gray's Papaya** (402 Ave of the Americas, 539 Eighth Ave, and 2090 Broadway), **Old Town Bar** (45 E 18th St), and **Papaya King** (179 E 86th St)

Huitlacoche (Mexican specialty): **Rosa Mexicano** (1063 First Ave and 61 Columbus Ave)

Hummus, best: **Hoomoos Asli** (100 Kenmare St)
Ice cream: **Ciao Bella Cafe** (27 E 92nd St), **Emack & Bolio's** (389 Amsterdam Ave, 56 Seventh Ave, and 151 W 34th St, Macy's Herald Square), **Petrossian Cafe and Boutique** (911 Seventh Ave), **Petrossian Restaurant** (182 W 58th St), and **Serendipity 3** (225 E 60th St)
Ice cream, caramel (occasional): **Gramercy Tavern** (42 E 20th St)
Ice cream, nougatine (by request): **Payard Patisserie** (1032 Lexington Ave)
Ice cream soda, Jack Daniel's: **Judson Grill** (152 W 52nd St; by request)
Ice cream sundae: **Brooklyn Diner USA** (212 W 57th St)
Jambalaya: **107 West** (2787 Broadway)
Juice, fresh-squeezed: **Candle Cafe** (1307 Third Ave) and **Good Health Cafe** (324 E 86th St)
Kebabs: **Turkish Cuisine** (631 Ninth Ave) and **Turkish Kitchen** (386 Third Ave)
Kielbasa: **First Avenue Meat Products** (140 First Ave)
Kielbasa spring roll: **Pat Pong** (93 E 7th St)
Knishes: **Murray's Sturgeon Shop** (2429 Broadway)
Lamb, rack of: **Cafe des Artistes** (1 W 67th St) and **Gotham Bar and Grill** (12 E 12th St)
Lamb shank: **Bolo** (23 E 22nd St), **Lawrence Scott** (1363 First Ave), **Molyvos** (871 Seventh Ave), and **Park Bistro** (414 Park Ave S; occasional)
Lamb stew: **Bouterin** (420 E 59th St) and **Pamir** (1437 Second Ave)
Lasagna: **Noie Italian Bistro** (271 Bleecker St) and **Via Emilia** (240 Park Ave S)
Latino hot drinks: **Mosaico** (175 Madison Ave)
Latkes: **Just Like Mother's** (11060 Queens Blvd, Forest Hills, Queens)
Lemonade: **Hadom** (137 Seventh Ave S), **Lexington Candy Shop** (1226 Lexington Ave), and **Pyramida** (401 E 78th St)
Liver, chopped: **Fischer Brothers** (230 W 72nd St) and **Second Avenue Kosher Delicatessen and Restaurant** (156 Second Ave)
Lobster: **Docks Oyster Bar and Seafood Grill** (2427 Broadway and 633 Third Ave)
Lobster bisque (catering): **Neuman & Bogdonoff** (212/228-2444; by request)
Lobster, live: **Blue Ribbon Sushi** (119 Sullivan St)
Lobster roll: **Pearl Oyster Bar** (18 Cornelia St)
Macaroni and cheese: **Shelly's New York** (104 W 57th St)
Marinara sauce: **Patsy's** (236 W 56th St)
Meat (best prices): **Empire Purveyors** (901 First Ave)
Meat (best service): **H. Oppenheimer Meats** (2606 Broadway) and **Jefferson Market** (450 Ave of the Americas)
Meat (cold-cut selection): **Schaller and Weber** (1654 Second Ave)
Meat (German deli): **Schaller and Weber** (1654 Second Ave)
Meat (grill-ready): **Les Halles** (411 Park Ave S)
Meat (prime): **Jefferson Market** (450 Ave of the Americas)
Meatballs: **Il Gattopardo** (33 W 54th St)
Meatloaf: **Ouest** (2315 Broadway)
Meats and poultry (reasonably priced): **Empire Purveyors** (901 First Ave)
Mexican foodstuffs: **Kitchen Market** (218 Eighth Ave)
Meze (Turkish tapas-like appetizer): **Beyoglu** (1431 Third Ave)
Milkshake: **Comfort Diner** (214 E 45th St)
Moussaka: **Periyali** (35 W 20th St)
Mousse, chocolate (the best!): **Bistro Margot** (26 Prince St)

Mousse, white chocolate, in a bittersweet chocolate basket: **Manhattan Ocean Club** (57 W 58th St)

Mozzarella and ricotta: **Russo and Son** (344 E 11th St)

Mozzarella, smoked: **Joe's Dairy** (156 Sullivan St)

Muffins: **Between the Bread** (145 W 55th St), **Manhattan Muffins** (11 John St), **Muffins & More** (114 Fourth Ave), and **Muffins Cafe** (22 Columbus Ave)

Muffins, corn: **107 West** (2787 Broadway)

Muffins, pear-walnut: **Soutine Bakery** (104 W 70th St)

Mushrooms, grilled portobello: **Giovanni 25** (25 E 83rd St)

Mushrooms, wild: **Grace's Marketplace** (1237 Third Ave)

Mussels: **Jubilee** (347 E 54th St) and **Markt** (401 W 14th St)

Nachos: **Benny's Burritos** (93 Ave A and 113 Greenwich Ave)

Napoleon: **Ecco** (124 Chambers St)

Natural foods: **Whole Food** (2421 Broadway)

Noodles: **Honmura An** (170 Mercer St) and **Sammy's Noodle Shop & Grill** (453 Ave of the Americas)

Noodles, Asian: **Republic** (37 Union Sq W)

Noodles, cold with hot sesame sauce: **Sung Chu Mei** (615 Hudson St)

Noodles, green tea: **Ten Ren's Tea Time** (79 Mott St)

Noodles, Shanghai-style: **Shun Lee Palace** (155 E 55th St)

Nuts: **A. L. Bazzini Co.** (339 Greenwich St)

Oatmeal: **Sarabeth's Kitchen** (1295 Madison Ave, 423 Amsterdam Ave, and 945 Madison Ave, at Whitney Museum)

Olive oils: **Oliviers & Co.** (249 Bleecker St)

Olives: **International Grocery** (543 Ninth Ave)

Onion rings: **Cornerstone Grill** (327 Greenwich St), **Home Restaurant** (20 Cornelia St), **Lola** (30 W 2nd St), **Palm One** (837 Second Ave), **Palm Too** (840 Second Ave), and **Palm West Side** (250 W 50th St)

Organic foods: **Angelica's** (147 First Ave) and **Urban Organics** (718/499-4321)

Oyster stew: **Grand Central Oyster Bar Restaurant** (Grand Central Station)

Oysters: **Cafe des Artistes** (1 W 67th St)

Oysters Rockefeller (occasional): **City Hall** (131 Duane St)

Paella: **Bolo** (23 E 22nd St) and **Sevilla** (62 Charles St)

Panna cotta (dessert, occasional): **Gramercy Tavern** (42 E 20th St)

Pancakes: **Friend of a Farmer** (77 Irving Pl) and **Vinegar Factory** (431 E 91st St; Sunday brunch)

Pancakes, blue corn: **Mesa Grill** (102 Fifth Ave)

Pancakes, Dutch: **NL** (169 Sullivan St)

Pancakes, kimchi: **Dok Suni's** (119 First Ave)

Pancakes, potato: **Rolf's** (281 Third Ave)

Pancakes, raspberry: **Veselka** (144 Second Ave)

Panini: **Bar Veloce** (17 Cleveland Pl) and **Ino** (21 Bedford St)

Panino: **San Domenico** (240 Central Park S)

Pasta: **Arqua** (281 Church St), **Artusi** (36 W 52nd St), **Bottino** (246 Tenth Ave), **Cafe Pertutti** (2888 Broadway), **Caffe Buon Gusto** (236 E 77th St), **Cinque Terre** (22 E 38th St), **Col Legno** (231 E 9th St), **Fresco by Scotto** (34 E 52nd St), **Gabriel's** (11 W 60th St), **Il Valentino** (330 E 56th

St), **Paola's** (245 E 84th St), **Pinocchio** (1748 First Ave), and **Todaro Bros.** (555 Second Ave)

Pasta (inexpensive): **La Marca** (161 E 22nd St)

Pasta, angel hair: **Piemonte Homemade Ravioli Company** (190 Grand St) and **Nanni's** (146 E 46th St)

Pasta, fresh: **Teodora** (141 E 57th St)

Pasta, handmade egg: **Balducci's** (155-A W 66th St)

Pasta, Venetian: **Remi** (145 W 53rd St)

Pastrami: **Artie's** (2290 Broadway), **Carnegie Delicatessen and Restaurant** (854 Seventh Ave), and **Katz's Delicatessen** (205 E Houston St)

Pastrami, salmon: **Park Avenue Cafe** (100 E 63rd St)

Pastries: **Bleecker Street Pastry** (245 Bleecker St)

Pastries, charlotte russe (weekends): **Jon Vie Pastries** (492 Ave of the Americas)

Pastries, French: **La Bergamote** (169 Ninth Ave)

Pastries, Hungarian: **Hungarian Pastry Shop** (1030 Amsterdam Ave)

Pastries, Italian: **LaBella Ferrara Pastry & Caffe** (108-110 Mulberry St) and **Rocco Pastry Shop** (243 Bleecker St)

Pastries, Japanese traditional: **Minamoto Kitchoan** (608 Fifth Ave)

Paté: **Zabar's** (2245 Broadway)

Peanut butter: **Peanut Butter & Co.** (240 Sullivan St)

Penne with prosciutto: **Petak's** (1246 Madison Ave)

Petit fours: **Sea Grill** (19 W 49th St)

Pickles: **Pickle Guys** (49 Essex St)

Pickles, sour or half-sour: **Guss' Pickles** (85-86 Orchard St) and **Russ & Daughters** (179 E Houston St)

Pie, apple: **William Greenberg Jr. Desserts** (1100 Madison Ave) and **Yura** (1645 Third Ave and 1292 Madison Ave)

Pie, apple crumb: **Cupcake Cafe** (522 Ninth Ave)

Pie, banana cream: **Sarabeth's Kitchen** (423 Amsterdam Ave, 1295 Madison Ave, and 945 Madison Ave, at Whitney Museum)

Pie, cheddar-crust apple (autumn only): **Little Pie Company** (424 W 43rd St)

Pie, cherry crumb (summer only): **Magnolia Bakery** (401 Bleecker St)

Pie, duck shepherd's: **Balthazar** (80 Spring St)

Pie, key lime: **Little Pie Company** (424 W 43rd St) and **Union Square Cafe** (21 E 16th St; occasional)

Pie, pecan: **Magnolia Bakery** (401 Bleecker St)

Pie, shepherd's: **Landmark Tavern** (626 Eleventh Ave)

Pie, walnut sour-cream apple: **Little Pie Company** (424 W 43rd St)

Pies: **Anglers & Writers** (420 Hudson St) and **E.A.T.** (1064 Madison Ave)

Pig's feet (occasional): **Cafe Boulud** (20 E 76th St) and **Daniel** (60 E 65th St)

Pizza and calzone: **House of Pizza and Calzone** (132 Union St, Brooklyn) and **Lombardi's** (32 Spring St)

Pizza by the slice: **Pizza 33** (201 E 33rd St)

Pizza, designer: **Paper Moon Milano** (39 E 58th St)

Pizza, gourmet: **Apizz** (217 Eldridge St)

Pizza, grilled: **Gonzo** (140 W 13th St)

Pizza, Neapolitan: **Sal's and Carmine's Pizza** (2671 Broadway) and **Stromboli Pizzeria** (112 University Pl)

Pizza, Sicilian: **Sal's and Carmine's Pizza** (2671 Broadway)

Popovers: **Popover Cafe** (551 Amsterdam Ave)
Pork: **H. Oppenheimer Meats** (2606 Broadway)
Pork, braised: **Daniel** (60 E 65th St)
Pork, European-style cured: **Salumeria Biellese** (378 Eighth Ave)
Pork and chicken buns: **Lung Moon Bakery** (83 Mulberry St)
Pork chops, smoked: **Yorkville Packing House** (1560 Second Ave)
Pork shank: **Maloney & Porcelli's** (37 E 50th St)
Pot de crème: **Verbena** (54 Irving Pl)
Potato chips: **Vinegar Factory** (431 E 91st St)
Potatoes, huge stuffed baked: **Citarella** (1313 Third Ave and 2135 Broadway)
Potatoes, mashed: **Mama's Food Shop** (200 E 3rd St) and **Union Square Cafe** (21 E 16th St)
Pot-au-feu: **Cafe des Artistes** (1 W 67th St), **Le Bernardin** (155 W 51st St), and **Le Cirque 2000** (455 Madison Ave)
Pretzels and cookies, hand-dipped chocolate: **Evelyn's Chocolates** (4 John St)
Pretzels, Martin's: **Greenmarket** locations
Prime rib: **Fresco by Scotto** (34 E 52nd St) and **Smith & Wollensky** (201 E 49th St)
Produce, fresh: **Fairway Market** (2127 Broadway)
Profiteroles (24 hours notice): **Chez Ma Tante** (189 W 10th St)
Pudding, rice: **D'Artagnan, Marti Kebab** (238 E 24th St), **Rice to Riches** (37 Spring St), and **The Rotisserie** (152 E 46th St)
Quenelles: **La Caravelle** (33 W 55th St) and **Payard Patisserie** (1032 Lexington Ave)
Quiche: **Chez Laurence Patisserie** (245 Madison Ave)
Ravioli: **Di Palo Fine Food** (206 Grand St), **Osteria del Circo** (120 W 55th St), **Piemonte Homemade Ravioli Company** (190 Grand St), and **Ravioli Store** (75 Sullivan St)
Ravioli, steamed Vietnamese: **Indochine** (430 Lafayette St)
Rib chop: **Baldoria's** (249 W 49th St)
Ribs: **Brother Jimmy's Bar-B-Q** (1485 Second Ave), **Hog Pit** (22 Ninth Ave), **Sylvia's Restaurant** (328 Lenox Ave), and **Tennessee Mountain** (143 Spring St)
Ribs, baby back: **Baby Buddha** (753 Washington St), **Emily's** (1325 Fifth Ave), **Mesa Grill** (102 Fifth Ave), and **Ruby Foo's** (1626 Broadway and 2182 Broadway)
Ribs, braised, short, beef: **Daniel** (60 E 65th St) and **Deborah** (43 Carmine St)
Rice: **Rice** (227 Mott St)
Rice, fried: **Ollie's** (1991 Broadway)
Rice, sticky, with mango: **Vong** (200 E 54th St)
Risotto: **Four Seasons** (99 E 52nd St) and **Risotteria** (270 Bleecker St)
Rugelach: **Margaret Palca Bakes** (191 Columbia St, Brooklyn) and **Ruthy's Cheesecake and Rugelach Bakery** (75 Ninth Ave)
Salad bar: **Azure** (830 Third Ave) and **City Bakery** (22 E 17th St)
Salad, Caesar: **Pearl Oyster Bar** (18 Cornelia St) and **Post House** (28 E 63rd St)
Salad, egg: **Murray's Sturgeon Shop** (2429 Broadway)
Salad, lobster: **Sable's Smoked Fish** (1489 Second Ave)
Salad, seafood: **Gotham Bar & Grill** (12 E 12th St)

Salad, tuna: **Cosi Sandwich Bar** (numerous locations), **Murray's Sturgeon Shop** (2429 Broadway), and **Todaro Bros.** (555 Second Ave)

Salad, warm white bean: **Caffe Grazie** (26 E 84th St)

Salad, whitefish: **Barney Greengrass** (541 Amsterdam Ave)

Salmon filets, Norwegian: **Sea Breeze** (541 Ninth Ave)

Salmon, smoked: **Aquavit** (13 W 54th St), **Murray's Sturgeon Shop** (2429 Broadway), and **Sable's** (1489 Second Ave)

Salmon, truffle-crusted: **Montrachet** (239 West Broadway)

Sandwich, avocado: **Olive's** (120 Prince St)

Sandwich, bacon, lettuce & tomato: **Eisenberg's Sandwich Shop** (174 Fifth Ave) and **Good** (89 Greenwich Ave; summer only)

Sandwich, beef brisket: **Second Avenue Kosher Delicatessen and Restaurant** (156 Second Ave) and **Smith's Bar & Restaurant** (701 Eighth Ave)

Sandwich, cheese-steak: **BB Sandwich Bar** (120 W 3rd St)

Sandwich, chicken: **Ranch 1** (62 Pearl St and other locations)

Sandwich, croque monsieur: **Payard Patisserie** (1032 Lexington Ave)

Sandwich, flatbread: **Cosi Sandwich Bar** (numerous locations)

Sandwich, French dip: **Sandwich Planet** (534 Ninth Ave)

Sandwich, grilled cheese: **Grilled Cheese** (168 Ludlow St)

Sandwich, grilled chicken breast: **Ranch 1** (62 Pearl St and other locations)

Sandwich, grilled portobello: **Zoë** (90 Prince St)

Sandwich, loin of pork: **Bottino** (246 Tenth Ave)

Sandwich, pastrami on rye: **Katz's Delicatessen** (205 E Houston St)

Sandwich, pig (pulled pork): **Hard Rock Cafe** (221 W 57th St)

Sandwich, po'boy: **Two Boots** (37 Ave A and other locations)

Sandwich, *poulet roti* (roast chicken): **Chez Brigitte** (77 Greenwich Ave)

Sandwich, turkey: **Viand Coffee Shop** (1011 Madison Ave)

Sandwich wraps: **Emerald Planet** (2 Great Jones St)

Sandwiches (125 kinds): **Call Cuisine** (1032 First Ave)

Sardines, marinated (occasional): **Oceana** (55 E 54th St)

Satays: **Typhoon Brewery** (22 E 54th St)

Sauerkraut: **Katz's Delicatessen** (205 E Houston St)

Sausage, East European: **Kurowycky Meat Products** (124 First Ave)

Sausage, Italian: **Corona Heights Pork Store** (10704 Corona Ave, Queens)

Sausages, freshly made (over 40 kinds): **Salumeria Biellesse** (376 Eighth Ave; selection varies daily)

Scallops: **Le Bernardin** (155 W 51st St)

Schnecken: **William Greenberg Jr. Desserts** (1100 Madison Ave)

Scones: **Mangia** (50 W 57th St), **Muffin Shop** (222 Columbus Ave), and **Tea and Sympathy** (108-110 Greenwich Ave)

Sea bass, Chilean: **Cellini** (65 E 54th St)

Seafood dinners: **Le Bernardin** (155 W 51st St) and **Le Pescadou** (18 King St)

Shrimp Creole: **Jezebel** (630 Ninth Ave)

Shrimp, grilled: **Periyali** (35 W 20th St)

Sliders (mini burgers): **Sassy's Sliders** (1530 Third Ave)

Snacks, soups, and sandwiches: **Serendipity 3** (225 E 60th St)

Sorbet: **Atelier** (50 Central Park S), **AZ** (21 W 17th St), **Ciao Bella** (227 Sullivan St), **La Boite en Bois** (75 W 68th St), and **La Maison du Chocolat** (1018 Madison Ave; summer only)

Soufflé: **Capsouto Frères** (451 Washington St), **La Caravelle** (33 W 55th St), and **La Côte Basque** (60 W 55th St)

Souffé, chocolate: **Jean Georges** (1 Central Park W)

Soufflé, chocolate: **La Caravelle** (33 W 55th St)

Soufflé, Grand Marnier: **La Caravelle** (33 W 55th St) and **La Grenouille** (3 E 52nd St)

Soufflé, lime: **Gramercy Tavern** (42 E 20th St)

Soup, black bean: **Union Square Cafe** (21 E 16th St)

Soup, Charleston she-crab soup: **Gage and Tollner** (372 Fulton St, Brooklyn)

Soup, chestnut and fennel (seasonal and by request): **Picholine** (35 W 64th St)

Soup, chestnut with mushroom ravioli (seasonal): **Jean Georges** (1 Central Park W)

Soup, chicken: **Brooklyn Diner USA** (212 W 57th St), **Bubby's** (120 Hudson St), **Pastrami Queen** (1269 Lexington Ave), **Second Avenue Kosher Delicatessen and Restaurant** (156 Second Ave), and **Teresa's** (103 First Ave)

Soup, Chinese: **Chao Chow** (111 Mott St)

Soup, duck: **Kelley and Ping** (127 Greene St)

Soup, French onion: **La Bonne Soupe** (48 W 55th St) and **Le Singe Vert** (160 Seventh Ave)

Soup, hot and sour: **Shun Lee Cafe** (43 W 65th St)

Soup, hot yogurt: **Beyoglu** (1431 Third Ave)

Soup, kimchi chigae (spicy stew with beef, tofu, and pork): **Do Hwa** (55 Carmine St)

Soup, matzoh ball: **Inside** (9 Jones St) and **Second Avenue Kosher Delicatessen and Restaurant** (156 Second Ave)

Soup, minestrone: **Il Vagabondo** (351 E 62nd St) and **Trattoria Spaghetto** (232 Bleecker St)

Soup, noodle: **New Chao Chow** (111 Mott St)

Soup, pumpkin (seasonal): **Mesa Grill** (102 Fifth Ave)

Soup, raison d être: **Shopsin's General Store** (54 Carmine St)

Soup, split pea: **Cafe Edison** (228 W 47th St) and **Joe Jr.** (482 E 6th St and 167 Third Ave)

Soup, tomato: **Sarabeth's Kitchen** (423 Amsterdam Ave, 1295 Madison Ave, and 945 Madison Ave, at Whitney Museum)

Soup, white borscht (weekends): **Teresa's** (80 Montague St, Brooklyn)

Soybeans: **Soy** (102 Suffolk St)

Spaghetti: **Paolucci** (149 Mulberry St)

Spareribs, Chinese: **Fu's** (972 Second Ave) and **66** (241 Church St)

Spices: **Aphrodisia** (264 Bleecker St), **International Grocery** (543 Ninth Ave), and **Kalustyan's** (123 Lexington Ave)

Spinach pies, Greek: **Poseidon Bakery** (629 Ninth Ave)

Spring rolls, crab: **Vong** (200 E 54th St)

Squab, roasted stuffed: **Daniel** (60 E 65th St)

Squid, grilled stuffed: **I Trulli** (122 E 27th St)

Steak, Black Angus, and French fries: **Steak Frites** (9 E 16th St)

Steak, Cajun rib: **Morton's of Chicago** (551 Fifth Ave) and **Post House** (28 E 63rd St)

Steak frites: **Balthazar** (80 Spring St) and **Montparnasse** (230 E 51st St)

Steak, grilled ribeye: **Restaurant Charlotte** (145 W 44th St)

Steak, hanger: **Pastis** (9 Ninth Ave)

Steak, pepper: **Chez Josephine** (414 W 42nd St)

Steak, Porterhouse: **Manhattan Grille** (1161 First Ave), **Morton's of Chicago** (551 Fifth Ave), and **Porters New York** (216 Seventh Ave)

Steak tartare: **21 Club** (21 W 52nd St)

String beans, Chinese-style: **Tang Tang** (1328 Third Ave)

Strudel: **Mocca Hungarian** (1588 Second Ave)

Sundae, chocolate chip: **Washington Park** (24 Fifth Ave)

Sushi: **Avenue A Sushi** (103 Ave A), **Hatsuhana** (17 E 48th St), **Iso** (175 Second Ave), **Kuruma Zushi** (7 E 47th St, 2nd floor), **Nippon** (155 E 52nd St), **Sushihatsu** (1143 First Ave), **Takahachi** (85 Ave A), and **Ten Kai** (20 W 56th St)

Sushi, *omakase* ("astonish me"): **Taka** (61 Grove St)

Sweetbreads: **Metisse** (239 W 105th St)

Swordfish, charbroiled: **Morton's of Chicago** (551 Fifth Ave)

Tacos: **Gabriela's** (685 Amsterdam Ave), **Maya** (1191 First Ave), **Mexicana Mama** (525 Hudson St), and **Rosa Mexicano** (1063 First Ave and 61 Columbus Ave)

Tamales: **Rosa Mexicano** (1063 First Ave and 61 Columbus Ave) and **Zarela** (953 Second Ave)

Tapas: **Azafran** (77 Warren St), **Bolo** (23 E 22nd St), **El Cid** (322 W 15th St), **Il Buco** (47 Bond St), **ñ** (33 Crosby St), **Oliva** (161 E Houston St), **Pipa** (ABC Carpet & Home, 38 E 19th St), **Solera** (216 E 53rd St), and **Xunta** (174 First Ave)

Tart, apple: **Gotham Bar & Grill** (12 E 12th St), **Marquet Patisserie** (15 E 12th St), and **Quatorze Bis** (323 E 79th St)

Tart, chocolate: **Le Bernardin** (155 W 51st St)

Tart, fruit: **CeciCela** (55 Spring St) and **Payard Patisserie** (1032 Lexington Ave)

Tart, fruit and vegetable: **Once Upon a Tart** (135 Sullivan St)

Tart, lemon: **Margot Patisserie** (2109 Broadway)

Tart, mango: **Gotham Bar & Grill** (12 E 12th St)

Tart, peanut butter: **Marseille** (630 Ninth Ave)

Tartufo: **Erminia** (250 E 83rd St), **Il Corallo** (172-176 Prince St), **Il Vagabondo** (351 E 62nd St), **Manhattan Grille** (1161 First Ave), and **Sette Mezzo** (969 Lexington Ave)

Tempura: **Inagiku** (Waldorf-Astoria Hotel, 111 E 49th St)

Tequila: **Dos Caminos** (373 Park Ave S)

Tiramisu: **Biricchino** (260 W 29th St), **Caffe Dante** (79 MacDougal St), **Mezzogiorno** (195 Spring St), and **Torre di Pisa** (19 W 44th St)

Tong shui (Chinese soup): **Sweet-n-Tart Cafe** (76 Mott St)

Tonkatsu: **Katsuhama** (11 E 47th St)

Torte, sacher: **Bruno Bakery** (245 Bleecker St) and **Duane Park Patisserie** (179 Duane St)

Tripe *alla parmigiana:* **Babbo** (110 Waverly Pl)

Truffles: **Black Hound** (170 Second Ave), **La Maison du Chocolat** (25 E 73rd St), and **Teuscher Chocolates** (620 Fifth Ave and 25 E 61st St)

Turkey, fresh-roasted (Tuesday and Friday): **M&O Market** (124 Thompson St)

Veal chops: **Aperitivo** (29 W 56th St) and **Daniel** (60 E 65th St)

Veal stew (occasional): **Pierre au Tunnel** (250 W 47th St)

Vegan foods: **Whole Earth Bakery & Kitchen** (130 St. Marks Pl)

Vegetable terrine: **Montrachet** (239 West Broadway)
Vegetables, raw: **Estiatorio Milos** (125 W 55th St)
Vegetarian combo: **Hudson Falafel** (516 Hudson St)
Vegetarian items: **Vegetarian's Paradise** (144 W 4th St)
Vegetarian meals: **Natural Gourmet Cookery School** (48 W 21st St)
Venison (seasonal): **Chanterelle** (2 Harrison St)
Waffles, Belgian: **Le Pain Quotidien** (1131 Madison Ave), **Petite Abeille**
    (107 W 18th St), and **Cafe de Bruxelles** (118 Greenwich Ave)
Waffles, pumpkin: **Sarabeth's Kitchen** (1295 Madison Ave, 423 Amsterdam
    Ave, and 945 Madison Ave, at Whitney Museum)
Wagashi (gelatinous sweet confection): **Minimoto Kitchoan** (608 Fifth Ave)
Whiskeys, malt: **SoHo Wines & Spirits** (461 West Broadway)
Wine, French: **Park Avenue Liquors** (292 Madison Ave) and **Quality House**
    (2 Park Ave)
Wine, German: **First Avenue Wines & Spirits** (383 First Ave)
Zabaglione: **Il Monello** (1460 Second Ave)

Bagels

Absolute Bagels (2788 Broadway)
Bagel City (720 W 181st St)
Bagel Works (1229 First Ave)
Bagel Zone (50 Ave A)
Bagelry (1324 Lexington Ave, 1380 Madison Ave, and 1228 Lexington Ave)
Columbia Hot Bagels (2836 Broadway)
Ess-A-Bagel (359 First Ave and 831 Third Ave)
H&H Bagels (2239 Broadway and 639 W 46th St)
H&H Midtown Bagels East (1551 Second Ave)
Hot Bagels (168 Madison Ave)
Lenny's (2601 Broadway)
Mom's Catering (15 W 45th St)
Murray's Bagels (500 Ave of the Americas)
Pick-a-Bagel (1083 Lexington Ave)

Barbecues

Big Wong (67 Mott St): Chinese style
Biscuit BBQ Joint (367 Flatbush Ave, Brooklyn)
Blue Smoke (116 E 27th St): Danny Meyer does it again!
Brother Jimmy's (428 Amsterdam Ave): ribs, sandwiches, good sauce
Brothers Bar-B-Q (228 W Houston St): smoked ribs
Copeland's (547 W 145th St): Harlem setting
Daily Chow (2 E Second Ave): Mongolian
Dallas BBQ (1265 Third Ave, 27 W 72nd St, 21 University Pl, and 132
    Second Ave): big and busy, but only fair in quality
Pearson's Texas BBQ (71-04 35th Ave, Queens)
Shun Lee Cafe (43 W 5th St): classy Chinese
Sylvia's (328 Lenox Ave): reputation better than the food
Virgil's Real Barbecue (152 W 44th St): big, brassy, mass-production
Woo Chon (8-10 W 36th St): Korea

Breakfast

For the real morning meal power scenes, hotels are the preferred locations. The biggest names are:

Four Seasons, Fifty Seven Fifty Seven (57 E 57th St): excellent pancakes
Paramount (235 W 46th St)
Peninsula New York (700 Fifth Ave)
Regency (540 Park Ave)
Royalton (44W 44th St)

Other places with excellent day-starters:

Balthazar (80 Spring St)
Brasserie (100 E 53rd St)
Bright Food Shop (216 Eighth Ave)
Bubby's (120 Hudson St)
Bulgin' Waffles (49 /2 First Ave)
Cafe Botanica (Essex House, a Westin Hotel, 160 Central Park S)
Cafe Word of Mouth (1012 Lexington Ave)
Carnegie Delicatessen and Restaurant (854 Seventh Ave): The cheese
   blintzes only have a half-million calories.
City Bakery (3 W 18th St)
Columbus Bakery (474 Columbus Ave): sinful cheese Danishes and yummy
   croissants
Comfort Diner (214 E 45th St)
Cucina & Co. (MetLife Building, 200 Park Ave): commuter convenient
District (Muse Hotel, 130 W 46th St)
E.A.T. (1064 Madison Ave): breads are great (and expensive)
EJ's Luncheonette (447 Amsterdam Ave)
Ellen's Stardust Diner (1377 Ave of the Americas)
Fairway (2127 Broadway): fresh-tasting food in sizable portions
Fitzer's (Fitzpatrick Manhattan Hotel, 687 Lexington Ave): Irish breakfast
14 Wall Street Restaurant (14 Wall St):
Friend of a Farmer (77 Irving Pl): late pancake feast
Heartbeat (W New York Hotel, 149 E 49th St): breakfast for "well-being"
Home (20 Cornelia St): Greenwich Village
Jerry's (101 Prince St)
Kitchen/Market (218 Eighth Ave): south of the border
Kitchenette (80 West Broadway)
Lunchbox Food Company (357 West St)
Michael's (24 W 55th St)
Nadine's (99 Bank St)
Noho Star (330 Lafayette St)
Old John's (251 W 50th St): Lincoln Center area
Once Upon a Tart (135 Sullivan St)
One C.P.S. (Plaza Hotel, 1 Central Park S)
Pastis (9 Ninth Ave): haven for weekday breakfasts in the Meatpacking
   District
Payard Bistro (1032 Lexington Ave)
Pink Tea Cup (42 Grove St): country breakfasts
Popover Cafe (551 Amsterdam Ave)
Sarabeth's Kitchen (423 Amsterdam Ave, 1295 Madison Ave, and 945
   Madison Ave, at Whitney Museum)
Serafina (38 E 58th St): great egg dishes
Terrance Brennan's Seafood & Chop House (125 E 50th St)
Tivoli (515 Third Ave)
Tramway Coffee Shop (1143 Second Ave)

Veselka (144 Second Ave)
Viand (300 E 86th St, 673 Madison Ave, and 1011 Madison Ave): crowded, great value
Vietnam Banh Mi So 1 (369 Broome St)

If you are really hungry and price is no object, then head to **Norma's** in Le Parker Meridien Hotel (118 W 57th St) for all-day breakfast fare. What a choice: blueberry pancakes, molten chocolate French toast, red berry risotto oatmeal, buttermilk biscuits, seared rock lobster and asparagus omelet, mango-papaya brown-butter cinnamon crepes, smoothies, and much more. What a way to start the day!

Brunch

Annie's (1381 Third Ave)
Aquagrill (210 Spring St)
Balthazar (80 Spring St)
Blue Ribbon Bakery (33 Downing St)
Cafe Botanica (Essex House, a Westin Hotel, 160 Central Park S)
Cafe des Artistes (1 W 67th St): classy ambience and food
Cafe Habana (17 Prince St)
Cafe Luluc (214 Smith St, Brooklyn)
Cafe Habana (17 Prince St)
Capsouto Frères (451 Washington St)
Cendrillon (45 Mercer St): Filipino flavors
Chelsea Bistro & Bar (358 W 23rd St)
Church Lounge (2 Ave of the Americas)
Crystal Fountain (Grand Hyatt Hotel, Park Ave at Grand Central Station)
Cupping Room Cafe (359 West Broadway)
Danal (90 E 10th St): luscious French toast
Eighteenth & Eighth (159 Eighth Ave)
Eleven Madison Park (11 Madison Ave)
Emily's (1325 Fifth Ave): soul food
Five Points (31 Great Jones St)
Florent (69 Gansevoort St)
Friend of a Farmer (77 Irving Pl)
Good (89 Greenwich Ave)
Good Enough to Eat (483 Amsterdam Ave)
Grace's Trattoria (201 E 71st St): homey eatery inside Grace's Marketplace
Grill on the Park (101 W 57th St)
Iridium (44 W 63rd St): live gospel music
Lobster Club (24 E 80th St)
Mark's Restaurant (25 E 77th St): classy
Miss Elle's Homesick Bar and Grill (226 W 79th St)
Nadine's (99 Bank St)
Odeon (145 West Broadway)
Olive's (W New York Hotel, 201 Park Ave S)
Paris Commune (411 Bleecker St): Bohemian West Village bistro
Park Avenue Cafe (100 E 63rd St): American dim sum, Saturday only
Pig'n Whistle (922 Third Ave): traditional Irish breakfast, too
Provence (28 MacDougal St)

Prune's (54 E 1st St): inspired weekend brunch
River Cafe (1 Water Street, Brooklyn)
Sarabeth's Kitchen (1295 Madison Ave, 423 Amsterdam Ave, and 945 Madison Ave, at Whitney Museum)
Stingy Lulu's (129 St. Marks Pl)
Tabla (11 Madison Ave)
Tapika (950 Eighth Ave): Southwestern
Tartine (253 W 11th St)
Tavern on the Green (Central Park at 67th St): for entertaining out-of-town guests
Town (15 W 56th St)
Vinegar Factory (431 E 91st St)
Water Club (500 E 30th St)

When you are a little hungry and not too flush with cash, try **Sassy's Sliders** (1530 Third Ave, 212/828-6900). Sliders are bite-sized burgers—beef, turkey, veggie, chicken parmesan, barbequed chicken—that are grilled and served on a steamed bun for less than $1. Fries, great shakes, and soft ice cream are also available.

Burgers

AKA Cafe (49 Clinton St)
Bar 89 (89 Mercer St)
Beer Bar at Cafe Centro (MetLife Building, 200 Park Ave)
Better Burger (565 Third Ave)
Big Nick's (2175 Broadway): You'll love it!
Billy's (948 First Ave)
Blue Ribbon Bakery (33 Downing St)
Brasserie 360 (200 E 60th St): convenient for Bloomingdale's shoppers
Burger Heaven (20 E 49th St, 536 Madison Ave, and 9 E 53rd St)
Cafe de Bruxelles (118 Greenwich Ave)
Chelsea Grill (135 Eighth Ave)
Chumley's (86 Bedford St)
Corner Bistro (331 W 4th St)
DB Bistro Moderne (City Club Hotel, 55 W 44th St)
Fanelli (94 Prince St)
44 (Royalton Hotel, 44 W 44th St)
Great Jones Cafe (54 Great Jones St)
Hamburger Harry's (145 W 45th St)
Hard Rock Cafe (221 W 57th St)
Home Restaurant (20 Cornelia St)
J.G. Melon (1291 Third Ave)
Jackson Hole Burgers (232 E 64th St, 521 Third Ave, 1611 Second Ave, 1270 Madison Ave, and 517 Columbus Ave)
Keens Steakhouse (72 W 36th St)
Knickerbocker Bar and Grill (33 University Pl)
McDonald's (160 Broadway): atypically classy
Michael Jordan's, the Steak House (Grand Central Station)
Odeon (145 West Broadway)

Old Town (45 E 18th St)
P.J. Clarke's (915 Third Ave)
Patroon (160 E 46th St)
Popover Cafe (551 Amsterdam Ave)
Prime Burger (5 E 51st St)
Rare (Shelburne Hotel, 303 Lexington Ave)
Rue 57 (60 W 57th St)
Smith & Wollensky (797 Third Ave)
21 Club (21 W 52nd St)
Union Square Cafe (21 E 16th St)
Wollensky's Grill (201 E 49th St)
Zoë (90 Prince St)

Cheap Eats

Some of the better deals in town:

A (947 Columbus Ave)
AKA Cafe (49 Clinton St)
Alias (76 Clinton St)
Alouette (2588 Broadway)
Avenue (520 Columbus Ave)
Bagel Restaurant (170 W 4th St)
Bereket (187 E Houston St)
Beyoglu (1431 Third Ave)
Big Nick's (2175 Broadway)
Bistro Margot (26 Prince St)
Burger Joint (Le Parker Meridien, 119 W 56th St)
Cabana Carioca (123 W 45th St)
Cafe Cafe (470 Broome St)
Cafe Edison (Hotel Edison, 228 W 47th St)
Cafe Lalo (201 W 83rd St)
Cafe Orlin (41 St. Marks Pl)
Cafe Riazor (245 W 16th St)
Caffe Vivaldi (32 Jones St)
Carmine's (2450 Broadway)
Casa Adela (66 Ave C)
Chips Mexican Grill & Restaurant (42-15 Queens Blvd, Queens)
City Bakery (3 W 18th St)
Coffee Shop (29 Union Sq W)
Comfort Diner (214 E 45th St)
Confetti (5 E 38th St)
Corner Bistro (331 W 4th St)
Cosette (163 E 33rd St)
Cucina Della Fontana (368 Bleecker St)
Cucina Stagionale (275 Bleecker St)
Cupcake Cafe (522 Ninth Ave)
Curry & Curry (153 E 33rd St)
Dakshin Indian Bistro (741 Ninth Ave)
Danal (90 E 10th St)
Dining Commons (City University of New York Graduate Center, 365 Fifth Ave, 8th floor)
Dokpa (136 W Houston St)

Dom's (202 Lafayette St)
East Village Cheese (40 Third Ave)
Edgar's Cafe (255 W 84th St)
El Cid (322 W 15th St)
Euzkadi (108 E 4th St)
F&B (269 W 23rd St)
Frank (88 Second Ave)
Frank's (85 Tenth Ave)
Gennaro (665 Amsterdam Ave)
Golden Unicorn (18 East Broadway)
Gray's Papaya (402 Ave of the Americas, 539 Eighth Ave, and 2090 Broadway)
Hallo Berlin Wine & Beer Garden (402 W 51st St)
Havana Chelsea (188 Eighth Ave)
Havana New York (27 W 38th St)
Hoi An (135 West Broadway)
Home (20 Cornelia St)
Il Bagatto (192 E Second Ave)
Inside (9 Jones St)
Ivy's Cafe (154 W 72nd St)
Jasmine (1619 Second Ave)
Jean Claude (137 Sullivan St)
John's Pizzeria (278 Bleecker St and other locations)
Kai Kai Thai Eatery (78 E 1st St)
Katz's Delicatessen (205 E Houston St)
Kitchenette (80 West Broadway)
La Flor de Broadway (3401 Broadway)
Le Gamin (183 Ninth Ave, 27 Bedford St, 132 W Houston St, and 536 E 5th St)
Le Tableau (511 E 5th St)
Lil' Frankie's Pizza (19 First Ave)
Little Havana (30 Cornelia St)
Luke's Bar & Grill (1394 Third Ave)
Manhattan Fruit Exchange (Chelsea Market, 75 Ninth Ave)
Market Diner (572 Eleventh Ave)
McDonald's (160 Broadway)
Miss Elle's Homesick Bar and Grill (226 W 79th St)
Munson Diner (600 W 49th St)
Nam (110 Reade St)
Nam Phuong (19 Ave of the Americas)
National Cafe (210 First Ave)
Natural Restaurant (88 Allen St)
Nha Trang (87 Baxter St)
107 West Restaurant (2787 Broadway)
Pakistan Tea House (176 Church St)
Pantry (179 Ave B)
Paul's Place (131 Second Ave)
Peep (177 Prince St)
Phi Lan (249 E 45th St)
Pho Bang (6 Chatham St)
Pigalle (790 Eighth Ave)
Pommes Frites (123 Second Ave)

Popover Cafe (551 Amsterdam Ave)
Pret à Manger (287 Madison Ave)
Prime Burger (5 E 51st St)
Rose of Bombay (326 E 6th St)
Sapporo (152 W 49th St)
Second Avenue Kosher Delicatessen and Restaurant (156 Second Ave)
Shopsin's General Store (63 Bedford St, at Morton St): an original!
Sirtaj (36 W 26th St)
Sosa Borella (460 Greenwich St and 832 Eighth Ave)
Spring Street Bakery (30 Spring St)
Spring Street Natural Restaurant (62 Spring St)
Supper (156 E 2nd St)
Suzie's (163 Bleecker St)
Sweet-n-Tart Cafe (76 Mott St)
Sylvia's (328 Lenox Ave)
Tanti Baci Flower Room (135½ Seventh Ave S)
Tartine (253 W 11th St)
Tavern on Jane (31 Eighth Ave)
Tossed (295 Park Ave S)
Turkish Cuisine (631 Ninth Ave)
Uncle Moe's (14 W 19th St)
Urban Roots (51 Ave A)
Veronica (240 W 38th St)
Veselka (144 Second Ave)
Viand Coffee Shop (300 E 86th St, 673 Madison Ave, and 1011 Madison Ave)
Vietnam Restaurant (11 Doyers St)
Zula Restaurant (1260 Amsterdam Ave)
Zum Schneider (107-109 Ave C)

There is nothing like a bowl of real French onion soup for a pick-me-up on a cool day. One of the best can be had at **Le Singe Vert** (160 Seventh Ave, 212/366-4100).

Cheese Plates

Artisanal (2 Park Ave)
Babbo (110 Waverly Pl)
Chanterelle (2 Harrison St)
Craftbar (47 E 19th St)
Daniel (60 E 65th St)
Eleven Madison Park (11 Madison Ave)
Georgia's (597 Metropolitan Ave): fresh mozzarella made daily
Gramercy Tavern (42 E 20th St)
Jean Georges (Trump International Hotel, 1 Central Park W)
La Caravelle (33 W 55th St)
La Grenouille (3 E 52nd St)
Osteria del Circo (120 W 55th St): tasting of the classic Italian pecorino (sheep's milk) cheeses
Picholine (35 W 64th St)
Solera (216 E 53rd St)

Tasting Room (72 E 1st St)
Verbena Restaurant (54 Irving Pl)

Coffeehouses

Coffeehouses are very hot! You can relax, enjoy good company, and drink coffee beverages at the following.

Basset Cafe (123 West Broadway)
Big Cup (228 Eighth Ave)
Bleecker Street Pastry (245 Bleecker St)
Cafe La Fortuna (69 W 71st St)
Cafe Lalo (201 W 83rd St)
Cafe Mozart (154 W 70th St)
Caffe Biondo (141 Mulberry St)
Caffe Dante (79 MacDougal St)
Caffe Roma (385 Broome St)
Caffe Vivaldi (32 Jones St)
Chez Laurence Patisserie (245 Madison Ave)
City Bakery (22 E 17th St)
Cupcake Cafe (522 Ninth Ave)
Cupping Room Cafe (359 West Broadway)
Dean & Deluca (9 Rockefeller Center)
Dolci on Park (12 Park Ave)
Espresso Madison (33 E 68th St)
Ferrara's Cafe (195 Grand St)
French Roast (458 Ave of the Americas)
Hungarian Pastry Shop (1030 Amsterdam Ave)
Java 'n Jazz (868 Broadway)
Le Figaro Cafe (184 Bleecker St)
Le Pain Quotidien (1131 Madison Ave; 38 E 19th St, at ABC Carpet Home; and other locations)
Lipstick Cafe (885 Third Ave)
Once Upon a Tart (135 Sullivan St)
Oren's Daily Roast (many locations)
Sarabeth's Kitchen (1295 Madison Ave, 423 Amsterdam Ave, and 945 Madison Ave, at Whitney Museum)
Sensuous Bean (66 W 70th St)
71 Irving (71 Irving Pl)
Starbucks (many locations)
Timothy's Coffees of the World (100 Park Ave and 1285 Ave of the Americas): reading material, too!
Veselka Coffee Shop (144 Second Ave)
Xando Coffee and Bar (2160 Broadway)

Do you feel like taking in a bit of cafe life downtown? Here are some suggestions for color, charm, and conviviality:
Cafe Borgia II (161 Prince St, Soho)
Caffe Dante (79-81 MacDougal St, Greenwich Village)
Caffe Sha Sha (510 Hudson St, West Village)
Wild Lily Tea Room (511A W 22nd St, Chelsea)

Crepes

Cosette (163 E 33rd St)
Jean Georges (Trump International Hotel, 1 Central Park W)
Le Gamin (183 Ninth Ave, 27 Bedford St,132 W Houston St, and 536 E 5th
   St)
Mon Petite Cafe (801 Lexington Ave)
Serendipity 3 (225 E 60th St)
Vong (200 E 54th St)

Deli Food

Artie's Delicatessen (2290 Broadway)
Back Stage III (807 Lexington Ave)
Barney Greengrass (541 Amsterdam Ave)
Ben's Kosher Deli (209 W 38th St)
Carnegie Delicatessen and Restaurant (854 Seventh Ave)
E.A.T. (1064 Madison Ave)
Ess-a-Bagel (831 Third Ave and 359 First Ave)
Fine & Schapiro (138 W 72nd St)
Katz's Delicatessen (205 East Houston St)
Junior's (Grand Central Station)
Second Avenue Kosher Delicatessen and Restaurant (156 Second Ave)
Stage Deli (834 Seventh Ave and 1481 Second Ave)
Third Avenue Delicatessen (276 Third Ave)

Desserts

Bouley (120 West Broadway)
Cafe Lalo (201 W 83rd St): best European-style cafe!
Cafe Pertutti (2862 Broadway): a waist-expanding experience
Cafe Sabarsky (Neue Galerie, 1048 Fifth Ave)
Caffe Biondo (141 Mulberry St): Little Italy's star
Cupcake Cafe (522 Ninth Ave)
Delices de France (289 Madison Ave): name says it all
Dolci on Park Caffe (12 Park Ave): undiscovered gem
Ferrara (195 Mulberry St): Italian gelati
Gramercy Tavern (42 E 20th St)
Le Cirque 2000 (New York Palace Hotel): world famous!
Les Delices West (370 Columbus Ave): fine French pastries
Les Friandises (972 Lexington Ave): fabulous chocolate mousse cake
Lo Spuntino (117 Mulberry St): ice cream specialties
Magnolia Bakery (401 Bleecker St): wonderful cupcakes and more
Once Upon a Tart (135 Sullivan St)
Palm Court (Plaza Hotel, 768 Fifth Ave): vintage New York
Payard Bistro (1032 Lexington Ave): You'll pay a bit more and enjoy it
   more, too!
Petrossian (182 W 58th St)
Rocco (181 Thompson St)
Serendipity 3 (225 E 60th St): an institution for the young-at-heart
Veniero's (342 E 11th St)
Zabar's Cafe (2245 Broadway): big treats, low prices

A very unlikely place for a restaurant turns out to be a very unlikely surprise! The **Lunchbox Food Company** (357 West St, 646/230-9466) is a streamlined diner with excellent food at reasonable prices, plus extra-friendly service and delicious sweets to go! You'll find both a breakfast and lunch menu, with excellent sandwiches and salads. At dinner time, the menu expands to steaks, tacos, chicken, seafood, and more. In keeping with the times, a nice selection of cheeses is available. Brunch is served on Saturdays and Sundays.

Dim Sum

The serving of small tea pastries called "dim sum" originated in Hong Kong and has become a delicious Chinatown institution. Although dim sum is usually eaten for brunch, some restaurants also serve it as an appetizer before dinner. Dim sum items are brought to your table on rolling carts, and you simply point at whatever looks good. This eliminates the language barrier and encourages experimentation. When you're finished, the small plates you've accumulated are counted and the bill is drawn up. Some of the most popular dim sum dishes include:

Cha Siu Bow (steamed barbecued pork buns)
Cha Siu So (flaky buns)
Chun Guen (spring rolls)
Dai Tze Gau (steamed scallop and shrimp dumplings)
Don Ta (baked custard tarts)
Dow Sah Bow (sweet bean-paste-filled buns)
Fancy Fans (meat-filled potsticker triangles)
Floweret Siu Mai (meat-filled dumplings)
Four-color Siu Mai (meat-and-vegetable-filled dumplings)
Gau Choi Gau (pan-browned chive and shrimp dumplings)
Gee Cheung Fun (steamed rice-noodle rolls)
Gee Yoke Go (savory pork triangles)
Ha Gau (shrimp dumplings)
Jow Ha Gok (shrimp turnovers)
Pot Sticker Kou The (meat-filled dumplings)
Satay Gai Tran (chicken satay)
Siu Mai (steamed pork dumplings)
Tzay Ha (fried shrimp ball on sugarcane)

For the most authentic and delicious dim sum in New York, try the following:

Dim Sum Go Go (5 East Broadway)
Golden Unicorn (18 East Broadway): an especially fine selection
H.S.F. (46 Bowery and 578 Second Ave)
Jing Fong (20 Elizabeth St)
Mandarin Court (61 Mott St)
Nice Restaurant (35 East Broadway)
Oriental Pearl (103 Mott St)
Ping's (22 Mott St)
Ruby Foo's (2182 Broadway and 1626 Broadway)
Shun Lee Cafe (43 W 65th St)
Silver Palace (50 Bowery)
Sixty-Six (241 Church St)

Sun Hop Shing Tea House (21 Mott St)
Sweet-n-Tart Restaurant (20 Mott St)
Tai-Hong-Lau (70 Mott St)
Triple 8 Palace (59 Division St)

Diners

There are not many classic diners left in Manhattan. The best of the survivors are:

Broadway Diner (590 Lexington Ave)
Brooklyn Diner USA (212 W 57th St): outstanding
Ellen's Stardust Diner (1650 Broadway)
Empire Diner (210 Tenth Ave)
Lunchbox Food Company (357 West St)
Market Diner (572 Eleventh Ave)
Moondance Diner (80 Ave of the Americas)
Munson's Diner (600 W 49th St)

Dining and Dancing

Cafe Pierre (Pierre Hotel, 2 E 61st St): refined
Decade (1117 First Ave): modern food, 1960s and 1970s music
Supper Club (240 W 47th St): vintage 1940s with big bands
Tavern on the Green (Central Park W at 67th St): great setting
World Yacht Cruises (Pier 81, W 41st St at Hudson River): nonstop party

Dining Solo

Some of these restaurants have dining counters, others are tranquil and suitable for single diners:

Aquavit (13 W 54th St)
Babbo (110 Waverly Pl)
Broadway Diner (590 Lexington Ave)
Cafe de Bruxelles (118 Greenwich Ave)
Cafe SFA (Saks Fifth Avenue, 611 Fifth Ave)
Carnegie Delicatessen and Restaurant (854 Seventh Ave)
Caviar Russe (538 Madison Ave)
Chez Napoleon (365 W 50th St)
Coffee Shop (29 Union Sq)
Col Legno (231 E 9th St)
Cupcake Cafe (522 Ninth Ave)
Elephant & Castle (68 Greenwich St)
Gotham Bar & Grill (12 E 12th St)
Grand Central Oyster Bar Restaurant (Grand Central Station, lower level)
J.G. Melon (1291 Third Ave)
Jackson Hole Burgers (232 E 64th St, 521 Third Ave, and 1611 Second Ave)
Joe's Shanghai (9 Pell St)
Kitchenette (80 West Broadway)
La Bonne Soupe (48 W 55th St)
La Caridad 78 (2199 Broadway)
Lipstick Cafe (885 Third Ave)
Matthew's (1030 Third Ave)
Mayrose (920 Broadway)

Pepolino (281 West Broadway)
Raoul's (180 Prince St)
Republic (37 Union Square W)
Sarabeth's Kitchen (1295 Madison Ave, 423 Amsterdam Ave, and 945 Madison Ave, at Whitney Museum)
Savoy (70 Prince St)
Second Avenue Kosher Delicatessen and Restaurant (156 Second Ave)
Stage Deli (834 Seventh Ave and 1481 Second Ave)
Sushihatsu (1143 First Ave)
Trattoria dell'Arte (900 Seventh Ave)
Tropica (MetLife Building, 200 Park Ave)
Union Square Cafe (21 E 16th St)
Verbena (54 Irving Pl)
Viand Coffee Shop (300 E 86th St, 673 Madison Ave, and 1011 Madison Ave)
Village Natural (123 Greenwich Ave)
Zoë (90 Prince St)

Dog Friendly

Brew Bar (327 W 11th St)
Cafe Pick Me Up (145 Ave A)
Chelsea Lobster Company (156 Seventh Ave)
Christina's (606 Second Ave)
11th Street Bar (510 E 11th St)
Girasole (151 E 82nd St)
Time Cafe (87 Seventh Ave)
Verbena (54 Irving Pl)
Zum Schneider (107-109 Ave C)

Don't Bother

Too many restaurants spoil the real reason for dining out: to get a good meal in a comfortable setting at a fair price. With so many great choices in Manhattan, why waste time and money on mediocre ones? Many restaurants on the following list are well known and popular, but I feel you can get better value elsewhere.

Angelo of Mulberry Street: The portrait of former president Reagan is their only claim to fame.
B Bar & Grill: The servers are as disinterested as you will be in the food.
Bice: very "in," very noisy, very unimpressive
Chiam: charming in every way except the most important—the food
Cipriani Downtown: expensive journey to Italy
City Crab: The amateurish service and mediocre food are enough to make anyone crabby.
City Grill: big menu, big crowd, not so big taste
Crispo: You may be attracted by the reasonable prices, but the anticipation is far better than the reality.
Cub Room: needs a lot of mothering with the tasteless food
Demarchelier: very ordinary
Django: The great French guitarist Django Reinhardt would have been underwhelmed by this rather uninspiring spot.

Foley's Fish House: An exciting view overlooking Times Square is spoiled by unexciting chow.

Frére Jacques: unrealized potential as a French dining destination

Gage & Tollner: great ambience and reputation, but not really worth the trip to Brooklyn

Giovanni Venti Cinque: haughty treatment and high prices

Giorgio's of Gramercy: utterly unmemorable

Great American Health Bar: Ugh!

Island Burgers and Shakes: overpraised, unattractive hole-in-the-wall

Jekyll & Hyde: for ghoulish appetites

Le Clown: I'd be clown if I claimed there was anything appealing about this bare-boned bistro.

Le Veau d'Or: Heaven help the stranger.

Lexington Avenue Grill: poor service

Lotus: dark, deafening, and disappointing

Lupa: very uneven in both food and service

Maroons: Jamaican and Southern cooking that strays far from its origins.

Meet: This Meatpacking District eatery strikes out as a place to meet or eat meat.

Metrazur: The train left a long time ago!

Mickey Mantle's: a strikeout

Old Homestead: "Old" is the best description.

Rothmann's Steakhouse & Grill: Why waste bucks at this amateurish place when there are so many good alternatives?

Savoy: uncomfortably cute, unappealing plates

Swifty's: unpleasant greeting, snobby atmosphere

Triomphe: small in size, value, and service

Union Pacific: The culinary ride is not always smooth.

Vanderbilt Station: Alfred G. Vanderbilt wouldn't have wasted his time at this stop.

Village: uninspired cooking in an uninspired space

Waikiki Wally's: Hawaii is nothing like this place . . . thank goodness! Macadamia nut growers would be aghast at the namesake chicken.

By all means, include a visit to **Jarnac** (328 W 12th St, 212/924-3413). Tony Powe's jewel is typically French, and features great food with the added treat of a gracious host. Try to make the 3-course *prix fixe* Sunday night dinner ($35).

Eating at the Bar or Pub

AZ (21 W 17th St)

Beacon (25 W 56th St)

Belgo Nieuw York (415 Lafayette St)

Cafe de Bruxelles (118 Greenwich Ave)

China Grill (52 W 53rd St)

Cipriani Dolci (Grand Central Station)

D'Artagnan (152 E 46th St)

Delmonico's (56 Beaver St)

Emerald Inn (205 Columbus Ave): pre-Lincoln Center

Fanelli (94 Prince St)
Five Points (31 Great Jones St)
Gotham Bar & Grill (12 E 12th St)
Grace (114 Franklin St)
Gramercy Tavern (42 E 20th St)
Hallo Berlin (402 W 51st St)
Keens Steakhouse (72 W 36th St)
Markt (401 W 14th St)
Mesa Grill (102 Fifth Ave)
Old Town Bar & Restaurant (45 E 18th St)
Patroon (160 E 46th St)
Penang (109 Spring St)
Petrossian (182 W 58th St)
Rain (100 W 82nd St)
Redeye Grill (890 Seventh Ave)
The Steakhouse at Monkey Bar (Elysee Hotel, 60 E 54th St)
Typhoon Brewery (22 E 54th St)
Union Square Cafe (21 E 16th St)
Wollensky's Grill (205 E 49th St)
Zoë (90 Prince St)

Family-style Dining

Becco (355 W 46th St)
Carmine's (2450 Broadway)
Da Umberto (107 W 17th St)
Golden Unicorn (18 East Broadway)
Marchi's (251 E 31st St)
Sambuca (20 W 72nd St)
Szechuan Hunan (1588 York Ave)
Tony's di Napoli (1606 Second Ave)

Fireside

All-State Cafe (250 W 72nd St)
American Park at the Battery (Battery Park)
Barbetta (321 W 46th St)
Bayard's (1 Hanover Square)
Beekman Bar & Books (889 First Ave)
Chelsea Bistro & Bar (358 W 23rd St)
Chumley's (86 Bedford St)
Commune (12 E 22nd St)
Cornelia Street Cafe (29 Cornelia St)
Gramercy Tavern (42 E 20th St)
Hunter's (1397 Third Ave)
I Trulli (122 E 27th St)
Keens Steakhouse (72 W 36th St)
La Bohême (24 Minetta Lane)
Maratti (135 E 62nd St)
March (405 E 58th St)
Marchi's (251 E 31st St)
Molly's Pub and Shebeen (287 Third Ave)
Moran's Chelsea (146 Tenth Ave)

One If By Land, Two If By Sea (17 Barrow St)
René Pujol (321 W 51st St)
Savoy (70 Prince St)
Shaffer City Oyster Bar & Grill (5 W 21st St)
Vivolo (140 E 74th St)
Water Club (500 E 30th St)
Ye Waverly Inn (16 Bank St)

Food Tips From Distant Lands:

- **Chinese**: The most popular Chinese cuisines are **Cantonese** (heavy on fish, dim sum a specialty); **Chiu Chow** (thick shark's fin soup, sliced goose, China's "Sicilian" cuisine); **Hakka** (salted, use of innards); **Hunan** (spicy, try fried chicken with chili); **Peking** (Peking duck and beggar's chicken are the best known); **Shanghai** (freshwater hairy crab is very popular); and **Szechuan** (spiciest of all, simmering and smoking are common cooking methods).
- **Indian**: Not necessarily hot; north Indian food features wheat bread and curries. Fish and chicken are cooked in a tandoor clay oven.
- **Indonesian**: Satays (skewered chicken and beef, barbecued and served with peanut sauce) are the main dishes.
- **Japanese**: Most popular foods are sushi (raw fish atop light, vinegary rice), sashimi (slices of raw fish), tempura (deep-fried vegetables and fish), and teppanyaki (beef, seafood, garlic, and veggies cooked on a central griddle). Try them with sake (rice wine) or Japanese beers such as Sapporo.
- **Korean**: Table-top griddles are used for barbecuing beef slices for a dish called bulgogi.
- **Malaysian**: The best-known dish is laska, a creamy, coconut-based soup with noodles, shrimp, and chicken.
- **Singaporean**: This cuisine combines cultures: fried mee (thick yellow noodles) and satay (skewered and barbecued meat). Coconut is featured in sweet rice cakes and laska.
- **Taiwanese**: Heavy on fish and other seafoods cooked in hot pots and enhanced by chili- and sesame-flavored oil condiments.
- **Thai**: Thai food can be very spicy! The national dish is tom yum gung, a soup made with chili, lemon grass, and coriander and topped with shrimp, chicken, or squid.
- **Vietnamese**: You'll find French-inspired dishes like fried frog legs, sausage, and salami cold cuts platter. Spring rolls wrapped in lettuce

---

Foreign Flavors

Some commendable ethnic establishments do not have full write-ups in this chapter. Here are the best of the more exotic eateries, arranged by cuisine:

Afghan: **Afghanistan Kebab House** (764 Ninth Ave) and **Pamir** (1437 Second Ave)

African: **La Baraka** (153 Broadway), **Lamu** (39 E 19th St), **Métisse** (239 W 105th St), and **Sugar Bar** (354 W 72nd St)

Arabian: **Layla** (211 West Broadway)

Argentine: **Chimichurri Grill** (606 Ninth Ave) and **Sosa Borella** (460 Greenwich St and 832 Eighth Ave)

Armenian: **Bistro Monk** (309 E 5th St)

Asian: **Pacific East** (318 W 23rd St) and **Rain** (100 W 82nd St)

Australian: **Eight Mile Creek** (240 Mulberry St)

Austrian: **Cafe Sabarsky** (Neue Galerie, 1048 Fifth Ave) and **Wallsé** (344 W 11th St)

Belgian: **Cafe de Bruxelles** (118 Greenwich Ave) and **Petite Abeille** (400 W 14th St)

Brazilian: **Cabana Carioca** (123 W 45th St), **Churrascaria Plataforma** (316 W 49th St), **Circus** (808 Lexington Ave), **Emporium Brazil** (15 W 46th St), **Ipanema** (13 W 46th St), and **Riodizio** (417 Lafayette St)

Caribbean: **Bambou** (243 E 14th St), **Cabana** (1022 Third Ave), **Caribe** (117 Perry St), **Caridad** (4311 Broadway), **Negril Village** (70 W 3rd St), and **Tropica** (MetLife Building, 200 Park Ave)

Chilean: **Pomaire** (371 W 46th St)

Chinese: **Au Mandarin** (200-250 Vesey St), **Baby Buddha** (753 Washington Ave), **Big Wong** (67 Mott St), **Broadway Cottage** (2690 Broadway), **Chin Chin** (216 E 49th St), **China Fun West** (246 Columbus Ave), **Fu's** (1395 Second Ave), **Golden Unicorn** (18 East Broadway), **Grand Sichuan International** (229 Ninth Ave, 745 Ninth Ave, and 227 Lexington Ave), **H.S.F.** (46 Bowery), **Hunan Park** (721 Columbus Ave), **Joe's Shanghai** (9 Pell St), **Kam Chueh** (40 Bowery), **Lozoo** (140 W Houston), **Mr. K's** (570 Lexington Ave), **Natural Restaurant** (88 Allen St), **New Hong Kong City** (11 Division St), **Oriental Garden** (14 Elizabeth St), **Oriental Pearl** (103 Mott St), **Ping's Seafood** (22 Mott St), **Shanghai Cuisine** (89-91 Bayard St), **Shun Lee Palace** (155 E 55th St), **Shun Lee West** (43 W 65th St), **Sixty-Six** (241 Church St), **Sunny East** (21 W 39th St), **Tang Pavilion** (65 W 55th St), **10 Pell St** (10 Pell St), and **Wu Liang Ye** (36 W 48th St)

Cuban: **Cafe Con Leche** (424 Amsterdam Ave), **La Caridad** (2199 Broadway), **Little Havana** (30 Cornelia St), **National Cafe** (210 First Ave), **Sucelt Coffee Shop** (200 W 14th St), and **Victor's Cafe** (240 Columbus Ave)

Dutch: **NL** (169 Sullivan St)

East European: **Caviarteria** (Delmonico Hotel, 502 Park Ave), **Danube** (30 Hudson St), **Firebird** (365 W 46th St), **Petrossian** (182 W 58th St), **Sammy's Roumanian** (157 Chrystie St), and **Veselka Coffee Shop** (144 Second Ave)

Ethiopian: **Ghenet** (284 Mulberry St), **Meskerem** (468 W 47th St), **Queen of Sheba** (650 Tenth Ave), and **Zula** (1260 Amsterdam Ave)

Filipino: **Elvie's Turo-Turo** (214 First Ave)

French: see restaurant write-ups

French-Moroccan: **Chez Es Saada** (42 E 1st St)

German: **Hallo Berlin** (402 W 51st St), **Heidelberg Restaurant** (1648 Second Ave), **Rolf's** (281 Third Ave), **Silver Swan** (41 E 20th St), and **Zum Schneider** (107 Avenue C)

Greek: **Avra** (141 E 48th St), **Estiatorio Milos** (125 W 55th St), **Gus's Place** (149 Waverly Pl), **Ithaka** (48 Barrow St), **Likitsakos Market** (1174 Lexington Ave), **Meltemi** (905 First Ave), **Molyvos** (871 Seventh Ave), **Periyali** (35 W 20th St), **Snack** (105 Thompson St), **Thalassa** (179

Franklin St), **Uncle Nick's** (747 Ninth Ave), and **Viand Coffee Shop** (300 E 86th St, 673 Madison Ave, and 1011 Madison Ave)

Hungarian: **Mocca Hungarian Restaurant** (1588 Second Ave)

Indian: **Banjara** (97 First Ave), **Bay Leaf** (49 W 56th St), **Bengal Express** (789 Ninth Ave), **Bombay Dining** (320 E 6th St), **Bukhara Grill** (230 E 58th St), **Chola** (232 E 58th St), **Dawat** (210 E 58th St), **Diwan** (148 E 48th St), **Haveli** (100 Second Ave), **Jewel of India** (15 W 44th St), **Marichu** (342 E 46th St), **Mirchi** (29 Seventh Ave S), **Rose of India** (308 E 6th St), **Salaam Bombay** (317 Greenwich St), **Shaan** (57 W 48th St), **Surya** (302 Bleecker St), **Tabla** (11 Madison Ave), **Taj Mahal** (328 E 6th St), **Tamarind** (41-43 E 22nd St), **Thali** (28 Greenwich Ave), and **Utsav** (1185 Ave of the Americas)

Indonesian: **Bali Nusa Indah** (651 Ninth Ave)

Irish: **Bellew** (167 E 33rd St), **Landmark Tavern** (626 Eleventh Ave), **Neary's** (358 E 57th St), and **Thady Con's** (915 Second Ave)

Italian: see restaurant write-ups

Jamaican: **Jamaican Hot Pot** (2260 Adam Clayton Powell, Jr. Blvd) and **Maroons** (244 W 16th St)

Japanese: **Benihana** (120 E 56th St), **Bond Street** (6 Bond St), **Chikubu** (12 E 44th St), **Donguri** (309 E 83rd St), **Hatsuhana** (17 E 48th St), **Honmura An** (170 Mercer St), **Inagiku** (Waldorf-Astoria, 301 Park Ave), **Iso** (175 Second Ave), **Japonica** (100 University Pl), **Jewel Bako** (239 E 5th St), **Kai** (822 Madison Ave), **Kiiroi Hana** (23 W 56th St), **Kuruma Zushi** (7 E 47th St), **Mana** (646 Amsterdam Ave), **Menchanko-Tei** (39 W 55th St), **Minimoto Kitchoan** (608 Fifth Ave), **Nadaman Hakubai** (Kitano Hotel, 66 Park Ave), **Nobu** and **Nobu Next Door** (105 Hudson St), **Omen** (113 Thompson St), **Ozu** (566 Amsterdam Ave), **Sakagura** (211 E 43rd St), **Seryna** (11 E 53rd St), **Sugiyama** (251 W 55th St), **Sushihatsu** (1143 First Ave), **Sushi Samba** (275 Park Ave S and 877 Seventh Ave S), **Sushisay** (38 E 51st St), **Sushi Yasuda** (204 E 43rd St), **Tatany 52** (250 E 52nd St), and **Toraya** (17 E 71st St)

Korean: **Cho Dang Gol** (55 W 35th St), **Do Hwa** (55 Carmine St), **Dok Suni's** (119 First Ave), **Gam Mee Oak** (43 W 32nd St), **Hangawi** (12 E 32nd St), **Jin Dal Lae** (494 Amsterdam Ave), **Kang Suh** (1250 Broadway), **Kori** (253 Church St), **Kum Gang San** (49 W 32nd St), **New York Kom Tang** (32 W 32nd St), **Won Jo** (23 W 32nd St), **Woo Chon** (8-10 W 36th St), and **Woo Lae Oak Soho** (148 Mercer St)

Lebanese: **Al Bustan** (827 Third Ave)

Malaysian: **Malaysia and Indonesia** (18 Doyers St), **Malaysia Restaurant** (48 Bowery), and **Penang** (109 Spring St)

Mediterranean: **Marseille** (630 Ninth Ave), **Mezze** (10 W 44th St), **Provence** (38 MacDougal St), **Spartina** (355 Greenwich St), and **Zanzibar** (240 E 27th St, 7E)

Mexican: **Alamo** (304 E 48th St), **El Parador Cafe** (325 E 34th St), **El Rey del Sol** (232 W 4th St), **El Teddy's** (219 West Broadway), **Ernesto Restaurant** (2277 First Ave), **Fresco Tortillas** (766 Ninth Ave), **La Hacienda** (219 E 116th St), **L-Ray** (64 W 10th St), **Maya** (1191 First Ave), **Mexicana Mama** (525 Hudson St), **Mexican Radio** (112 First Ave), **Mi Cocina** (57 Jane St), **Miracle Grill** (415 Bleecker St), **Rinconcito Mexicano** (307 W 39th St), **Rosa Mexicano** (1063 First Ave and 61 Columbus Ave), **Taqueria de Mexico** (93 Greenwich Ave), **Tortilla Flats** (767 Washington St), **Zarela** (953 Second Ave), and **Zocalo** (174 E 82nd St)

Middle Eastern: **Al Bustan** (827 Third Ave), **Bread from Beirut** (24 W 45th St), **Cleopatra's Needle** (2485 Broadway), **Habib's Place** (438 E 9th St), **Layla** (211 West Broadway), **Lemon Tree Cafe** (769 Ninth Ave), and **Moustache** (265 E 10th St)

Moroccan: **Acquario** (5 Bleecker St), **Chez Es Saada** (42 E 1st St), **Cookies and Couscous** (230 Thompson St), **Lofti's** (358 W 46th St), **L'Orange Bleue** (430 Broome St), **Marseille** (630 Ninth Ave), and **Zitoune** (46 Gansevoort St)

Pan-Latino: **Cabana Carioca** (123 W 45th St), **Calle Ocho** (446 Columbus Ave), **Circus** (808 Lexington Ave), **Flor's Kitchen** (149 First Ave), **Ideya** (349 West Broadway), **Isla** (39 Downing St), **Paladar** (161 Ludlow St), **Patria** (250 Park Ave S), **Pipa** (ABC Carpet & Home, 38 E 19th St), and **Victor's Cafe** (236 W 52nd St)

Persian: **Persepolis** (1423 Second Ave)

Polish: **Christine's** (208 First Ave), **Teresa's** (103 First Ave), and **Veselka Coffee Shop** (144 Second Ave)

Portuguese: **Alfama** (551 Hudson St), **O Lavrador** (138-40 101st Ave), and **Pó** (322 Spring St)

Puerto Rican: **La Taza de Oro** (96 Eighth Ave)

Russian: **Firebird** (363 W 46th St), **Moscow** (137 E 55th St), **Russian Samovar** (256 W 52nd St), and **Uncle Vanya** (315 W 54th St)

Scandinavian: **Christer's** (145 W 55th St)

Scottish: **St. Andrews** (120 W 44th St)

Senegalese: **Africa Restaurant** (346 W 53rd St) and **Keur-Famba** (126 W 116th St)

South American: **Bolivar** (206 E 60th St), **Cafe Habana** (17 Prince St), **Calle Ocho** (446 Columbus Ave), **Churrascaria Plataforma** (316 W 49th St), **Ideya** (349 West Broadway), **L-Ray** (64 W 10th St), and **Patria** (250 Park Ave S)

Southwestern: **Agave** (140 Seventh Ave S)

Spanish: **Azafran** (77 Warren St), **Bolo** (23 E 22nd St), **Cafe Riazor** (245 W 16th St), **El Cid** (322 W 15th St), **El Faro** (823 Greenwich St), **Flor de Mayo** (484 Amsterdam Ave), **Marichu** (342 E 46th St), **Solera** (216 E 53rd St), and **Toledo** (6 E 36th St)

Sri Lanka: **Lakruwana** (358 W 44th St)

Swedish: **Aquavit** (13 W 54th St) and **Christer's** (145 W 55th St)

Thai: **Holy Basil** (149 Second Ave), **Peep** (177 Prince St), **Pongsri Thai** (106 Bayard St), **Regional Thai Sa-Woy** (1479 First Ave), **Royal Siam Thai** (240 Eighth Ave), **Siam Cuisine** (1411 Second Ave), **Siam Grill** (586 Ninth Ave), **Thai House Cafe** (151 Hudson St), **Thailand Restaurant** (106 Bayard St), **Topaz** (127 W 56th St), and **Vong** (200 E 54th St)

Tibetan: **Lhasa** (96 Second Ave), **Tibetan Kitchen** (444 Third Ave), **Tibetan Shambala** (488 Amsterdam Ave), and **Tsampa** (212 E 9th St)

Turkish: **Ali Baba** (206 E 34th St), **Beyoglu** (1431 Third Ave), **Layla** (211 West Broadway), **Pasha** (70 W 71st St), **Turkish Cuisine** (631 Ninth Ave), **Turkish Kitchen** (386 Third Ave), and **Uskudar** (1405 Second Ave)

Vietnamese: **Blue Velvet 1929** (227 First Ave), **Cyclo** (203 First Ave), **La Soirée d'Asie** (156 E 64th St), **Le Colonial** (149 E 57th St), **Me Kong** (44 Prince St), **Miss Saigon** (1425 Third Ave), **Monsoon** (435 Amsterdam Ave), **Nam Phuong** (19 Ave of the Americas), **New Viet Huong** (77 Mulberry St), **Nha Trang** (87 Baxter St), **Orienta** (205 E 75th St), **Pho Viet Huong** (73 Mulberry St), **Rain** (100 W 82nd St), **River** (345 Amsterdam Ave), and **Vietnam** (11 Doyers St)

French Bistros

Balthazar (80 Spring St)
Banania Cafe (241 Smith St, Brooklyn)
Bar Tabac (128 Smith St, Brooklyn)
Cafe Boulud (20 E 76th St)
Chelsea Bistro & Bar (358 W 23rd St)
Epiceris (170 Orchard St)
Flea Market Cafe (131 Ave A)
Fleur de Sel (5 E 20th St)
Jean Claude (137 Sullivan St)
Jo Jo (160 E 64th St)
Le Gigot (18 Cornelia St)
Le Jardin Bistro (25 Cleveland Pl)
Montrachet (239 West Broadway)
Pastis (9 Ninth Ave)
Payard Patisserie and Bistro (1032 Lexington Ave)
Raoul's (180 Prince St)
Rive Gauche (560 Third Ave)

Game

Aquavit (13 W 54th St)
Aureole (34 E 61st St)
Babbo (110 Waverly Pl)
Barbetta (321 W 46th St)
Blue Hill (75 Washington Pl)
Bouterin (420 E 59th St)
Cafe Boulud (Surrey Suites Hotel, 20 E 76th St)
Cafe des Artistes (1 W 67th St)
Chanterelle (2 Harrison St)
Daniel (60 E 65th St)
Danube (30 Hudson St)
Eleven Madison Park (11 Madison Ave)
Il Cantinori (32 E 10th St)
Il Mulino (86 W 3rd St)
Jean Georges (Trump International Hotel, 1 Central Park W)
La Caravelle (Shoreham Hotel, 33 W 55th St)
Le Cirque 2000 (New York Palace Hotel, 455 Madison Ave)
Le Périgord (405 E 52nd St)
Les Halles (411 Park Ave S)
March (405 E 58th St)
Mesa Grill (102 Fifth Ave)
Montrachet (239 West Broadway)
Park Bistro (414 Park Ave)
Picholine (35 W 64th St)
Primavera (1578 First Ave)
The Steakhouse at Monkey Bar (Elysee Hotel, 60 E 54th St)
Union Square Cafe (21 E 16th St)

Healthy Fare

Healthy fare can be found at the following restaurants, some of which have special menus:

American Cafe and Health Bar (160 Broadway)
Angelica Kitchen (300 E 12th St)
Blanche's Organic Cafe (22 E 44th St and 972 Lexington Ave)
Dine by Design (252 Elizabeth St)
Four Seasons (99 E 49th St): expensive
Heartbeat (149 E 49th St)
Herban Kitchen (290 Hudson St)
Honmura An (170 Mercer St)
Josie's Restaurant and Juice Bar (300 Amsterdam Ave)
Other Foods (47 E 12th St)
Popover Cafe (551 Amsterdam Ave)
Quantum Leap Natural Food (88 W 3rd St)
Republic (37 Union Sq W)
Spring Street Natural Restaurant (62 Spring St): your best bet
Time Cafe (380 Lafayette St)
Zen Palate (663 Ninth Ave and other locations)

High-tech Eateries

The Internet has begat cyber-cafes. Computer terminals make food seem secondary at these:

Alt.coffee (137 Avenue A)
Internet Cafe (82 E Third St)

Have you ever been to a restaurant where the meal was quite good but you left in no hurry to revisit? **Aix** (2398 Broadway, 212/874-7400) is, for me, one of those. Chef Didier Virot, a Jean-Georges protégé, does his best with foie gras, lobster, lamb, and the like. Guests are presented with tasteless cotton candy at the conclusion of the meal. Why, I don't know. Aix has received good words from some of my fellow reviewers, but I am still not that impressed.

Hotel Dining

One of the biggest changes on the restaurant scene in Manhattan over the last decade has been the resurgence of hotel dining. No longer are on-premises eateries just for the convenience of registered guests. Now they are destinations for those who desire a less trendy scene with a bit more atmosphere. Here are some of the best.

Algonquin (59 W 44th St): **Round Table Room** and **Oak Room** (evening cabaret)
Carlyle (35 E 76th St): **Dumonet** (pricey)
City Club (55 W 44th St): **DB Bistro Moderne** (Daniel Boulud's urbane bar-restaurant)
Elysee (60 E 54th St): **The Steakhouse at Monkey Bar** (great history and excellent American cuisine)
Essex House, a Westin Hotel (160 Central Park S): **Cafe Botanica** (casual) and **Alain Ducasse** (very expensive)
Four Seasons (57 E 57th St): **Fifty Seven Fifty Seven** (superb dining)
Giraffe (365 Park Ave S): **Sciuscia**
Hilton New York (135 Ave of the Americas): **New York Marketplace** (casual, deli-like) and **Etrusca** (Italian, dinner only)

Inn at Irving Place (54 Irving Pl): **Lady Mendl's** (very proper)

Kimberly (145 E 50th St): **Olica** (superb dining) and **Vue** (supper club)

Kitano (66 Park Ave): **Nadaman Hakubai** (Japanese) and **Garden Cafe**

Library (299 Park Ave): **Branzini**

Lowell (28 E 63rd St): **Pembroke** and **Post House** (very good meat and potatoes, next door)

Mark, The (25 E 77th St): **Mark's Restaurant** (one of the very best French)

Marriott Marquis (1535 Broadway): **The View** (top floor, revolving), **Encore** (casual), and **JW Steakhouse**

New York Palace Hotel (455 Madison Ave): **Le Cirque 2000** (a New York one-and-only by Sirio Maccioni) and **Istana** (lobby)

Pierre (2 E 61st St): **Cafe Pierre** (stately and beautiful)

Plaza, The (768 Fifth Ave): **Palm Court** (vintage New York), **Oak Room** (serious), **Oyster Bar** (seafood), **One C.P.S.** (trendy)

Plaza Athenee (37 E 64th St): **Arabelle** (dignified)

Regency (540 Park Ave): **540 Park Restaurant** (power scene) and **The Library** (informal)

Regent Wall Street (55 Wall St): **55 Wall St** (delightful setting, great American food)

Ritz-Carlton Battery Park (2 West St): **2 West** (new American)

Ritz-Carlton Central Park (50 Central Park S): **Atelier** (French)

Royalton (44 W 44th St): **44** (chic, favorite of publishing moguls)

St. Regis (2 E 55th St): **Astor Court** (you can't do better)

Shelburne Hotel (303 Lexington Ave): **Rare** (elegant burger spot)

Sheraton Manhattan (790 Seventh Ave): **Russo's Steak & Pasta**

Sheraton New York (811 Seventh Ave): **Streeter's** (cafe) and **Hudson's Sports Bar & Grill**

Shoreham (33 W 55th St): **La Caravelle** (elegant French)

SoHo Grand (310 West Broadway): **Grand Bar & Lounge** (upscale bar menu)

Stanhope Park Hyatt (995 Fifth Ave): **Melrose** (continental American)

Surrey Suites Hotel (20 E 76th St): **Cafe Boulud** (French-American)

Trump International (1 Central Park W): **Jean Georges** (*the* Donald's personal gem)

Waldorf-Astoria (301 Park Ave): **Bull & Bear** (British atmosphere), **Inagiku** (Japanese), and **Oscar's** (cafeteria)

Wales (1295 Madison Ave): **Sarabeth's Kitchen** (delightful)

Warwick (63 W 54th St): **Ciao Italia**

Westin New York (270 W 43rd St): **Shula's Steak House** (hearty)

W New York (541 Lexington Ave): **Heartbeat** (healthy American)

W New York Times Square (1567 Broadway): **Blue Fin** (seafood)

Kosher

New York City has the largest concentration of kosher restaurants outside of Israel. They range from tiny bagel stands to elegant restaurants that can hold their own with New York's best. The better establishments are frequented by kosher business people entertaining non-kosher clients. The kosher status should be discreet and indiscernible to non-kosher diners. Here are some of the better-known kosher restaurants.

Abigael's (1407 Broadway): Arguably, this is the best kosher restaurant in the city. Chef Jeffrey Nathan is a media star (TV, cookbook author).

Baruch Cafe (115 Lexington Ave): On the corner along Indian food row, this is a fast-food deli and grill with a sushi bar.

Ben's Kosher Deli (209 W 38th St): huge portions; event catering

Box Tree (250 E 49th St): possibly the most expensive and elegant kosher restaurant

Cafe Classico & Gourmet Caterers (35 W 57th St): Mediterranean kosher

Caravan of Dreams (405 E 6th St): natural, raw, and vegetarian, East Village kosher restaurant

Circa NY (22 W 33rd St): now an upscale self-serve lunch spot

Circa 26 (601 W 26th St, 8th floor): elegant dairy spot

Colbeh (43 W 39th St): Persian kosher

Date Palm Cafe (15 W 16th St): light vegetarian and dairy fare in a museum complex

Diamante Cafe (8 E 48th St): maybe the busiest lunch spot in New York; something for everyone, from sushi to pizza

Diamond Dairy (4 W 47th St): on the mezzanine overlooking the Diamond Exchange

Domani Ristorante (1590 First Ave): elegant, romantic, and expensive Italian dining

Dougie's Bar-B-Que & Grill (247 W 72nd St): The ribs are as good as kosher gets.

Dougie's Dairy (222 W 72nd St): dairy twist on Dougie's (above)

Dovid's Kosher Food Stand (27 William St): Finding Dovid's is not easy, but it is one of the few remaining choices downtown.

Eden Wok (127 W 72nd St): great kosher Chinese restaurant with sushi bar

EEE's Bakery & Cafe (105 E 34th St): wraps, soups, salads

Essex on Coney Downtown (17 Trinity Pl): Heir to the old Kosher Deli, this branch of the Brooklyn store (hence the name) is an authentic choice downtown, where there are otherwise few choices.

Estihana (221 W 79th St): simple, delicious, and reasonably priced

Gusto Va Mare (237 E 53rd St): upscale Italian dairy cuisine

Haikara Grill (1016 Second Ave): kosher Japanese steakhouse

Judaica Treasures (226 W 72nd St): A hidden treasure in the back and basement of a Judaica store, this is a remarkably good cafe.

Le Marais (150 W 46th St): This French steakhouse sets the standard; it's noisy, crowded, dark, and good.

Levana Restaurant (141 W 69th St): This is some of the most creative cooking in town; catch the goose and venison festivals. Chef Michael Hennessey teaches cooking and knows the kosher diner.

Mendy's (Grand Central Food Court, The Galleria at 57th Street, 30 Rockefeller Center, and 61 E 34th Street): At nearly every quintessential New York landmark there's a Mendy's Jewish Deli.

Mr. Broadway (1372 Broadway): Chinese, sushi, deli, and Mediterranean cuisine

My Most Favorite Dessert Company (120 W 45th St): Expensive pasta, fish, salads, and desserts are all delectable. Service could be *much* better, however.

Penguin (258 W 15th St): The whole family works at this small Middle Eastern/Jewish cafe.

Prime Grill (60 E 49th St): very expensive steakhouse; poor reservation policy

Shallots (550 Madison Ave): excellent seasonal cuisine and superb location

Vegetable Garden (48 E 41st St): light spot

Tevere 84 (155 E 84th St): old family recipes and great traditions
Va Bene (1589 Second Ave): superb pastas
Village Crown Italian (94 Third Ave): fish, dairy, vegetarian, and pasta specialties
Village Crown Moroccan (96 Third Ave): Moroccan grill specialties
Wolf & Lamb (10 E 48th St): steakhouse and other meat delicacies

Late Hours

The city that never sleeps . . .

24 hours:

Bereket (187 East Houston St)
Big Nick's (2175 Broadway)
Cafeteria (119 Seventh Ave)
Coffee Shop (29 Union Square W): open 23 hours, to be exact
Empire Diner (210 Tenth Ave)
Florent (69 Gansevoort St): only on weekends
French Roast (78 W 11th St and 2340 Broadway)
Gray's Papaya (2090 Broadway)
Green Kitchen (1477 First Ave)
Han Bat (53 W 35th St)
Kum Gang San (49 W 32nd St)
Lahore (132 Crosby St)
L'Express (249 Park Ave S)
Market Diner (572 Eleventh Ave)
Odessa (119 Ave A)
Sarge's Deli (548 Third Ave)
Veselka Coffee Shop (144 Second Ave)
Viand Coffee Shop (1011 Madison Ave)
Won Jo (23 W 32nd St)

Munching at the Museums

Some of the more appealing possibilities while digesting art and culture:

American Folk Art Museum (45 W 53rd St): Cafe
American Museum of Natural History (Central Park W at 79th St): Garden Cafe
Asia Society (Park Ave at 70th St): Garden Court Cafe
Guggenheim Museum (1071 Fifth Ave): Museum Cafe
International Center of Photography (1133 Ave of the Americas): Cafe
Jewish Museum (1109 Fifth Ave): Cafe Weissman
Metropolitan Museum of Art (1000 Fifth Ave): Museum Restaurant, Great Hall Balcony Bar, Museum Bar and Cafe, and Roof Garden Espresso and Wine Bar (warm weather only)
Neue Galerie (1048 Fifth Ave): Cafe Sabarsky
Scandinavia House Galleries (58 Park Ave): Cafe AQ
Whitney Museum of American Art (945 Madison Ave): Sarabeth's Kitchen

Offbeat

Looking for something a bit different? Here are some ideas:

Afghan Kebab House (764 Ninth Ave and 1345 Second Ave): kebab
Barney Greengrass (541 Amsterdam Ave): You're in the 1940s!
Becco (355 W 46th St): family dining

Brother Jimmy's Bar-B-Q (1461 First Ave): great ribs
Coco Pazzo (23 E 74th St): crazy chef!
Great Jones Cafe (54 Great Jones St): eclectic
Khyber Pass (34 St. Mark's Pl): Afghan
Landmark Tavern (626 Eleventh Ave): historic
Nobu and Nobu Next Door (105 Hudson St): Oriental delight
Noho Star (330 Lafayette St): diner
Rao's (455 E 114th St): way uptown
Sammy's Roumanian (157 Chrystie St): Lower East Side
Sylvia's (328 Lenox Ave): soul food
Veselka Coffee Shop (144 Second Ave): Polish-Ukrainian

Though **Viand Coffee Shop** (673 Madison Ave, 212/751-6622) hardly qualifies as one of New York's gourmet restaurants, it is one of the city's best values for good, solid food. The place is tiny and crowded but incredibly well organized. Service is efficient and prompt. Personnel are unfailingly polite and genuinely happy to see you. Breakfasts are a particularly good value. Service is rapid, and takeouts are handled with dispatch. (You might even call ahead.) At lunch, the turkey is really good; they go through nearly a dozen of them a day. Burgers and BLTs are wonderful, too.

Old-timers

How far back do you want to go?

1794: **Bridge Cafe** (279 Water St)
1851: **Bayard's** (1 Hanover Square)
1854: **McSorley's Old Ale House** (15 E 7th St)
1864: **Pete's Tavern** (129 E 18th St)
1865: **Landmark Tavern** (626 Eleventh Ave)
1868: **Old Homestead** (56 Ninth Ave)
1870: **Billy's** (948 First Ave): oldest family-run restaurant in Manhattan
1879: **Gage & Tollner** (372 Fulton St, Brooklyn)
1885: **Keens Steakhouse** (72 W 36th St)
1887: **Peter Luger** (178 Broadway, Brooklyn)
1888: **Katz's Delicatessen** (205 East Houston St)
1890: **P.J. Clarke's** (915 Third Ave)
1906: **Barbetta** (321 W 46th St)
1907: **Plaza Hotel restaurants** (768 Fifth Ave)
1913: **Grand Central Oyster Bar Restaurant** (Grand Central Station, lower level)
1914: **Cafe des Artistes** (1 W 67th St)
1920: **Ye Waverly Inn** (16 Bank St)
1926: **Palm One** (837 Second Ave)
1927: **Minetta Tavern** (113 MacDougal St)

Outdoor Bars

Baraza (349 Amsterdam Ave)
Barramundi (147 Ludlow St)
Beer Bar at Cafe Centro (35 E 13th St)
Bubby's (120 Hudson St)
Bull McCabe's (29 St. Marks Pl)
Caliente Cab Co. (61 Seventh Ave S)

Casimir (103-105 Ave B)
Chelsea Brewing Company (Pier 59, West St at 18th St)
Cibar (56 Irving Pl)
Europa Grill (599 Lexington Ave)
55 Wall (55 Wall St)
Finnegan's (1361 First Ave)
Hallo Berlin (626 Tenth Ave)
International Bar (120½ First Ave)
Iris and B. Gerald Cantor Roof Garden (Metropolitan Museum of Art, 1000 Fifth Ave)
Luna Park (1 Union Square E)
Martini's Restaurant & Bar (810 Seventh Ave)
Metro Grill Roof Garden (Hotel Metro, 45 W 35th St)
Miracle Grill (112 First Ave and 415 Bleecker St)
O'Flaherty's Ale House (56 Irving Pl)
Revival (129 E 15th St)
Ryan's Irish Pub (151 Second Ave)
St. Bart's (109 E 50th St)
Sweet & Vicious (133 Ave C)
White Horse Tavern (567 Hudson St)

A visit to **American Park** (inside Battery Park, opposite 17 State St, 212/809-5508) might well be more for the spectacular view of the harbor and Statue of Liberty than for the food!

Outdoor Dining

A taste of the outdoors in a garden, patio, or on the sidewalk:
American Park at the Battery (Battery Park)
Aquagrill (210 Spring St)
Aureole (34 E 61st St)
AZ (21 W 17th St)
Barbetta (321 W 46th St)
Barolo (398 West Broadway)
B Bar & Grill (40 E 4th St)
Bello Giardino (71 W 71st St)
Blue Water Grill (31 Union Sq W)
Bottino (246 Tenth Ave)
Bouterin (420 E 59th St)
Bryant Park Grill (25 W 40th St)
Cafe la Fortuna (69 W 71st St)
Caffe Bianco (1486 Second Ave)
Caffe Dante (79 MacDougal St)
Chelsea Commons (242 Tenth Ave)
Cheyenne Diner (411 Ninth Ave)
Chez Ma Tante (189 W 10th St)
Cloister Cafe (238 E 9th St)
Da Silvano (260 Ave of the Americas)
Dia Center for the Arts (548 W 22nd St)
Druids (736 Tenth Ave)

Empire Diner (210 Tenth Ave)
Fletcher Morgan Provisions (864 Lexington Ave)
Gascogne (158 Eighth Ave)
Gigino's (Wagner Park, 20 Battery Pl)
Grocery (288 Smith, Brooklyn)
Grove (314 Bleecker St)
Hatsuhana (17 E 48th St)
Home (20 Cornelia St)
Il Gattopardo (33 W 54th St)
I Trulli (122 E 27th St)
Il Monello (1460 Second Ave)
Jackson Hole Burgers (232 E 64th St)
Jean Georges (Trump International Hotel, 1 Central Park W)
La Bohême (24 Minetta Lane)
La Vidâ (222 E 39th St)
Le Jardin Bistro (25 Cleveland Pl)
Le Madri (168 W 18th St)
Lombardi's (32 Spring St)
Luna Park (1 Union Square E)
March (405 E 58th St)
Mezzogiorno (195 Spring St)
Miracle Grill (112 First Ave)
One If By Land, Two If By Sea (17 Barrow St)
Paladar (161 Ludlow St)
Pampa (768 Amsterdam Ave)
Pastis (9 Ninth Ave)
Patois (255 Smith St, Brooklyn)
Patroon (160 E 46th St, 3rd floor)
Pete's Tavern (129 E 18th St)
Porters New York (216 Seventh Ave)
Provence (38 MacDougal St)
Radio Perfecto (190 Ave B)
Rialto (265 Elizabeth St)
River Cafe (1 Water St, Brooklyn)
San Pietro (18 E 54th St)
Sel et Poivre (853 Lexington Ave)
Spring Street Natural Restaurant (62 Spring St)
Sugar Hill Bistro (458 W 145th St)
Tabla (11 Madison Ave)
Tartine (253 W 11th St)
Tavern on the Green (Central Park W at 67th St)
Terrace in the Sky (400 W 119th St)
Time Cafe (380 Lafayette St)
Trattoria dell'Arte (900 Seventh Ave)
Verbena (54 Irving Pl)
Water Club (500 E 30th St)
White Horse Tavern (567 Hudson St)
Yaffa (97 St. Mark's Pl)

Oyster Bars

Blue Ribbon (97 Sullivan St)
Docks Oyster Bar and Seafood Grill (2427 Broadway and 633 Third Ave)

Grand Central Oyster Bar Restaurant (Grand Central Station, lower level)
Pearl Oyster Bar (18 Cornelia St)
Plaza Oyster Bar (Plaza Hotel, 768 Fifth Ave)
Shaffer City Oyster Bar & Grill (5 W 21st St)

The decidedly modern and cool **Blue Fin** (1567 Broadway, Times Square, 212/918-1400), is part of the W New York Times Square hotel. You'll find a fair sushi selection, a raw bar, a delicious lobster sandwich, caviar, and an extended seafood menu with outstanding dishes created by chef Paul Sale. Just about everything except a warm, cozy feeling.

Personal Favorites

Everybody has a list of favorite places, and I am happy to share mine:

Blue Ribbon (97 Sullivan St): value for your buck
Cafe des Artistes (1 W 67th St): restful
Gabriel's Bar & Restaurant (11 W 60th St): sophisticated
Gotham Bar & Grill (12 E 12th St): Everything is good.
Gramercy Tavern (42 E 20th St): the "in" place
Il Mulino (86 W 3rd St): Italian heaven!
Jackson Hole Burgers (232 E 64th St, 521 Third Ave, 1611 Second Ave, 1270 Madison Ave, and 517 Columbus Ave): the best burgers
La Bohême (24 Minetta Ln): unpretentious
La Caravelle (33 W 55th St): Everything seems important here.
La Grenouille (3 E 52nd St): beautiful
La Métairie (189 W 10th St): cozy
Le Périgord (405 E 52nd St): impeccable
March (405 E 58th St): imaginative
Mark's (The Mark Hotel, 25 E 77th St): the way hotel dining should be
One If By Land, Two If By Sea (17 Barrow St): romantic
Park Side (107-01 Corona Ave, Queens): Come here to eat!
Piccolo Angolo (621 Hudson St): like family friends
Post House (28 E 63rd St): macho meals
Primavera (1578 First Ave): superb service
River Cafe (1 Water St, East River, Brooklyn): Oh, that view!
Smith & Wollensky (797 Third Ave): old-time charm
Union Square Cafe (21 E 16th St): justly famous
Wong Kee (113 Mott St): basic Chinatown

Picnic Lunches

Chelsea Market Baskets (Chelsea Market, 75 Ninth Ave)
China Fun (1239 Second Ave and 246 Columbus Ave)
Citarella (1250 Ave of the Americas)
Dean & Deluca (560 Broadway, 9 Rockefeller Center, 75 University Pl)
Mark's (The Mark Hotel, 25 E 77th St)
Murray's Cheese Shop (257 Bleecker St)
One C.P.S. (Plaza Hotel, 768 Fifth Ave)
2 West (Ritz-Carlton Battery Park, 2 West St)
Virgil's Real Barbecue (152 W 44th St)
Word of Mouth (1012 Lexington Ave)

Pizza

Angelo's (117 W 57th St)
Antonio Restaurant (140 W 13th St)
Apizz (217 Eldridge St)
Arturo's Pizzeria (106 W Houston St)
Coffee Shop (29 Union Sq W)
Da Ciro (229 Lexington Ave)
Da Nico (164 Mulberry St)
Denino's (524 Port Richmond Ave, Staten Island)
Fred at Barney's New York (10 E 61st St)
Grimaldi's (19 Old Fulton St)
Il Corallo (176 Prince St)
Isola (485 Columbus Ave)
Joe's (233 Bleecker St and 7 Carmine St)
John's Pizzeria (278 Bleecker St, 260 W 44th St, and 408 E 64th St)
La Bohême (24 Minetta Lane)
Le Madri (168 W 8th St)
Lemon Tree Cafe (769 Ninth Ave)
Lento's (7003 Third Ave)
Lil' Frankie's Pizza (19 First Ave)
Lombardi's (32 Spring St)
Luca Lounge (220 Ave B)
Luigi's (1701 First Ave)
Mezzogiorno (195 Spring St)
Mona Lisa (190 Bleecker St)
Naples 45 (200 Park Ave)
Nick & Toni's Cafe (100 W 67th St)
Orso (322 W 46th St)
Osteria del Circo (120 W 55th St)
Patsy's Pizza (2291 First Ave)
Sal's & Carmine's Pizza (2533 Broadway)
Serafina (29 E 61st St and 38 E 58th St)
Spazzia (366 Columbus Ave)
Stromboli Pizzeria (112 University Pl)
Sullivan Street Bakery (73 Sullivan St)
Totonno's Pizzeria Napolitano (1544 Second Ave)
Trattoria dell'Arte (900 Seventh Ave)
Two Boots (36 Ave A, 514 2nd St, and 74 Bleecker St)
Zito's East (211-13 First Ave)

Talk about overhype! There's been much ink and conversation about a relatively new pizza establishment, **Otto** (1 Fifth Ave, 212/995-9559). It has a good wine list. But the rest! Service is straight out of *Animal House*, the bread arrives with a paper covering, and the pizzas just aren't that great. In fact, the antipasti, *formaggi*, and gelato are better than the pizza.

Power Meals

Alain Ducasse (Essex House, a Westin Hotel, 155 W 58th St)
Cafe des Artistes (1 W 67th St)
Cafe Pierre (Pierre Hotel, 2 E 61st St)

Carlyle Hotel (35 E 76th St)
Four Seasons (99 E 52nd St)
Gabriel's Bar and Restaurant (11 W 60th St)
Il Mulino (86 W 3rd St)
Jean Georges (Trump International Hotel, 1 Central Park West)
La Caravelle (3 W 55th St)
La Grenouille (3 E 52nd St)
Le Bernardin (155 W 51st St)
Le Cirque 2000 (New York Palace Hotel, 58 E 65th St)
Maloney & Porcelli (37 E 50th St)
Michael's (24 W 55th St)
Morton's of Chicago (551 Fifth Ave)
Nobu and Nobu Next Door (105 Hudson St)
Palm One (837 Second Ave)
Park Avenue Cafe (100 E 63rd St)
Peninsula New York Hotel (700 Fifth Ave)
Primavera (1578 First Ave)
Regency Hotel (540 Park Ave)
Sette Mezzo (969 Lexington Ave)
Shula's Steak House (270 W 43rd St)
Smith & Wollensky (797 Third Ave)
The Steakhouse at Monkey Bar (Elysee Hotel, 60 E 54th St)
Terrance Brennan's Seafood & Chop House (125 E 50th St)
21 Club (21 W 52nd St)

Pre-theater

It is best to let your waiter know when you sit down that you are attending the theater so that service can be adjusted accordingly. Also, if it is raining, allow extra time for getting a taxi. Some restaurants have specially priced pre-theater dinners.

Acacia (217 E 59th St)
Aquavit (13 W 54th St)
Arqua (281 Church St)
Avenue (520 Columbus Ave)
Barbetta (321 W 46th St)
Beacon (25 W 56th St)
Becco (355 W 46th St)
Cafe Botanica (Essex House, a Westin Hotel, 160 Central Park S)
Cafe des Artistes (1 W 67th St)
Cafe Un Deux Trois (123 W 44th St)
Carmine's (2450 Broadway and 200 W 44th St)
Chez Josephine (414 W 42nd St)
Dawat (210 E 58th St)
Esca (402 W 43rd St)
Fifty Seven Fifty Seven (57 E 57th St)
Firebird (365 W 46th St)
44 (Royalton Hotel, 44 W 44th St)
Four Seasons (99 E 52nd St)
Garrick (242 W 49th St)
Gino (780 Lexington Ave)
Hell's Kitchen (679 Ninth Ave)

Indochine (430 Lafayette St)
La Boite en Bois (75 W 68th St)
La Caravelle (Shoreham Hotel, 33 W 55th St)
Limoncello (777 Seventh Ave)
Marchi's (251 E 31st St)
Ollie's Noodle Shop and Grill (200-B W 44th St, 2315 Broadway, and 1991 Broadway)
Orso (322 W 46th St)
Picholine (35 W 64th St)
Red Cat (227 Tenth Ave)
Sandwich Planet (534 Ninth Ave)
Tavern on the Green (Central Park W at 67th St)
Thalia (828 Eighth Ave)
Tropica (MetLife Building, 200 Park Ave)
Westside Sushi (717 Ninth Ave)

Prix-fixe Lunches

Cafe Boulud (20 E 76th St)
Eleven Madison Park (11 Madison Ave)
Gotham Bar and Grill (12 E 12th St)
La Caravelle (Shoreham Hotel, 33 W 55th St)
Le Cirque 2000 (New York Palace Hotel, 455 Madison Ave)
Nobu (105 Hudson St)
21 Club (21 W 52nd St)
Vong (200 E 54th St)

Pubs and Good Bars

To feel the real flavor of New York, visit a pub on St. Patrick's Day. However, these spots feature good brew, good times, and good company every day.

Anotheroom (149 West Broadway)
APT (419 W 13th St): hidden
Arlene's Grocery (93 Stanton St)
AZ (21 W 17th St): Asian-fusion lounge
Balcony Bar (Metropolitan Museum of Art, 1000 Fifth Ave): culture
Baraonda (1439 Second Ave): international
Bar East (1733 First Ave): down-to-earth
Barrow's Pub (463 Hudson St)
Bemelman's Bar (Carlyle Hotel, 35 E 76th St): old-school hotel bar
Billy's (948 First Ave)
Blarney Rock Pub (137 W 33rd St)
Blue Elephant (1409 Second Ave): restaurant
Blue Fin (W New York Times Square, 1567 Broadway): best pre-theater
Boat Basin Cafe (W 79th St at Hudson River): view with a bar
Campbell Apartment (Grand Central Station, off west balcony): unique
Carnegie Hill Brewing Company (1600 Third Ave)
Cellar Bar (Bryant Park Hotel, 40 W 40th St): hotel bar
Chelsea Brewing Company (Pier 59, West St at 18th St): big place, big steaks
Chibi's Bar (238 Mott St): Japanese hideaway

Chumley's (86 Bedford St): an old speakeasy in the Village
Citarella (1240 Ave of the Americas): classy restaurant bar
Coda (Hanover Trust, 34 E 34th St): bar in a bank
Commonwealth Grill & Brewery (35 W 48th St): German lagers
Corner Bistro (331 W 4th St): eat
Danube (30 Hudson St): Austrian
d.b.a. (41 First Ave): relaxed, best bar list (130 single-malt Scotches, 50 tequilas, etc.)
Eleven Madison Park (11 Madison Ave)
Feinstein's at the Regency Hotel (540 Park Ave): sophisticated cocktail-sipping and people watching
Frank's (85 Tenth Ave)
Ginger Man (11 E 36th St): huge beer selection
Good World Bar & Grill (3 Orchard St)
Grand Bar (SoHo Grand Hotel, 310 West Broadway): recently renovated hotel bar
Heartland Brewery (1285 Ave of the Americas and 35 Union Square W): try the charcoal stout
Hudson Bar and Books (636 Hudson St): reading
Jack Dempsey (61 Second Ave): books plus fireplace
Jeremy's Ale House (254 Front St)
Jimmy's Corner (140 W 44th St): pre-theater bar
Keens Steakhouse (72 W 36th St)
Landmark Tavern (626 Eleventh Ave): good afternoon bar
Lenox Lounge (288 Malcolm X Blvd): Harlem lounge and jazz club
The Library (Regency Hotel, 540 Park Ave): class
Living Room (W New York Times Square, 1567 Broadway): tourists
McQuaid's Public House (589 Eleventh Ave)
Morgan's Bar (235 Madison Ave): great ambience
Night Cafe (938 Amsterdam Ave)
No Idea (30 W 20th St)
Noche (1604 Broadway): restaurant
North Star Pub (93 South St): authentic English style
Old Town Bar (45 E 18th St): burgers
Park, The (118 Tenth Ave): people watching
Peculiar Pub (145 Bleecker St): 500 beers!
Peter McManus Cafe (152 Seventh Ave)
Pete's Tavern (66 Irving Pl): New York's oldest continuously operating pub
P.G. Kings (18 W 33rd St): a beautiful bar
Pianos (158 Ludlow St): busy
P.J. Clarke's (915 Third Ave)
Pussycat Lounge (96 Greenwich St): dancing
Rao's (455 E 114th St)
Rise (Ritz-Carlton New York Battery Park, 2 West St, 14th fl): view
Route 85A (85-A Ave A): a true bar
Rudy's Bar & Grill (627 Ninth Ave)
Sakagura (211 E 43rd St): Japanese restaurant bar
66 Water (66 Water St): bar, restaurant, club, gallery
Smith's Bar and Restaurant (701 Eighth Ave): drink standing up
Smoke Jazz Club & Lounge (2751 Broadway): best jazz bar
The Steakhouse at Monkey Bar (Elysee Hotel, 60 E 54th St)
Subway Inn (143 E 60th St): cheapo

Swift Hibernian Lounge (34 E 4th St): 26 beers on tap
Tabla Bar (11 Madison Ave): fancy bar menu
Tavern at the Tonic (108 W 18th St)
Times Square Brewery (160 W 42nd St): in the middle of it all
Town Bar (Chambers Hotel, 15 W 56th St): good service
12:31 (12 E 31st St): cozy
Uncle Ming's (225 Ave B, 2nd floor): mysterious
Wall Street Kitchen & Bar (70 Broad St): 128 beers on tap
Waterfront Ale House (540 Second Ave): great Belgian beer, good food
Westside Brewing Company (340 Amsterdam Ave)
Whiskey, The (1567 Broadway): see and be seen
Wollensky's Grill (205 E 49th St)
Xunta (174 First Ave): tapas bar

Romantic

Some great places for hand-holding (or whatever):
Aureole (34 E 61st St)
Barbetta (321 W 46th St)
Bouterin (420 E 59th St)
Bridge Cafe (279 Water St)
Cafe des Artistes (1 W 67th St)
Cafe Pierre (Pierre Hotel, 2 E 61st St)
Cafe Trévi (1570 First Ave)
Caffe Reggio (119 MacDougal St)
Caffe Vivaldi (32 Jones St)
Capsouto Frères (451 Washington St)
Casa la Femme (150 Wooster St)
Chanterelle (2 Harrison St)
Chez Josephine (414 W 42nd St)
Danal (90 E 10th St)
Enoteca at I Trulli (122 E 27th St)
Erminia (250 E 83rd St)
Firebird (365 W 46th St)
Four Seasons (99 E 52nd St)
Il Buco (47 Bond St)
Il Cortile (125 Mulberry St)
King Cole Bar (St. Regis Hotel, 2 E 55th St)
La Bohême (24 Minetta Ln)
La Caravelle (33 W 55th St)
La Côte Basque (60 W 55th St)
Lady Mendl's Tea Parlour (Inn at Irving Place, 56 Irving Pl)
La Grenouille (3 E 52nd St)
La Métairie (189 W 10th St)
Le Cirque 2000 (New York Palace Hotel, 455 Madison Ave)
Le Périgord (405 E 62nd St)
March (405 E 58th St)
Mark's (The Mark Hotel, 25 E 77th St)
One If By Land, Two If By Sea (17 Barrow St)
Palm Court (Plaza Hotel, 768 Fifth Ave)
Paola's (347 E 85th St)
Provence (38 MacDougal St)

River Cafe (1 Water St, Brooklyn)
Scalinatella (201 E 61st St)
Tavern on the Green, Crystal Room (Central Park W and 67th St)
Water Club (East River at E 30th St)
Zoë (90 Prince St)

Sandwiches

There are thousands—yes, thousands—of places that serve sandwiches in Manhattan, and most of them are pretty ordinary. But the following turn out exceptionally good combinations for eating in or taking out:

Alcazar (163 First Ave)
America (9 E 18th St)
Amy's Bread (672 Ninth Ave)
Bread Market & Cafe (485 Fifth Ave)
Cafe Gitane (242 Mott St)
Cafe Journal (47 E 29th St)
Call Cuisine (1032 First Ave): 125 kinds of sandwiches
Carnegie Delicatessen and Restaurant (854 Seventh Ave)
City Bakery (3 W 18th St)
Cleaver Company (229 West Broadway)
Cosi Sandwich Bar (11 W 42nd St, 685 Third Ave, 38 E 45th St, 61 W 48th St, 1633 Broadway, 165 E 52nd St, and 60 E 56th St)
Cucina & Co. (MetLife Building, 200 Park Ave)
Deb's (200 Varick St)
Delices de France (289 Madison Ave)
E.A.T. (1064 Madison Ave)
Eisenberg's Sandwich Shop (174 Fifth Ave)
Good and Plenty to Go (410 W 43rd St)
Hudson Caterers Cafe (145 Hudson St)
Italian Food Center (186 Grand St)
La Boulangère (49 E 21st St)
La Fromagerie (1374 Madison Ave)
La Sandwicherie (842 Greenwich St)
Lunch Basket (403 W 24th St)
Mama Joy's (2892 Broadway)
Manganaro's Hero Boy (105 Sullivan St)
Mangia (50 W 57th St)
Melampo Imported Foods (105 Sullivan St)
Once Upon a Tart (135 Sullivan St)
Peppe Rosso to Go (149 Sullivan St)
Popover Cafe (551 Amsterdam Ave)
Sandwich Planet (534 Ninth Ave)
Sosa Borella (460 Greenwich St and 832 Eighth Ave)
Sullivan Street Bakery (73 Sullivan St)
Telephone Bar and Grill (149 Second Ave)
Terramare (22 E 65th St)
Union Square Cafe (21 E 16th St)

Seafood

Aquagrill (210 Spring St)
Aquavit (13 W 54th St)

Blue Fin (W New York Times Square, 1567 Broadway)
Blue Ribbon (97 Sullivan St)
Blue Water Grill (31 Union Square W)
Bridge Cafe (279 Water St)
Captain's Table (860 Second Ave)
Citarella (1313 Third Ave and 2135 Broadway)
Docks Oyster Bar and Seafood Grill (2427 Broadway and 633 Third Ave)
Esca (402 W 43rd St)
Estiatorio Milos (125 W 55th St)
Grand Central Oyster Bar Restaurant (Grand Central Station, lower level)
Kuruma Zushi (7 E 47th St)
Le Bernardin (155 W 51st St)
Manhattan Ocean Club (57 W 58th St)
Mary's Fish Camp (64 Charles St)
Mermaid Inn (96 Second Ave)
Milos Estiatorio (125 W 55th St)
Oceana (55 E 54th St)
Ocean Grill (384 Columbus Ave)
Oriental Garden (14 Elizabeth St)
Pearl (18 Cornelia St)
Primola (1226 Second Ave)
Remi (145 W 53rd St)
RM (33 E 60th St)
Sea Grill (19 W 49th St)
Tropica (MetLife Building, 200 Park Ave)
Wild Tuna (1081 Third Ave)
W.K. Seafood (42 Bowery)

Fish lovers: **Esca** (402 W 43rd St, 212/564-7272) is one of the very best. Located in the Theater District, with an emphasis on Southern Italian seafood and pastas, this attractive establishment is deservedly always crowded.

Shopping Breaks

To replenish your energy, here are some good places to eat located in the major Manhattan stores:

ABC Carpet & Home (888 Broadway, 212/473-3000): **Le Pain Quotidien** (bakery & cafe) and **Pipa** (South American)
Barney's New York (660 Madison Ave, 212/833-2200): **Fred's** (upscale)
Bergdorf Goodman (men's store, 745 Fifth Ave, 212/753-7300): **Cafe 745**
Bergdorf Goodman (women's store, 754 Fifth Ave, 212/753-7300): **Cafe on 5** (5th floor) and **Goodman** (plaza level)
Bloomingdale's (1000 Third Ave, 212/705-2000): **40 Carrots** (basement), **59 & Lex** (midlevel), **Le Train Bleu** (6th floor), and **Showtime Cafe** (7th floor)
Bodum (413 W 14th St, 212/367-9125): **Coffee and Tea Bar**
Burberry (9 E 57th St, 212/407-7100): **Mad Tea Cup**
Lord & Taylor (424 Fifth Ave, 212/391-3344): **An American Place** (5th floor, American cuisine) and **Signature Cafe** (6th floor, American)
Macy's (151 W 34th St, 212/695-4400): **Au Bon Pain** (street level and 8th

floor), **Cucina Express Marketplace** (cellar level), **Emack and Bolio** (4th floor), **Grill Restaurant & Bar** (cellar level), **Naples** (cellar level), **Sago Cafe** (4th floor), and **Starbucks** (3rd floor)

Saks Fifth Avenue (611 Fifth Ave, 212/753-4000): **Cafe SFA** (8th floor, tasty and classy)

Takashimaya (693 Fifth Ave, 212/350-0100): **Tea Box Cafe** (lower level, Oriental flavor)

Under the weather? How about some chicken soup? Here are a few of the best bowls in the city:

Artie's Delicatessen (2290 Broadway)
Brooklyn Diner USA (212 W 57th St)
Carnegie Delicatessen and Restaurant (854 Seventh Ave)
Citarella (2135 Broadway and 1313 Third Ave)
Fine & Schapiro (138 W 72nd St)
Kitchenette (80 West Broadway)
Second Avenue Kosher Delicatessen and Restaurant (156 Second Ave)
Zabar's (2245 Broadway): Saul Zabar himself is there to make sure it's just like his grandmother's.

Soups

Chez Laurence Patisserie (245 Madison Ave)
Hale and Hearty Soups (849 Lexington Ave)
Seaport Soup Company (76 Fulton St)
Second Avenue Kosher Delicatessen and Restaurant (156 Second Ave)
Soup Kitchen International (259-A W 55th St)
Sweet-n-Tart Cafe (76 Mott St)
Tea Den (940 Eighth Ave)
Veselka Coffee Shop (144 Second Ave)

Southern Flavors and Soul Food

Acme Bar and Grill (9 Great Jones St)
Amy Ruth's (113 W 116th St)
Bayou (308 Lenox Ave)
Biscuit BBQ Joint (367 Flatbush Ave, Brooklyn)
Brother Jimmy's Bar-B-Q (1485 Second Ave)
Bubby's (120 Hudson St)
Cafe Con Leche (424 Amsterdam Ave)
Cajun (129 Eighth Ave)
Chantale's Cajun Kitchen (510 Ninth Ave)
Charles' Southern Style Kitchen (2841 Frederick Douglass Blvd)
Comfort Diner (214 E 45th St and 142 E 86th St)
Copeland's (547 W 145th St)
Emily's (1325 Fifth Ave)
Great Jones Cafe (54 Great Jones St)
Jezebel (630 Ninth Ave)
Jimmy's Uptown (2207 Adam Clayton Powell, Jr. Blvd)
Londel's (2620 Frederick Douglass Blvd)
M&G Soul Food Diner (383 W 125th St)
Mama's (222 Sullivan St and 200 E 3rd St)
Manna's (2331 Frederick Douglass Blvd)

Mekka (14 Ave A)
Miss Maude's Spoonbread Too (547 Lenox Ave)
107 West (2787 Broadway)
Pink Tea Cup (42 Grove St)
Shark Bar (307 Amsterdam Ave)
Sister's Cuisine (1931 Madison Ave)
Sylvia's (328 Lenox Ave)
T.J.'s Southern Gourmet (92 Chambers St)

Sports Bars

Jimmy's Bait Shack (1644 Third Ave): football
McCormack's (365 Third Ave): soccer
Mustang Sally's (324 Seventh Ave): basketball
Park Avenue Country Club (381 Park Ave S)
Play-by-Play (4 Penn Plaza)
Proof (239 Third Ave)
Runyon's (932 Second Ave)
Sporting Club (99 Hudson St): basketball
Vazac's Horseshoe Bar (108 Ave B): hockey

Steak restaurants come and go, especially lately. Many of the new steakhouses are quite good, but a true pioneer, **Smith & Wollensky** (797 Third Ave, 212/753-1530), continues to stand out as one of the very best. Steak and chop lovers will enjoy the comfortable atmosphere, top-quality meat, and informed service. Look around at the tables; some of New York's biggest deals have been made here.

Steaks

Steaks are in, big-time. For meat-and-potato lovers, here is the best beef in town:

Angelo and Maxie's (233 Park Ave S): reasonable prices
Ben Benson's Steak House (123 W 52nd St)
Bistro le Steak (1309 Third Ave): inexpensive and good
Bull & Bear (Waldorf-Astoria, 301 Park Ave)
Churrascaria Plataforma (Belvedere Hotel, 316 W 49th St)
Cité (120 W 51st St)
Dan Maxwell's Steakhouse (1708 Second Ave): good value, good eating
Del Frisco's Double Eagle Steak House (1221 Ave of the Americas)
Frank's (85 Tenth Ave)
Frankie and Johnnie's (269 W 45th St)
Gage & Tollner (372 Fulton St, Brooklyn)
Gallagher's (228 W 52nd St)
Keens Steakhouse (72 W 36th St)
Le Marais (150 W 46th St): kosher
Les Halles (411 Park Ave S)
Maloney & Porcelli (37 E 50th St)
Manhattan Grille (1161 First Ave)
MarkJoseph Steakhouse (261 Water St)
Michael Jordan's, the Steak House NYC (Grand Central Station)
Morton's of Chicago (551 Fifth Ave)

Palm One, Palm Too, and **Palm West** (837 Second Ave, 840 Second Ave,
    and 250 W 50th St)
Patroon (160 E 46th St): outrageously expensive
Peter Luger (178 Broadway, Brooklyn): a tradition since 1887
Pietro's (232 E 43rd St)
Post House (Lowell Hotel, 28 E 63rd St)
Ruth's Chris Steak House (148 W 51st St and 885 Second Ave)
Shula's Steak House (270 W 43rd St): Former football coach Don Shula's
    steakhouse franchise comes to Manhattan.
Smith & Wollensky (797 Third Ave)
Soho Steak (90 Thompson St)
Sparks Steakhouse (210 E 46th St)
Steak Frites (9 E 16th St)
Strip House (13 E 12th St)
Terrance Brennan's Seafood & Chop House (125 E 50th St)

Sushi hints:

- Older and smaller sushi outposts are usually the best.
- Always sit at the sushi bar.
- Vinegared ginger pieces are for cleansing your palate between courses.
- It is okay to use your hands, but always pass the chopsticks.
- It is always proper to eat a piece in just one bite.
- Spearing food with chopsticks is "out."
- The proper way to dip hand rolls into the soy sauce/wasabi mixture is
  to immerse the fish side only, not the rice.
- Rice should never be cooler than body temperature.
- Sushi may be fresher at lunch than dinner
- Start a sushi meal with a few slices of sashimi (especially tuna) accom-
  panied by beer, sake, or whiskey.
- Sake, a wine distilled from rice, goes well with sushi.
- And finally, an insider tip: a light scotch and soda with a bit of ice is a
  refreshingly astringent accompaniment to sushi.

Sushi

During the boomtime of the 1980s, sushi bars were the fast-food joints of
the fashionable set. New Yorkers still love to wrap their chopsticks around
succulent bits of raw fish on rice. Although many are content to order plates
concocted by the chef, true aficionados prefer to select by the piece. To tailor
your next sushi meal to your own tastes, here's what you need to know:

Amaebi (sweet shrimp)
Anago (sea eel)
California roll (avocado and crab)
Hamachi (yellowtail)
Hirame (halibut)
Ika (squid)
Ikura (salmon roe)
Kappa maki (cucumber roll)
Maguro (tuna)
Nizakana (cooked fish)

Saba (mackerel)
Sake (salmon)
Tekka maki (tuna roll)
Toro (fatty tuna)
Umeshiso maki (plum roll)
Unagi (freshwater eel)
Uni (sea urchin)

Give any of these a try for sushi:

Aki (181 W 4th St)
Avenue A Sushi (103 Ave A)
Blue Ribbon Sushi (119 Sullivan St)
Bond Street (6 Bond St)
Catch 21 (31 E 21st St)
Genki Sushi New York (565 Fifth Ave)
Hatsuhana (17 E 48th St)
Honmura An (170 Mercer St)
Inagiku (Waldorf-Astoria, 301 Park Ave)
Iso (175 Second Ave)
Japonica (100 University Pl)
Jewel Bako (239 E 5th St)
Kuruma Zushi (7 E 47th St, 2nd floor)
March (405 E 58th St)
Nadaman Hakubai (Kitano Hotel, 66 Park Ave)
Nippon (155 E 52nd St)
Nobu and Nobu Next Door (105 Hudson St)
Otabe (68 E 56th St)
Ruby Foo's (2128 Broadway)
Sapporo East (245 E 10th St)
Shabu-Tatsu (216 E 10th St)
Sugiyama (251 W 55th St)
Sushi a Go-Go (1900 Broadway)
Sushi Bar (256 E 49th St)
Sushi Hana (1501 Second Ave)
Sushi of Gari (402 E 78th St)
Sushi Rose (248 E 52nd St)
Sushi Samba 7 (87 Seventh Ave)
Sushi Seki (1143 First Ave)
Sushi Yasuda (204 E 43rd St)
Sushi Zen (57 W 46th St)
Takahachi (85 Ave A)
Takino Japanese (1026 Second Ave)
Ten Kai (920 W 56th St)
Tomoe Sushi (172 Thompson St)
Toraya (17 E 71st St)
Yama (92 W Houston St, 40 Carmine St, and 122 E 17th St)

Takeout

Cucina Vivolo (138 E 74th St)
It's a Wrap (2012 Broadway)
Kumquat (1 Fifth Ave)

Lorenzo and Maria's Kitchen (1418 Third Ave)
Musette (228 Third Ave)
Pepe Verde (559 Hudson St)
Sushi a Go-Go (1900 Broadway)
Tossed (295 Park Ave S)

Teatime

A few interesting sidelights on an increasingly popular pastime in this country: afternoon tea.

- The English drink has quite a bit of milk and sugar. Lump sugar is the proper way to go; granulated sugar is considered very ordinary.
- Afternoon tea is usually served between 4 p.m. and 5 p.m. It is rumored to have been originated by Anna, the Seventh Duchess of Bedford, in 1840, when she felt peckish in the middle of the afternoon.
- The only time it is correct to drink tea at a meal is after breakfast or at "high tea." High tea can be a hearty meal, served about 6 p.m., and is consumed at a table. It replaces dinner in England and would probably be called supper in our country.
- Instructions for preparing tea: Warm the teapot with warm water. Put one heaping teaspoon of fresh tea into the warmed pot for each cup to be served, plus "one for the pot." Add freshly boiled water, stir with a spoon, and let steep for five minutes. Pour the tea through a strainer into a second prewarmed teapot, and you are ready to go. If you first pour the milk into the cups and then add the tea, you'll protect the cups from damage.
- If you're wondering what kind of tea to serve, Darjeeling is considered the finest of Indian black teas.
- Afternoon tea is rarely served at home. At hotels and restaurants, it is often served with crumpets in the winter or scones topped with clotted cream and strawberries in the summer ("cream tea").

Now you're ready for an invitation to take tea with the Queen!

Anglers and Writers (420 Hudson St)
Astor Court (St. Regis Hotel, 2 E 55th St)
Barclay Restaurant (Inter-Continental Hotel, 111 E 48th St)
Cafe SFA (Saks Fifth Avenue, 611 Fifth Ave, 8th floor)
Carlyle Hotel Gallery (35 E 76th St)
Ceci Cela (55 Spring St)
Cocktail Terrace (Waldorf-Astoria Hotel, 301 Park Ave)
Danal (90 E 10th St)
Fifty Seven Fifty Seven (Four Seasons Hotel, 57 E 57th St)
Firebird (365 W 46th St)
Gold Room (New York Palace Hotel, 455 Madison Ave)
Gotham Lounge (Peninsula New York Hotel, 700 Fifth Ave)
Ito En (822 Madison Ave)
King's Carriage House (251 E 82nd St)
Kitano Hotel (66 Park Ave)
Lady Mendl's (56 Irving Pl)
Le Train Bleu (Bloomingdale's, 1000 Third Ave)
Lowell Hotel (28 E 63rd St)
Mark, The (25 E 77th St)
Mayfair Regent Hotel (610 Park Ave)

Oak Room (Algonquin Hotel, 59 W 44th St)
Palm Court (Plaza Hotel, 768 Fifth Ave)
Payard Patisserie (1032 Lexington Ave)
Pembroke Room (Lowell Hotel, 28 E 63rd St)
Plaza Athenee (37 E 64th St)
Podunk (231 E 5th St)
Regency Hotel (540 Park Ave)
Rotunda (Pierre Hotel, 2 E 61st St)
Salon de Thé (Fauchon, 442 Park Ave)
Serendipity 3 (225 E 60th St)
Stanhope Park Hyatt Hotel (995 Fifth Ave)
Sweet Melissa (276 Court St)
Sweet Tea Room (Mackenzie-Childs, 824 Madison Ave)
Tea and Sympathy (108 Greenwich Ave)
Tea Box Cafe (Takashimaya, 693 Fifth Ave)
Toraya (17 E 71st St)
T Salon (11 E 20th St)
21 Club (21 W 52nd St)
Yaffa's Tea Room (19 Harrison St)

Your fluency could impress the waiter and your date.

bruschetta (brew-SKET-uh or brew-SHET-uh): toast rubbed with garlic and annointed with olive oil
ceci (CHEH-chee): chickpea
challah (CKHAH-la): egg enriched loaf; holy bread
chayote (chi-OH-tay): pear-like South American fruit
chipotle (chih-POHT-lay): dried smoked jalapeno chile
coq au vin (COKE oh-VANH): female chicken braised in red wine
duck a l'orange (DUCK a-lo-RAHNGE): orange duck
foie gras (FWAH GRAH): fatty liver of a force-fed goose
haricots verts (AH-ree-co VAIR): green beans
knaidlach (kuh-NAYD-lackh): Yiddish for matzo balls
kreplach (KREP-lackh): boiled, meat-filled dumplings
maraschino (ma-ruh-SKEE-no or ma-ruh-SHEE-no): denatured cherries
mascarpone (mah-scar-POE-nay): sweet, creamy fresh cheese
mirepoix (meer-PWAH): sauteed mixture of chopped carrots, onions, and celery
paella (pie-AY-ah): Spanish rice dish
prix fixe (PREE FEEKS): fixed price
radicchio (ruh-DEEK-yo): crisp, red-leafed chicory
saveur (sa-VUR)
steak au poivre (STAKE oh PWAHV): peppercorn-crusted steak
tagliatelle (tahl-yuh-TELL-ay): quarter-inch-wide ribbons of fresh pasta
tomatillo (toh-mah-TEE-yoh): small green tomatoes
vichyssoise (vee-shee-SWAHZ): pureed soup of leeks and potatoes, served cold

---

Top-rated Restaurants

The following appear in most listings of the best.
Alain Ducasse (Essex House, a Westin Hotel, 155 W 58th St)

Aureole (34 E 61st St)
Babbo (110 Waverly Pl)
Barbetta (321 W 46th St)
Bouley (120 West Broadway)
Cafe Boulud (20 E 76th St)
Cafe des Artistes (1 W 67th St)
Chanterelle (2 Harrison St)
Craftbar (47 E 19th St)
Daniel (60 E 65th St)
Danube (30 Hudson St)
Four Seasons (99 E 52nd St)
Gotham Bar & Grill (12 E 12th St)
Gramercy Tavern (42 E 20th St)
Il Mulino (86 W 3rd St)
Jean Georges (Trump International Hotel, 1 Central Park W)
La Caravelle (33 W 55th St)
La Côte Basque (60 W 55th St)
La Grenouille (3 E 52nd St)
Le Bernardin (155 W 51st St)
Le Cirque 2000 (New York Palace Hotel, 455 Madison Ave)
Le Périgord (405 E 52nd St)
Manhattan Ocean Club (57 W 58th St)
March (405 E 58th St)
Montrachet (239 West Broadway)
Nobu and Nobu Next Door (105 Hudson St)
Oceana (55 E 54th St)
Park Avenue Cafe (100 E 63rd St)
Peter Luger (178 Broadway, Brooklyn)
Post House (Lowell Hotel, 28 E 63rd St)
Primavera (1578 First Ave)
River Cafe (1 Water St, Brooklyn)
71 Clinton Fresh Food (71 Clinton St)
Sugiyama (251 W 55th St)
Sushi of Gari (402 E 78th St)
Union Square Cafe (21 E 16th St)

Looking for a relatively inexpensive, non-dressy place for Sunday brunch? **Good** (89 Greenwich Ave, 212/691-8080), is a very good choice.

Vegetarian

Restaurants where vegetarian dishes are available.

Angelica Kitchen (300 E 12th St)
Bachué (36 W 21st St)
Benny's Burritos (113 Greenwich Ave and 93 Avenue A)
Cafe Boulud (20 E 76th St)
Candle Cafe (1307 Third Ave)
Caravan of Dreams (405 E 6th St)
Chola (232 E 58th St)
Good Earth (169 Amsterdam Ave)
Good Health Cafe (324 E 86th St)
Hangawi (12 E 32nd St)

Integral Yoga (299 W 13th St)
Le Potager (Cafe Boulud, 20 E 76th St)
Nature Works (200-A W 44th St)
Planet One (76 E 7th St)
Quantum Leap (88 W 3rd St)
Quintessence (353 E 78th St, 566 Amsterdam Ave, and 263 E 10th St)
Sanctuary (25 First Ave)
Snack (105 Thompson St)
Souen (28 E 13th St and 210 Ave of the Americas)
Spring Street Natural Restaurant (62 Spring St)
Surya (302 Bleecker St)
Two Boots (37 Ave A and other locations)
Union Square Cafe (21 E 16th St)
Vege Vege II (544 Third Ave)
Vegetable Garden (233 Bleecker St)
Village Natural (46 Greenwich Ave)
VP 2 (144 W 4th St)
Whole Earth Bakery and Kitchen (130 St. Marks Pl)
Zen Palate (633 Ninth Ave, 2170 Broadway, and 34 Union Sq E)

View

Contrary to the axiom that good food generally does not come with a good view, the food at all of these "rooms with a view" is good.

Alma (187 Columbia St, Brooklyn): magical rooftop garden
American Park (Battery Park, off State St)
Delegates' Dining Room (United Nations, First Ave at 42nd St, visitors' entrance)
River Cafe (1 Water St, Brooklyn): A window seat affords the famous view of the downtown skyline you've always seen on postcards and in movies.
Tavern on the Green (Central Park W at 67th St): magical!
The View (Marriott Marquis Hotel, 1535 Broadway): revolves high above Times Square
Top of the Tower (3 Mitchell Pl): an art deco penthouse delight
Water Club (500 E 30th St, at East River): Try the view with Sunday brunch.
World Yacht Cruises (Pier 81, W 41st St at Hudson River): Manhattan from the water

Wine Bars

Artisanal (2 Park Ave)
Barbaluc (135 E 65th St)
Eleven Madison Park (11 Madison Ave)
Enoteca I Trulli (124 E 27th St)
Harry's at Hanover Square (1 Hanover Sq)
Il Posto Accanto (192 E 2nd St)
I Tre Merli (463 West Broadway)
Morrell's Wine Bar (1 Rockefeller Plaza)
Paradou (8 Little West 12th St)
Proseccheria (447 Third Ave)
Punch & Judy (26 Clinton St)
Rhone (63 Gansevoort St)
Veritas (43 E 20th St)

New York Restaurants: The Best in Every Price Category

ACAPPELLA
1 Hudson St (at West Broadway)   212/240-0163
Lunch: Mon-Fri; Dinner: Mon-Sat   www.acappella-restaurant.com
Moderately expensive

Acappella is a classy, upscale (in atmosphere, food, and pricing) Tribeca diningroom with a highly professional staff that provides a very special dining experience. It's a good place for a romantic interlude, for an important business lunch, or to experiment with some unique Northern Italian dishes. You'll find pastas, risotto, calamari, fish, veal scaloppine, veal chops, breaded breast of chicken and prime steak on the menu. Forget the ordinary desserts and splurge on the homemade Italian cheesecake or chocolate truffle torte.

ALAIN DUCASSE
Essex House, a Westin Hotel
155 W 58th St   212/265-7300
Dinner: Mon-Sat   www.alain-ducasse.com
Extremely expensive

A meal here is definitely an experience. Alain Ducasse, the most highly starred chef in the world, has finally let New Yorkers taste his magic. In a magnificent setting, it is thoughtful to the last detail (even a stool at chairside for a lady's bag), with superb table settings and a rarefied atmosphere. The staff almost outnumbers the diners (just 65 are seated per meal). I counted over 20 at work in the bustling kitchen alone. The restaurant also has a cozy alcove where special diners can see how all the famous dishes are put together. There is no question that dining here will be something you'll long remember, but methinks more for the size of the tab than for the taste of the spit-roasted chicken breast or grilled Arizona beef. To be fair, there are some great dishes, like the veloute of sweet pear with crab fingers appetizer or several knockout chocolate desserts. Different seasonal menus are a part of the dining experience. And the candy cart is magnificent! But with prices in the range of several hundred dollars—even for lunch—and wine tabs that would make a Wall Street baron think twice, most folks will reflect that Alain Ducasse was fun to see and experience but would hesitate for a return visit, unless they won the lottery. For a party of up to 12, you can reserve a private dining room with your own waiter, sommelier, pre-menu consultation, and private entrance.

ALOUETTE
2588 Broadway (bet 97th and 98th St)   212/222-6808
Dinner: Daily   www.alouettenyc.com
Moderate

Looking for a bustling eatery on the Upper West Side where prices are within reason and the food is good? Well, Alouette is made even more desirable by a friendly and helpful staff. Seating is provided in smallish quarters on the street floor, and more tables are available on the mezzanine. Lots of French specialities to start: pate de foie gras de canard, onion soup *gratinee,* escargots, and a delicious warm goat cheese *tartelette.* Seafood dishes are available, but it is in the steak category that Alouette really shines. Hanger steak and sirloin are both excellent choices, with superb *pommes frites* (as you would expect) and a coconut-infused spinach side dish! Pretend you are in Paris and enjoy the cheese plate for dessert.

AMERICA
9 E 18th St (bet Fifth Ave and Broadway)   212/505-2110
Lunch, Dinner: Daily; Brunch: Sat, Sun   www.arkrestaurants.com
Inexpensive to moderate

This place is *big!* The room is big, the menu is big, the portions are big, the noise level is big. The good news is that the tab is relatively small at this touristy stop. Kids will love the burgers, chili, pasta, pizza, and great sandwiches. Mom and Dad have their items, too: omelets, Boston brown bread, Buffalo wings, New Mexican black bean cakes, roast turkey, and South Carolina crab cakes. Super desserts include Tollhouse cookies, Death by Chocolate, key lime pie, ice cream, and more. This is not gourmet dining, but it's vintage America-at-the dinner-table—a really *big* dinner table.

Arezzo (46 W 22nd St, 212/206-0555) is a high-priced Tuscan eatery that does some really delicious dishes. They should at these prices ($34 veal chops!). What really caught my attention was the warm flourless chocolate cake. And here I thought that desserts were supposed to be a cool meal finisher!

ANGELS RISTORANTE
1135 First Ave (bet 62nd and 63rd St)   212/980-3131
Daily: 11:30 a.m.-11:30 p.m.   www.angelsnyc.com
Moderate

For over a decade Angels has been one of the most popular East Side Italian restaurants. They bring consistency to their homemade pastas, breads, cheeses, salads, and exotic appetizers. Entree offerings include a variety of fish and meat dishes. Known for huge portions and good service, Angels is an experience not to be missed. Stroll around the corner and take home a variety of homebaked goodies, ready-to-eat pastas, and sandwiches from **Wings on Angels** (deliveries, 212/371-8484). They cater such estimable establishments as Gracie Mansion and the New York Public Library.

ANNIE'S
1381 Third Ave (bet 78th and 79th St)   212/327-4853
Breakfast: Mon-Fri; Lunch, Dinner: Daily
Inexpensive to moderate

Doesn't anyone go out for breakfast or lunch on Saturday? It would seem that way in Manhattan, with most restaurants pulling the shades until dinnertime. Not at Annie's. The daily brunch menu finds this place hopping with neighborhood regulars who know they can get a good meal at a sensible price. On the brunch menu are tasty eggs, omelets, frittatas, cereals, and homemade baked items. Regular lunch and dinner menus feature tasty soups and salads, sandwiches, pastas, steaks, chicken, burgers, seafood, and delicious beef short ribs. If you can imagine desserts under $7 in inflated New York, then look at what Annie offers: homemade apple pie, tarts, old-fashioned strawberry shortcake, gelati, and sorbets. No wonder this is such a popular place. Even standing in line is a pleasure when you get value like this! Free delivery is available from 65th to 96th streets, between East End and Fifth avenues.

AQUAVIT
13 W 54th St (bet Fifth Ave and Ave of the Americas) 212/307-7311
Lunch: Mon-Sat (cafe); Mon-Fri (atrium);
Dinner: Daily; Smorgasbord: Sun (12-3)
Expensive

Aquavit presents an attractive, wholesome background for some very tasty (and expensive) Scandinavian dishes. The setting is a feast for the eyes, the platters a feast for the tummy. One has a choice of eating upstairs in the slightly less expensive cafe or in the several areas downstairs, including one with a waterfall. From here, the diner looks eight stories skyward in a dramatic atrium (the former John D. Rockefeller townhouse). Major alterations have been made to the menu, which is now prepared by chef Marcus Samuelsson. Cafe specialties include herring, gravlax, and delicious salmon (poached or pan-fried). Open-faced sandwiches are also available. Outstanding dishes in the diningroom include pan-roasted loin of beef, loin of Arctic venison, Arctic char, and rack of lamb. For dessert, try warm chocolate ganache.

ARABELLE
Hotel Plaza Athenee
37 E 64th St (bet Madison and Park Ave)   212/734-9100
Breakfast: Daily; Lunch, Dinner: Tues-Sat; Brunch: Sun
Moderately expensive to expensive   www.arabellerestaurant.com

Dining in this attractive room is a civilized experience. This room is elegant and charming, and the adjacent lounge is one of the classiest places in Manhattan. For starters, try real French onion soup (in the lounge), sauteed Hudson Valley foie gras, or sashimi ahi tuna. If you still have room, entree winners are pan-roasted Atlantic halibut, beef tenderloin, and a tasty Maine lobster salad. By all means, try the warm valrhona chocolate soufflé (order at the start of a meal) for dessert. The attentive waiters here look like they have been doing this their whole life.

ARTISANAL
2 Park Ave (at 32nd St)   212/725-8585
Lunch, Dinner: Daily
Moderate to moderately expensive

Imagine a combination bistro, brasserie, and fromagerie, and you'll have a clear picture of this exciting operation. Being a cheese lover, I found the menu and the attractive in-house takeout cheese counter first-rate. But there is much more! A wonderful shrimp and avocado salad is a great way to start. Pricey seafood platters include lobster, clams, scallops, oysters, shrimp, sea urchin, and more. Several fondues are offered, including a classic Swiss and a wonderful stilton and sauterne. Seafood specialties include soft-shell crabs, cod, and Dover sole; heartier appetites will be satisfied with grilled lamb chops, several steak items, and daily offerings. Cruise the cheese counter and load up your plate from a selection of 250 of the world's best for dessert. Seating is comfortable in a spacious room, service is highly informed and refined, and the energy level is high.

A TAVOLA
1095 Lexington Ave (at 77th St)   212/744-1233
Breakfast, Lunch, Dinner: Daily
Inexpensive to moderate

An inexpensive Italian diner on the high-rent Upper East Side? Yes sir, and they serve excellent food. A small kitchen turns out dozens of hot and cold appetizers, soups, stews, seafood, sandwiches, poultry, pastas, and more. They serve complete Italian meals with tasty Italian breads and just about anything else your heart desires. There's nothing fancy in the decor, the service is homey and informal, and the owners seem sincerely happy to welcome you. The breakfast menu offers juices, fresh fruit, omelets, lox and bagels, cereals, and griddle items. Don't ask me how they manage to do it all so well, but this is a real find . . . and the price is right. Their tartufo is as good any I have tasted in Italy.

ATELIER
Ritz-Carlton Central Park, 50 Central Park S (at Ave of the Americas)
Breakfast, Lunch, Dinner: Daily   212/521-6125
Expensive

With a great location right on Central Park, a name that denotes top quality and service, and a room that is executed in sparkling good taste, Atelier has joined the ranks of the city's best hotel restaurants. The menu features the freshest in every category, the accent is definitely continental, with a tip of the chef's hat to the Alsace region. The salads are delicious and meats formidable, but it is in the seafood department that the place really shines. This is definitely an expense-account room or one for wealthy widows to cement a relationship. A tasting menu, with little change from a $100 bill, is available, as well as a nice selection of caviar (don't ask the price!). Any memories of the once-glorious Rumplemeyer's—which occupied the same location and went down badly in its later days—are dispelled by Atelier's innovative desserts. If you have time, the soufflés are *really* ritzy! But there is lighter fare, like tarts and apple crumb, for those whose portfolios are not quite what they used to be. Oh yes, the staff here are very nice and not the least bit snobbish, as well they might be.

AUREOLE
34 E 61st St (bet Madison and Park Ave)   212/319-1660
Lunch: Mon-Fri; Dinner: Mon-Sat   www.aureolerestaurant.com
Expensive

I am not a big fan of Aureole. Not that it isn't a fine restaurant; at the prices they charge, it should be. Owner-chef Charlie Palmer usually does a fine job with the preparation of his dishes. They are beautifully served by personnel who are more than a little impressed that they work here. If you manage to get seated (without questionable waits at the bar) and are lucky enough to sit on the first floor, with its seasonal garden views, you are fortunate. Best bets are the game dishes. Desserts look better than they taste. Personally, I can think of other places to spend your hard-earned bucks where the staff will appreciate your business. On the plus side, the four-course *prix fixe* luncheon is a good value.

AZ   212/691-8888
21 W 17th St (bet Fifth Ave and Ave of the Americas)
Dinner: Daily   www.aznyc.com
Moderate (lunch); expensive (dinner)

Fusion dining seems to be on the way out, but AZ defies the trend, with executive chef Patricia Yeo doing unusual things in a rather unique atmosphere. Three dining floors include a large private room on the second floor. The rooftop dining area, complete with a retractable sun-roof ceiling, is by far the most interesting place to dine. The menu changes daily. If you can understand the strange combination of Asian and Eastern influences with an American touch, then you'll be able to eat here comfortably. There surely are enough servers to take care of every need. Unusual touches: an elevator to whisk you to the rooftop, and a hot fudge sundae for dessert (in a place like this?). Well, dear readers, AZ is different!

BABBO
110 Waverly Pl (near Washington Square)   212/777-0303
Dinner: Daily   www.babbonyc.com
Moderate to moderately expensive

For many years 110 Waverly Place has been one of my favorite dining addresses. First it was the legendary Coach House, and now it is the magnificent Italian watering spot Babbo, which means "daddy" in the native tongue. Surely it has become one of the most respected houses of fine Italian dining in New York, and a reservation here is one of the toughest in Manhattan. The townhouse setting is warm and comfortable, the service is highly professional, and an evening here is one you will savor for a long time! Most everything is good, but I especially recommend pork tenderloin, sweetbreads, grilled ribeye steak for two, and beef cheek ravioli. Wonderful desserts include chocolate hazelnut cake, pistachio and chocolate *semifreddo*, and the ever-popular cheese plate. Best of all is the assortment of homemade gelati and sorbetti, served in small cups that really whet the appetite.

A great place for those who want a special selection of wine along with their French dinner is **Bandol Bistro & Wine Bar** (181 E 78th St. 212/744-1800). With a romantic decor, extremely friendly personnel, and an interesting menu, you can be assured of a delicious dinner. They are open daily for dinner from 5 p.m., lunch on Saturday, and for brunch on Sunday.

BALDORIA
249 W 49th St (bet Eighth Ave and Broadway)   212/582-0460
Lunch: Mon-Fri; Dinner: Mon-Sat   www.baldoriamo.com
Moderately expensive

New Yorkers in the know head way uptown to Rao's, on 114th Street. Although getting a reservation at Rao's can be a problem, an offshoot of this famous Italian eatery has opened in midtown, and it is a definite winner. The seasonings and sauces at Baldoria make almost every dish memorable. There are mussels and clams to start, wonderfully fresh seasonal salads, a good selection of pastas, and especially delectable spaghetti dishes. Their lemon chicken is one of the best I have ever tasted. If the fresh peach semifreddo is on the menu, try it for dessert; otherwise I'd recommend Italian cream puffs with espresso cream and chocolate caramel sauce. The place is busy, but an abundance of personnel will make sure you are well taken care of.

> You've no doubt heard a lot about **Balthazar** (80 Spring St, 212/965-1414), but maybe you didn't know that it is one of the best breakfast houses in Manhattan. Give it a try. You'll see many familiar faces!

BALTHAZAR
80 Spring St (at Crosby St)   212/965-1414
Breakfast, Lunch, Dinner: Daily; Brunch: Sat, Sun
(afterhours menu after midnight)   www.balthazarny.com
Moderate

A certain chemistry hurtles some restaurants into the big time very early in their existence. This happened in spades at Balthazar. Despite the over-taxing of every aspect of their operation, they realized that the food must be good—even very good—if their reputation and popularity were to last. In a comfortable setting with tile floors, old mirrors, ceiling fans, and an unat-tractive yellow tin roof, the harried help scoot around trying to please diners, who almost need earplugs in order to concentrate on the tasty dishes. Seafood—steamed halibut, grilled brook trout, seared salmon, and the like—is especially good. Don't miss the steak *frites*. An attractive baked goods section sits right by the front door, and a seafood bar serves oysters, clams, and lobster until the wee hours. A nice selection of cheese is available, along with tasty desserts like apple tart a la mode. If you want to see or be seen, this is a hot spot. The takeout menu includes soups, salads, and sand-wiches on delectable breads.

BARBETTA
321 W 46th St (bet Eighth and Ninth Ave)   212/246-9171
Lunch, Dinner, Supper: Tues-Sun   www.barbettarestaurant.com
Moderate to expensive

Barbetta is one of those special places you'll find only in New York. And owner Laura Maioglio is one of those very special people you will only find in New York. It is an elegant restaurant serving Piemontese cuisine. Piemonte is located in the northern part of Italy, and the cuisine reflects that charming part of the country. You can dine here in European elegance. One of New York's oldest restaurants, Barbetta will celebrate its 100th anniversary in 2006. It's still owned by the family who founded it. One of the special attractions is dining alfresco in the garden during the summer. The main dining room and private party rooms are magnificent! They offer an a la carte luncheon menu, as well as a four-course pre-theater dinner menu, which includes fish specialties, *scottiglia,* and a number of other selections served expeditiously so that you can make opening curtain. If you have more time and can enjoy a leisurely dinner, think about the *crespelle* (almost a meal in itself), handmade ravioli, or the fabulous quail's nest of *fonduta* with white truffles. Barbetta specializes in fish and game dishes that vary daily. Try the squab prepared with foie gras and chestnuts. Other selections include rabbit, beef braised in red wine with polenta, and a delicious rack of venison. Sixteen desserts are prepared daily, including several chocolate offerings and an assortment of cakes, tarts, and fruits, as well as panna cotta—one of the best in the city. Barbetta's extraordinary wine list, featuring 1,630 wines, is six-time winner of *Wine Spectator's* Best-of Award of Excellence.

BAYARD'S
1 Hanover Square (bet Pearl and Stone St)   212/514-9454
Dinner: Mon-Sat   www.bayards.com
Expensive

This is a most unusual and hard-to-find setting for a restaurant. The building is India House, a private club in the Financial District for members only during lunch. The facilities open to the general public at night and for private parties. The decor is New England nautical, and the rooms are exceptionally nice. This would be a good place to celebrate a special occasion. Prices are high but so is value. The dishes are high-quality, and an enormous selection is available. Chef Eberhard Müller is also at home on a farm, growing his own produce. Appetizers range from sauteed foie gras to a selection of chilled oysters from both coasts. On to the marvelous Maine lobster salad or seared Atlantic salmon. Your choice from among a dozen desserts includes a cheese dish, soufflés, homemade sorbets, and ice cream. Service is very professional, and a tour of Bayard's private party rooms is an extra treat.

BEACON
25 W 56th St (bet Fifth Ave and Ave of the Americas)
Lunch: Mon-Fri; Dinner: Daily   212/332-0500
Moderately expensive   www.beaconnyc.com

In a huge space divided into intimate sections, Beacon serves some of the tastiest open-fire cooked dishes in the city. If you can get a seat in the room by the open kitchen ("the pit"), it is a fascinating show. With over 200 seats and an expansive menu for lunch and dinner, the staff have been well trained to provide superior service. Over a dozen appetizers (from grilled quail to oysters on the half shell), sandwiches, salads, steaks, chops, seafood, and pasta are available at noon. In the evening the seafood selection increases, as do the meat offerings. The wood-roasted chops and veal dishes are special. Several game dishes are listed on the dinner menu. Dessert soufflés add a festive ending to a great meal. All breads and rolls are made in-house and are available for purchase.

BELLINI
208 E 52nd St (bet Second and Third Ave)   212/308-0830
Lunch: Mon-Fri: Dinner: Mon-Sat   www.bellinirestaurantnyc.com
Moderately expensive

You might call the cuisine at this classic Italian beauty "all in the family." The head lady at Bellini is Donatella Arpaia. Her father, the well-known chef Lello Arpaia, and brother Dino are also in the restaurant business. Donatella has successfully stepped out on her own with Bellini. Her menus take into account the current interest in healthy platters. Specialties include thinly sliced raw tuna with dill, grilled sirloin steak, and a number of Neapolitan specialties. Even the appetizers, which include grilled portobello mushrooms, and fresh salads are a treat. For traditionalists, the Bellini gnocchi, served with a Bolognese sauce, is sure to please. For dessert, you can't miss with warm chocolate hazelnut cake. In addition to the glamorous owner, other attractions include businesslike waiters, tables far enough apart to permit conversation, and a noise-dampening ceiling—amenities that are missing in so many of today's better restaurants.

BEN BENSON'S STEAK HOUSE
123 W 52nd St (bet Ave of the Americas and Seventh Ave)
Lunch: Mon-Fri; Dinner: Daily   212/581-8888
Moderately expensive   www.benbensons.com

With all the new steakhouses in Manhattan, it is easy to overlook the old reliables. For years, Ben Benson's Steak House has been a favorite of the meat-and-potato set, and with justification. The atmosphere is macho-clubby, and the food is uniformly good. Unlike some other steakhouses, service here is courteous and efficient. The menu is what you would expect: sirloin steak, filet mignon, T-bone, prime rib, chops, and the like. But Ben Benson's also offers seafood, chicken, calves liver, and chopped steak. A special veal chop steak-style offers 22 ounces of indulgence without the guilt. The soups are great! Wonderful potatoes, onion rings, or healthy spinach complete the stomach-filling experience. Lunchtime specials include lobster cakes, grilled chicken breast, roast beef hash, and chicken pot pie. Don't come looking for bargains. Ben treats you well, and you pay well for what you get!

My initial impression of **Beppe** (45 E 22nd St, 212/982-8422) was only so-so. Recently, however, things have improved. The Tuscan food, including family-style meals, is pretty good. Fried chicken and spareribs may not exactly be Tuscan, but both are delicious.

BIENVENUE
21 E 36th St (bet Fifth and Madison Ave)   212/684-0215
Lunch: Mon-Fri; Dinner: Mon-Sat
Moderate

The neighborhood knows and loves this reliable, smallish French bistro, which serves exceptionally good food in large portions at moderate prices. There is absolutely no "attitude" here, just informed and gracious folks taking care of busy tables. Snails, fresh salads, delicious onion soup, and specialty patés all make good starters. (Be sure to bring a healthy appetite.) On to chicken in red wine sauce, monkfish, crab cakes, beef bourguignon, roast loin of pork, or other daily specials. Profiteroles are my dessert choice. This comfortable, professional operation has been doing things right since 1971, and that is quite an accomplishment!

BIG NICK'S
2175 Broadway (at 77th St)   212/362-9238
24 hours   www.bignicks.citysearch.com
Inexpensive

For those readers who believe this volume deals only in pricey places, that is simply not true! Take Big Nick's, for example. This place is unfancy, inexpensive, untrendy, and relatively unknown . . . except among those who want good food at low prices and really don't care about atmosphere! Breakfasts are super, and they serve lots of salads and sandwiches for lunch. The burgers are sensational. There is a special selection for diet-watchers. Filo pastries and meat, cheese, and spinach pies are all specialties. There are pizzas, baked potatoes served any way you want, delicious cakes and pies, homemade baklava, and yogurt. The service is friendly, and they offer free delivery. They've been at it since 1962 with no publicity.

BISTRO LES AMIS
180 Spring St (at Thompson St)   212/226-8645
Lunch, Dinner: Daily   www.bistrolesamis.com
Moderate

Bistro les Amis is a delightful bistro worth stopping by to enjoy in the middle of a Soho shopping or gallery excursion. In the warmer months, doors open to the sidewalk, and the passing parade is almost as inviting as the varied menu. The French onion soup with gruyere is a must; salmon marinated with fresh dill and herbs is just as good. Lunch entrees include sandwiches and fresh salads. In the evening, seafood and steak dishes are available. The steak *frites* with herb butter are first-class. There's nothing very fancy about this bistro—just good food with an extra touch of friendly service.

Unique Dining Available in the Kitchen (for a price):

Alain Ducasse (Essex House, a Westin Hotel, 155 W 58th St, 212/265-7300)

Le Cirque 2000 (New York Palace Hotel, 455 Madison Ave, 212/303-7788)

Park Avenue Cafe (100 E 63rd St, 212/644-1900)

Patroon (160 E 46th St, 212/883-7373)

BLUE HILL
75 Washington Pl (at Ave of the Americas)   212/539-1776
Dinner: Mon-Sun   www.bluehillnyc.com
Moderate to moderately expensive

Dramatic it is not. Comfortable it is barely. Solid it is in spades. Blue Hill, named after a farm in the Berkshires inhabited by one of the owner's family, reflects the chefs' solid upbringing with David Bouley. The smallish menu, with only a half dozen appetizers and entrees, does include some spectacular standouts and changes periodically. If your evening involves intimate conversation, forget Blue Hill, as eavesdropping is rampant. The chocolate bread pudding ("chocolate silk") is the best and really the only dessert worth the calories. This is one of those spots that elderly members of your family may especially enjoy, as it is very civilized.

BLUE RIBBON
97 Sullivan St (bet Spring and Prince St)   212/274-0404
Daily: 4 p.m.-4 a.m.
Moderate

This place deserves a blue ribbon in just about every respect except for quiet, leisurely dining. Blue Ribbon is one of the most popular spots in Soho, with a bustling bar scene and a line waiting for its limited number of tables. Regulars appreciate the exceptional food served in this unpretentious restaurant. There is a raw bar to attract seafood lovers, along with clams, lobster, crab, boiled crawfish, and the house special "Blue Ribbon Royale." One can choose from two dozen appetizers, including barbequed ribs, smoked trout, caviar, and chicken wings. Entrees are just as wide-ranging: sweetbreads, catfish, tofu ravioli, fried chicken and mashed potatoes, burgers, and much more. How the smallish kitchen can turn out so many dishes is amazing, but they certainly do it well. Don't come here for a relaxed evening; this is strictly an all-American culinary experience. Those who experience hunger pangs after midnight will appreciate the late hours. Try the sushi at another Blue Ribbon operation, **Blue Ribbon Sushi** (119 Sullivan St, 212/343-0404).

BLUE RIBBON BAKERY
35 Downing St (at Bedford St)   212/337-0404
Lunch, Dinner: Daily
Moderate

Another Blue Ribbon operation is this cafe and bakery. The rustic breads are excellent, and there is much more. Downstairs, customers may dine in a fantastic grotto-like atmosphere, complete with two small diningrooms, a wine cellar, and wonderful fresh-bread aroma. The upstairs and downstairs menus feature sandwiches, grill items, veggies and yummy desserts, including profiteroles. The wonderful veal stew is a must!

BLUE SMOKE
116 E 27th St (bet Lexington Ave and Park Ave S)   212/447-7733
Lunch, Dinner: Daily   www.bluesmoke.com
Moderate

Leave it to Danny Meyer to take advantage of a real void in the Manhattan dining scene. There are legions of barbecue lovers who find it difficult to get real down-home ribs with all the trimmings in the Big Apple. Blue Smoke is not just a barbecue place; it is a scene, with an ultra-busy bar attracting the trendsetters. In addition to ribs, you'll find chili, smoked beef brisket, tasty sandwiches, pit beans, and more. The sticky toffee pudding sounds better than it tastes. Oh well, the place is fun and different, and Meyer can add another star to his culinary crown.

BLUE WATER GRILL
31 Union Square W (at 16th St)   212/675-9500
Lunch, Dinner: Daily; Brunch: Sun   www.brguestrestaurants.com
Moderate

This seafood restaurant really knows the ocean and all the edible creatures that inhabit it! The Blue Water Grill is a highly professional operation, with superbly trained personnel operating in a building that once served as a bank and is now a *very* bustling restaurant. Wonderful appetizers include lobster bisque, Cape Cod steamers, real Maryland crab cakes. Tuna, salmon, swordfish, and mahi-mahi are prepared several ways. Lobsters and oysters (several dozen varieties) are fresh and tasty. For those who want to stick to shore foods, there are pastas, chicken dishes, and grilled filet mignon. A half dozen sensibly priced desserts include key lime tart and warm valhrona chocolate cake with vanilla ice cream.

BOLO
23 E 22nd St (bet Broadway and Park Ave S)   212/228-2200
Lunch: Mon-Fri; Dinner: Daily   www.bolorestaurant.com
Moderate to moderately expensive

The menu here is not a copy of the namesake restaurant at the Ritz Hotel in Madrid, but it does encompass contemporary Spanish as well as Southwestern flavors in an attractive and comfortable setting. The atmosphere and personnel are upbeat, as the folks here want your meal to be both tasty and fun. The dozen or so tapas are delicious. The logistics are a miracle, with a tiny kitchen turning out a bevy of wonderful, sometimes seasonal, dishes.

The best chefs in Manhattan:
Mario Batali (Babbo)
David Bouley (Bouley)
Daniel Boulud (Daniel)
Tom Colicchio (Gramercy Tavern)
Scott Conant (L'Impero)
Alain Ducasse (Alain Ducasse)
Troy Dupuy (La Caravelle)
Cornelius Gallagher (Oceana)
Gabriel Kreuther (Atelier)
Marcus Samuelsson (Aquavit)
Tom Valenti (Ouest)
Jean-Georges Vongerichten (Jean Georges)
Michael White (Fiamma Osteria)

BOULEY
120 West Broadway (at Duane St)   212/964-2525
Lunch, Dinner: Daily   www.bouley.net
Expensive

Subdued, plush, elegant, quiet, refined, professional, and delicious—all of these words describe one of the great places to dine in Manhattan. Even the original carved door is back! David Bouley is at his best when he is in the kitchen, and this restaurant in Tribeca is a tribute to his genius. All manner of nice touches make a meal here a never-to-be-forgotten experience, like the placing of a silver cover on the dish of a diner who must leave the table for a moment. Tasting menus are offered, as are seasonal offerings. There are a dozen appetizers and just as many enticing entrees. Don't miss the potato puree! Cheeses are a specialty, as are fabulous desserts like hot valrhona chocolate soufflé. Before and after some courses, small surprises arrive at the table.

David Bouley is one of the most innovative and talented food-business professionals in Manhattan. His **Bouley** and **Danube** restaurants set a high standard of excellence. Now, through his catering operation, David's remarkable food can be brought right to you at a country field or a city loft. Every detail will be coordinated, and the staff will work with you on your custom menu. Call 212/962-2902 to arrange for private dining at the restaurants or for an off-premises event.

BOUTERIN
420 E 59th St (near First Ave)   212/758-0323
Dinner: Daily   www.bouterin.com
Moderately expensive

In one of the most pleasant dining settings in Manhattan, Antoine Bouterin has created a French country restaurant with style and class. The flowers and accessories in the room add to the enjoyment of the *provençal* theme. And what goodies he produces: homemade paté, crab cakes with red pepper sauce, hearty lamb stew, red snapper with shallot crust, and bouillabaisse Marseille-style are just a few of the treats. By all means save room for the signature dessert: Grandmother's Floating Island, with fresh berries. For the health conscious, vegetarian dishes are available.

BRASSERIE
100 E 53rd St (bet Park and Lexington Ave)   212/751-4840
Breakfast: Mon-Fri; Lunch, Dinner: Daily
Moderate   www.restaurantassociates.com

For years the Brasserie was a round-the-clock operation, but alas the night owls now have to get their orders in a bit earlier. In attractive quarters, with sexy lighting and a bar that offers all manner of goodies, the Brasserie now closes at 1 a.m. During its 18-hour day, you can find good, if not exceptional, food with a variety of choices, most with a French flair. Among them are grilled dishes, short ribs, *pot-au-feu,* steamed mussels with *frites,* and daily specials. But the real winners here are good old onion soup, burgers, and salad nicoise. Desserts (except the beignets) are tasteless. If you like to make a grand entrance, the central staircase provides a perfect setting.

Hungry Bloomingdale's shoppers can retreat to **Brasserie 360** (200 E 60th St, 212/688-8688), where a bi-level restaurant features a French brasserie with a Belgian flavor on the first level and a sushi bar upstairs. I'd recommend *coq au vin* downstairs and very good sushi upstairs.

BRASSERIE 8½
9 W 57th St (bet Fifth Ave and Ave of the Americas)   212/829-0812
Lunch: Mon-Sat; Dinner: Daily; Brunch: Sun (summer hours vary)
Moderately expensive   www.restaurantassociates.com

The interior almost beats the dining at this dramatic restaurant. Descending a long spiral staircase, you enter a spectacular room filled with comfy chairs, an attractive bar, a wall of Luger stained glass, and a collection of signed Matisse prints. Even the tableware is pleasing. Main-course winners include roasted Chilean sea bass, crab cakes, roast chicken, grilled sea scallops, grilled veggie salad, and Maine lobster salad. Specials are offered daily. The Friday seafood bouillabaisse is worth a special visit. Great desserts include chocolate soufflé with malt ice cream. On top of everything, these folks really seem happy to greet their diners.

BRAVO GIANNI
230 E 63rd St (bet Second and Third Ave)   212/752-7272
Lunch: Mon-En; Dinner: Mon-Sun
Moderately expensive

Fans of Bravo Gianni—and there are many—may be upset that I've included it in this book. They want to keep it a secret. It's so comfortable and the food so good that they don't want it to become overcrowded and spoiled. But it doesn't look like there's any real danger of that happening as long as Gianni himself is on the job. The not-too-large room is pleasantly appointed, with beautiful plants on every table. The atmosphere is intimate.

And what tastes await you! You can't go wrong with any of the antipasto selections or soups. They have the best ravoli in town. But save room for the *tortellini alla panna* or the *fettuccine con ricotta;* no one does them better. I can recommend every dish on the menu, with top billing going to the fish dishes and rack of lamb. Marvelous desserts, many of them made in-house, will surely tempt you. Legions of loyal customers come back again and again, and it's easy to see why.

BRIDGE CAFE
279 Water St (under Brooklyn Bridge)   212/227-3344
Lunch: Mon-Fri: Dinner: Daily; Brunch: Sun   wwwbridgecafe.com
Moderate

Who knows? You might see former mayor Ed Koch in here; like so many other dyed-in-the-wool New Yorkers, he knows this is one of Manhattan's treasures. As a matter of fact, the Bridge Cafe—located north of South Street Seaport, beneath the Brooklyn Bridge—has been in operation since 1794, making it the oldest business establishment in the city. Over the decades (nay, centuries!) it has housed its share of brothels and saloons. Great seasonal dishes include grilled shrimp salad, pumpkin ravioli, and braised brisket of beef. There is nothing fancy about this place—just good food with especially pleasant personnel. Don't leave without trying the key lime pie. On Sundays the French toast will get you off to a great start!

BROOKLYN DINER USA
212 W 57th St (bet Broadway and Seventh Ave)   212/977-1957
Breakfast, Lunch, Dinner, Late Supper: Daily
Moderate   www.thefiremangroup.com

Brooklyn Diner USA (which is located in Manhattan) is worth a visit. With all-day dining, expansive menu, pleasant personnel, better-than-average diner food, and reasonable prices, this place is a winner. You can find just about anything your heart desires: breakfast fare, sandwiches (the cheeseburger is a must), salads, hearty lunch and dinner plates, homemade desserts, and good drinks. Their muffins are moist, flavorful, and outrageously good. A tile floor and comfortable booths add to the ambience.

BRYANT PARK GRILL
25 W 40th St (bet Fifth Ave and Ave of the Americas)
Lunch: Mon-Fri; Dinner: Daily; Brunch: Sat, Sun   212/840-6500
Moderate   www.arkrestaurants.com

A handy location in midtown, a refreshing view of Bryant Park, and a sensible menu with prices that are comfortable for families make this a popular destination. Although the menu changes with the seasons, one can count on a good selection of soups, salads, steak, and seafood items at lunch and dinner. A *prix fixe* pre-theater menu is available daily from 5 to 7 with three courses—handy for those going to shows nearby. The $25 *prix fixe* weekend brunch is popular, too. Personnel here are unusually friendly and especially child-oriented.

BUTTER
415 Lafayette St (bet E 4th St and Astor Pl)   212/253-2828
Dinner: Mon-Sat   www.butterrestaurant.com
Moderately expensive

Noisy and fun, Butter prides itself on turning out exceptional dishes. The appetizer menu includes oysters, rare tuna, and sweetbreads. For entrees, I can recommend any of the seafood dishes and the outstanding grilled organic ribeye. Creamed spinach is done the way it should be! A dozen desserts will appeal to the sweet tooth. The warm mocha bread pudding with chocolate caramels and caramel ice cream is a must, if it's on the menu. Informal downstairs dining is available.

CAFE ATLAS
40 Central Park S (bet Fifth Ave and Ave of the Americas)
Dinner: Daily; Brunch: Sun   212/759-9191
Moderate to moderately expensive

This room has changed its focus about as often as Ivana Trump changes outfits, but perhaps the current look will last for awhile. The attractive setting (overlooking Central Park), the friendly personnel (especially the manager), and a simple menu combine to make dining here a pleasure. Lobster roll and mushroom strudel are suggested appetizers. There are plates and platters from the garden (vegetables, quail eggs), from the sea (lobster, shrimp, oysters), from the land (smoked duck, country paté, *jambon de bayonne*), and from the farm (an artisan cheese selection). All are priced by the plate or platter. Braised short ribs is an outstanding entree. There is also a $17 burger, pork loin, seared sea scallops, and steak. I liked the *dulce de leche* cake with coffee ice cream for dessert.

CAFE BOTANICA
Essex House, a Westin Hotel
160 Central Park S   212/247-0300, 212/484-5120 (direct)
Breakfast, Lunch, Dinner: Daily; Brunch: Sun
Moderate

Chalk up another winner for the increasing number of good dining spots in Manhattan hotels. The Essex House features two top-quality restaurants. Cafe Botanica overlooks Central Park, offering magnificent table settings to go along with the tasty fare. Villeroy and Boch's "Botanica" pattern is the theme. Along with the colorful chairs and the light and airy feel of the room, the china makes the terrace area of the restaurant one of Manhattan's most attractive diningrooms. Spicy crab cakes or a selection of cold appetizers will get you started well. There are great pizzas, pastas, and seafood dishes. It's a wonderful spot for a special lunch—the closest thing to a private diningroom in Central Park!

CAFE BOULUD
Surrey Hotel
20 E 76th St   212/772-2600
Lunch: Tues-Sat; Dinner: Daily
Moderately expensive   www.danielnyc.com

If you are one of the "ladies who lunch" or like to look at those who do, then this is the place for you. It's not that the food isn't quite good (it is); it is the attitude I find unappealing. Once seated, however, you'll find the menu innovative. There are vegetarian selections (like vegetable couscous), world cuisines (every season highlights a different area), traditional French classics and country cooking, and menu items inspired by the "rhythm of the seasons" (crab salad with avocado and fennel is an example). A two- or three-course *prix fixe* menu is available at lunch. Dinner prices are higher, but remember this place belongs to *the* Daniel Boulud. The room is rather drab, but then again you are in the home of one of the nation's best chefs. Unfortunately he isn't in the kitchen here, because he is busy doing great things at Daniel.

D'Artagnan (152 E 46th St, 212/687-0300) has long been famous for high-quality organic poultry and game meats from around the world. At the first-floor copper-topped bar you'll find fabulous foie gras, pork-free mousses, patés and terrines, sausages, duck, salads, sandwiches, and more. Upstairs is a cozy diningroom with attentive service and many of the same menu items featured downstairs. Prices are reasonable, the French bread is fresh, and the *fondant au chocolat* is a magnificent dessert.

CAFE CENTRO
MetLife Building
200 Park Ave (45th St at Vanderbilt Ave)   212/818-1222
Lunch: Mon-Fri; Dinner: Mon-Sat
Moderate   www.restaurantassociates.com

In a rather large room that's very attractively appointed and broken up into appealing spaces, Restaurant Associates (a major player in the city) has created a purely American restaurant. One is greeted by a gas-fired working rotisserie and a beautiful open kitchen that's spotlessly clean and efficient. There are *prix fixe* dinners, if you so desire. The menu changes daily, but I can always find such favorites as chicken pie *bisteeya* (with almonds, raisins, and orange-flower essence), which is not a normal chicken pot pie but a light and tasty dish. There is a raw bar, a hefty seafood platter, excellent steaks and French fries, and daily roasts. Crusty French bread is laid out in front of you. Other specialties include sea bass, penne pasta, and a moist, flavorful roasted chicken. The pastry chef obviously has a chocolate bias (good for him!). *La marquise au chocolat,* bittersweet chocolate mousse, *soufflé chaud au chocolat,* valrhona bittersweet chocolate ice cream, and crème brûlée with caramel sauce are just a sampling. Adjoining the diningroom is a busy beer bar that serves light sandwiches and appetizers.

CAFE DES ARTISTES
1 W 67th St (near Central Park W)   212/877-3500
Lunch: Mon-Fri; Dinner: Daily; Brunch: Sat, Sun
Moderate   www.cafenyc.com

George Lang has created an absolute masterpiece at his West Side landmark, just off Central Park. Cafe des Artistes is truly a great dining destination. There are several dining levels and some hidden tables, giving each diner the impression of being in a small, cozy establishment. Beautiful murals by Christy complement the charming decor. The personnel are wonderfully accommodating, and the food is absolutely delicious. Try the unusual Sunday brunch. Some of the mouthwatering selections on the changeable menu include smoked salmon Benedict and delicious French toast. Dinner appetizers include salmon four ways (smoked, poached, dill-marinated, and tartare), *foie gras de canard,* and an array of delightful salads. For the main course, there is swordfish, rack of lamb with basil crust, duck confit, and much more. By all means don't overlook desserts. A great dessert plate samples several different treats. A dessert buffet occupies the center of the front room. Three-course *prix fixe* lunches and dinners are offered. This is a lovely, romantic place at any time, but I especially recommend Cafe des Artistes for an after-theater supper. An addition is **The Parlor**. It is most attractive, with a turn-of-the-century zinc bar from Paris, plus several inlaid chessboard tables on which patrons may play.

CAFE INDULGE
561 Second Ave (at 31st St)   212/252-9750
Breakfast, Lunch, Dinner: Daily: Brunch: Sat, Sun
Inexpensive to moderate

The fresh-baked goods are tasty, reasonably priced and attractive. I'd particularly recommend the flourless chocolate cake and the devil's food cake with chocolate frosting. But there is much more at this cozy, unpretentious hideaway! The breakfast three-egg omelets are excellent, and nearly three dozen varieties are offered. Breakfast pastries, especially scones, are also excellent. Sugar-free muffins will please dieters. For light meals you'll find wraps, salads, sandwiches, pastas, and more. Burgers are a specialty, as are smoothies and a variety of cafe drinks. For a special treat, try the grilled portobello-mushroom sandwich. Dinners at comfortable prices include steaks, lamb chops, grilled chicken, baked meatloaf, lasagna, and filet of sole.

It's no wonder that **Cafe Lalo** (201 W 83rd St, 212/496-6031) is a madhouse during the noon and afternoon hours. For delicious, reasonably priced sandwiches and other light meals, this room is first-rate. The selection of desserts can only be described as awesome!

CAMAJE
85 MacDougal St (bet Bleecker and Houston St)   212/673-8184
Daily: 12 noon-12 midnight; Brunch: Sat, Sun   www.camaje.com
Inexpensive

Abigail Hitchcock and Patrick Woodside know how to cook a great meal. In tiny quarters (capacity 20 or so), this cozy French bistro can evoke memories of some wonderful little place you may have discovered in Paris. Camaje is one of those New York restaurants that few know about; however, diners who know it return often. From the moment delicious crusty bread arrives to the excellent homemade desserts, everything is wholesome and tasty. I don't think I've ever had a better sandwich than their shrimp salad and avocado. There's three-onion soup gratinee, smoked trout salad, a half-dozen sandwiches, crostini, small plates, meat and fish entrees, and veggie side dishes. You can create your own three-ingredient crepe, if you desire. By all means, try one of their crepes *sucrées* for dessert; my favorite was a chocolate ice cream crepe with caramel sauce. Another plus is the large selection of quality teas. For a change, their iced tea is the real thing.

Beware of Restaurant Pricing Ripoffs!
- Check the price of wine you selected. Also check its vintage when delivered to the table.
- Bottled water is grossly overpriced.
- Check to see if gratuities have been added to the bill, and double-check the math.
- Daily specials are usually more expensive than regular menu items.
- Ask if an offered birthday cake is really complimentary.
- Add up the items on your bill to see if the addition is correct.
- Be sure to read the fine print about surcharges.

CANDELA
116 E 16th St (near Irving Pl)   212/254-1600
Dinner: Mon-Sun; Brunch: Sun   www.candelarestaurant.com
Moderate

All that is missing here is King Arthur arriving on horseback with his Knights of the Round Table! As you might guess from the name of this unique establishment in the Union Square area, Candela is awash with candles . . . everywhere. The effect is quite dramatic, with a high ceiling and brick walls. Waiters are attired in ill-fitting and ugly outfits. But the American menu is special, the service is prompt and efficient, and the dishes are fairly priced. The winners here: excellent salads, a superb seafood platter (three tiers for two or more hungry patrons), and tasty homemade pasta dishes. Try the standout valrhona chocolate cake with malted-milk-ball ice cream and dark chocolate and milk chocolate malt sauces. Despite the high energy and noise levels, you'll not regret your visit. Private parties may be held here during the day.

If you know someone who works for **Condé Nast,** ask to meet him or her for lunch at the fabulous cafeteria on the fourth floor of their building at 4 Times Square. (Breakfast is also offered.) In a titanium-sheathed room designed by Frank Gehry, one can find nearly everything to make a memorable meal: a tempting salad bar, hot and cold entrees, sandwiches, good-looking desserts and much more. The cost is inexpensive (about $6 for an average lunch), but you can't pay; only Condé Nast employees can pick up the very reasonable tab. The parade of models is quite something! But so is the whole scene.

CAPSOUTO FRÈRES
451 Washington St (south of Canal St; entrance at 135 Watts St)
Lunch: Tues-Fri; Dinner: Daily; Brunch: Sat, Sun   212/966-4900
Moderate   www.capsoutofreres.com

Capsouto Frères just gets better and better. In 1891, when the building here was constructed, this was an "in" area. Now it is "hot" all over again, and the Landmark Building is still a beauty. Serving contemporary French cuisine, three brothers and their mother operate a classic establishment, complete with ceiling fans, wooden tables, good cheer, and tasty plates. At noon a special *prix fixe* lunch is offered, or you can order from an a la carte menu laden with salads, fish, meat, and pasta dishes. In the evening, they offer more of the same, along with quail, duckling, and first-rate sirloin steak. They are known for their signature dessert soufflés. This bistro is a great setting for a casual, let-your-hair-down evening with good friends who like to live it up!

CARMINE'S

2450 Broadway (bet 90th and 91st St)	212/362-2200
Lunch, Dinner: Daily	
200 W 44th St (bet Seventh and Eighth Ave)	212/221-3800
Lunch, Dinner: Daily	
Moderate	www.carminesnyc.com

Time to treat the whole gang? Or the whole family? Call Carmine's for reservations and show up famished. You won't be disappointed! Carmine's presents Southern Italian-style family dining with huge portions and zesty seasonings. Not only are the platters full, they are delicious. If you are coming with fewer than a half-dozen friends or family, show up early. The wait can be as long as an hour, as they will not reserve tables for smaller parties after 7 p.m. Menu choices run the gamut of pastas, chicken, veal, seafood, and tasty Italian appetizers such as calamari. Wall signs explain the offerings. There is also a delivery menu.

CARNEGIE DELICATESSEN AND RESTAURANT

854 Seventh Ave (at 55th St)   212/757-2245, 800/334-5606
Breakfast, Lunch, Dinner: Daily (7 a.m.-4 a.m.)
No credit cards
Moderate   www.carnegiedeli.com

There's no city on earth with delis like New York's, and the Carnegie is one of the best. Its location in the middle of the hotel district makes it perfect for midnight snacks. Everything is made on the premises, and free delivery is offered between 7 a.m. and 3 a.m. within a five-block radius. Where to start? Your favorite Jewish mother didn't make chicken soup better than the Carnegie's homemade variety. It comes with matzo balls, golden noodles, rice, kreplach, or kasha. There's more: Great blintzes. Open-faced sandwiches, hot and delicious. Ten different deli and egg sandwiches. A very juicy burger with all the trimmings. Lots of fish dishes. Corned beef, pastrami, and rare roast beef. An unequaled choice of egg dishes. Salads. Side orders of everything from hot baked potatoes to potato pancakes. Outrageous cheesecake topped with strawberries, blueberries, or cherries (or just served plain). Desserts from A to Z—even Jell-O.

CHANTERELLE

2 Harrison St (at Hudson St)   212/966-6960
Lunch: Tues-Sat; Dinner: Mon-Sat   www.chanterellenyc.com
Expensive

This is a must! For over 20 years I have been a great admirer of Chanterelle. Karen and David Waltuck have created something unique and special for Manhattan diners. All the ingredients are here: magnificent decor, extremely professional service, wonderful food, and owners who look after every detail. Of course, nothing this good comes cheaply, and Chanterelle's dinners can be tough on the pocketbook. However, the *prix fixe* lunch is a real treat. As the menu changes often, there are many specials; I'd ask Karen (who is out front) or David (in the kitchen) to suggest a menu. The seafood dishes are extra special. Their grilled seafood sausage is rightfully famous. If you have room for dessert, the cheese selection is superb, as is the cheesecake. As if all of this were not enough, the petit fours (served with coffee) make all others seem mundane.

CHELSEA BISTRO & BAR
358 W 23rd St (bet Eighth and Ninth Ave)   212/727-2026
Lunch: Mon-Fri; Dinner: Daily
Moderate

Cozy up to a working brick fireplace! Chelsea offers a number of trendy eating establishments, and this is one of the best. It used to be a cave, but now it is a bustling bistro. In a comfortable space that includes an attractive glass-enclosed French garden room, this well-run house has a menu that will please both adventurous and conservative diners. For appetizers, there is a cassoulet of snails, grilled baby calamari, and a tart of goat cheese and onions. Seafood entrees include lightly smoked Atlantic salmon and Chilean sea bass. The nicoise salad is hard to beat; other specialties include hanger steak in red wine sauce, dry-aged ribeye steak for two, roasted duck, and marinated chicken. All items are seasonal. At dessert time, the tarts really shine. Ask about daily specials.

CHEZ JACQUELINE
72 MacDougal St (bet Bleecker and Houston St)   212/505-0727
Dinner: Daily; Brunch: Sat, Sun
Moderate   www.chezjacqueline.com

Chez Jacqueline is a very popular neighborhood French bistro, and no wonder. The atmosphere and service are appealingly relaxed. All ages seem to be happy here: young lovers hold hands, and seniors have just as good a time on a special evening out. Popular appetizers are fish soup, snails, and goat cheese salad. As you might expect from a French house, the rack of lamb and veal dishes are excellent. My favorite is the hearty beef stew in red wine, tomato and carrot sauce. For dessert, try the caramelized apple tart.

CHEZ MICHALLET
90 Bedford St (at Grove St)   212/242-8309
Dinner: Daily; Brunch: Sun   www.michallet.com
Moderate

Imagine you are sitting at the window of a quaint little restaurant in a picturesque French countryside village. The place has 14 tables, the decor is eclectic, the kitchen is tiny . . . but the food and service are wonderful. All this is true at Chez Michallet, except you are looking out on the corner of Bedford and Grove streets in Greenwich Village. What a charming place! The friendly waiters couldn't be more helpful in explaining the varied menu: steak, salmon, duck, lamb, veal, chicken, fish . . . anything your heart desires. Desserts are good as well. Choose from tarts, a great chocolate truffle cake, crème brûlée, profiteroles, and fresh berries. For a perfectly satisfying and relaxing evening, this spot is hard to beat. There is also a special pre-theater menu.

CHIN CHIN
216 E 49th St (bet Second and Third Ave)   212/888-4555
Lunch: Mon-Fri; Dinner: Daily
Moderate to moderately expensive

Chin Chin is a very classy Chinese restaurant whose ambience and price reflect a superior cooking style. There are two rooms and a garden in back. The soups and barbecued spareribs are terrific starters. The Szechuan jumbo prawns are sensational. I'd concentrate on the seafood dishes, though you might also try the wonderful Peking duck dinner, with choice of soup, crispy duck skin with pancakes, fried rice, poached spinach, and homemade sorbet and ice cream. The menu is much the same for lunch or dinner. A reasonable *prix fixe* lunch is available.

CINNABAR
235 W 56th St (at Eighth Ave)   212/399-1100
Lunch, Dinner: Daily
Moderate

What, an attractive Chinese restaurant? Yes, and more. Not only is Cinnabar clean, cool, and inviting, but the food is also excellent Chinese! Dim Sum is the big thing, but there is much more on the very extensive menu. Recommended dishes: spring rolls, wonderful jumbo sweet and sour shrimp, Peking duck, roasted cashew chicken, and Yang Chow pan-fried noodles. Takeout and delivery are available; the address is convenient to hotels in the Central Park area.

CITARELLA
1240 Ave of the Americas (at 49th St)   212/332-1515
Lunch: Mon-Fri; Dinner; Mon-Sat   www.citarella.com
Moderately expensive

The name Citarella is synonymous with quality seafood at their retail stores. Now they have brought ocean-fresh magic to a restaurant in midtown. With two levels for dining, a bar with some of the most pleasant and informed tenders in town, and a sushi bar that stays open until midnight, this is a great place for diners desiring a large fish selection. (If there is a meat-and-potato person in your party, the steak entree is also very good.) To start, I strongly suggest the creamy clam chowder, which is as good as any I have ever tasted—including the famous chowders of my native West Coast. On to bass, cod, halibut, lobster, pompano, scallops, or swordfish. Daily specials are dazzlingly recited. The sushi menu is outstanding. A dozen desserts are listed, including a warm vanilla cake with vanilla-bean ice cream taking top honors. This wonderful addition to Manhattan's dining scene is giving the overpriced Le Bernardin a run for its money.

CITY BAKERY
3 W 18th St (at Fifth Ave)   212/366-1414
Breakfast, Lunch, Dinner: Daily
Moderate

The taste buds become excited the minute you walk into the bustling City Bakery (which is really not a bakery but a buffet operation). Your eyes and stomach will lust after the fresh-looking salad bar, the tempting hot entrees, a chocolate room, hearty sandwiches, yummy pastries, and much more. In addition, a bar menu is available at happy hour. I am impressed with the well-trained personnel, who keep displays well stocked, tables clean, and checkout counters running efficiently. For a casual, moderately priced meal in unfancy surroundings, this is a good deal.

COMPASS
208 W 70th St (at Amsterdam Ave)   212/875-8600
Lunch: Mon-Fri; Dinner: Daily; Brunch: Sun
Moderately expensive   www.compassrestaurant.com

In a room that has seen lots of ups and downs, chef Neil Annis has put his excellent training at Lespinasse to use in creating a new look and taste at this expansive space. The excellent food is complemented by the superb service staff put together by general manager Al Lopez. The well-trained personnel are unfailingly polite and efficient. Most everything on the menu is good, but especially the swordfish steak, honey-glazed roast pork loin, and fillet of skate wing. A tasty selection of over a dozen cheeses for dessert is the perfect complement to an outstanding meal. A nice touch at the end: a cup of hot chocolate served with lemon marshmallows. The Upper West Side has another winner here!

COOKE'S CORNER
618 Amsterdam Ave (at 90th St)   212/712-2872
Dinner: Daily
Moderate

If you are tired of pretense, glitter, and affectation, then hurry to this small-ish room, where you will feel like you're having dinner at a good friend's home. This same feeling extends to the kitchen, where the food is lovingly prepared. I started with sizzling tiger shrimp, but appetizers at neighboring tables looked just as inviting. Entrees include tasty maple-glazed salmon, four-hour braised beef (which I could eat every night), and an always good rack of lamb with yummy potato pancakes. If gelato is on the menu, order it; I enjoyed every last calorie. Cheers to a cozy, clean, and comfortable place.

When a craving strikes for some great pastries and quiches, but you want to feel comfortable in your grubbies, I'd suggest a trip to **Ceci Cela** (55 Spring St, 212/274-9179), where Laurent Dupal and Herve Grall dish up some of the area's best breakfasts and light lunches.

COUNTRY CAFE
69 Thompson St (bet Spring and Broome St)   212/966-5417
Lunch, Dinner: Daily; Brunch: Sat, Sun   www.countrycafesoho.com
Moderate

You have to know about this tiny Soho establishment to find it! But once inside, you'll appreciate the no-nonsense approach to French country dining. The service and atmosphere could easily be transplanted to any small village in France. The menu would fit right in as well, with items like homemade country paté with onion and fruit chutney; a fabulous country salad with croutons, lardons, blue cheese, and walnuts; vegetable couscous; snails in garlic butter; and steak *au poivre* with homemade French fries. The latter are the real thing, believe me! I love the informality of the place, the sizable portions, and the obvious delight the young staff takes in showing guests what it is like to be treated by some real homebodies. *Bon appetit!*

CRAFTBAR
47 E 19th St   212/780-0880
Lunch: Mon-Fri; Dinner: Daily
Expensive

You can pretend you are a chef here! Unlike any restaurant you've ever seen, Craftbar is worth visiting for a number of reasons. The atmosphere is conducive to good eating, the help is particularly friendly. Most of all, the way you order is unique. The menu is divided into sections: fish and shell-fish, meats, vegetables, mushrooms, potatoes, grains, and beans. You can put together any combination you might find appealing, and the plates won't overwhelm your appetite. Chef-owner Tom Colicchio has Gramercy Tavern roots, and the expertise shows. Even the dessert selection is great: wonderful cheeses, pastries, custards, fruits, ice creams, and sorbets (with many sauces available). If you're not terribly hungry, or if there are picky eaters in the family, head to Craftbar.

CUCINA & CO.
MetLife Building, lobby
200 Park Ave (45th St at Vanderbilt Ave), lobby   212/682-2700
Breakfast, Lunch, Dinner: Mon-Fri
(takeout open 7 a.m.-9 p.m.; Sat: 8-4) www.restaurantassociates.com
Moderate

Hidden between two hyped restaurants (Tropica and Cafe Centro) in the bowels of the huge MetLife Building, Cucina & Co. is a treasure. The take-out counter is one of the best in mid-Manhattan: all sorts of prepared foods, sandwiches, salads, great cookies and cakes, breads, and whatever else you might want to take back to the home or office. Adjoining is a bustling, crowded, noisy cafe that serves first-class food at reasonable prices for such a prime location. You will find delicious burgers (served on sesame brioche rolls), baked pastas, quiches, seafood, health food dishes, and a good selection of dessert items. The service is fast, the quality of the food top-notch, and the personnel highly professional. They have to be in order to serve so many people in the rush hours. I heartily recommend this place, especially for lunch. Another Cucina location in prime real estate is at 30 Rockefeller Center (212/332-7630).

CUCINA STAGIONALE
289 Bleecker St (at Seventh Ave)   212/924-2707
Lunch, Dinner: Daily
Inexpensive

When you serve good food at a low price, word gets around. So it's no wonder there's a line in front of this small Greenwich Village cafe almost any time of day. Its name translates as "seasonal kitchen," and the seasonal specialties are real values. It's a bare-bones setup, with seating for only a few dozen hungry folks. Service is impersonal and nonprofessional, but who cares at these prices? Innovative Italian cuisine—tasty, attractive, and filling—is served here, and you can do very well on a slim budget. Recommended appetizers include smoked salmon with endive and radicchio, and sauteed wild mushrooms. For a few pennies more, you can get a large dish of linguine or ravioli. I'm constantly asked about inexpensive places that serve quality food, and I have no hesitation recommending this spot. One word of warning: don't go if it's raining, because you'll probably have to wait outside to get seated.

For a terrific quick business lunch in midtown, book a table at **Cité** (120 W 51st St, 212/956-7100). The personnel here are among the friendliest in Manhattan. The Cité salad with bleu cheese, toasted pecans, and truffle vinaigrette dressing is just right for those who want something light and delicious.

CUPPING ROOM CAFE
359 West Broadway (bet Broome and Grand St)   212/925-2898
Breakfast, Lunch: Mon-Fri; Dinner: Daily; Brunch: Sat, Sun
Moderate   www.cuppingroomcafe.com

It is easy to see why the Cupping Room Cafe is one of the most popular places in Soho to meet and dine. In a noisy, convivial atmosphere, with close-together tables and a bar where you can drink and/or eat, all the news of the area is exchanged here. The diverse food offerings at lunch and dinner include pastas, seafood, chicken, steaks, and vegetarian dishes. But breakfast and brunch are where they really shine: freshly baked pastries, fruit and cheese, waffles, pancakes, wonderful French toast, and eggs and omelets. Eggs Benedict can be customized. For the lighter diner, there are soups, sandwiches, burgers, and salads. Be sure to ask about daily dessert items; most are delicious, fresh, reasonably priced, and caloric.

DANAL
90 E 10th St (bet Third and Fourth Ave)   212/982-6930
Lunch: Tues-Fri; Dinner: Tues-Sun; Brunch: Sat, Sun;
Tea: Fri-Sat (by reservation)
Moderate

Here are my guidelines for a good eating spot: The bread is fresh, crisp, and warm. Vegetables are not overcooked. Salads are cool, and the house salad is not just a pile of lettuce. If homemade ice cream is served, it is rich and creamy and has no ice particles in it. Finally, the owner is on the job. Danal meets all of the above criteria with flying colors. The location is the East Village, on a safe, quiet street. The atmosphere is what the owner calls "country French." I would call it homey mix-and-match. The service is understated and friendly, with no pretense. The dishes are uniformly delicious, served in right-sized portions. Entrees at Danal are typical French Mediterranean bistro fare. The menu varies every day but features something tasty for any appetite.

DANIEL
60 E 65th St (bet Madison and Park Ave)   212/288-0033
Dinner: Mon-Sat   www.danielnyc.com
Expensive

Daniel Boulud is a master! He should be immensely proud of his four-star, $10 million classical French country restaurant. Despite all the hype and intense scrutiny of every aspect of his dream, this accomplished chef has achieved perfection. If you are ready to have an absolutely superb dining experience and bucks don't matter, then join the often long waiting list for a table in the space of the former Mayfair Hotel lobby and the old Le Cirque restaurant. The setting is a reminder of the original 1920s look, with neo-classical details. The result is an unusually pleasant feeling, with the light and hum of the room adding to the joy of each delicious platter. The wait staff is highly professional and knowledgeable. Signature dishes change by the season. It might be a duo of roasted beef tenderloin and braised short ribs (the best I have ever tasted), morels filled with braised duck and lamb's quarter greens, roasted quail, or roasted filet of venison. Desserts are works of art. Don't miss the cheese selection! Every time I visit this restaurant I don't want the meal to end. I can't think of a higher compliment.

The delicious foie gras burger at **DB Bistro Moderne** (55 W 44th St) tipped the price scale at $29. Now comes a wallet-gouging burger from the renowned **Old Homestead Steakhouse** (56 Ninth Ave, 212/242-9040). This 20-ounce beauty, made from Kobe beef, breaks the bank at $41!

DANUBE
30 Hudson St (bet Duane and Reade St)   212/791-3771
Dinner: Mon-Sat   www.thedanube.net
Expensive

If you are looking for a purely Austrian-inspired restaurant, then this may not satisfy. But if you want a dining experience with a touch of Austria, done with class in magnificent surroundings, then by all means book a reservation here. The decor is spectacular. An odd-sized room has all the ingredients of a plush European drawing room: Venetian stucco, ebony paneling, velvet and ultrasuede fabrics, beautiful lighting fixtures. Tyrolean wine soup, great Austrian cheese ravioli, and roasted sweet organic beets make great starters. Beef cheeks are braised in a wine sauce with chive spatzle. The veal wiener schnitzel with Austrian crescent potatoes will have you dreaming about Vienna's Imperial Hotel. I could make an entire meal from the great dessert offerings here. Between courses, special items periodically arrive at the table. By the time you leave, you will appreciate the magic created in this kitchen.

DA UMBERTO
107 W 17th St (at Ave of the Americas)   212/989-0303
Lunch: Mon-Fri; Dinner: Mon-Sat
Moderate to moderately expensive

Da Umberto is for serious Italian diners. This Tuscan trattoria is a feast for the eyes as well as the palate. A groaning table of inviting antipasto dishes greets guests; one could easily make an entire meal just from this selection. All of the platters look so fresh and healthy! Umberto Assante himself is around much of the time, ensuring that the service is as good as the food. One can look into the glass-framed kitchen at the rear to see how real professionals work. The three-color salad is a house specialty. On to well-prepared pastas, fish, veal, game (in season), or chicken. Your waiter will have many specials, like calamari *ritieni,* to detail. If you have room, the chocolate truffle cake and tiramisu are the best of the dessert selections.

DAWAT
210 E 58th St (bet Second and Third Ave)   212/355-7555
Lunch: Mon-Sat; Dinner: Daily   www.restaurant.com/dawat
Moderate

Ms. Madhur Jaffrey, a highly respected cookbook author, creates innovative Indian dishes that set Dawat apart as one of the best Indian restaurants in the city. There are numerous good seafood choices, including a sensational shrimp entree called Shrimp Konju Pappaas. Chicken, goat, and lamb dishes are other favorites, as is as an attractive choice of vegetarian dishes. Different varieties of excellent breads are available. Don't pass up Jaffrey's desserts, which are unusually good for an Indian restaurant.

DB BISTRO MODERNE
55 W 44th St (bet Fifth Ave and Ave of the Americas)   212/391-2400
Lunch: Mon-Sat; Dinner: Mon-Sun   www.danielnyc.com
Moderate to moderately expensive

Renowned restaurant impressario Daniel Boulud has done it again! His latest venture is, for him, a much more casual dining experience. Even burgers are served, and they are very good. (At $29, they should be!) Of course, this is no ordinary hamburger. It is ground sirloin filled with short ribs, foie gras and black truffles, served on a parmesan bun and accompanied by delicious, light *pommes soufflés* presented in a silver cup. Diners have their choice of two rooms with a bar-type arrangement in between them that is comfortable for singles. The stylish menu is divided into sections like *thon* (tuna), *saumon* (salmon), *canard* (poultry), and *boeuf* (beef), offering several items in each category. For dessert, the cheese selection is a real winner, as are any of Daniel's specialties using berries and other fresh fruit.

DEL FRISCO'S DOUBLE EAGLE STEAK HOUSE
McGraw-Hill Building
1221 Ave of the Americas (at 49th St)   212/575-5129
Lunch: Mon-Fri; Dinner: Daily
Moderately expensive to expensive

Del Frisco's provides a good meal with accommodating service in a high-ceilinged setting where prices seem a bit high as well. Fresh, warm bread is brought to the table as you enjoy a fresh seafood appetizer or great beefsteak-tomato and sliced-onion salad. Steaks, chops, veal dishes, and lobster are all first-rate, while accompanying side dishes are large and uneven. Desserts are made in-house: bread pudding with Jack Daniel's sauce, crisp chocolate soufflé cake with raspberries, and strawberries Romanoff with vanilla ice cream. All are winners. This establishment is inviting, except when it comes to price. Isn't $15.95 for a shrimp cocktail a bit steep? To be frank, I also found myself wondering whether all dishes are freshly cooked for each diner.

DINING COMMONS
City University of New York Graduate Center
365 Fifth Ave (at 34th St), 8th floor   212/817-7953
Breakfast, Lunch: Mon-Fri (express coffee shop on 1st floor)
Inexpensive

The Dining Commons offers excellent food in comfortable surroundings at affordable prices. Continental breakfasts—featuring muffins, Danishes, croissants, bagels, and more—are available. Lunches feature deli sandwiches, salads, and some hot entrees. It is possible to eat heartily for under $10, and both eat-in and takeout are available. The facility is open to faculty, students, and the general public. Students get a discount with CUNY identification cards. This is no run-of-the-mill fast-food operation. Restaurant Associates does a particularly good job of offering tasty, adequate portions without fancy touches.

DOCKS OYSTER BAR AND SEAFOOD GRILL
2427 Broadway (bet 89th and 90th St)   212/724-5588
Lunch: Mon-Sat; Dinner: Daily; Brunch: Sat, Sun

633 Third Ave (at 40th St)   212/986-8080
Lunch: Mon-Fri; Dinner: Daily; Brunch: Sun
Moderate

For those who appreciate a great raw bar, Docks is the place to anchor! Sail right up Broadway or to a larger location on Third Avenue. At both lunch and dinner you'll find fresh swordfish, lobster, tuna, Norwegian salmon, red snapper, and other seafood specials. The crab cakes are outstanding. At dinner, the raw bar offers four oyster and two clam selections. All this comes with cole slaw and choice of potatoes. Vegetables are a la carte. For a lighter meal, try steamers in beer broth or mussels in tomato and garlic. Delicious smoked sturgeon and whitefish are available. Docks has a special New England clambake on Sunday and Monday night. For dessert, the chocolate mud fudge is a fitting way to finish your culinary cruise. The atmosphere is congenial, and so are the professional waiters.

Whenever you see a place jammed to the rafters with customers, you know that something good must be going on. For weekend brunches, **Eighteenth and Eighth** (159 Eighth Ave, 212/242-5000) is the place to be. The decor is bare bones, but the food is excellent and the service extra friendly. Besides, prices are right, and delivery and takeout are available.

ELEVEN MADISON PARK
11 Madison Ave (at 24th St)   212/889-0905
Lunch: Mon-Sat; Dinner: Daily; Brunch: Sun
Expensive

When Danny Meyer opens a restaurant, you can be assured it will have class. Eleven Madison Park is no exception. In a soaring space previously used for business meetings, an attractive dining facility has been created with an intimate wine bar and several private meeting rooms. The cuisine is described as "New York with a French accent." Appetizers are heavy on the seafood side: a seasonal shellfish assortment, flash-seared squid, tuna *cru,* and a salad of Maine lobster. Foie gras is a specialty. Braised shoulder of pork, seared Arctic char, and prime aged rib of beef are excellent main-course choices. Save room for the chocolate soufflé or lemon *assiette*! A meal here would not be complete without a journey into the past glory of this building and area by studying the archival photographs featured throughout.

ELIO'S
1621 Second Ave (at 84th St)   212/772-2242
Dinner: Daily
Moderate to moderately expensive

Elio's is *the* classic clubby Upper East Side diningroom for those who are recognizable, as well as those who aspire to be! In not so fancy surroundings, with waiters who greet old friends as if they are part of the family, tasty platters of beef carpaccio, clams, mussels, stuffed mushrooms, and minestrone are offered as starters. Lots of spaghetti and risotto dishes follow, along with seafood (their specialty), liver, scaloppine, and the usual Italian assortment. Half the fun is watching the not-so-subtle eye contact among diners. But the food is excellent, and it is easy to see why Elio's has become a neighborhood favorite.

ELLEN'S STARDUST DINER
1650 Broadway (at 51st St)   212/956-5151
Breakfast, Lunch, Dinner: Daily   www.ellensstardustdiner.com
Inexpensive to moderate

You come here for the good food and the singing wait staff! Ellen's fits right into the neighborhood. A casual, fun, and noisy spot, it serves satisfying food the traditional American way. Trains are the theme of the decor; a track circles the balcony, with a locomotive and cars that would thrill any railroad buff. The breakfast menu includes bagels and muffins, along with tasty buttermilk pancakes, Belgian waffles, French toast, and omelets. For the rest of the day, comfort foods are the order: salads and sandwiches, chicken pot pie, meatloaf, barbecue baby back ribs, turkey, and steak. Burgers are served with whiffle-ball fries that are tasty if delivered warm. (Send them back if they're not.) There is more: egg creams, shakes, malts, and a nice selection of caloric desserts. Be sure to ask them to make your shake "thick"! Delivery is available.

Folks wait even in cold, wet weather at **EJ's Luncheonette** (1271 Third Ave, 212/472-0600), where breakfast, lunch, and dinner are served daily. You'll find great flapjacks, waffles, omelets, sandwiches, burgers, baked items, salads, and everything in between. In addition to a huge menu, especially at breakfast, you'll enjoy the very reasonable prices. Free delivery, too!

EL PARADOR
325 E 34th St (nr First Ave)   212/679-6812
Lunch, Dinner: Daily
Moderate

A restaurant that has been in business for four decades in New York is obviously doing something customers like. At El Parador, delicious Mexican food is served in a fun atmosphere at down-to-earth prices. Moreover, they are some of the nicest folks in the city. Warm nachos are put on the table the minute you arrive; from there, you have a choice of specialties. There are quesadillas, Spanish sausages, and black bean soup to start. Delicious shrimp and chicken dishes follow. Create your own tacos and tostaditas, if you like.

How about stuffed jalapenos? El Parador has over 50 brands of premium tequila and what many consider the best margaritas in New York. It really is the granddaddy of New York Mexican restaurants.

ETATS-UNIS
242 E 81st St (bet Second and Third Ave)   212/517-8826
Dinner: Daily
Moderate to moderately expensive

Etats-Unis is like a large family diningroom. There are only 14 tables and a busy kitchen where the Rapp family produces some of the best food this side of your grandmother's! Appetizers, entrees, and desserts (usually about five of each) change every evening and are uniformly delicious. It's very wholesome food, not cute or fancy but served professionally in portions that are substantial but not overwhelming. Fresh homemade bread is an attraction. Try date pudding or chocolate soufflé for dessert. The tab is not cheap, but in order to support an operation with limited hours and few tables, the Rapps have to make every meal count. A bar/cafe across the street is open for lunch. The entire room is available for private parties.

F&B GÜDTFOOD
269 W 23rd St (bet Seventh and Eighth Ave)   646/486-4441
Sun, Mon: 12-10:30; Other days: 12-11   www.gudtfood.com
Inexpensive

Güdtfood means "good food," of course. This place is unlike any other. There are no tables, which means you eat counter style. And what do you eat? European street food like fish and chips, steak *frites*, Belgian *pommes*, lots of hot dogs, Swedish meatballs . . . you get the idea. Kids menus and healthy vegetarian items are also available. For dessert there is Danish rice pudding, French ice cream, and French sorbets. The people-watching is pretty good, and the prices are even better! A great place for kids' parties.

FIAMMA OSTERIA
206 Spring St (bet Ave of the Americas and Sullivan St) 212/653-0100
Lunch: Mon-Sat; Dinner: Daily; Brunch: Sun
Moderate to moderately expensive   www.brguestrestaurants.com

Some restaurants just make you feel good when you enter. Located on a busy Soho street, Fiamma is one of them. They have a flair for tasty Italian dishes that include fresh seafood, excellent chicken, tender meat, and wonderful pastas like ricotta cheese tortelli and handmade pasta quills. The duck breast is tender, appealing, and not as rich as that offered elsewhere. As for desserts, imagine choosing from a dark chocolate praline cake, a caramel zabaglione with a milk-chocolate rum center, or homemade gelati and sorbets. A delicious selection of Italian cheeses is also available.

FIFTY SEVEN FIFTY SEVEN
Four Seasons Hotel, lobby level
57 E 57th St   212/758-5757
Breakfast, Lunch, Dinner: Daily; Brunch: Sun
Moderate to moderately expensive   www.fourseasons.com

When the name Four Seasons is on the door, you can be assured that the service on the inside is something special. So it is at Fifty Seven Fifty Seven, one of Manhattan's star hotel diningrooms. The room is highlighted by handsome cherry floors with mahogany inlays, ceilings of Danish beechwood, and bronze chandeliers. The tabletops match the floor in material and design. Served in an informal yet elegant atmosphere, the food has the authority of classic American cooking. The menu changes by season, featuring some exceptionally well-thought-out pasta entrees. I'd also recommend the bison. Taste and personal attention, not the ego of a famous chef, are what makes this room tick. A thoughtful touch is the offer of rapid service for breakfast guests.

FLEUR DE SEL
5 E 20th St (bet Fifth Ave and Broadway)   212/460-9100
Lunch: Mon-Sat; Dinner: Daily
Moderately expensive (lunch), expensive (dinner)

Some restaurants immediately create a buzz, and Fleur de Sel is one of them. Chef-owner Cyril Renaud does interesting and exciting things with a constantly changing menu. The plates are all well presented. The charming exposed-brick room features some of Renaud's own oil paintings. Lobster salad with avocado is different and delicious. Entrees tend to be on the rich, exotic side, so if your meat-and-potato husband is looking for a basic kind of a dinner, send him elsewhere. However, those with more adventurous palates will find marinated beef cheeks tender and delicious. To be honest, I found Fleur de Sel worthy of a visit but not the unabashed raves it has received from all sides. By the way, the chocolate tart soufflé with vanilla ice cream and white chocolate caramel ganache are magnificent. Dinner is *prix fixe* and costs $52.

44 & X HELL'S KITCHEN
622 Tenth Ave (at 44th St)   212/977-1170
Dinner: Daily; Brunch: Sat, Sun
Moderate to moderately expensive

The Hell's Kitchen area is an unlikely place for a first-rate restaurant, but this one qualifies in spades! Boasting a menu of "reinvented American classics" served in a rather sterile white-on-white atmosphere, this spot literally sparkles with tasty dishes presented in a most professional manner. There is an abundance of polite, well-trained servers and helpers; your every desire seems to be their uppermost concern as they parade their clever *Heaven* (on the front) and *Hell* (on the back) T-shirts. The bisque of butternut squash was so good I just about licked the bowl. Other classy starters: Mediterranean chopped salad, pan-seared scallops, and crab fritters. Don't miss the buttermilk fried chicken, the super burger with outstanding fries, a hefty casserole of Maine lobster, comfortable tomato meatloaf, or melt-in-your-mouth barbecued salmon. Delicious apple crisp and white chocolate bread pudding are stars on the dessert menu.

FOUR SEASONS
99 E 52nd St (bet Park and Lexington Ave)   212/754-9494
Lunch: Mon-Fri; Dinner: Mon-Sat   www.fourseasonsrestaurant.com
Expensive

If you ever find yourself entertaining a visitor of style and substance from abroad who has never tasted an American meal, the magnificent Four Seasons restaurant would be the top choice. It is elegant and awe-inspiring in its simplicity and charm. Two separate dining areas—the Grill Room and the Pool Room—are different in menu and appeal. The dark suits (translation: business and media heavy hitters) congregate at noon in the Grill Room, where the waiters know them by name and what they like (baked potatoes, great salads, steak tartare, burgers). The Pool Room, set beside an actual marble pool, is more romantic and feminine. Ladies who lunch and couples who want to dine with the stars are right at home here with superb service, a wonderful duck entree, and a dessert menu that can only be described as obscene. Individual soufflés in coffee cups are a splendid treat.

FRANK'S
85 Tenth Ave (at 15th St)   212/243-1349
Lunch: Mon-Fri; Dinner: Daily   www.franksnyc.com
Moderate

The Molinari family—the third generation in a business that started in 1912—has kept up the quality and appeal of this popular spot. Customers are usually folks with large appetites! Reservations are suggested, as the place is very popular. There are great pastas, huge steaks, superb prime rib, fresh fish, veal, lamb, and really good French fries. New York cheesecake is the best dessert choice.

Soups, salads, sandwiches, and wonderful pastry items can be had for lunch at **Financier Patisserie** (62 Stone St, 212/344-5600). The taste is good and the drain on the pocketbook small.

FRANK'S TRATTORIA
371 First Ave (bet 21st and 22nd St)   212/677-2991
Lunch, Dinner: Daily   www.frankstrattoria.com
Inexpensive

It's true in New York, just as it is anywhere else in the country, that no one knows great, cheap places to eat better than the boys in blue. Manhattan's finest are some of the best customers of this modest trattoria, and it is easy to see why. The menu runs the gamut of Florentine dishes, each prepared to order and served piping hot (as is the bread, which is always a good sign). There is a large seafood selection, plus steaks, chops, and chicken. You can choose from over 20 pizzas, served whole or by the piece. Everyone here is informal and friendly, and Frank is delighted that the good word about his place has spread beyond the neighborhood regulars.

FRESCO BY SCOTTO
34 E 52nd St (bet Madison and Park Ave)   212/935-3434
Lunch: Mon-Fri; Dinner: Mon-Sat   www.frescobyscotto.com
Moderate to moderately expensive

Things are hopping at Fresco, especially during the noon hour. Even with the pressure of folks in a hurry, the staff is courteous and efficient. They take rightful pride in serving outstanding dishes prepared by executive chef Stefano Battistini. His background shows with the kinds of plates offered: delicious homemade pastas, a number of grilled dishes (including great grilled veal chops), eggplant and zucchini pie, a 32-ounce steak, and braised short ribs that will melt in your mouth. Wonderful potato side dishes include garlic mashed, basil whipped, mashed sweet, and smashed Yukon Gold potatoes. For dessert, try the key-lime panna cotta or bombolini filled with vanilla cream. After a meal here, you will understand why modern Tuscan cuisine is so popular. Next door, **Fresco on the Go** (40 E 52nd St) offers homemade muffins, croissants, scones, sticky buns, Danishes, Belgian waffles, homemade pancakes, granola and yogurt, eggs to order, and espresso or cappuccino for breakfast. Lunch consists of sandwiches (meatball, eggplant parmesan, prosciutto and mozzarella), pizzas, soups, salads, fresh pastas, homemade desserts, and ice cream. Private parties from 20 to 150 are welcome all day long.

You'll always see a crowd at **French Roast** (78 W 11th St, 212/533-2233) in Greenwich Village, and for good reason. The food is good, the price is right, the service is prompt, and the place is open 24 hours a day.

GABRIEL'S BAR & RESTAURANT
11 W 60th St (bet Broadway and Ninth Ave)   212/956-4600
Lunch: Mon-Fri; Dinner: Mon-Sat   www.gabrielsbarandrest.com
Moderate

Here's a winner for dining in the Lincoln Center area. You are greeted by an extremely friendly host, Gabriel Aiello, while "Gabriel . . . Gabriel" plays in the background. And what good food and drink! Delicious bread. Fresh melon and blood-orange mimosa. A fine assortment of Italian appetizers. Then on to really first-class pastas (like tagliatelle with peppers), chicken, steaks, and grilled seafood dishes. The in-house gelati creations are among New York's best, as is the flourless chocolate torte. To cap it all off, Gabriel's offers a selection of more than a dozen unusual teas (like peach melba, raspberry, and French vanilla). Gabriel doesn't have to blow his own horn; his satisfied customers are happy to do it for him! Private party facilities are available.

GASCOGNE
158 Eighth Ave (at 18th St)   212/675-6564
Lunch: Tues-Fri; Dinner: Daily; Brunch: Sat, Sun
Moderate   www.gascognenyc.com

Hearty appetites and southwest French cooking spell happiness with a capital *H* at this intimate Chelsea bistro. There's no fuss or fancy affectations by the capable and friendly waiters, who will happily explain the fine points of the rather limited menu. Salads are popular. Foie gras lovers will be in heaven. The main-course menu features duck, cassoulet, quail, and roasted rabbit. Seafood dishes are especially tasty. All desserts are made in-house and show imagination. There are sorbets, fruit tarts, soufflés, and some unusual ice cream flavors (prune, Armagnac, and chocolate mint). A small dining area is available downstairs, but it is rather claustrophobic. The garden is charming. If you are longing for an extensive French dining experience, take a look at the *prix fixe* menu. By the way, Gascony is the only region in the world where Armagnac, a brandy distilled from wine, is produced.

GENNARO
665 Amsterdam Ave (bet 92nd and 93rd St)   212/665-5348
Dinner: Daily
Cash only
Moderate

When patrons line up outside in the freezing rain or blistering heat, you know that what's inside must be special. And it is at Gennaro, a 12-table sliver of a place on the Upper West Side. Known mainly to those who inhabit the neighborhood, this find offers very friendly service, delicious food, and moderate prices. There is a $20 minimum per person, and no credit cards are accepted. Listen to the evening specials before ordering, as there are always some attractive possibilities. The menu is mainly Italian-Mediterranean, with specialties like Tuscan cannelloni bean soup, potato gnocchi, grilled Italian sausage, and grilled salmon with honey mustard sauce. Spinach is delicious and mashed potatoes melt in your mouth. For old-timers who remember the flourless chocolate cake at the Coach House, Gennaro's taste-alike is equally superb.

GINO
780 Lexington Ave (at 61st St)   212/758-4466
Lunch, Dinner: Daily
Cash only (checks accepted if known on premises)
Moderate

As you survey the crowd at this famous New York institution, you can tell immediately that the food is great. Why? Because this Italian restaurant is filled with native New Yorkers. You'll see no tourist buses out front. The menu has been the same for years: a large selection of popular dishes (over 30 entrees) from antipasto to soup, pasta to fish. There are daily specials, of course, but you only have to taste such regulars as chicken a la Capri, Italian sausages with peppers, or scampis a la Gino to get hooked. Gino's staff has been here forever, taking care of patrons in an informed, fatherly manner. The best part comes when the tab is presented. East Side rents are always climbing, but Gino has resisted price hikes by taking cash only and serving delicious food that keeps the tables full. No reservations are accepted, so come early.

GIORGIONE
307 Spring St (bet Greenwich and Hudson St)   212/352-2269
Lunch: Mon-Fri; Dinner: Daily; Brunch: Sat, Sun
Moderate

You know when the name Deluca (as in Dean and Deluca) is involved, it will be a quality operation. So it is here, with Giorgio Deluca one of the partners in this attractive high-tech establishment that features shiny metal-top tables and an inviting pizza oven that turns out some of the best pies in the area. This is a very personal restaurant, with Italian dishes like you'd find in mother's kitchen in the Old Country: carpaccio, prosciutto, ravioli, risotto, and linguine. The minestrone is as good as I have tasted anywhere. Pizzas come in eight presentations. You can finish with a platter of tasty Italian cneeses or pick from the appealing dessert trolley. A raw bar is also available.

GOLDEN UNICORN
18 East Broadway (at Catherine St)   212/941-0911
Breakfast, Lunch, Dinner, Dim Sum: Daily
Inexpensive

Golden Unicorn prepares the best dim sum outside of Peking! This bustling, two-floor, Hong Kong-style Chinese restaurant serves delicious dim sum every day of the week. Besides delicacies from the rolling carts, diners may choose from a wide variety of Cantonese dishes off the regular menu. Pan-fried noodle dishes, rice noodles, and noodles in soup are house specialties. Despite the size of the establishment (they can take care of over 500 diners at one time), you will be amazed at the fast service, cleanliness, and (most of all) prices. This is one of the best values in Chinatown.

GONZO
140 W13th St (bet Ave of the Americas and Seventh Ave)
Lunch: Sat, Sun; Dinner: Tues-Sun   212/645-4606
Moderate

It is a wonder that more restaurants don't understand that what diners really want is tasty food served in a fun atmosphere with competent service. All of this is available at Gonzo, one of the lately popular places in Manhattan. Seating is available in front, at the bar, and in the smallish, attractive back room. Grilled pizzas are the big thing here, and a number of them are available at a modest tab. There are also chopped salads, sliced meat and cheese plates, real Italian pastas, and a nice selection of meat and fish entrees. My choices: braised shortribs of beef that literally falls off the bone, and fresh grilled whole fish, which varies each day. Veggie lovers will savor a dozen or more side dish offerings, a number of them grilled. Chef/owner Vincent Scotto knows what the younger crowd likes, and he caters to them. I could go back time and time again for the espresso gelato.

Googie's Italian Diner (1491 Second Ave, 212/717-1122) is a fun place, especially when you can eat outdoors. Breakfast is served until 7 p.m. There is a large selection of soups, sandwiches, salads, and pastas at lunch and dinner. Moderately priced entrees include a wide selection of comfort foods. Kids will enjoy special drinks from the soda fountain.

GOOD
89 Greenwich Ave (bet Bank and 12th St)   212/691-8080
Lunch: Tues-Fri; Dinner: Tues-Sun; Brunch: Sat, Sun
Moderate   www.goodrestaurantnyc.com

Good bills itself as featuring "country cuisine of the Americas," with some Latin influences, whatever that means. No matter. They do a really good job with an eclectic menu that includes salads (the crispy chicken salad is tops), sandwiches (burgers, BLT), and other offerings like Colombian stew, smoked barbecued pulled pork, sauteed fresh tuna, and Atlantic salmon cakes. At dinner, add sauteed farm chicken and flank steak. Meatless dishes are served at lunch and dinner. Desserts run the gamut from toasted coconut pound cake sundaes to butterscotch banana pudding. But the real treats are the homemade orange sour cream doughnuts. Superb! Brunch includes doughnuts, fresh-baked buttermilk biscuits, homemade maple granola with yogurt, eggs with a Mexican twist, pancakes, sandwiches, salads, and more. The place is tiny, the service homey, and the atmosphere neighborly. It's worth a try, especially on Sunday.

GOOD ENOUGH TO EAT
483 Amsterdam Ave (at 83rd St)   212/496-0163
Breakfast, Lunch: Mon-Fri; Dinner: Daily, Brunch: Sat, Sun
Inexpensive

New York is a weekend breakfast and brunch town, and you cannot do better than Good Enough to Eat in both categories. Savor the apple pancakes, four-grain pancakes with walnuts and fresh bananas, and chocolate chip and coconut pancakes. There is more: French toast, waffles, six kinds of omelets, four scrambled egg dishes, corned beef hash, homemade Irish oatmeal, fresh-squeezed orange juice, and homemade sausage. The lunches in this homey and noisy room—which has been open for over two decades, with tile floor and wooden tables and bar—feature inexpensive and delicious salads, burgers (juicy and delicious), pizzas, and sandwiches. More of the same is served for dinner, plus meatloaf, turkey, pork chops, fish, and roast chicken plates. A children's menu is available, and an outdoor cafe is popular in nice weather. This is comfort food at its best, all the way through wonderful home-made pies, cakes, and ice creams for dessert.

GOTHAM BAR & GRILL
12 E 12th St (bet Fifth Ave and University Pl)   212/620-4020
Lunch: Mon-Fri; Dinner: Daily   www.gothambarandgrill.com
Moderately expensive

The Gotham Bar & Grill is recognized as one of New York's best. Dining here can be summed up in one word: exciting! It is not inexpensive, but every meal I have had here has been worth the tab. However, there is a really good *prix fixe* lunch deal. Alfred Portale is one of the most talented chefs in the city. The modern, spacious, high-ceilinged space is broken by direct spot lighting on the tables. Fresh plants lend a bit of color. There are great salads (try the seafood), excellent free-range chicken, and superior grilled salmon and roast cod. Each entree is well seasoned, attractively presented, and delicious. The rack of lamb is one of the tastiest served in the area. Desserts are all made in-house; try the vanilla crème brûlée or the Gotham chocolate cake.

GRAMERCY TAVERN
42 E 20th St (bet Park Ave S and Broadway)   212/477-0777
Lunch, Dinner: Daily
Expensive

It is no mystery why Gramercy Tavern is one of New York's most popular restaurants. When you combine an outstanding and innovative operator like Danny Meyer, a highly trained staff, an unusually attractive space, and reasonable prices with excellent food, the public will respond. Every detail is in superb taste. The ceiling is a work of art, the private party room is magnificent, and there isn't a bad seat in the house. Singles are in heaven here, and the light menu (including a fabulous cheese selection) adds strength to possible conquests. The menu changes often, but you can't go wrong with the large selection of seafood appetizers and entrees. If the roasted loin and braised shank of lamb is on the menu, grab it! How does lemon soufflé tart with ginger ice cream and lemon confit sound for dessert? If you are entertaining out-of-town guests, I'd highly recommend this place for a showcase dinner. The Tavern menu also has some delicious offerings, like a wood-grilled veggie Dagwood or grilled pork tenderloin sandwich.

GRAND CENTRAL OYSTER BAR AND RESTAURANT
Grand Central Station (lower level)   212/490-6650
Mon-Fri: 11:30-9:30; Sat: 12-9:30   www.oysterbarny.com
Moderate

Native New Yorkers know about the nearly century-old institution that is the Oyster Bar at Grand Central. A midtown destination once popular with commuters and residents, it has been restored and is doing quite nicely again. (They serve over 2,000 folks a day!) The young help are most accommodating, and the drain on the pocketbook is minimal. The menu boasts more than 72 seafood items (with new entrees daily), 20 to 30 varieties of oysters, a super oyster stew, clam chowder (Manhattan and New England), oyster pan roast, bouillabaisse, coquille St. Jacques, Maryland crab cakes (Wednesday special), Maine lobsters, 75 wines by the glass, and marvelous homemade desserts.

GRANGE HALL
50 Commerce St (at Barrow St)   212/924-5246
Lunch: Mon-Fri; Dinner: Daily; Brunch: Sat, Sun
Moderate

Hidden away on a picturesque corner in the West Village, this charmer is an ex-speakeasy! Inside you will find peace and relaxation, as well as excellent "comfort" food. The menu changes by season, but you can count on homemade soups, a large selection of small dishes (as appetizers or in addition to your main dish), fresh salads, and ample, delicious entrees. The latter can be ordered simple (entree and accompaniment, as listed on the menu) or complete (with soup or salad). Things start off right with a loaf of warm homemade bread, and all other items are served either piping hot or chilly cold, as they should be. I was particularly taken with the appetizer selection: unusual items like spicy string beans, hand-cut yam fried potatoes, freshly made sausage, wild rice and wheat berry medley, and baked eggplant steaks. Your choices may not be the same, but will no doubt be equally inventive! Desserts are also prepared in-house, and the accommodating help makes the experience almost like eating at home. You'll love the ambience.

GUIDO'S (SUPREME MACARONI CO.)
511 Ninth Ave (at 39th St)   212/502-4842
Lunch: Mon-Fri; Dinner: Mon-Sat
No credit cards
Inexpensive

You might wonder what you're doing having lunch in the back room of a macaroni factory on Ninth Avenue. Well, this is no typical back room and no ordinary macaroni factory! Up front, as you walk in, is a display of 23 brands of macaroni. That was the original business (dating back to 1947), but now it's just a sideline. The real draw is the smallish restaurant in the back, which is as busy as Times Square. Tom Scarola is the third-generation family member who runs this unusual operation. Whether you're coming for lunch or dinner, make sure to have a reservation. You might rub shoulders with some celebrities. Even if they're not here in person, their pictures (along with blue-checkered tablecloths and wine bottles on the ceiling) create a special atmosphere at Guido's. You don't want to miss the lobster, rigatoni with vodka sauce, shrimp *francese,* veal sorrentino, or the house specialty, chicken *alla Guido.* The pasta is freshly made, authentic, inexpensive, and delicious. Finish with an assortment of mixed pastries and fresh cakes, along with a special espresso, and you will have had a marvelous meal. Lunch specials include four chicken, veal, and shrimp entrees, as well as linguini or spaghetti with all the trimmings.

For a later breakfast served daily, you can't do better than **Grey Dog's Coffee** (33 Carmine St, 212/462-0041). This is also a good bet for catering for office meetings or other gatherings. A complete breakfast goes for as little as $8.50, which is a New York bargain.

HATSUHANA
17 E 48th St (bet Fifth and Madison Ave)	212/355-3345
237 Park Ave (at 46th St)	212/661-3400
Lunch: Mon-Fri; Dinner: Mon-Fri	www.hatsuhana.com
Moderate	

Hatsuhana has deservedly become known as the best sushi house in Manhattan. One can sit at a table or at the bar and get equal attention from the informed help. There are several dozen appetizers, including broiled eel in cucumber wrap and chopped fatty tuna with aged soybeans. Next, try the salmon teriyaki or any number of tuna or sushi dishes. Forget about desserts and concentrate on the exotic appetizer and main-dish offerings.

HEARTBEAT
W New York Hotel
149 E 49th St (at Lexington Ave)   212/407-2900
Breakfast: Daily; Lunch: Mon-Fri: Dinner: Mon-Sat
Moderate to moderately expensive   www.myriadrestaurantgroup.com

What a winning combination: a menu overflowing with dishes that are good for you, and an overseer like Drew Nieporent, one of America's culinary greats. Here in the W Hotel, Heartbeat looks as good as it tastes! The place is a cozy and comfortable extension of the lounge area just outside. This is not my kind of food, but if you obsess over your waistline, this is the place to visit. There are chilled oysters and sliced raw tuna for lunch. For dinner you will find meat dishes like beef tenderloin and organic chicken with lemon grass. The cuisine at Heartbeat is healthy, pure, and full-flavored. You can even get organic fruit for dessert.

HOUSTON'S
378 Park Ave S (at 27th St)   212/689-1090
Lunch, Dinner: Daily   www.houstons.com
Moderate

In a warm and clubby atmosphere, Houston's serves wonderful American food and more. Every day brings a different soup specialty. The regular menu offers a large selection of appetizers (like Chicago-style spinach and arti-choke dip), seasonal vegetables, big salads (their grilled chicken salad is a specialty), and sandwiches (the burgers are super). Entrees include rotisserie chicken, pork chops, steaks, ribs, a veggie platter, crab cakes, and more. Desserts are the weakest part of the menu. There is an active bar business with a wide selection of wines and beers. Houston's is popular with the young business set; the energy created by an unusually pleasant and fun staff makes this a great spot for casual dining any time of the day or evening.

I COPPI
432 E 9th St (bet First Ave and Ave A)   212/254-2263
Lunch: Sat, Sun; Dinner: Daily
Moderate

A husband and wife team, Lorella Innocenti and John Brennan, have created a charming Tuscan restaurant in the East Village with tasty food to match the appealing atmosphere. As readers of this publication know, I am keen on good bread. The folks here have brought talent from the Old Country to insure that the breads are authentic. A brick pizza oven adds a special touch. Outstanding luncheon dishes on a menu that changes seasonally may include Tuscan-style omelets or thin egg noodles with *Bolognese* sauce. Pastas, grilled striped bass, roasted rabbit, and grilled sirloin steak are excellent dinner choices, if offered. Save room for gelati, sorbet, or Tuscan cheese for dessert. The heated and canopied outdoor garden is especially inviting. No need to rush uptown to fancier and pricier Tuscan restaurants; this one is as professional as I have found anywhere in the city

---

Hype feeds on hype, and this is no more true than in the restaurant busi-ness. Once a place gets a reputation as being very "in" with hard-to-get reservations, folks can't wait to say they've eaten there. One such spot is **The Harrison** (355 Greenwich St, at Harrison St, 212/274-9310). (Note: This is Greenwich Street, not Avenue.) The room is busy and attractive, the service quite professional (neatly dressed, on-the-ball help), and some dishes are quite tasty. But by no means does it break new ground.

IL BAGATTO
192 E 2nd St (bet Ave A and B)   212/228-0977
Dinner: Tues-Sun (closed Aug)
Inexpensive
Cash only

One of Manhattan's best bargains, Il Bagatto is the place to come if you're feeling adventurous. Housed in tiny digs in an area you would hardly call compelling, the doors open to an extremely popular Italian trattoria. The owners have discovered the rules of success: being on the job and ensuring that every dish tastes just like it came out of mama's kitchen. About a dozen tables upstairs (and in the lounge) are always filled, so it's best to call ahead for reservations. There's delicious spaghetti, homemade gnocchi with spinach, tortellini with meat sauce (made from their own secret recipe), and wonderful tagliolini with seafood in a light tomato sauce. Other menu offer-ings include chicken, thin slices of beef, salads, and always a few specials. They deliver, too.

IL CORTILE
125 Mulberry St (bet Canal St and Hester St)   212/226-6060
Lunch, Dinner: Daily   www.ilcortile.com
Moderate

Little Italy is more for tourists than serious diners, but there are some exceptions. Il Cortile is an oasis of tasty Italian fare in an attractive and romantic setting. A bright and airy garden area in the rear is the most pleasant part of the restaurant. The menu is typical Italian, with just about anything you could possibly want. Entree listings include fish, chicken and veal dishes, plus excellent spaghetti, fettuccine, and ravioli. Sauteed vegetables like bitter broccoli, hot peppers, mushrooms, spinach, and green beans are specialties of the house. One thing is for certain: the waiters zip around like they are on roller skates. Service is excellent and expeditious. If you can fight your way through the gawking visitors, you will find Il Cortile worth the effort!

IL GATTOPARDO
33 W 54th St (bet Fifth Ave and Ave of the Americas)   212/246-0412
Lunch: Mon-Fri; Dinner: Mon-Sat
Expensive

Yes, Il Gattopardo is expensive, but it's certainly worth the tariff. This is the kind of place that appeals to serious gourmets, as food and service leave little to be desired. The room is not fancy; it is, in fact, rather claustrophobic. In nice weather, the outdoor patio is charming. Very interesting appetizers that vary from time to time include beef and veal meatballs wrapped in cabbage, scallops and shrimp salad, and parmigiana of baby artichokes. Among the many pastas, homemade cavatelli with shellfish ragu is great. Main-course highlights include neapolitan meat loaf, herb-crusted rack of lamb, fish and shellfish stew, and much more. For dessert, warm chocolate cake with ice cream is sinful. Il Gattopardo's atmosphere is so pleasant you will really be sad to see the meal conclude.

With more folks visiting Cuba, there is renewed interest in the cuisine of this country. One of the best Manhattan locations for creating your own paella or to taste delicious Havana-style barbecued ribs with mango ginger sauce is **Havana Central** (22 E 17th St, 212/414-4999). Jeremy Merrin, a hands-on partner, welcomes diners with counter service at breakfast and lunch, and tables at dinner. The price is right, and vegetarians will feel right at home.

IL GIGLIO
81 Warren St (bet West Broadway and Greenwich St)   212/571-5555
Lunch: Mon-Fri; Dinner: Mon-Sat   www.ilgigliorestaurant.com
Moderate

If you can find this place, you will be delighted to discover a bright, clean, classy operation that serves absolutely great Northern Italian food. Smallness is a virtue here, as the two dozen tables are looked after by a crew of highly trained, tuxedo-clad waiters, most of whom have been on the premises since its opening. Specials are almost as numerous as menu items (be sure to ask for prices), and by all means look over the display of fresh fruits, desserts, and other goodies by the entrance. The scampi and veal dishes are superb, and few places in Tribeca (or elsewhere in Manhattan) do pasta any better. Moreover, all desserts are made in-house.

IL MULINO
86 W 3rd St (bet Sullivan and Thompson St)   212/673-3783
Lunch: Mon-Fri; Dinner: Mon-Sat
Moderately expensive

Those who live to eat will want to pay attention to this entry. Never mind that reservations usually must be made a week or so in advance. Never mind that it's always crowded, the noise level is intolerable, and the waiters nearly knock you down as you wait to be seated. It's all part of the ambience at Il Mulino, one of New York's best Italian restaurants. Your greeting is usually "Hi, boss," which gives you the distinct impression that the staff are accustomed to catering to members of the, uh, "family." When your waiter finally comes around, he'll reel off a lengthy list of evening specials with glazed eyes. On the other hand, a beautiful, mouth-watering display of daily specials is arrayed on a huge entrance table. After you're seated, the waiter delivers one antipasto after another while he talks you into ordering one of the fabulous veal dishes with portions bountiful enough to feed King Kong. Osso buco is a favorite dish. By the time you finish one of the luscious desserts, you'll know why every seat in the small, simple diningroom is kept warm all evening.

ILO
Bryant Park Hotel
40 W 40th St (bet Fifth Ave and Ave of the Americas)   212/642-2255
Lunch: Mon-Fri: Dinner: Daily; Brunch: Sat, Sun
Expensive   www.ilorestaurant.com

The name *Ilo* means joyful in Finnish, and this restaurant lives up to that description in the quality of its food. However, don't come here expecting lavish surroundings; it is a rather plain room, no flowers on the tables, but the tabletop items (especially the glassware) are all very classy. Ilo is another of the very trendy smallish restaurants attached to smallish hotels. Pricey appetizers are uniformly delicious; artichoke soup with wild mushrooms is particularly good. (It should be at $15 a bowl.) Owner/chef Rick Laakkonen is a master when it comes to sauces, and it shows with dishes like charred fillet of pork, pan-roasted pheasant, and grilled sturgeon. At lunch, appetizers like white asparagus salad or terrine of smoked duck foie gras are enough for a satisfying meal. A selection of artisanal cheeses is a perfect climax to the evening, as are several other desserts. Service is very attentive and pleasant. However, at $110 a person, the tasting menu is, to put it mildly, grossly overdone.

IL POSTINO
337 E 49th St (bet First and Second Ave)   212/688-0033
Lunch: Mon-Sat; Dinner: Daily
Expensive

It is nice to splurge on occasion if what you get is really worth the extra bucks. Well, Il Postino does have a rather hefty price structure, but the offerings rival the best of them! The setting is comfortable and not showy. You'll be impressed by the captains, who can recite a lengthy list of specials without hesitation. You have your choice of ground-level tables or a slightly raised balcony; I have found the latter to be more comfortable. An extraordinarily tasty bread dish and assorted small appetizer plates get things off to a good start. Next, sensational pastas—like linguine with three kinds of clams or fresh made tagliolini with mushrooms—should not be missed. The chicken in a baked crust is very satisfying; also the roasted loin of veal for two is top-grade. The sorbets, whose taste is straight from the homeland, finish a memorable gourmet experience. Incidentally, lunch is equally tasty and easier on the wallet.

IL RICCIO
152 E 79th St (bet Third and Lexington Ave)   212/639-9111
Lunch, Dinner: Daily
Moderate

Nothing fancy here, just darn good Italian fare. Il Riccio is consistent, so you can count on leaving satisfied and well fed. Spaghetti with crabmeat and fresh tomato is one of my favorites. So is thinly sliced beef with truffled pecorino cheese and breaded rack of veal. Also offered are Dover sole and grilled sardines with broccoli. The patio is a small and comfortable place to dine in nice weather. Service is unfailingly pleasant. Fruit tarts are homemade and delicious, and marinated peaches (when available) are the signature dessert.

IL VAGABONDO
351 E 62nd St (bet First and Second Ave)   212/832-9221
Lunch: Mon-Fri; Dinner: Daily
Inexpensive

Many folks consider this their favorite restaurant! Il Vagabondo is a good spot to recommend to your visiting friends. This bustling restaurant has been a favorite with knowledgeable New Yorkers since 1965. The atmosphere is strictly old-time, complete with white tablecloths, four busy rooms, and an even busier bar. You may have spaghetti, ravioli, an absolutely marvelous minestrone, chicken parmigiana, or sliced beef. There is no pretense at this place. It is a great spot for office parties and folks with slim pocketbooks. You will see happy faces, compliments of a delicious meal and the extremely reasonable bill. Save room for the great "bocce-ball dessert" (*tartufo*). Il Vagabondo, you see, is the only restaurant in New York with an indoor bocce court!

JACKSON HOLE BURGERS
232 E 64th St (bet Second and Third Ave)	212/371-7187
521 Third Ave (at 35th St)	212/679-3264
1611 Second Ave (at 84th St)	212/737-8788
1270 Madison Ave (at 91st St)	212/427-2820
517 Columbus Ave (at 85th St)	212/362-5177
69-35 Astoria Blvd, Jackson Heights	718/204-7070
35-01 Bell Blvd, Bayside	718/281-0330
Lunch, Dinner: Daily	www.jacksonholeburgers.com
Inexpensive	

You might think that a burger is a burger. But having done hamburger taste tests all over the city, I've chosen Jackson's as one of the best. Each one weighs at least seven juicy, delicious ounces. You can get all kinds of them; pizza burger, Swiss burger, English burger, or a Baldouni® burger (mushrooms, fried onions, and American cheese). Or try an omelet, Mexican items, salads, or grilled chicken breast. The atmosphere isn't fancy, but once you sink your teeth into a Jackson Hole burger, accompanied by great onion rings or French fries and a homemade dessert, you'll see why I'm so enthusiastic. Free delivery and catering are available.

JACQUES
204 E 85th St (bet Second and Third Ave)   212/327-2272
Lunch, Dinner: Daily; Brunch: Sat, Sun
Moderate

It is easy to understand why this bistro is so popular with folks in the neighborhood. It is cozy, friendly, moderately priced, and serves great food. In addition, Jacques himself is one of the friendliest proprietors in town. All of the classic French dishes are available: onion soup, mussels and fries, steak *au poivre,* great fries, crème brûlée, cheeses, and a wonderful chocolate soufflé with Tahitian vanilla ice cream. There are also several outstanding seafood dishes. Mussels are prepared six different ways. Added treats: this bistro is intimate, makes a great place for private parties, and offers music on Friday and Saturday evening.

JEAN GEORGES
Trump International Hotel
1 Central Park W (bet 60th and 61st St)   212/299-3900
Lunch: Mon-Fri; Dinner: Mon-Sat (cafe open daily for breakfast);
Brunch: Sun   www.jean-georges.com
Very expensive

Jean-Georges Vongerichten has created a new French dining experience in a setting that can only be described as cool, calm, and calculating. I mean *calculating* in the sense that one is put into a frame of mind to sample *haute cuisine* at its best in a very formal diningroom that's awash with personnel who seem to be looking for something to do. In keeping with any operation bearing the Trump name, the hype at Jean Georges has been momentous. But to be honest, if price is unimportant, you just can't do better. The cafe, Nougatine, is a bit less intimidating. The menu changes regularly. Come ready to be educated!

JEAN-LUC
507 Columbus Ave (bet 84th and 85th St)   212/712-1700
Dinner: Daily
Moderate to moderately expensive

If energy, noise, and making the scene are important to you, then this is a place to try. Jean-Luc, despite some strange decorative touches, does have one particularly strong suit: the wait and service personnel are superbly energized. A dirty plate or a half-filled glass is taken care of immediately. Ed "Jean-Luc" Kleefield is on the spot, making sure that the right people get the right treatment. (If you're not known here, you may have to wait for awhile.) This Upper East Side attraction has some exceptionally tasty dishes: steamed artichokes with a flavorful vinaigrette dressing, Black Angus filet mignon (though the mounds of French fries taste like they came from McDonald's),

New Zealand rack of lamb served on white beans and diced vegetable stew, and many excellent seafood items. Alas, for a French operation, the bread basket is noticeably poor, and their profiteroles with a chocolate ganache sauce were just so-so, as were other desserts.

Il Monello (1460 Second Ave, 212/535-9310) is the place for a good traditional Italian lunch or dinner, seven days a week. The pastas are outstanding.

JIMMY SUNG'S
219 E 44th St (bet Second and Third Ave)   212/682-5678
Lunch, Dinner: Daily   www.jimmysungs.com
Moderate

For over two decades Jimmy Sung has been a talented player in the highly competitive world of Chinese restaurants in Manhattan. Sung's can seat over 250 customers in the main area, and seven exceptionally attractive private diningrooms can accommodate groups of various sizes. The cuisine includes Hunan, Canton, Shanghai, and Manchurian dishes that range from mild to very spicy. Some of Jimmy's favorites: vegetarian pie with house pancakes, Japanese sushi, sauteed frog legs with garlic sauce, and seafood combination. An experienced staff of chefs and waiters provide a personal touch to this busy spot. The next time the office gang plans a get-together, put Jimmy Sung's at the top of the list. On top of everything, prices are very affordable.

JOHN'S PIZZERIA
278 Bleecker St (at Seventh Ave)   212/243-1680
260 W 44th St (bet Eighth Ave and Broadway)   212/391-7560
408 E 64th St (bet First and York Ave)   212/935-2895
Daily: Open at 11:30 a.m., closing hours vary
Moderate   www.johnspizzeria.com

Pete Castelotti (there is no John) is known as the "Baron of Bleecker Street." However, he has expanded his John's Pizzeria chain to the Upper West Side and the Upper East Side so that more New Yorkers can taste some of the best brick-oven pizza in the city. John's offers 55 (count 'em) varieties, from cheese and tomatoes to a gut-busting extravaganza of cheese, tomatoes, anchovies, sausage, peppers, meatballs, onions, and mushrooms. If homemade spaghetti, cheese ravioli, or manicotti are your preference, John's does all these well, too. The surroundings on Bleecker Street are a bit shabby. Things are higher-class uptown; in fact, the 44th Street location is a former church. The renovation is spectacular, and the space is huge. Imagine tackling a giant pizza *bianca* in such a hallowed space!

JUBILEE
347 E 54th St (bet First and Second Ave)   212/888-3569
Lunch: Mon-Fri; Dinner: Daily; Brunch: Sun   www.jubileeny.com
Moderate

Jubilee is a pleasant, satisfying, and unique French bistro, serving well-prepared food in a refined atmosphere. Authentic French dishes include rack of lamb, grilled steak with marvelous French fries, and duck cassoulet. Mussels, a specialty of the house, are served several ways: curried, with chicken-mushroom sauce, marinière, vinaigrette, or *farcies a la Provencale*. Try the cozy and romantic table in the rear for tasty desserts like Cointreau crème brûlée or molten chocolate mousse cake.

JUDSON GRILL
152 W 52nd St (bet Ave of the Americas and Seventh Ave)
Lunch: Mon-Fri; Dinner: Mon-Sat   212/582 5252
Moderate (bar), moderately expensive (main room)

With chef Bill Telepan in the kitchen, this huge operation has taken on a decidedly upbeat feel. The place is constantly packed. If a lighter meal is what you want (handy for pre-theater), try eating in the bar area. You'll find sirloin burgers, tuna tartare, and ravioli, plus other treats like great onion rings and a hearty cheese selection. For heavier lunches or dinners, a highly interesting selection of appetizers is offered: grilled garlic-duck sausage, terrine of New York State foie gras, and a nice selection of salads. For entrees, there is a wide choice of seafood, roasted veal loin chops, duck breast, and some healthy veggie dishes. Don't pass up Judson's French fries! My dessert favorite: warm bittersweet chocolate cake with praline ice cream.

KATZ'S DELICATESSEN
205 E Houston St (at Ludlow St)   212/254-2246
Sun-Tues: 8 a.m.-10 p.m.; Wed, Thurs: 8 a.m.-11 p.m.;
Fri. Sat: 8 a.m.-3 a.m.
Inexpensive

If you're experiencing hunger pangs on the Lower East Side, try Katz's Delicatessen. It is a super place with some of the biggest and best sandwiches in town, hand-carved and overstuffed. Mainstays include pastrami, hot dogs, and potato pancakes. The atmosphere goes along with the great food, and the prices are reasonable. Go right up to the counter and order—it is fun watching the no-nonsense operators slicing and fixing—or sit at a table where a seasoned waiter will take care of you. Try dill pickles and sauerkraut with your sandwich. Incidentally, Katz's is a perfect way to sample the unique "charm" of the Lower East Side. While you wait for a table or discover that the salt and pepper containers are empty and the catsup is missing, you'll know what I mean. Catering (at attractive rates) and private party facilities are available.

KEENS STEAKHOUSE
72 W 36th St (bet Fifth Ave and Ave of the Americas)
Lunch: Mon-Fri; Dinner: Daily   212/947-3636
Moderate   www.keenssteakhouse.com

With glamorous new places opening every week and people always wanting to follow the crowd, we sometimes forget about older restaurants that consistently do a good job. One of them is Keens Steakhouse, a unique New York institution. I can remember going there decades ago when those in the garment trade made Keens their lunch headquarters. This has not changed. Keens still has the same attractions: the bar reeks of atmosphere, and there are great party facilities and fine food to match. Keens has been a fixture in the Herald Square area since 1885. For some time it was for "gentlemen only," and although it still has a masculine atmosphere, ladies now feel comfortable and welcome. The famous mutton chop with mint is the house specialty, but other delicious dishes include veal, steak, lamb, and fish. For the light eater, especially at lunch, there are some great salads. Lobster has been added to the menu. They do seasonal single malt Scotch tastings from fall to spring and stock one of the largest single malt collections in New York. If you have a meat-and-potato lover in your party, this is the place to bring him. Make sure to save a little room for the deep-dish apple pie.

Egg Cream

A New York invention, the egg cream is generally credited to Louis Auster, a Jewish immigrant who owned a candy store at Stanton and Cannon streets during the early part of the century. Mostly to amuse himself, he started mixing carbonated water, sugar, and cocoa until he got a drink he liked. It was such a hit that Schraft's reportedly offered him $20,000 for the recipe. Auster wouldn't sell and secretly continued making his own syrup in the back room of his store. When he died, his recipe went with him. Some years later, Herman Fox created another chocolate syrup, which he called Fox's U-Bet. Fox's brand is regarded as the definitive egg cream syrup to this day.

KING'S CARRIAGE HOUSE
251 E 82nd St (bet Second and Third Ave)   212/734-5490
Lunch: Mon-Sat; Dinner: Daily
Moderately expensive

Even folks in the immediate neighborhood don't know about this sleeper. King's is indeed an old carriage house, remade into a charming two-story dining salon that your mother-in-law will love. The mood is Irish manor house, with the menu changing every evening. In a quaint setting with real wooden floors, you dine by candlelight in a very civilized atmosphere. The luncheon menu stays the same: salads, sandwiches, and lighter fare. Afternoon tea is a treat. The continental menu in the evening may feature grilled items (like loin of lamb); on Sundays, it is a roast dinner (leg of lamb, loin of pork, chicken, or tenderloin of beef). The *prix fixe* menu is a really good value. Personally, I found the Stilton cheese with a nightcap of ruby port absolutely perfect for dessert, but you may prefer chocolate truffle cake or rhubarb tart.

LA BOITE EN BOIS
75 W 68th St (near Columbus Ave)   212/874-2705
Lunch: Tues-Sat; Dinner: Daily; Brunch: Sun
No credit cards
Moderate

You don't have to pronounce the name of this restaurant properly to have a good time! It packs them in every evening for obvious reasons. Owner Alan Brossard, an ex-chef, has hit upon a winning combination: delicious food, personal service, and moderate prices. Salads are unusual, and the country paté is a great beginner. For an entree, I recommend fillet of snapper, roast chicken with herbs, or *pot-au-feu*. The atmosphere is intimate, and all the niceties of service are operative from start to finish. Desserts are made in-house; I suggest one of their sorbets. Call for reservations, since La Boite en Bois is small and popular.

LA CARAVELLE
Shoreham Hotel
33 W 55th St (bet Fifth Ave and Ave of the Americas)
Lunch: Mon-Fri; Dinner: Mon-Sat   212/586-4252
Expensive   www.lacaravelle.com

I have been a diner here for decades! With the incessant hype of new places and dishes, it is comforting to know that there are still some old reliables where things have always been good and remain that way. Such is La Caravelle, where chef Troy Dupuy offers many of the same dishes that have made this deluxe French palace famous: quenelles in a rich lobster sauce, roasted crispy duck, fillet of Dover sole, sauteed foie gras, mouth-watering roast chicken, and a very popular crab salad. Of course, there are newer dishes, but every time I come here I opt for something tried and true. As you would expect, service is extremely gracious, befitting the warm and luxurious interior of the room. Don't leave without trying one of the rich soufflés or peanut crunch with white chocolate mousse. If you want to leave it up to the chef, he'll take good care of you with his fabulous *menus d'inspiration*. Congratulations to Rita and Andre Jainmet for keeping a great tradition going.

LA CÔTE BASQUE
60 W 55th St (near Fifth Ave)   212/688-6525
Lunch: Mon-Sat; Dinner: Mon-Sun   www.lacotebasque.net
Expensive

Yes, it's expensive. *Quite* expensive (*prix fixe*). But dining at La Côte Basque is an experience worth every dollar. I doubt whether there is a room anywhere in the world more attractive and comfortable than this one. With gorgeous murals, superb lighting, and a magnificent open setting (no high banquettes), La Côte Basque is a feast for the eyes and the palate. The service is ultra-professional, as one would expect. There are marvelous appetizers like Petrossian caviar, sauteed wild mushrooms, seared duck liver, and oak-smoked salmon. Entrees include superb quenelles, roasted duckling with honey, and a special cassoulet by chef-owner Jean-Jacques Rachou. The desserts, like the fabulous soufflés belong in a museum of beauty and good taste. As if this weren't enough, a box of dessert goodies is placed temptingly in front of you. What an evening!

LA GRENOUILLE
3 E 52nd St (at Fifth Ave)   212/752-1495
Lunch, Dinner: Tues-Sat   www.la-grenouille.com
Expensive

After charming Manhattan for four decades, La Grenouille remains a special place that must be seen to be believed. Beautiful fresh flowers herald a unique, not-to-be-forgotten dining experience. The food is as great as the atmosphere, and although prices are high, it's worth every penny. Celebrity-watching adds to the fun. You'll see most of the famous faces at the front of the room. The professional staff serves a complete French menu. Be sure to try the cold hors d'oeuvres, which are a specialty of the house. So are the lobster dishes, sea bass, and poached chicken. Nowhere in New York are sauces any better. Don't miss the superb dessert soufflés. The tables are very close together, but what difference does it make when the people at your elbows are so interesting?

LA LUNCHONETTE
130 Tenth Ave (at 18th St)   212/675-0342
Lunch, Dinner: Daily
Inexpensive to moderate

La Lunchonette proves that you don't have to be fancy to succeed, as long as you serve good food. In an unlikely location, this popular spot offers some of the tastiest French dishes around: snails, sauteed portobello mushrooms, and lobster bisque to start, and omelets, grilled lamb sausage, sauteed calves liver, and more for entrees. On Sunday evenings, live music is a feature. You'll be pleasantly surprised when the bill comes!

The **Hungarian Pastry Shop** (1030 Amsterdam Ave, 212/866-4230) is a cafe *and* bakery! The wonderful cakes (linzer tarts are my favorite) are only part of the appeal. The cafe serves all sorts of waist-expanding items, along with delicious Viennese coffee.

LA MÉTAIRIE
189 W 10th St (bet 4th and Bleecker St)   212/989-0343
Lunch, Dinner: Daily; Brunch: Sat, Sun
Moderate   www.lametairie.com

Once just a tiny hole in the wall, La Métairie ("a small communal farm") has expanded into a delightful place to dine in the Village. The atmosphere is still cozy, the food exceptional, the service prompt and accommodating. Moreover, the price is right! The kitchen offers a wide choice of French dishes. Specialties of the house include wild boar stew with fresh noodles, bouillabaisse, and rack of lamb.

LANDMARK TAVERN
626 Eleventh Ave (at 46th St)   212/757-8595
Daily: Noon-midnight; Brunch: Sun
Inexpensive

How about a cozy meal by a fireplace or potbellied stove? Landmark Tavern is open friendly hours for sandwich platters, a variety of salads, fresh seafood, steaks, and roast prime rib of beef. The real treat here is Sunday brunch, a unique tradition since 1868. Normal brunch items are available, but so is shepherd's pie (ground lamb sauteed with herbs), delicious lamb steaks, and English-style fish and chips. There is the added pleasure of sampling their famous soda bread, made fresh every hour and served with imported jams and marmalade. Corned beef hash is a favorite. Great homemade desserts like Irish soda bread pudding and Jack Daniel's cake will make you want to come back every Sunday. The bar is friendly, the help is harried, and the atmosphere reeks of nostalgia. More important, the food is delicious, and prices are a bargain.

LA PETITE AUBERGE
116 Lexington Ave (at 28th St)   212/689-5003
Lunch: Mon-Fri: Dinner: Daily
Moderate

Genuine French cooking in this area is not easily found, but this smallish restaurant is worth a casual lunch or dinner visit. No pretense here! Extra friendly personnel will lead you through the usual French favorites, like onion soup and escargots. But there is much more: frog legs, roast duck, filet mignon, rack of lamb, and filet of sole. Delicious chocolate mousse is a fine way to finish a satisfying meal.

LA RIPAILLE
605 Hudson St (at 12th St)   212/255-4406
Lunch, Dinner: Daily; Brunch: Sun
Moderate

This small, bright, romantic Parisian-style bistro (complete with fireplace) makes a cozy spot for an informal meal. The chef puts his heart into every dish. Entrees are done to perfection; the seafood is always fresh (try bass in champagne and fine herbs), and they do an excellent job with rack of lamb and duck *magret*. White chocolate is a house favorite; at least half of the dessert offerings use it as an ingredient. Proudly displayed at the front of the room are rave notices from a number of New York gourmets.

Italian Specialties

Bruschetta: slices of crispy garlic bread, usually topped with tomatoes and basil

Carpaccio: thin shavings of raw beef topped with olive oil and lemon juice or mayonnaise

Risotto: creamy rice-like pasta, often mixed with shellfish and/or vegetables

Saltimbocca: Thinly sliced veal is topped with prosciutto and sage, then sauteed in butter and slow-simmered in white wine. The name means "jumps in your mouth."

Zabaglione: a dessert sauce or custard made with egg yolks, marsala, and sugar; also known as *sabayon* in France

---

LAYLA
211 West Broadway (at Franklin St)   212/431-0700
Dinner: Tues-Sat   www.myriadrestaurantgroup.com
Moderate to moderately expensive

Leave it to Drew Nieporent to do something different. His exotic Layla is just that: good food with a Mediterranean flair. Don't be put off by the exotic menu, as the patient personnel will make sure you have a pleasurable meal. There is tabbouleh, hummus, and other dishes from this part of the world. A family-style feast is available, as is a belly-dancing show. You may feel out-of-shape after seeing the performers!

LE BERNARDIN
155 W 51st St (near Seventh Ave)   212/489-1515
Lunch: Mon-Fri; Dinner: Mon-Sat   www.le-bernardin.com
Expensive

There has to be one place that tops every list, and among seafood palaces Le Bemardin holds that spot. Owner Maguy LeCoze and chef Eric Ripert make this house extremely attractive to the eye and very satisfying to the stomach. Wonderfully fresh oysters and clams are a great way to start.

Whatever your heart desires from the ocean is represented on the entree menu. What distinguishes La Bernardin is presentation. Signature dishes (a different one each night) include yellowfish tuna (appetizer), monkfish, halibut, and skate. *Prix fixe* lunch is $47; dinner is $84. The changeable dessert menu usually includes a cheese assortment and superb chocolate dishes.

LE BIARRITZ
325 W 57th St (bet Eighth and Ninth Ave)   212/245-9467
Lunch: Mon-Fri; Dinner: Mon-Sat   www.lebiarritz.com
Moderate

Happily, nothing changes here. New York is full of neighborhood restaurants, and Le Biarritz is one of the best. It seems like home every evening as regulars claim most of the seats in this warm, smallish eatery. The place has been at the same location and in the same hands for nearly four decades. Gleaming copper makes any eating establishment look inviting, and here you can see a first-rate collection of beautiful French copper cooking and serving pieces. If you're in the mood for escargots to start, the chef prepares them well. You might also try French onion soup or crepes a la Biarritz (stuffed with crabmeat). Entrees include frog legs *provençale*, duck in cherry sauce with wild rice, and all kinds of chicken, lamb, beef, veal, and fish dishes, each served with fresh vegetables. Desserts are homemade and very good. The reasonably priced dinners include soup, salad, and choice of dessert. I recommend Le Biarritz if you are going to a Broadway show or an event at Lincoln Center.

LE CIRQUE 2000
New York Palace Hotel
455 Madison Ave (bet 50th and 51st St)   212/303-7788
Lunch: Mon-Sat; Dinner: Daily   www.lecirque.com
Expensive

Certain restaurants are legends, and Le Cirque is one of them. There are also restaurateurs who are legends, such as owner Sirio Maccioni. His personality, combined with a reputation for outstanding food and beautiful people as guests, has made this establishment a must-do. This man is pure genius—showman, culinary master, and superb host. The theme is circus: colorful blue and red decor, magnificent china, fun touches in the two diningrooms, bar, and banquet facilities (for 250). Very talented executive chef Pierre Schaedelin presides over a kitchen staff of 55 (along with pastry chef Luis Robledo-Richards), $250,000 stoves, and a private area for special guests to eat in the midst of it all. The Sultan of Brunei footed most of the bill for the $3 million kitchen and furnishings. The food is superb. Even the soufflés, which usually take extra time to prepare, appear at a moment's notice. Don't miss a chance to savor a memorable meal at this palace!

LE GIGOT
18 Cornelia St (bet Bleecker and 4th St)   212/627-3737
Lunch, Dinner: Tues-Sun; Brunch: Sat, Sun
American Express and cash only
Moderate

I can't imagine a more pleasant dinner on a chilly New York evening than one prepared at this tiny, 30-seat bistro in the bowels of the Village. Most taxi drivers have never heard of Cornelia Street, so allow extra time if you come by cab. Once you're here, the cozy atmosphere and warm hospitality of the ladies who greet and serve combine with hearty dishes that will please even the most discerning diner. My suggestion for a memorable meal: bouillabaisse or, in the winter, *le boeuf Bourguignon* (beef stew in red wine with shallots, bacon, carrots, mushrooms, and potatoes). All of this for a truly modest price. Snails or patés make delicious starters. Equally tasty desserts like upside-down apple tarts and flambéed bananas with cognac are offered. Le Gigot is a lot less expensive than its counterpart in Paris but just as appealing.

Once one of the really hot spots in Chelsea, **Le Madri** (168 W 18th St, 212/727-8022) is now tamer but still offers excellent pastas and delicious prime rib of beef. Although Italy is the dominant culinary flag flown here, the mood actually is more international. The wood-burning oven in the center of the room adds special ambience!

LE PÉRIGORD
405 E 52nd St (bet First Ave and East River)   212/755-6244
Lunch: Mon-Fri; Dinner: Daily   www.leperigord.com
Expensive

Civilized is the word to describe Le Périgord. It is like dining in one of the great rooms of Manhattan in the "good old days," but with a distinctively modern presence. From gracious host Georges Briguet to the talented chef, everything here is class personified. Gentlemen must wear jackets. Every captain and waiter has been trained to perfection. Fresh roses and Limoges dinner plates adorn every table. But this is just half the pleasure of a meal here. Every dish, from the magnificent cold appetizer buffet that greets guests to the spectacular dessert cart, is tasty and memorable. You may order a la carte, of course. Soups are outstanding. Dover sole melts in your mouth. A fine selection of game is available in winter. Roasted free-range chicken, served with the best potato dish I have ever tasted (*bleu de gex* potato gratin), should not be missed; neither should the roasted spiced duck breast. The chocolate mousse is without equal in Manhattan. The luxurious setting of Le Périgord makes one appreciate what gracious dining is really all about.

LE REFUGE
166 E 82nd St (bet Third and Lexington Ave)   212/861-4505
Lunch: Sat, Sun; Dinner: Daily; Brunch: Sat, Sun
Moderate   www.lerefuge.com

In any other city, Le Refuge would be one of the hottest restaurants in town. But aside from folks in the neighborhood, few seem to have heard of it. This charming, three-room French country restaurant offers excellent food, professional service, and delightful surroundings. The front room is cozy and comfortable, and the rear sections provide nice views and pleasant accommodations. A back garden is open in the summer. This is another house where the owner is the chef, and as usual, it shows in the professionalism of the presentations. Specialties of the house: duck with fresh fruit, bouillabaisse *de crustaces,* and couscous Mediterranean with shrimp. Finish off your meal with crème brûlée, profiteroles *au chocolate,* or chocolate truffle cake. A delightful *prix fixe* brunch is served on weekends. The antique bar in the front room is open from 5 p.m. to 8 p.m.

LES HALLES

411 Park Ave S (bet 28th and 29th St)	212/679-4111
Daily: noon to midnight	www.leshalles.net
Moderate	

Las Halles has struck a responsive chord on the New York restaurant stage. Probably this is because this establishment provides the necessary ingredients in today's restaurant sweepstakes: tasty food in an appealing atmosphere at reasonable prices. Specialties like blood sausage with apples, lamb stew, and fillet of beef are served in hefty portions with fresh salad and delicious French fries. Harried waiters try their best to be polite and helpful, but they are not always successful, as tables turn over more rapidly than at most fast-food outlets. If a week in Paris is more of a dream than a reality, then you might settle for mussels (ten ways), snails, onion soup, and classic cassoulet at this busy establishment. Unless you love tarts, the dessert selection is a disappointment. (Note: Their butcher shop by the front door is open daily.) A quieter **Les Halles Downtown** (15 John St, 212/285-8585) has much the same menu.

Soho visitors should not miss a visit to **Mercer Kitchen** (Mercer Hotel, 99 Prince St, 212/966-5454), where a raw bar, salad bar, pizza oven, and rotisserie are just some of the features. The restaurant is open for breakfast, lunch, and dinner.

LES ROUTIERS

568 Amsterdam Ave (bet 87th and 88th St)	212/874-2742
Dinner: Mon-Sun	www.les-routiers.com
Moderate	

This charming small French bistro set amid scruffy-looking storefronts is a happy find on the Upper West Side. This is the real thing, with a changing contemporary French menu and genuine ambience. There are snails and mussels with wine, patés, duck, seafood, steaks, breast of chicken—all those things you might find in the French heartland. Salads are almost a meal in themselves. An enticing selection of sweet things is available; look at the dessert table as you come in.

L'IMPERO

45 Tudor City Pl (bet 42nd and 43rd St)	212/599-5043
Lunch: Mon-Fri: Dinner: Mon-Sat	www.limpero.com
Expensive	

Tucked away in Tudor City Place, L'Impero is like a Tiffany jewel wrapped up in that famous blue box. This 1928 landmark room is for serious diners. The theme is rustic Italian, but the menu will appeal to diverse tastes. The pastas are uniformly delicious: homemade fettuccine and spaghetti are recommended. Their tuna, poached in olive oil, is superb. I particularly enjoyed choosing a cheese plate from a mouth-watering selection of nearly a dozen varieties. The gelati is authentic. For a different dessert you might try sesame cannoli, orange mascarpone mousse, or blood orange sorbet. Get a rich relative to pick up the check, especially if you succumb to the magnificent tasting menu.

MALONEY & PORCELLI
37 E 50th St (bet Park and Madison Ave)   212/750-2233
Lunch, Dinner: Daily   www.maloneyandporcelli.com
Expensive

The lawyers for whom this restaurant is named need to get reasonable with their prices. No argument that the food is very good, but the tab is simply outrageous. Admittedly, their bread basket is exceptional. Pizzas and crab-cakes with ratatouille and pastrami salmon are delicious appetizers. I have seldom tasted a better sirloin steak. (It *should* be, at that price!) Equally tasty lobster is even more expensive. Don't pass up the "Angry Lobster"! If this is a business meal, go for it. Don't leave without trying the chocolate brownout cake. The supervisory staff could lower their noses a notch or two, but the floor staff is pleasant and accommodating. I hope these talented foodies don't go the way of one of the former tenants (Gloucester House), who found out the hard way that pockets do indeed have bottoms!

MANGIA È BEVI
800 Ninth Ave (at 53rd St)   212/956-3976
Lunch, Dinner: Daily   www.mangiaebevirestaurant.com
Inexpensive to moderate

This is definitely not the spot for a relaxing, intimate, refined meal. But it is a top choice for delicious food at unbelievably low Manhattan prices. The noise level is almost unbearable, the tables allow you to instantly become friendly with strangers, and the waiters are very casual and surprisingly helpful. The abundant antipasto platter, overflowing with nearly a dozen choices, is a house specialty. This rustic trattoria also features a large selection of pastas, fish, meat dishes, salads and a bevy of in-season veggies. Brick-oven pizza lovers will be in seventh heaven with pleasing combinations and equally pleasing prices. There's nothing special about desserts, except the homemade tiramisu. It is easy to see why colorful Mangia è Bevi is one of the most popular destinations along Ninth Avenue.

MANHATTAN GRILLE
1161 First Ave (at 64th St)   212/888-6556
Lunch: Mon-Fri; Dinner: Daily; Brunch: Sun
Moderate to moderately expensive   www.manhattangrille.com

This classy continental steakhouse has been a hit for quite some time. It is indeed an attractive, pleasant place to dine. The steaks are large and delicious, as are the lamb chops and prime rib. Even the seafood, especially the filet of sole, is worth trying. Among the veal dishes, veal piccata is particularly good. Accompany your choice with excellent cottage fries. For dessert, the *tartufo* equals any I've tasted in Italy (except Tre Scalini's in Rome), and the cheesecake melts in your mouth. A pre-theater menu is available daily before 6:15 p.m.

MANHATTAN OCEAN CLUB
57 W 58th St (bet Fifth Ave and Ave of the Americas)   212/371-7777
Dinner: Daily   www.manhattanoceanclub.com
Expensive

As is true of all of his operations, Alan Stillman has created a unique restaurant in the Manhattan Ocean Club. In a dramatic two-story room, diners are treated to a wide selection of seafood dishes expertly prepared by chef Jonathan Parker. Depending on availability, the menu may include lobster, swordfish, mahi-mahi, salmon, grouper, blackfish, and more. Poultry and meat dishes are available, but you should come here for fish. The must-have dessert is their famous chocolate box. All of this comes at a price, but rarely is a seafood dinner presented so magnificently.

French Specialties

Bouillabaise: French seafood stew
Confit: goose, duck, or pork that has been salted, cooked, and preserved in its own fat
Coulis: a thick, smooth sauce, usually made from vegetables but sometimes from fruit
En croute: anything baked in a buttery pastry crust or hollowed-out slice of toast
Foie gras: duck or goose liver, usually made into a paté
Tartare: finely chopped and seasoned raw beef, often served as an appetizer

---

MARCH
405 E 58th St (bet First Ave and Sutton Pl)   212/754-6272
Lunch, Dinner: Mon-Sun
Expensive

If you want to be spoiled, start here. This attractive, romantic, and renovated townhouse with high ceilings and teak floors offers regal dining in three rooms on lower levels, plus a summer rooftop terrace. Executive chef Wayne Nish and partner Joseph Scalice (who oversees the front of the house) have raised the art of dining to perfection. Create your own *prix fixe* meal of up to seven courses from over 30 choices. It is well worth the tab, for the sky is the limit when it comes to service and quality. The fact that March remains so busy is a tribute to the format. An attractive, glass-enclosed back porch overlooks a small garden in this Sutton Place neighborhood. Jackets are required.

MARCHI'S
251 E 31st St (near Second Ave)   212/679-2494
Dinner: Mon-Sat (special hours for private parties)
Moderate   www.marchirestaurant.com

This must be one of the best-kept secrets in New York. Though there's no sign out front, Marchi's has been a New York fixture since 1930, when it was established by the Marchi family in an attractive brownstone townhouse. The Marchis, joined by their three sons, are still on hand, lending a homey flavor to the restaurant's three diningrooms and garden patio (a great spot for a private dinner). It's almost like eating at your favorite Italian family's house, especially since there are no menus. Bring a hearty appetite to take full advantage of a superb feast. The first course is a platter of antipasto—including radishes, *finocchio,* and Genoa salami—plus a salad of tuna, olives, and red cabbage. The second is an absolutely delicious homemade lasagna. The third is crispy deep-fried fish. Side orders of cold beets and string beans with fish are light and tempting. The entree is delicious roast chicken and veal served with fresh mushrooms and a tossed salad. Dessert consists of fresh fruit, cheese, lemon fritter, and sensational *crostoli* (crisp fried twists sprinkled with powdered sugar). The price tag is reasonable. Come to Marchi's for a unique, leisurely meal and an evening you will long remember. In the summer, outdoor dining is available.

MARKJOSEPH STEAKHOUSE
261 Water St (off Peck Slip)   212/277-0020
Lunch: Mon-Fri; Dinner: Mon-Sat   www.markjosephsteakhouse.com
Moderately expensive

If the trendy uptown steakhouses turn you off, then head downtown—with good directions, as Water Street turns into Pearl Street near this location—to a comfortable, homey neighborhood room that is high on quality meat and low on attitude. The room is filled with folks in casual garb, more interested in delving into a huge, juicy steak, than wondering who's sitting at the next table. Some of the personnel (including a few who came over from Peter Luger) are all business. If you're dining with a group or family, the seafood combination platter (lobster, shrimp, clams, calamari, and mussels) is a great place to start. Porterhouse steak and filet mignon are highly recommended. Baked or hash brown potatoes are great side dishes. At lunch, the half-pound burgers are wonderful, as is the signature steak sandwich. If there's still room for dessert, I'd opt for the tartufo.

MARK'S RESTAURANT
The Mark Hotel
25 E 77th St   212/879-1864
Breakfast, Lunch, Dinner: Daily; Brunch, Sun
Moderately expensive   www.themarkhotel.com

You'd be hard-pressed to find better hotel dining than this fine French-American restaurant. Refined, professional service, beautiful appointments, fresh flowers, and gorgeous china add up to a delightful experience. The menu is seasonal, with fresh seafood always available. Imported caviars and oysters are a specialty. A pre-theater menu is offered from 6 to 7 p.m. You don't have to be a hotel guest to partake of this room's charm. Afternoon tea here is an occasion!

MARKT
401 W 14th St (at Ninth Ave)   212/727-3314
Lunch: Mon-Fri; Dinner: Daily; Brunch: Sat, Sun
Moderate

In a building that once housed a fish market, Markt presents an attractive, large, and noisy room with a distinctive Belgian flavor. The huge bar is a good place to get a feel for the restaurant. A menu feature is *waterzooi,* a classic Belgian stew that can be prepared with chicken and veggies, fresh fish, or lobster. The several lobster dishes offered are among the best in the house. You'll also find seafood, Belgian beef stew, rabbit, steak, and more. A raw bar offers a good selection of shrimp, crab, lobster, and periwinkles, as well as a variety of oysters. Mussels are popular, too. Don't pass up the great Belgian fries. Dessert specials vary every day, but the trio of Belgian dark, white, and milk chocolate mousse is tops.

MARSEILLE
630 Ninth Ave (at 44th St)   212/333-3410
Lunch: Mon-Fri; Dinner: Daily; Brunch: Sat, Sun
Moderate to expensive (tasting menu)   www.marseillenyc.com

You might think that you are in the rough-and-tumble city of Marseille, but in reality you are still in the Hell's Kitchen area of Manhattan. There is a distinct Mediterranean feel here, with a tile floor and rather plain apricot-colored walls. Early in the evening the place is filled with theatergoers, and after they clear out, the neighbors arrive at this brasserie. You won't want to miss the three-meat *meze* plates (there are four of these available) or the *haricots verts* salad to start. Proceed to melt-in-your-mouth short ribs, beef cheeks, or Moroccan tuna. Note the very attractive presentations; there's not too much food, but it looks extremely appetizing on the plate. Service is informed and not pushy. Bouillabaisse is available. Crunchy peanut butter tart with sorbet is the signature dessert, but I found the toffee-soaked date sponge cake with caramel ice cream a better choice. An expensive seven-course tasting menu is also available.

MÉTISSE
239 W 105th St (bet Amsterdam Ave and Broadway)   212/666-8825
Dinner: Mon-Sun
Moderate

This French bistro does all the good things you would expect, but it is the atmosphere that adds so much to a dinner here. The place is quiet and restful, the waiters unobstrusive, the cuisine satisfying, and the check reasonable. Salads are fresh, entrees varied (many seafood dishes, steaks, and chops). For dessert, napoleons will top off a fine meal.

MEZZOGIORNO
195 Spring St (near Ave of the Americas)   212/334-2112
Lunch, Dinner: Daily   www.mezzogiorno.com
Moderate

Florence, Italy, is one of the world's most charming cities, not only because of its abundance of great art, but also for the wonderful small restaurants on every street corner. At Mezzogiorno, a Florence-style trattoria in New York, the food is comparably good (though some of the art is questionable). The place is busy and noisy, and tables are so close together that conversation is impossible. The decor is nearly best described as "modern Florence." Check out the unusual writing on the ceiling, done by master fresco artist Pontormo. Better yet, keep your eyes on the food. The salad selection is outstanding, and their lasagna is one of the best. Mezzogiorno is also famous for pizza. You'll find all the ingredients for a wonderful make-believe evening in Florence.

MICHAEL JORDAN'S THE STEAK HOUSE NYC
23 Vanderbilt Ave (at Grand Central Terminal)   212/655-2300
Lunch, Dinner: Daily   www.theglaziergroup.com
Moderately expensive

Grand Central Station has come back to life, and Michael Jordan's establishment is one more reason to visit this historic building even if you are not catching a train. Michael and his partners have provided another good New York steakhouse. The menu is very much what you would expect: steaks, chops, lobster, and salmon. You'll fill up on the sizable portions, but if you feel especially hungry, try the sliced tomatoes and sweet onion appetizer. Forget about calories and try the special French fries as a side dish. For a change, desserts are reasonably priced. They include brownie ice cream sundae and a fabulous 12-layer chocolate cake.

MINETTA TAVERN
113 MacDougal St (near Bleecker St)   212/475-3850
Lunch, Dinner: Daily
Moderate

Would you like to take your guests to a Northern Italian restaurant where the coat-and-tie, meat-and-potato set feels comfortable? Well, Minetta Tavern—established in 1937 and serving excellent food for generations in Greenwich Village—is the place to go. Located on the spot where Minetta Brook wandered through Manhattan in the early days, this tavern was made famous by Eddie "Minetta" Sieveri, a friend of many sports and stage stars of yesteryear. Dozens of old pictures adorn the walls of this intimate, scrupulously clean tavern, where professional personnel serve no-nonsense Italian food at attractive prices. Grilled mushrooms, steamed clams, or homemade tortellacci are good ways to get the juices flowing. If you'd like something a bit heftier, veal and various chicken dishes are available. Chocolate mousse cake, profiteroles, and other pastries cap off a satisfying meal.

The Wall Street area is fascinating, even if the security precautions make it sometimes difficult to move around. While exploring downtown, looking at Ground Zero or the many other places of interest, take time to enjoy a pleasant meal. One of the more attractive places to have a casual lunch is **Casis On Stone** (52 Stone St, 212/425-3663). Their Mediterranean offerings include salads that are particularly tasty, and steak frites that are exceptional. Outdoor seating is provided in nice weather, and a takeout menu is available.

MONTRACHET
239 West Broadway (bet White and Walker St)   212/219-2777
Lunch: Fri; Dinner: Mon-Sat   www.myriadrestaurants.com
Moderately expensive

Montrachet has been a fixture for years in Tribeca, and its popularity well deserved. When you enter this charming restaurant you'll leave behind the rather shabby neighborhood. You'll find superb dishes of seafood, game, and meat prepared by chef Chris Tegesualdi. The menu changes periodically, but you can hope that such specialties as truffle-crusted salmon or foie gras are available when you visit. The signature dessert, crème brûlée, is one of the best in the city. Service here is highly professional, and the *prix fixe* lunch on Friday is a winner.

MORAN'S CHELSEA
146 Tenth Ave (at 19th St)   212/627-3030
Lunch, Dinner: Daily   www.moransny.com
Moderate

In a building that's nearly 200 years old, Moran's has seen a lot of history, including time as a speakeasy and as a Jewish lodging house during Prohibition days. Time has been good to this exceptionally charming tavern, complete with fireplaces in every room, hardwood paneling, large and attractive party facilities, and a cozy bar, all done with touches of copper everywhere you look. The old tin roof adds a special dimension. On to the food: fresh seafood, aged chops, lobster, crab cakes, prime rib, and shepherd's pie are just a few of the specialties. You'll also find excellent burgers, fresh salads, and a few pastas. If you are looking for a unique venue for a party or celebration in groups of 20 to 250, I'd strongly suggest you take a look here. The personnel are friendly and accommodating.

Looking for a quick bite in midtown? Try **Lyn's Cafe** (12 W 55th St, 212/397-2020). You'll find breakfast items, fresh baked goods, sandwiches, health foods, good soups and burgers, pizzas, and more. I especially liked the selection of jumbo muffins.

MORTON'S OF CHICAGO
551 Fifth Ave (at 45th St)   212/972-3315
Lunch: Mon-Fri; Dinner: Mon-Sun
Moderately expensive to expensive

Now this is a real steakhouse. These folks are experts, with units all over the country. Every member of the highly efficient staff has been trained in the Morton's manner. At the start of your meal, you are shown a cart with samples of entree items: fresh vegetables, lobster, and whatever else happens to be featured. Every dish is fully explained. Appetizers are heavy in the seafood department: shrimp, oysters, smoked salmon, sea scallops. Attractive and appetizing salads include sliced beefsteak tomatoes and purple onions. The steaks and chops are so tender you can cut them with a fork. They arrive promptly, too, which is not the case in many steakhouses. There are several potato choices, including wonderful hash browns. Sauteed spinach with mushrooms and steamed broccoli and asparagus are fresh and tasty. Top it all off with a delicious soufflé—chocolate, Grand Marnier, lemon, or raspberry —that's large enough for two hungry diners.

MR. K'S
570 Lexington Ave (at 51st St)   212/583-1668
Lunch, Dinner: Daily   www.mrksnyc.com
Moderately expensive to expensive

In Washington, D.C., Mr. K's was the power diningroom for politicos, especially Republican practitioners of that art. The New York branch has not yet achieved the same distinction. However, this is a very classy Chinese diningroom. All manner of goodies will whet the appetite: Shanghai spring rolls, dumplings, and a delicious seafood dish of sauteed crab, shrimp, and scallops. Of course, there is chicken and corn chowder; in my opinion, no Chinese dinner is complete without it. What else? Share an assortment of plates with your table partners: lemon chicken, Peking duck, honey-braised pork ribs, sesame beef, crispy sea bass, and sesame prawns with shiitake mushrooms. If you like hot dishes, go for the firecracker prawns with Szechuan sauce!

NICOLA'S
146 E 84th St (bet Lexington and Third Ave)   212/249-9850
Dinner: Daily
Moderately expensive

Upper-crust New Yorkers who like a clubby atmosphere and good food (which are not often found together) love this place! In a setting of rich wood with framed familiar faces on the walls, and a noise level that sometimes reaches that of a Broadway opening, no-nonsense waiters serve delicious platters of pasta, veal, chicken, fish, and steak. There are daily Italian specials in every category, and each is inviting. It is difficult to come up with really good home fries in a busy restaurant, but Nicola's are sensational! Concentrate on the main part of your meal, as desserts show little imagination.

Mama's (222 Sullivan St, 212/505-8123, and 200 E 3rd St, 212/777-4425) is an inexpensive and tasty destination for homemade dishes like meatloaf, grilled salmon, and fried, roasted and grilled chicken. Sides include mashed potatoes, macaroni and cheese, honey-glazed sweet potatoes, green beans, Swiss chard, and turnips. Don't miss the banana cream pie! Takeout, delivery, and catering are available.

92
Wales Hotel   212/828-5300
45 E 92nd St (at Madison Ave)
Lunch: Mon-Fri: Dinner: Daily; Brunch: Sat, Sun
Moderate

If you're in the mood to escape fancy diningrooms, complicated dishes, and overbearing service, 92 is the place to go. The hamburger and turkey burger fit right into the brasserie setting. Salads are fresh and satisfying. Special dishes are featured nightly and change seasonally, like chicken pot pie, crab cakes, and pork tenderloin. If all of this sounds interesting, bring the family and save room for dessert (strawberry shortcake in season, banana cream pie, and a root beer float), which is by far the best part of the experience.

NOBU
105 Hudson St (near Franklin St)   212/219-0500
Lunch: Mon-Fri; Dinner: Daily   www.myriadrestaurantgroup.com

NOBU NEXT DOOR
105 Hudson St (near Franklin St)   212/334-4445
Dinner: Daily
Moderately expensive

These two restaurants are a must-visit for anyone who likes Japanese cuisine. There is a bevy of talent here: the management expertise of Drew

Nieporent, the setting by the David Rockwell Group, and most of all, the great cuisine of Chef Nobu Matsuhisa. You receive a traditional Japanese welcome as you progress to the comfortable sushi bar. The menu includes hot and cold dishes, special dinner entrees (salmon, scallops, chicken, tenderloin of beef), plus tempura, sashimi, and sushi dinners. There's also kushiyaki (two skewers), salads, soups, sushi rolls, and desserts like the bento box (warm valrhona chocolate soufflé cake). The ambience is unique, the people-watching is as fabulous as the food, and the pricey tab is worth every penny. To take care of the overflow crowds, Nobu Next Door serves equally good dishes with a no-reservations policy. It also has a raw bar and a fine selection of noodle dishes.

NOCHE
1604 Broadway (bet 48th and 49th St)   212/541-7070
Lunch: Mon-Fri; Dinner: Mon-Sat
Moderate

You might feel like you need a road map when you first enter this place, because Noche is big! Located in Times Square, it features a pan-Latin menu, has a number of bars, four open levels and entertainment, and it is busy. Good food at reasonable prices has made Noche very popular. You might even have the feeling you are in Latin America, with dishes like ceviche, tamales, Cuban sandwiches, tacos, flatbreads, and more. Desserts include a rich coffee custard topped with chipped pistachio cream or a classic cake made with three milks. You won't find a place like this in Des Moines—or anywhere else for that matter—so if you have a bit of tropical wanderlust in your system, this is the place to sate it.

OCEAN GRILL
384 Columbus Ave (bet 78th and 79th Ave)   212/579-2300
Lunch, Dinner: Daily; Brunch: Sun (menu also available
     for Sat lunch)   www.brguestrestaurants.com
Moderate

Ocean Grill is one of the few good seafood restaurants on the Upper West Side, and in nice weather, the passing parade from outside tables is fun. The place, which is quite popular with young professionals, is noisy, too. The food is good, not great, with littleneck clams topping the list. For a party, chilled shellfish platters—offering a selection of lobster, clams, oysters, shrimp, and more—are appropriate. A wood-burning grill offers Atlantic salmon, yellowfin tuna, Pacific mahi-mahi, East Coast swordfish, and more. A moderately priced "sunset" menu is available, with such attractions as lobster club sandwich or seafood Cobb salad. For brunch, blueberry, banana, and buttermilk pancakes are a good bet.

OCEANA
55 E 54th St (bet Park and Madison Ave)   212/759-5942
Lunch: Mon-Fri; Dinner: Mon-Sat   www.oceanarestaurant.com
Expensive

When you save enough dough to take a cruise, you want to do it the right way and book passage on a really fabulous ship. Well, the same is true if you want a really first-rate seafood meal, with price no object. Oceana is just that kind of place. This midtown townhouse offers several floors of classy dining, with relatively new chef Cornelius Gallagher putting out a terrific *prix fixe* dinner at a terrific price ($58). The menu changes frequently, and the seafood catches are so fresh they practically swim to the table. The "Life in the Ocean" appetizer is quite a spread: baby eel, bluefin toro, geoduck and razor clams, oysters, scallops, and caviar! For entrees I'd suggest striped bass, haddock *basquaise,* and crispy Atlantic skate. Don't miss the dessert course! The crème brûlée and doughnut filled with ice cream are winners. If you really want to splurge, a six-course feast ($110 a head) is the best catch of all!

OLICA
145 E 50th St (bet Lexington and Third Ave)   212/583-0001
Lunch: Mon-Fri; Dinner: Mon-Sat   www.olicanyc.com
Moderate to moderately expensive

It's sometimes difficult for a new restaurant to top an excellent predecessor in the same location, but Olica has succeeded. In what used to be the home of L'Actuel, Olica has created an absolutely first-class diningroom, with wonderful modern French food and great service. A few dishes survive from the former operation, while Olica's new and seasonal items are presented in a classy, appetizing manner. How about fettuccine with asparagus and morels to start? Or Alsatian pizza with onions, bluefin tuna and wasabi? Good seafood entrees include seared salmon or cod, roasted sea bass, and filet of sole. Braised sweetbreads is another winner. Three great chocolate dessert choices: bittersweet chocolate mousse, warm molten chocolate cake, and chocolate *mille feuille* with orange flavoring and chocolate sorbet. A good cheese selection is also available.

OLIVES NEW YORK
W Union Square Hotel
201 Park Ave S (at 17th St)   212/353-8345
Breakfast: Daily; Lunch: Mon-Fri; Dinner: Daily; Brunch: Sat, Sun
Moderate   www.toddenglish.com

The trendy crowd here seems to like the New England influence of Todd English's open-kitchen charmer. A spirited and jazzy atmosphere combines with superbly trained personnel and great food to make a pleasant dining experience. Portions are big, with delicious pastas high on the list. If your tastes are not too fancy, the burgers are very good, and the peanut-butter pancakes at brunch are "to die for." For dessert I'd recommend a vanilla, chocolate, or pecan soufflé.

ONE C.P.S.
Plaza Hotel
1 Central Park S (at 59th St)   212/583-1111
Lunch: Mon-Fri; Dinner: Daily; Brunch: Sat, Sun   www.onecps.com
Moderately expensive

There is hardly a setting that's more "New York" than the former Edwardian Room of the Plaza Hotel, overlooking Central Park and the ever-present horse-drawn carriages. Many a romantic interlude has taken place here, and lots of famous people (like Donald Trump, who had a special table in the corner when he owned the hotel), have dined in the magnificent room. Now top restaurateur Alan Stillman and chef David Burke have turned it into a handsome brasserie with huge red-shaded chandeliers and a dramatic, uncovered mosaic flooring. Lots of attractions here: very fresh seafood, tender steaks and fancy dishes like caviar and foie gras. Families will find just about anything to suit a variety of tastes, and the memories of the setting will be everlasting.

ONE IF BY LAND, TWO IF BY SEA
17 Barrow St (bet Seventh Ave and 4th St)   212/228-0822
Dinner: Daily   www.oneifbyland.com
Expensive

If romance is the intent of your evening out, then I heartily recommend this restaurant. The candlelight, fireplace, flowers, and background piano music all add to the ambience. One If By Land, Two If By Sea is housed in an 18th-century carriage house once owned by Aaron Burr. Allow extra time to find this place, as Barrow Street (one of the West Village's most charming) is generally unknown to taxi drivers. Besides, there's no sign out front! Tables at the front of the balcony are particularly appealing. You can't go wrong with rack of lamb or breast of duck. Individual beef Wellington is usually excellent, as is the spice-roasted lobster. A *prix fixe* seven-course tasting menu is available. Their classic crème brûlée is a favorite dessert.

O'NIEAL'S GRAND STREET
174 Grand St (bet Centre and Mulberry St)   212/941-9119
Lunch, Dinner, Late Night Menu: Daily   www.onieals.com
Moderate

This legendary and historic speakeasy, with its secret tunnel to the old police headquarters, evokes memories of days long past. Housed beneath a 150-year-old hand-carved mahogany ceiling, this bar, lounge, and restaurant is reminiscent of another time. Recently, Onieal's achieved additional celebrity, as a backdrop on HBO's *Sex and the City*. Try something light from the ever-popular bar menu, like barbecued oysters or pan-seared scallops with orange sesame dipping sauce. They also serve some of the best burgers in the city. You'll find pan-seared yellowfin tuna, chicken Cobb salad, hangar steak *au poivre*, risotto, pastas, and more. For dessert, try the Four Devils chocolate soufflé cake (named after the four devils intricately carved on the ceiling). Service at Onieal's is friendly and efficient.

ORSO
322 W 46th St (bet Eighth and Ninth Ave)   212/489-7212
Mon, Tues, Thurs, Fri: noon-11:45; Wed, Sat: 11:30 a.m.-11:45 p.m.;
Sun: noon-11:30   www.orsorestaurant.com
Moderate

This restaurant features the same menu all day long, which is great for those with unusual dining hours and handy for theatergoers. Orso is one of the most popular places on midtown's "restaurant row," so if you're thinking about a six o'clock dinner, be sure to make reservations. The smallish room is cozy and comfortable. It's watched over by a portrait of Orso, a Venetian dog who is the mascot for this Italian bistro. The kitchen is open in the back, allowing diners to see the experienced staff at work. The changing menu offers many good appetizers, including cold roast veal and fried artichokes. A variety of pizzas and some excellent pasta dishes are also offered. For an entree, you can't go wrong with the popular calves liver. The mascarpone cheesecake, one of many homemade desserts, will finish off a great meal. A special Sunday brunch menu is available.

Asian Specialties

Dim sum: a whole meal of succulent nibblers, such as steamed dumplings, shrimp balls, and savory pastries

Egg foo yung: thick, savory pancakes made of eggs, vegetables, and meat, often slathered with a rich, broth-based sauce

General Tso's chicken: breaded and deep-fried chicken chunks tossed in a spicy-sweet sauce

Moo shu: stir-fried shredded meat, vegetables, and seasonings, scrambled with eggs and rolled (usually by the diner) inside thin pancakes

Peking duck: After air is pumped between a duck's skin and flesh, the bird is coated with honey and hung up until the skin dries and hardens. The duck is then roasted, cut into pieces, and served with scallions and pancakes or steamed buns.

Sashimi: sliced raw fish served with daikon (Japanese radish), wasabi (Japanese horseradish), fresh ginger, and soy sauce

Sukiyaki: stir-fried pieces of meat (and sometimes vegetables, noodles, or tofu) flavored with soy sauce, dashi (Japanese fish stock), and mirin (sweet rice wine)

Sushi: raw fish or vegetables placed atop vinegared rice or served inside rolls wrapped in nori (sheets of dried seaweed)

Tempura: fried, battered seafood and vegetables

Teriyaki: beef or chicken marinated in a sauce of rice wine, soy sauce, sugar, and seasonings, then grilled or stir-fried

---

OSTERIA DEL CIRCO
120 W 55th St (bet Ave of the Americas and Seventh Ave)
Lunch: Mon-Fri; Dinner: Daily   212/265-3636
Moderately expensive   www.osteriadelcirco.com

Were it not for the fact that the owners are the sons of legendary Sirio Maccioni (of Le Cirque fame), this establishment might just be written off as another Italian restaurant. But here we have three brothers—Mario, Marco, and Mauro (and mother Egidiana)—operating a classy establishment with a friendly, circus-themed ambience and atypical Italian menu. The tastiest items include great pizzas, satisfying soups, and unusual pastas. A unique dessert is an Italian favorite called *bomboloncini:* very small vanilla-, chocolate- and raspberry-filled doughnuts. The menu changes seasonally.

OUEST
2315 Broadway (at 84th St)   212/580-8700
Dinner: Daily   www.ouest.com
Moderate

If there ever was a question about how a really good restaurant would fare on the Upper West Side, the answer has been found in Ouest. The place is overflowing with happy locals enjoying one of the best rooms in the city. The comfortable booths, the open kitchen, the cozy (if dark and noisy) balcony, and the pleasant serving staff combine to make Thomas Valenti's jewel first-class. This is not surprising, as Valenti got good experience at Alison on Dominick Street and Butterfield 81 on the Upper East Side. The bistro menu is just as inviting as the semicircular tables, with appetizer choices like oyster pan roast with Yukon gold potatoes, goat cheese ravioli, or several fresh salads. The braised short ribs melt in your mouth, and the bacon-wrapped pork tenderloin would be welcome on my plate every night! Nightly specials include braised lamb shanks on Monday and Tuesday, and meatloaf like your mother served on Sunday, of course! From delicious warm bread to the rich chocolate cake with chocolate mousse inside for dessert, the whole experience here is pure pleasure.

OUR PLACE
1444 Third Ave (at 82nd St)   212/288-4888
Lunch, Dinner: Daily   www.ourplaceuptown.com
Moderate

Our Place is not a typical Chinese restaurant! Classy service, moderate prices, and delicious food have been its trademarks for over a decade. Appreciative Upper East Siders have kept its two spotlessly clean diningrooms filled for nearly every meal. Now the place has been renovated. Single diners obviously enjoy the atmosphere and feel comfortable here. You'll find many of your favorite Chinese dishes on the menu. I've enjoyed wonton soup, moo shu pork, tangerine beef, Szechuan chicken, duck-wrapped lettuce with pine nuts, and home-style chicken casserole. Free delivery is offered in a wide area. Prices are as comfortable as the chairs.

PALM ONE
837 Second Ave (at 44th St)
212/687-2953

PALM TOO
840 Second Ave (at 44th St)
212/697-5198

PALM WEST SIDE
250 W 50th St (bet Eighth Ave and Broadway)
212/333-7256

Lunch: Mon-Fri; Dinner: Daily   www.thepalm.com
Expensive

Even with all the excellent new steakhouses in Manhattan, steak and lobster lovers still have a special place in their hearts for the Palm, which started as a speakeasy in 1926. All three locations have much the same atmosphere. They're noted for huge, delicious steaks, chops, and lobsters. Don't miss the terrific Palm fries—homemade potato chips—or try a combination of fries and onion snakes. These are earthy spots, so don't get too dressed up. Indolent waiters are part of the scene.

PAMIR
1437 Second Ave (bet 74th and 75th St)   212/734-3791
Dinner: Daily
Moderate

Pamir is among Manhattan's best ethnic restaurants. Turnovers are an Afghan specialty, and Pamir offers several. If you like extra-spicy food like that served in the native country, they will gladly oblige. Excellent Afghan bread comes with each entree. Lamb is prepared many ways: seasoned lamb with rice, almonds, and pistachios; chunks of lamb in an onion-and-garlic-flavored spinach sauce; lamb and eggplant cooked with tomatoes, onions, and spices; and lamb marinated in spices, broiled on a skewer. All are worth a try. Several vegetarian dishes are also available. Eat heartily from the start, because desserts are zilch. The restaurant is unpretentious, the desire to please is sincere, and prices are modest.

PAOLA'S
245 E 84th St (bet Second and Third Ave)   212/794-1890
Lunch: Mon-Sat; Dinner: Daily
Moderate

There is a new look at Paola's, a wonderful place for a romantic evening! The Italian home cooking is first-class, with Paola herself in the kitchen looking after the food. Great homemade filled pastas, superb veal dishes, and tasty hot vegetables (like baby artichoke hearts) are house specialties. Be advised that they don't spare on the garlic! Mirrors reflect the warmth and flicker of candles, and the lady of the house will charm any guest. To top off your reasonably priced meal, try the rich chocolate mousse.

PARIS COMMUNE
411 Bleecker St (bet Bank and 11th St)   212/929-0509
Dinner: Daily; Brunch: Sat, Sun
Moderate

Paris Commune is a popular gathering spot in the West Village, where regulars outnumber visitors every night. The Mediterranean-American menu includes pastas, salads, steaks, and seafood. There are only 17 tables, and the staff is prompt and efficient. Dining by candlelight with an adjoining fireplace is a big attraction! The weekend brunch features spectacular French toast, along with the usual fare. Delicious dishes include a great vegetable frittata. Their homemade cheesecakes are good and rich.

PARK AVENUE CAFE
100 E 63rd St (at Park Ave)   212/644-1900
Lunch: Mon-Fri; Dinner: Daily; Brunch: Sat (Sept-May), Sun
Moderately expensive

The Park Avenue Cafe, with windows on Park Avenue, is a showpiece for expert restaurateur Alan Stillman (who also has his hand in the Post House, Cité, Manhattan Ocean Club, and Smith & Wollensky). He obviously is a man of eclectic tastes. Chef David Burke does unusual things that please most diners while puzzling some with less sophisticated palates. The basically American menu is served by very professional waiters who appear to have been influenced sartorially by Larry King. The signature dish is a swordfish chop served with a tart lemon sauce. The people watching is great, and conversations at adjacent tables can be fascinating. (It's not eavesdropping when you can't help it!) Desserts are sensational!

PARK BISTRO
414 Park Ave S (bet 28th and 29th St)   212/689-1360
Lunch: Mon-Fri; Dinner: Mon-Sun
Moderate

These days it is fun to go to a place with smiling faces, and the Park Bistro is that! This small, homey jewel of a diningroom specializes in authentic

French cuisine from the Provence region. From the start, when warm and tasty bread is placed before you, to the finishing touch of rich and luscious homemade desserts (like chocolate napoleon), you are surrounded by attentive service and magnificent food. Don't miss the hanger steak or lamb stew. A professional team runs this place, and it shows.

PARK SIDE
107-01 Corona Ave (51st Ave at 108th St, Corona, Queens)
Lunch, Dinner: Daily   718/271-9274
Moderate

Do you want to show someone who claims to know everything about New York a spot he or she doesn't know? Would you like to eat on your way to or from LaGuardia or Kennedy airport? Do you want a special meal in an unusual setting? Well, all of the above are excellent reasons to visit Park Side, in Queens. I make an exception in including a restaurant not in Manhattan because it is exceptional. Joseph Oliva runs a first-class, spotlessly clean restaurant that serves wonderful Italian food at prices that make most New York restaurateurs look like highway robbers. Start with garlic bread and then choose from two dozen kinds of pasta and an opulent array of fish, steak, veal, and poultry dishes. The meat is all prime-cut and fresh—nothing frozen here. You'll also find polite, knowledgeable waiters in an informal atmosphere. Get a table in the garden room or the Marilyn Monroe room upstairs. Eat to your heart's content, and then be pleasantly amazed at the tab.

PASTIS
9 Ninth Ave (at Little West 12th St)   212/929-4844
Breakfast, Lunch, Dinner: Daily   www.pastisny.com
Moderate

Even in New York you've never experienced a scene like this. In what was once a garage, a large area has been gutted and converted into a bar and dining space, with touches that make it look like it has been around for a long time. Keith McNally, who knows how to hype a restaurant like no one else, has turned a spot in the Meatpacking District—an area with little parking and absolutely no glamour—into one of the most high-energy rooms in Manhattan. The huge bar is a sea of hundreds of young Turks—and some not so young—who come to see and be seen. The diningroom, if you can get in, serves reasonably good food to hordes who love the unbelievable noise level and the classic bistro fare. A nice touch is a large long table in the center of the dining space for singles and others who do not want to wait in the reservation line. The menu includes oysters on the half shell, omelets, shellfish stew, roast lobster and chicken, braised beef, pates, good French fries, and their "Floating Island" dessert. The first question you will ask is "How did they cram all these people into this place?" After a few minutes, you'll understand that's part of the attraction. Pastis offers delivery, too.

PATSY'S
236 W 56th St (bet Broadway and Eighth Ave)   212/247-3491
Lunch, Dinner: Daily   www.patsys.com
Moderate

For over half a century, the Scognamillo family has operated this popular eatery, specializing in Neapolitan cuisine. At present, the son and a grandson are taking care of the front of the house, while another grandson is following the family tradition in the kitchen. "Patsy" was an immigrant gentleman chef whose nickname graces a two-level restaurant. Each floor has its own cozy atmosphere and convenient kitchen. The family makes sure that every guest is treated as if they are in a private home; courtesy and concern are the name of the game. A full Italian menu is available, with numerous specials that include a different soup and seafood entree each day. If you can't find what you like among the two dozen pasta choices, you are in deep trouble! There are *prix fixe* lunch and dinner (pre-theater) menus as well.

PAYARD PATISSERIE
1032 Lexington Ave (bet 73rd and 74th St)	212/717-5252
Lunch, Tea, Dinner: Mon-Sat (bakery 7 a.m.-11 p.m.)	
Moderate	www.payard.com

Francois Payard has created a winner! Everything about this place is appetizing: the look of the bakery cases as you enter, the attractively presented appetizers and entrees, the informed service by the well-trained staff. Payard is a combination French bistro and pastry shop, and it works to perfection. When you pair an expert pastry chef like Francois with executive chef Philippe Bertineau, you're going to get the very best. If you want to take some goodies home, choose from croissants, muffins, tea cakes, seasonal tarts, individual pastries, gateaux, petit fours, biscuits, handmade candies, and superb chocolates. Classic and seasonal ice creams and sherbets are offered. Prepared soups, salads, sandwiches, and other goodies are also available for takeout. But don't miss the opportunity to dine here, as Payard offers terrific appetizers, superb salads, homemade foie gras, seafood dishes, traditional bouillabaisse, caramelized sweetbreads, steaks, and more.

PERSHING SQUARE
90 E 42nd St (at Park Ave)	212/286-9600
Breakfast, lunch, dinner: Daily; Brunch: Sat, Sun	
Moderate	www.pershingsquare.com

In a space just opposite Grand Central Station, Pershing Square is serving throngs of hungry local and traveling New Yorkers. The odd-shaped room is full of energy and conversation, much of it relating to the broad variety of menu offerings. For those who missed breakfast before boarding their train, Pershing Square offers Irish oatmeal, eggs Benedict, vanilla-bean brioche French toast, and great buttermilk pancakes. Omelets are a specialty. Lunch and dinner items include seafood dishes, boneless beef short ribs, roast chicken, steaks, and pastas. The grilled hamburger with a selection of cheeses and really good, crisp steak fries is a winner any time of day. Weekend brunches feature the daily menu items. More serious seafood dishes, like yellowfin tuna with white Tuscan bean ragout and pan-seared Atlantic salmon, are popular for dinner. Try chocolate mousse cake for dessert. A friendly wait staff and an attractive bar are pluses.

PETER LUGER STEAK HOUSE
178 Broadway (at Driggs Ave), Brooklyn	718/387-7400
Lunch, Dinner: Daily	www.peterluger.com
Expensive	

The place is a bit of a dump and nobody goes here for the ambience or service, but if it's steak you want, you simply can't do better. The menu makes it simple: your choices are steak for one, steak for two, steak for three, and steak for four. The creamed spinach and steak sauce are out of this world, although the French fries are uninspired and the wine selection is slim. Tell your waiter to go easy on the whipped cream if you order dessert. Peter Luger is only a stone's throw from Manhattan (take the very first right off the Williamsburg Bridge), and the staff is accustomed to ordering cabs. Reservations are suggested well in advance.

PICHOLINE
35 W 64th St (bet Broadway and Central Park W)   212/724-8585
Lunch: Sat; Dinner: Daily
Moderately expensive to expensive

You'll want to come back here every season! Terrance Brennan is a work-horse, and it shows in his attractive restaurant. The warm atmosphere is a perfect backdrop for the seasonal, Mediterranean-inspired plates. The many pluses include outstanding service, delicious homemade breads, perfectly done fish dishes, superbly prepared game, one of the best cassoulets in the city, and daily classic cuisine specials. If you're having a party at Lincoln Center, the wine room and small private party room are fabulous settings for a memorable evening. I always look forward to the magnificent cheese cart for dessert. Jackets are required for gentlemen.

PIETRO'S
232 E 43rd St (bet Second and Third Ave)   212/682-9760
Lunch: Mon-Fri; Dinner: Mon-Sat (closed Sat in summer)
Expensive

Pietro's is a steakhouse featuring Northern Italian cuisine. Everything is cooked to order. The menu features great salads (they claim to make New York's best Caesar salad), steaks, chops, seafood, chicken, and an enormous selection of veal dishes. Tell your companion not to bother dressing up. Bring an appetite, however, because portions are huge. Although steaks are the best known of Pietro's dishes, you will also find ten chicken and ten veal selections (marsala, cacciatore, scaloppine, piccata, *francaise*, etc.). For meat-and-potato lovers, there are nine potato dishes. Prices border on expensive and service is boisterous, but you'll certainly get your money's worth. By the way, Pietro's is very child-friendly.

PINOCCHIO
1748 First Ave (bet 90th and 91st St)   212/828-5810
Dinner: Tues-Sun; Brunch: Sun
Moderate

There's no pretense at this place, which is for serious Italian diners. Mark Petrillo is now presides over this tiny 12-table etablishment nestled on the Upper East Side. And now his wife, Regina, has opened **Geppetto** at 307 E 84th Street! He still serves the wonderful home-style Italian food his larger original house was known for. There are numerous specials every night, and I would suggest letting the boss order for you. You'll always find great pastas—like cheese-filled ravioli, tortellini Pinocchio (meat-filled tortellini with cream, peas, and prosciutto)—several spaghetti dishes, and fettuccine alfredo. Just one question: can't this innovative kitchen do better than tiramisu for dessert?

P.J. CLARKE'S
915 Third Ave (at 55th St)   212/317-16165
Lunch, Dinner: Daily   www.pjclarkes.com
Moderate

P.J. Clarke's can rightfully be called a Manhattan institution. Every day at lunch or dinner the regulars are joined by hordes of visitors, guzzling at the bar, eyeing the raw bar, or fighting for a table in the back room. None is disappointed. The platters are sizable, the burgers great, and the seafood fresh. Service is highly professional, and the price is right. Daily specials include wonderful meatloaf with mashed potatoes on Thursday. Upstairs you'll be taken with the decor at the Sidecar, which has its own kitchen and separate entrance.

If you are worn out after a stressful day, try **The Pump**, an energy food restaurant (40 W 55th St, 212/246-6844). Healthy sandwiches, salads, and energy-filled plates are available daily for eat-in, takeout, and delivery. Shakes are mixed with fruit, juice, and nonfat frozen yogurt. A special protein shake will surely pump you up!

PLAZA HOTEL PALM COURT
768 Fifth Ave (at 59th St)   212/546-5350
Breakfast, Lunch: Mon-Sat; Tea, Supper: Daily; Brunch: Sun
Moderate   www.fairmont.com

Feeling nostalgic? Some rooms, like some people, just get better with age, and happily this is one of them. If just one place in the city could be singled out as the embodiment of all that folks dream of as the New York of yesteryear—romantic and carefree, delicious and proper—it would have to be the Palm Court at the Plaza Hotel. The great and near-great have laughed and loved here with the likes of Eloise and Auntie and Uncle, creating thousands of memories of special times. You can enjoy breakfast, luncheon salads, wonderful teas with tea sandwiches, and caloric goodies. A harpist plays at teatime. There are also super snacks, seafood salads, assorted smoked fish, and some unusual sandwiches and pastries. The fabulous Sunday buffet—the largest and most glamorous in the city—is a popular New York tradition. Many three-generation families show the young ones where they used to go in the "good old days." A real treat, day or night, and a must for visitors.

PÓ
31 Cornelia St (bet Bleecker and 4th St)   212/645-2189
Lunch: Wed-Sun; Dinner: Daily
Moderate

Steve Crane has found the formula for a successful eating establishment. The space is crowded, but tables are not on top of each other. The service is family-friendly, informed, and quick. The food is hearty, imaginative and unusually tasty. The portions are king-size. The prices are right. No wonder the place is always busy! As I have noted before, if the bread is good, chances are what follows will be also. Pó has hearty, crunchy, fresh Italian bread. The pastas are huge: tagliatelle, tortellini, linguine, and always a special or two. The tasting menus offer great value, with a six-course meal for only $40.

Pastas and some heavier entrees (like grilled salmon) are available for lunch, along with inventive sandwiches like marinated portobello with roasted peppers. An unusual and satisfying dessert called *affogato* consists of coffee gelato in chilled cappuccino with chocolate and caramel sauce.

POST HOUSE
Lowell Hotel
28 E 63rd St   212/935-2888
Lunch: Mon-Fri; Dinner: Daily
Moderately expensive

Although there are many new steakhouses, this one deserves to take its place as one of Manhattan's gems. This great restaurant, not on the list for calorie counters, is an "in" social and political hangout on East 63rd Street that serves excellent food in comfortable surroundings. The guest list usually includes many well-known names and easily recognizable faces. They are attracted, of course, by the good food and warm ambience. Hors d'oeuvres like crabmeat cocktail, lobster cocktail, and stone crabs are available in season, but the major draws are steak and lobster. Prices for the latter entrees are definitely not in the moderate category; ditto for lamb chops. However, the quality is excellent, and the cottage fries, fried zucchini, hash browns, and onion rings are superb. Save room for the chocolate box (white and dark chocolate mousse with raspberry sauce). If you can walk out under your own steam after all this, you're doing well!

Mexican Specialties

Fajitas: marinated beef, shrimp, chicken, and/or vegetables served in warm tortillas (often wrapped by the diner)
Ceviche: citrus-marinated raw fish
Chilis rellenos: mild to spicy chili peppers stuffed with cheese and fried in egg batter
Chorizo: spicy pork sausage
Empanadas: meat-filled pastries surrounded by a fat-laden crust
Enchiladas: soft corn tortillas filled with meat, vegetables, or cheese and topped with salsa and cheese
Paella: an elaborate saffron-flavored rice dish that includes a variety of seafood and meats
Tamales: chopped meat and vegetables encased in cornmeal dough

---

PRIMAVERA
1578 First Ave (at 82nd St)   212/861-8608
Lunch: Mon-Fri; Dinner: Daily   www.primaveranyc.com
Expensive

Primavera is one of my favorite places, and it just gets better! Nicola Civetta, the owner, is the epitome of class; his wife, Peggy, is equally charming. They know how to make you feel at home and present a superb Italian meal. Don't come if you're in a hurry, though. This place is for relaxed dining. I could wax eloquently with descriptions of the dishes, but you can't go wrong no matter what you order. Let Nicola choose for you, as there are specials every day. To top it all off, they have one of the most beautiful desserts anywhere: a gorgeous platter of seasonal fruit that looks too good to eat. Primavera is always busy, so reservations are a must. A beautiful private party room is available.

PROVENCE
38 MacDougal St (at Prince and Houston St)   212/475-7500
Lunch, Dinner: Daily   www.provence-soho.com
Moderate

Here's a sliver of France in Manhattan! You won't quickly forget a visit to Provence, a Greenwich Village charmer. Tasty and wholesome food is professionally served at sensible prices. Garlic is another reason you won't forget this bistro. If you like its taste, you'll love Provence! The French-country menu is served in several spaces: one noisy room by the bar, another more romantic area in the back, and a comfortable outside patio. You'll find dishes typical of the Provence region (fish and steamed vegetables) on the menu. If you like some of the signature dishes (*pot-au-feu*, cassoulet, bouillabaisse), call ahead to find out what is featured that evening. Wonderful French fries come with some dishes. Top it all off with some great desserts!

RAFAELLA
381 Bleecker St (bet Charles and Perry St)   212/229-9885
Dinner: Daily
Moderate

One gets a bit nervous looking at a huge menu in a small establishment. How can they do well by all of those dishes? Well, though the menu is indeed all-encompassing, you needn't worry here. There are a dozen appetizers (from baked oysters to stuffed mushrooms), four soups, and over two dozen pasta dishes. Their risotto is especially delicious. There are also more than 30 entrees (and many specials), some from the grill. Choosing from a half-dozen tasty dessert dishes will complete your opportunity for a great meal at a reasonable price. This Village find is very popular with locals, so reservations are highly recommended. The youngish staff seems pleased to be of service and are particularly helpful in guiding you through the maze of goodies.

Attention Tribeca residents and visitors! Don't miss a visit to **Bubby's Pie Co.** (120 Hudson St, 212/219-0666). First of all, the regular menu items are tasty and reasonably priced. The Sunday brunch is delicious and a real scene for the locals! Then there are the great pies: mile-high apple, sour cherry, key lime, and chocolate peanut butter pie. Homemade cakes, too! Delivery in the Tribeca area is free.

RAIN
100 W 82nd St (at Columbus Ave)   212/501-0776
1059 Third Ave (bet 62nd and 63rd St)   212/223-3669
Lunch, Dinner: Daily
Moderate

There's no need to cross the Pacific Ocean; a visit to Rain will do the trick, at least in the culinary department. You will be treated to Vietnamese, Malaysian and Thai fare, some of which is, naturally, quite spicy. Spring (and summer) rolls are a personal favorite, and the ones here are superb. Of course, there is more to start: soups, broths, noodles, and Thai crab cakes. Popular entree items include crispy snapper, stir-fried spicy jumbo shrimp, stir-fried prawns, cracked lobster, shrimp, and green curry chicken.

RAO'S
455 E 114th St (near First Ave)   212/722-6709
Dinner: Mon-Fri
No credit cards
Inexpensive

Getting these people on the phone is next to impossible! Don't be put off by rumors about Rao's, such as two-month waits for reservations. If you want to go to Rao's—an intimate old-time (1896) Italian restaurant—you should plan a bit in advance, however. The place is crowded all the time for two reasons: the food is great, and prices are ridiculously low. Don't walk or take a car; hail a taxi and get out in front of the restaurant, which is in Spanish Harlem. When you're ready to leave, they'll call a taxi to pick you up. Frankie is a gregarious and charming host who makes guests feel right at home and will even sit at your table while you order. Be prepared for leisurely dining. While you're waiting, enjoy the excellent bread and warm atmosphere. Believe it or not, the Southern fried chicken (Rao's style) is absolutely superb; it would be my number-one choice. (Hint: Try appearing unannounced at the door or call the same day, as tables are often available on the spur of the moment.)

RAOUL'S
180 Prince St (bet Sullivan and Thompson St)   212/966-3518
Dinner: Daily   www.raoulsrestaurant.com
Moderate

There are dozens of good places to eat in Soho, and Raoul's is one of the best. This long, narrow restaurant used to be an old saloon. There are paper tablecloths and funky walls covered with a mishmash of posters, pictures, and calendars of every description. The bistro atmosphere is neighborly, friendly, and intimate, the prices moderate, and the service attentive. The trendy clientele runs the gamut from jeans to mink. The house favorites are steak *au poivre* and paté *maison.* Raoul's is a natural for those whose days begin when the rest of us are ready to hit the sack.

RAYMOND'S CAFE
88 Seventh Ave (bet 15th and 16th St)   212/929-1778
Lunch, Dinner: Daily; Brunch: Sat, Sun
Moderate

Some of the old haunts in the Chelsea area have lost their appeal, but Raymond's still has a lot going for it. Chef Raymond is obviously a perfectionist. The place is spotlessly clean with an up-to-date look, and the food is well presented and very tasty. Choices range from pastas and sandwiches at noon to delicious hot and cold appetizers, fresh seafood items, and a great grilled salmon steak at dinner. The weekend brunch features omelets, linguini dishes, and warm chicken salad. A private dining room is available, and there is free delivery within eight blocks. The early-bird dinner is a three-course bargain!

(THE FAMOUS) RAY'S PIZZA OF GREENWICH VILLAGE

465 Ave of the Americas (at 11th St)   212/243-2253
Sun-Thurs: 11 a.m.-2 a.m.; Fri, Sat: 11 a.m.-3 a.m.
Inexpensive

Ray's is so popular that guests have asked to ship pizzas to midwestern relatives (and they will)! You must be named "Ray" to be in the pizza biz in Manhattan—or so it seems. None of the pizzerias in the Big Apple are any better than this one, supposedly featuring the *real* Ray. The pizza is gourmet at its best, and you can create your own from the many toppings offered. You can have a slice, a whole pizza, or a Sicilian square, all fresh. Kids love the baby pizzas. You won't leave hungry, as pizzas are a generous 18 inches. Take-and-bake personal pizzas—ten-inch pies that are all natural and hand-made, with real cheese—bake in your oven in 12 minutes and are sold only at this location! Free delivery is available.

REDEYE GRILL

890 Seventh Ave (at 56th St)   212/541-9000
Lunch: Mon-Fri; Dinner: Daily; Brunch: Sat, Sun
Moderately expensive   www.redeyegrill.com

From the day it opened, this "home of the dancing shrimp bar" has been a busy place! The name attracted my attention, because I am a frequent coast-to-coast redeye flyer. When I first entered the place, I could see I had a lot of company. Owner Sheldon Fireman knows how to appeal to the eye, taking a cue from his very successful nearby Trattoria dell'Arte antipasto bar. Specialties include shrimp done in all shapes and sizes, smoked salmon, a huge seafood appetizer platter (at a huge price), a smoked maki and sashimi bar, grilled fish and pastas. You can even find weiner schnitzel, burgers, smoked fish, and egg dishes. The personnel are hip and helpful, but the scene is the major attraction here. Live jazz is featured Tuesday through Saturday.

REMI

145 W 53rd St (bet Ave of the Americas and Seventh Ave)
Lunch: Mon-Fri; Dinner: Daily   212/581-4242
Moderate   www.remi.citysearch.com

Come here for the best seafood risotto in town! Remi operates in a spectacular space in midtown, handy to hotels and theaters. In an unusually long room dominated by a dramatic 120-foot Venetian wall painting by Paulin Paris, the food soars as high as the setting. In warm weather, the doors open up and diners can enjoy sitting at tables in the adjoining atrium. Waiters, chairs, and wall fabrics all match in attractive stripes. Antipasto like roasted quail wrapped in bacon will get you off to a delicious start. Main dishes are not of the usual variety. The spaghetti, linguine, and ravioli (stuffed with ginger and tuna) can match any house in Venice. Of course, there are fish and meat dishes for more mainstream appetites. The warm chocolate-cake dessert (*cioccolatissimo*) is superb. Paddle on down (Remi means "oars") for a first-class experience! Takeout and delivery are available.

RENÉ PUJOL

321 W 51st St (bet Eighth and Ninth Ave)   212/246-3023
Lunch, Dinner: Mon-Sat   www.renepujol.com
Moderate

First things first: order a chocolate soufflé right away for dessert! René Pujol is a very attractive French restaurant that makes an ideal spot for a pre-theater dinner or a private party. It's always busy, and it's obvious that a large number of customers are regulars, which always speaks well of a restaurant. One reason for René Pujol's success is that it's a family enterprise. The owners (daughter and son-in-law of the retired René Pujol) are on the job, and the waiters are superb. Housed in an old brownstone, the restaurant has two warmly decorated, cozy, and comfortable diningrooms, complete with a working fireplace in winter. There are attractive private party rooms upstairs, too. The menu is vintage French, with filet mignon, grilled Atlantic salmon, and tasty tarts being the specialties of the house. They boast an award-winning wine list, too!

RISTORANTE GRIFONE
244 E 46th St (bet Second and Third Ave)   212/490-7275
Lunch: Mon-Fri; Dinner: Mon-Sat   www.citysearch.com/nyc/grifone
Moderate to moderately expensive

New Yorkers get so hyped up about trendy new places that they tend to forget about some of the old-timers that quietly continue to do a good job. Grifone is one of those. If you are looking for an attractive, comfortable, and cozy place to dine—one with impeccable service and great food—then try Grifone. Seemingly only neighborhood regulars have heard of it. The menu is Northern Italian; there are so many daily specials that you probably won't even look at the printed sheet. A takeout menu is available as well. Quality never goes out of style.

RIVER CAFE
1 Water St (Brooklyn Bridge), Brooklyn   718/522-5200
Lunch: Mon-Sat; Dinner: Daily; Brunch: Sun
Moderately expensive

The River Cafe isn't in Manhattan, but it *overlooks* Manhattan and features American cuisine. And that's the main reason to come here. The view from the window tables is fantastic, awesome, romantic—you name it. There's no other skyline like it in the world. And so the River Cafe—just across the East River in the shadow of the Brooklyn Bridge—remains an extremely popular and sophisticated place. Call at least a week in advance to make reservations, and be sure to ask for a window table. This is a true Yankee, flag-waving special-occasion restaurant that's proud of its American cuisine. The seafood, lamb, and steak entrees are particularly good, and desserts are rich and fresh. The Brooklyn Bridge, done in dark chocolate, is a dessert you will never forget. Don't forget to bring your camera.

RM
33 E 60th St (bet Madison and Park Ave)   212/319-3800
Lunch: Mon-Fri; Dinner: Mon-Sat   www.restaurantrm.com
Expensive

If seafood is your thing, then rm is your place! For a $55 *prix fixe* (less for a vegetarian meal) you'll enjoy manageable (read smallish) plates in a handsome setting with a highly professional staff. Chef-owner Rich Moonen, who's been at Le Cirque and Oceana, should be proud to have his lowercase initials on this establishment, where the halibut, pike, and skate are done to perfection. Choices vary according to the season, but you can be assured that the sea scallops appetizer and banana rice crispy pillbox dessert will nicely bookend the main course. A large and appealing selection of green, oolong, and black teas will top off a meal that exudes freshness in quality, variety, and presentation. Upstairs bar/lounge guests can choose from an a la carte menu.

ROLF'S
281 Third Ave (at 22nd St)   212/477-4750
Lunch, Dinner: Daily
Moderate

In a city without many good German restaurants, Rolf's is worth remembering. It's a colorful spot whose several dozen tables and wooden benches fit in perfectly with the eclectic decor. Faux Tiffany lampshades, old pictures, tiny lights, strings of beads, and what-have-you add up to a charming and cozy spot for tasty German dishes. The schnitzels, goulash, sauerbraten, boiled beef, veal shanks, and bratwurst are served in ample portions with delicious potato pancakes and sauerkraut. For pancake lovers there are German, apple, and potato varieties, with applesauce on the side. For dessert, save room for homemade apple strudel or Black Forest cake.

ROSA MEXICANO
1063 First Ave (at 58th St)   212/753-7407
61 Columbus Ave (at 62nd St)   212/977-7700
Lunch: Daily (Columbus Ave location); Dinner: Daily (open late)
Moderate to moderately expensive   www.rosamexicano.com

This is, quite simply, classic Mexican cuisine. Start with the guacamole *en molcajete;* prepared fresh at the table, it is the best around. There are also great appetizers, like small tortillas filled with sauteed shredded pork, small shrimp marinated in mustard and chili vinaigrette, and raviolis filled with sauteed chicken and served with tomato and onion. Main-course entrees include tasty (and huge) crepes filled with shrimp, and a multi-layered tortilla pie with all manner of goodies. Grilled specialties like beef short ribs and skewered marinated shrimp are tempting possibilities. Even the desserts are first-class. Choose from a traditional flan, cornmeal custard smothered with chocolate sauce, and layered chocolate mousse cake with a hint of chili. The atmosphere is friendly, the energy level high, and the dining top-drawer.

ROUGE
135 E 62nd St (bet Lexington and Park Ave)   212/207-4601
Lunch: Mon-Fri; Dinner: Daily   www.rougeny.com
Moderate

When you step into this vintage Upper East Side townhouse, expecting a lavish French menu with equally lavish prices, you might well be surprised. Yes, the menu is seriously continental, but the prices are unusually reasonable. Chef David Ruggiero has transformed a two-level home into a staid but comfortable setting for some delicious dishes. Filling salads and great seafood platters, like a risotto with scallops or slow-roasted salmon, are amazingly tasty and affordable. There is much more: a special *rouge* burger (not the usual variety), tender braised beef short ribs, and oven-roasted baby chicken. At dinner, unusual appetizers like fricassee of baby octopus and sashimi of fluke will whet any appetite. Heartier platters include double-rib lamb chops and roasted sweetbreads of veal. The dessert cheese selection is tempting. The only disappointment for this chocolate lover was the degustation of the chocolate platter; nothing on it was memorable. Instead, opt for a dessert crepe.

ROY'S NEW YORK
New York Marriott Financial Center Hotel
130 Washington St   212/266-6262
Breakfast: Daily; Lunch: Mon-Fri; Dinner: Mon-Sat
Moderate to moderately expensive   www.roysrestaurant.com

Whenever I am in Hawaii, I try to dine at one of Roy Yamaguchi's restaurants because of the food and trained staff. I have never seen operations run as efficiently as Roy's. This large one in Manhattan's Financial District brings to 22 the number he oversees all around the globe. The menu blends ideas from Europe (where Roy was trained) with popular ingredients from Asia and the Pacific. The changing menu includes items like wonderful coconut shrimp on a stick with pineapple chili sauce, grilled Szechuan baby back pork ribs, Chinese-style barbecued chicken pizza, Hong Kong steamed fish with wok veggies, and Hawaiian-seared mahi-mahi. Top it all off with a hot chocolate soufflé or fresh fruit cobblers. Seats at the counter overlooking the kitchen provide an extra dimension to the meal.

RUBY FOO'S
2182 Broadway (at 77th St)   212/724-6700
1626 Broadway (at 49th St)   212/489-5600
Lunch, Dinner: Daily   wwwbrguestrestaurants.com
Moderate

What a scene this is! Upper West Siders, who lack a great choice of moderately priced and fun places to dine, have discovered Ruby Foo's in a big way. The two-level facility, which seats about 400 people, is packed. You'd better call for reservations or be prepared to spend an eternity at the bar. The same is true at the newer Times Square location. The place is billed as a dim sum and sushi palace; the best dishes are in the latter category. However, if you and your tablemates share baby back ribs with spicy black bean sauce, you will go home happy. There is a large selection of maki rolls: spicy tuna, fresh crabmeat, spicy grilled shrimp and pineapple, tempura vegetable, and many more. The seven different sushi platters are well-selected and great for a party. Hand rolls, soups, salads, and rice dishes are also featured. The crowd is hip, the noise level high, the food very good, and the value outstanding.

RUE 57
60 W 57th St (at Ave of the Americas)   212/307-5656
Lunch, Dinner: Daily; Brunch: Sat, Sun
Moderate (lunch) to moderately expensive (dinner)

With an extremely convenient location, friendly and accommodating service, and pleasant atmosphere, this Parisienne brasserie is one busy place. When you combine a menu that encompasses soups and salads, oysters and clams, sushi, steaks, varied entrees (like salmon, chicken, risotto, and ravioli), plus special plates each day of the week, you have a winning attraction.

The young ones will enjoy the great burgers. Lovers of Japanese cuisine will find sushi, sashimi, maki, and temaki. Don't pass up the beefsteak tomato salad with onions and Roquefort!

SAN PIETRO
18 E 54th St (bet Fifth and Madison Ave)   212/753-9015
Lunch, Dinner: Mon-Sat   www.sanpietro.net
Moderately expensive

A visit to classy San Pietro is like a vacation in southern Italy. The Bruno brothers have brought the joys of this part of the world to their upscale restaurant, a popular one with society mavens and the well-heeled. Fresh fruit and veggies are legendary here, as is the linguine with anchovy juice. Spaghetti dishes are also a specialty, as is *scialatelli*. Chicken dishes are especially well crafted. On the down side, waiters can be offhand and even snooty if they think you're not a big tipper, and desserts leave a lot to be desired. However, if you want to see how the other half lives while enjoying tasty Italian dishes, San Pietro might just be your ticket!

SARABETH'S KITCHEN
423 Amsterdam Ave (at 80th St)   212/496-6280
Breakfast, Lunch, Dinner: Daily

1295 Madison Ave (at 92nd St)   212/410-7335
Breakfast, Lunch, Dinner: Daily
Moderate

SARABETH'S AT THE WHITNEY
Whitney Museum of American Art
945 Madison Ave (bet 74th and 75th St)   212/570-3670
Lunch: Tues-Fri; Brunch: Sat, Sun   www.sarabeth.com
Moderate

I am reminded of the better English tearooms when visiting one of Sarabeth's locations. Swinging it is not. Reliable it is. The big draw is the homemade quality of all the dishes, including the baked items and excellent desserts. They also make gourmet preserves and sell them nationally. Menu choices include excellent omelets, porridge, or fresh fruit for breakfast, a fine assortment of light items for lunch, and fish, game, or meat dishes for dinner. The chocolate mousse cake, chocolate soufflé, warm berry bread pudding, and homemade ice cream are splendid desserts. Service is rapid and courteous. Look in on their bakery at 75 Ninth Avenue, too.

SAVORE
200 Spring St (at Sullivan St)   212/431-1212
Lunch, Dinner: Daily; Brunch: Sat, Sun
Moderate

Soho has no shortage of restaurants, many of them with an attitude that goes along with the area. Savore has none of this. You come here for good, fresh food served in a casual and friendly atmosphere. It is a particularly attractive destination in nice weather, when tables are placed outside for people-watching along with dining. The menu offers a large selection of pastas, from buckwheat tagliatelle with pheasant ragout to hand-cut spaghetti with basil and roasted tomato. In true Tuscan fashion, salads are served after the main course. I am partial to their crème brûlée, which features a wonderful coffee flavor.

SCALINI FEDELI
165 Duane St (bet Greenwich and Hudson St)   212/528-0400
Lunch: Mon-Fri; Dinner: Mon-Sat
Expensive

An out-of-the-way room that used to house Bouley, this very upscale Italian restaurant is for those who want a truly classy and classic meal. The offerings are exotic: seared foie gras and roasted apples, soft egg-yolk ravioli with ricotta and spinach, chanterelle cannelloni . . . all to start! Then delicious braised short ribs of beef, breast of Muscovy duck, and wonderful tuna. Desserts are equally fabulous, like a flourless chocolate cake (cooked to order) with a trio of gelati or a warm caramelized apple tart in a baked fillo crust. Luncheons are a bit lighter. *Prix fixe* menus are the order of the day. As you look around this sedate establishment, you'll be impressed by the relative youth of some of the gourmet diners. A nice, private wine cellar room is available for parties.

If You Must Smoke

New York says "no" to smoking in bars and restaurants, but I have found an exception! **Uncle Jack's Steakhouse** (39-40 Bell Blvd, Bayside, 718/229-1100) allows smoking because of an exemption stating that if an establishment receives 10% of its revenues from tobacco sales (Uncle Jack's sells cigarettes and several types of cigars) or related rentals, smoking is then permitted. Uncle Jack's also allows smoking around a big table in a separate room.

SCREENING ROOM
54 Varick St (below Canal St)   212/334-2100
Lunch: Tues-Fri; Dinner: Daily; Brunch: Sun
Moderate   www.thescreeningroom.com

Movie lovers and gourmets can satisfy both passions at this innovative Tribeca watering hole. The atmosphere is informal and congenial, with an emphasis on traditional American dishes that look and taste terrific. As a starter, I loved the pan-fried artichokes. But there's also smoked trout, pan-roasted quail, a number of healthy salads, and a very popular macaroni dish with spinach, leeks, tomatoes, and parmesan. On to salmon, grilled duck, or venison (order some crushed baked potatoes, too). Dessert selections are topped by a great lemon-caramel ice box cake and a scrumptious "Fallen Chocolate Cake" with a chocolate *touille* and espresso ice cream. You might go to sleep during the flicks! A late-night menu is available.

SEA GRILL
19 W 49th St (at Rockefeller Plaza)   212/332-7610
Lunch: Mon-Fri; Dinner: Mon-Sat   www.restaurantassociates.com
Moderately expensive

You'll pay for the setting as well as the food at this renovated Rockefeller Center seafood house, which overlooks the ice-skating rink in winter and features open-air dining in nice weather. Take advantage of the seafood bar (clams, oysters, shrimp, mussels, crab, and lobster) to start. The well-prepared but somewhat pricey main courses include tasty crab cakes, salmon, and Dover sole. I loved the desserts, especially the mile-high valrhona chocolate parfait (caramel cinnamon crème *anglaise,* pecan *croccante,* and chocolate sorbet). Rockefeller Center has been spruced up, and Sea Grill is one of its gems. Now if they could just lighten up on the prices!

SECOND AVENUE KOSHER DELICATESSEN
AND RESTAURANT
156 Second Ave (at 10th St)   212/677-0606
Sun-Thurs 7 a.m.-midnight (Fri. Sat till 3 a.m.)
Inexpensive   www.2ndavedeli.com

You've heard all about the great New York delicatessens; now try one of the really authentic ones, located in the historic East Village. From the traditional *k*'s—knishes, kasha varnishkes (buckwheat groats with pasta), and kugel—to boiled beef and chicken in the pot (with noodles, carrots, and matzo balls), no one does it quite like the Lebewohl family. Portions are enormous. Homemade soups, three-decker sandwiches (tongue and hot corned beef are sensational), deli platters, complete dinners—you name it, they've got it. The smell is overwhelmingly appetizing, the atmosphere is "caring Jewish mother," and they don't mind if you take out your meal instead of dining in the colorful back room. Don't leave without trying the chopped liver and warm apple strudel.

SERENDIPITY 3
225 E 60th St (bet Second and Third Ave)   212/838-3531
Sun-Thurs: 11:30 a.m.-12:30 a.m.;   www.serendipity3.com
Fri: 11:30 a.m.-1 a.m.; Sat: 11:30 a.m.-2 a.m.
Moderate

The young and young-at-heart rate Serenpidity 3 *numero uno* on their list of "in" places, as it has been for a half century. In an atmosphere of nostalgia set in a quaint, two-floor brownstone, this full-service restaurant offers a complete selection of delicious entrees, sandwiches, salads, and pastas. The real treats are the fabulous desserts, including favorites like hot fudge sundaes and frozen hot chocolate. You can even take home frozen hot chocolate mix! An added pleasure is the opportunity to browse a shop loaded with trendy gifts, books, clothing, and accessories. If you are planning a special gathering for the teen members of your clan, make this the destination!

SETTE MEZZO
969 Lexington Ave (at 70th St)   212/472-0400
Lunch, Dinner: Daily
Cash only
Moderate

Sette Mezzo is small, professional, and busy, and it makes a great spot for people-watching on Sunday evenings! There are no affectations in decor, service, or food preparation. This is strictly a business operation, with the emphasis on serving good food at reasonable prices. Don't worry about wearing your best gown or a suit and tie; many diners are informally dressed, enjoying a variety of Italian dishes done to perfection. At noon the menu is tilted toward lighter pastas and salads. In the evening, all of the grilled items are excellent. Fresh seafood is a specialty. Ask about the special pasta dishes; some of the combinations are marvelous. For more traditional Italian plates, try breaded rack of veal, stuffed baked chicken, or fried calamari and shrimp. All desserts are made in-house. They include several caloric cakes, tasty lemon tarts, sherbet and ice cream, and (take it from an expert) one of the best *tartufos* you've ever sinned over.

71 CLINTON FRESH FOOD
71 Clinton St (at Rivington St)   212/614-6960
Dinner: Daily
Moderately expensive

The area is anything but fancy, the place is tiny, and tables are close together. Never mind. The food, wait staff, and dining experience at 71 Clinton are all superb. Wylie Dufresne and his associates present dishes pleasing to both the eye and the tummy. There's a crisp potato, applewood-smoked bacon, and goat-cheese tart to start. Don't overlook the venison and sliced hanger steak entrees. Seafood offerings include poached monkfish, seared sea scallops, and crisp sea bass. For dessert, I loved the warm chocolate cake with peanut butter center served with vanilla ice cream.

Clinton Street on the Lower East Side may seem an unlikely place for "in" gourmet restaurants. The trend started with **71 Clinton Fresh Food**, which is excellent. **Alias** (76 Clinton St, 212/505-5011) followed several years later, with chef and co-owner Scott Ehrlich doing the honors. For what it is worth, unless you are a very sophisticated gourmet, I'd skip this one. The menu is pretentious, and the neighborhood certainly isn't the most desirable in the evening.

Check out these additional Clinton locations for good eats. They're not Gucci fancy, but all are darn good:

Azul (152 Stanton St, 646/602-2004): Mediterranean bistro
Lansky (104 Norfolk St, 212/677-9489): ribs; formerly Ratner's
WD50 (50 Clinton St, 212/477-2900): very "in".

SHELLY'S NEW YORK
104 W 57th St (near Seventh Ave)   212/245-2422
Lunch, Dinner: Daily; Brunch: Sun   www.shellysnewyork.com
Moderate

Shelly Fireman is the consummate restaurant innovator. His various spots, scattered around New York, are dramatic and unique, but all have a common thread: good food. Shelly's is no exception. In a space that was once a booming Horn and Hardart Automat (where you got your food through little mailbox-like windows), a bustling eatery combines a cafe, a wine and raw bar, an American bar, and several unique diningrooms. In nice weather, the open sidewalk windows showcase New York characters by the dozens. Inside, you'll find a grand array of oysters from both coasts, littleneck clams, lobster, salads and sandwiches, moderately priced entrees, steaks, and prime rib. Stone crab claws are featured year round. Don't miss the unusual and somewhat risque art scattered around the premises. A penthouse and roof garden terrace can accommodate up to 500 guests. Shelly has outdone himself!

SHUN LEE CAFE/SHUN LEE WEST
43 W 65th St   212/769-3888, 212/595-8895
Lunch: Sat, Sun; Dinner: Daily
Moderate

Dim sum and street-food combinations are served in an informal setting at
Shun Lee Cafe, which adjoins Shun Lee West, an excellent old Chinese
restaurant. A waiter comes to your table with a rolling cart and describes the
various goodies. The offerings vary, but don't miss stuffed crab claws if they
are available. Go on to the street-food items: delicious roast pork, barbecued
spare ribs, a large selection of soups and noodle and rice dishes, and a menu
full of mild and spicy entrees. Sauteed prawns with ginger and boneless
duckling with walnut sauce are great choices. A vegetarian dish of shredded
Chinese vegetables is cooked with rice noodles and served with a pancake
(like moo shu pork, but without the meat). It's a fun place where you can try
some unusual and delicious Chinese dishes. For heartier appetites, Shun Lee
West is equally good. Some of the best Chinese food in Manhattan is served
here. If you come with a crowd, family-style dining is available. Prices are a
bit higher at the restaurant than in the cafe.

SHUN LEE PALACE
155 E 55th St (bet Lexington and Third Ave)   212/371-8844
Lunch, Dinner: Daily   www.shunleepalace.com
Moderate to moderately expensive

There are all manner of Chinese restaurants in Manhattan: The colorful
Chinatown variety. The mom-and-pop corner operations. The over-Ameri-
canized establishments. The grand Chinese diningrooms. Shun Lee Palace
belongs in the latter category, possessing a very classy and refined look. Here
you are offered a delicious journey into the best of this historic cuisine.
You can dine rather reasonably at lunch; a four-course *prix fixe* experience
is available. Ordering from the menu (or from your captain) can be a bit
pricier, but the platters are worth it. Specialties include beggar's chicken (24
hours advance notice required), curry prawns, short ribs braised in rock
candy, and Beijing duck. There's much more, including casserole specials
and spa cuisine. Yes, this is just about the nearest thing Manhattan has to a
real Chinese palace.

Hit these places near closing time to score sweet deals on the day's left-
overs:
  Amy's Bread (75 Ninth Ave, 672 Ninth Ave, and 972 Lexington Ave)
  Balthazar (80 Spring St)
  Healthy Pleasures (489 Broome St, 93 University Pl, and 2493 Broad-
    way)
  Sushi Rose (248 E 52nd St, 2nd floor)

SISTINA
1555 Second Ave (at 80th St)   212/861-7660
Lunch, Dinner: Daily
Moderate

The philosophy of this family operation is that the joy is in the eating, not
the surroundings, and for that they get top marks. Because the atmosphere is

pretty plain Jane, one comes to Sistina for the food, and it can't be beat for classy Italian cooking. The specialty of the house is seafood; the Mediterranean red snapper and salmon are excellent dishes. There are also the usual choices of pasta, veal, and chicken, as well as daily specials.

66

66 Leonard St (entrance is at 241 Church St, bet Leonard and
   Worth St)   212/925-0202
Lunch, Dinner: Daily
Moderate to moderately expensive

Leave it to Jean-Georges Vongerichten to do something different, colorful, delicious, and thoroughly professional. This time he's turned his attention to Chinese food, served in a downtown setting that is clean, bold, attractive, and comfortable. Bright red banners add a special note. A long communal dining table also serves as a bar with intriguing back lighting. The Asian personnel are competent and attractive, though their uniforms are drab. Sensibly sized portions of appetizers, dim sum, noodles and rice, vegetables, seafood, poultry, and fish leave one looking forward to the main dishes, which are likewise exciting and tasty. Especially recommended are barbecued beef short ribs, stir-fried shrimp, Chinese chive dumplings, black bass, and lemon-sesame chicken. Modestly priced (for Jean Georges) desserts include almond tofu, frozen mandarin orange segments, and a nice selection of sorbets and ice cream. This is definitely not your usual Chinese restaurant; in my opinion, it is a must-try.

SMITH & WOLLENSKY

797 Third Ave (at 49th St)   212/753-1530
Lunch: Mon-Fri; Dinner: Daily   www.smithandwollensky.com
Moderate to moderately expensive

When visitors to the Big Apple want a taste of what this great city is all about, there is no better spot than Smith & Wollensky. This place captures what sets New York apart from every other city in the world. There is lots of space (two floors) and an abundance of talented and helpful personnel. I always grade a place on the quality of their bread, and Smith & Wollensky's is great. There is no better lobster cocktail offered anywhere in the city. New outposts around the country (like Miami's South Beach) add to the authenticity of this house, along with the wonderful steaks, prime rib, lamb chops, and more. Every man in the family will love the place, and the ladies will appreciate the special attention paid to them. Come here when you and your guests are really hungry.

SPARKS STEAKHOUSE

210 E 46th St (bet Second and Third Ave)   212/6874855
Lunch: Mon-Fri; Dinner: Mon-Sat
Moderately expensive

You come here to eat, period. This is a well-seasoned and popular beef restaurant with little ambience. For years, businessmen have made an evening at Sparks a must, and the house has not let time erode its reputation. You can choose from veal and lamb chops, beef scaloppine, and medallions of beef. There are a half-dozen steak items, like steak *fromage* (with Roquefort), prime sirloin, sliced steak with sauteed onions and peppers, and top-of-the-line filet mignon. Seafood dishes are another specialty. Rainbow trout, filet of tuna, and halibut steak are as good as you'll find in most seafood houses. The lobsters are enormous, delicious, and expensive. Skip the appetizers and desserts, and concentrate on the main dish. Private party rooms are available.

SPRING STREET NATURAL RESTAURANT
62 Spring St (at Lafayette St)   212/966-0290
Daily: 11:30 a.m.-midnight; Fri-Sat until 1 a.m.
Moderate

Even before eating "naturally" became a big thing, Spring Street Natural Restaurant was a leader in the field. That tradition continues today after 30 years. In attractive surroundings, their kitchen provides meals prepared with fresh, unprocessed foods, and most everything is cooked to order. Neighborhood residents are regular customers, so you know the food is top-quality. Specials are offered every day, with a wide variety of organic salads, pastas, vegetarian meals, free-range poultry, and a large selection of fresh fish and seafood. Try wonderful roasted salmon with creamy risotto and baby asparagus stalks. The best is saved for last: Spring Street believes in great desserts, like chocolate walnut pie, honey raspberry blueberry pie, and honey pear pie. The latter two are made without sugar and dairy products.

STRIP HOUSE
13 E 12th St (bet Fifth Ave and University Pl)   212/328-0000
Dinner: Daily   www.theglaziergroup.com
Moderately expensive

The Strip House is a classy steakhouse with a sexy red ambience. If anything separates this place from others in this macho business, it is the attitude of the personnel. Everyone here is friendly, helpful, and informed. Besides, the food is quite good. On the broiled side, there are New York strips and porterhouse steaks, filet mignon, rib chops, Colorado lamb rack, and lobster. Of course, there is more: seafood, chicken, and linguine. Daily specials might include duck breast, bouillabaisse, veal chops, Dover sole, and rabbit. Steamed littleneck clams make a nice appetizer, and a side of crisp goose-fat potatoes is tasty. I even liked the truffled cream spinach! The toughest part of dining here is choosing dessert. What a great selection: chocolate profiteroles, chocolate fondue, and crepe soufflé.

TABLA
11 Madison Ave (at 25th St)   212/889-0667
Lunch: Mon-Fri: Dinner: Daily
Moderate (downstairs) to expensive (upstairs)

In the New York restaurant world, no one is more respected than Danny Meyer. He takes his establishments and the city he calls home very seriously. His restaurants have become legends, with Gramercy Tavern and Union Square Cafe always at the top of the city's most popular venues. Tabla is a different story. Those who like Indian food will find the upstairs room dramatic in decor and quite different in taste, with the option of a *prix fixe* menu. Downstairs, you'll find home-style Indian cooking and an a la carte menu. Personally, I find it far more appealing than the uneven fusion of American and Indian dishes served upstairs. In any case, desserts are the best part of the evening!

TAO

42 E 58th St (bet Madison and Park Ave)   212/888-2288
Lunch: Mon-Fri; Dinner: Daily
Moderate

Tao is billed as an Asian bistro, but it is much more than that. In a huge space that once served as a theater, a dramatic dining setting has been created with a huge Buddha looking down as you enjoy really wonderful food at surprisingly reasonable prices. The hordes of diners can be accommodated on two levels; a sushi bar and several regular bars are also available. Reservations are strongly recommended, as the thirty-somethings make this their regular headquarters. A number of small plates are available to start, including such goodies as Thai stuffed shrimp and squab lettuce wraps. By all means save room for a delicious steak: kobe beef or filet mignon cooked at your table on a hot stone, or a marvelous wok-seared New York sirloin with shitake mushrooms. It literally melts in your mouth. For dessert, the molten chocolate cake with coconut ice cream. You'll love this place!

TARTINE

253 W 11th St (at 4th St)   212/229-2611
Lunch: Tues-Fri; Dinner: Tues-Sun; Brunch: Sat, Sun
Cash only
Moderate

Tartine will be your kind of place if you don't mind: (1) waiting outside in the rain, cold, or heat; (2) bringing your own drinks; (3) paying cash; (4) having your dirty fork laid back down in front of you for the next course. All of this, of course, is secondary to the fact that this tiny spot (about 30 chairs) serves some of the tastiest dishes in the Village. There are soups, salads, quiches, and omelets, plus chicken, meat, and fish entrees at pleasing prices. The French fries are a treat. Desserts and pastries are baked on the premises. For about half the price of what you would pay uptown, you can finish your meal with splendid custard-filled tarts, a fabulous hazelnut-covered chocolate ganache, strawberry shortcake, or thinly sliced warm apples with cinnamon on puff pastry with ice cream. There is always a wait at dinner, which is a good sign, since neighbors know what's best!

TASTE

1411 Third Ave (at 80th St)   212/717-9798
Breakfast, Lunch: Mon-Fri; Dinner: Daily; Brunch: Sat, Sun
Moderate to moderately expensive (dinner)   www.elizabar.com

Leave it to Eli Zabar! When it comes to quality food (with prices to match), there is no equal in Manhattan. Taste is his latest restaurant, and it has all the pluses and minuses you've come to expect from this gentleman. Breakfast is a normal experience. Lunch is served buffet-style, with ample selections of dozens of attractive dishes. Dinners change nightly and can feature such winners as sauteed duck livers, roasted artichoke hearts, wild Pacific salmon, pork chops, and quail. The brunch menu is large: matzoh-ball soup, whole-grain pancakes, omelets, roasted beef hash and egg, sandwiches (try Eli's turkey club), and much more on the buffet table. A wine bar, serving good wines by the glass that aren't too expensive, is an added feature. With his market just below, it looks like Taste is getting really fresh food. And the breads, as you would expect, are superb.

TASTING ROOM
72 E 1st St (bet First and Second Ave)   212/358-7831
Dinner: Tues-Sat
Inexpensive to moderate

Don't blink or you will miss this tiny treasure! Renée (in front) and chef-husband Cohn Alevras (in the kitchen) treat just 25 guests for dinner with an ever-changing menu of very tasty dishes, along with a huge cache of wines —300 labels and over 2,000 bottles. I even noticed a large offering of great Oregon wines from the Willamette Valley. The menu is unusual: you can order either a small tasting plate or a larger share plate. The latter is fun if you are dining with a group. You'll find such sophisticated dishes as duck foie gras terrine, roasted partridge, chili-braised pork, and citrus-cured fresh cod. Whatever they have on the night you are there, rest assured it will be fresh and individually done. Renée is a charming hostess. Finish your meal with a piece of her mother's cheesecake featuring wine-poached apricots and cherries topped with healthy bee pollen.

Dining in Harlem has improved. Here are some favorites:

Amy Ruth's (113 W 116th St): good breakfasts

Bayou (308 Lenox Ave): Creole cuisine

Copeland's (547 W 145st St): Try the Sunday gospel brunch.

Jimmy's Uptown (2207 Adam Clayton Powell, Jr. Blvd.): Latin and soul food

Londel's Supper Club (2620 Eighth Ave): jazz entertainment on weekends

Miss Maude's Spoonbread Too (547 Lenox Ave): pork chops and spoonbread, of course

Native (161 Lenox Ave, 212/665-2525): French-Moroccan

Rao's (455 E 114th St): famous Italian landmark

Revival (2367 Frederick Douglass Blvd, 212/222-8338): soul food

Settepani (196 Malcolm X Blvd, 917/492-4806): deli and bakery specialties

Sylvia's (328 Lenox Ave): now larger, with soul food and entertainment

Yvonne (301 W 135th St, 212/862-1223): Southern specialties

TAVERN ON THE GREEN
Central Park W (at 67th St)   212/873-3200
Lunch, Dinner: Daily   www.tavernonthegreen.com
Moderate to moderately expensive

There's no place like this back home! With Tavern on the Green, Warner LeRoy created a destination attraction. The setting in Central Park, with lights twinkling on nearby trees and glamorous inside fixtures, makes for dining experiences that residents and visitors alike never forget. Even though the operation is big and busy, the food and the service are usually first-rate. Chef Gary Coyle has a big job keeping this place hopping. If you are planning an evening that must be extra special, make reservations in the Crystal Room. Your out-of-town relatives will love it! Seasonal menus can be viewed online.

TERRANCE BRENNAN'S SEAFOOD & CHOP HOUSE

Benjamin Hotel   212/715-2400
565 Lexington Ave (at 50th St)
Breakfast, Lunch, Dinner: Daily
Moderate (breakfast) to expensive (lunch, dinner)

Admittedly, the service is pretentious and the prices are high. But those are the only negatives at Terrance Brennan's. The food—especially the sirloin, filet mignon, porterhouse, ribeye, and lamb chops—is superb. So are seafood dishes like tuna mignon, wild striped bass, bay scallops, and lobster. Both the seafood and meat dishes are offered with a large array of sauces and butters (try the truffle). Side dishes include huge baked potatoes with all the trimmings, onion rings, whipped potatoes, sauerkraut, broccoli, macaroni and cheese, and more. Salads are prepared tableside. Shellfish and raw bars are added features, with caviar by the ounce also available. For dessert, the baked Alaska, served flaming at the table, is the odds-on favorite. Surrounded by a fruit soup, it is delicious. If you want to throw your budget to the wind, this is the place to go for a hefty and satisfying meal.

Looking for an unusual place for a private event? Try the vaults at **Vine** (25 Broad St, 212/344-VINE). Here you can dine on tasty food in the historic PaineWebber building.

THOM

60 Thompson St (bet Spring and Broome St)   212/219-2000
Breakfast, Lunch, Dinner: Daily; Brunch: Sat, Sun
Moderately expensive

No matter where you live or are staying in the New York area, a trip to Thom, at the Thompson Hotel in Soho, is a must. When it comes to attractive personnel, no place can equal it. The scene is trendy and noisy, with eyes fixed on the extremely skinny black-clad male waiters and the less clad female waiters—a show in itself. But it is the food you'll come for, and I can vouch that you won't be disappointed. Good choices include roast chicken and medallions of veal. The only downside is the poor synchronization of the dishes by the kitchen.

TOCQUEVILLE

15 E 15th St (bet Union Square W and Fifth Ave)   212/647-1515
Lunch: Mon-Sat; Dinner: Daily   www.tocquevillerestaurant.com
Moderately expensive

Tocqueville is a smallish restaurant tended with TLC by the husband-and-wife team of Jo-Ann Makovitzky and Marco Moreira. The result is outstanding. Innovative dishes are featured in a constantly changing menu. "Billy Bi soup" (mussels in broth) is a superb way to start. On to the 60-second seared dry-aged sirloin. The warm apple tart is a wonderful finish. You'll have an absolutely fabulous meal, made all the more pleasant by a well-trained and accommodating staff. I'd fault only the not-very-warm bread and rather spartan decor, but those are minor flaws. This talented pair also operates **Marco Polo Caterers** (same phone number as Tocqueville), which offers an outstanding selection for home or business affairs. The owners will personally deliver the delicious food, and they can also take care of rental items, flowers, photographers, and professional service staff.

TONY'S DI NAPOLI

1606 Second Ave (at 83rd St)	212/861-8686
147 W 43rd St (Times Square)	212/221-0100

Lunch: Daily (Sat, Sun only from 2 p.m. at Second Ave location);
    Dinner: Daily   www.tonysdinapoli.com
Moderate

Tony's is not to be missed for great family-style dining. The kids will love it, as will your hungry husband or wife, and so will your grandparents! The place is colorful, noisy, and busy. The Times Square location is a bit more subdued. Huge platters of appetizers, really delicious salads, pastas, chicken and veal dishes, broiled items, and fish come piping hot and ready for the whole crew to dig into. Most everyone finds that they can't eat it all; you'll see lots of take-home boxes exiting these locations. Even the dessert menu is gigantic: cheesecakes, strawberry shortcake, sundaes, sorbets, and *tartufo* (almost the real thing). An outrageous fresh Godiva cappuccino is made with vanilla custard ice cream, espresso, cappuccino liquor, and topped with Godiva chocolate liqueur. Sheer fun, believe me!

TRATTORIA DELL'ARTE

900 Seventh Ave (at 57th St)	212/245-9800

Lunch: Mon-Fri; Dinner: Daily; Brunch: Sat, Sun
Moderate   www.trattoriadellarte.com

I like to recommend this bustling spot across the street from Carnegie Hall. The natives already know about Trattoria Dell'Arte, as the place is bursting at the seams every evening. A casual cafe is at the front, seats are available at the antipasto bar in the center, and the diningroom is in the rear. One would be hard-pressed to name a place at any price with tastier Italian food than is served here. The antipasto selection is large, fresh, and inviting; you can choose a platter with various accompaniments. There are daily specials, superb pasta dishes, grilled fish and meats, and salads. Wonderful pizzas are available every day. Special spa cuisine from Italy is a feature. The atmosphere and personnel are warm and pleasant. I recommend this place without reservation—although you'd better have one if you want to sit in the diningroom.

TRIBECA GRILL

375 Greenwich St (at Franklin St)	212/941-3900

Lunch: Mon-Fri; Dinner: Daily; Brunch: Sun
Moderate   www.myriadrestaurantgroup.com

It hardly seems possible this place is over a decade old! Please note the address is Greenwich *Street,* not Avenue. The setting is a huge old coffee-roasting house in Tribeca. The inspiration is Robert DeNiro. The bar comes from the old Maxwell's Plum restaurant. The kitchen is first-class. The genius is savvy Drew Nieporent. Put it all together, and you have a winner. No wonder the people watching is so good here! Guests enjoy a spacious bar and dining area, fabulous private screening room upstairs, a collection of paintings by Robert DeNiro, Sr., and banquet facilities for private parties. The food is stylish and wholesome. Excellent salads, seafood, veal, steak, and first-rate pastas are house favorites. One of the top dishes is seared tuna with sesame noodles. The tarts, tortes, and mousses also rate with the best. Their wine list (1,500 selections!) is world-class.

TROPICA
MetLife Building
200 Park Ave (45th St at Vanderbilt Ave), lobby   212/867-6767
Lunch, Dinner: Mon-Fri   www.restaurantassociates.com
Moderate

Realizing that most New Yorkers have limited time to spend over lunch, Tropica provides speedy and efficient service in addition to very tasty food. Dinner hours are a bit more relaxed in this bright, charming, tropical seafood house, which is hidden away on the concourse of the MetLife Building in midtown. Featured entrees include excellent tuna (in the sushi and sashimi assortment) and seafood salads. The molten chocolate cake easily wins best-dessert honors. Stick to the fish and shellfish, and you'll be more than satisfied.

T SALON & EMPORIUM
11 E 20th St (bet Fifth Ave and Broadway)   212/358-0506
Daily: 9-8   888/nyc-teas
Moderate   www.tsalon.com

Given the renewed interest in tea, the unusual and enchanting T Salon will captivate tea addicts, as well as those who just want to experiment on an occasional basis. You will find green teas (light-colored Oriental tea with a delicate taste), oolong teas (distinctively peachy flavor), black teas (heavy, deep flavor and rich amber color), as well as white and red teas. A specialty here is tea blending. The T Salon is home of the new tea bag "pyramid pouch." Proper afternoon tea with scones, sandwiches, and pastries is served daily. One can choose from 500 different teas. One of Manhattan's largest tea selections is sold upstairs, as are all kinds of attractively displayed and reasonably priced tea accessories. They host bridal and baby showers, book signings, and special events. This is one of the more unusual operations in Manhattan, again proving that no other city in the world is quite like the Big Apple!

TURKISH KITCHEN
386 Third Ave (bet 27th and 28th St)   212/679-6633
Lunch: Mon-Fri; Dinner: Daily
Moderate

This Turkish delight has great ethnic food and is absolutely spotless. Moreover, the staff exudes TLC! There are all kinds of Turkish specialties, like zucchini pancakes, *istim kebab* (baked lamb shanks wrapped with eggplant slices), hummus, and tasty baked and grilled fish dishes. You can wash it all down with sour cherry juice from Turkey or *cacik,* a homemade yogurt. Turkish music is the Tuesday entertainment feature. This family-run Gramercy-area operation is one of the best.

21 CLUB
21 W 52nd St (bet Fifth Ave and Ave of the Americas)   212/582-7200
Lunch: Mon-Fri; Dinner: Mon-Sat   www.21club.com
Expensive to very expensive

You know about 21. It has been around for a long time and has certainly established a reputation as a place to see and be seen. I can remember fascinating lunches there with my uncle, who was a daily diner. Alas, things have changed. Yes, there is still a gentleman at the door to give you the once over. Yes, jackets, please. Yes, there are still the 21 classics on the menu, even a not-so-lowly burger at $21.50. Yes, the atmosphere is still quite special. But there it ends, as far as I am concerned. The service is haughty, and the food is just okay. More has been added: Upstairs at 21, an attractive, small-ish salon that charges absolutely exorbitant prices, with a quiet ambience that is appealing. If your out-of-town guests simply *must* see this place and you're feeling flush, then go. Otherwise, the memories are better!

2 WEST
Ritz-Carlton Battery Park Hotel
2 West St (at Battery Pl)　　　　　　　　　　　　　917/790-2525
Breakfast, Lunch, Dinner: Daily
Moderately expensive

The view is the thing here! Not that the food isn't very good, but the edibles are outclassed by the visual sights. The park and water view combines with the gorgeous glass pieces and artwork indoors to make a memorable feast for the eyes. The serving pieces are just as attractive, too. When you combine all of this with extremely fast and informed service and good food, I have no complaints. This room is just one of the hotel's dining choices, all of them done to Ritz-Carlton's standards of perfection. You'll find a rich selection of plates carefully designed and presented with local ingredients. I like the dessert plate; the chocolate tart is exceptional. If you're looking for a special place for afternoon tea, the adjoining Lobby Lounge is perfect.

JAMES BEARD HOUSE
167 W 12th St (bet Ave of the Americas and Seventh Ave)　212/675-4984
www.jamesbeard.org

This is a real chefs' place! The legendary James Beard had his roots in Oregon, so anything to do with his life is of special interest to this author. He was a familiar personality on the Oregon coast, where he delighted in serving the superb seafood for which the region is famous. When Beard died in 1985, his Greenwich Village brownstone was put on the market and purchased by a group headed by Julia Child. Now the home is run by the nonprofit James Beard Foundation as a food and wine archive, research facility, and gathering place. It is the nation's only such culinary center. There are nightly dinners anyone can attend at which some of our country's best regional chefs show off their talents. For foodies, this is a great opportunity to have a one-on-one with some really interesting folks. Call for scheduled dinners.

TYPHOON BREWERY
22 E 54th St (bet Fifth and Madison Ave)　　　　　　212/754-9006
Lunch: Mon-Fri; Dinner: Mon-Sat
Moderate

A bit of Bangkok has come to midtown Manhattan with this booming Thai eatery and brewery. The ground floor houses a huge bar with a vast selection of handcrafted American beers on draft and others (domestic and imported) in bottles. Daily specials are offered. A raw bar offers oysters from both coasts, as well as littleneck clams. All five Thai flavors—salty, sweet, sour, bitter and spicy—are featured on the menu. Take your choice of selections in each category. Family-style platters add to the fun: great squid with garlic, delicious lemon-grass chicken, superb seared monkfish in sour tamarind broth. Desserts aren't bad for a Thai house. Typhoon brûlées (Thai coffee crème, coconut jelly, apple tofu) head the list. It's crowded and fun but no place for those wearing hearing aids.

UNION SQUARE CAFE
21 E 16th St (bet Fifth Ave and Union Square W)   212/243-4020
Lunch, Dinner: Daily
Moderate

This is one of New York's most popular restaurants—and with good reason. The Stars and Stripes fly high here, as Union Square Cafe is very much an American restaurant. The clientele is as varied as the food. Conversations are often oriented toward the publishing world, as well-known authors and editors are in attendance at lunch. The menu is creative, the staff unusually down-to-earth, and the prices very much within reason. Owner Danny Meyer offers such specialties as oysters Union Square, hot garlic potato chips, and wonderful black bean soup. For lunch, try the yellowfin tuna burger served on a homemade poppyseed roll. Dinner entrees from the grill are always delicious (tuna, shell steak, veal). I go here just for the warm banana tart with honey-vanilla ice cream and macadamia nut brittle. Try a light afternoon cheese plate at the bar. A Yankee winner!

UNITED NATIONS DELEGATES DINING ROOM
United Nations Headquarters
First Ave at 46th St   212/963-7626, 212/963-7099 (banquets)
Lunch: Mon-Fri (open nights and weekends for special functions)
Moderate

Don't let the name or the security keep you away! The public can enjoy the international food and special atmosphere here. Conversations at adjoining tables are conducted in almost every language. The setting is charming, overlooking a patio and the river. The room is large and airy, the service polite and informed. Although there is a large selection of appetizers, soups, salads, entrees, and desserts on the regular menu, the best deal is the Delegates Buffet. A huge table of salads, baked specialties, seafoods, meats, vegetables, cheeses, desserts, and fruits await the hungry noontime diner. Some rules do apply: jackets required, no jeans permitted, and photo ID is needed. (The room is used for private gatherings in the evening.) There isn't a more appetizing complete daily buffet available in New York than this one. All of the dishes are attractively presented and very tasty.

VERITAS
43 E 20th St (near Park Ave S)   212/353-3700
Dinner: Daily   www.veritas-nyc.com
Moderately expensive

Good things come in small packages! With only 55 seats—all of them kept warm for every meal—getting to enjoy chef Scott Bryan's refreshingly simple dishes is worth the wait. The world-class wine cellar stocks 1,300 bottles, ranging from $18 to $25,000. Like the food, the room is done in superb taste; every color and surface spells quality. Top dishes include seared foie gras, crisp sweetbreads, roast saddle of lamb, and roasted organic chicken that will melt in your mouth. Warm chocolate cake is a must for dessert. The praline parfait and cheese selection are also top-notch. Veritas proves that someone has finally gotten the word that complex food combinations, in most cases, just don't work. Simpler is better!

VERONICA RISTORANTE
240 W 38th St (bet Seventh and Eighth Ave)   212/764-4770
Breakfast, Lunch: Mon-Fri
Inexpensive to moderate

Some time ago a friend who works in the Garment District told me about a fantastic Italian restaurant but wouldn't divulge the name or location because he was afraid I'd put it in my book. This piqued my interest, so I did some investigating. The restaurant turned out to be Veronica, a tiny place in the heart of the Garment District that's open only for breakfast and lunch. Run by Andrew Frisari and his wife, Ceil Hermes, this marvelous cafeteria-style restaurant serves sensational home-cooked food. There is veal parmesan, mouth-watering homemade lasagna, delicious tortellini, and chicken salad. Other favorites are pasta primavera and lemon chicken with artichokes and wine. Low-fat and cholesterol-free items are featured. The clientele is sophisticated, the atmosphere informal and homey. Try the homemade cheesecakes or other great desserts. Most items are available for takeout, individual orders, parties, and special occasions.

VICEVERSA
325 W 51st St (bet Eighth and Ninth Ave)   212/399-9291
Lunch: Mon-Fri; Dinner: Mon-Sat   www.viceversarestaurant.com
Moderate to moderately expensive

ViceVersa is one of the most popular spots in the Theater District, mainly because their Italian heritage shows in the tasty preparation of every dish. The menu changes periodically. You'll find antipasti treats like pan-sauteed shrimp wrapped with smoked prosciutto and slow-roasted rabbit salad. I'd recommend the green spinach tagliatelle and homemade spaghetti as pastas. For the main course, seared salmon, grilled swordfish, beef tenderloin, and veal medallions are among the better dishes. Homemade gelato is a good dessert choice. In nice weather, an outdoor patio is particularly inviting. It is a good idea to call ahead for reservations, particularly if you are going to an evening show.

VINEGAR FACTORY
431 E 91st St (bet York and First Ave)   212/987-0885
Brunch: Sat, Sun   www.elizabar.com
Moderate

Savvy Upper East Siders quickly learned that weekend brunch at Eli Zabar's Vinegar Factory is delicious. The taste buds spring to alertness as you wander the packed aisles of the Vinegar Factory (a great gourmet store) on your way upstairs for Saturday or Sunday brunch. Don't expect bargain prices; after all, this is an Eli Zabar operation. But the quality is substantial. Wonderful breads (Eli is famous for them), a fresh salad bar, omelets, pizzas, pancakes, blintzes, and huge sandwiches are the order of the day. Your kids will love the massive portions, and you'll appreciate the fast, friendly service.

A Burger Hideaway!

Buried in the back lobby of Le Parker Meridien Hotel (119 W 56th St, 212/708-7414) is the **Burger Joint**, a busy, bare-bones room with freshly ground burgers that go for $4.50 and are as good as you'll find anywhere in the area. Crisp fries and brownies, too!

VIVOLO

140 E 74th St (bet Park and Lexington Ave)	212/737-3533
Lunch: Sun-Fri; Dinner: Daily	www.vivolonyc.com
Moderate	

Angelo Vivolo has created a neighborhood classic in an old townhouse converted into a charming two-story restaurant with cozy fireplaces and professional service. His empire includes **Cucina Vivolo** (138 E 74th St, 212/717-4700), a specialty food shop next door at 138 East 74th Street, and **Anche Vivolo** (222 East 58th Street, 212/308-0112), in the Bloomingdale's area. There are great things to eat at all three places. You can sit down and be pampered, have goodies ready for takeout, or place an order for delivery to your front door free of charge (from 66th to 80th streets between York and Fifth avenues). The Cucina menu offers wonderful Italian specialty sandwiches, made with all kinds of breads, as well as soups, cheeses, sweets, espresso, and cappuccino. A boxed lunch is also available. In the restaurant proper there are daily specials, pastas, stuffed veal chops, and much more. The capellini primavera pasta is the house favorite. Vivolo serves over 60 scaloppine preparations. Their secret is simple: they use vegetable oil when sauteeing scaloppine and add butter when finishing the sauce. (Butter burns at the high temperatures required of sauteeing.) Save room for the cannoli *alla Vivolo,* a pastry filled with ricotta cream. A special *prix fixe* menu is available from 5 to 6:30 p.m.

VONG

200 E 54th St (bet Second and Third Ave)	212/486-9592
Lunch: Mon-Fri; Dinner: Daily	www.jean-georges.com
Moderate to moderately expensive	

The atmosphere here is Thai-inspired, with romantic and appetizing overtones. The ladies will love the colors and lighting, and the gentlemen will remember the great things Vong does with peanut and coconut sauces. I could make a meal of appetizers like chicken and coconut milk soup, prawn satay with oyster sauce, and raw tuna wrapped in rice paper. Order crispy squab or venison medallions, if available. A vegetarian menu is offered. For dessert try sticky rice with tamarind-glazed mango and taro ice cream, passionfruit soufflé with passionfruit ice cream, or lemon-grass tart with crushed raspberries. Dining here is a lot cheaper than a week at Bangkok's Oriental Hotel and just as delicious!

WALKER'S
16 N Moore St (at Varick St)   212/941-0142
Lunch, Dinner: Daily
Inexpensive

If you are looking for a glimpse of what old Manhattan was like, you'll love Walker's. In three crowded rooms, at tables covered with plain white paper so that diners can doodle with crayons, you will be served hearty food at agreeable prices. The regular menu includes homemade soups, salads, omelets (create your own), sandwiches, and quiches. Their burgers are big and satisfying. A dozen or so daily specials include fish and pasta dishes. For those coming from uptown, it is a bit of a project to get here. For those in the neighborhood, it is easy to see why Walker's is a community favorite, especially on Sunday jazz nights.

Charlie Palmer's three-course *prix fixe* restaurants **Kitchen 22** (36 E 22nd St, 212/228-4399) and **Kitchen 82** (461 Columbus Ave, 212/875-1619) are drawing crowds. Although the food is not gourmet style, it is a good value, and the diningroom staffs are friendly and accommodating. After some operational problems are ironed out, Palmer could become a leader in the current desire to eat better for less money.

WALLSÉ
344 W 11th St (at Washington St)   212/352-2300
Dinner: Daily; Brunch: Sat, Sun   www.wallse.com
Moderate to moderately expensive

Vienna it is not, but Kurt Gutenbrunner has brought a somewhat Austrian flavor to the West Village. The two diningrooms are sparse but comfortable. The staff is pleasant and helpful, adding immeasurably to the dining experience. Appetizers like sauteed foie gras with string beans and pistachios and squash soup with black mushrooms are seasonal favorites. Yes, there is Wiener schnitzel with parsley potatoes that comes off rather well. The roast potatoes are outstanding. Great pastries for dessert: apple strudel, poached dumplings, and Salzburger Nockerl. Of couse, I'd rather be at Hotel Sacher in Vienna, but then getting to Wallsé is a lot less expensive.

WASHINGTON PARK
24 Fifth Ave (at 9th St)   212/529-4400
Dinner: Daily   www.washingtonparknyc.com
Moderately expensive

Jonathan Waxman may finally have found the right recipe for this stellar location, which has previously had its ups and downs (mainly the latter). Washington Park is a breath of fresh air in an inviting room, with some tables looking out on the fascinating passing scene of the Village and lower Fifth Avenue. The menu changes daily, with the word from servers that everything is strictly fresh and seasonal. Some favorites remain, however, like the wonderful chicken and fries, so moist and tasty you'll think the dish came from your own backyard barbecue. Salads are first-rate, and the numerous seafood offerings would do credit to any house on the waterfront. If red-pepper pancakes, smoked salmon, and caviar are on the menu, go for it!

Desserts will be the highlight of the evening: tarts, cobblers, chocolate layer cake, and more. Let's hope the double-chocolate and bourbon-baked Alaska will still be around. Eight delicious cheeses are available. For a satisfying casual bistro experience with some real taste surprises, Washington Park is a very good bet.

WATER CLUB
500 E 30th St (at East River)   212/683-3333
Lunch: Mon-Sat; Dinner: Daily; Buffet Brunch: Sun
Moderately expensive   www.thewaterclub.com

Warning! Do not fill up on the marvelous small scones that are made fresh in the Water Club's kitchen and served warm. They are absolutely the best things you have ever tasted, but they will undoubtedly diminish your appetite for the excellent meal to follow. The Water Club presents a magnificent setting right on the river. The place is large and noisy, with a fun atmosphere that is ideal for special occasions. (They also have excellent private party facilities.) There is nightly piano music, as well as accommodations for a drink or light meal on the roof, weather permitting. A large selection of seafood appetizers is available. Entrees include numerous fish dishes, and you will also find meat and poultry items. Homemade ice cream and sorbet and fresh-baked apple crisp (served at Sunday brunch), will round off a special meal. The Water Club's chocolate chocolate chocolate molten cake with layered mousse is great. Be advised that getting here from the north can be confusing. (Exit FDR Drive at 23rd Street and make two left turns.)

Here's one the kids will love! Dark tunnels, Martian men and women, interactive games, plus good food and drink—all can be found at **Mars 2112** (1633 Broadway, 212/582-2112). Menu offerings include out-of-this-world Interstellar Shrimp, Meteor Talapia, Pavonis Mons Chinese Chicken Salad, and much more!

WOO CHON
10 W 36th St (off Fifth Ave)   212/695-0676
Daily: 10:30 a.m.-5 a.m.
Moderate

This Korean restaurant, which rarely closes, is sparkling clean, friendly, and inviting. For a group dinner, order a variety of beef, pork, or shrimp dishes and have fun broiling them at your table. The sizzling seafood pancake is a winner! Accompanying dishes add a special touch to your meal. In addition to marinated barbecue items, there are such tasty delights as Oriental noodles and vegetables, traditional Korean herbs and rice served in beef broth, a variety of noodle dishes, and dozens of other Far East treats. If you are unfamiliar with Korean food, the helpful personnel will explain the dishes and how to eat them.

WOO LAE OAK SOHO
148 Mercer St (bet Prince and Houston St)   212/925-8200
Lunch, Dinner: Daily   www.woolaeoaksoho.com
Moderate to moderately expensive

This is one of the better Korean restaurants in the city, although it would be out-of-place in the native country. In attractive Soho surroundings, one can choose from a large selection of hot and cold appetizers, as well as traditional Korean specialties. The best include Dungeness crab wrapped in spinach crepes and tuna tartare served over sliced Korean pears. Rice and side dishes such as stir-fried peppers, radish *kimchi,* and raw garlic are also available. The big draws are the barbecued items, cooked right at the table and done with class. Available for barbecuing are slices of beef, short ribs, chicken, lamb, pork, scallops, shrimp, squid, tuna, veggies, and much more. The personnel are very helpful to beginners and seem genuinely pleased when diners show interest in their unusual menu.

ZARELA
953 Second Ave (bet 50th and 51st St) 212/644-6740
Lunch: Mon-Fri; Dinner: Daily www.zarela.com
Moderate

Not all Mexican dining is of the fast food variety! Zarela Martinez proves this in her family-style Mexican restaurant, which sets the standard for this type of cuisine in Manhattan. For lunch you'll find such tempting dishes as *flautas* (rolled chicken tacos), *tamales del dia,* guacamole, and delicious salads. A number of seafood, chicken, and meat dishes are also available, and a $25 *prix fixe* menu offers guests an opportunity to try a number of different flavors. At dinner more *antojitos* are featured, including different varieties of fresh and dried chiles with assorted fillings and sauces. You'll also find sauteed shrimp, tuna steak, roasted half duck, pan-fried liver, and vegetable dishes. Even the desserts are great: chocolate crepes or Mexican fruit bread pudding with applejack-brandy butter sauce.

ZOË
90 Prince St (bet Broadway and Mercer St) 212/966-6722
Lunch: Tues-Fri; Dinner: Daily; Brunch: Sat, Sun
Moderate www.zoerestaurant.com

Zoë occupies an old building, and the original tiles and columns still show. The setting is attractive and particularly enjoyable for younger diners, who like to sit at the chef's counter and watch the interactive kitchen. There is a wood-burning grill, a wood-fueled pizza oven (used for lunch), and a rotisserie. The grill features delicious double-cut pork chops, yellowfin tuna, steaks, and chops. The menu is contemporary American, with seasonal changes. It's worth saving room for the chocolate desserts!

III. Where to Find It: Museums, Tours, and Other Experiences

A Week in New York

You could spend an entire lifetime in New York and still never see and do everything this fabulous city has to offer. If you're here for a week (or even a month), you obviously have a lot of choices to make!

The first thing you need to know when planning an itinerary is that some areas are better visited on certain days—Soho on Saturday and the Lower East Side on Sunday, for example. Others shut down on the weekend (the Financial District), Saturday (the Lower East Side), Sunday (Soho and most of midtown), or Monday (many major museums and theaters). If your time is limited, pick a couple of things you really want to do or places you really want to see and build your days around them. Check the hours they're open and plan accordingly.

If you're at a loss, look through this chapter to get a good sense of the possibilities. If you still don't know where to start, I've sketched an outline of possible itineraries for seven days in New York. I do not mean to imply that the places I've included are necessarily "better" than others, nor do I recommend attempting everything I've listed on any given day. Part of the pleasure of New York is wandering, lingering, and taking your time.

MONDAY (Upper West Side)
- Breakfast "to go" from Fairway (2127 Broadway) or Zabar's (2245 Broadway)
- Cathedral Church of St. John the Divine (Amsterdam Ave at 112th St)
- Columbia University, main campus (entrance off 116th St at Broadway and Amsterdam Ave)
- American Museum of Natural History and the Rose Center for Earth and Space (Central Park W between 77th and 81st St)
- Henry Luce III Center at the New-York Historical Society (2 W 77th St)
- Late lunch at Tavern on the Green's Crystal Room (inside the park near 67th St at Central Park W)
- Stroll through Central Park
- Wander through the new AOL-Time Warner Center (Columbus Circle)
- Lincoln Center (Columbus Ave between 62nd and 65th St)
- Museum of American Folk Art galleries (Columbus Ave bet 65th and 66th St)
- Dinner at Ouest (2315 Broadway)

TUESDAY (midtown)
- Macy's (151 W 34th St)
- H&M (640 Fifth Ave)
- New York Public Library (Fifth Ave bet 40th and 42nd St)
- International Center of Photography (1133 Ave of the Americas)
- Saks Fifth Avenue (611 Fifth Ave)
- Early lunch at Tropica (MetLife Building, 200 Park Ave)
- Rockefeller Center (49th to 51st St bet Fifth Ave and Ave of the Americas)
- American Folk Art Museum (45 W 53rd St)
- Museum of Arts and Design (40 W 53rd St)
- Carnegie Hall (153 W 57th St)
- Dinner at Trattoria dell'Arte (900 Seventh Ave)
- Empire State Building observation deck (Fifth Ave between 33rd and 34th St)

WEDNESDAY (midtown and northern Manhattan)
- United Nations (First Ave between 45th and 46th St)
- Visit Pier 1 Imports (461 Fifth Ave, 71 Fifth Ave, and 1550 Third Ave)
- Ford Foundation Gardens (320 E 43rd St)
- Lunch at Grand Central Oyster Bar Restaurant (Grand Central Station, 42nd St and Vanderbilt Ave, lower level)
- 12:30 tour of Grand Central Terminal (offered by the Municipal Art Society)
- The Cloisters (Fort Tryon Park)
- Dyckman Farmhouse Museum (4881 Broadway)
- Dinner at Barbetta (321 W 46th St)
- Show at the Apollo Theater (253 W 125th St)

THURSDAY (Museum Mile)
- Breakfast at Sarabeth's Kitchen (1295 Madison Ave)
- Museum of the City of New York (1220 Fifth Ave)
- Jewish Museum (1109 Fifth Ave)
- Cooper-Hewitt National Design Museum (2 E 91st St)
- Solomon R. Guggenheim Museum (1071 Fifth Ave)
- Lunch at the Museum Cafe in the Guggenheim Museum
- Metropolitan Museum of Art (Fifth Ave between 80th and 84th St)
- Whitney Museum of American Art (945 Madison Ave)
- Frick Collection (1 E 70th St)
- Asia Society (Park Ave at 70th St)
- Bloomingdale's (1000 Third Ave)
- Dinner at Tony Di Napoli (1606 Second Ave)

FRIDAY (Financial District)
- Ferry from Battery Park to Statue of Liberty and Ellis Island
- National Museum of the American Indian (1 Bowling Green)
- Museum of Jewish Heritage (18 First Pl)
- South Street Seaport (pick up half-price theater tickets, too)
- Lunch at Nobu (105 Hudson St)
- Museum of American Financial History (28 Broadway)
- Federal Hall National Memorial (Wall St at Nassau St)
- St. Paul's Chapel (211 Broadway)
- Woolworth Building (233 Broadway)
- City Hall Park (Broadway at Chambers St)

- Brooklyn Bridge
- Pre-theater dinner at Orso (322 W 46th St)
- Theater

SATURDAY (Chelsea, West Village, and Soho)
- ABC Carpet and Home (888 Broadway)
- Gallery hopping on and around West 22nd Street in Chelsea
- Visit Bed Bath & Beyond (620 Ave of the Americas)
- Dia Center for the Arts (548 W 22nd St)
- Wander down Hudson Street or Avenue of the Americas in West Village
- Gallery hopping and shopping on and around West Broadway in Soho
- Dinner at Blue Ribbon (97 Sullivan St)

SUNDAY (Lower East Side and Chinatown)
- Lower East Side shopping; Fine & Klein (19 Orchard St) is a must
- Brunch at Katz's Delicatessen (205 Houston St)
- Lower East Side Tenement Museum (97 Orchard St)
- Eldridge Street Synagogue (12 Eldridge St)
- Museum of Chinese in the Americas (70 Mulberry St)
- Dinner in Chinatown at the Golden Unicorn (18 East Broadway)

Note: for further information on any of these suggestions, please refer to detailed individual listings elsewhere in the book.

Auction Houses

Whether you're in the market for rare antiques or just looking for a fun experience, New York's auction houses can be a real treat. Look in the Weekend section of the Friday *New York Times* or the Arts and Leisure section of the Sunday *Times* for advertisements about auctions and previews at the auction houses listed below and others. The classified section of the *New York Times* also has an auction section, and all of Manhattan's auction houses are listed in the Manhattan Yellow Pages under "Auctioneers."

Before you go, think carefully about what it is that you're doing. If you just want to learn a little about the art world, simply show up, hang back, and take it all in. If you're even remotely serious about making a purchase, however, make sure you know the rules of the game. I strongly advise you to obtain the auction's illustrated catalog and take full advantage of auction previews. Attend some of the lectures and courses offered at the auction houses listed below to learn about a particular period or medium.

Finally, a word of warning: the people at most auctions in New York are professionals. They know what they are looking for, they know what they want to pay, and sometimes they know each other. Auctions in New York are a one-of-a-kind experience and can be lots of fun. Just don't go expecting to beat the professionals.

CHRISTIE'S
20 Rockefeller Plaza (49th St bet Fifth Ave and
Ave of the Americas)   212/636-2000

This British auction house specializes in fine arts and antiques. Upcoming auctions are often open to the public for preview. Call ahead for schedule details. Check too at **Christie's East** (219 E 67th St).

SOTHEBY'S

1334 York Ave (at 72nd St)   212/606-7000

Arguably the most elite auction house in the world, this British institution also specializes in fine art and antiques. Like Christie's, Sotheby's is open for auction previews. Look for **Sotheby's Arcade**, a junior version of the parent house.

Christie's and Sotheby's really dominate the auction world, both in New York and around the globe. Other reputable houses in New York include **Doyle New York** (212/427-2730), **Tepper Galleries** (212/677-5300), **Swann Auction Galleries** (212/254-4710), and **Guernsey's** (212/794-2280).

Films

Like any city, New York has a multitude of theaters for first-run movies. Indeed, many movies open in New York and Los Angeles before they open anywhere else. (Depending on the size of the crowds they draw, some never do open anywhere else.) *The New Yorker, Time Out New York, New York* magazine, and the *New York Times'* Friday Weekend section and its Sunday Arts and Leisure section are all good places to look for what is playing and where at any given time. You can also call 212/777-FILM (3456) for information about what movies are showing at virtually every theater in Manhattan and to purchase tickets by credit card at many of those theaters. If you're online, go to www.moviephone.com or newyork.citysearch.com.

If you want to combine an excellent dinner with a first-run movie for a surprisingly reasonable price, head for the **Screening Room** at 54 Varick Street in Tribeca (212/334-2100). If you're looking for an old movie, a foreign film, an unusual documentary, a 3D movie (in the Sony IMAX Theater), or something out of the ordinary, try calling one of the following theaters. Most numbers connect you with a recording that lists current movies and times, ticket cost and directions.

American Museum of Natural History's IMAX Theater: 175-208 Central Park West (212/769-5034)
Angelika Film Center and Cafe: 18 W Houston St (212/995-2000)
Anthology Film Archives: 32 Second Ave (212/505-5181)
Asia Society: 725 Park Ave (212/327-9276)
Austrian Cultural Forum: 11 E 52nd St (212/319-5300)
Film Forum: 209 W Houston St (212/727-8110)
Florence Gould Hall at the French Institute: 55-B 59th St (212/355-6160)
Japan Society: 333 E 47th St (212/752-0824)
Lincoln Plaza Cinema: 1886 Broadway (212/757-2280)
Loews Lincoln Square Theater: 890 Broadway (212/336-5000)
Makor: 25 W 67th St (212/601-1000)
Millenium: 66 E 4th St (212/673-0090)
Museum of Modern Art's Gramercy Theater: 127 E 23rd St (212/777-4900)
Museum of Television and Radio: 25 W 52nd St (212/621-6800)
Quad Cinema: 34 W 13th St (212/255-8800)
Symphony Space: 2537 Broadway (212/864-5400)
Walter Reade Theater at Lincoln Center: 165 W 66th St (212/875-5600)
Whitney Museum of American Art: 945 Madison Ave (212/570-3676)

Like everything, the price of movie tickets in New York tends to be higher than elsewhere in the country. If you purchase tickets over the phone and thus incur a per-ticket surcharge, you'll spend more than $20 for two adults! In fact, you can spend $20 for two tickets at some movie theaters even if you buy at the box office. The second-run theaters, film societies, and museums usually charge a little less than the first-run theaters, however. For free open-air movies in the summer, try Bryant Park, Seward Park, and other parks throughout the city.

Finally, New York is home to dozens of popular film festivals. Probably the best known is the Film Society of Lincoln Center's **New York Film Festival,** held in late September and early October. This annual event showcases 20 films and gets more popular every year. Call the Walter Reade Theater box office at 212/875-5600 for more information. Look in *New York* magazine, *Time Out New York, The New Yorker,* or any daily newspaper for information on upcoming films and festivals.

Photo Ops!

Of course there are thousands of great backdrops in New York, but here are a couple enduring favorites:

- **The LOVE block** (Ave of Americas at 55th St)
- **Prometheus statue** (Fifth Ave between 50th and 51st St)
- **Rockefeller Plaza ice rink** (off Fifth Ave, between 49th and 50th St)
- **Statue of Liberty** (Battery Park)
- **Wall Street bull** (Broadway at Bowling Green)
- **Washington Arch** (Washington Square Park, Greenwich Village)

Flea Markets

Craft and street fairs pop up all over New York on weekends in spring, summer, and fall. If you hear about or just stumble onto one, by all means do some browsing. Real New Yorkers go to these, so you'll get a very different sense of the city and the people who live here than you would walking around midtown on a weekday. You'll also find everything from woven baskets made by somebody's relatives in Nigeria to socks and underwear sold at steep discounts. You'll also find some great food. That said, however, many street fairs have begun to look alike, and some neighborhoods have grown weary of them. Moreover, I suggest watching your pockets in a crowd.

In addition to these craft and street fairs, New York also has several regularly scheduled flea markets, as well as Greenmarkets. (See the "Fruits, Vegetables" section of Chapter IV for more information on these wonderful markets.) Take cash, don't be embarrassed to haggle a bit, and look around before buying anything—sometimes you'll see the same item at more than one place. Collectors and treasure hunters often go at the beginning of the day when selections are best, while bargain hunters usually wait until the end of the day when dealers may lower prices. Remember there are no guarantees or refunds.

The flea markets in the following list all are relatively well-established. Be forewarned that virtually all of them shrink a bit in the colder months and some may disappear without notice. You might look under "Flea Markets" in the special "Antiques" classified listing in the Friday *New York Times'* Weekend section before setting out.

Annex Antiques Fair and Flea Market—Assuming developers haven't bought out all the real estate, you'll find this sprawling market in parking lots on both sides of Avenue of the Americas from 26th to 27th streets. The antiques section is closer to 27th Street, while the flea market is closer to 26th Street and is open from 9 a.m. to 5 p.m. on Sunday only. Admission to the antiques section is $1, and the flea market is free. Both are open from 9 a.m. to 5 p.m. on Saturday and Sunday.

Intermediate School 44 Flea Market—Inside and outside Public School 44 on Columbus Avenue between 76th and 77th streets, this fading but still popular market is held on Sundays from 10 a.m. to 5:30 p.m. Look for one of the city's Greenmarkets here, too.

Public School 183 Flea Market—Open Saturdays from 9 a.m. to 5:30 p.m., this decidedly upscale flea market is known for antiques and jewelry as well as a terrific Greenmarket. It's held at Public School 183, on 67th Street between First and York avenues.

Union Square Farmers Market—This is the grandfather of all Green-markets. Open for business on Wednesdays, Fridays, and Saturdays at the north end of Union Square (between Broadway and Park Avenue South on 17th Street), this popular market offers all sorts of fresh goodies: seasonal produce, baked goods, jams, jellies, and flowers.

Galleries

When people think of art, they sometimes think only of museums. While the art museums in New York are exceptional, anybody interested in art ought to think about visiting commercial galleries, too. Galleries are places where potential buyers and admirers alike can look at the work of contemporary and 20th-century artists (a few galleries specialize in older work) at their own pace and without charge. Let me stress "admirers alike." A lot of people are afraid to go into galleries because they think they'll be expected to buy something or be treated poorly if they don't know everything there is to know about art. That just isn't true, and an afternoon of gallery hopping can be fun.

First decide what kind of art you want to see. New York has long been considered the center of the contemporary art world, and it follows that the city is home to literally hundreds of galleries of all sizes and styles. In general, the more formal and conventional galleries are on or close to Madison Avenue on the Upper East Side and along 57th Street. (You need to look up to find a lot of them, particularly on 57th Street.) Some of the less formal, avant-garde galleries tend to be in Soho on West Broadway, between Broome and Houston streets; on Greene Street between Prince and Houston streets; and on Prince Street, between Greene Street and West Broadway. Some of the latter are also in Tribeca. As a general rule, artists who have yet to be discovered go where the rents are lower, and then more established artists and galleries follow. In recent years, the west end of Chelsea, in the blocks around the Dia Center for the Arts (at 22nd Street and Tenth Avenue), as well as the northwest corner of the West Village on 14th Street (also known as the Meatpacking District), and now even the Lower East Side on and around Rivington Street have joined the list of gallery hot spots. In fact, Chelsea alone is home to almost 200 galleries!

If you want to get a sense of the diversity of the New York gallery scene, sample a couple galleries in each neighborhood. For a free directory of galleries and their specialties, write the Art Dealers Association of America (575 Madison Avenue, New York, NY, 10022) or call 212/940-8590. You can also ask at any gallery for a free copy of the *Art Now Gallery Guide,* a monthly listing of exhibits at several hundred Manhattan galleries.

Galleries are typically known for the artists they showcase. If you are interested in the work of just one artist, both the *New Yorker* and *New York* magazine contain listings of gallery shows by artists' names. Be sure to look at the dates, as shows sometimes change quickly. *Time Out New York* has a list of galleries by neighborhood in its "Arts" section, complete with descriptions of current shows. The Sunday *New York Times'* Arts and Leisure section contains several pages of advertisements from various galleries and reviews of new shows. The Friday *Times'* Weekend section also devotes space to reviews and advertisements, as do *Art in America* and *Arts* magazines.

> Most galleries are open Tuesday through Saturday from 10 or 11 a.m. to 5 or 6 p.m. Some close for a few weeks in summer.

Museums

New York is home to some of the most famous, interesting, and unusual museums in the world. With a few exceptions, I've limited the following list to museums in Manhattan, but that does not mean that museums in the other boroughs aren't worth exploring. The recently renovated **New York Transit Museum** in Brooklyn (718/243-8601) is a must-see for train and subway buffs, while the **Brooklyn Museum of Art** (718/638-5000) is among the oldest and largest art museums in the country and has one of the best Egyptian collections in the world. The **New York Hall of Science** in Queens (718/699-0005), the **Museum of the Moving Image** in Queens (718/784-0077), the **Staten Island Children's Museum** (718/273-2060), the **Bronx Zoo** (718/367-1010), and the **New York Botanical Garden** (718/817-8700) also have lots of fans. The **Liberty Science Center** (201/200-1000), just across the Hudson River in Jersey City, New Jersey, is quite popular as well.

I've also not given full writeups of some of the smaller museum gallery spaces in Manhattan, such as the **Drawing Center** (212/219-2166), the **French Institute-Alliance Française** (212/355-6100), the **Americas Society Gallery** (212/249-8950), the **Japan Society** (212/832-1155) the **Grolier Club** (212/838-6690), the **China Institute** (212/744-8181), the **Austrian Cultural Forum** (212/319-5300), and **Tibet House** (212/807-0563). They, too, are worth visiting, and you'll find a listing of their current exhibitions in the "Museums" section of *Time Out New York.*

Even if you aren't a museum person, take a look at the following museum outlines. I can't imagine that you won't find at least one that strikes a chord. Most of them have gift shops, the larger and more interesting of which I've described in the "Museum and Library Shops" section in Chapter VI. For a list of the best museums for children, see the "Where to Go with Children" section in Chapter VII. For a complete list of museums offering free admission or special free hours, see the "New York for Free" section in Chapter VII. For museums off the beaten path, I've provided suggestions about how to get there.

As a general rule, I suggest calling ahead. Some of the smaller museums and galleries close for days or even weeks while new exhibits are being mounted, and they sometimes change their hours. If you want to find out about current exhibits, look in the front of the *New Yorker,* the back of *New York* magazine, the "Museums" section of *Time Out New York, Museums New York,* or *Where New York* magazine, which is distributed free in most Manhattan hotel rooms.

Turn Off That Phone!
  New York City law requires that cell phones be turned off in all museums, galleries, theaters, and concerts. The fine for an ill-timed ring from your purse or pocket is $50! Now if they would just extend the ban to include restaurants and public transportation . . .

AMERICAN BIBLE SOCIETY
1865 Broadway (at 61st St)   212/408-1200

  The American Bible Society is dedicated to making the Christian Bible readily available to people in this country and around the world. Founded in 1816, ABS has distributed nearly seven billion Bibles and portions of Scripture. If you're interested in religious history, the small gallery on the second floor of its remodeled headquarters is well worth the trip. Changing exhibits offer insight into various biblical subjects as well as such related topics as the art and purposes of stained glass. In the adjacent research library, you'll find a portion of a Torah scroll found after the flooding of Kai Feng Eu in China in 1643. Many kinds of Bibles—from annotated study Bibles to richly illustrated ones for children—are sold in the first-floor gift shop. **Hours:** Monday through Wednesday from 10 to 6, Thursday from 10 to 7, and Saturday from 10 to 5. **Admission:** free.

AMERICAN FOLK ART MUSEUM
43 W 53rd St (bet Fifth Ave and Ave of the Americas)   212/265-1040

  Although the small gallery space across from Lincoln Center remains open, the stunning new eight-story home of the American Folk Art Museum puts most of the collection back in midtown (where it began) with the Museum of Arts and Design and the renovated and expanded Museum of Modern Art. The skinny building is itself a work of art, with various galleries on the top four floors, a skylight capping the building, and art integrated throughout its many interesting spaces. The permanent and changing exhibitions offer stunning examples of 18th- and 19th-century folk art, as well as the work of self-taught artists from the 20th and 21st centuries. The enormous painted copper St. Tammany Weathervane is a particular treat, as is the two-story box of carved duck decoys by the open staircase. **Hours:** Tuesday through Saturday from 10 to 6 (Friday until 8). **Admission:** $9 for adults, $7 for students and seniors, and free for children under 12 and everyone between 6 and 8 p. m. on Friday.

AMERICAN MUSEUM OF NATURAL HISTORY
Central Park West (bet 77th and 81st St)   212/769-5100

  If ever there was a perfect answer for what to do with children on a rainy day, this sprawling collection of 30 million (yes, *million!*) artifacts and specimens is it. You could spend an entire day on any one of the museum's four floors. (The main entrance puts you on the second floor.) Obtain a floor plan at the information desk and decide what you want to see, especially if time is limited. I also advise taking advantage of the coat check and going during the week to avoid often overwhelming weekend crowds. Exhibits include dinosaur and fossil halls; the Oceans Hall, with a whale suspended from the ceiling; a hall devoted to African mammals, including elephants; a display allowing some hands-on exploration of the natural world in New York itself; gems and minerals (keep an eye out for the Star of India sapphire); the Hall of Biodiversity; and fascinating displays about cultures from all over the globe. The rebuilt Hayden Planetarium and Rose Center for Earth and Space, and the Millstein Hall of Oceans are among the new and updated parts of the museum.

Guided tours of the museum's highlights are scheduled frequently throughout the day. You'll find a decidedly downscale cafeteria and the more pleasant Garden Cafe on the lower level, and another cafe on the fourth floor. The refurbished park on the north side of the museum is a grand place for a picnic. Request information about the IMAX Theater (212/769-5034) at the information desk. It costs extra, but whatever is showing is bound to be excellent. **Hours:** Sunday through Thursday from 10 to 5:45 (Friday until 8:45). **Admission:** $12 for adults, $9 for students and senior citizens, and $7 for children between 2 and 12 is suggested. Indeed, those amounts are solicited as if mandatory, but pay whatever you feel is appropriate.

"Drachmas, Doubloons, and Dollars: The History of Money" is the **American Numismatic Society**'s permanent display, housed since 2001 in the **Federal Reserve Bank** (33 Liberty Street, between Nassau and William streets). Those wanting to study coins of a particular period or region should call the society's main offices in northern Manhattan (212/234-3130) to arrange a personal visit.

ASIA SOCIETY
725 Park Ave (at 70th St)   212/288-6400

The Asia Society is a nonprofit organization founded in 1956 in order to foster mutual understanding between Asian nations and the United States. Housed in this recently renovated and expanded building on swanky Park Avenue, the Asia Society is the leading institution in the United States dedicated to fostering an understanding of Asia and the Pacific. The society mounts traditional and contemporary art exhibitions, performances, films, lectures, and conferences to highlight the diversity of this remarkable part of the world. Free tours of the exhibitions are given daily (twice on Friday and Saturday). The galleries are well designed, the atmosphere is peaceful, and there are lots of great spaces for sitting and contemplating. A wonderful gift shop is to the left of the admissions desk. **Hours:** Tuesday through Sunday from 11 to 6 (Friday until 9). **Admission:** $7 for adults, $5 for students and senior citizens, and free to children under 16.

BARD GRADUATE CENTER FOR STUDIES IN THE
DECORATIVE ARTS, DESIGN, AND CULTURE
18 W 86th St (bet Central Park W and Columbus Ave)   212/501-3000

A welcome newcomer to the New York art world, the Bard Graduate

Center devotes three floors of its elegant beaux-arts townhouse to changing exhibitions of decorative arts. As is the case in many smaller museums and galleries in New York, half the pleasure of a visit here is simply being inside the building itself. Call ahead to learn about tours and public lectures. **Hours:** Tuesday through Sunday from 11 to 5 (Thursday until 8). **Admission:** $3 for adults, $2 for students and senior citizens, free for children under 12 accompanied by an adult.

CHILDREN'S MUSEUM OF MANHATTAN
212 W 83rd St (bet Broadway and Amsterdam Ave)   212/721-1234

"CMOM," as the locals call it, has lots of buttons to push, ladders to climb, and things to sort, touch, and examine. There's an early childhood center and play space for children four and under, as well as an imaginative exhibit and WordPlay exploration space. Older preschoolers and kids in early elementary school will appreciate the interactive media center, complete with a professional television studio. Kids five and over will also like the arts and crafts workshops, and everyone will love the daily book readings at 2:30. You know you're headed for a child-friendly place when a ramp instead of stairs leads up to the front entrance, but strollers must be checked at the entrance and food is not allowed in the museum. **Hours:** Wednesday through Sunday from 10 to 5. **Admission:** $6 for adults and children, $3 for senior citizens, free for children under one. Many workshops and performances cost an additional small sum.

THE CLOISTERS
Fort Tryon Park   212/923-3700

Perhaps the finest medieval art museum in the world, The Cloisters is also one of the quietest and most beautiful places in all of Manhattan. Built on land donated by John D. Rockefeller, Jr. in the late 1930s, the museum incorporates large sections of cloisters and other pieces of buildings brought to the United States from southern France by sculptor George Grey Barnard. His collection was purchased by the Metropolitan Museum of Art with money donated for that purpose by Rockefeller in 1925, making The Cloisters a branch of the Metropolitan. The truly spectacular collection also includes carved wood and ivory, tapestries, and sculptures. The museum is quiet, peaceful, and rarely crowded, and its outdoor terrace and medieval gardens offer a great view of the Hudson River and the Palisades. A cafe is open in warmer months. Though it takes about an hour each way, the M4 bus brings you right to the front entrance from Madison Avenue in midtown and back again via Fifth Avenue (the A subway line to 190th Street takes half the time). **Hours:** Tuesday through Sunday from 9:30 to 5:15 (4:45 from November through February). **Admission:** $12 for adults, $7 for students and senior citizens, free for children under 12 when accompanied by an adult. The fee entitles you to same-day admission to the Metropolitan Museum of Art.

COOPER-HEWITT NATIONAL DESIGN MUSEUM/
SMITHSONIAN INSTITUTION
2 E 91st St (bet Fifth and Madison Ave)   212/849-8400

Founded by three granddaughters of Peter Cooper (their last name was Hewitt) as the Cooper Union Museum for the Arts of Decoration just before the turn of the century, this exceptional museum became part of the Smithsonian Institution in 1967 and was moved into Andrew Carnegie's Fifth Avenue mansion in 1976. Drawing from a permanent collection of almost a quarter million pieces involving every imaginable aspect of design, the museum's exhibitions change frequently. Outstanding lectures, workshops, tours, and gallery talks are developed around the exhibitions. They are often free but usually require advance reservations (call 212/849-8389 for more information). Of course, a big part of the pleasure of a visit to the Cooper-Hewitt is seeing the Carnegie Mansion itself, including the spectacular Great Hall (where an organ was once played at 8 a.m. every morning to wake up the household) and Carnegie's personal library (which now houses the gift shop). Take time to look around (and up!), and in warmer months visit the outside garden, behind the reception desk. **Hours:** Tuesday from 10 to 9, Wednesday through Friday from 10 to 5, Saturday from 10 to 6, and Sunday from noon to 6. **Admission:** $5 for adults, $3 for senior citizens and students over 12, free for children under 12 accompanied by an adult and for Smithsonian Associates. It's also free to everybody on Tuesday evening from 5 to 9.

In the years that I've been writing this book, the large gallery space on the first and ground floors of 580 Madison Avenue has been home to the IBM Gallery and the Freedom Forum's Newseum. IBM long ago closed its gallery, and the Newseum moved to the Washington, D.C. area several years ago, but now the space has a new tenant. The **Dahesh Museum of Art** originally opened in a tiny space on Fifth Avenue, where it displayed the wondrous collection of a longtime Lebanese art collector. Soon the Dahesh will reopen in this much larger space, complete with an auditorium, gift shop, and cafe. It promises to become a midtown favorite!

DIA CENTER FOR THE ARTS
548 W 22nd St (bet Tenth and Eleventh Ave)   212/989-5566

This renovated warehouse is the anchor for the burgeoning art scene in Chelsea and an exhibition space for large-scale projects designed specifically for it. Those interested in Minimalism, Conceptualism, and Earth Art know that Dia has been a major force in supporting the careers of many of the world's most innovative contemporary artists. If those schools are your thing, the four floors of this museum and its rooftop will be a real treat. Dia also sponsors lectures, poetry readings, and conferences, as well as several long-term installations. These include the Dan Flavin Art Institute in Bridgehampton, the Cy Twombly Gallery in Houston, and the Andy Warhol Museum in Pittsburgh. A new 300,000-square-foot facility in an old factory up the Hudson River in Beacon, New York, recently opened as well. **Hours:** Wednesday through Sunday from noon to 6. **Admission:** $6 for adults, $3 for students and senior citizens.

DYCKMAN FARMHOUSE MUSEUM
4881 Broadway (at 204th St)   212/304-9422

This is the last surviving example of the sort of farmhouse built all over New York well into the 19th century. It is a real treat for anybody interested in the city's history in the decades following the Revolutionary War. The Dyckman family emigrated to what were then the American colonies from the Netherlands in the 17th century and had a thriving orchard in this area before the Revolutionary War. They were forced to flee during the war, and both their home and orchard were occupied and ultimately destroyed by British troops. When they returned to the area in 1784, the Dyckmans built this remarkable example of a Dutch-American farmhouse and later used the surrounding area for grazing cattle on their way to market downtown. The adjoining outbuildings no longer exist, but the house itself has been preserved. You'll find several rooms with period furniture (some of which actually belonged to the Dyckmans) on the first and second floors and a kitchen in the basement.

Probably the most interesting room in the house is the Relic Room, which houses a display of Revolutionary War artifacts, including a general's uniform, cannonballs, and bayonets. All items on display were excavated at the beginning of this century. The cherry tree and flowers on the lovely grounds surrounding the house come alive during spring and early summer, and you'll find all sorts of seasonal activities throughout the year. You can get to Dyckman House from midtown by taking the A subway line to 207th Street and walking south to 204th Street on Broadway. (It's actually only a block, as there are no 205th and 206th streets.) You can also get there by taking the M1 bus up Madison Avenue to 125th Street and transferring to the M100, which will drop you off at the front door. **Hours:** Wednesday through Sunday from 10 to 4. **Admission:** $1 for adults, free for children under 12.

EL MUSEO DEL BARRIO
1230 Fifth Ave (near 105th St)   212/831-7272

El Museo del Barrio—Spanish for "Museum of the Neighborhood"—is the only museum in New York devoted to the art and culture of Puerto Rico and Latin America. Located at the southern end of Spanish Harlem and the northern tip of Museum Mile, El Museo occupies part of the old Heckscher Building, on the block between 104th and 105th streets. El Museo, a special place devoted to the people and cultures of the surrounding community, gained notoriety for its recent Frida Kahlo exhibit. It routinely features permanent and changing exhibitions of contemporary and traditional art, and sponsors all sorts of festivals, lectures, workshops, and outreach programs. Plans for expansion seem to be on hold at the moment, but this is a thriving, imaginative place. **Hours:** Wednesday through Sunday from 11 to 5. Call for extended summer hours from May through September. **Admission:** free, but they suggest a contribution of $5 for adults, $3 for students with ID and senior citizens, free for children under 12.

ELLIS ISLAND MUSEUM OF AMERICAN IMMIGRATION
Ellis Island   212/363-3200

When you think of immigration to the United States, Ellis Island instantly comes to mind. At least one in every four Americans today can trace one or more relatives who came through the immigration processing center on the island between 1892 and 1954. Whether or not you're one of them, this is a New York "must see" museum. Located in the shadow of the Statue of Liberty in New York Harbor, Ellis Island was all but abandoned until a major portion was restored and opened to the public in 1990 as a National Park. (The restoration of another 30 buildings, including a hospital complex, is now underway.) Walk through the moving display of photographs and artifacts brought to this country by immigrants, and you'll inevitably come across someone telling his children or grandchildren about what his family brought when they came to this country. Other displays include one that retraces the steps the immigrants took once they arrived on the island and another that discusses immigration in the U.S. through the present.

An Academy Award-winning film by the late Charles Guggenheim— *Island of Hope, Island of Tears*—is shown frequently and is well worth watching. To get to Ellis Island, take the Circle Line ferry from Battery Park. The ticket booth is in Castle Clinton, and the ferry makes stops at both Ellis Island and the Statue of Liberty. The best time to go is early in the morning on a weekday, as lines can get pretty long in the afternoon and on weekends due to crowds and security screenings. (For information on ferry sailings, call 212/269-5755.) The least expensive and most efficient way to get to Battery Park is by taking the 1 or 9 subway line to the South Ferry stop (be sure to get in one of the front cars, as only a few doors open at this stop) or the 4 or the 5 to the Bowling Green stop. **Hours:** 9 to 5 in winter and 8:30 to 6:45 in summer, although the last ferry leaves earlier and those times are subject to change. The Museum and the Statue of Liberty are closed on July 4 and December 25. **Admission:** $10 for adults, $8 for senior citizens over 62, and $4 for children 3 to 17. Time permitting, admission to both Ellis Island and the Statue of Liberty is included in the price of a ferry ticket.

EQUITABLE GALLERY
787 Seventh Ave (bet 51st and 52nd St)   212/554-4818

Perhaps the nicest of several gallery spaces in the lobbies of midtown office buildings, this is located in the righthand corner of the Equitable Center's soaring atrium. It includes four interconnected rooms that play host to a variety of consistently well-conceived exhibitions. While you're here, make sure to rest your feet in the unusually pleasant and peaceful sitting area in the building's atrium while looking at Roy Lichtenstein's five-story *Mural with Blue Brushstroke*. **Hours:** Monday through Friday from 11 to 6, Saturday from noon to 5. **Admission:** free.

FORBES MAGAZINE GALLERIES
62 Fifth Ave (bet 12th and 13th St)   212/206-5548

Given the appeal of *The Antiques Roadshow* on PBS, it's amazing there aren't lines out the door of this Greenwich Village gem every day! More than 10,000 toy soldiers and other figurines, 500 toy boats and submarines, a tremendous collection of Monopoly games from as early as 1920, and 400 items from the House of Faberge (including nine eggs) are among the treasures on display in these recently renovated galleries. Everything on display was collected by the late Malcolm Forbes and his sons. It's worth noting that strollers are prohibited, children under 16 are not allowed without an adult, and no more than four children can accompany each adult. **Hours:** Tuesday, Wednesday, Friday, and Saturday from 10 to 4. (Call ahead to make a reservation if you want to join one of the guided tours offered on Thursday or to make sure the museum has not closed for a private luncheon or tour.) **Admission:** free.

FRAUNCES TAVERN MUSEUM
54 Pearl St (at Broad St)   212/425-1778

If you're interested in Colonial and early U.S. history and culture, you'll really enjoy this often overlooked museum. The site of General George Washington's farewell address to his officers in 1783 and an anti-British meeting place before and during the Revolutionary War, this tavern has seen many generations and much history come and go through its doors. The latest renovation brought a new restaurant downstairs, but upstairs you'll still find period rooms (including the room in which General Washington gave his address) with changing exhibitions on all sorts of topics in early American history and culture. Make sure to ask about movies, special events, and walking tours. **Hours:** Tuesday, Wednesday, and Friday from 10 to 5, Thursday from 10 to 7, Saturday from 11 to 5. **Admission:** $3 for adults, $2 for children and senior citizens, and free for children under 6.

FRICK COLLECTION
1 E 70th St (bet Fifth and Madison Ave)   212/288-0700

This exceptionally elegant and peaceful mansion displays the late Henry Clay Frick's collection of paintings, sculpture, rugs, furniture, porcelain, and other artwork. Take time to wander around and look at the building itself —the moldings, the floors, the ceilings, the light fixtures, and the stairs—as well as the art. Built in 1914, this is one of the last great mansions on Fifth Avenue. Unlike the guards at a lot of other museums, the sentinels here are very knowledgeable and obviously proud of the building and the collection. If you ask, they'll even tell you about the giant heat lamps that are brought out every night for the plants and flowers in the inner garden! Because the museum's temperature is kept at a constant 70 degrees, you'll be glad they require that all coats be checked (at no charge). Special exhibitions are often held downstairs, so be sure to ask what's current. Although this is not a place to take children (those under ten are not allowed), this beautiful and uncrowded museum is a real treat for art buffs and oglers alike. A free audio tour of the permanent collection is available in six languages, and a 22-minute slide presentation about the collection runs throughout the day. **Hours:** Tuesday through Saturday from 10 to 6, Sunday from 1 to 6. **Admission:** $12 for adults, $8 for senior citizens, and $5 for students with ID.

HISPANIC SOCIETY OF AMERICA
Audubon Terrace (Broadway bet 155th and 156th St)   212/926-2234

Founded as a public museum and research library in 1904, this little-known place is home to a diverse and impressive collection of art and artifacts from the Iberian Peninsula (Spain and Portugal). The building itself, located directly across from the dramatic El Cid statue in the middle of Audubon Terrace, is beautiful and the collection astonishing. You'll find seals from the Roman Empire, a 15th-century silver processional cross from Barcelona, and paintings by such masters as Goya, Velázquez, and El Greco. Make sure to look at the beautiful tiles and mosaics in the walls on your way up the stairs between floors. You can take the M4 bus up Madison Avenue or the M5 bus up Avenue of the Americas to the museum and then take either back to Fifth Avenue in midtown. You can also take the 1 subway line from the West Side to 157th Street. **Hours:** The museum and library are open Tuesday through Saturday from 10 to 4:30. The museum is also open on Sunday from 1 to 4. The library is closed in August. **Admission:** free.

INTERNATIONAL CENTER OF PHOTOGRAPHY
1133 Ave of the Americas (at 43rd St)   212/857-0000

If you're interested in photography, put the International Center of Photography (ICP) gallery at the top of your list of places to visit. Devoted to displaying photography as both art and historical record, this gallery has changing exhibits of work by photographers from all over the world, as well as photographs drawn from the center's permanent collection. Complete with a new cafe downstairs, this is a pleasant, unhurried spot to spend an afternoon without leaving midtown. **Hours:** Tuesday through Thursday from 10 to 5, Friday from 10 to 8, and Saturday and Sunday from 10 to 6. **Admission:** $10 for adults, $7 for students and senior citizens, $1 for children under 12, and "pay what you wish" for everyone on Friday evening from 5 to 8.

INTREPID SEA-AIR-SPACE MUSEUM
Pier 86 (46th St at Hudson River)   212/245-0072

The water in the Hudson River is not particularly inviting and getting over here can seem like a big production, but the trip is well worth the effort if you're interested in aircraft carriers, submarines, space exploration, and the like. The centerpiece is the giant *U.S.S. Intrepid,* an aircraft carrier that served in both World War II and the Vietnam War. The *U.S.S. Edison* (a destroyer used in Vietnam) and the *U.S.S. Growler* (a guided-missile submarine) are also here. You can either take a self-guided audio tour or wander around by yourself, although the *Growler* and parts of the *Edison* are open only for scheduled guided tours. Galleries, display halls, video screens, and theaters are scattered throughout the complex. Kids will particularly like the two flight simulators (available for a significant extra charge) in the back of the *Intrepid* and in the planes up on the deck.

You won't have much trouble finding the museum, as the *Intrepid* dominates this part of the river. The ticket booth and gift store are inside the main entrance, past the tanks, as is McDonald's. The best way to get to the museum from midtown is the M42 bus on 42nd Street (make sure it says "Piers" on the front). And stay aboard when it turns south on Eleventh Avenue, as it will then loop back around. **Hours:** Daily from 10 to 6 from April 1 to September 30; Tuesday through Sunday from 10 to 5 the rest of the year. The ticket booth closes at 4 (5 in summer), and tours finish at 6. **Admission:** $14 for adults; $10 for veterans, reservists, college students, students between 12 and 17 with ID cards, and senior citizens; $7 for children between 6 and 11; $2 for children under 6. Disabled patrons are admitted at half price, and active-duty military personnel are admitted free of charge.

JEWISH MUSEUM
1109 Fifth Ave (at 92nd St)   212/423-3200

Operated by the Jewish Theological Seminary of America and housed in yet another elegant Fifth Avenue mansion (donated for the purpose by Felix Warburg's widow in 1947), the Jewish Museum displays the largest collection of Jewish art and Judaica in the United States. Some of the museum's collection was rescued from European synagogues and Jewish communities before World War II, and all of it is extremely well displayed. Renovated and expanded a decade ago, the museum has a large permanent exhibit tracing the Jewish experience—called "Culture and Continuity: the Jewish Journey"

—on the third and fourth floors, as well as a variety of changing exhibits. A plaster sculpture by George Segal commemorating the Holocaust is a particularly moving part of the exhibit. It is tucked in a corner at the end and ought not be missed. Families will want to visit the children's gallery and ask about special family programs and workshops. They'll also want to check out the new, interactive audioguide for families, available free with admission. Cafe Weissman, in the museum's basement, is a pleasant place for a light lunch or snack. **Hours:** Sunday through Wednesday from 11 to 5:45, Thursday from 11 to 8, and Friday from 11 to 3. The museum is closed on major Jewish holidays. **Admission:** $10 for adults, $7 for students and senior citizens, free for children under 12, and "pay what you wish" for everyone between 5 and 8 on Thursday evening.

LOWER EAST SIDE TENEMENT MUSEUM
90 Orchard St (at Broome St)   212/431-0233

Founded in 1988, this unique museum is making an enormous contribution to the preservation of American social history and the urban immigrant experience. In the visitors center are permanent and changing exhibits, an oral history video, and a slide show tracing the history of the tenement building across the street at 97 Orchard Street. The really exciting part of this museum, however, is the tenement building. Home to as many as 7,000 people from more than 20 nations between 1863 and 1935, the tenement has had five of its apartments restored to different periods in their history. The most recent addition, the so-called Levine Apartment, shows what life was like in the apartment and dress shop of an 1897 textile worker. Together, these apartments offer a glimpse of life in one of these incredibly crowded places (or what it is like for hundreds of thousands who still live this way).

The museum's docents—who lead two different tours of the tenement Tuesday through Sunday every 40 minutes in the afternoon—are enormously well informed and dedicated. The Confino Program, a living-history tour in which families can interact with an actress portraying a resident of the Confino apartment, is also offered on Saturday and Sunday on the hour from noon to 3. Reservations are strongly encouraged (and required in advance for groups of ten or more). **Hours:** Tuesday through Sunday from 11 to 6 (extended hours in warmer months). **Admission:** $9 for adults, $7 for senior citizens and students, free for children under five. That fee includes admission to an audiovisual history of the site and a tour of the tenement building. Admission to the Confino Program is $8 for adults and $6 for students and senior citizens. Educational walking tours are offered on weekends for an additional charge.

MERCHANT'S HOUSE MUSEUM
20 E 4th St (bet Bowery and Lafayette St)   212/777-1089

Home to a hardware merchant and his family for 100 years, this 1832 rowhouse now offers its visitors a glimpse of life in an age when Greenwich Village was considered the suburbs. The house is filled with the family's original possessions and all the latest "modern" equipment of the period, including pipes for gas lighting. It is the only family home in New York City to survive intact, both inside and out, from the 1830s. The great effort and dedication of staff and volunteers has made that survival possible, and those of us interested in the history of this grand city ought to be deeply grateful. A self-guided tour is available inside the front door, while docent-led tours are available Saturday and Sunday afternoons. **Hours:** Thursday through Monday from 1 to 5. **Admission:** $5 for adults, $3 for students and senior citizens, and free for children under 12. The money goes to support the building's ongoing restoration.

METROPOLITAN MUSEUM OF ART
Fifth Ave (bet 80th and 84th St)   212/535-7710

The Met, as it is known to New Yorkers (not to be confused with the Metropolitan Opera), is one of those places you can visit a hundred times and never see the same thing twice. Whether you're interested in Egyptian tombs, Greek and Roman sculpture, paintings by the great Renaissance masters, African masks, Chinese and Asian art, Tiffany windows, or arms and armor from the Crusades, the Met has a lot worth seeing. Start by picking up a floor plan at one of the information desks in the main hall and mapping out your visit. Make sure to ask for a "Dining Guide" of the museum's five restaurants, bars, and cafes. Although the Met often has extremely popular special exhibits, I sometimes head for places with fewer people in order to wander and gaze at my own pace. If you want to avoid the crowds (almost 5 million people come through every year), the best time to visit is on weekday mornings. (In fact, it gets so crowded on Sundays that strollers are banned altogether, as they are during special exhibitions.) Self-guided audio tours in English and other languages are available at an extra charge.

The Met also sponsors films, lectures, gallery talks, concerts, and other special programs. Call 212/879-5500 for information on gallery and museum tours, as well as upcoming schedules and programs, or pick up a seasonal program at one of the information desks. If you come to New York frequently and like to visit the Met and its gift shops, consider becoming a National Associate. For a small annual fee, people who live outside a 200-mile radius of New York City can get free admission to both the Met and The Cloisters, a 10% discount at the Met's many gift shops, seasonal schedules, and a subscription to the museum's magazine. **Hours:** Sunday, Tuesday, Wednesday, and Thursday from 9:30 to 5:30; Friday and Saturday from 9:30 to 9. **Admission:** $12 for adults, $7 for senior citizens and students, and free for children under 12 when accompanied by an adult. The fee entitles you to same-day admission to The Cloisters.

What Happened to the Morgan Library?

One of my favorite little-known New York treasures, the library built by J. Pierpont Morgan to house his personal collection of art, manuscripts, books, and furniture, closed in May 2003 for a three-year renovation and expansion. It is scheduled to open again in early 2006.

MORRIS-JUMEL MANSION
65 Jumel Terrace (at 160th St, east of St. Nicholas Ave) 212/923-8008

Built in 1765 as a summer house for Colonel Roger Morris and his wife, this graceful Georgian country house sits atop a hill overlooking the East River. It briefly served as General George Washington's headquarters in 1776 and later was home to Madame Eliza Jumel and her second husband, Aaron Burr. (Rumor has it that Madame Jumel's ghost has been spotted yelling at neighborhood children to be quiet from the second floor balcony!) Throughout the house you'll find exceptional period furniture, including a 19th-century French mahogany directoire sleigh bed said to have belonged to Napoleon Bonaparte when he was First Consul of France. The surrounding neighborhood has definitely seen better days, but the mansion itself has been renovated. The grounds are particularly attractive in the spring and early summer. Take the M2 bus up Madison Avenue to the front of the mansion on Edgecombe Avenue, or take the A or C subway line to 163rd Street. **Hours:** Wednesday through Sunday from 10 to 4. **Admission:** $3 for adults, $2 for senior citizens over 60 and students with ID, free for children under 10.

MOUNT VERNON HOTEL MUSEUM & GARDEN
421 E 61st (bet First and York Ave)   212/838-6878

Known until recently as the Abigail Adams Smith Museum, this terrific little time capsule will transport you back to the days when midtown Manhattan was a country escape for New Yorkers living at the southern end of the island. Constructed in 1799 as a carriage house and converted into the Mount Vernon Hotel in 1826, this museum shows what life in the building and in the city was like circa 1830. The staff and volunteer docents are enthusiastic and knowledgeable, and someone is always available to answer questions and point out interesting features of the hotel. If you're interested in social history or antiques, put this well-run and interesting museum at the top of your itinerary. **Hours:** Tuesday through Sunday from 11 to 4 (Tuesday evenings in June and July until 9). The museum is closed in August. **Admission:** $5 for adults, $4 for senior citizens and students, free for children under 12.

MUSEUM AT FIT
Seventh Ave (at 27th St)   212/217-5800

This out-of-the-way exhibit space is located inside the Fashion Institute of Technology (FIT), a highly regarded school for fashion and design. If you're interested in fashion, it's worth seeing their display here. Exhibits change frequently and might seem a bit esoteric to laymen, but they are often quite interesting and always well presented. **Hours:** Tuesday through Friday from noon to 8, Saturday from 10 to 5. **Admission:** free.

While the Museum of Modern Art has gotten all the publicity for its temporary relocation and renovation, another Manhattan-based museum has also made a temporary move to Queens. The **Museum for African Art**—the only independent museum dedicated exclusively to the rich and diverse art of the African continent—has pulled up stakes on its Soho location and is now at 36-01 43rd Avenue, near the temporary MoMA in Long Island City, for the next several years. Be sure to check out the museum's gift shop and its weekend programs. Call 718/784-7700 for hours and directions.

MUSEUM OF AMERICAN FINANCIAL HISTORY
28 Broadway (bet Morris St and Battery Pl)   212/908-4110

Now affiliated with the Smithsonian Institute, this often overlooked gem of a museum offers visitors insight into the financial history of our country. Appropriately housed in the basement of the former site of John D. Rockefeller's Standard Oil Company headquarters (and Alexander Hamilton's law offices before that), it is not exactly a kid-friendly sort of place. But if you're interested in the way our economy works, the Museum of American Financial History is a great place to start your tour around Wall Street. A real highlight: a working ticker-tape machine will actually spit your name out at the end of your visit. Be sure to check out the unusually well-conceived gift shop. **Hours:** Tuesday through Saturday from 10 to 4 (closed on national and stock market holidays). **Admission:** $2 donation requested.

MUSEUM OF AMERICAN ILLUSTRATION
128 E 63rd St (bet Park and Lexington Ave)   212/838-2560

Located on the first floor of the Society of Illustrators' townhouse offices, this gallery houses changing exhibits of advertising, artistic, and other works by professional illustrators. Most of the exhibits center around the society's annual juried competitions for illustrators in a variety of categories. A small museum shop offers books by and for illustrators, exhibition catalogs, and other items. **Hours:** Tuesday 10 to 8, Wednesday through Friday from 10 to 5, Saturday noon to 4. **Admission:** free.

MUSEUM OF ARTS AND DESIGN
40 W 53rd St (bet Fifth Ave and Ave of the Americas)   212/956-3535

This is an exciting, vibrant place with a new name—it was formerly the American Craft Museum—and big plans for a new location as well (a redesigned 2 Columbus Circle). Dedicated to what its director calls "celebrating materials and creative processes," the museum is a showcase for the work of established and emerging designers, artists, and craftspeople. In addition to various changing exhibitions, the museum offers numerous hands-on workshops, public programs, and family classes for members and non-members alike. An expanded store adjacent to the entrance has a marvelous selection of unusual items from a wide assortment of contemporary American craftspeople. **Hours:** daily from 10 to 8 (Thursday until 8). **Admission:** $8 for adults, $5 for students and senior citizens, and free for children under 12.

Oregon Connections

Most New Yorkers likely couldn't place my home state of Oregon on a map if their lives depended on it, but like every other state in the nation, Oregon has made numerous contributions to this great city. Legendary chef James Beard had Oregon roots and brought our Pacific seafood to many of his menus. The 10,000-year-old Willamette meteor—on display in the Hall of the Universe at the Rose Center for Earth and Space—came from Oregon and remains sacred to the Confederated Tribes of the Grande Ronde. An Oregon architect—Brad Cloepfil, of Allied Works Architecture in Portland—has lately been chosen to redesign the Huntington Hartford building on Columbus Circle as a new home for the Museum of Arts and Design.

MUSEUM OF CHINESE IN THE AMERICAS
70 Mulberry St (at Bayard St), 2nd floor   212/619-4785

Designed in the shape of a 15-sided traditional Chinese lantern, this recently opened successor to the Chinatown History Museum is a small but wonderfully interesting place in the heart of Chinatown. Its stated mission is to reclaim, preserve, and broaden the understanding of the incredibly diverse story of Chinese people in the Americas. The museum's fascinating permanent exhibit—"Where Is Home? Chinese in the Americas"—combines the extraordinary with the ordinary to give visitors a glimpse into that story. If you're visiting Chinatown, this museum offers some perspective on the world bustling around you on the streets below. **Hours:** Tuesday through Sunday from noon to 5. **Admission:** $3 for adults, $1 for senior citizens and students, free for children under 12.

MUSEUM OF THE CITY OF NEW YORK
1220 Fifth Ave (bet 103rd and 104th St)   212/534-1672

This grande dame was dealt a serious blow in 2002 when Mayor Michael Bloomberg decided to install the Board of Education in the recently reno-vated Tweed Courthouse instead of making it this museum's new home. But don't let its location deter you! Overlooked by tourists and New Yorkers alike, this treasure is dedicated to the history of the city from the earliest European settlement through the present, and it offers something for just about every-one. Permanent exhibits include period rooms, an exquisite silver collection, toys and dollhouses, a firefighting gallery, an enormous number of model ships, and an exhibit on Broadway. The actual bedroom and dressing rooms from the home of John D. Rockefeller, Sr., on the museum's fifth floor, are truly breathtaking sights for anyone who likes antiques. Changing exhibits cover everything from the history of theater in New York to the city's differ-ent ethnic groups. The museum also offers an exceptionally diverse array of walking tours, children's programs, lectures, classes, and other events. Call the number listed above for more information, or pick up a seasonal sched-ule at the information desk right inside the entrance. **Hours:** Wednesday through Saturday from 10 to 5, Sunday from noon to 5. **Admission:** Sug-gested contributions of $7 for adults, $4 for senior citizens, students, and chil-dren, and $12 for families are strongly encouraged.

MUSEUM OF JEWISH HERITAGE: A LIVING MEMORIAL TO THE HOLOCAUST
18 First Pl (adjacent to Battery Park)   212/968-1800

A newcomer to the New York museum scene, this exceptional place fills a real void in the city. In addition to being a museum (and, when a $60 mil-lion expansion is completed, a classroom and theater space as well), it is also a memorial to Holocaust victims and survivors. New York is, after all, the heart of Jewish history and culture in the United States, and it is fitting that such a thoughtfully conceived and carefully constructed museum has its home here. The museum is composed of three parts, one on each floor. The first floor is dedicated to Jewish life a century ago, the second to the persecution of Jews and the Holocaust, and the third to modern Jewish life and renewal. A well-done eight-minute video sets the tone for your visit. This may not be a place for young children, and visitors should be prepared to take their time.

Two additional notes: the view of New York Harbor, Ellis Island, and the Statue of Liberty from the museum's third floor is extraordinary, and a visit to the gift shop is worthwhile. Security is very tight, and the rule against food in the galleries is strictly enforced. The museum was designed in the shape of a hexagon to memorialize the six-pointed Star of David and commemorate the 6 million Jews killed in the Holocaust. You'll recognize it immediately from its shape and the black gate surrounding the site, adjacent to Robert

Wagner, Jr. Park at the southern end of Battery Park City. **Hours:** Sunday through Wednesday from 10 to 5, Thursday from 10 to 8, and Friday from 9 to 3 (until 5 during Daylight Savings Time). The museum closes early on the eve of Jewish holidays and is closed on all major Jewish holidays. **Admission:** $7 for adults, $5 for students and senior citizens. Advance tickets can be purchased by calling 212/945-0039.

Where is MoMA?

The **Museum of Modern Art** (MoMA) has moved temporarily out to Queens while its 53rd Street home undergoes extensive renovations. As a result, the city's art lovers have been beating a path to **MoMA QNS**, in the former Swingline staple factory in Long Island City. It really isn't hard to find: take the 7 subway from Times Square to 33rd Street and Queens Boulevard or catch the Artlink bus, a free weekend shuttle. (Call 212/708-9750 for schedule information.) While you're out there, you might stop by the temporarily relocated **Museum for African Art** (36-01 43rd Avenue, 718/784-7700) as well. By the way, MoMA is scheduled to reopen in Manhattan in 2005.

THE MUSEUM OF SEX
233 Fifth Ave (at 27th St)   866/667-3969

I agonized about whether to include this newcomer in the otherwise dignified list of museums in this chapter, particularly because it is the single most expensive museum in Manhattan. The entire affair (excuse the pun) is a bit tawdry, and the museum seems to exist on a shoestring. But crowds are streaming to the place and its first exhibit at least tried very earnestly to take itself seriously. So if you aren't shy about what really can only be described as at least softcore pornography, you may want to visit this two-floor museum just south of midtown. The free audiophone is worth using. Be forewarned that nobody under 18 is allowed in the museum. **Hours:** Monday, Tuesday, Thursday, and Friday from 11 to 6:30, Saturday from 10 to 9, and Sunday from 10 to 6:30. **Admission:** $17 for adults, $14 for students and seniors, and $12 for everyone on weekdays before 2.

MUSEUM OF TELEVISION AND RADIO
25 W 52nd St (bet Fifth Ave and Ave of the Americas) 212/621-6800

Television fans of all ages will definitely not want to miss this terrific place. Several galleries display changing exhibits on every imaginable aspect of television and radio, but the real reason to come here is to watch a favorite television show. The museum's extensive collection includes 110,000 radio and television programs and advertisements, many of which are periodically screened for the public and all of which are available for individual viewing. Indeed, the museum's computerized catalog makes more than six decades of radio and television shows immediately accessible. Give the museum a call to find out what's going on or stop by the front desk to reserve your own screening. I suggest going on a weekday, as the museum gets crowded on weekends. **Hours:** Tuesday through Sunday from noon to 6 (Thursday until 8). The theater stays open on Friday until 9. **Admission:** $10 for adults, $8 for students with ID and senior citizens, $3 for children under 14.

NATIONAL ACADEMY OF DESIGN
1083 Fifth Ave (bet 89th and 90th St)   212/369-4880

Founded in 1825, this museum, fine-arts school, and artists' association was modeled after the Royal Academy in London. In addition to workshops and classes for artists, the National Academy of Design has changing exhibits of American and European paintings and other art. During the academy's "annual exhibition," some pieces are actually put up for sale. The museum occupies a surprisingly large townhouse, and wandering its three floors of galleries is a real pleasure. Winslow Homer, Thomas Eakins, and John Singer Sargent are just a few artists who have been members of the academy and whose work is part of its permanent collection. A small museum shop featuring work by artist members sits inside the museum's lobby. For information on lectures and other programs, call 212/369-4880 or pick up a seasonal schedule at the museum's information desk in the lobby. For information about the school itself, call 212/996-1908. **Hours:** Wednesday and Thursday from noon to 5, Friday through Sunday from 11 to 6. **Admission:** $8 for adults, $4.50 for students, children under 16 and senior citizens.

NATIONAL MUSEUM OF THE AMERICAN INDIAN
1 Bowling Green (at the foot of Broadway)   212/514-3700

Opened in 1994, the George Gustav Heye Center here at the southern tip of Manhattan hosts the National Museum of the American Indian. It replaced the old Museum of the American Indian on Audubon Terrace and is the first of what will soon be three museums showcasing the Smithsonian's enormous collection of North, Central, and South American Indian art and artifacts. Construction of what will be the crown jewel of this trio is well underway on the National Mall in Washington, D.C. The changing exhibits are consistently well conceived and interesting. The spectacular building—the former Customs House—is worth visiting in and of itself. Take time to look up at the intricate detail in the ceilings, especially in the rotunda and library, and make sure to go down the exquisite (if a bit worn) staircase. Also be sure to visit at least one of the museum's two gift shops. **Hours:** daily (except Christmas) from 10 to 5 (Thursday until 8). **Admission:** free.

NEUE GALERIE
1048 Fifth Ave (at 86th St)   212/628-6200

It isn't every day that a new museum opens in the heart of Fifth Avenue's Museum Mile, but then Ronald Lauder—the man responsible for bringing this boutique museum to life—isn't your ordinary art collector. Lauder is the former U.S. Ambassador to Austria and current chairman of Estee Lauder International. He and the late Serge Sabarsky—a longtime New York art dealer and namesake of the museum's popular Viennese cafe—shared a love of early 20th-century German and Austrian art. The museum is a reflection of that love, showcasing fine and decorative works in its two floors of gallery space. As with many museums in this part of New York, one of the pleasures of a visit is the turn-of-the-century mansion in which it is housed. Note that the museum is closed Tuesday through Thursday, although the cafe and shops are open. **Hours:** Friday from 11 to 9, Saturday through Monday from 11 to 6. **Admission:** $7 for adults, $5 for students and seniors. Children under 16 must be accompanied by an adult, and children under 12 are not admitted.

NEW MUSEUM OF CONTEMPORARY ART
583 Broadway (bet Houston and Prince St)   212/219-1222

This showcase for contemporary artists is worth a visit if you're in Soho. Its changing exhibits feature individual artists and thematic collections, which tend to be well displayed and conceived. The museum is known for its multi-disciplinary approach to art, focusing on group and solo shows accompanied by educational public programs. The museum, which recently announced plans to create a new 60,000-square-foot facility at 235 Bowery, offers gallery talks and group tours tailored to the age and interests of participants. **Hours:** Tuesday through Sunday from noon to 6 (Thursday until 8). **Admission:** $6 for adults, $3 for students and senior citizens, and free for those under 18 and for everyone on Thursday evening from 6 to 8.

NEW YORK CITY FIRE MUSEUM
278 Spring St (bet Hudson and Varick St)   212/691-1303

This museum, located in a turn-of-the-century firehouse, is dedicated to the history of firefighting and fire prevention. In addition to a relatively modern fire engine, a quite old ladder truck, a hand-pulled hand pump from 1820, and many other fire apparatuses, the museum displays pictures from fire stations all over New York, a collection of 19th-century leather fire buckets, and an assortment of badges. The darkest hour in the New York City Fire Department's history—the terrorist attacks of September 11, 2001—is also remembered with an exhibition and a memorial to those brave fallen heroes who saved so many lives on that dreadful day. Older kids will love looking at the equipment, and most things are quite well displayed. Although the museum hopes to create a climbing and "hands-on" exploring space for younger children in the future, "hands-off" is the rule now. The museum is a bit out of the way, although less so since Soho has become a major tourist destination. Call ahead to make sure your visit won't coincide with that of a large school group. **Hours:** Tuesday through Saturday from 10 to 5, Sunday from 10 to 4. **Admission:** Suggested contribution of $5 for adults, $2 for students and senior citizens, and $1 for children under 12.

NEW YORK CITY POLICE MUSEUM
100 Old Slip (bet Water and State St)   212/480-3100

Almost a century ago, this beautiful building just off the East River was built for the New York City Police Department's 1st Precinct. Now, 30 years after the precinct moved out from under a cloud of scandal, the NYPD has come back home with this excellent museum. Permanent exhibits include century-old mug shots; notorious criminals and the tools of their trade; police vehicles and uniforms; and a tribute to every NYPD officer killed in the line of duty throughout the city's history, including those who perished on September 11, 2001. Regular Saturday programs allow children to meet and interact with police officers and various NYPD units. The Firearms Training Simulator on the top floor allows visitors to test their judgment and response time in life-and-death situations through an interactive exhibit also used to train NYPD officers. And don't miss everyone's favorite photo op: the jail cell, complete with bunks and a latrine. The museum's two-level gift shop, located on the east end of the first floor, is the only source in New York for officially licensed NYPD merchandise. **Hours:** Tuesday through Sunday from 10 to 5. **Admission:** a donation is suggested.

NEW-YORK HISTORICAL SOCIETY
2 W 77th St (at Central Park West)   212/873-3400

For two centuries, the New-York Historical Society has been what the *New York Times* once described as "New York City's archive and attic." The grand old institution is a real treasure trove, with more than half a million books; 2 million maps, manuscripts, and other documents; thousands of pieces of art; and John James Audubon's watercolor "Birds of America" series. While I'm a big fan of the Museum of the City of New York and encourage anyone interested in New York's history to spend time there, the New-York Historical Society also has tremendously deep archives and mounts a wide array of interesting exhibits in its grand and recently renovated space. The Luman Reed Gallery (complete with Thomas Cole's *The Course of the Empire* and many of Audubon's works) and the library (open to those 18 and older) are great treats, as are the jam-packed display cases in the remarkable Henry Luce III Center for the Study of American Culture on the museum's fourth floor. Ric Burns' documentary on New York, which the Historical Society co-produced, is screened here daily, as are three films related to the September 11, 2001, terrorist attacks on the World Trade Center. **Hours:** Tuesday and Thursday through Sunday from 10 to 6 and Wednesday from 10 to 9 (the library is open from 10 to 5 but closed on Sunday). **Admission:** Suggested donation of $6 for adults and $4 for senior citizens and children.

The **New York Transit Museum** has a small gallery and shop tucked behind the Grand Staircase in the Shuttle Passage of Grand Central Station. If you're a subway or train buff, a trip here can be great fun. It's open on weekdays from 8 to 8 and on weekends from 10 to 4. If that piques your interest, hop on a 2, 3, 4, or 5 subway line to Borough Hall Station in Brooklyn and visit the newly renovated main museum (Boerum Place at Schermerhorn Street). Call 718/243-8601 for more information.

NEW YORK UNEARTHED
17 State St (opposite Battery Park)   212/748-8628

The word *archeology* conjures up visions of Egyptian deserts or Central American rain forests, but a great deal of archeology is done right in New York City. At this tiny and often overlooked branch of the South Street Seaport Museum, New York Unearthed offers glimpses into the city's history with displays of artifacts dug up in the area. They include imported ceramics from the 1760s, items from a silversmith's home and shop on Wall Street circa 1790, things thrown down the privy of a Sullivan Street tenement in the late 19th century, and even a plate and cup from a 1950s lunch counter. Downstairs you'll find a laboratory where archeologists work on new pieces, a tremendous picture of the ways in which the East River waterfront has changed, and a provocative display of what might be unearthed from contemporary New York one day in the future. To reach the museum, head up Pearl Street from the northeastern side of Battery Park. **Hours:** Monday through Friday from noon to 5, mornings by appointment. **Admission:** free.

NICHOLAS ROERICH MUSEUM
319 W 107th St (just off Riverside Dr)   212/864-7752

Located in an aged but still elegant townhouse on an unusually pleasant block between Riverside Drive and Broadway, this museum is dedicated to the life and work of Russian-born artist-philosopher-author-educator Nicholas Roerich. History buffs may remember him as author of the Roerich Pact, a 1935 agreement signed by President Franklin Roosevelt and the leaders of 20 Latin American countries stipulating that a banner be flown over museums, monuments, and other cultural institutions in war and peace alike, declaring them to be protected, neutral territory. You'll find a number of books written by and about Roerich in several languages, but the real reason to come to this museum is the large collection of unusual paintings of the Himalayas, various religious scenes, and other subjects by Roerich. The displays are quite informal, but it's a pleasant place that's off the beaten track. Seasonal schedules of poetry readings, concerts, and other events are available in the front hall, as are postcard reproductions of Roerich's paintings. **Hours:** Tuesday through Sunday from 2 to 5. **Admission:** free.

PAINEWEBBER GALLERY
1285 Ave of the Americas (bet 51st and 52nd St)   212/713-2885

The folks at PaineWebber have set aside the east end of their wood-paneled lobby for a variety of changing exhibits. Much like those at the gallery in the Equitable Center's lobby, the exhibits here are often high quality. Look for printed exhibit information on either side of the lobby immediately inside the entrance. **Hours:** Monday through Friday from 8 to 6. **Admission:** free.

ROSE MUSEUM
Weill Recital Hall entrance of Carnegie Hall
154 W 57th St (just off Seventh Ave)   212/247-7800

Actually just a handsome, wood-paneled room with well-lit display cases, this small museum is home to a permanent exhibit on the history of Carnegie Hall and the people who have made their careers here. In addition, a temporary exhibit coinciding with a special event or anniversary changes annually. The museum, located on the second floor of Carnegie Hall, is open to ticket-holders one hour before performances and during intermissions, and it's also accessible to the general public during the day. **Hours:** weekdays (except Wednesday) from 11 to 4:30. **Admission:** free.

SCANDINAVIA HOUSE GALLERIES
58 Park Ave (near 38th St)   212/879-9779

The charming Scandinavia House, on Park Avenue just south of Grand Central Station, is home to several small galleries with changing exhibitions from or related to the five Scandinavian countries. You'll also find a beautiful gift shop and AQ Cafe on the first floor, as well as a terrific children's room on the fourth floor that, unfortunately, is open only on Friday and Saturday to the general public (Tuesday through Thursday to members). **Hours:** Tuesday through Saturday from noon to 6. **Admission:** suggested contribution of $3 for adults, $2 for students and senior citizens.

SOLOMON R. GUGGENHEIM MUSEUM
1071 Fifth Ave (bet 88th and 89th St)   212/423-3500

Housed in an enormous white spiral designed by Frank Lloyd Wright, the Solomon R. Guggenheim Museum is as famous for its building as for its collection. That is saying a lot, given a collection of 20th-century art that is arguably the best in the world: Chagall, Miro, Calder, Kandinsky, Picasso, and Gauguin are just a few of the artists whose work you'll come across. Special exhibits featuring world-renowned collections and artists are mounted regularly and gallery talks and other special events are held here. Unfortunately, the Guggenheim has fallen on financial hard times, forcing the closure of its branches in Soho and Las Vegas, as well as cancellation of plans to build a soaring new space on the East River. **Hours:** Saturday through Wednesday from 10 to 5:45, Saturday from 10 to 8. **Admission:** $12 for adults, $8 for senior citizens over 65 and students with ID. Children under 12 are admitted free but must be accompanied by an adult. Admission on Friday between 6 and 8 is "pay what you wish."

Think of New York, and one of the first images that comes to mind is the skyline and its many skyscrapers. New York doesn't have the tallest building anymore. It may not even have the most tall buildings of any city. But this is where skyscrapers were born, and it's only fitting that the city is home to a museum dedicated to the subject. The **Skyscraper Museum** has bounced around several times since its inception in 1996, but, rather ironically, it now has a home on the *ground floor* of the Ritz-Carlton New York Hotel in Battery Park City, across the street from the Museum of Jewish Heritage. Call 212/968-1961 for more information.

SOUTH STREET SEAPORT MUSEUM
209 Water St (at east end of Fulton St)   212/732-7678

This is not a museum in the traditional sense but rather a collection of exhibits, ships, stores, and restaurants spread throughout 11 square blocks of what was once the city's bustling port and economic center. You can walk around the South Street Seaport complex and look at everything from a distance without paying a dime, but admission to the museum includes the four-masted *Peking*, a light ship called the *Ambrose,* a tall ship called the *Wavertree* (which is being restored), several galleries with changing exhibitions, a printer's shop, and a children's center with hands-on workshops and displays. These places are worth the price of admission, particularly since your money supports educational outreach, historical research and preservation, and urban archaeological programs. Stop by the visitors center just inside the entrance or the ticket booth on Pier 16 to get a map and more information. On any given day (particularly in warmer months), you'll find all sorts of special tours and activities throughout this fascinating complex. **Hours:** daily from 10 to 6 (Thursday until 8) between April 1 and September 30; daily (except Tuesday) from 10 to 5 between October 1 and March 31. Restaurants and some stores stay open longer in summer. **Admission:** $5 for adults, and free for children under 12.

STUDIO MUSEUM IN HARLEM
144 W 125th St (bet Malcolm X and Adam Clayton Powell, Jr. Blvd)
212/864-4500

This light and modern space is a real jewel. The name reflects its original mission to be a studio for working artists. It has evolved into a premier museum of visual art, exhibiting the work of local, national, and international artists of African descent. Renovations and expansions have made the museum's presence on 125th Street in the heart of Harlem even stronger. The museum mounts exhibits from its permanent collection and plays host to traveling ones. It also offers lectures, gallery talks, performances, and other interpretive programs throughout the year. To get to the museum from midtown, take the M101 bus up Third Avenue to the corner of 125th Street and Malcolm X Boulevard. To return, board the M101 bus downtown from the opposite corner. You can also take a number of subway lines to 125th Street, although all require a brief walk to the museum. **Hours:** Sunday and Wednesday through Friday from noon to 6, Saturday from 10 to 6. **Admission:** suggested donation of $7 for adults, $3 for students and senior citizens with identification, and free to children under 12 and everyone on the first Saturday of every month.

THEODORE ROOSEVELT BIRTHPLACE
28 E 20th St (bet Broadway and Park Ave)   212/260-1616

Tucked on a side street in a neighborhood often overlooked by New Yorkers and visitors alike (although the street was once among the city's most elegant), this wonderful brownstone is a reconstruction of Theodore Roosevelt's childhood home. The original building was torn down in 1916 but rebuilt by the President's sisters and wife using original blueprints and the house next door as a model. The rooms were then furnished and decorated largely as they had been in Teddy's childhood. Operated as a National Historic Site, the home is entered through the servants' entrance on the ground floor. Visitors browse a collection of pictures, clothing, and other items that belonged to the Roosevelt family in a wonderful wood-paneled room, then are taken through the living quarters on the second and third floors by a National Park Service guide. If you're interested in presidential history and the late 19th and early 20th centuries, or if you want to see how the wealthy lived in the 1850s and 1860s, put this museum on your itinerary. **Hours:** Monday through Friday from 9 to 5 (tours begin on the hour until 4). Special concerts are often held on Sundays at 2. **Admission:** Tours cost $3 for adults and senior citizens, free for children under 18.

UKRAINIAN MUSEUM
203 Second Ave (bet 12th and 13th St)   212/228-0110

Founded by the Ukrainian National Women's League of America in 1976 and housed in the top two floors of a townhouse on the northern edge of the East Village, this out-of-the-way place is a real find for anybody interested in the Ukraine and the heritage of its people. The best time to visit is roughly the two-month period around Easter, when the museum displays its extraordi-nary collection of *pysanky,* the elaborately decorated Ukrainian Easter eggs that were once used as talismans to ward off evil spirits. Pysanky workshops and demonstrations occur during this period. The educational program includes Ukrainian folk craft courses and workshops, which are offered throughout the year. You'll find Ukrainian costumes and folk craft objects on permanent exhibit. Changing exhibitions are mounted from the museum's fine arts and documentary collections or from loans. A small gift shop is located on the fifth floor. **Hours:** Wednesday through Sunday from 1 to 5. **Admission:** $3 for adults, $2 for senior citizens and students, free for children under 12.

WHITNEY MUSEUM OF AMERICAN ART
945 Madison Ave (at 75th St)   212/570-3676

This museum has a decidedly modern focus, although the Whitney's collection includes works by American artists from throughout this country's history. Several exhibits run concurrently, some focusing on a single artist and others built around a theme. If you're interested in gallery talks, special events, or what's on display at any given time, pick up a *This Week at the Whitney* schedule outside the museum's main entrance or drop by the information desk inside the front door. Also look here for some innovative family programs. A branch of Sarabeth's Kitchen, long a popular East Side restaurant, is located on the museum's lower level. If you want a brief retreat from the crowds, find one of the comfortable benches in the museum's stairwells. **Hours:** Tuesday, Wednesday, Thursday, Saturday, and Sunday from 11 to 6, Friday from 1 to 9. **Admission:** $12 for adults, $9.50 for students with ID and senior citizens over 62, free for children under 12 and free for everybody on Friday evening from 6 to 9.

The small **Whitney Gallery and Sculpture Court at Altria** is located in the lobby of 120 Park Avenue, directly across 42nd Street from Grand Central Station. The gallery is open weekdays from 11 to 6 (until 7:30 on Thursday), and admission is free. The sculpture court, which doubles as a pleasant sitting area, is open Monday through Saturday from 7:30 a.m. to 9:30 p.m., Sunday from 11 to 7. Call 917/663-2453 for more information.

Grand Central Station, the **Hayden Planetarium**, and the **Millstein Hall of Ocean Life** at the American Museum of Natural History, and many of the city's parks are just a few of the places around town that have had dramatic facelifts. However, the work has just begun. Renovations and expansions are underway or planned at the **Museum of Modern Art**, the **Museum of Jewish Heritage, the Morgan Library**, and the **Museum of Arts and Design**. A new **Staten Island Ferry** terminal is being built, as is a new home for **Jazz at Lincoln Center**, and a **National Jazz Museum** in Harlem. Part of the **Farley Post Office** is being converted into shops and a new home for Amtrak. Plans are in the works for the **Rubin Museum of Art** at the old Barney's store in Chelsea. Even the **United Nations** is due for a facelift! Not everything is rosy, however. Plans to give the **Museum of the City of New York** a new home in the Tweed Courthouse were shelved when Mayor Bloomberg came into office. Financial troubles at the **Guggenheim** forced the museum to close its Soho branch and cancel plans for an East River location. The **Whitney** recently cancelled a planned expansion as well.

YESHIVA UNIVERSITY MUSEUM
15 W 16th St (bet Fifth Ave and Ave of the Americas)   212/294-8330

The Yeshiva University Museum has moved from the far reaches of Manhattan to the Center for Jewish History, just north of Greenwich Village. It houses an exceptional collection of paintings, books, religious artifacts, and other items related to Jewish life and culture. The museum mounts changing exhibitions in this beautiful and peaceful space. Look for special holiday events and workshops for adults, children, and families, as well as guided tours and gallery talks. **Hours:** Sunday, Tuesday, Wednesday and Thursday from 11 to 5. The museum is closed on major Jewish holidays. **Admission:** $6 for adults, $4 for children and senior citizens, and free for children under 5.

Places of Worship

Manhattan is home to some of the oldest, largest, and most famous churches and synagogues in the United States. These places, many of which are Episcopal churches—a relic of the city's life under British colonial rule—are integral to the social and architectural history of the city. Many of them allow people to come in and look around. Remember that you are in a place of worship and should always behave respectfully. Here are some of my favorites.

ABYSSINIAN BAPTIST CHURCH
132 W 138th St (bet Frederick Douglass and
Adam Clayton Powell, Jr. Blvd)   212/862-7474

This church is one of the oldest in Harlem, and is home to one of the city's largest congregations. It was made famous by the late Adam Clayton Powell, Jr., its longtime minister and a U.S. congressman.

CATHEDRAL CHURCH OF ST. JOHN THE DIVINE
Amsterdam Ave at 112th St   212/316-7540

This magnificent Episcopal cathedral has been under construction for more than a century and will be among the largest Christian houses of worship in the world when (and if) it is completed sometime in this new century. The stonework, art, and stained glass are exceptional, as is the combination of Gothic, Romanesque, and Byzantine architectural styles. Even if you are not particularly interested in cathedrals, architecture, or religion, this somewhat out-of-the-way marvel is a must-see. To give you some sense of its scale, the Statue of Liberty could fit comfortably inside the main sanctuary. The rose window over the entrance is 40 feet in diameter! The Cathedral Shop, in what will one day be the north transcept, has an eclectic assortment of books and gifts.

CENTRAL SYNAGOGUE
Lexington Ave at 55th St   212/838-5122

This reform synagogue is the oldest continuously used synagogue in the city. Completed in 1872, it was designed by Henry Fernbach and is a rare example of early Victorian religious architecture. The beautiful Moorish Revival exterior, complete with magnificent carved wooden doors and jaw-dropping tile work, is well worth a look. A fire in 1998 did extensive damage, but the congregation wasted no time rebuilding this gem while adding one of the city's most impressive organs.

CHURCH OF THE HOLY TRINITY
316 E 88th St (bet First and Second Ave)   212/289-4100

Near Gracie Mansion, this Episcopal church is a French Gothic marvel that dates back a hundred years. It's a favorite of classical music lovers because of its frequent winter concerts.

CHURCH OF THE TRANSFIGURATION
E 29th St (bet Fifth and Madison Ave)   212/684-6770

Known to older generations as "the little church around the corner," this Episcopal church is known to younger generations for its marvelous programs of the music of Vivaldi and other composers throughout the year. You'll find a lovely garden in front of this low-lying brick church and beautiful stained-glass windows inside.

FIRST PRESBYTERIAN CHURCH
12 W 12th St (at Fifth Ave)   212/675-6150

The direct decendant of the first Presbyterian congregation in the United States, this church was built in 1846 (the original church was on Wall Street). The sanctuary has wooden pews with doors, a beautifully carved wooden pulpit that towers over the congregation, and a glorious blue rose window.

GRACE CHURCH
802 Broadway (bet 10th and 11st St)   212/254-2000

Built in 1846, this exquisite Episcopal church is one of several in New York designed by James Renwick, Jr. It is an elegant Gothic presence in the neighborhood and one of the most important examples of early Gothic Revival architecture in the country. The church is best known for its daily prayer services, carved pulpit, and outstanding music.

HOLY TRINITY GREEK ORTHODOX CATHEDRAL
337 E 74th St (bet First and Second Ave)   212/288-3215

This magnificent brick cathedral may not look like much from the outside, but you'll think you're in ancient Greece once you go through the lovely wooden doors.

ISLAMIC CENTER OF NEW YORK
Third Ave (bet 96th and 97th St)   212/722-5234

Opened in 1991, this sleek mosque and its grounds are hard to miss. The mosque dominates the skyline here. A gift to New York's Muslim community from several Islamic countries, it was built at an angle so that it faces Mecca.

MARBLE COLLEGIATE CHURCH
Fifth Ave at 29th St   212/686-2770

This stately church was designed by Samuel Warner in 1854 and made famous by Dr. Norman Vincent Peale. It is an example of Early Romanesque Revival, and it draws its name from the Tuckahoe marble used in its construction. Its congregation is large and socially active.

RIVERSIDE CHURCH
490 Riverside Dr (bet 120th and 122nd St)   212/870-6700

A gift of John D. Rockefeller, Jr., this interdenominational church was inspired by the famous Chartres Cathedral in France and can seat up to 2,500 people. Its 22-story bell tower dominates the northern end of Morningside Heights, and the 74-bell carillon can be heard throughout the area. From long before the civil rights movement and the Vietnam War up to the present, this church has been a center of social activism.

ST. BARTHOLEMEW'S CHURCH
Park Ave (bet 50th and 51st St)   212/751-1616

Complete with a carved triple-arched portico (designed by architect Stanford White) and a mosaic dome, this brick and stone Episcopal church is a midtown landmark. It has a reasonably priced (by midtown standards) cafe open for lunch on weekdays.

If you want to find out when services are held at churches, synagogues, and other places of worship, the first section of the Saturday *New York Times* includes advertisements for Catholic, Protestant, Ethical Culture, Hindu, and Jewish services under the heading "Religious Services." The Manhattan Yellow Pages' extensive listings can be found under the headings "Churches," "Synagogues," and "Religious Organizations."

ST. MARK'S IN THE BOWERY
E 10th St at Second Ave   212/674-6377

Constructed on the site of Peter Stuyvesant's personal chapel in 1799, this understated but elegant Episcopal church has lovely yards on either side. It is now the East Village but was once Stuyvesant's farm or "Bouwerie" (Dutch for farm). Call 212/674-6377 for information about services.

ST. PATRICK'S CATHEDRAL
Fifth Ave (bet 50th and 51st St)   212/753-2261

Designed by James Renwick, Jr., more than a century ago, this astonishing building is the largest Roman Catholic church in the United States and the seat of the archdiocese of New York. The main organ has 9,000 pipes! The cathedral's steps along Fifth Avenue are a great place to rest your feet and watch the world go by.

ST. PAUL'S CHAPEL
Broadway (bet Fulton and Vesey St)   212/602-0874

As the dates on the gravestones in the surrounding cemetery might suggest, this Episcopal parish is housed in the oldest church building in the city. Its construction began in 1764 when New York was New Amsterdam and America was a British colony. Though the interior may initially strike visitors as surprisingly plain, it is exceptionally elegant, understated, and lit by Waterford crystal chandeliers. Look for George Washington's pew in the north aisle. It's also known for the physical, emotional, and spiritual sanctuary offered to people in the immediate aftermath of the September 11, 2001 terrorist attacks and still does today.

St. Paul's Chapel was a gathering place for thousands fleeing the destruction of the World Trade Center on September 11, 2001, a safe haven for rescue and clean-up workers. Today, in many ways, it is a living memorial to victims and survivors. An exhibit inside the church, "Out of the Dust: A Year of Ministry at Ground Zero," offers glimpses into the physical and psychological devastation of that terrible day and those that followed. The exhibit is open Monday through Saturday from 10 to 6 and on Sunday from 10 to 4. Admission is free.

ST. PETER'S LUTHERAN CHURCH
E 54th St at Lexington Ave   212/935-2200

The only really modern church on this list, St. Peter's is nestled under the towering Citicorp Center. The church has an extensive program of jazz, opera, and other music on Sunday and during the week.

ST. THOMAS EPISCOPAL CHURCH
Fifth Ave at 53rd St   212/757-7013

This beautiful church is best known for its magnificent music programs. The heart of these is the St. Thomas Choristers, who attend the country's only residential all-boy chorister school. They perform at many of the church's services. The incredibly ornate stone carvings on the church's exterior, its lovely doors and stately bell tower make it a real presence on Fifth Avenue.

SPANISH AND PORTUGUESE SYNAGOGUE
8 W 70th St (at Central Park W)   212/873-0300

Home of the orthodox Congregation Shearith Israel, founded in 1654 by descendants of Jews who fled the Spanish Inquisition, this synagogue was built in 1897. It contains remnants from its congregation's original synagogue, built on the Lower East Side in 1730. The Tiffany stained-glass windows are particularly impressive.

TEMPLE EMANU-EL
1 E 65th Street (at Fifth Ave)   212/744-1400

Built in 1929 and capable of seating 2,500 people, this is the largest Reform synagogue in the world. Stained-glass windows and mosaics grace the interior, and the limestone facade is a beautifully carved combination of Eastern and Western architectural styles. While the entrance is on East 65th Street, be sure to look at the doors on Fifth Avenue.

TRINITY CHURCH
Broadway at Wall St   212/602-0800

In the heart of the Financial District, this is the third Episcopal church to occupy a site on land donated by King William III of England in 1698. This building was completed in 1846, although the oldest headstones in its 2.5-acre graveyard date back to 1681. Alexander Hamilton is among the many historic figures buried here. Believe it or not, Trinity Church was the tallest building in Manhattan for much of the 19th century. The church offers a small museum, guided tours, and concerts, in addition to daily services.

Sights and Other Places Worth a Look

Some of the places that make New York unique don't fit neatly into "Museums," "Places of Worship," or any of the other categories included in this book. Many can be visited without a guide or a formal agenda—indeed, simply walking around and gazing is pleasurable. A diverse lot, the following list includes some of the most famous, interesting, and unusual sights and places in Manhattan. Unless otherwise noted, admission is free.

AFRICAN BURIAL GROUND
Foley Square Park (just north of City Hall)

A four-story black granite sculpture marks this otherwise unremarkable spot where the remains of 427 black New Yorkers from the 18th century were unearthed in 1991. This out-of-the-way cemetery was long forgotten until backhoes dug it up while doing renovations in lower Manhattan. A bronze medallion inscribed with the words of Maya Angelou's "Still I Rise" is on the ground.

ALWYN COURT APARTMENTS
Seventh Ave at 58th St

Of all the magnificent apartment buildings in New York, this is my favorite to look at from outside. Built between 1907 and 1909 and recently renovated, it's a block north of Carnegie Hall. You could spend hours studying the elaborate carved terra-cotta exterior. Its features include a crowned sala-mander—the symbol of Renaissance art patron Frances I, in whose style the building was built. For the best view, cross the street.

Columbus Circle Gets a Facelift

It wasn't so long ago that Columbus Circle, at the southwest corner of Central Park, was a dreary collection of underused and unattractive buildings like the old coliseum on the west side and the odd Huntington Hartford building on the east side. As this book goes to press, however, the much-anticipated **AOL-Time Warner Center** is about to open. With a seven-level luxury mall anchored by a 58,000-square-foot Whole Foods Market, the center will house such things as a 20,000-square-foot Williams-Sonoma Grande Cuisine store and demonstration kitchen, the new home for Jazz at Lincoln Center, and a luxury Mandarin Oriental hotel. Meanwhile, the redesigned Huntington Hartford building will soon house the **Museum of Arts and Design** (formerly the American Craft Museum).

BROOKLYN BRIDGE
East River (east of City Hall)

Spanning the East River between Manhattan and Brooklyn, this was the world's longest suspension bridge when built, and it remains one of the most spectacular. The 5,989-foot bridge took 15 years (1868–1883) and two generations of Roeblings to construct. After John Roebling, the engineer who designed the bridge, died from injuries sustained in an accident, his son Washington and wife Emily finished the project. To reach the bridge's bustling and historic promenade, go to the east side of the park surrounding City Hall and follow the bike signs. It's a surprisingly long walk—more than a mile from end to end—and a pretty noisy one too, but the views are well worth the effort. Climbers, take note: One of these days, it may be possible to sign up for a "climbing tour" of this amazing structure! In the meantime, just try to stay in the pedestrian lane and watch out for bicycle riders zooming by!

CARNEGIE HALL
Seventh Ave at 57th St

Named for steel magnate Andrew Carnegie, this magnificent concert hall opened in 1891 with the American conducting debut of Peter Ilyich Tchaikovsky. It underwent a $60 million renovation in the 1990s that dramatically improved acoustics. Actually, it restored the acoustics of old by taking out a piece of concrete that had been added during an earlier renovation! In addition, the seating capacity was expanded to more than 2,800. If you want to visit during the day, take a tour or stop by the Rose Museum at Carnegie Hall (see listing earlier in this chapter). For box office information, call 212/247-7800 or drop by the lobby after 11 a.m. **Hours**: Monday through Saturday from 11 to 6, Sunday from noon to 6.

CASTLE CLINTON NATIONAL MONUMENT
Battery Park (southern tip of Manhattan)

Probably the best known of Manhattan's seven National Parks—it's the gateway to two others and headquarters for them all—Castle Clinton is a red circular building in Battery Park. Built on what was once an island as part of a series of forts designed to defend New York Harbor at the beginning of the 19th century, Castle Clinton has been different things through the years: an entertainment center, an immigrant receiving station (8 million came through between 1855 and 1890), and home to the New York Aquarium. Castle Clinton is best known as the place to buy tickets for the short boat rides to Ellis Island and the Statue of Liberty. It's worth taking a few minutes to visit the small museum detailing the site's history inside the door to your right. **Hours**: daily from 9 to 5.

The More Things Change . . .

The last peep shows have moved out of Times Square and even the fish are moving out of the old Fulton Fish Market, but some things in New York haven't changed. If it's nostalgia you want, try the **Waldorf-Astoria** (301 Park Ave), the overpriced **21 Club** (21 W 52nd St), or the **Grand Central Oyster Bar Restaurant**, inside Grand Central Station. You might check out some of the old-time shops on the Lower East Side, too. Just don't go looking for the **Russian Tea Room**. After the building (at 150 W 57th St) was sold in 2002, the new owners—the United States Golf Association—unveiled plans to turn it into a golf museum just in time for the 2004 U.S. Open.

CENTRAL PARK ZOO
Central Park at Fifth Ave and 64th St (behind The Arsenal)

When people in New York hear the word *zoo,* they tend to think of the big one in the Bronx. But this animal-friendly replacement for the dilapidated and depressing zoo that was here for many years is well worth a visit for kids and grownups alike. Divided by climate into three sections this well-designed zoo includes an indoor rain forest, an outdoor temperate zone, and an indoor "Edge of the Icepack" exhibit. You'll find everything from a bat cave and a colony of leaf-cutter ants to Japanese snow monkeys and chinstrap penguins. There are even a couple of polar bears! The **Tisch Children's Zoo,** located just north of the main zoo, has lots of spaces for preschoolers to climb and explore. It sponsors classes, workshops, and other events for children and families on weekends and in warmer months. A visit on a winter weekday can be enjoyable, too. Call 212/861-6030 for information on classes, workshops and other events. The gift shop is nothing special unless you are big on stuffed polar bears, but the hot-dog-and-French-fries crowd will love the small cafe. **Hours:** daily from 10 to 5:30 (4:30 from November through March). The last tickets are sold half an hour before closing. **Admission:** $6 for adults, $1.25 for senior citizens, $1 for children between 3 and 12, free for children under 3. Children under 16 must be accompanied by an adult.

CHELSEA MARKET
15th St bet Ninth and Tenth Ave

The huge brick building in this long-maligned section of Manhattan once housed the original Oreo cookie factory. It's now home to one of the city's most fashionable and popular shopping destinations. It isn't shoes or silks or antiques folks get in line for down here but food: fresh vegetables, soups, breads—you name it and you'll find it here. Look for kitchen stores, wine, and other shops as well, along with the offices of companies like NY1 News, Major League Baseball Productions, and Oxygen Media. And thanks to the recent purchase across the street, the already enormous Chelsea Market is expanding.

CHELSEA PIERS
Along the Hudson River (bet 17th and 23rd St)

When built at the beginning of the 20th century, Piers 59, 60, 61, and 62 on the Hudson River in Chelsea quickly became the destination for such elegant passenger ships as the *Lusitania and* the *Ile de France.* Indeed, the *Titanic* was headed for the Chelsea Piers when she sank in 1912. But when the length of ships increased in the 1930s and 1940s, new piers were built near 44th Street and those in Chelsea were largely abandoned. Thanks to a visionary developer, the Chelsea Piers have sprung back to life. The Chelsea Piers Sports & Entertainment Complex encompasses 1.7 million square feet of golf (yes, there's a year-round outdoor driving range in Manhattan!); ice skating, rollerblading and roller-skating rinks; rock climbing; gymnastics; and other activities. There's more: two restaurants, a 1.2-mile esplanade, a maritime center, and Silver Screen Studios (home to NBC's *Law and Order*). It's really an amazing place. If you're interested in classes for just about every sport, membership at the sports center, or a one-time visit, call 212/336-6000.

CHRYSLER BUILDING
Lexington Ave (bet 42nd and 43rd St)

One of New York's most recognizable sights, this art deco building housed the Chrysler Corporation at the dawn of the automobile age. Its stainless-steel spire is easy to spot, but take a closer look at the radiator-cap gargoyles (based on the then-current 1929 Chrysler) and the racing cars built into the relief. The Chrysler Corporation no longer maintains offices here and the interior isn't particularly interesting, but the lobby is open to the public.

CITY HALL PARK
City Hall (bet Broadway and Park Row)

Not so long ago, a trip down to this area was to be avoided. Not anymore! City Hall has been beautifully renovated and, despite ongoing security concerns, the Governor's Room is again open to the public. Moreover, the park surrounding it has been restored and is absolutely magnificent. In this spot where General George Washington once encamped his troops, you can sit on comfortable benches, stroll through gardens, and admire the wonderful fountain, which was brought back to this site after an 80-year stint in Crotona Park in Brooklyn. **Hours:** The Governor's Room is open Fridays from 10 to 4 and by appointment. Call 212/788-6865 for more information.

CONSERVATORY GARDEN
Central Park (off Fifth Ave at 105th St)

In warmer months, this elegant and peaceful spot is alive with color— and, as it's a popular site for wedding pictures, with wedding parties as well. The fountains, benches, and entrance gates once were part of Cornelius Vanderbilt's Fifth Avenue mansion. On Saturdays in spring, summer, and early fall, the Central Park Conservancy offers tours of the garden.

When you're standing in City Hall Park, look north to the McKim, Mead, and White-designed **Municipal Building**. The five towers represent the five boroughs, but one is much higher than the others and is plated in gold. Guess which borough it represents! (Hint: you're standing in it.)

CUNARD BUILDING
25 Broadway (at Bowling Green)

Now serving as the Bowling Green branch of the U.S. Post Office, and often overlooked in this historic part of town, this building near the foot of Broadway was the longtime home of the Cunard Steamship Line. Although the Cunard building was not erected until 1921, the Cunard Line is perhaps best known for its steamship *Lusitania*, which was sunk by a German U-boat off the coast of Ireland in 1915. Stand across the street and look for the triads and nautilus in the relief and for Poseidon himself over the door.

ELDRIDGE STREET SYNAGOGUE
12 Eldridge St (bet Canal and Division St)

New York is full of time capsules, but this one, in what was once the largely Jewish Lower East Side but is now the edge of Chinatown, must be seen to be believed. This magnificently elaborate synagogue was home to more than a thousand worshipers at the turn of the 19th-century. Although the orthodox Congregation K'hal Adath Jeshurun hasn't missed a Sabbath since the synagogue opened in 1887, its numbers steadily shrank in the middle of this century, and the building fell into such disrepair that pigeons were living in the sanctuary. Thanks to a few visionary and committed people, the synagogue has been saved, and an $8.5 million capital campaign is well on its way. Call 212/219-0888 for more information or to schedule a tour of this special place. **Hours:** Drop-in tours are given on Sunday on the hour from 11 to 3 and on Tuesday and Thursday at 11:30 and 2:30. **Admission:** $5 for adults, $3 for students, senior citizens, and children. All money goes to the synagogue's restoration.

EMPIRE STATE BUILDING
Fifth Ave (bet 33rd and 34th St)

When people think of New York, this 102-story building is often the first image that comes to mind. Conceived as a great office building but almost bankrupted when it opened in 1931 because of the Great Depression, the Empire State Building soars above its neighbors here just south of midtown. The neighborhood and the building itself are a bit grimy these days, most of the staff are alternately bored or rude, and the deadly gunfire that erupted here in early 1997 still weighs heavily on everyone's mind. However, this New York landmark draws almost 3 million visitors a year, and the views from the top live up to every expectation (assuming it's a relatively clear day or night). For more information about the outdoor terrace on the 86th floor and the indoor observation deck on the 102nd floor, call 212/736-3100. Although many people beg off, I urge you to make the trip to the 102nd floor. The views are spectacular! **Hours:** daily from 9:30 to midnight (the last tickets are sold at 11:25 p.m.). **Admission:** Tickets to the terrace and observation deck cost $10 for adults, $4 for children under 12, military personnel, and senior citizens over 62.

FEDERATED HALL NATIONAL MEMORIAL
Wall St at Nassau St

Here's a history test: where was the nation's first capital? Not Washington, D.C., or even Philadelphia. It was New York City! The building that housed the entire federal government occupied this site. George Washington took his first oath of office and Congress debated the Bill of Rights here. Earlier, this site was home to New York's first city hall (dating back to 1703). Federal Hall was built in 1842 as the U.S. Customs House and is now a National Monument run by the National Park Service with exhibits on the site's incredible history. **Hours:** weekdays from 9 to 5.

FLATIRON BUILDING
Fifth Ave (bet Broadway and 23rd St)

This 22-story architectural oddity has been sitting at this intersection for a century. The prow of the building is said to sit on the windiest street corner in Manhattan. Its triangular shape and terra-cotta exterior have made it a familiar landmark, and the thriving neighborhood around it—the Flatiron District—carries its name.

FORD FOUNDATION GARDENS
320 E 43rd St (bet First and Second Ave)

The warm, multilevel garden in the Ford Foundation's glorious atrium is one of New York's great escapes, especially in the winter. The plants are watered with rain and steam condensation gathered in a cistern on the building's roof, and any coins thrown into the little pool are donated to UNICEF. **Hours:** weekdays from 9 to 5.

New York-ese

Many towns have their own special words and phrases that people from other places can't understand. Here are some of the ones commonly heard in New York:

Bridge and tunnel crowd: a disparaging term for visitors from New Jersey

Coffee regular: coffee with milk and sugar

The FDR: Franklin Roosevelt Drive, an expressway running the length of Manhattan's East Side along the East River

Fuhgeddaboudit: Forget about it, as in "Don't mention it." It can also mean "No way."

The Garden: Madison Square Garden

The Island: Long Island

Houston: a street in lower Manhattan, pronounced HOUSE-ton

The Met: the Metropolitan Opera or Metropolitan Museum of Art

Shlep: as a verb, to drag or haul something; as a noun, a jerk

Shmeer: a smear of cream cheese, usually on a bagel

Slice: a piece of pizza

Soda: any carbonated beverage

Standing on line: Nobody in New York seems to stand *in* line!

GRAND CENTRAL STATION
E 42nd St (bet Lexington and Vanderbilt Ave)

This stunningly beautiful beaux-arts station was built at the turn of the 19th-century during the great age of railroads. It replaced a station built by Cornelius Vanderbilt after steam engines were banned south of 42nd Street in 1854. Scores of commuter trains to Westchester County and Connecticut arrive and depart here. But the real reason for visitors to see Grand Central Station is the incredible cleaning and renovation it has undergone. To say that the project was long overdue is an understatement—the ceiling hadn't been cleaned since 1944! And the results are amazing. Retail space has doubled. Newcomers like **Michael Jordan's, the Steakhouse NYC** (yes, *that* Michael Jordan) have joined famous eateries like the **Grand Central Oyster Bar Restaurant**. Wine, lingerie, music, toy, and all sorts of other great shops line the Lexington Avenue Passageway and other spots throughout this grand place. **Grand Central Books** is one of my favorites. **Grand Central Market**, on the Lexington Avenue side of the station just south of the main lobby, is a destination in itself for those interested in fresh fruit, bread, seafood, meat, and the like. You'll even find New York's best food court—with great choices like **Cafe Spice, Mike's Take-Away, Masa's,** the **Shoebox Cafe,** and a **Two Boots** pizza outlet—as well as clean, safe public bathrooms downstairs and a small **Transit Museum** gallery and gift shop behind the west stairs.

Purists need not fear: Grand Central does not feel like a giant shopping mall. With its breathtaking ceiling, chandeliers, and carved marble details, this is first and foremost an elegant peephole into New York's past, present, and future. The Municipal Art Society offers a fascinating free tour of the station at 12:30 on Wednesdays. (See the "Tours" section of this chapter for more information.) The most dramatic entrance to Grand Central Station is through the driveway off Vanderbilt Avenue (a small street just east of Madison Avenue) at 43rd Street. Incidentally, the original waiting room off Park Avenue has been cleaned and renovated, too, and is well worth a visit. While you're at it, spend a couple minutes at the Whisper Gallery outside the Oyster Bar. Stand in opposite corners facing the wall and try to hear each other whisper! **Hours:** The terminal itself is open from 5:30 a.m. to 1:30 a.m. **Grand Central Market** is open from 7 a.m. to 9 p.m. on weekdays, 10 to 7 on Saturday, and 11 to 6 on Sunday. Store and restaurant hours vary.

GRANT'S TOMB
Riverside Park (Riverside Dr at 122nd St)

If you're an American history buff, you'll want to venture to the far reaches of the Upper West Side to visit this not-so-subtle final resting place of President (and General) Ulysses S. Grant and his wife, Julia. When you're up at this lonely place, inspired by Napoleon's tomb in Paris and run today by the National Park Service, it's hard to imagine that a quarter million people filed through City Hall during the 48 hours Grant lay in state, and that a million more lined Broadway to watch his coffin being transported. Call 212/666-1640 for more information. **Hours:** daily from 9 to 5.

GROUND ZERO
Between Church, West, Liberty, and Vesey St

Ground Zero. Just the words evoke graphic pictures in our collective memory—painful and unshakable memories of the terrorist attacks on the World Trade Center on September 11, 2001. This is the place where 26,000 people a day rode the elevators to the observation deck on the 104th floor of Tower 2, where tens of thousands of people came to work every day in a 16-square-acre office complex with the world's tallest "twin" towers. Today there is nothing but the retaining wall that continues to hold back the Hudson River and empty space—lots and lots of very empty space where thousands of men and women from 115 nations lost their lives, and fires burned for three months.

If you want to visit Ground Zero, the first thing you should know is that there isn't much to see. A thousand people working 24 hours a day for months on end removed 1.8 million tons of debris, and now "the bathtub" at the World Trade Center's foundation is a big, gaping hole. Although you can stand along Church Street and look through the fence, the best viewing is from the glass-enclosed back wall of the World Financial Center, directly across West Street from the site. Construction will eventually begin on a memorial and replacement for the World Trade Center, and indeed a design was recently chosen, but it no doubt will be a long and evolving process.

If you want to revisit the events of September 11, the memorials at the New York Fire Museum, the New York Police Museum, and St. Paul's Chapel are particularly moving. Almost hidden in the hustle and bustle just outside the police station in the Union Square subway station is a memorial that will take your breath away. Three films about that dreadful day are showing at the New-York Historical Society.

HAUGHWOUT BUILDING
Broadway at Broome St

Considered by many architectural historians to be the finest example of cast-iron construction in the country, the Haughwout was built in 1857 and contained one of Elisha Otis' first elevators. Originally home to E.V. Haughwout (pronounced how-it) & Company—a silver, china, and porcelain manufacturer and retailer—the building fell on hard times around the turn of the 20th-century and was almost demolished in the 1960s. Thanks to the Landmarks Preservation Commission and its current owners, however, it remains standing and is even restored to some of its original grandeur.

IRISH HUNGER MEMORIAL
Vesey St at North End Ave

A half-acre memorial to the 1.5 million people who died in the Irish potato famines of 1845–52, this quiet, peaceful spot is tucked away in the shadow of the World Financial Center, overlooking the Hudson River and New York Harbor. The path is made of stones from all of Ireland's 32 counties, and the little stone cottage in the middle comes from County Mayo. Be sure to look around the base of the memorial for moving words about the Irish famines and others throughout history.

JEFFERSON MARKET LIBRARY
425 Ave of the Americas (at 10th St)

I've included this courthouse-turned-public library because it looks like a castle in a fairy tale and people are always wondering exactly what it is. Built in 1877 and modeled after Mad King Ludwig's Neuschwanstein in Bavaria, it was saved from years of neglect and abuse by community activists and is now one of the city's nicest (and most used) public libraries. A wonderful community garden grows on its south side during warmer months. A bit of trivia: the library's bell, thought to be the second largest in New York, was rung in 1995 for the first time in 97 years. Prior to that it was rung to commemorate Admiral George Dewey's triumph in Manila Bay during the Spanish-American War. Thus the graffiti on the bell, which reads: "To hell with Spain—Remember the *Maine*—1898"! It's now rung every day on the hour.

LINCOLN CENTER
Columbus Ave bet 62nd and 65th St

Constructed between 1959 and 1969, this amazing complex includes Avery Fisher Hall, the New York State Theater, Alice Tully Hall, a wonderful public library and small gallery devoted to the performing arts, the Juilliard School of Music, the Guggenheim Bandshell, the Vivian Beaumont Theater, and the Metropolitan Opera House. Call the Lincoln Center events hotline at 212/546-2656 for current information.

MADAME TOUSSAUD'S
234 W 46th St (at Broadway)

For all the hype surrounding the opening of this London icon in the midst of Times Square, I really expected to hate it. The prices are outrageous and seem to climb by the month, the signs and layout are confusing, and they make you exit through an incredibly shlocky gift shop. But I must admit the wax museum itself is fun. From New Yorkers like Donald Trump and Rudolph Giuliani to sports greats like Billie Jean King, Pelé, and Michael Jordan, from world leaders like Nelson Mandela and the Dali Lama to movie stars like Susan Sarandon and Woody Allen, you'll see several hundred "familiar faces." If wax figures are your cup of tea, be sure to bring a camera: the photo ops are great! One word of warning: there is a lot of noise and gore in the section devoted to the period before the French Revolution, when Madame Toussaud was perfecting her craft. If you have children in tow, heed the signs and take the alternate route. Call 212/512-9600 for more information. **Hours:** daily from 10 to 8 (hours may be extended in summer and on holidays). **Admission:** $25 for adults, $19 for children 4 to 12, and $22 for senior citizens.

MADISON SQUARE GARDEN
31st to 33rd St bet Seventh and Eighth Ave

The only real sporting arena in Manhattan, Madison Square Garden plays host to everything from the Westminster Kennel Club's annual dog show and the Ringling Brothers and Barnum Bailey Circus to professional basketball's New York Knicks and hockey's New York Rangers. There have been three other Madison Square Gardens; the one at this location opened in 1968. Oddly enough, Penn Station—the terminal for Amtrak and New Jersey Transit, through which 750 trains pass every day—sits directly underneath "the Garden." You'll also find the Paramount Theater inside the complex. (For information about tours, see the "Tours" section of this chapter.) To find out what's going on at any given time, call 212/465-6741.

NEW AMSTERDAM THEATER
214 W 42nd St (at Broadway)

Regardless of how you view the Disney Company and its takeover of Times Square, the $36 million renovation of this historic theater is nothing short of amazing. Built for $1.5 million at the turn of the 19th-century, it housed the Ziegfeld Follies from 1913 to 1927 and later presented performers like Bob Hope and Jack Benny. Painted brown and used as a movie theater in the 1970s and early 1980s, the New Amsterdam finally shut its doors in 1983. Pigeons, cats, and mushrooms the size of dinner plates made it home for 15 years, until Disney started cleaning it out. The theater is now home to the enormously popular musical *The Lion King*. (If you're interested in touring the theater, see the "Tours" section of this chapter.)

NEW YORK PUBLIC LIBRARY
Fifth Ave bet 40th and 42nd St

The main branch of the extraordinary New York Public Library is a treasure trove for researchers and architecture fans alike. This beautiful building is adjacent to Bryant Park. The marble stairs and open areas outside—a favorite brown-bag lunch spot for people who work in the area—are dominated by statues of two lions, Patience and Fortitude. You'll find a gallery with changing exhibits and a terrific gift shop on the first floor. But the greatest treat for tourists and even hard-to-impress New Yorkers is the stunning renovation of the Rose Main Reading Room (actually two connected rooms) on the library's third floor. This is where the Gilded Age meets the computer age, and the results are splendid. The nonprofit group Friends of the New York Public Library offers frequent tours of exhibits and the library itself. (For more information, stop by the desk in the lobby or see the "Tours" section of this chapter.) You're also free to wander alone and marvel at this glorious place. Call 212/869-8089 for recorded information about the library, current exhibits, and special events. **Hours:** Monday, Thursday, Friday, and Saturday from 10 to 6; Tuesday and Wednesday from 11 to 7:30.

NEW YORK PUBLIC LIBRARY FOR THE PERFORMING ARTS
40 Lincoln Center Plaza

Wedged between the Metropolitan Opera House and the Vivian Beaumont Theater in Lincoln Center, this branch of the New York Public Library houses a tremendous collection of music, plays, and other material related to the performing arts. It is also home to a small gallery with changing exhibits and a huge range of free public programs featuring authors, musicians, artists, playwrights, and others. Call 212/642-0142 for current schedule information. **Hours:** Tuesday through Saturday from noon to 6 (Thursday until 8).

Because of security concerns in the aftermath of the September 11, 2001, attacks on the World Trade Center and our country's ongoing war on terrorism, the **New York Stock Exchange** is unfortunately no longer open to the public.

PLAZA HOTEL
59th St at Fifth Ave

On the south side of Central Park South, just west of Fifth Avenue, this elegant old hotel is a sentimental and architectural (and personal) favorite. A stroll through the lobby is pure class. You might even catch a glimpse of Eloise (or at least her portrait)!

RADIO CITY MUSIC HALL
Ave of the Americas at 50th St

This 6,200-seat art deco wonder was the largest theater in the world when it was built in the early 1930s as part of the Rockefeller Center complex. Its murals and art alone are worth a visit, but Radio City is best known for its long-running Christmas show, featuring the Rockettes. This is yet another New York institution that has been renovated and refurbished in recent years. Call 212/247-4777 or drop by the lobby to find out what's scheduled. (If you're interested in taking a tour, see the "Tours" section of this chapter.) **Hours:** weekdays and Saturday from 10 to 8, Sunday from 11 to 8.

ROCKEFELLER CENTER
47th to 52nd St bet Fifth and Seventh Ave

The 19 buildings in Rockefeller Center stretch for blocks, but the heart of it all is off Fifth Avenue, between 49th and 50th streets. All sorts of interesting shops, the famed statue of Prometheus, the ice-skating rink, the *Today Show* studios, and the beautiful Channel Gardens are all here in the shadow of 30 Rockefeller Plaza. "30 Rock" is the home of NBC's network studios. (For information about the NBC Studio Tour, see the "Tours" section of this chapter.) In December, Rockefeller Center is home to the nation's most photographed Christmas tree. A lot of renovations have been done in recent years, and people rave about the shopping. Wonderful as the complex and its world-famous views may be, however, I find the whole layout a bit confusing and Rockefeller Center itself worth only a brief picture-taking stop. Call 212/632-3975 for more information about the complex and special events.

There's Only One Real "Channel"!
Channel Gardens, home to some lovely displays throughout the year, got is name because it sits between a French and an English building.

ROOSEVELT ISLAND
In the East River, east of midtown

If you want an experience even most New Yorkers haven't had, along with amazing views of the city's skyline, take the tram to Roosevelt Island in the middle of the East River. It leaves regularly from its station on Second Avenue between 59th and 60th streets and costs $2 per person each way. Although they are only minutes from midtown Manhattan, the 7,500 people who live over here might as well be on another planet. Their island—which was at various times home to a hog pasture, a debtors' prison, and an insane asylum —is quiet, unhurried, and almost crime-free. For 10¢ you can take one of the elderly red buses that traverse the island from the tram station through the small shopping area to Lighthouse Park, on the island's northern end. Buy a map at the tram station and see the sights or just wander around. Be sure to walk along the island's west side to get a priceless view of the Manhattan skyline. Call 212/832-4555 for tram schedules and other information.

ROSE CENTER FOR EARTH AND SPACE
81st St at Central Park West (adjacent to the
American Museum of Natural History)

This much-anticipated companion to the Hayden Planetarium at the American Museum of Natural History has bells and whistles galore. In the Hall of the Universe, galaxies collide, supernovas explode, and telescopes beam back amazing images. In the Hall of Planet Earth, you can learn all about the Mothra Hydrothermal Field while tectonic plates collide and sulfide chimneys percolate with life. There's a fascinating multimedia display of the Big Bang, an exceptional display of relative scale in the universe, and even a "cosmic pathway" detailing the 13 billion-year evolution of our universe. Older children will be particularly taken with all the hands-on displays. Of course the centerpiece of the Rose Center is the retooled Hayden Planetarium.

The show is fascinating, but be forewarned that it may scare young children, and senior citizens might find all the standing and waiting required a bit much. Also be forewarned of the stratospheric cost: a strongly suggested $19 for adults to take in the Rose Center, Hayden Planetarium, and American Museum of Natural History—and you can't choose to bypass the museum. Call 212/769-5100 for more information. **Hours:** Sunday through Thursday from 10 to 5:45, Friday and Saturday from 10 to 8:45. Open daily except Thanksgiving and Christmas. **Admission:** varies depending on package selected, but a minimum of $10 for adults without the Hayden Planetarium's space show.

SCHOMBURG CENTER FOR RESEARCH
IN BLACK CULTURE
515 Malcolm X Blvd (at 135th St)

This branch of the New York Public Library is a stunningly comprehensive resource for scholars and others interested in the Harlem Renaissance, enduring African traditions, the civil rights movement, and a wide variety of topics associated with the African-American experience. It's also home to 300,000 prints and photographs, 10,000 pieces of art and artifacts, 5,000 hours of oral histories, and (as part of a 75-year loan) many of Malcolm X's personal papers. While its two galleries are small and not in the best shape, you'll often find unique exhibits here. The center's Langston Hughes Theater is used for performances and special programs. Call 212/491-2200 for more information. **Hours:** Monday through Wednesday from noon to 8, Thursday through Saturday from 10 to 6. (Since hours for the galleries and collections vary, call ahead to confirm they are open.)

SCIENCE, INDUSTRY, AND BUSINESS LIBRARY
188 Madison Ave (at 34th St)

Known around town as SIBL (as in the woman's name), this amazing library in the old B. Altman department store is among the most technologically advanced and user-friendly libraries in the world. Intended for use by the general public and business people, the library unites the New York Public Library system's collections of scientific, technological, mathematical, and business-related materials. This enormous archive comprises 1.2 million books, plus microfilm, microfiche, magazines, and journals. Whether you're interested in patents and trademarks, labor history, advertising practices, or how the Small Business Administration works, this is where to look for information. But don't expect to browse the stacks. With the exception of a circulating collection of 40,000 books on the first floor, everything is housed in electronically operated moving stacks at the core of the building. Each of the library's 500 seats is wired for laptop computer use, and 100 computer stations allow you to search electronic databases or go online. If you're interested in learning how to surf the Internet, sign up for one of the library's free classes, offered through its Electronic Training Center. Call 212/592-7000 for more information. **Hours:** Tuesday through Thursday from 10 to 8, Friday and Saturday from 10 to 6.

SEVENTH REGIMENT ARMORY
643 Park Ave (at 66th St)

Most New Yorkers know this as a giant exhibition space in a prime location, but the Seventh Regiment Armory is also what the *New York Times* once called "a bit of New York in a bottle." The Seventh Regiment was founded in 1806 as a volunteer militia. Its members, a Who's Who of New York throughout the 19th-century, built this armory as their headquarters in 1879. It includes rooms designed by famed architect Stanford White and decorated by Louis Comfort Tiffany, as well as paintings by such artists as Thomas Nast. Though it is used for all sorts of exhibits, including the prestigious Winter Antiques Show, the Armory was called into service by the National Guard after September 11, 2001, and may serve that role again in the future.

SONY WONDER TECHNOLOGY LAB
Madison Ave at 56th St

A brilliant public-relations and merchandising ploy, this four-story interactive wonderland is a huge favorite among preteens and teenagers. Whether you want to try your hand at surgery or making a music video, you'll definitely find something to do and explore here. The lab was recently renovated and is often very crowded, especially on weekends and in summer. Call 212/833-8100 for more information. **Hours:** Tuesday through Saturday from 10 to 6 (Thursday until 8), Sunday from noon to 6.

SOUTH STREET SEAPORT
209 Water Street (at Fulton St)

This is the only place I've included in both the "Museums" section and this one, because it's a little of both. The main entrance to this popular area is at the east end of Fulton Street, but the area stretches for several blocks between Water Street and the East River. If you've ever been to Boston's Quincy Market or Baltimore's Inner Harbor, you'll recognize the concept of upscale shops, food courts, restaurants, and history all wrapped into one. South Street was one of the city's most important ports for many years, and this district was created more than two decades ago to preserve that history. You can stroll cobblestone streets, look at the early 19th-century buildings along Schermerhorn Row, and gaze at the tall ships. Alternatively, you can buy a ticket to tour the ships and visit the seaport's galleries and children's center. (For a few extra dollars you also can take a cruise of New York Harbor in the warmer months.) A new TKTS discount ticket booth is here as well, just south of the main plaza on the corner of John and Front streets. Call 212/732-7678 for information about South Street Seaport and its special events. **Hours:** South Street Seaport Museum is open daily from 10 to 6 (Thursday until 8) in summer and daily (except Tuesday) from 10 to 5 in winter. Many shops and restaurants in the area stay open much later.

STATEN ISLAND FERRY
At the foot of Whitehall St in lower Manhattan

There are no better views of New York than those from the decks of these legendary ferryboats. The 22-minute trip is free, and boats leave from both sides every half hour during the week (a bit less frequently on weekends and holidays). The ferry terminal on the Manhattan side is a pretty grim place, but a replacement is in the works. To get to the ferry, take the 1 or 9 subway to the South Ferry stop in Battery Park. Call 718/727-2508 for more information.

STATUE OF LIBERTY
In New York Harbor (south of Battery Park)

This 151-foot gift to the United States from France was built on Liberty Island in New York Harbor in 1886 and has been among New York's most recognized sights ever since. (Before the statue was erected, the island was used as a fort and later for hanging pirates!) Generations of immigrants remember seeing Lady Liberty and her raised torch when they arrived at nearby Ellis Island. The Emma Lazarus sonnet "The New Colossus" ("Give me your tired, your poor/Your huddled masses yearning to breathe free"), which is carved onto its base, still expresses the most noble instincts of our country. A small exhibit tells you about the statue's construction. To reach the Statue of Liberty, you must ferry over from Castle Clinton in Battery Park. For more information about the ferry (which also goes to Ellis Island), call 212/269-5755. For recorded information about the Statue of Liberty, call 212/363-3200. Be forewarned: go early, particularly in warmer months, as lines can grow very long and security is tight. **Hours:** 9 to 5 in winter, 8:30 to 6:45 in summer (although the last boat leaves Castle Clinton at about 3). The Statue of Liberty is closed on July 4 and December 25. **Admission:** $10 for adults, $8 for senior citizens over 62, and $4 for children from 4 to 12. Time permitting, admission to both Ellis Island and the Statue of Liberty is included in the price of a ferry ticket.

STEINWAY & SONS
109 W 57th St (bet Ave of the Americas and Seventh Ave)

New York is full of hidden treasures, and this is one of them. Part showroom and part monument to beauty and grace, this is not a place to bring kids or big groups. The 1925 building itself is magnificent and the pianos so elegant you don't need to be a music lover to appreciate their beauty and craftsmanship. Just down the street from Carnegie Hall, this also is the home of the Steinway "bank"—a collection of several dozen prime Steinway grand pianos from which visiting pianists can choose for their performances. Call 212/246-1100 for more information. **Hours:** weekdays from 9 to 6, Saturday from 9 to 5, and Sunday from noon to 5.

TIMES SQUARE
42nd St at Broadway

When I first began writing this book, Times Square was among the most unpleasant places in Manhattan. It was synonymous with petty crime, pornography, and filth. Not anymore. In fact, it is increasingly hard to believe it's the same place. The Disney Company has reinvented West 42nd Street with the stunning success of *The Lion King* in the lovingly restored New Amsterdam Theater. A growing number of tourist-oriented restaurants, megastores, hotels, and entertainment venues have opened here, including a McDonald's with 7,500 light bulbs in its marquee! The Times Square subway station, the city's busiest, has been redesigned, refurbished, and fitted for a 53-foot porcelain mural by Roy Lichtenstein! The Times Square Business Improvement District runs a great tourist information center on Seventh Avenue between 46th and 47th streets. Despite all the positive changes, however, be warned that the "new" Times Square still leaves something to be desired. It's wildly crowded with out-of-towners, the food is almost uniformly bad, prices are sky-high, and service tends to run from surly to incompetent.

TRUMP TOWER
Fifth Ave (bet 56th and 57th St)

This 66-floor building is named for flamboyant financier Donald Trump. Its six-story pink marble atrium—complete with galleries, shops, restaurants, outdoor gardens (on levels 4 and 5), and a dramatic waterfall—is open to the public and almost always crowded. Apartments begin on the 30th floor; tenants enter and leave via a separate entrance to avoid the crowds. **Hours:** daily between 8 a.m. and 10 p.m.

Where Did They Go?
Much has been made about the remarkable redevelopment of Times Square and the closure of its dozens of peep shows. When Peep-o-Rama, the last of them, closed in the summer of 2002 to make room for a new office tower, it signaled the end of an era. But don't be fooled: many of those businesses are still around. They've just moved a couple of blocks west to Eighth Avenue!

UNITED NATIONS
First Ave bet 42nd and 47th St

The flags of member nations fly along the entire length of this complex, and you'll hear all sorts of languages spoken inside the UN and on surrounding streets. The main visitors' entrance, between 45th and 46th streets, is well marked and manned by UN guards. The park and plaza inside the gate offer wonderful views of the East River and comfortable benches. Once you've passed through a security checkpoint inside the main building, you can wander the enormous lobby, eat in the Delegates' Dining Room, take a formal tour, or head downstairs to visit the UN post office and a great assortment of shops. An information desk in the main lobby provides daily schedules of meetings and events. Remember that those who work here are busy overseeing world affairs, so look around and ask questions but be quiet and respectful. For information about UN tours and other programs, call 212/963-7713. **Hours:** weekdays from 9 to 5; Saturday, Sunday, and holidays from 9:15 to 5 (closed weekends in January and February).

VENETIAN ROOM
French Cultural Mission
972 Fifth Ave (at 79th St)

The building now houses the French Cultural Service's mission and is hardly ever noticed by tourists headed to the nearby Metropolitan Museum of Art, but this grand townhouse was designed 100 years ago for Payne and Helen Hay Whitney by architect Stanford White. While its rooms are now largely occupied by French bureaucrats, the home's almost indescribably elegant Venetian Room (just inside the main entrance) has been painstakingly rebuilt from the contents of 75 crates that were packed and stored in a stable when Helen Hay Whitney died in 1944. Furnished largely with items purchased by the Whitneys and White on a trip to Europe in 1905, the room was designed to allow visitors a chance to catch their breath before ascending the stairs to the townhouse's main living areas. Ask the guard for a wonderful booklet about the room and its reconstruction, and you might even be allowed in for a minute or two. On your way out, look in the main foyer at *The Marble Boy,* a sculpture White bought in 1905 that many experts believe to be the work of Michelangelo. Call 212/439-1400 for more information and to confirm hours. **Hours:** Friday from 12:30 to 2:30.

WASHINGTON ARCH
Washington Square Park (at the foot of Fifth Ave)

Thanks to movies like *When Harry Met Sally,* you've probably seen this marble triumphal arch. Erected at the end of the 19th century at the foot of Fifth Avenue, just south of 8th Street, the marble arch replaced a wooden structure commemorating the inauguration of George Washington, who was sworn in as our nation's first president in New York.

WOOLWORTH BUILDING
233 Broadway (bet Barclay St and Park Pl)

Constructed of 17 million bricks, 28,000 tons of tile, and 53,000 pounds of bronze and iron hardware, this national landmark is among the city's most impressive office buildings. It's also become one of the city's hottest residential properties, as the upper floors have been converted into condominiums. The cathedral-like lobby has extraordinary mosaics on its vaulted ceilings; it is a definite "don't miss" if you're in the area, although only a small part is open to the public for security reasons. Dime-store king F.W. Woolworth paid $13.5 million in cash to have his namesake building erected in 1913, and it reigned as the world's tallest structure for more than a decade. Study the details and try to spot (under the south balcony) the gargoyle of Woolworth himself counting his nickels and dimes. **Hours:** The lobby is open 24 hours a day.

WORLD FINANCIAL CENTER
On the Hudson River (bet Vesey and Albany St)

In the heart of Battery Park City, the World Financial Center amazingly still stands after the destruction on September 11, 2001 of the nearby World Trade Center. A proud but haunted survivor in this scarred area, the World Financial Center's Winter Garden was restored with 2,000 new panes of glass and more than a million pounds of Italian marble before reopening in September 2002. Ironically, the east windows of the World Financial Center, just upstairs from the Winter Garden, now offer the best view of Ground Zero. You'll find upscale stores and restaurants, great views of the Hudson River, and some pleasant sitting areas both indoors and out. You'll also find the water taxi to Liberty State Park, not to mention some of the city's best children's playgrounds, just outside the World Financial Center along the Hudson River. Call 212/945-0505 for information about events and programs.

Tickets

Nowhere else in the world will you find such a wealth of performing arts. And no trip to New York is complete without taking in at least one play, musical, ballet, concert, or opera.

The trick, of course, is getting tickets. People have written entire books about how and where to get tickets, and others have made lucrative careers out of procuring them for out-of-towners. I've provided a variety of approaches for getting theater tickets and to find out about other performances. Keep your eye out for student and other discounts, but be forewarned that good deals for the best shows and performances are few and far between.

Ten Ways to Tell if You're a Real New Yorker:

1. You say "the city" and expect everyone to know you mean Manhattan.
2. You've never been to the Statue of Liberty or the Empire State Building.
3. You can argue for hours about how to get from Columbus Circle to Battery Park but can't find Wisconsin on a map.
4. You think Central Park is "nature."
5. You've never bought a bagel at a grocery store.
6. You believe that being able to swear at people in their native tongue makes you multilingual.
7. You think that making eye contact is an act of aggression.
8. You rent a car to go shopping at Ikea, Home Depot, and Fairway's store in upper Manhattan.
9. You've worn out a car horn.
10. You think having an "early dinner" means eating at 8 p.m.

BROADWAY

People may have different things in mind when they say they want to see a show. Some have their hearts set on great seats at a Saturday night performance of the hottest show on Broadway, while others are willing to sit anywhere to see anything. A lot of people fall somewhere between those extremes. In addition, some are willing to pay whatever it takes to see the show they want, while others just won't go if they can't pay less than full price. If the main purpose of your visit is to see a particular show (or shows), and you don't happen to know a star or producer (who often get blocks of seats set aside every night), make sure you have the tickets you want before leaving so you're not disappointed.

Look in the Sunday Arts and Leisure section or the Friday Weekend section of the *New York Times,* the front pages of a current *New Yorker,* the Theater section of *Time Out New York,* or the back pages of a current *New York* magazine to find out where the play or musical you want to see is being performed. The front section of the Manhattan Yellow Pages has a list of Broadway and off-Broadway theaters and a map of the Theater District. **The Broadway Line** (888/276-2392 or 212/302-4111) tells you what is playing and where, and also gives a quick plot summary.

Box Offices and Phone Orders—If you want to save a little money and pick your seat, go directly to the theater's box office with cash or a major credit card. Ask to see a diagram of the theater if it isn't posted, although most theaters are small enough to ensure that everybody has a good view. The best time to try is midweek. You can also check with the box office to learn if it releases day-of-performance "rush" tickets (most do, usually around 10 a.m.).

If you're willing to spend a little extra and let a computer pick what is in theory the "best available" seat, call the number or go to the website listed and have your credit card ready. Most numbers will be for **Telecharge** (212/239-6200) or **TicketMaster's Broadway Performance Line** (212/307-4100). Both services charge a per-ticket handling fee in addition to the ticket price. Other options include stopping by the Broadway Ticket Center at the tourist information center in the Embassy Theater (on Seventh Avenue between 46th and 47th streets). Open from 8 to 8 every day, it is one source where you can get tickets to every Broadway show.

Be forewarned: full-price tickets to Broadway shows typically cost between $50 and $80. Moreover, if the play or musical you want to see is really hot, it may be sold out the entire time you're in New York. In fact, a few really hot ones may be sold out months in advance.

One of the inquiries I get most often is, "Where can I find a really reliable ticket broker?" Well, I have the answer with **Americana Tickets** (800/833-3121 or 212/581-6660). For over 60 years, this business has been the one pointed to over and over for outstanding service. The third generation of the Radler family are outstanding people to deal with! Just a few of the advantages: premium seating for all theater, entertainment, concert, and sporting events in New York and worldwide; expert, professional agents; unique cancellation and exchange privileges; special offers for individuals and groups; hotel theater-desk locations (Marriott Marquis, Sheraton New York, Crowne Plaza Manhattan); great hours (8 a.m. to 8 p.m. seven days a week); and complimentary hotel, restaurant, limousine and sightseeing reservations. For more information try www.americanatickets.com; e-mail: jonathan@americanatickets.com; FAX: 212/262-9627.

CareTix—If you have your heart set on a particular show and cost is no option, Broadway Cares/Equity Fights AIDS sells house seats for sold-out Broadway and off-Broadway shows for twice the box-office price. The extra money goes to a good cause and is a tax-deductible contribution for you. Call 212/840-0770, ext. 230, for more information.

TKTS Outlets—If you want to see a Broadway show but are flexible and have some free time, go to one of the TKTS outlets in Manhattan. Operated by the Theater Development Fund, these outlets sell whatever tickets happen to be left for various shows on the day of performance for half price or less (plus a $3 per-ticket charge). The most popular TKTS outlet is in Duffy Square, at 47th Street and Broadway. It's open from 3 to 8 Monday through Saturday (from 2 on Tuesday, when performances start an hour earlier at many theaters), from 10 to 2 on Wednesday and Saturday for matinee tickets, and from 11 to 7 on Sunday. A less crowded TKTS outlet is at the intersection of Front and John streets, just below South Street Seaport's main plaza. It's open Monday through Saturday from 11 to 6 and Sunday from 11 to 3:30. A list of shows for which tickets are available is posted in the window. Matinee tickets at this location go on sale the day *before* a performance. You must pay with cash or travelers checks at both places.

The **Theater Development Fund** also offers extremely good deals on tickets to theater and other performances to its members. If you're a student, member of the clergy, teacher, union member, performing artist, or member of the armed forces (retired or serving), send a stamped, self-addressed envelope for an application to Theater Development Fund, Attention: Application, 1501 Broadway, New York, NY 10036. All Broadway theaters offer a small number of deeply discounted tickets to people in wheelchairs and their companion or attendant. Call the theater box office directly for more information. Finally, standing-room-only tickets are sometimes available for sold-out performances on the day of the performance for between $10 and $20. Again, call the theater box office for more information.

A great new addition to the New York theater world is **Theater Row**, a wonderfully conceived and renovated "multiplex" of off-Broadway theaters on 42nd Street between Ninth and Tenth avenues (212/714-2442). Other off-Broadway—and off-off and *really* way out—venues include:

Center Stage, NY: 48 W 21st St (212/929-2228)
The Flea: 41 White St (212/226-0051)
Soho Rep: 46 Walker St (212/941-8632)

Off-Broadway and off-off-Broadway—In part because staging a Broadway production has become almost prohibitively expensive, off-Broadway and off-off-Broadway theater have really taken *off*. Thanks to a glut of talented actors and actresses in New York, such theater is typically excellent and often quite innovative. The front section of the Manhattan Yellow Pages lists off-Broadway theaters. Descriptions of what's playing off-Broadway and off-off-Broadway are published every Sunday in the *New York Times* Arts and Leisure section, in the back of *New York* magazine, and in *Time Out New York*. Tickets for off-Broadway and off-off-Broadway productions tend to be significantly less expensive, and TKTS outlets and twofers sometimes offer discounts.

OPERA AND CLASSICAL MUSIC

No other city in the world has as much music to choose from as New York. *Time Out New York* has an excellent listing of classical and opera performances, including locations, times, and ticket prices. Many New York-related websites, including several listed in the "For More Resources" section of Chapter VII, have comprehensive listings as well. Call the **92nd Street Y** (212/996-1100) if you're interested in chamber music or recitals by top performers. Otherwise, here's how to find schedule and ticket information at New York's top venues:

Carnegie Hall—You'll find individual musicians, out-of-town orchestras, and chamber music ensembles performing at Carnegie Hall all year. Call CarnegieCharge (212/247-7800) between 11 and 6. A money-saving tip: on Saturday morning at 11, the box office releases 70 tickets at only $10 apiece for the week's main-hall performances.

Metropolitan Opera—The internationally renowned Met's season runs from fall through spring, and ticket sales are broken into three periods. Call the box office (212/362-6000), but be aware that orchestra seats can cost as much as $150! For a real bargain, bring cash only to the Metropolitan's box office at 10 a.m. on Saturday, when standing-room-only tickets for the upcoming week's performances are sold for $16 each.

New York City Opera—The season for this exceptional but often overshadowed opera runs through summer and early fall. For schedule and ticket information, call the box office (212/870-5570) or try TicketMaster (212/307-4100). Standing-room-only tickets are sometimes available for $8 on the morning of a performance from the New York State Theater's box office in Lincoln Center.

New York Philharmonic—The Philharmonic's season runs from September through June. For schedule and ticket information, call CenterCharge (212/721-6500), the box office (212/721-6500), or the New York Philharmonic information line (212/875-5656). If you're a student, call around 10:30 on the morning of a performance to see if they have any $10 "rush" tickets available.

Can You Go Out in New York and Still Get to Bed Before Midnight?

The answer is yes, particularly with the introduction of "Tuesdays at 7" on Broadway and the earlier weekday curtain times at the New York Philharmonic. My advice for those accustomed to late curtain times in New York: check your tickets. The times they are a-changin'!

DANCE AND BALLET

Ballet and dance companies have experienced tough times financially in recent years, but New York still is home to several world-class companies and a great many smaller ones. They include:

Alvin Ailey American Dance Theater: 212/767-0590
American Ballet Theater: 212/362-6000
Dance Theater of Harlem: 212/690-2800
Dance Theater Workshop: 212/691-6500
New York City Ballet: 212/870-5570
Paul Taylor Dance Company: 212/431-5562

Time Out New York has a particularly good section on dance, including reviews and a day-by-day calendar of large and small performances by local and visiting companies. A number of major companies—including Paul Taylor, Alvin Ailey, and the Dance Theater of Harlem—now perform at various times at the City Center of Music and Dance (131 West 55th Street), although Alvin Ailey is scheduled to open its own facility in 2004. Call CitiTix (212/581-1212) for information about tickets and upcoming performances.

TELEVISION SHOW TAPINGS

Fine arts aside, there is one other kind of ticket everybody wants to get in New York: those that allow you to become part of the television studio audience for one of the many talk shows filmed here. I've listed some of the most popular shows (in alphabetical order) and rules for getting free tickets.

Late Nite with Conan O'Brien—Tickets can be obtained by sending a postcard to NBC Tickets/Late Nite, 30 Rockefeller Plaza, New York, NY 10112 or by calling 212/664-3056. You can specify the date you want (tapings are usually done on Tuesday through Friday evenings), but are not allowed more than four tickets per group. There is a four- to five-month wait, and children under 16 are not admitted. A limited number of standby tickets are distributed on taping days (usually Tuesday, Thursday, and Friday) at 9 a.m. in the NBC lobby, on 50th Street between Fifth Avenue and Avenue of the Americas. One ticket is given per person, and it does not guarantee admission.

Late Show with David Letterman—These are among the hottest tickets in town, and you must be at least 16 to qualify for them. Send a postcard to The Late Show Tickets, 1697 Broadway, New York, NY 10019 or go to www.cbs.com. Include your name, address, and phone number. Two tickets are allotted per postcard. (Don't send more than one postcard, as duplicates are discarded.) Expect to wait at least six to eight months and probably longer. Standby tickets are sometimes distributed at 11 on the morning of a show by calling 212/247-6497 (*not* in person, as used to be the case). If you hear a recording, you'll know tickets have run out. Shows are taped Monday through Thursday. Bring picture ID and a jacket. (Dave insists that the theater be kept at 52° all year!) Call 212/975-5853 for more information.

The major television networks all have street-level studios for their morning shows. Look for NBC's **Today Show** crowd on the sidewalk at 49th Street between Fifth Avenue and Avenue of the Americas. CBS's **Early Show** crowd gathers at the General Motors Building (Fifth Avenue at 59th Street), as do those who want to see **NFL Today** on Sunday mornings during football season (much to the irritation of neighbors in nearby apartment buildings). ABC's **Good Morning America** crowd assembles in Times Square at 44th Street and Broadway, CNN's **American Morning** originates in a former bank branch at Avenue of the Americas and West 51st Street. People often show up before dawn, although cameras don't starting rolling until 7 a.m.

Saturday Night Live—Year in and year out, these remain the hardest tickets of all to get. A lottery is held every August from postcards collected during the preceding 12 months, and each winner gets two tickets. If you want to be included in the lottery, send a postcard to Saturday Night Live, NBC Tickets, 30 Rockefeller Plaza, New York, NY 10112. Standby tickets for the 8 p.m. dress rehearsal and the 11:30 p.m. live show are available at 9:15 a.m. on the day of the show (but show up around 5 a.m. if you really want them) at the 49th Street entrance to 30 Rockefeller Plaza. They do not guarantee entrance, and only one ticket is distributed per person over 16.

The View—The wait for these tickets is roughly nine months, and they aren't sent to you until about three weeks in advance of the show you're going to see. If that doesn't complicate your planning, send a postcard to The View, 320 West 66th Street, New York, NY 10023, or register online at www.abcnews.go.com/theview. Include your name, address, and a daytime phone number. The show is taped Monday through Friday from 11 to noon at ABC Studios on West 66th Street. Standby tickets are distributed on a first-come, first-serve basis at 9:30 each weekday morning. You must be at least 18 to be in this audience.

Tours

No matter what your interest, price range, or schedule, New York has a tour for you. If you're interested in having a tour organized for your group,

Doorway to Design (212/221-1111), **Manhattan Passport** (212/861-2746), **New York Inside/Out** (212/861-4114), and **Viewpoint International** (212/246-6000) are all reputable outfits. The tours listed here, however, are do-it-yourself affairs. They're divided into three categories: tours of New York, tours of specific sights and neighborhoods, and individuals and organizations that put together walking tours of various areas. Some of the tours in the other three categories simply require you to show up and pay a couple of dollars, while others require reservations in advance and can be costly. Some are well established and reliable, while others are new or eccentric and may not be around by the time you read this. As with just about everything else, my advice is to call in advance. You can always contact the **Guides Association of New York** (212/969-0666) for advice about the kind of tour or guide you're looking for, as well as a list of members and their specialties. One last piece of advice: if you're going to join a big tour—which is often the best option for people with limited time—realize that you're going to look like a tourist and be herded around.

TOURS OF NEW YORK

Big Apple Greeter—A volunteer service, this outfit will hook you up with a personal guide to New York. If you're looking for a really personalized introduction to this sometimes overwhelming city, or a particular neighborhood, Big Apple Greeters may be right for you. Best of all, it's free! You must give as much notice as possible, and tell them what part of New York you would like to see. Call 212/669-8159 for more information.

Circle Line—Particularly on warm days, the three-hour boat trip around the island of Manhattan on one of Circle Line's boats is a real treat. In addition to nice breezes, you'll get a good idea of how Manhattan is laid out. A guide offers commentary as the boat makes its way down the Hudson River, into New York Harbor, up the East River, across the top of the island via the Harlem River, and back down the Hudson. Trips depart Pier 83 (43rd Street at the Hudson River) daily between mid-March and December, with more trips added at the height of the season. In warmer months, tours also depart from Pier 16 at South Street Seaport. Tickets cost $24 for adults, $19 for senior citizens, and $12 for children under 12. Shorter tours are also available. Call 212/563-3200 for more information or a brochure.

Gray Line—If you're overwhelmed by New York and want to be shown the highlights from the safety and anonymity of a tour bus, try a Gray Line tour. The company offers a wide range of part-day and full-day bus tours to various parts of Manhattan, including a marathon eight-and-a-half-hour "Manhattan Comprehensive" that goes from Harlem to Wall Street and even out to the Statue of Liberty and Ellis Island. Most tours run at least once a day, and some are offered in French, German, Italian, Portuguese, and Spanish, as well as English. Gray Line also offers package tours to places like West Point, factory outlets north of the city, Niagara Falls, and even Washington, D.C. Tickets are available at the Gray Line office in the Port Authority Bus Terminal (42nd Street at Eighth Avenue), the Times Square Business Improvement District's tourist information center (Seventh Avenue between 46th and 47th streets), and many hotel concierge desks. Call 800/669-0051 or 212/445-0848 for more information or a brochure.

New York Sightseeing/Gray Line—This is a terrific way to see many of the city's major sights without having to pay for taxis or brave the public transportation system. Somewhat like the Tour Mobile in Washington, D.C., Gray Line's open-air double-decker buses and trolleys run every half hour between Battery Park, South Street Seaport, the Empire State Building, and three dozen other places. Tickets start at $35 for adults and $25 for kids, and they're good for as many stops as you want to make. Tickets are available at the Gray Line office in the Port Authority Bus Terminal (42nd Street at Eighth Avenue), the Times Square Business Improvement District's tourist information center (Seventh Avenue between 46th and 47th streets), and many hotel concierge desks. Schedules change by season. Call 800/669-0051 or 212/445-0848 for more information.

Sailing Up, Sailing Down

The Hudson and East rivers, long the economic engines of this region, became very polluted in the second half of the 20th century and were little used when I first began writing this book 20 years ago. No longer! Whether it's basic transportation or a nostalgic sail on a 100-year-old schooner, there are many options for getting out on the water. They include:

The Adirondack—This modern copy of a 19th-century pilot boat is docked at Pier 62 in the Chelsea Piers complex (on the Hudson River at 23rd Street). Call 800/701-7245 for more information.

New York Water Taxi—This water-taxi makes regular stops for commuters and tourists alike at various West Side and lower Manhattan locations. Call 212/742-1969 for more information.

New York Waterway—Also a water-taxi service, this one runs between various East River locations and Pier 11 near Wall Street.

The Pioneer—This wonderful 1885 coastal schooner is docked at South Street Seaport. Call 212/748-8786 for more information.

The Ventura—This 1921 sloop is docked in North Cove at the World Financial Center in Battery Park City. Call 212/786-1204 for more information.

NY Waterway—Ninety-minute New York Harbor cruises, a harbor cruise combined with a "hop-on, hop-off" bus tour, twilight cruises, and more are available from NY Waterway (Pier 78, 38th Street at Hudson River). Prices for the harbor cruise, which runs throughout the year, are $19 for adults, $16 for senior citizens, and $9 for children. Prices vary for the other tours, which run only in warmer months. Call 800/533-3779 for more information.

TOURS OF SPECIFIC PLACES AND AREAS

ARTime—This outfit puts together "Saturday in the Galleries" tours of Soho and Chelsea galleries. Tours are centered around particular themes and geared to elementary school children and their families. It's run by two art historians whose background includes working with children at the Brooklyn Museum. Ninety-minute tours cost $20 for each child-adult pair and $5 for each additional child. Call 718/797-1573 for more information.

Carnegie Hall—Lincoln Center may have the Metropolitan Opera and the

New York Philharmonic, but Carnegie Hall remains synonymous with classical music. If you want to take a look around during the day, one-hour tours are offered on weekdays at 11:30, 2, and 3. The tour costs $6 for adults, $5 for students and senior citizens, and $3 for children under 12. Call 212/903-9765 for more information, or drop by the house manager's window inside the Carnegie Hall lobby at 153 West 57th Street, just off Seventh Avenue. The box office opens at 11 a.m.; advance reservations are not accepted. Tours meet inside the lobby.

At various times of year, dozens of New York's cultural institutions —including such heavyweights as the Metropolitan Museum of Art and lesser known spots like the Caribbean Cultural Center—host special **"Insiders' Hour"** tours. The New York City Opera, the New York Philharmonic, Jazz at Lincoln Center, Carnegie Hall, and even WNET (the area's flagship PBS station) all offer such tours as well. Look for a complete list at **NYC & Company** (810 Seventh Avenue) or call 800/692-8474.

Cathedral Church of St. John the Divine—If you're interested in Gothic architecture or just want to see one of the most amazing places in all of New York, I urge you to take a tour of this beautiful cathedral-in-progress. Located on Amsterdam Avenue at 112th Street, this Episcopal church makes a real effort to welcome people of all faiths. Regular tours cost $3 and meet at a table in the back of the narthex, inside the main doors. They begin at 11 a.m. Tuesday through Saturday and at 1 p.m. Sunday after morning services. Although the "vertical tour" of the cathedral's hidden areas was canceled after a serious fire, it may be available again by the time you read this. Inquire if you're interested, because it's simply wonderful! Call 212/316-7540 for more information.

Central Park—The Central Park Conservancy leads a wide array of free tours in Central Park, including an hour-long "Views from the Past" tour of the lower park offered at 1 p.m. on Saturday throughout the year and a tour of the Conservatory Garden (at 105th Street and Fifth Avenue) on Saturday in the summer and early fall. Call the visitor information center at The Dairy (212/794-6564) daily (except Monday) between 10 and 4 for more information on those and other tours. Another possibility is the Central Park Bicycle Tour, a two-hour romp through "New York's front yard." For $35 per adult and $20 for children, you get a tour and a bicycle. For reservations or more information, call 212/541-8759. **The Audubon Society** (212/310-6660) gives birdwatching tours in the park. Check with the city's **Urban Park Rangers** (212/360-2774) to see if any free walking tours are scheduled.

Central Park occupies 843 acres—a larger area than the principality of Monaco—and contains more than 500,000 trees and shrubs.

Eldridge Street Synagogue—This stunning synagogue was built by Eastern European immigrants at 12 Eldridge Street (between Canal and Division streets) on the Lower East Side in 1887. The building fell into disrepair in the middle of last century and is now being renovated. Fascinating tours are offered every Sunday on the hour between 11 and 3 and on Tuesday and Thursday at 11:30 and 2:30. Admission, which helps pay for the renovation, is $5 for adults and $3 for students, senior citizens, and children. They also have all sorts of specially designed tours and talks for student groups and children. Call 212/219-0888 for more information.

Federal Reserve Bank—More than 20 countries keep their gold buried in the bedrock of Manhattan at the Federal Reserve Bank. Daily tours of this incredible institution are free, but reservations must be made at least a week in advance, and children under 16 are not allowed. Be sure to look for the American Numismatic Society's display on the history of money. Call 212/720-6130 for more information. The Federal Reserve Bank is located on Liberty Street between Nassau and Williams streets in lower Manhattan.

Gracie Mansion—Thanks to Fiorello LaGuardia, New York is the only city in the U.S. with an official mayoral residence. Built in 1799, this historic mansion is one of the oldest continuously occupied homes in New York (well, sort of—current mayor Michael Bloomberg actually lives in an East Side townhouse). It's located in Carl Schurz Park, overlooking the East River (at 88th Street and East End Avenue). Morning and afternoon tours are offered on Wednesday by appointment in warmer months. Call 212/570-4751 for more information or a reservation (which is required). Reservations must be made far enough in advance to allow tickets to be mailed. A contribution of $7 for adults and $4 for senior citizens is suggested.

Grand Central Station—In addition to excellent walking tours, the Municipal Art Society conducts a 90-minute free tour of this beautiful building every Wednesday at 12:30. I highly recommend this popular tour. Grand Central Station is one of the city's real landmarks, and the society's tour conveys a sense of its grandeur and history while allowing you to see features most commuters don't even know exist. The tour meets at the information booth on the main concourse directly across from the grand staircase. Call 212/935-3960 for more information. The Grand Central Partnership also offers a free tour of the neighborhood on Friday at 12:30 p.m. It meets at the Whitney Museum's small gallery, directly across 42nd Street from Grand Central Station.

Harlem—Whether you want to visit a jazz club, stop by historic buildings like the Morris-Jumel Mansion and the Apollo Theatre, or go to church on Sunday morning to hear a gospel choir, **Harlem Your Way!** (212/690-1687), specializes in customized tours for individuals and groups, family reunions, and other events.

Lincoln Center—Tours of the magnificent auditoriums and concert halls at Lincoln Center are given at least four times a day between 10 and 4:30. Because the schedule is set only a day in advance, you must call on the day you want to tour the complex to find out when they're being offered. The tour costs $12.50 for adults, $9 for students and senior citizens, and $6 for children 6 to 12. (If that seems steep, check out the prices of opera and concert tickets!) Lincoln Center stretches from 62nd to 65th streets along Columbus Avenue. The tour office is on the mezzanine level of the Metropolitan Opera House, directly in back of the main square. Call 212/875-5350 for more information or a brochure.

Lower East Side—This shopper's tour is sponsored by the Historic Orchard Street Shopping District (a merchants association). You'll learn about this wonderful area's shops and retailing history. The tour meets on Sunday at 11 at Katz's Delicatessen (East Houston at Ludlow Street) from April through December. It lasts about an hour and is free. Call 212/226-9010 for more information.

Lower East Side Tenement Museum—I can't say enough about this wonderful museum and its docents. In addition to tours of the restored apartments in the tenement at 97 Orchard Street, the museum offers fascinating tours exploring the surrounding area's rich and diverse ethnic heritage on weekends in warmer months. Though not cheap they're well worth the price. Tours leave from the museum's offices at the corner of Orchard and Broome streets. Call 212/431-0233 for more information.

Madison Square Garden—If you've always wanted to see the New York Knicks' locker room, this tour's for you! It's offered daily on the hour from 10 to 3. Be aware that schedules are frequently abbreviated because of events at the Garden. Tickets cost $16 for adults and $12 for children 12 and under, and are available at the Garden's box office. Call 212/465-5800 for more information.

The **New York Landmarks Conservancy** has published several books detailing self-guided walking tours in such neighborhoods as Lower Manhattan, the Upper East Side, Harlem, and the Flatiron District. Call 212/995-5260 for more information or visit the conservancy at 141 Fifth Avenue.

Metropolitan Opera—The Metropolitan Opera Guild offers 90-minute tours of this extraordinary place between the start of the opera season (around the end of September) and the end of the ballet season (in or around June) on weekday afternoons and Saturday mornings. Reservations should be made well in advance, but you can always call at the last minute to see if space is available or go on a standby basis. Tickets cost $8 for adults and $4 for full-time students. Call 212/769-7020 between 10 and 4 on weekdays for more information or a brochure.

NBC Experience/Studio Tour—Children under six are not admitted, but anybody else can take an hour-long tour of NBC's television studios for $17.50 per person ($15 per person if you're with a group of four or more). They've added lots of high-tech bells and whistles to this tour, but the quality still varies dramatically, depending on chance (what famous person happens to be getting off the elevator as you're getting on) and whether some big news event is breaking. The tour leaves every 15 minutes daily from 8:30 to 5 from NBC's lobby on 50th Street between Fifth Avenue and Avenue of the Americas. Call 212/664-7174 for more information.

New Amsterdam Theater—Tours of this beautifully restored theater— home of *The Lion King*—offer a glimpse into Broadway's past and present. They're offered hourly on Monday and Tuesday between 10 and 5. Tickets are available at the theater's box office and cost $10 for adults and $5 for children under 12. Tours meet at the box office on 42nd Street between Seventh and Eighth avenues. Call 212/282-2907 for more information.

New York Public Library—An informative free tour of the grand New York Public Library is offered free Monday through Saturday at 11 and 2. It leaves from the Friends of the Library desk, to the right of the library's main entrance on Fifth Avenue at 41st Street. Tours of the changing exhibits in the library's

Gottesman Hall are also offered Monday through Saturday at 11 and 2. Call the library's volunteer office at 212/930-0501 for more information or to schedule a tour for groups of ten or more.

Radio City Music Hall—If you want to get inside this art deco treasure but don't want to attend a concert or other event, try one of the daily "Stage Door" tours. Tours run about an hour and are offered at various times, depending on the season. The cost is $16 for adults and $10 for children under 12. Call 212/247-4777 for more information. Tickets are available inside the main lobby, on the corner of Avenue of the Americas and 50th Street.

Rockefeller Center—An hour-long tour begins at the NBC Experience Store on 49th Street between Fifth Avenue and Avenue of the Americas. You'll be given headphones so you can hear your tour guide over the hustle and bustle of this sprawling complex in the heart of midtown. It costs $10 for adults and $8 for children from 6 to16 and senior citizens. Call 212/664-7174 for more information.

Scene on TV Tour—This 90-minute bus tour of sites from such television shows as *Law and Order*, *Seinfeld*, and even *I Love Lucy* leaves several times on Saturday and Sunday from the Times Square Information Center (on Seventh Avenue between 46th and 47th streets). Call 212/410-9830 for information and schedules.

Schomburg Center for Research in Black Culture—Tours of the collection and galleries in this rich cultural resource on the corner of Malcolm X Boulevard and 135th Street are offered by appointment only, Monday through Saturday (except Thursday) between 10 and 2. Call 212/491-2207 for information and reservations.

34th Street—The 34th Street Partnership sponsors a free 90-minute tour of the neighborhood around the Empire State Building on Thursdays at 12:30. The tour meets at the Fifth Avenue entrance of the Empire State Building, between 33rd and 34th streets. Call 212/868-0521 for more information.

Trinity Church—A guided tour of this historic church at Broadway and Wall Street leaves from the pulpit inside the sanctuary at 2 p.m. daily. The tour is free, but donations are accepted. Call 212/602-0800 for more information.

United Nations—If you want to peek inside the chambers of the United Nations General Assembly and learn more about this incredible organization, tours begin about every half hour between 9:30 and 4:45 seven days a week (weekdays only in January and February). The tour costs $8 for adults, $7 for senior citizens, $6 for students, and $5 for children in grades 1 through 8. Children under five are not allowed on the tours, which last from 45 minutes to an hour and are offered in languages other than English. The visitors' entrance to the United Nations is on First Avenue, between 45th and 46th streets, and the tour desk is directly across from the entrance, past the main lobby and down the hall. Call 212/963-7713 for more information.

Yankee Stadium—Even in the off-season, baseball fans can tour the dugout, press box, and clubhouse of "the House that Ruth Built" (which is, by the way, in the Bronx). If you're alone or with a few other people, simply show up at the stadium's press gate at noon daily (except on game days). If you're with a group of 12 or more, advance reservations are required. Tours cost

$10 for adults and $5 for children and senior citizens. Call 718/579-4531 for more information.

> Babe Ruth hit his first home run in Yankee Stadium in the first game ever played there, on April 18, 1923.

WALKING TOURS

Time Out New York lists scheduled walking tours in its "Around Town" section each week. Among the potential sources:

Adventure on a Shoestring—The name pretty much sums up Howard Goldberg's marvelous organization, now celebrating four decades in the business. Scores of interesting and often offbeat tours of the city and surrounding areas are offered for only $5 per person. Ethnic neighborhoods, historic areas, and the Brooklyn Bridge on its birthday—complete with cake and candles—are among the selections. Call 212/265-2663 for more information.

Big Onion Walking Tours—Seth Kamil and his band of guides—most of them graduate students in American history from Columbia University and New York University—share their vast knowledge of New York through a wide array of walking tours. Governor's Island, George Washington's New York, Historic Catholic New York, and the Civil War and Draft Riots are just a few of the many topics. You can even take a wildly popular tour of the Lower East Side on Christmas Day. Most tours cost $10 for adults and $8 for senior citizens and students. Some are a bit more and all can be arranged for private parties. All tours last between two and two-and-a-half hours. While some of the guides are more charismatic than others, all are well informed. Call 212/439-1090 for more information or to get on their mailing list.

Joyce Gold's History Tours of New York City—Nowhere in the United States are past and present so closely quartered as in New York, and few people are better able to convey that than historian Joyce Gold. Her scheduled tours—which include such topics as the American Revolution, the Gilded Age of J. P. Morgan, and the Jewish Lower East Side—are usually given on weekends in warmer months and cost $12. She is also available for private tours. Call 212/242-5762 for more information and a current schedule.

Municipal Art Society—This terrific advocacy group offers a wide array of thematic and area-specific walking tours for people interested in the city's architecture and history. Most tours are led by historians. The diverse topics include architectural oddities, immigrant New York, downtown skyscrapers, and subway art and design. Tours are offered on different days at various places. Most last 90 minutes and cost $10 to $15 for adults (less for students and senior citizens). Call 212/439-1049 for general information or to get on the mailing list.

Museum of the City of New York—This museum's walking tours are very much in tune with the tenor of life in the city. Typically held every other Sunday from April to October, tours are led by experts and cost $15. Registration is required. For more information or to get on the mailing list, call the museum's education department at 212/534-1672, ext. 206.

92nd Street Y—This amazing institution offers walking tours to complement its frequent lectures and other programs, as well as open houses in historic areas. Prices vary, guides are knowledgeable, and tours are well run. They fill up quickly, and reservations are required. Call 212/415-5628 for more information or to get on the mailing list.

Seth Kamil, Eric Wakin, and Kenneth Jackson—founders of Big Onion Walking Tours—have written a wonderful book outlining self-guided walking tours of New York. It's loaded with interesting details about this wonderful city. **The Big Onion Guide to New York City: The Historic Tours** is sold in bookstores, or you can call 212/439-1090 to order copies.

River-to-River Downtown Walking Tours—I don't know of a better guide for a "river to river" walk through lower Manhattan than Ruth Alscher-Green, a retired high school teacher and lifelong New Yorker. A two-hour tour costs $35 for one person and $50 for two, and special rates are offered for groups and senior citizens. Call 212/321-2823 for more information or to get on her mailing list.

Urban Explorations—Landscape designer Patricia Olmstead offers thoughtful and informative walking tours of Battery Park City, Soho, Chinatown, the Flower District, the area around the 96th Street Mosque, and just about any other neighborhood or district you want to see. She specializes in garden tours and will happily design an itinerary or private tour if nothing in her repertoire suits you or your group. Most tours are conducted on weekends and cost $12 for adults and $10 for students, senior citizens, and repeat customers. Call 718/721-5254 for more information or to get on her mailing list.

Urban Park Rangers—The city's Department of Parks and Recreation employs Urban Park Rangers, who give wonderful weekend walking tours of Central Park and other parks throughout Manhattan and the outer boroughs. Tours are free, and many are designed for children or families. Call 212/360-2774 to get on their mailing list or 888/697-2757 for recorded information.

IV. Where to Find It: New York's Best Food Shops

The food shops found in this section represent the finest in Manhattan —and perhaps in the world. No city has the variety of fine food outlets found in New York; I would encourage you to try the specialty stores as well as the wonderful larger gourmet emporiums. When kitchen time is limited, you'll be able to pick up ready-to-serve items in many of these places. In addition, fine catering is offered by numerous stores. Amazingly, prices in most of these shops are quite reasonable.

Asian

ASIA MARKET
71½ Mulberry St (bet Canal and Bayard St)   212/962-2020
Daily: 8-7

Fresh fruit and vegetables, plus exotic herbs and spices from all over Asia, are the main attraction at Asia Market. You'll find items from Thailand, Indonesia, Malaysia, the Philippines, Japan and China, plus a staff ready to explain how to prepare dishes from these countries. The Asia Market provides produce to some of New York's best restaurants.

Bakery Goods

AMY'S BREAD
672 Ninth Ave (Hell's Kitchen)   212/977-2670
Mon-Fri: 7:30 a.m.-11 p.m.; Sat: 8 a.m.-11 p.m.; Sun: 9 a.m.-6 p.m.

75 Ninth Ave (Chelsea Market)   212/462-4338
Mon-Fri: 7:30 a.m.-8 p.m.; Sat: 8 a.m.-7 p.m.; Sun: 10 a.m.-6 p.m.

972 Lexington Ave (Upper East Side)   212/537-0270
Mon-Fri: 7:30 a.m.-7 p.m.; Sat: 8 a.m.-7 p.m.; Sun: 9 a.m.-6 p.m.

As the aroma of freshly baked bread and sweets drifts onto Ninth Avenue, locals and tourists alike line up outside of Amy's Hell's Kitchen location to sample the many treats for sale. An oasis in the heart of midtown, Amy's Bread is a cross between a Parisian *boulangerie* and a cozy Midwestern kitchen. Of course, you should come for the bread—Amy's signature semolina with golden raisin and fennel, the green olive picholine, or just a simple French baguette. One could eat three meals a day and in-between snacks at Amy's Bread. Just to name a few goods, there are grilled sandwiches, sticky buns, old-fashioned double layer cakes, and decadent brownies. The staff provides consistent, friendly service.

A. ORWASHER BAKERY
308 E 78th St (at Second Ave)   212/288-6569
Mon-Sat: 7-7; Sun: 9-4   www.orwashers.com

Orwasher has occupied the same location and been run by the same family for nearly a century. Many of its breads are made from recipes handed down from father to son. You'll find Old World breads that once were commonly made in the local immigrant bakeries but are now extremely rare. Over 30 varieties are always available. Hearth-baked in brick ovens and made with natural ingredients, the breads come in a marvelous array of shapes and sizes—triple twists, cornucopias, and hearts, just to name a few. Be sure to sample the onion boards, rye, cinnamon raisin bread, and challah, available on Friday. It's almost as good as the home-baked variety. Best of all is raisin pumpernickel, which comes in small rolls or loaves and is sensational when warm. The Irish soda bread is also special!

BREAD MARKET & CAFE
485 Fifth Ave (bet 41st and 42nd St)   212/370-7356
Mon-Fri: 6-6; Sat: 7-5

Freshness is the key here! The bread is baked fresh daily in their rotating oven. You'll find very good San Francisco sourdough, French baguettes, sourdough focaccia, ciabatta, German pumpernickel, and much more. They make a wide variety of excellent sandwiches. Free delivery is offered.

CAFE LALO
201 W 83rd St (at Amsterdam Ave)   212/496-6031
Mon-Thurs: 8 a.m.-2 a.m.; Fri: 8-4; Sat: 9-4;
Sun: 9 a.m-2 a.m.   www.cafelalo.com

In my opinion, this is the best dessert shop in town. You will be reminded of a fine European pastry shop as you enjoy cappuccino, espresso, cordials, and a large selection of delicious desserts. Cafe Lalo offers more than 100 choices, including cakes, cheesecakes, tarts, and pies! Yogurt and ice cream are also available, and soothing music makes every calorie go down sweetly. Breakfasts and brunches are all a treat.

CHARLES & LAUREL DESSERTS
537 Greenwich St (at Houston St)   212/229-9339
Mon-Fri: 9-5 (phone orders only; no drop-in sales)

You've found a real winner! Charles and Laurel Desserts, a mother and son operation since 1990, is essentially a wholesale business but will take phone orders from readers of this volume. Among treats in store here: the best semisweet chocolate brownies in town, blondies, innovative bar cookies (like raspberry truffle brownies and espresso caramel hazelnut bars), tortes, mini bundt cakes, loaf cakes, and much more. Charles and Laurel have a personal and corporate gift division that ships delicious treats anywhere.

COLUMBUS BAKERY
474 Columbus Ave (at 83rd St)   212/724-6880
Daily: 8 a.m.-l0 p.m.

The Upper West Side has a quality bakery it can call its own! Columbus Bakery sells great rosemary rolls, delicious onion rolls (great for burgers), multigrain breads, really crusty sourdoughs, wonderful cakes and pastries, and more. You can eat in or take out, but what a pleasure just to sit here and smell those fresh loaves. Catering is available.

CREATIVE CAKES
400 E 74th St (at First Ave)   212/794-9811
Mon-Fri: 8-4:30; Sat: 9-11

Being in the "creative cake" business myself, I know all about making special concoctions. Creative Cakes knows how to have fun using fine ingredients and ingenious patterns. Cake lovers are fans of the fudgy chocolate cake with frosted buttercream icing and sensational designs. Among other things, Bill Schutz has replicated the U.S. Customs House in cake form for a Fourth of July celebration. Prices are reasonable, and the results are sure to be a conversation piece at any party.

DUFOUR PASTRY KITCHENS
25 Ninth Ave (at 13th St)   212/929-2800
Mon-Fri: 9-5

This area is now one of New York's hottest! The air at Dufour is full of pastry dough, so don't wear your best black outfit. Moreover, all items are frozen, so you'll have to bake them yourself (instructions included). But these are the only drawbacks! You'll find delicious and sensibly priced pastry items of high quality at Dufour, which counts many fancy uptown restaurants among its customers. Chocolate and regular puff-pastry dough are available in sheets and in bulk. Wonderful hors d'oeuvres include bite-size, hand-filled "party bites" in flavors like fresh mushroom paté, Swiss cheese and spinach.

It's a cake shop *and* a bakery! The wonderful cakes—linzer tarts are my favorite—are only a part of the appeal of the **Hungarian Pastry Shop** (1030 Amsterdam Ave, 212/866-4230). The cafe serves all sorts of waist-expanding items, along with delicious Viennese coffee.

FERRARA CAFE
195 Grand St (bet Mulberry and Mott St)   212/226-6150
Daily: 8 a.m.-midnight (Sat to 1 a.m.)

This store in Little Italy is one of the largest little *pasticcerias* in the world. The business deals in wholesale imports and several other ventures, but the sheer perfection of their confections could support the whole business. Certainly, the atmosphere would never suggest that this is anything but a very efficiently run Italian bakery. Its Old World Caffe is famous for numerous varieties of pastry, gelati, and coffee.

No trip to the greater New York area is complete without a visit to the world's largest dairy store: **Stew Leonard's**, the "Disneyland of dairy stores." There are three of them: in Norwalk, CT (100 Westport Ave, 203/847-7213), Yonkers, NY (1 Stew Leonard Rd, 914/375-4700), and Danbury, CT (99 Federal Rd. 203/790-8030). They can also be visited online at www.stewleonards.com.

These are like no other stores you have ever visited, being supermarkets that feature dancing cows, singing milk cartons, and a petting zoo for starters. Visitors each year purchase more than 10 million quarts of milk, 500 tons of hamburger, 1,500 tons of poultry products, 4 million hot dogs, and 800 tons of bananas. There's an in-house fish-smoking facility, a 300-seat restaurant, live lobster tanks, a kosher bakery, a garden center, and a huge open-air farmer's market. Stew Leonard's attracts 13 million customers a year because it is one of the friendliest and most unusual stores in the country.

GERTEL'S BAKE SHOP
53 Hester St (bet Essex and Ludlow St) 212/982-3250
Sun-Thurs: 7-5:30; Fri: 7-2

You simply must try Gertel's blackout cake! Customers who come here are almost evenly divided between those who call it Ger*tel's* (accent on the last syllable) and those who call it *Ger*tel's (as in girdles). Regardless, all agree that their cakes and breads are among the best in New York. Locals prefer the traditional babkas, strudels, and kuchens, but I find the chocolate rolls and aforementioned blackout cake to be outstanding. Tables are available for enjoying baked goods, coffee, or a light lunch. From the regulars at these tables, one can glean the choicest shopping tidbits on the Lower East Side. A final tip: every Thursday and Friday, Gertel's makes potato kugels. People claim to have come all the way from California for a Thursday kugel! During a slow week, you can occasionally find one left over on a Sunday. (Note: They will ship anywhere in the U.S.)

GLASER'S BAKE SHOP
1670 First Ave (bet 87th and 88th St) 212/289-2562
Tues-Fri: 7-7; Sat: 8-7; Sun: 8-3
Closed July and part of Aug

If it's Sunday, it won't be hard to find Glaser's. The line frequently spills outside as people queue up to buy the Glaser family's fresh cakes and baked goods. One isn't enough of anything here. Customers always walk out with arms bulging. The Glasers have run their shop as a family business since 1902 at this same location, and they're justifiably proud of their breads, cakes, cookies (try the chocolate chip!), and wedding cakes.

H&H BAGELS
2239 Broadway (at 80th St) 212/595-8000
639 W 46th St (bet Eleventh and Twelfth Ave) 212/765-7200
Daily: 24 hours www.hhbagels.com

If you find yourself out and about at 2 a.m., you can get a fresh hot bagel without having to wait on H&H's long daytime line. Regardless of the hour, you can satisfy your hot bagel craving day or night at H&H, which bakes the best bagels in Manhattan. They ship worldwide; call 800/NY-BAGEL for mail order.

KOSSAR'S BIALYS
367 Grand St (at Essex St)   212/473-4810
Sun-Thurs: 6 a.m.-10 p.m.; Fi: 6-3:30; Sat: 6 a.m.-9 p.m.

Tradition has it that the bialy derives its name from Bialystoker, where they were first made. Kossar's brought the recipe over from Europe almost a century ago, and their bialys, bagels, horns, and onion boards are fresh from the oven. The taste is Old World and authentic.

Now this one is a real find! For some of the best-tasting pastries in town, hurry down to **La Bergamote** (169 Ninth Ave, 212/627-9010). Their offerings taste great and look absolutely fabulous, too. You'll get raves from your guests!

LE PAIN QUOTIDIEN
1131 Madison Ave (bet 84th and 85th St)   212/327-4900
Mon-Fri: 7-7; Sat, Sun: 8-7

833 Lexington Ave (bet 63rd and 64th St)   212/755-5810
Mon-Fri: 7-7; Sat, Sun: 8-7

100 Grand St (at Mercer St)   212/625-9009
Daily: 8-7

38 E 19th St (bet Park Ave and Broadway)   212/673-7900
Daily: 8-7

1336 First Ave (bet 71st and 72nd St)   212/717-4800
Mon-Fri: 7-7; Sat, Sun: 8-7

50 W 72nd St (bet Columbus and Park Ave S)   212/712-9700
Mon-Fri: 7-7; Sat, Sun: 8-7   www.painquotidien. com

Le Pain Quotidien traces its roots to Brussels, Belgium. It is a country-style bakery with long, wooden communal tables that serve customers for breakfast, lunch, and light afternoon meals. European breads and pastries are sold at the counter. The meals offered are simple and the service very refined. You'll find delicious croissants, *pain au chocolate,* brioche, heaping bread baskets, Belgian sugar waffles, wonderful sandwiches (like Scottish smoked salmon with dill and Parisian ham with three mustards), an unusual Tuscan platter, crisp salads, and a wonderful board of French cheeses. Don't pass up the Belgian chocolate brownies!

LITTLE PIE COMPANY
424 W 43rd St (at Ninth Ave)   212/736-4780
Mon-Fri: 8-8; Sat: 10-7; Sun: 12-7

Former actor Arnold Wilkerson started baking apple pastries for private orders in his own kitchen. Now he and educator Michael Deraney operate a unique shop that makes handmade pies and cakes using fresh seasonal fruits. Although they specialize in apple pie (available every season), they also make fresh peach, cherry, blueberry, and other all-American fruit-pie favorites, along with cream, meringue, and crumb pies. Stop by for a hot slice of pie a la mode and a cup of cider. Also available are delicious brownies, bars, muffins, applesauce carrot cake, white coconut cakes, chocolate cream pies, and cheesecakes with wild blueberry, cherry, and orange toppings. No preservatives are used! Little Pie Company has two other locations: a large eat-in American bakery at 407 West 14th Street (212/414-2324) and a spot in Grand Central Terminal (212/983-3538).

MAGNOLIA BAKERY
401 Bleecker St (at 11th St)   212/462-2572
Mon-Fri: 9 a.m.-11:30 a.m.; Sat, Sun: 10 a.m.-12:30 a.m.

What a charming spot this is! Everything is made right on the premises: layer cakes, pies, cupcakes, brownies, cookies, icebox desserts, banana pudding, and ice cream (a new addition). Birthday cakes are a specialty that come in various types and sizes. You won't go away hungry!

MOISHE'S HOMEMADE KOSHER BAKERY
115 Second Ave (bet 6th and 7th St)   212/505-8555
Sun-Thurs: 7 a.m.-9 p.m.; Fri: 7-5

Jewish bakery specialties are legendary, and they are done to perfection at Moishe's. The cornbread is prepared exactly as it was in the old country (and as it should be now). The pumpernickel is dark and moist, and the ryes are simply scrumptious. The house specialty is black Russian pumpernickel, which cannot be bested in any old-fashioned Russian bakery. The cakes and pies are special, too! The owners are charming and eager to please, and they run one of the best bakeries in the city, with the usual complement of bagels, bialys, cakes, and pastries. By all means, try the challah; Moishe's produces the best. The chocolate layer cakes are also superb. (Note: There is no cornbread or white bread on Fridays.)

MURRAY'S BAGELS
500 Ave of the Americas (bet 12th and 13th St)   212/462-2830
Mon-Fri: 6:30 a.m.-9 p.m.; Sat, Sun: 6:30 a.m.-7 p.m.

242 Eighth Ave (bet 22nd and 23rd St)   646/638-1335
Daily: 7 a.m.-10 p.m.

Delicious hand-rolled, kettle-boiled and baked bagels—14 kinds of them! — are the feature here, but there is much more. You'll also find smoked fish, spreads and schmears, deli items for sandwiches, plus soups and pastries. All of this is available to eat on-premises, for catering platters, or free home delivery (within limits).

When you mention cheesecakes, natives in the know immediately sing the praises of **Junior's** (386 Flatbush Ave, 718/852-5257), a Brooklyn restaurant that's famous for it. Now you can get Junior's delicious treats, in many shapes and flavors, at Grand Central Terminal (near the waiting room on the main concourse or in Junior's restaurant, on the lower level).

PATISSERIE LANCIANI
414 W 14th St (bet Ninth and Tenth Ave)   212/989-1213
Mon-Fri: 8-8; Sat: 8-6; Sun: 9-4

For those who haven't yet sampled the delicacies at Patisserie Lanciani, a quick review of Joseph Lanciani's extensive credentials is in order. For starters, you may have sampled his work while he was chief pastry chef at the Plaza (a major recommendation in itself). Lanciani's cakes, cookies, pastries, tortes, and mousses defy description.

PIECE OF CAKE
1370 Lexington Ave (bet 90th and 91st St)   212/987-1700
Mon-Fri: 8-8; Sat, Sun: 9-8 (closed weekends in summer)
                                       www.pieceofcakebakery.com

This delightful bakery and cafe is a welcome change of pace from Starbucks and other chains. Breakfast, lunch, and dinner are available, although simply snacking any time of day is encouraged. Various cakes, cookies, tarts, cupcakes, and coffees are among the offerings. Stop in for a tasty treat, order a birthday cake, or bring the kids for cupcake decorating parties. The food is good, the prices reasonable, and the atmosphere warm and inviting. The husband-and-wife team of Fred and Vivian Kenvin—he's behind the counter, she's in the kitchen—have created a real winner!

POSEIDON GREEK BAKERY
629 Ninth Ave (bet 44th and 45th St)   212/757-6173
Tues-Sat: 9-7

Poseidon is a family-run bakery that produces Greek specialties. Tremendous pride is evident here. When a customer peers over the counter and asks about something, the response is usually a long description and sometimes an invitation to taste. There is homemade baklava, strudel, *katalf*, *trigona*, *tiropita* (cheese pie), spanakopita, *saragli*, and phyllo. They have cocktail-size frozen spinach, cheese, vegetable, and meat pies for home or parties. Poseidon was founded in 1922 by Greek baker Demetrios Anagnostou. Today it is run by grandson Anthony Fable, his wife Lili, and their son Paul, to the same exacting standards. Poseidon's handmade phyllo is world-renowned.

Attention all bakers! **N.Y. Cake & Baking Distributors** (56 W 22nd St, 212/675-CAKE) is a treasure house of cake and chocolate supplies. The selection is vast, prices reasonable, and you'll find everything in the baking world for sale here.

SILVER MOON BAKERY
2740 Broadway (at 105th St)   212/866-4717
Mon-Fri: 7:30 a.m.-8 p.m.; Sat, Sun: 9-7

Here you can find delicious French, German, and Italian breads, French pastries and cakes, tarts, French macaroons, challah, brioche (fresh fruit, raspberry, raisin, and chocolate chip), muffins, scones, and much more. There are a few tables where you can enjoy a sandwich or quiche (pizzas, too, on Sunday) and watch the passing parade.

STICKY FINGERS
121 First Ave (at 7th St)   212/529-2554
Daily: 7 a.m.-8 p.m.

This is an old-fashioned bakery with one of the best reputations in town. The diverse ethnic makeup of the neighborhood is reflected in the variety of breads. The quality is endorsed by neighborhood locals with roots in Italy, Poland, the Ukraine, and Russia, who claim the peasant bread tastes as good as grandma's (or even great-grandma's)! The dark, moist pumpernickel tastes nothing like the commercial variety. The Italian breads are authentic. The Jewish contingent is represented by bagels and bialys. Each group thinks Sticky Fingers is their bakery. Could there be a higher compliment? There are also cakes, focaccia, muffins, scones, brownies, fruit bars, and very special cupcakes!

STREIT MATZOH CO.
150 Rivington St (bet Clinton and Suffolk St) 212/475-7000
Sun-Thurs: 9-4:30

Matzoh is a thin, wafer-like cracker. According to tradition, it came out of Egypt with Moses and the children of Israel when they had to flee so swiftly there was no time to let the bread rise. Through the years, matzoh was restricted to the time around Passover, and even when matzoh production became automated, business shut down for a good deal of the year. But not today and not in New York. Streit produces matzoh throughout the year, pausing only on Saturday and Jewish holidays to clean the machines. Streit allows a peek at the production, which is both mechanized and extremely primitive. Matzoh is baked in enormous thin sheets that are later broken up. If you ask for a batch that's baking, they might break it right off the production line.

SULLIVAN STREET BAKERY
73 Sullivan St (bet Spring and Broome St) 212/334-9435
Daily: 7-7

533 W 47th St (bet Tenth and Eleventh Ave) 212/265-5580
Daily: 7-7

Getting fresh, crusty, warm French loaves here is a must. If you savor really fresh authentic Italian country bread, this is also the place to go. Their sourdough is used by a number of restaurants, so you know it is first-rate. Sullivan Street Bakery carries the only flatbread Pizza Bianca Romana (six feet long) in Manhattan. Raisin-walnut bread is one of their specialties.

SYLVIA WEINSTOCK CAKES
273 Church St (bet Franklin and White St) 212/925-6698
Mon-Fri: 9-4 (by appointment only)

Sylvia Weinstock has been in the cake business for over two decades, so she knows how to satisfy customers who want the very best. Her trademark is floral decorations, which are almost lifelike! Although weddings are a specialty (two months notice is required), she will produce a masterpiece for any occasion, including hand-molded sugar figures.

VESUVIO BAKERY
160 Prince St (bet West Broadway and Thompson St) 212/925-8248
Mon-Sat: 7-7

Tony Dapolito was born and bred (no pun intended) in his family's store in Soho. Since that time, the expertise in baking has grown along with the bakery's claim to fame as Soho's heart and soul. When he's not manning the ovens, Tony serves on the community planning board and disperses Soho lore to customers. Visitors unaware of Dapolito's status (it doesn't remain a secret for long) come for the bread, biscuits, and rolls, whose reputation reaches far beyond Soho. After all, it isn't every commercial bakery that eschews sugar, shortening, and preservatives and still manages to produce the tastiest Italian bread around. Try the pepper biscuits or whole-wheat brick-oven baked bread.

At **Patisserie Margot** (1212 Lexington Ave, 212/772-6064 and 2109 Broadway, 212/721-0076) you'll find some of the most delicious cakes and tarts in Manhattan. Prices are not cheap, but you can always begin with their sizable number of miniatures, like mini fruit tarts, eclairs, cream puffs, and chocolate squares. Wedding cakes are available by special order. The Broadway location is inside the Ansonia Hotel.

WHOLE EARTH BAKERY & KITCHEN
130 St. Mark's Pl (bet First Ave and Ave A)   212/677-7597
Daily: 9 a.m.-midnight

This is a completely vegan establishment. It's the only Manhattan bakery using organic flours and organic, unprocessed sweeteners. They feature great pizza, lasagna, and soup, with daily selections of savory foods. Catering is available.

YONAH SCHIMMEL'S KNISHES
137 E Houston St (bet First and Second Ave)   212/477-2858
Sun-Thurs: 9-7; Fri, Sat: 9 a.m.-10 p.m.

Yonah Schimmel has been selling knishes for so long that his name is legendary. National magazines have written articles about him. Schimmel started out dispensing knishes among the pushcarts of the Lower East Side, and a Yonah Schimmel knish is still a unique experience. It doesn't look or taste anything like the mass-produced things sold at supermarkets, lunch stands, and New York ballgames. The knish made here has a thin, flaky crust —almost like strudel dough—surrounding a hot, moist filling, and it is kosher. The best-selling filling is potato, but kasha (buckwheat), spinach, and a half-dozen others are also terrific. No two knishes come out exactly alike, since each is handmade.

ZITO BAKERY
259 Bleecker St (bet Ave of the Americas and Seventh Ave)
Mon-Sat: 7 a.m.-8 p.m.; Sun: 7-3   212/929-6139

Those in the know, know Zito's. They flock here at sunrise to buy bread straight from the oven. Greenwich Village residents love Zito's because the bread crust is crunchy perfection—a sharp contrast to the soft, delicate inside. Two best sellers are the whole-wheat loaf and the Sicilian loaf.

Anthony John Zito is proudest of the house specialties: Italian, whole-wheat, and white breads. The breads are also sold at **Zito's East** (211-213 First Ave, 212/473-3400).

Is your sweet tooth aching? Since 1894, **Veniero's** (342 E 11th St, 212/674-7070, www.venierospastry.com) has been serving Italian pastries, cakes, and gelato to satisfied customers. The quarters still have many of the original details, including hand-stamped metal ceilings and etched glass doors. And what choices: cannolis, cream puffs, profiteroles, eclairs, napoleons, *millefoligie*, fruit tarts, biscotti, butter cookies, pasticiotti, and *pastacroce*. Cakes by the slice include Gran Marnier, truffle, cheesecakes, mocha espresso, sacher torte, *zuppa inglese*, tiramisu, mousse cakes, strawberry shortcake, and even chocolate banana strawberry shortcake. What a way to go!

Beverages

B&E QUALITY
511 W 23rd Ave (bet Tenth and Eleventh Ave)　　　　212/243-6559
Mon-Thurs: 8:30-6:30; Fri, Sat: 8:30-7

If you are planning a party and want to make a quantity purchase of beer and soda, this is a good place to go. They are a wholesale distributor but will pass along savings to retail customers. Some 800 beers from around the world are available, as well as kegs from over 15 breweries.

NEW YORK BEVERAGE WHOLESALERS
207 E 123rd St (bet Second and Third Ave)　　　　212/831-4000
Mon-Fri: 8:30-6; Sat: 8:30-5　　　　　　　　　www.nybeverage.com

The *buy*-words here: tremendous variety, great prices. This outfit has one of the largest retail beer selections in Manhattan, with over 500 brands available, plus soda, mineral and natural waters, iced teas, and seltzers. They will deliver to your door, supply specialty imports, and work with you on any quantities needed.

RIVERSIDE BEER AND SODA DISTRIBUTORS
2331 Twelfth Ave (at 133rd St)　　　　　　　　　212/234-3884
Mon-Sat: 9-5

This place mainly supplies wholesalers and large retail orders, but they are not averse to serving retail customers. Once you've made the trek up here, you might as well take advantage of the discount and buy in quantity.

British

MYERS OF KESWICK
634 Hudson St (bet Horatio and Jane St)　　　　　212/691-4194
Mon-Fri: 10-7; Sat: 10-6; Sun: noon-5

Peter and Irene Myers are to English food what Burberry, Church, and Laura Ashley are to English clothing. They've made it possible for you to visit "the village grocer" for imported staples and fresh, home-baked items you'd swear came from a kitchen in Soho—the London neighborhood, that is. Among the tins, a shopper can find Heinz treacle sponge pudding, trifle mix, ribena, mushy peas, steak and kidney pie, Smarties, Quality Street toffee, lemon barley water, chutneys, jams and preserves, and all the major English teas. Fresh goods include sausage rolls, steak and kidney pie, Scotch eggs, and British bangers. There are also cheeses (the double Gloucester is outstanding) and chocolates. For Anglophiles and expatriates alike, Myers of Keswick is a *luverly* treat.

Candy

CHOCOLATE BAR
48 Eighth Ave (bet Jane and Horatio St)   212/366-1541
Mon-Fri: 8:30 a.m.-10 p.m.; Sat: 9 a.m-10 p.m.; Sun: 10-7
                                                www.chocolatebarnyc.com

If, like your author, you are a chocoholic, you'll love the yummy brownies, handmade truffles, chocolate-covered peanut butter and jelly bars, cookies, and much more at the Chocolate Bar. Some of the best-known pastry chefs in New York, like Jacques Torres, contribute their talents to help customers expand their waistlines. Treats are available for eat-in or takeout.

DYLAN'S CANDY BAR
1011 Third Ave (at 60th St)   646/735-0078
Mon-Thurs: 11-9; Fri, Sat: 11-11; Sun: 11-7
                                                www.dylanscandybar.com

Ralph Lauren's daughter, Dylan, and partner Jeff Rubin, are in the candy business in a big way. Dylan's is a huge candy emporium, delighting grownups as much as kids. You'll find an old-fashioned soda fountain with custom-made ice cream flavors, a candy spa (for goodies like chocolate bath salts), the world's largest lollipop, 21 colors of M&Ms, Pez dispensers, and much more. This is a two-level operation, with stairs that look like gummies! A private party room with all kinds of candy activities—like designing your own candy picture frame—is available. The candy selection includes about 5,000 types of sweets from all over the world.

Although it is not in Manhattan, **Jacques Torres Chocolate** (66 Water St, Brooklyn, 718/875-9772) is a chocolate factory worth visiting. One can see chocolates being made, shop at Jacques' factory outlet store, and watch Jacques bake special goodies on Saturdays. They're open Monday through Saturday from 9 to 7.

ECONOMY CANDY
108 Rivington St (bet Essex and Ludlow St)   212/254-1531
Sun-Fri: 9-6; Sat: 10-5   800/352-4544 (outside New York)
                                                www.economycandy.com

The same family of owners has been selling everything from penny candies to beautiful gourmet gift baskets at Economy Candy since 1937. What a selection of dried fruits, candies, coffees, teas, jams, cookies, crackers, and chocolates, and even sugar-free goodies! The best part is the price. You can buy gourmet items like oils, vinegars, and patés without busting your party budget. Mail orders are filled efficiently and promptly; an online catalog is available.

LA MAISON DU CHOCOLAT

1018 Madison Ave (bet 78th and 79th St)   212/744-7117
Mon-Sat: 10-7; Sun: 12-6

30 Rockefeller Plaza   212/265-9404
Mon-Sat: 9:30-7; Sun: 11-6

What a place! Over 40 delicious variations of light and dark chocolates are available under one roof. They carry French truffles, plain and fancy champagnes, orangettes, coffee beans, chocolate-covered almonds, caramels, candied chestnuts, and fruit paste. There's even a tea salon that serves pastries and drinks. Everything is made in Paris, and La Maison du Chocolat is the first branch of the store outside of France. Prices are a cut above the candy-counter norm, but then so are exotic flavors like September raspberries, freshly grated ginger root, raisins flamed in rum, marzipan with pistachio and kirsch, and caramel butter. What a way to go!

Superb chocolates:

Burdick Chocolates: 800/229-2419 (mail order or delivery)
Christopher Norman Chocolates: 212/677-3722 (factory); carried at Dean & Deluca, Balducci's, Henri Bendel, and Whole Foods Market
Fifth Avenue Chocolatiere: 510 Madison Ave, 212/935-5454
L.A. Boss: 230 Park Ave (Helmsley Building), 212/949-4054
Laderach Chocolatier Suisse: 800/231-8154; carried at Macy's, Bloomingdale's, Balducci's at Lincoln Square
La Maison du Chocolat: 1018 Madison Ave, 212/744-7117
Leonidas: 485 Madison Ave, 212/980-2608
Manhattan Fruitier: 105 E 29th St, 212/686-0404
Neuchatel Chocolates: 758 Fifth Ave (Plaza Hotel), 212/751-7742 and 60 Wall St, 212/480-3766
Richart Design et Chocolat: 7 E 55th St, 212/371-9369
Teuscher Chocolates of Switzerland: 25 E 61st St, 212/751-8482 and 620 Fifth Ave, 212/246-4416

LEONIDAS

485 Madison Ave (bet 51st and 52nd St)   212/980-2608
Mon-Fri: 9-7; Sat: 12-7; Sun: 12-6

3 Hanover Sq (one block south of Wall St)   212/422-9600
Mon-Fri: 7-6

This is a U.S. franchise of the famous Belgian confectionary company and a haven for those who appreciate exquisite sweets. Over 80 varieties of confections—milk, white, and bittersweet chocolate pieces, chocolate orange peels, solid chocolate medallions, fabulous fresh cream fillings, truffle fillings, and marzipan—are flown in fresh every week. Leonidas' pralines are particularly sumptuous. Jacques Bergier, the genial owner, can make the mouth water just describing his treasure trove. Best of all, prices are reasonable. The Hanover Square location features a European-style espresso bar. A new retail location, **Manon Cafe** (120 Broadway, 212/766-6100) serves coffee, espresso, and cappuccino as well as Leonidas' Belgian chocolates.

LI-LAC CANDY SHOP
120 Christopher St (bet Bleecker and Hudson St)   212/242-7374
Mon-Fri: 10-8; Sat: 12-8; Sun: 12-5

Grand Central Terminal (42nd St at Vanderbilt Ave)   212/370-4866
Mon-Fri: 7 a.m.-9 p.m.; Sat: 10-7; Sun: 11-6

Since 1923, Li-Lac has been *the* source for fine chocolate in Greenwich Village. The most delicious creation is Li-Lac's chocolate fudge, made fresh every day. If you tire of chocolate, maple walnut fudge is every bit as good. Then there are pralines, mousses, French rolls, nuts, glacé fruits, and hand-dipped chocolates, all made on premises.

MONDEL CHOCOLATES
2913 Broadway (at 114th St)   212/864-2111
Mon-Sat: 11-7; Sun: 12-6

Mondel has been a tasty gem in the neighborhood for about a half-century. Owner Florence Mondel's father founded the store. The aroma is fantastic! The chocolate-covered ginger, orange peel, nut barks, and turtles are especially good. I order their nonpareils every month or so. A dietetic chocolate line is offered.

NEUCHATEL CHOCOLATES
Plaza Hotel, 758 Fifth Ave (at 58th St)   212/751-7742
Daily: 9 a.m.-9:30 p.m.

60 Wall St (bet William and Pearl St)   212/480-3766
Mon-Fri: 10-5:30

Neuchatel Chocolates is a class act—and you pay for the high quality. A discount is offered for orders over $1,000, and it's not difficult to earn it! The finest Swiss chocolates are prepared by hand from family recipes. The taste has been likened to velvety silk. There are 70 varieties of chocolate, with the house specialty being handmade truffles. The marzipan and pralines with fruit or nuts are also worth trying. Neuchatel's origins are Swiss, but the chocolates are created fresh in New York.

I still like to go to real old-time places! Established in 1925, **Lexington Candy Shop** (1226 Lexington Ave, 212/288-0057) continues to provide great breakfasts, burgers, ice cream, and candy.

NEUHAUS CHOCOLATES
Saks Fifth Avenue
611 Fifth Ave (at 50th St), 8th floor   212/940-2891
Mon-Sat: 10-7 (Thurs till 8); Sun: 12-6

NEUHAUS CHOCOLATE BOUTIQUE
922 Madison Ave (bet 73rd and 74th St)   212/861-2800
Mon-Fri: 10:30-6:30; Sat: 11-6

Grand Central Terminal (42nd St at Vanderbilt Ave)   212/972-3740
Mon-Fri: 10-7; Sat: 11-6   www.neuhauschocolate.com

In 1857, the same year my great-grandfather started his one-man store on the riverfront in Portland, Oregon, Jean Neuhaus established a pharmacy and confectionery shop in Belgium. Succeeding generations have produced some of the finest handcrafted, enrobed, and molded-design bittersweet, dark, and milk chocolates in the world. At Neuhaus' New York outlets, chocolates are still imported from Belgium. The showpiece is the Astrid Praline, named after the beloved late queen of Belgium; it is a sugar-glazed delight! Candy is sold in bulk, bars, pre-packs, and holiday and seasonal collections. Be sure to check out their fine assortment of truffles.

I make no bones about being a candy freak. One of the best candy bars available is the Ultimate Candy Bar at **Garrison Confections** (119 W 23rd St, 212/929-2545).

TEUSCHER CHOCOLATES OF SWITZERLAND
25 E 61st St (at Madison Ave)   212/751-8482
Mon-Sat: 10-5:45

620 Fifth Ave (Rockefeller Center)   212/246-4416
Mon-Sat: 10-6; Thurs: 10-7:30; Sun: 11-5

www.teuscherchocolate.com

If there was an award for "most elegant chocolate shop," it would have to go to Teuscher. These are not just chocolates; they're imported works of art. Bernard Bloom, who owns these Teuscher stores, imports chocolates weekly from Switzerland. They are packed into stunning handmade boxes that add to the decor of many a customer's home. The truffles are almost obscenely good. The superb champagne truffle has a tiny dot of champagne cream in the center. The cocoa, nougat, butter-crunch, muscat, orange, and almond truffles each have their own little surprise. Truffles are the stars, but Teuscher's marzipan, praline chocolates, and mints (shaped like sea creatures) are of similar high quality.

Catering, Delis, Food to Go

AGATA & VALENTINA
1505 First Ave (at 79th St)   212/452-0690
Daily: 8 a.m.-8:30 p.m.

This is a very classy expanded gourmet shop with an ambience that will make you think you're in Sicily. There are all kinds of good things to eat, with one counter more tempting than the next. In summer they have a sidewalk cafe. You'll love the great selection of gourmet dishes, bakery items, seafood, magnificent fresh vegetables, meats, candies, and gelati. Extra virgin olive oil is a house specialty. They have recently made their prices more attractive.

AZURE
830 Third Ave (at 51st St)   212/486-8080
Daily: 24 hours

What a salad bar! Azure's 125 feet of hot and cold offerings is a sight. Of course, there is more: homemade soups, hot Italian sandwiches, stuffed baked potatoes, pizzas, sushi, and great muffins. This place also offers healthy Mongolian grill fare.

BALDUCCI'S
155-A W 66th St (bet Broadway and Amsterdam Ave) 212/653-8320
Daily: 8 a.m.-9 p.m.

The Balducci name is synonymous with food in Manhattan, especially when it comes to fresh fruits and veggies. The Balduccis started the empire in 1946, offering fabulous selections of cakes and pastries, coffees, breads, meats, seafood, prepared entrees, domestic and imported cheeses, and much more. You'll find a huge selection of Italian foodstuffs: focaccia, fresh-cut pastas and ravioli, sauces, *taralli,* and more. In the fresh produce area you'll find spectacular displays of vegetables and fruits, in season or not. It all looks so inviting! This uptown store carries on the family's quality tradition, with attractive displays and decor. Delivery is locally available.

BARNEY GREENGRASS
541 Amsterdam Ave (bet 86th and 87th St)   212/724-4707
Tues-Sun: 8-6 (takeout)
Tues-Fri: 8:30-4; Sat, Sun: 8:30-5 (restaurant)
closed first two weeks of Aug

Barney Greengrass is synonymous with sturgeon to New Yorkers. This family business has occupied the same locale since 1929. Barney has been succeeded by his son Moe and grandson Gary, but the same quality gourmet smoked fish is still sold over the counter, just as it was in Barney's day. Greengrass lays claim to the title of "Sturgeon King," and few would dispute it. While sturgeon is indeed king, Barney Greengrass also has other smoked-fish delicacies: Nova Scotia salmon, belly lox, and white fish. There is also caviar, pickled herring, and kippered salmon salad. The dairy-deli line—including vegetable cream cheese, great homemade cheese blintzes, homemade salads and borscht, and a smashing Nova Scotia salmon with scrambled eggs and onions, is world-renowned. In fact, because so many customers couldn't wait to get home to unwrap their packages, Greengrass started a restaurant next door.

BARRAUD CATERERS
405 Broome St (at Centre St)   212/925-1334
Mon-Fri. 10-6 (office hours)

Owner Rosemary Howe has an interesting background. She was born in India, grew up British, and is therefore familiar with Indian and Anglo-Indian food. Her training in developing recipes is on the French side. Because she grew up in the tradition of afternoon tea, she knows finger sandwiches and all that goes with them. Her menus are unique. All breads are menu-specific, every meal is customized from a lengthy list, a wine consultant is available, and consultations on table etiquette are given. Dinners focused on cheese and wine are a specialty. This is a real hands-on operation, with Rosemary taking care of every detail of your special brunch, tea, lunch, or dinner.

BUTTERFIELD MARKET
1114 Lexington Ave (bet 77th and 78th St)   212/288-7800
Mon-Fri: 8-8; Sat: 8-5:30; Sun: 7:30-5

Upper East Siders have enjoyed the goodies at Butterfield for nine decades. Highlights of this popular market include an excellent prepared foods section, a good selection of quality specialty items, tasty pastries, attractive gift baskets, an excellent cheese selection, and a diet-busting candy and sweets section. Catering is a specialty, and service is personal and informed.

CAVIARTERIA
502 Park Ave (at 59th St)   212/759-7410, 800/4-CAVIAR
Mon-Thurs: 9-7; Fri, Sat: 9-9; Sun: 12-4:30

Caviarteria is the largest distributor of caviar in the U.S. It is known for high-quality products at reasonable prices. Much of the business is done by phone; shipments are packed with ice and handled responsibly. You will find paté de foie gras, Scottish and Swedish smoked salmon platters, sturgeon, and homemade biscotti. There is an on-premises restaurant and a caviar- and champagne-tasting bar. Delivery and catering are added services. Specialties include a Caspian caviar sampler, Caviarteria *club du roi* sandwiches, caviar crepes, and Caviarteria carpaccio. Owner Bruce Sobol is right on the job, accounting for the superior operation of this shop.

CHARLOTTE'S CATERING
146 Chambers St (bet Greenwich St and West Broadway) 212/732-7939
Mon-Fri: 10-6

Quality is Number One here! Charlotte's has developed an outstanding reputation for catering, with no detail too small for their careful attention. Their client list reads like a who's who, including Chase Manhattan, Lincoln Center, and Tiffany's. Charlotte's is a full-service catering establishment, from menus and music to flowers and waiters' outfits. Come here when you want real experts to handle wedding receptions, dinner dances, teas, luncheons, business meetings or dinners, and so forth. Specialties include wonderful tapas, a spa buffet menu, and outrageous desserts.

CHELSEA MARKET
75 Ninth Ave (bet 15th and 16th St)   212/243-6005
Mon-Sat: 8-9; Sun: 10-8

In a complex of 18 former industrial buildings, including the old Nabisco Cookie Factory of the late 1800s, an 800-foot-long concourse houses one of the most unusual marketplaces in the city. The space is innovative, including a waterfall supplied by an underground spring. Among the nearly two dozen shops, you'll find **Amy's Bread** (big choice, plus a cafe), **Bowery Kitchen Supplies** (kitchen buffs will go wild!), **Chelsea Wholesale Flower Market** (really fresh cut flowers), **Chelsea Wine Vault** (climate-controlled), **Cleaver Company** (catering and event planning), **Ronnybrook Farm Dairy** (fresh milk and eggs), **buonItalia** (great Italian basics), **Hale & Hearty Soups** (dozens of varieties), the **Lobster Place** (takeout seafood), **Sarabeth's Bakery**, **Frank's Butcher**, **Manhattan Fruit Exchange** (bulk buying), plus bagels, ice creams, rugelach, meats, hospitality products, and more. **Ruthy's Cheesecake and Rugelach Bakery** (212/463-8800) is outstanding!

DEAN & DELUCA
560 Broadway (at Prince St)   212/431-1691
Mon-Sat: 10-8; Sun: 10-7   www.deananddeluca.com

This is one of the great gourmet stores in the country. Long a tradition for smart food buyers, Dean & Deluca is now housed in a store four times as large as its original location. The temptations are extraordinary: fresh produce, a huge selection of cheeses, fresh bakery items, takeout dishes, coffees, magnificent pastries and desserts, housewares, books, and all kinds of meat, poultry, and fish products. An espresso and cappuccino bar by the door is very popular. This part of the operation has been expanded into convenient smaller locations at 75 University Place, the Paramount Hotel (235 W 46th Street), and 9 Rockefeller Plaza. A takeout shop and newsstand has opened across from the flagship store on Broadway. Professional kitchen equipment is available to wholesale and retail customers, and a catering kitchen is on-premises.

Some excellent, reasonably priced catering outfits and their specialties:

Artie's (2290 Broadway, 212/579-5959): carved turkey, cold salad platters, and reuben sandwiches

City Market Cafe (1100 Madison Ave, 212/535-2070): sandwiches, grilled panini, homemade soups, and smoothies

D&D Deli & Grocery (67 Spring St, 212/941-5770): cold cuts, Italian and Oriental specialties, and roasted items

Food NY (156 W 56th St, 212/265-5551): sandwiches, wraps, tossed salads, and a pasta bar

Murray's Bagels (500 Ave of the Americas, 212/462-2839 and 242 Eighth Ave, 646/638-1335): bagels and lox, smoked fish, spreads and schmears, soups, and cold-cut platters

---

DELMONICO GOURMET FOOD MARKETS

320 Park Ave (at 50th St)	212/317-8777
55 E 59th St (bet Madison and Park Ave)	212/751-5559
375 Lexington Ave (at 42nd St)	212/661-0150
24 hours	

Each of these markets has gourmet groceries, fresh produce, pastries, bakery, a huge selection of cheese, and much more. This is a good place to know about if you are planning a catered event for your office or home. If you're on your own, you can't help but be tempted. I like the ultra-clean surroundings and accommodating help. Don't miss the charcuterie selection and large salad bars.

FAIRWAY

2127 Broadway (at 74th St)	212/595-1888
Daily: 24 hours (closed midnight Sun to 7 a.m. Mon)	
2328 Twelfth Ave (at 133rd St)	212/234-3883
Daily: 8 a.m.-11 p.m.	

The popular institution known as Fairway made its name with an incredible selection of fruits and vegetables. They offer produce in huge quantities at very reasonable prices. The uptown store is newer and larger, stocking a wonderful array of cheeses, meats, bakery items and more. Additions to the Broadway store include an on-premises bakery, a cafe, organically grown produce, expanded fish and meat departments, and a catering service. Fairway operates its own farm on Long Island and has developed a good relationship with area produce dealers. Both stores offer a full line of organic and natural grocery, health, and beauty items. As you make your rounds on the Upper West Side, you can't go wrong by carrying a Fairway bag on one arm and a Zabar's bag on the other.

Some of the better possibilities for takeout meals by neighborhood:

Chelsea: **Chelsea Ristorante**, Italian (108 Eighth Ave, 212/924-7786); **Le Zie**, Italian (172 Seventh Ave, 212/206-8686)

East Side: **Indian Tandoor Oven**, Indian (175 E 83rd St, 212/628-3000); **Luke's Bar & Grill**, burgers (1394 Third Ave, 212/249-7070); **Mangiarini**, Italian (1593 Second Ave, 212/734-5500); **Vermicelli**, Vietnamese (1492 Second Ave, 212/288-8868); **Viand**, diner (673 Madison Ave, 212/751-6622)

East Village: **Il Bagatto**, Italian (192 E 2nd St, 212/228-3703); **Second Avenue Kosher Delicatessen and Restaurant**, deli (156 Second Ave, 212/677-0606)

Gramercy: **Curry Leaf**, Indian (99 Lexington Ave, 212/725-5558); **Republic**, Pan-Asian (37 Union Square W, 212/627-7172); **Tossed**, deli (295 Park Ave S, 212/674-6700)

Lower East Side: **East Side Cafe**, diner (189 East Broadway, 212/387-0366), **Lombardi's**, pizza (32 Spring St, 212/941-7994)

Midtown East: **Angelo's**, Italian (1043 Second Ave, 212/521-3600); **Hatsuhana**, Japanese (17 E 48th St, 212/355-3345); **Patsy's Pizza**, Italian (509 Third Ave, 212/689-7500); **Wollensky's Grill**, steaks (205 E 49th St, 212/753-0444)

Midtown West: **Angelo's**, Italian (117 W 57th St, 212/333-4333); **Mangia**, Italian (50 W 57th St, 212/582-5882); **Topaz Thai**, Thai (127 W 56th St, 212/957-8020)

Morningside Heights: **Miss Mamie's Spoonbread Too**, Southern (366 W 110th St, 212/865-6744); **107 West**, American (2787 Broadway, 212/864-1555)

Soho: **Balthazar Bakery**, French (80 Spring St, 212/965-1785); **Spring Street Natural Restaurant**, health (62 Spring St, 212/966-0290)

Tribeca: **Bubby's**, American (120 Hudson St, 212/219-0666); **Gigino**, Italian (323 Greenwich St, 212/431-1112)

Upper West Side: **Aegean**, Greek (221 Columbus Ave, 212/873-5057); **Barney Greengrass**, deli (541 Amsterdam Ave, 212/724-4707); **City Market Cafe**, deli (2077 Broadway, 212/579-9100); **Francesco**, Italian (186 Columbus Ave, 212/721-0066); **Gennaro**, Italian (665 Amsterdam Ave, 212/665-5348)

West Village: **Cafe Asean**, Southeast Asian (117 W 10th St, 212/633-0348); **Do Hwa**, Korean (55 Carmine St, 212/414-1224); **Risotteria**, Italian (270 Bleecker St, 212/924-6664)

FINE & SCHAPIRO

138 W 72nd St (bet Broadway and Columbus Ave)
Daily: 9 a.m.-10 p.m.   212/877-2874, 212/877-2721
www.fineandschapiro. com

Ostensibly a kosher delicatessen and restaurant, Fine & Schapiro also offers great dinners for at-home consumption. Because of the quality of their foods, they term themselves "the Rolls-Royce of delicatessens." That description is very apt. Fine & Schapiro dispenses a complete line of cold cuts, hot and cold hors d'oeuvres, catering platters, and magnificent sandwiches—try the pastrami! Everything that issues from Fine & Schapiro is perfectly cooked and artistically arranged. The sandwiches are masterpieces; the aroma and taste are irresistible. Chicken in the pot and stuffed cabbage are two of their best items.

FISHER & LEVY
Citicorp Center
875 Third Ave (at 53rd St, concourse level)   212/832-3880
Mon-Fri: 7:30-3:30 (call before 3 p.m. for dinner delivery)
                                             www.fisherlevy.com

Chip Fisher and partner Thom Hamill have served the corporate catering needs of Manhattan with high-quality style and service for nearly two decades. They take care of big parties and solitary diners alike. Fisher & Levy begins the day with delicious breakfast items like coffee crumb cake slices and fresh-baked blueberry scones. For lunch, dive into a juicy filet mignon sandwich with grilled red peppers or roasted turkey breast with honey glaze. In addition to delicious pizza, their small retail store in the food court at Citicorp Center offers sandwiches, soups, interesting pastas and vegetable salads, Cobb salad, and such desserts as homemade bread pudding. Other desserts include gooey brownies, raspberry rugelach, and fabulous all-butter cookies.

GARDEN OF EDEN
162 W 23rd St (bet Ave of the Americas and
    Seventh Ave)   212/675-6300
310 Third Ave (bet 23rd and 24th St)   212/228-4681
7 E 14th St (bet University Pl and Fifth Ave)   212/255-4200
Mon-Sun: 7 a.m.-10 p.m.   www.gardenofedengourmet.com

These stores are real farmer's and gourmet markets! The food items are fresh, appetizing, and priced to please. Moreover the stores are immaculate and well organized, and the personnel are exceptionally helpful. You'll find breads and bakery items, cheeses, veggies, meat, seafood, pastas, desserts and more. All manner of catering services are available, including suggestions for locations, rentals, and service. Platters of cheese, meats, fruit, vegetables, fish, paté, and breakfast are offered. **Garden of Eden Cafe** (14 E 33rd St, 212/576-9961) is now open.

GLORIOUS FOOD
504 E 74th St (bet East River and York Ave)   212/628-2320
Mon-Fri: 9-5   www.gloriousfood.com

Glorious Food is at the top of many New Yorkers' list when it comes to catering. They are a full-service outfit, expertly taking care of every small detail of your event. In business for over a quarter of a century, they have met most every challenge. Give 'em a try!

GOURMET GARAGE
453 Broome St (at Mercer St)   212/941-5850
Daily: 7 a.m.-9 p.m.

301 E 64th St (at Second Ave)   212/535-6271
Daily: 7 a.m.-8:30 p.m.

2567 Broadway (at 96th St)   212/663-0656
Daily: 7 a.m.-10 p.m.

117 Seventh Ave S (bet 10th and Christopher St)   212/699-5980
Daily: 7 a.m.-10 p.m.   www.gourmetgarage.com

A working-class gourmet food shop is the best way to describe Gourmet Garage. These stores carry a good selection of in-demand items—including fruits and veggies, cheeses, breads, pastries, coffees, meats, and olive oils—at low prices. Organic foods are a specialty.

GRACE'S MARKETPLACE
1237 Third Ave (at 71st St)   212/737-0600
Mon-Sat: 7 a.m.-8:30 p.m.; Sun: 8-7   www.gracesmarketplace.com

Founded by Grace Balducci Doria, the late Joe Doria, Sr., and their family, Grace's Marketplace is one of the city's most popular food emporiums. Products, service, and ambience are strictly top of the line. You'll find smoked meats and fish, cheeses, fresh pastas, homemade sauces, produce, a full range of baked goods, candy, coffee, tea, dried fruits, pastries, gourmet groceries, prepared foods, prime meats, and fresh seafood. They are also known for quality gift baskets and catering. Get a taste of Puglia at their restaurant, **Grace's Trattoria** (201 East 71st Street, 212/452-2323). No visit to New York is complete without an excursion to Grace's!

One of Manhattan's best food courts is located on the lower level of **Grand Central Station** (42nd St bet Park and Lexington Ave). You'll find some of the city's best food purveyors, along with comfortable tables and chairs.

GREAT PERFORMANCES
287 Spring St (bet Hudson and Varick St)   212/727-2424
Mon-Fri: 8:30-5:30   www.greatperformances.com

Great Performances has been creating spectacular events in the New York area for 20 years with the help of folks from the city's artistic community. Each division of this full-service catering company has a team of expert staff. They take pride in recruiting and maintaining the best and brightest the industry has to offer. Their people bring creativity, personality, and technical expertise to each event. From intimate dinner parties to gala dinners for thousands, Great Performances is a complete event-planning resource.

H&H MIDTOWN BAGELS EAST
1551 Second Ave (bet 80th and 81st St)   212/734-7441
Daily: 24 hours

Delicious bagels are made fresh right on the premises, and if you're lucky, you'll get 'em warm! But there is more: homemade croissants, assorted Italian cookies, soups, cold cuts, sandwiches, salads, salmon, lox, sturgeon, and pickled herring. The emphasis is on carryout, but tables are available for those who can't wait to dive in.

KELLEY & PING
127 Greene St (bet Houston and Prince St)   212/228-1212
Daily: 11:30 a.m.-11 p.m. (closed 4-5:30)   www.kelleyandping.com

One of the fastest growing categories in foreign flavors is the exotic cuisine of Asia. Thai, Chinese, Vietnamese, Japanese, Malaysian, and Korean foods are popular in restaurants and on home diningroom tables. Kelley & Ping specializes in groceries and housewares from this part of the world. A restaurant is now a major part of the operation, and they do catering, too. If you have questions about how to prepare Asian dishes, these are the folks to ask.

LUCKY DELI
138 Fifth Ave (bet 18th and 19th St)   212/675-0640
Daily: Open 24 hours

Manhattan has plenty of great delis and markets, many of which offer a good sandwich and salad selection. But few do it better than Lucky Deli. Fancy it is not. For quality, selection, and reasonable prices, however, it is among the best. You will find over two dozen classic sandwiches, a dozen grilled and hot sandwiches, seven triple-decker jobs (with French fries), and 55 specialty combination sandwiches, all served on your choice of bread. In addition, there are a dozen salad platters, a sushi bar, and homemade soup. Free delivery is available, and corporate catering is a specialty.

MANGIA
50 W 57th St (bet Fifth Ave and Ave of the Americas)   212/582-5882
Mon-Fri: 7 a.m.-8 p.m.; Sat: 8-7
16 E 48th St (bet Fifth and Madison Ave)   212/754-7600
Mon-Fri: 7-7
40 Wall St (bet Broad and William St)   212/425-4040
Mon-Fri: 7 a.m.-5:30 p.m.   www.mangianet.com

At Mangia, the old European reverence for ripe tomatoes and brick-oven bread endures. This outfit offers four distinct services: corporate catering, with anything needed for an office breakfast or luncheon; a juice bar; a carry-out shop with an antipasto bar, soups, salads, sandwiches, entrees, sweets, and cappuccino; and a restaurant with full menu and made-to-order pastas. Prices are competitive, and delivery service is offered.

NEWMAN & LEVENTHAL
45 W 81st St (bet Central Park W and Columbus Ave)
By appointment only   212/362-9400

Having been a kosher caterer for nearly a century, this firm is known for unique menus and top quality. Be prepared to pay well for outstanding food.

NINTH AVENUE INTERNATIONAL FOODS
543 Ninth Ave (at 40th St)   212/279-1000
Mon-Fri: 8-6:30; Sat: 8-6

Ninth Avenue is one great wholesale market of international cookery. Accordingly, Ninth Avenue International Foods is both a spice emporium and an excellent source for rudiments on which to sprinkle the spices. Here you will sacrifice frills for some of the best prices and freshest foodstuffs in town. Lamb and kid can be special-ordered.

PETAK'S
1246 Madison Ave (bet 89th and 90th St)   212/722-7711
Daily: 7:30 a.m.-8 p.m.; Sun: 9-8

Richard Petak, third-generation member of a family that has owned appetizer businesses in the South Bronx and New Jersey, made the leap to Manhattan. His "appy shop" was the first in the Carnegie Hill neighborhood in a long time. No neighborhood has truly arrived until it has a gourmet shop, and Petak's fills that need. There are all the appy standbys, such as salads (60 of them!), corned beef, pastrami, smoked fish, and all sorts of takeout foods. The store offers full corporate catering, a sushi chef, picnic hampers, and a full-service cafe/restaurant.

PRANZO FINE FOODS
1500 Second Ave (at 78th St)   212/439-7777
Mon-Fri: 7 a.m-9 p.m.; Sat, Sun: 7-8

In addition to delicious food, there are two more reasons to shop at Pranzo: extended hours and free delivery (from 60th to 96th streets on the East Side). Prices are not inexpensive, but quality is apparent in the wide selection of appetizers and entrees. Their custom-made sandwiches, served on a variety of specialty breads, are excellent. Table service in the retail store and a very good catering service are available.

RUSS & DAUGHTERS
179 E Houston St (bet Allen and Orchard St)
Mon-Sat: 9-7; Sun: 8-5:30   212/475-4880, 800/RUSS-229
www.russanddaughters.com

One of my favorite places! A family business in its fourth generation, Russ & Daughters has been a renowned New York shop since it first opened its doors. They carry nuts, dried fruits, lake sturgeon, salmon, sable, and herring. Russ & Daughters has a reputation for serving only the very best. Six varieties of caviar are sold at low prices. Their chocolates are premium quality. They sell wholesale and over the counter, and ship anywhere. Many a Lower East Side shopping trip ends with a stop at Russ & Daughters. It is clean, first-rate, friendly—what more could you ask?

I know this is a Manhattan-only guide, but some places in the boroughs simply must be mentioned. One of them is **Sahadi** (187 Atlantic Ave, Brooklyn, 718/624-4550). For the very best prepared foods, hummus, nuts, dried fruits, olives, coffee, and more at great prices, this Middle Eastern shop is a real find.

SABLE'S SMOKED FISH
1489 Second Ave (bet 77th and 78th St)   212/249-6177
Mon-Fri: 8:30-7:30; Sat: 7:30-7:30; Sun: 7:30-5

Kenny Sze was the appetizers manager at Zabar's for many years, and he learned the trade well. He brings that knowledge to the Upper East Side, where he offers wonderful smoked salmon, famous lobster salad, sturgeon, caviar (good prices), cold cuts, cheeses, coffees, salads, fresh breads, and prepared foods. Sable's catering service can provide platters (smoked fish, cold cuts, and cheese), jumbo sandwiches, whole hams, cured meat, and more. Free delivery is offered in the immediate area, and they'll ship anywhere in the U.S. Cold cuts and chicken dishes are specialties. Tables for eat-in are available.

SALUMERIA BIELLESE
378 Eighth Ave (at 29th St)   212/736-7376
Mon-Fri: 6:30-6; Sat: 9-5

This Italian-owned grocery store (with a restaurant in back) is also the only French charcuterie in the city. If that isn't contradiction enough, consider that the loyal lunchtime crowd thinks it's dining at a hero shop when it's really enjoying the fruits of a kitchen that serves many fine restaurants in the city. To understand how all this came about, a lesson in New York City geography is necessary. In 1945, when Ugo Buzzio and Joseph Nello came to this country from the Piedmontese city of Biella, they opened a shop a block away from the current one in the immigrant neighborhood Hell's Kitchen. (Today, this gentrified area is known as Clinton.) The two partners almost immediately began producing French charcuterie. Word spread rapidly among the chefs of the city's restaurants that Salumeria Biellese was producing a quality product that could not be duplicated anywhere. Buzzio's son Marc is one of three partners who run the business today.

If you're looking for a small but well-stocked specialty food market in the Lincoln Center area, try **Hadleigh's** (1900 Broadway, 212/580-0669). They show a lot of food products in a small space, and there are a few tables where you can eat their goodies right on the spot.

SARGE'S
548 Third Ave (bet 36th and 37th St)   212/679-0442
Daily: 24 hours   www.sargesdeli.com

It isn't fancy, but Sarge's could feed an army, and there's much to be said for the taste, quality, and price. Sarge's will cater everything from hot dogs to hot or cold buffets for almost any size crowd. Prices are gauged by the number of people and type of food, but there are remarkably reasonable package deals. Sarge's also caters deli items and has an excellent selection of cold hors d'oeuvre platters, offering everything from canapes of caviar, sturgeon, and Nova Scotia salmon to shrimp cocktail. To make the party complete, Sarge's can supply utensils, condiments, and staff. Delivery is available.

SONNIER & CASTLE FOOD
532 W 46th St (bet Tenth and Eleventh Ave)   212/957-6481
Hours by appointment   www.sonnier-castle.com

These folks are full-service caterers who can provide assistance in finding locations, designer flowers, entertainment, and anything else a customer might need for a special gathering. Russ Sonnier and David Castle are young enough to be inventive and aggressive, yet mature enough to do a first-class job. Their menus can incorporate French, Italian, Asian, and Mediterranean influences. They are also exclusive caterers for **Hudson Studios** (601 W 26th St, Suite 1330, 212/459-9762), an event space.

TAYLOR'S PREPARED FOODS AND BAKE SHOPS
523 Hudson St (bet 10th and Charles St)   212/378-2890
Daily: 7 a.m.-10 p.m.

175 Second Ave (bet 11th and 12th St)   212/378-2892
Mon-Fri: 7 a.m.-11 p.m.; Sat, Sun: 8 a.m.-11 p.m.

228 W 18th St (bet Seventh and Eighth Ave)   212/378-2895
Mon-Fri: 6:30 a.m.-8 p.m.; Sat, Sun: 7:30-7

156 Chambers St (bet West Broadway and Greenwich St)
Daily: 7-7   212/378-3401

These stores sell delicious pies and cakes, baked items like muffins and bagels, assorted salads, and hot takeout entrees. Breakfasts are a treat. A catering service for both informal and elegant affairs is available. Production companies may pick up their items as early as needed.

One of the must-visits in Paris is **Fauchon,** a famous market that upscale French shoppers swear by. Well, Fauchon has come to Manhattan with shops at 442 Park Avenue (212/308-5919), in the Drake Swissotel, at 1000 Madison Ave (212/570-2211), and 1383 Third Ave (212/517-9600). There are candies, gelati, panini, sauces, teas, foie gras, smoked salmon, Iranian caviar, and quiches. For an afternoon respite, tea and sandwiches are offered. There is a certain haughty air about the place, but then . . . it *is* Fauchon.

TODARO BROS.
555 Second Ave (bet 30th and 31st St)   212/532-0633
Mon-Sat: 6:30 a.m.-10 p.m.; Sun: 6:30 a.m.-9 p.m.
                                            www.todarobros.com

This is food heaven! An icon in the Kips Bay/Murray Hills area since 1917, Todaro Bros. carries the very best in specialty foods. Great lunch sandwiches, fresh mozzarella, sausages, and prepared food are offered daily. Count on the fresh fish and meat to be of the highest quality. The cheese department offers a huge variety of imported cheese. The shelves are stocked with artisanal oil, vinegar, pasta, condiments, coffee, fresh produce, and exquisite pastries.

VINEGAR FACTORY
431 E 91st St (near York Ave)   212/987-0885
Daily: 7 a.m.-9 p.m.   www.elizabar.com
Brunch: Sat, Sun: 8-4

Located on the site of what used to be a working vinegar factory, this operation of Eli Zabar's has bearable prices on fresh produce, pizzas, fish, flowers, meats, desserts, seafood, cheeses, baked goods (including Eli's great bread), coffee, deli items, paper goods, books, and housewares. Breakfast and brunch (on weekends) are available on the balcony. This is one of the most intriguing food factories around! Catering is also offered.

ZABAR'S
2245 Broadway (at 80th St)   212/787-2000
Mon-Fri: 8-7:30; Sat: 8-8; Sun: 9-6
Mezzanine (housewares): Mon-Sat: 9-7; Sun: 9-6   www.zabars.com

Zabar's is perhaps the foremost food-retailing operation in Manhattan. The Zabar family has been in the food business for decades, and Saul Zabar is carrying on the family tradition in a superb manner. Zabar's is known for vast assortments, great prices, and quality products. You will not find a better housewares department than their huge mezzanine operation. At street level there is an inviting bakery section, a huge showing of cheeses, a mouth-watering deli section, a renowned coffee selection (their coffee trade is among the largest in the world), sushi, prepared foods, smoked fish, appetizers, gift baskets, candy, and a value-priced cafe. A visit to Manhattan is not complete without a trip to Zabar's, while for residents, it is a part of daily life. Hats off to Saul Zabar and managers Scott Goldshine and David Tait.

There are good dogs and bad dogs. Here are two of my favorite hot dog spots, both on Manhattan's Lower East Side: **Crif Dogs** (113 St Marks Pl, at Ave A, 212/614-2728) and **Dawgs on Park** (178 E Seventh St, at Ave B, 212/598-0667). The ones at Crif Dogs are skinless pork/beef combos, while those at Dawgs on Park are all-beef Hebrew Nationals. Be sure to load up on the sauerkraut and onions at the latter.

Cheese

ALLEVA DAIRY
188 Grand St (at Mulberry St)   212/226-7990, 800/4-ALLEVA
Mon-Sat: 8:30-6; Sun: 8:30-3

Alleva, founded in 1892, is the oldest Italian cheese store in America. The Alleva family has operated the business from the start, always maintaining meticulous standards. Robert Alleva oversees the production of over 4,000 pounds of fresh cheese a week: *parmigiano, fraschi, manteche, scamoize,* and *provole affumicale.* The ricotta is superb, and the authentic mozzarella tastes like it was made on a side street in Florence. A mail-order catalog is available.

DIPALO FINE FOODS
206 Grand St (at Mott St)   212/226-1033
Mon-Sat: 9-6:30; Sun: 9-4

One word describes the cheeses and pastas offered at DiPalo: superb. It's worth a trip to the Lower East Side for the goodies and the friendly greetings.

EAST VILLAGE CHEESE
40 Third Ave (bet 9th and 10th St)   212/477-2601
Mon-Fri: 8:30-6:30; Sat, Sun: 8:30-6

Value is the name of the game here. For years this store has prided itself on selling cheese at some of the lowest prices in town (cash only). They claim similar savings for whole bean coffee, fresh pasta, extra virgin olive oil, quiche, paté, and a wide selection of fresh bread. Good service is another reason to shop here.

IDEAL CHEESE SHOP
942 First Ave (at 52nd St)   212/688-7579
Mon-Sat: 8:30-6 (closed Sat at 5 in summer)   800/382-0109
                                                        www.idealcheese.com

A great place! Hundreds of cheeses from all over the world are sold here. As a matter of fact, the owners are constantly looking for new items, just as is done in the fashion business. Though recently relocated, this store has been in operation since 1954, and many Upper East Siders swear by its quality and service. Members of the founding family are on hand to answer questions or prepare special platters and baskets. A catalog is available, and they will ship anywhere in the U.S.

JOE'S DAIRY
156 Sullivan St (bet Houston and Prince St)   212/677-8780
Tues-Fri: 9-6; Sat: 8-6

This is the best spot in town for fresh mozzarella. Anthony Campanelli makes it smoked, with prosciutto, and more.

Cheese Hints
- Remove cheese from the refrigerator one hour before serving.
- Offer guests at least three varieties.
- Start with a younger cheese and end with a blue cheese.
- Crackers are the best item to serve with cheese.

MURRAY'S CHEESE SHOP
257 Bleecker St (at Cornelia St)   212/243-3289
Mon-Sat: 8:30-7:30; Sun: 9-5   www.murrayscheese.com

This is one of the best cheese shops in Manhattan. Founded in 1940, Murray's offers wholesale and retail international and domestic cheeses of every description. Frank Meilak is the man to talk to behind the counter. Boy, does this place smell good! But that isn't all. There is also a fine selection of cold cuts, pasta, antipasto, bread, sandwiches, and specialty items. Owner Rob Kaufelt has built on the traditions of the city's oldest cheese shop. Special attractions include great cheese and other party platters, gift baskets, and wholesale charge accounts for locals. Mail order is big; a catalog is available.

Chinese

GOLDEN FUNG WONG BAKERY
41 Mott St (at Pell St)   212/267-4037
Daily: 7:30-8:30

Golden Fung Wong is the real thing. Everyone from local Chinatown residents to the city's gourmands extol its virtues. The pastries, cookies, and baked goods are traditional, authentic, and delicious. Flavor is not compromised in order to appeal to Western tastes. The bakery features a tremendous variety, and it has the distinction of being New York's oldest and largest "real" Chinese bakery.

KAM MAN FOOD PRODUCTS
200 Canal St (bet Mott and Mulberry St)   212/571-0330
Daily: 9-9   www.kammanfood.com

Kam Man is the largest Oriental grocery store on the East Coast. In addition to Chinese foodstuffs, they carry Japanese, Thai, Vietnamese, Malaysian, and Filipino products. Native Asians should feel right at home in this store, where all types of traditional condiments are available. All necessities for the preparation and presentation of Asian foods can be found, from sauces and spices to utensils and cookware. Tableware, too! For the health-conscious, Kam Man stocks a wide selection of teas and traditional Chinese herbal medicines. Prices are very reasonable. You needn't speak Chinese to shop here.

TONGIN MART
91 Mulberry St (at Canal St)   212/962-6622
Daily: 9-8

If a home-cooked Chinese dinner is on your itinerary, there's no better source than this store in Chinatown. Tongin Mart boasts that 95% of its business is conducted with the Chinese community. They have an open and friendly attitude, and great care is taken to introduce customers to the wide variety of imported Oriental foodstuffs, including Japanese, Thai, and Filipino products.

Coffee, Tea

BELL BATES HEALTH FOOD CENTER
97 Reade St (bet Church St and West Broadway)   212/267-4300
Mon-Fri: 9-7; Sat: 10-6   www.bellbates.com

Bell Bates is a hot-beverage emporium specializing in organic and natural foods and all manner of teas and coffees. The selection is extensive and prices are competitive. Bell Bates considers itself a complete food source, stocking health foods, vitamins, nuts, dried fruit, spices, herbs, and gourmet items, along with freshly ground coffees and teas. Ask for the marvelous Mrs. Sayage.

EMPIRE COFFEE AND TEA COMPANY
568 Ninth Ave (bet 41st and 42nd St)   212/268-1220
Mon-Fri: 8-7; Sat: 9-6:30; Sun: 11-5   www.empirecoffeetea.com

Midtown java lovers have all wandered in here at one time or another. Empire carries an enormous selection of coffee (75 different types of beans), tea, and herbs. Because of the aroma and array of the bins, choosing is almost impossible. Empire's personnel are very helpful, but a perusal of their free catalog before entering the shop might save you some time. Fresh coffee beans and tea leaves are available in bulk; everything is sold loose and can be ground. Empire also carries a wide selection of teapots and coffee and cappuccino machines. Gourmet gift baskets, too!

JAVA GIRL
348 E 66th St (bet First and Second Ave)   212/737-3490
Mon-Fri: 6:45-7; Sat, Sun: 8:30-7

The aroma of fresh-ground coffee that greets you upon entering this tiny spot is overwhelming! For fine coffees, teas, and pastries, look no further.

McNULTY'S TEA AND COFFEE COMPANY
109 Christopher St (bet Bleecker and Hudson St)
Mon-Sat: 10-9; Sun: 1-7   212/242-5351, 800/356-5200
                                  www.mcnultys.com

McNulty's has been supplying choosy New Yorkers with coffee and tea since 1895. Over the years they have developed a complete line that includes spiced and herbal teas, coffee blends ground to order, and coffee and tea accessories. They have a reputation for personalized gourmet coffee blends and work hard to maintain it. That reputation will take its toll on the pocketbook, but the blends are unique and the personal service is highly valued. McNulty's maintains an extensive file on customers' special blends.

Types of Coffee Drinks

A "tall" is any 12-ounce espresso drink, while a "grande" is any 16-ounce espresso drink. A "double" is any espresso drink with a second shot added. Finally, a "skinny" is any drink that uses nonfat milk.

Americano: a two-ounce shot of espresso with hot water; substitutes for drip coffee

Caffe Latte: a two-ounce shot of espresso combined with steamed milk and a spoonful of milk froth on top

Caffe Mocha: a latte with an ounce of chocolate flavoring (either powder or syrup)

Cappuccino: a unique coffee drink, layered with equal parts steamed milk, coffee, and foamed milk; may be topped with cinnamon, nutmeg, chocolate sprinkles, or powder

Espresso: a coffee beverage produced by using pressure to rapidly infuse ground coffee beans with boiling water

Flavored Caffe Latte: A latte with an ounce of Italian syrup with almond, hazelnut, and vanilla among the more popular flavors. Some like their espresso flavored with liqueurs.

Granita: Made with a granita machine, or *granitore*, these frozen Italian drinks can be made with espresso and milk or fresh fruits and juices.

M. ROHRS' HOUSE OF FINE TEAS AND COFFEES
303 E 85th St (near Second Ave)   212/396-4456
Mon-Thurs: 6 a.m.-9:30 p.m.; Fri, Sat: 6 a.m.-10 p.m.;
Sun: 6 a.m.-9 p.m.   www.rohrs.com

In 1996, M. Rohrs' turned a century old and Donald Wright became the new owner. He has expanded the lines of tea and coffee, and honey, jam, cookies, and chocolate are also offered. Rohrs' has a bar for espresso and ten types of brewed coffees. This is truly a village store in the big city. Wright, himself a great lover of coffee, claims to drink seven cups a day. He vows to carry on the store's tradition of Old World charm in its second century. Rohrs' will ship coffee and gift baskets anywhere.

PORTO RICO IMPORTING COMPANY
201 Bleecker St (main store)   212/477-5421, 800/453-5908
Mon-Sat: 9-9; Sun: 12-7

40½ St. Marks Pl (coffee bar)   212/533-1982
Mon-Fri: 8-8; Sat: 9-8; Sun: 12-7

107 Thompson St (coffee bar)   212/966-5758
Mon-Thurs: 8-6; Fri: 8-7; Sat: 10-7; Sun: 10-6   www.portorico.com

In 1907, Peter Longo's family started a small coffee business in the Village. Primarily importers and wholesalers, they were soon pressured to serve the local community, so they opened a small storefront as well. As that operation gained a reputation for the best and freshest coffee available, it developed a loyal corps of customers. Since much of the surrounding neighborhood consists of Italians, the Longo family reciprocated their loyalty by specializing in Italian espressos and cappuccinos, as well as health and medicinal teas. Dispensed along with such teas are folk remedies and advice to mend whatever ails you. Today, the store remains true to its tradition. Peter has added coffee bars, so now it is possible to sit and sip from a selection of 150 coffees and 225 loose teas while listening to folklore or trying to select the best from the bins. All coffees are roasted daily in their own facility. (Hint: The inexpensive house blends are every bit as good as some of the more expensive coffees.)

Want to try some Asian snacks? Here are some to get started:
- Asian street food at **United Noodles** (349 E 12th St, 212/614-0155)
- Calcutta wraps at **Kati Roll Co.** (99 MacDougal St, 212/420-6517)
- "Original" noodles at **ONY** (357 Ave of the Americas, 212/414-8429)
- Malaysian bread and tea at **Tea & Tea** (157 Second Ave, 212/614-0138)

SENSUOUS BEAN OF COLUMBUS AVENUE
66 W 70th St (at Columbus Ave)   212/724-7725, 800/238-6845
Mon, Tues, Fri: 8:30-7; Wed, Sat: 8:30-6; Thurs: 8:30-9;
Sun: 9:30-6   www.sensuousbean.com

In business long before the coffee craze started, this legendary coffee and teahouse carries 72 varieties of coffee and 52 teas. A coffee-of-the-month club is offered; after customers purchase ten pounds of coffee, they receive one pound free! The bulk bean coffees and loose teas come from all around the world. Teas from England, France, Germany, Ireland, and Taiwan are featured. They carry a large variety of green, white, chai, herbal, and rooibos teas, along with many organic and fair-trade coffees.

TEN REN TEA GINSENG CO.
75 -79 Mott St (at Canal St)   212/349-2286
Daily: 10-8

This company was founded a half century ago and is the largest tea grower and manufacturer in East Asia. They sell green, oolong, jasmine, and black teas, plus tea sets and all manner of accessories. Various kinds of ginseng are also available. Ten Ren means heavenly love, and you might well fall in love with one of their flavors. Some can set you back $100 a pound!

TORAYA
17 E 71st St (bet Fifth and Madison Ave)   212/861-1700
Mon-Sat: 10-6

For Japanese pastries, teas, sandwiches, sweets, and an absolutely restful atmosphere, Toraya is outstanding.

Foreign Foodstuffs (the best)

Chinese, Thai, Malaysian, Philippine, Vietnamese
Asia Market* (71½ Mulberry St)
Bangkok Center Grocery (104 Mosco St, at Mott St)
Chinese American Trading Company (91 Mulberry St)
Fong Inn Too (46 Mott St)
Hong Keung Seafood & Meat Market (75 Mulberry St)
Hung Chong Imports (14 Bowery)
Kam Kuo Foods (7 Mott St)
Kam Man Food Products* (200 Canal St)
Ten Ren Tea Ginseng Co* (75 Mott St)
Thuan-Nguyen Market (84 Mulberry St)

English
Myers of Keswick* (634 Hudson St)

German
Schaller & Weber* (1654 Second Ave)

Indian
Foods of India (121 Lexington Ave)

Italian
DiPalo Fine Foods* (200 Grand St)
Todaro Bros.* (555 Second Ave)

Japanese
Katagiri & Company* (224 E 59th St)

Korean
Han Mi Reum (25 W 32nd St)

Middle Eastern
Kalustyan's (123 Lexington Ave)

Polish
East Village Meat Market (139 Second Ave)

West African
West African Grocery (535 Ninth Ave)

*Detailed write-ups of these shops can be found in this chapter.

Fruits, Vegetables

GREENMARKET

130 E 16th St (office)   212/686-0404
Bowling Green (Broadway at Battery Pl)   www.cenyc.org
Tompkins Square (7th St at Ave A)
St. Mark's Church (10th St at Second Ave)
Abingdon Square (12th St at Hudson St)
Liberty Park (Liberty St bet Church and Broadway)
Union Square (17th St at Broadway)
Tucker Square (Columbus Ave bet 65th and 66th St)
77th St (W 77th St at Coumbus Ave)
97th Street (W 97th St bet Amsterdam and Columbus Ave)
175th St (W 175th St at Broadway)
Balsley Park (Ninth Ave at 57th St)

Tribeca (Greenwich St bet Chambers and Duane St)
Dag Hammarskjold Plaza (47th St at Second Ave)
South Street Seaport (Fulton St bet Water and Pearl St)
Rockefeller Center (Rockefeller Plaza at 50th St)
Columbia University (Broadway at 116th St)

Starting in 1976 with just one location, these unique open-air markets have been springing up in various neighborhoods. They are sponsored and overseen by a nonprofit organization. Bypassing the middle man means that prices are significantly less than at supermarkets. Another great advantage is that all produce (over 600 varieties), baked goods, flowers, and fish come straight from the source. When the supply is gone, the stand closes for the day. Come early for the best selection. Call the above number to find out the address of the nearest Greenmarket and when it will be open. Most are seasonal, operating from 8 to 3, although some stay open all year. (Note: Markets are not open every day, and hours may vary.)

Gift and Picnic Baskets

MANHATTAN FRUITIER
105 E 29th St (bet Park and Lexington Ave)   212/686-0404
Mon-Fri: 9-5; Sat: deliveries only   www.manhattanfruitier.com

Most fruit baskets are pretty bad, but this outfit makes tasty, great-looking masterpieces using fresh seasonal and exotic fruits. You can add such comestibles as hand-rolled cheddar cheese sticks, biscotti, and individually wrapped chocolates. Locally handmade truffles and fresh flowers are also available. Delivery charges in Manhattan are very reasonable.

Best pies in Manhattan:

Apple: **City Bakery** (3 W 18th St, 212/366-1414) and **William Greenberg Jr. Desserts** (1100 Madison Ave, 212/744-0304)

Apple crumb: **Cupcake Cafe** (522 Ninth Ave, 212/465-1530)

Banana cream (seasonal): **Sarabeth's Kitchen** (423 Amsterdam Ave, 212/496-6280, 1295 Madison Ave, 212/410-7335, and 75 Ninth Ave, 212/989-2424)

Cherry crumb: **Glaser's Bake Shop** (1670 First Ave, 212/289-2562)

Chocolate peanut butter: **Bubby's** (120 Hudson St, 212/219-0666)

Classic pies: **Tuscan Square** (16 W 51st St, 212/977-7777): call ahead

Pecan: **Magnolia Bakery** (401 Bleecker St, 212/462-2572) and **Sweet Chef Southern Styles Bakery** (122 Hamilton Place, 212/862-5909)

Pinolata: **Sullivan Street Bakery** (73 Sullivan St, 212/334-9435)

Sour cream apple-walnut, key lime (and seven other kinds): **Little Pie Company** (424 W 43rd St, 212/736-4780)

Strawberry rhubarb: **Buttercup Bake Shop** (973 Second Ave, 212/350-4144)

SANDLER'S
530 Cherry Ln, Floral Park, NY   212/279-9779, 800/75-FRUIT
Mon-Fri: 9-5   www.sandlers.com

Sandler's is a key source for scrumptious candies, delicacies, and some of the best chocolate-chip cookies, even if they are not located in Manhattan. Yet they are even better known for gift baskets filled with fancy fresh fruits, natural cheeses, and gourmet delicacies. No one does it better!

Where to Shop for Caviar

We aim to please all palates and pocketbooks in this volume, including sophisticated tastes.

Bubble Lounge (228 West Broadway): the real thing, plus hundreds of champagnes and wines

Caviar Russe (538 Madison Ave): a luxury spot

Caviarteria (502 Park Ave): I like everything about this place, especially the friendly attitude of Bruce Sobol.

Firebird (365 W 46th St): re-creation of a pre-revolutionary Russian mansion

Petrossian (182 W 58th St): Providing ambience befitting the caviar set, this is a spectacular place to dine.

Zabar's (2245 Broadway): If price is important, then make this your first stop.

Types of Caviar

Beluga: roe is large, firm, and well-defined, with a smooth, creamy texture

Osetra: strong, with a sweet, fruity flavor

Sevruga: subtle, clean taste with crunchy texture

Greek

LIKITSAKOS
1174 Lexington Ave (bet 80th and 81st St)   212/535-4300
Daily: 7 a.m.-9 p.m.   www.likitsakos.com

Likitsakos is one of the better places in New York for Greek and international specialties, including salads, fruits, vegetables, grains, dips, and appetizers.

Health Foods

GOOD EARTH FOODS
1330 First Ave (bet 71st and 72nd St)   212/472-9055
Mon-Fri: 9-7:30; Sat: 9-6; Sun: 12-6

Good Earth has the reputation of being one of the best-stocked health-food stores in New York. The helpful and knowledgeable sales personnel will vehemently deny they are overpriced, but a quick price comparison shows otherwise. Just as surely, a visit will confirm their reputation for having one of the largest and freshest stocks. Good Earth offers delivery anywhere in the city.

HEALTHY PLEASURES
93 University Pl (bet 11th and 12th St)   212/353-FOOD
Daily: 7:30 a.m.-11:30 p.m.   www.healthypleasures.com

You instantly feel healthy just walking in this place—and what a selection! Healthy Pleasures is a full-scale deli/health-products emporium and then some, with entree items (like roasted chicken, lasagna, and fish) for takeout, healthy platters (organic steamed vegetables, salads, and soups), and delicious sandwiches. The soups have no added fat or dairy products and are full of organic veggies. Delivery is free, an all-natural catering service is available, and a daily breakfast-to-go menu features fresh juice, all-natural muffins and bagels, organic and decaf coffees, and herbal teas.

INTEGRAL YOGA NATURAL FOODS
229 W 13th St (bet Seventh and Eighth Ave)   212/243-2642
Mon-Fri: 9-9:30; Sat, Sun: 9-8:30

www.integralyoganaturalfoods.com

Selection, quality, and health are abundant in this clean, attractive shop, which features a complete assortment of natural foods. Vegetarian items, packaged groceries, organic produce, bulk foods, and baked items are all available at reasonable prices. A juice bar, salad bar, and deli are on the premises. They occupy the same building as a center that offers classes in yoga, meditation, and philosophy. They have a vegetarian, vitamin, and herb shop across the street (234 W 13th St, 212/645-3051), with a nutritional consultant on staff.

LIFETHYME NATURAL MARKET
408-410 Ave of the Americas (bet 8th and 9th St)   212/420-9099
Mon-Fri: 8 a.m.-10 p.m.; Sat, Sun: 9 a.m.-10 p.m.

You'll find one of the area's largest selections of organic produce at this natural supermarket. In addition there is an organic salad table, over 5,000 health-related books, a deli serving natural foods, a "natural cosmetics" boutique, a complete vegan bakery, and an organic juice bar. Located in two renovated 1839 brownstones in the heart of the Village, this busy shop also discounts vitamins, does catering, and offers custom-baked goods for dietary needs.

Highlights in natural foods:

Bell Bates (97 Reade St, 212/267-4300): herbs, coffees
Bennie's (321½ Amsterdam Ave, 212/874-3032): large selection
Commodities Natural Market (165 First Ave, 212/260-2600): cheeses, good prices
Good Earth Foods (1330 First Ave, 212/472-9055): very fresh commodities
Health Nuts (2611 Broadway, 212/678-0054): salad bar
Healthy Pleasures (93 University Pl, 212/353-3663): organic meats, produce
Integral Yoga Natural Foods (229 W 13th St, 212/243-2642): organic produce, baked items, yoga classes in same building
Lifethyme Natural Market (410 Ave of the Americas, 212/420-9099): salad bar, produce
Uptown Whole Foods (2421 Broadway, 212/874-4000): one of Manhattan's best; juice bar and kosher items
Whole Foods Market (250 Seventh Ave, 212/924-5969): salad bar, flowers, large choice

UPTOWN WHOLE FOODS
2421 Broadway (at 89th St)   212/874-4000
Daily: 8 a.m.-11 p.m.

This is Manhattan's premier health food supermarket. Organic produce, fresh juices, discounted vitamins, and a full line of healthy supermarket products are featured. They deliver in Manhattan and ship anywhere in the world. A takeout deli offers rotisserie chicken, vegetarian entrees, and even popcorn. The deli and salad bar are organic and kosher.

No question about it: the best yogurt in Manhattan is the coffee flavor served at **Forty Carrots** on the metro level at **Bloomingdale's** (1000 Third Ave).

WHOLE FOODS MARKET
250 Seventh Ave (at 24th St)   212/924-5969
Daily: 8 a.m.-10 p.m.   www.wholefoodmarket.com

This Chelsea newcomer is big . . . and healthy. It is really a supermarket where everything's natural, including bakery items, seafood, meat, cheese, sushi, prepared foods, and ethnic items. There is also a floral department, and they carry all-natural body and nutritional products at sensible prices.

Ice Cream and Such

CONES, ICE CREAM ARTISANS
272 Bleecker St (at Seventh Ave)   212/414-1795
Mon-Thurs, Sun: 1-11 p.m.; Fri, Sat: 1 p.m.-1 a.m.

The D'Aloisio family brought their original Italian ice cream recipes to Manhattan . . . and boy, are they good! Cones specializes in creamy gelato made with all-natural ingredients. Thirty-six flavors (try the coffee mocha chocolate chip) are carried, and fat-free fruit flavors are available. All are made daily on the premises, ensuring freshness and creamy goodness, and can be packed for takeout.

The best ice cream in Manhattan:
Chinatown Ice Cream Factory (65 Bayard St. 212/608-4170)
Ciao Bella (27 E 92nd St and 285 Mott St, 212/431-3591): gelato and
    sorbets
City Bakery (3 W 18th St, 212/366-1414): elegant flavors
Cold Stone Creamery (253 W 42nd St, 212/398-1882): hyper-creamy
Cones, Ice Cream Artisans (272 Bleecker St, 212/414-1795): 36 flavors
    of ice cream and sorbet
Custard Beach (2 World Financial Center, 212/786-4707): many flavors
    of frozen custard
Emack & Bolio's (389 Amsterdam Ave, summer only, 212/362-2747 and
    56 Seventh Ave, 212/727-1198): vanilla bean ice cream
Il Caboratorio del Gelato (95 Orchard St, 212/343-9922): gelato, sorbet
Il Gelatone (397 Third Ave, 212/481-2092): gelato
NYC Icy (21 Ave B, 212/979-9877): Italian ices
Payard Patisserie (1032 Lexington Ave, 212/717-5252): top-grade
    gelato

Indian

K. KALUSTYAN'S
123 Lexington Ave (bet 28th and 29th St)
212/685-3451, 800/352-3451
Mon-Sat: 10-8; Sun: 11-7   www.kalustyans.com

In 1944, Kalustyan's opened as an Indian spice store at its present location. After all this time, it is still a great spot. Many items are sold in bins or bales rather than prepackaged containers. The difference in cost, flavor, and freshness compared to regular grocery stores is extraordinary. The best indication of freshness and flavor is the store's aroma! Kalustyan's is both an Indian store and an Orient export trading corporation with a specialty in Middle Eastern and Indian items. There is a large selection of dried fruit, nuts, and mixes.

Italian

RAFFETTO'S CORPORATION
144 W Houston St (bet Sullivan and MacDougal St)   212/777-1261
Tues-Fri: 9-6:30; Sat: 9-6

You can go to a gourmet market for pasta, but why not go straight to the source? Raffetto's has been producing all kinds of fresh-cut noodles and stuffed pastas since 1906. Though most of the business is wholesale, Raffetto's will sell their noodles, ravioli, mini-ravioli, tortellini, manicotti, gnocchi, and fettuccine to anyone. Variations include Genoa-style ravioli with meat and spinach, and Naples-style ravioli with cheese. Over ten kinds of homemade sauces prepared by Mrs. Raffetto herself, as well as daily bread, dry pasta, and bargain-priced olive oils and vinegars are featured.

RAVIOLI STORE
75 Sullivan St (bet Spring and Broome St)   212/925-1737
Mon-Sat: 10-7; Sun: 11-5   www.raviolistore.com

Since 1989, this factory has been producing one of New York's most unique ravioli and gourmet pasta products. Goat cheese ravioli in a black peppercorn pasta is one of about a dozen unusual raviolis at this factory outlet. A variety of fresh pastas are available daily, along with sauces and cheeses.

Japanese

KATAGIRI & COMPANY
224 E 59th St (bet Second and Third Ave)   212/755-3566
Mon-Wed, Sat: 10-7; Thurs, Fri: 10-9   www.katagiri.com

Are you planning a Japanese dinner? Do you have some important clients you would like to impress with a sushi party? Katagiri features all kinds of Japanese food, sushi ingredients, and utensils. You can get some great party ideas from the helpful personnel.

SUNRISE MART
4 Stuyvesant St (at Third Ave), 2nd floor   212/598-3040
Sun-Thurs: 10 a.m.-11 p.m.; Fri, Sat: 10 a.m.-12 a.m.

In a part of the East Village that is home to an increasing number of young

Japanese and stores that cater to them, this all-purpose grocery store does a bustling business. Japanese is spoken more often than English, and many packages bear nothing but Japanese calligraphy. In addition to a wide range of snack foods and candy, the store sells fruits, vegetables, meats, fish, and other grocery items. They also carry bowls, chopsticks, and items for the home. Sunrise Mart rents Japanese language videos, too. A Japanese bakery, **Panya Bakery** (10 Stuyvesant St, 212/777-1930), is next door.

Kosher

SIEGEL'S KOSHER DELI AND RESTAURANT
1646 Second Ave (bet 85th and 86th St)   212/288-3632
Mon-Fri: 11-11; Sat: 10-10; Sun: 10 a.m.-11 p.m.

If you are looking for a top kosher deli and gourmet appetizer store on the Upper East Side, you can't do better than Siegel's. They keep long hours (Sundays, too), and they also deliver. Featured are fresh, decorated turkey dishes; overstuffed sandwich platters; barbecued, roasted, and fried chicken platters; hors d'oeuvre selections; smoked fish platters; fresh baked breads and salad trays; and a large selection of cakes, cookies, and fruit platters. The number of menu items is awesome, with nearly two dozen sandwiches, ten kinds of soups, dozens of salads, and side dishes ranging from potato and meat knishes to kugel and kishka.

Liquor, Wine

ACKER, MERRALL & CONDIT
160 W 72nd St (bet Broadway and Columbus Ave)   212/787-1700
Mon-Sat: 9 a.m.-10 p.m.   www.ackerstore.com

This is the oldest operating wine and liquor store in America, having opened its doors in 1820. And what a place Acker, Merrall & Condit (AMC, for short) continues to be! There are in-store wine tastings Friday and Saturday afternoons. Wine seminars are offered to companies. Wine parties can be arranged in private residences for special occasions. Free delivery is available in Manhattan. This service-oriented firm stocks a good inventory of American wines and specializes in purchases from Bordeaux and the Rhine. The Wine Workshop—Acker, Merrall & Condit's special-events affiliate—offers wine-tasting classes and dinners that range in price from $40 to $1,295.

A handy wine-delivery service, **Winesby.com** (23 Jones St, 212/242-5144), offers a selection of over 60 bottles.

BURGUNDY WINE COMPANY
143 W 26th St (bet Ave of the Americas and Seventh Ave)
Mon-Sat: 10-7   212/691-9092
                                      www.burgundywinecompany.com

One of the great pleasures of shopping in New York is knowing that there is a store for just about every specialty. The customer is the winner because the selection is huge and the price range is broad. Such is the case with Burgundy Wine Company, a compact and attractive store in Chelsea. These folks are specialists in fine Burgundies, Rhones, and Oregon wines, with over 2,000 labels to choose from. There are some great treasures in their cellars;

ask the knowledgeable personnel. Tastings are offered all day Saturday, and Monday through Friday from 5 p.m. to 7 p.m.

CROSSROADS WINES AND LIQUORS
55 W 14th St (at Ave of the Americas)   212/924-3060
Mon-Sat: 9-8:45   www.crossroadswines.com

Crossroads carries 3,000 wines from all the great wine-producing countries. They stock rare, unique, and exotic liquors as well. Crossroads will special-order items, deliver, and help with party and menu planning. Best of all, their prices are as low as their attitude is low-key.

GARNET LIQUORS
929 Lexington Ave (bet 68th and 69th St)   www.garnetwine.com
Mon-Sat: 9-9   212/772-3211, 800/USA-VINO (out of state)

You'll love Garnet's prices, which are among the most competitive in the city for specialty wines. If you're in the market for champagne, Bordeaux, Burgundy, Italian, or other imported wine, check here first, as selections are impressive. Prices are good on other wines and liquors, too.

If you want to learn more about wine, then take a specialty course at one of the following:
Harriet Lembeck's Wine & Spirit Programs (212/252-8989)
International Wine Center (212/627-7170)
Peter Kump's New York Cooking School (212/847-0770)
Vintage New York (212/226-9463)
Wine Workshop (212/875-0222)

ITALIAN WINE MERCHANTS
108 E 16th St (bet Union Square E and Irving Pl)   212/473-2323
Mon-Fri: 10-7; Sat: 11-7   www.italianwinemerchant.com

If Italian wines are your thing, then Italian Wine Merchants might be your desired destination. You will find Italian wines exclusively, with specialties in cult wines and tightly allocated wines, many from undiscovered producers. Just wait until you see the place; it is class personified!

K&D FINE WINES AND SPIRITS
1366 Madison Ave (bet 95th and 96th St)   212/289-1818
Mon-Sat: 9-9   www.kdwine.com

K&D is an excellent wine and spirits market on the Upper East Side. Hundreds of top wines and liquors are sold at competitive prices. Major ads in local newspapers occasionally highlight special bargains.

MORRELL & COMPANY
1 Rockefeller Plaza (at 49th St bet Fifth Ave and Ave of the Americas)
Mon-Sat: 10-7   212/688-9370
www.morrellwine.com

Charming and well informed, Peter Morrell is the wine expert at this small, jam-packed store, which carries all kinds of wine and liquor. The stock is overwhelming, and a good portion of it must be kept in the wine cellar. However, it is all easily accessible, and the Morrell staff is amenable to helping you find the right bottle. The stock consists of spirits, including brandy liqueurs, and wine vintages ranging from old and valuable to young and inexpensive. While you are here, check out the **Morrell Wine Bar Cafe**, whose menu is inviting!

QUALITY HOUSE
2 Park Ave (bet 32nd and 33rd St)   212/532-2944
Mon-Fri: 9-6:30; Sat: 10-4; closed Sat in July, Aug
                                    www.qualityhousewines.com

Quality House boasts one of the most extensive assortments of French wine in the city, an equally fine offering of domestic and Italian wines, and selections from Germany, Spain, and Portugal. True to their name, this is a quality house, not a bargain spot. Delivery is available and almost always free.

SHERRY-LEHMANN
679 Madison Ave (bet 61st and 62nd St)   212/838-7500
Mon-Sat: 9-7   www.sherrylehmann.com

Sherry-Lehmann is one of New York's best-known wine shops, with an inventory of over 7,000 wines from all over the world. Prices run the gamut from $5 to $10,000 a bottle. This firm has been in business for seven decades, and it offers special services for their customers.

SOHO WINES AND SPIRITS
461 West Broadway (bet Prince and Houston St)   212/777-4332
Mon-Sat: 10-8   www.sohowines.com

Stephen Masullo's father ran a liquor store on Spring Street for over 25 years. When the neighborhood evolved into the Soho of today, sons Stephen, Victor, and Paul expanded the business and opened a stylish Soho establishment for wine (on West Broadway). Now they are celebrating their own 25th anniversary! The shop is lofty. In fact, it looks more like an art gallery than a wine shop. Bottles are tastefully displayed, and classical music plays in the background. Soho Wines also has one of the largest selections of single malt Scotch whiskeys in New York. Services include party planning and wine-cellar advice, and they carry items of interest to the neighborhood.

VINO
121 E 27th St (bet Lexington Ave and Park Ave S)   212/725-6516
Mon-Sat: 1-10   www.vinosite.com

If Italian wine is your passion, then Vino is your store. You will find over 500 labels, many very reasonably priced. The staff is extra friendly, and if you come at the right time, you might even get a sample sip

VINTAGE NEW YORK
482 Broome St (at Wooster St)   212/226-9463
2492 Broadway (at 93rd St)   212/721-9999
Mon-Sat: 11-9; Sun: 12-9   www.vintagenewyork.com

Never on Sunday? Don't believe it! This is one of the places to buy wine on Sunday. They are considered part of a winery (Rivendell), so it is all perfectly legal. Over 250 other wines are also available, so if you are suddenly in need of wine for a Sunday brunch, these stores are where to go. Sampling is available daily.

Meat, Poultry

FAICCO'S ITALIAN SPECIALTIES
260 Bleecker St (at Ave of the Americas)   212/243-1974
Tues-Thurs: 8:30-6; Fri: 8:30-7; Sat: 8-6; Sun: 9-2

An Italian institution, Faicco's carries delectable dried sausage, cuts of pork, and sweet and hot sausage. They also sell an equally good cut for barbecue and an oven-ready rolled leg of stuffed pork. Pork loin, a house specialty, is locally famous. They now carry veal cutlets, veal chops, ground veal, veal for stew, a large selection of olive oils, and every ingredient needed to make an antipasto. If you're into Italian-style deli, try Faicco's first. And if you're pressed for time, take home some heat-and-eat chicken rollettes: breasts of chicken rolled around cheese and dipped in a crunchy coating. Prepared hot foods to take home—including lasagna, baby back ribs, and eggplant parmesan—are also available.

GIOVANNI ESPOSITO & SONS MEAT MARKET
500 Ninth Ave (at 38th St)   212/279-3298
Mon-Sat: 8-7:30

Whatever you need in the way of meat, you'll find it here at good prices. Their homemade Italian sausages are a specialty, and every kind you can imagine—breakfast, sage, garlic, smoked, hot dogs—is available. The cold cuts selection is awesome: bologna, liverwurst, pepperoni, salami, ham, turkey breast, American and Muenster cheese, and much more. Hosting a dinner? You'll find pork roasts, crown roasts, pork chops, spare ribs, slab bacon, tenderloins, sirloin steaks, short ribs, filet mignon, London broil, corned brisket, leg of lamb, and standing rib roast. Free home delivery is available in midtown for "modestly minimum orders."

There are eight grades of beef, but only the top three are worthy of comment:

Prime: the highest and best tasting; young beef, tender and juicy, with 8%-10% fat

Choice: medium grade, usually found in supermarkets; young, with a moderate degree of marbling, less than 5% fat

Select: older beef, least amount of marbling, leaner, but I do not recommend this grade

---

JEFFERSON MARKET
450 Ave of the Americas (at 10th St)   212/533-3377
Mon-Sat: 8 a.m-9 p.m.; Sun: 9-8

Quality and personal service are the bywords here. Originally a prime meat and poultry market, Jefferson has grown into an outstanding full-line store. Second-generation family management ensures hands-on attention to service. Prime meats, fresh seafood, select produce, fancy groceries, Bell and Evans chicken, and fresh salads are all tempting. There are deli, cheese, produce, and fish sections. Delivery service is available. If you don't feel like cooking dinner, let Louis or John Montuori send you home with some delicious hot or cold prepared foods.

KUROWYCKY MEAT PRODUCTS
124 First Ave (bet 7th and 8th St)   212/477-0344
Mon-Sat: 8-6; closed Mon in July, Aug

Erast Kurowycky came to New York from Ukraine in 1954 and opened this tiny shop the same year. Almost immediately it became a mecca and bargain spot for the city's Poles, Germans, Hungarians, Russians, Lithuanians, and Ukrainians. Many of these East European nationalities still harbor centuries-old grudges, but they all come to Kurowycky, where they agree on at least two things: the meats are the finest and prices are the best available. A third-generation family member, Jaroslaw Kurowycky, Jr., now runs the shop. Hams, sausages, meat loaves, and breads are sold. There are also condiments, including homemade Polish mustard, honey from Poland, sauerkraut, and a half-dozen other Ukrainian specialties.

A West Village must: **Florence Meat Market** (5 Jones St, 212/242-6531).

LOBEL'S PRIME MEATS
1096 Madison Ave (bet 82nd and 83rd St)   212/737-1373
Mon-Sat: 9-6: closed Sat in summer   www.lobels.com

Lobel's runs periodic sales on some of the best cuts of meat in town (poultry and veal, too). Because of their excellent service and reasonable prices, few carnivores in Manhattan haven't heard of the shop. The staff has published five meat cookbooks, and they are always willing to explain the best use for each cut. It's hard to go wrong, since Lobel carries only the best. They will ship all over the country. Great hamburgers, too!

OPPENHEIMER PRIME MEATS
2606 Broadway (bet 98th and 99th St)   212/662-0246, 212/662-0690
Mon-Fri: 9-7; Sat: 8-6

Reliable and trustworthy, Oppenheimer is a first-rate source for prime meats in New York. Under the ownership of Robert Pence, an experienced butcher and chef, the traditions of Harry Oppenheimer have been carried forward. It's an old-fashioned butcher shop offering the kind of service and quality you'll never find at a supermarket. Prime dry-aged beef, milk-fed veal, free-range poultry, and game are all sold at competitive prices. Delivery is available throughout Manhattan.

OTTOMANELLI'S MEAT MARKET
285 Bleecker St (bet Seventh Ave and Jones St)   212/675-4217
Mon-Fri: 8:30-6:30; Sat: 7:30-6   www.wildgamemeatsrus.com

Looking for the unusual? The stock-in-trade here is rare gourmet fare. Among the weekly offerings are boar's head, whole baby lambs, game rabbits, and pheasant. They also stock buffalo, ostrich, rattlesnake, alligator meat, suckling pig, and quail. Quality is good, but service from the right person can make the difference between a good cut and an excellent one. Other family members run similar operations in other sections of town, but this is the original and most noteworthy. They gained their reputation by offering full butcher services and a top-notch selection of prime meats, game, prime-aged steaks, and milk-fed veal. The latter is available as Italian roasts, chops, and steaks, and their preparation by Ottomanelli's is unique. Best of all, they will sell it by the piece for a quick meal at home.

PREMIER VEAL
555 West St (off West Side Hwy, two blocks south of 14th St)
Mon-Fri: 4 a.m.-1 p.m.   212/243-3170
www.premierveal.com

Mark Hirschorn worked various business jobs from Albany to Aspen before deciding to join the family's wholesale veal distribution center. As he says, he's been on both sides of the counter. This makes Hirschorn a wholesaler who has a good eye for what sells in restaurants while running a business that is friendlier than most to individual customers. Premier Veal offers veal and lamb stew, Italian cutlets, shoulder or leg roasts, and veal pockets for stuffing, all at wholesale prices with no minimum order. Of course, if you're trekking to West Street, it might be economical to make the order as large as possible. Hirschorn suggests that three or four customers go in together on a few loins. A loin weighing 26 pounds breaks down to 16 or 24 steaks and chops, and the price is a fraction of what a butcher shop charges.

SCHALLER & WEBER
1654 Second Ave (bet 85th and 86th St)   212/879-3047
Mon-Fri: 9-6; Sat: 8:30-6   www.schallerweber.com

Once you've been in this store, the image will stay with you because of the sheer magnitude of cold cuts on display. Schaller & Weber is *Babes in Toyland* for delicatessen lovers, and there is not a wall or nook that is not covered with deli meats. Besides offering a complete line of delicatessen items, Schaller & Weber stocks game and poultry, and they claim to be a butcher shop as well. Try the sausage and pork, which they will bake, prepare, smoke, or roll for you.

Charcuterie
Faicco's Italian Specialties (260 Bleecker St)
Salumeria Biellese (378 Eighth Ave)

TARTARE
653 Ninth Ave (at 46th St)   212/333-5300
Mon-Thurs: 11-9; Fri: 11-8; Sat, Sun: 12-7

Tartare is an offshoot of Piccinini Brothers, a well-known and highly respected meat purveyor for many years. This shop offers great prepared meats to go, a number of side dishes, chicken, filet mignon, and much more. A butcher shop is on the premises, and even the desserts are first-class. This is a real find!

YORKVILLE PACKING HOUSE
1560 Second Ave (at 81st St)   212/628-5147
Mon-Sat: 8-7:30; Sun: 10-5

Yorkville used to be a bastion of Eastern European ethnicity and culture before becoming the Upper East Side's swinging singles playground. Here and there, remnants of Old World society remain. Yorkville Packing House is patronized by Hungarian-speaking little old ladies in black, as well as some of the city's greatest gourmands. The reason is simple: except for its neighbors, these prepared meats are available nowhere else in the city and possibly on the continent. The shop offers a vast variety of sausages and salami. Smoked meats include pork shoulder and tenderloin. Goose is a mainstay of Hungarian cuisine, so there is goose liverwurst, smoked goose, and goose liver. Fried bacon bits and bacon fried with paprika (another Hungarian staple) are other popular offerings, and there's more: preserves, jams, spices, ground nuts, jellies, prepared delicacies, head cheese, breads, and takeout meals. All of it is authentic.

Nuts

KADOURI & SONS
51 Hester St (at Essex St)   212/677-5441
Sun-Thurs: 8-6; Fri: 8-3

Kadouri & Sons is a wholesale and retail operation where everything sold is natural and healthful. The main staples are nuts and dried fruits. The almonds and their derivatives are especially good. Kadouri also carries candies, beans, canned items, and spices. Prices are wholesale, no matter how small the purchase. Specialty items from Israel—including pickles, jams, and soups—are available.

Organic

TERRE 47
47 E 12th St (bet University Pl and Broadway)   212/358-0103
Daily: 7:30 a.m.-10 p.m. (closed 4 to 5)

A self-described "organic cafe," Terre 47 does a good job with in-house lunch and dinner servings. They also offer free delivery ($12 minimum) between 11 a.m. and 3 p.m. Hungry stay-at-homers can choose from a menu full of healthy dishes. Selections include oatmeal and homemade granola for breakfast and soups, breads, salads, and sandwiches later in the day. Try such tasty organic appetizers as summer rolls, whole steamed soybeans, and roasted yams. Daily entrees include grilled fish, roasted veggie napoleon, vegetable curry, and a homemade veggie burger on whole wheat or rye.

Pickles

GUSS' PICKLES
85-86 Orchard St (bet Broome and Delancey St)   917/701-4000
Sun-Thurs: 9-6; Fri: 9-3

Guss' is *the* pickle outfit in Manhattan! In the famous huge barrels outside and in the refrigerator inside, you'll find half-sour pickles, sour pickles, hot pickles, sweet peppers, pickled tomatoes, sweet kraut, sauerkraut, olives, relishes, and much more. There is no other place like this!

Seafood

CATALANO'S FRESH FISH MARKET
Vinegar Factory
431 E 91st St (bet York and First Ave)   212/987-0885
Mon-Sun: 7 a.m.-9 p.m.

Joe Catalano is that rare blend of knowledge and helpfulness. He feels that the only way to attract new customers is to educate them. Catalano's customers, including many local restaurants, rely on him to select the best items for their dinner menus. This he does with a careful eye toward health, price, and cookery. Catalano's at the Vinegar Factory also has a good selection of poached fish, plus crawfish and soft-shell crabs in season. On cold winter days, don't miss the Manhattan clam chowder.

CENTRAL FISH COMPANY
527 Ninth Ave (bet 39th and 40th St)   212/279-2317
Mon-Fri: 8-6:30; Sat: 8-5:30

Central doesn't look like much from the outside, but the stock is so vast that it's easier to list what is not available than what is. They have 35 fish species in stock at any given time, including fresh imported sardines from Portugal. Assisting customers through this whale of a selection are some of the friendliest and most knowledgeable salespeople I've encountered. Louis and Anthony Riccoborno and Calogero Olivri are skillful guides who stock all manner of fresh and frozen fish and seafood products. That includes fish that even the most devoted seafood lover might have trouble identifying. Prices are among the most reasonable in town.

Best appetizers:

Barney Greengrass (541 Amsterdam Ave): the "sturgeon king"
Caviarteria (502 Park Ave): small caviar heaven
Dean and Deluca (560 Broadway, Paramount Hotel at 235 W 46th St, 9 Rockefeller Center, and 75 University Pl)
Murray's Sturgeon Shop (2429 Broadway): old-time reliability
Russ & Daughters (179 E Houston St): the very best, with a personal touch
Zabar's (2245 Broadway): There's no place in the world like it!

CITARELLA
2135 Broadway (at 75th St)   212/872-0383
1313 Third Ave (at 75th St)   212/874-0383
1250 Ave of the Americas (bet 49th and 50th St)   212/332-1599
Mon-Sat: 7 a.m.-9 p.m.; Sun: 9-7   www.citarella.com

Citarella has both the Upper West Side and the Upper East Side covered. They offer huge assortments in a number of categories at their three locations:

- 100 varieties of imported and domestic fish and shellfish
- 90 cuts of pork, lamb, and prime beef
- 160 different appetizers
- 20 varieties of smoked fish and foie gras
- 35 varieties of pastas
- 250 different cheeses
- 100 pastry items: tarts, cakes pies, mousses
- 300 varieties of fruits and vegetables
- 100 different bread items

Delivery service and house accounts are offered, and there is much more: catering, specialty groceries, and housewares. The location on Avenue of the Americas is "to go" only.

DOWNEAST SEAFOOD
402 W 13th St (bet Ninth Ave and Hudson St)
Mon-Fri: 10-3; Sat: 10 a.m.-12 p.m.   212/243-5639

Two excellent reasons to shop here: they have just about any seafood-related item you could possibly want, and their prices are usually about 30% to 40% below retail. Also, there is free delivery in Manhattan with orders of $75 or more. A good catch!

If you can put up with periodic poor service at **Pisacane Midtown Seafood** (940 First Ave, 212/752-7560), this wholesale/retail seafood operation is worth a visit.

JAKE'S FISH MARKET
2425 Broadway (bet 89th and 90th St)   212/580-5253
Daily: 8-8

The menu at Jake's: platters for takeout and delivery; fresh fish, cut kosher upon request; prepared foods, including a seven-course weekend dinner with a menu that changes weekly; cooked lobsters; and clams and oysters on the half shell.

LEONARD'S SEAFOOD AND PRIME MEATS
1385 Third Ave (bet 78th and 79th St)   212/744-2600
Mon-Fri: 8-7; Sat: 8-6; Sun: 11-6

Leonard's, a family-owned business since 1910, has expanded its inventory. You'll find oysters, crabs, striped bass, halibut, salmon, live lobsters, and squid. In addition, there are farm-fresh vegetables and organic dairy products. Their takeout seafood department sells codfish cakes, and crab cakes; hand-sliced Norwegian, Scottish, or Irish smoked salmon; lobsters; and some of the best Manhattan clam chowder in Manhattan! Barbecued poultry, cooked and prepared foods, and aged prime meats (beef, lamb, and veal) round out Leonard's selection. They also make beautiful platters of boiled shrimp, crab-meat, or smoked salmon for parties. This service-oriented establishment provides fast, free delivery.

MURRAY'S STURGEON SHOP
2429 Broadway (bet 89th and 90th St)   212/724-2650
Sun-Fri; 8-7; Sat: 8-8

Murray's is the definitive stop for fancy smoked fish, fine appetizers, and caviar products. Choose from sturgeon, Eastern and Norwegian salmon, whitefish, kippered salmon, sable, homemade salads, pickled herring, and schmaltz. The quality is excellent, and the prices are fair. Murray's also offers kosher cold cuts, dried fruits, and nuts.

ROSEDALE FISH AND OYSTER MARKET
1129 Lexington Ave (at 79th St)   212/861-4323
Mon-Fri: 8-7; Sat: 8-6

Rosedale opened for business in 1906, and its present owner is the son of the founder. Quality seafood is in good supply at all times. Takeout fish dishes and salads are tasty and unusual. All are individually prepared, and their high quality is matched by equally high prices. Many of the city's restaurants and caterers consider Rosedale the best fish source in New York. Free delivery is offered in most areas.

Spices

ANGELICA'S TRADITIONAL HERBS & FOODS
147 First Ave (at 9th St)   212/677-1549
Mon-Wed, Fri, Sat: 1-7; Sun: 1-5

The scent of Angelica's is heavily organic and home-remedy medicinal. This East Village shop caters to folks who want fresh, high-grade spices, essential oils, teas, and coffees. The bulk of the business is in medicinal herbs, dried fruits and nuts, and related books. They claim to be the largest and best-stocked herb retailer in the country.

APHRODISIA
264 Bleecker St (bet Ave of the Americas and Seventh Ave)
Mon-Sat: 11:30-7; Sun: 12:30-5:30   212/989-6440

Aphrodisia is stocked from floor to ceiling with nearly every herb and spice imaginable. Eight hundred of them are neatly displayed in glass jars. Some of the teas, potpourri, dried flowers, and oils (200 of them!) are really not what one might expect. The general accent is on folk remedies, but most every ingredient for ethnic cooking can be found here as well. Aphrodisia also conducts a mail-order business.

Some of Manhattan's best street vendors:

Classy edibles: **M.D. Rahman's Kwik Meal** (45th St at Ave of the Americas)

Crepes: **Crepe Cafe** (53rd St bet Fifth Ave and Ave of the Americas)

Falafel: **Prince of Egypt** (47th St at Ave of the Americas)

German meats: **Hallo Berlin** (54th St at Fifth Ave)

Grilled hot dogs: **Hot Dog King** (49th St at Ave of the Americas)

Kebabs: **"3 Rice"** (44th St at Ave of the Americas)

Pastrami: **Gabriel the Pastrami Guy** (50th St bet Ave of the Americas and Seventh Ave)

Roasted chestnuts (53rd St bet Fifth Ave and Ave of the Americas)

V. Where to Find It:
New York's Best Services

One of the many reasons I love New York is that you can find someone —and usually several someones—for every need imaginable. Whether you need a chair re-caned, a doll repaired, a party planned, or stained glass restored, I can recommend an expert who will take care of you with great skill and quality service. I can also direct you to places to rent formal wear, televisions, and even a personal assistant. On top of it all, I can point you to the right hotel at the right price.

Air Conditioning

AIR-WAVE AIR CONDITIONING COMPANY
Mon-Fri: 9-5 (Sat in spring and summer)   212/545-1122
www.airwaveac.com

If the dog days are getting you down or you want to plan ahead to make sure that they don't, give these folks a call. Air-Wave has been in business for half a century and comes highly recommended. They have sold tens of thousands of units over the years: top brands like Friedrich, Carrier, Westinghouse, and Panasonic. They will deliver and install the same day!

Animal Adoptions

AMERICAN SOCIETY FOR THE PREVENTION
OF CRUELTY TO ANIMALS
424 E 92nd St (bet First and York Ave)   212/876-7700, ext. 4120
Mon-Sat: 11-7; Sun: 11-5   www.aspca.org

This is one of the oldest animal protection organizations in the world, and these folks take pet adoptions very seriously. You'll need to fill out an application, go through an interview, bring two pieces of identification (at least one with a photograph), provide two references that the ASPCA staff can call, and offer proof of employment. The whole process sometimes takes longer than you might wish—but then *they're* sure *you're* serious, and you can go home with a good pet who needs a loving home. Adoption fees for dogs and cats start at $75; puppies and kittens are a bit more. The fee includes a veterinarian's exam, vaccinations, and spaying or neutering. Animal cruelty law enforcement and an on-site animal hospital are also offered.

BIDE-A-WEE HOME ASSOCIATION
410 E 38th St (bet First Ave and FDR Dr)   212/532-4455
Mon-Sat: 10-6; Sun: 10-5   www.bideawee.org

Bide-a-wee means "stay awhile" in Gaelic. This is a warm, friendly place staffed with volunteers who will match you with the perfect pet: puppies and kittens, dogs and cats. The adoption fee includes age-appropriate shots and spaying or neutering. A full-service veterinary clinic (212/532-5884) is open to the public, as is an outreach department offering pet-assisted therapy, bereavement counseling, and volunteer opportunities.

Animal Services

ANIMAL MEDICAL CENTER
510 E 62nd St (bet FDR Dr and York Ave)   212/838-8100
Daily: 24 hours   www.amcny.org

If your pet becomes ill in New York, try the Animal Medical Center first. This nonprofit organization handles all kinds of veterinary work reasonably and competently with board-certified specialists. They handle over 60,000 cases a year and have over 80 veterinarians on staff. The care is among the best offered anywhere in the city. They suggest calling for an appointment first; emergency care costs more.

BISCUITS & BATH
1535 First Ave ("Doggy Gym")   212/794-3600
227 E 44th St ("Doggy Village")   212/692-2323
Doggy Walking   212/737-2345
Daily: 7-7

One could refer to these places as Doggy City! They offer grooming, training, workshops and seminars, vet care, dog walking, day and overnight care, swimming, and even Sunday brunches. Prices have come down, so the place is now more pocketbook friendly, too.

CAROLE WILBOURN
299 W 12th St (bet Seventh and Eighth Ave)   212/741-0397
Mon-Sat: 9-6   www.thecattherapist.com

Want to talk to the author of *Total Cat, Cats on the Couch,* and *Cat Talk*? Need a fascinating speaker? Carole Wilbourn is an internationally known cat therapist who has the answer to most of your cat problems. Carole makes house calls from coast to coast and can take care of many cat problems with just one session and a follow-up phone call. She does international consultations, takes on-site appointments at Westside Veterinary Center, and is available for speaking engagements.

DOGGIE DO AND PUSSYCATS, TOO!
567 Third Ave (bet 37th and 38th St)   212/661-9111
Mon-Fri: 8-7; Sat: 9-6

You will find top-notch grooming facilities, an exclusive collection of custom-tailored coats and sweaters, European-designed collars, and much more. Doggie measurements are kept on file. Their posh boarding facility,

Ritzy Canine Carriage House (148 E 40th St, 212/949-1818), is a five-star hotel for the most pampered dogs and cats. It features a glass-enclosed penthouse play-exercise room, a *chef d'hotel* for special dietary requirements, and a veterinarian in residence.

EAST VILLAGE VETERINARIAN
241 Eldridge St (at Houston St)   212/674-8640
Daily: 9-3:30 (Wed, Sun till noon)

This is the only practicing homeopathic veterinary clinic in New York City. It features a complete homeopathic dispensary, with over a thousand remedies in stock. It is also a full-service animal hospital with an emphasis on prevention.

FIELDSTON PETS   718/796-4541
Mon-Sat: 9-7   www.pawsacrossamerica.com

Bash Dibra is a warm, friendly man who speaks dog language. Known as the "dog trainer to the stars" (clients include Mariah Carey, Martin Scorsese, Henry Kissinger, and Matthew Broderick), Bash is an animal behaviorist. If your dog has bad manners, Bash will teach it to behave. He believes in "tandem training"—training owners to train their dogs—because it's the owner who'll be in charge. Bash's experience in training a pet wolf gave him unique insight into the minds of dogs, and his success in bringing the most difficult pets to heel has made him a regular on the talk-show circuit. In addition to training sessions, dog and cat grooming is available.

LE CHIEN
Trump Plaza
1044 Third Ave (bet 61st and 62nd St)   212/752-2120
Mon-Sat: 8-7   www.lechiennyc.com

Occupying two floors of Trump Plaza, Le Chien is a luxurious pet spa offering day spa grooming and attentive boarding services. A boutique carries a fabulous selection of custom imported accessories, as well as Le Chien's own fragrance lines.

NEW YORK DOG SPA & HOTEL
145 W 18th St (bet Ave of the Americas and Seventh Ave)
32 W 25th St (bet Ave of the Americas and Broadway)
212/243-1199 (both locations)   www.dogspa.com

This is a full-service hotel for dogs, offering boarding, day care, massage, training, vet services, and more. I wonder if they have a frequent guest program for dogs!

PET CARE NETWORK
Daily: 9-6 and by appointment   212/580-6004
                                                      www.nycpetinfoline.com

Pet Care Network, a kennel alternative established in 1985, offers all the comforts of home to your pet (dogs, cats, birds) in 35 separate New York apartment homes. Your pet will receive individual, exclusive care by caring "dog people" or "cat people." There are no cages. These folks are bonded and insured.

SUTTON DOG PARLOUR
311 E 60th St (bet First and Second Ave)   212/355-2850
Daily: 7-7

Sutton has been around for nearly four decades, so you know it is a responsible establishment. Here you will find dog grooming; boarding and daycare; supplies for dogs, cats, and birds; and even a private outdoor park for your loved one to use. Sutton also boards birds, with each housed in its own large cage. A radio in the bird room keeps them up-to-date on world affairs—a necessity, of course!

Sometimes it is handy and even necessary to have a vet make a house call. One of the best is **Dr. Amy Attas** (212/581-7387).

Antique Repairs

MICHAEL J. DOTZEL AND SON
402 E 63rd St (at York Ave)   212/838-2890
Mon-Fri: 8-4:30

Dotzel specializes in the repair and maintenance of antiques and precious heirlooms. They won't touch modern pieces or inferior antiques, but if your older piece is made out of metal and needs repair, this is the place for the job. They pay close attention to detail and will hand-forge or hammer metal work, including brass. If an item has lost a part or if you want a duplication of an antique, it can be re-created. Dotzel also does stripping and replating, but since it isn't always good for an antique, they may try to talk you out of it.

SANO STUDIO
767 Lexington Ave (at 60th St), Room 403   212/759-6131
Mon-Fri: 10-5 (by appointment); closed Aug

Mrs. J. Baran presides over this fourth-floor antique repair shop, and she has an eye for excellence. That eye is focused on the quality of the workmanship and goods to be repaired. Both must be the best. Baran is a specialist who limits herself to repairing porcelain, pottery, ivory, and tortoise-shell works and antiques. She has many loyal adherents.

Someone broke your prized piece of glassware? Don't worry—just call **Augustine ("Gus") Jochec** (597 York Ave, 212/517-3287).

Appliance Repair

AUDIOVISION
1386 Second Ave (bet 71st and 72nd St)   212/639-1733
Mon-Fri: 10-7; Sat: 10-5

Audiovision has been in business for two decades, providing top-quality radio and TV repairs (guaranteed for three months) on all major brands. Pickup and delivery, installation, and hookup are also provided.

Appraisals

ABIGAIL HARTMANN ASSOCIATES
415 Central Park W (at 101st St)   212/316-5406
Mon-Fri: 9-6 (by appointment); also available on weekends
                                                    www.ah-haa.com

This firm specializes in fine and decorative art appraisals for insurance, donation, or other reasons. Their highly principled and experienced staff does not buy, sell, or receive kickbacks. (This can be a common practice with some auction houses, insurance companies, and galleries.) Fees are by the hour, consultations are available, and the friendly personnel can also provide restoration, framing, shipping, and storage contacts.

Art Services

A. I. FRIEDMAN
44 W 18th St (bet Fifth Ave and Ave of the Americas)   212/243-9000
Mon-Fri: 9-7; Sat: 10-7; Sun: 11-6   www.aifriedman.com

Those who want to frame it themselves can take advantage of one of the largest stocks of ready-made frames in the city at A. I. Friedman. Nearly all are sold at discount. In addition to fully assembled frames, they sell do-it-yourself frames that come equipped with glass and/or mats. Custom framing is also available.

If you need a painting restored, call the **American Institute for Conservation of Historic and Artistic Works** (202/452-9545). They will be able to direct you to legitimate conservators.

ELI WILNER & COMPANY
1525 York Ave (bet 80th and 81st St)   212/744-6521
Mon-Fri: 9:30-5:30   www.eliwilner.com

Eli Wilner's primary business is period frames and mirrors. He keeps over 3,300 19th- and early 20th-century American and European frames in stock and can locate any size or style. Wilner can create an exact replica of a frame in his inventory to your specifications. With a staff of over 25 skilled craftsmen, Wilner also does expert restoration of frames. With such clients as the Metropolitan Museum of Art and the White House, Wilner's expertise speaks for itself

GUTTMANN PICTURE FRAME ASSOCIATES
180 E 73rd St (bet Lexington and Third Ave)   212/744-8600
Mon-Thurs: 9-5

Though the Guttmanns have worked on frames for some of the nation's finest museums, including the Metropolitan, they stand apart from other first-class artisans in that they are not snobby or picky about the work they will accept. They will restore, regild, or replace any type of picture frame. They are masters at working with masterpieces but are equally at home restoring or framing a Polaroid snapshot. Even better, they are among the few experts who don't price themselves out of the market. Bring a broken or worn-out frame, and they will graciously tell you exactly what it will cost to fix it.

J. POCKER & SON
135 E 63rd St (bet Park and Lexington Aye)   212/838-5488
Mon-Fri: 9-5:30; Sat: 10-5:30 (closed Sat in summer)

www.jpocker.com

Three generations of this family have been in the custom framing business, so rest assured that you will receive expert advice from a superbly trained staff. As a sidelight, Pocker offers a gallery specializing in English sporting and botanical prints. Pickup and delivery are offered.

JINPRA NEW YORK PICTURE FRAMING
1208 Lexington Ave (at 82nd St)   212/988-3903
Tues, Wed: 11-6; Fri: 11-7; Sat: 11-5:30

The proprietor of Jinpra is Wellington Chiang, and his service is as unique as his name. Jinpra provides art services (cleaning and gilding) in general and picture framing in particular. Chiang makes the high-quality frames himself; his artistry is evident in every piece he creates, including his murals.

JULIUS LOWY FRAME AND RESTORING COMPANY
223 E 80th St (bet Second and Third Ave)   212/861-8585
Mon-Fri: 9-5:30   www.lowyonline.com

Serving New York City since 1907, Lowy is the definitive firm for the conservation and framing of fine works of art and the oldest and largest such firm in the nation. Lowy's services include painting and paper conservation, professional photography, conservation framing, and curatorial work. They sell antique frames (Lowy has the largest inventory in the U.S.) and authentic reproduction frames (the broadest selection anywhere). In addition, Lowy provides complete conservation work, mat-making and fitting services. Their client base includes art dealers, private collectors, auction houses, corporate collections, institutions, and museums.

LEITH RUTHERFURD TALAMO
by appointment only   212/396-0399

Does your treasured painting have a dent? Did movers mishandle a painting? Has the masterpiece that hung over the fireplace darkened with age? Do you need help hanging or lighting a collection? All of these services —plus cleaning, relining, painting, and polishing frames—are done with expertise and class.

Babysitters

BABY SITTERS' GUILD
60 E 42nd St (bet Fifth and Madison Ave), Suite 912   212/682-0227
Daily: 9-9   www.babysittersguild.com

Established in 1940, the Baby Sitters' Guild charges high rates, but their professional reputation commends them. All guild sitters have passed rigorous scrutiny, and only the most capable are sent out on jobs. Believe it or not, the sitters can speak more than a dozen languages between them. They enforce a four-hour minimum and add on any travel expenses.

BARNARD COLLEGE BABYSITTING SERVICE
Millbank Hall
3009 Broadway (at 120th St), Room 11   212/854-2035
call for hours

Barnard College Babysitting Service is a nonprofit organization run by students at the undergraduate women's college affiliated with Columbia University. The service provides affordable child care for parents in the New York metropolitan area. At the same time, it allows students to seek convenient employment. Live-in help is also available. A minimum registration fee is required.

ELITE NANNIES
Mon-Fri: 9-5; 24-hour babysitting service   212/489-3900
www.elitenanny.com

Elite Nannies comes highly recommended and is used by some of the leading hotels in Manhattan. They provide qualified and experienced nannies, babysitters, housekeepers, baby nurses, and home companions. Babysitters are paid a flat hourly rate (minimum four hours), with no surcharge for the number or ages of the children. All of Elite's candidates have undergone an extensive background and reference check.

Nannies (all highly recommended):
Basic Trust (212/222-6602): day care
Fox Agency (212/753-2686): good record
Pavilion Agency (212/889-6609): very reliable

Beauty Services

Botox Treatment
Howard Sobel Skin & Spa (960-A Park Ave, 212/288-0060)
Laser Medicine (216 E 50th St, 212/888-3003)

Cellulite Treatment
Wellpath (1100 Madison Ave, 212/737-9604): up-to-date equipment

Cosmetic Surgery Consultant
Denise Thomas (212/734-0233)

Day Spas
Acqua Beauty Bar (7 E 14th St, 212/620-4329): Indonesian flavor
Ajune (1294 Third Ave. 212/628-0044): full-service, Botox, superb facials
Anushka Institute (241 E 60th St, 212/355-6404)
Aveda Institute (233 Spring St, 212/807-1492)
Avon Salon & Spa (725 Fifth Ave, 212/755-2866): eyebrow sculpting, reflexology
Away Spa (W New York Hotel, 541 Lexington Ave, 4th floor, 212/407-2970): sports massage
Bliss 57 (19 E 57th St, 212/219-8970) and **Bliss Soho** (568 Broadway, 2nd floor, 212/219-8970): oxygen facial
Brigette Mansfield European Day Spa (37 Union Sq W, 212/366-0706): a bit of the old country

Carapan Urban Spa and Store (5 W 16th St, 212/633-6220): Santa Fe spirituality

Catherine Atzen Day Spa (856 Lexington Ave, 212/517-2400)

Dorit Baxter Skin Care, Beauty & Health Spa (47 W 57th St, 3rd floor, 212/371-4542): salt scrub

Dr. Howard Sobel Skin and Spa (960 Park Ave, 212/288-0060): medical personnel on the premises

Elizabeth Arden Red Door Salon (611 Fifth Ave, 212/940-4000 and 691 Fifth Ave, 212/546-0200)

Ella Baché Day Spa (8 W 36th, 212/279-8562): eyelash perm

Equinox Wellness Spa (140 E 63rd St, 212/750-4671): facials, sports massage

Erbe (196 Prince St. 212/966-1445)

Estée Lauder Spa (Bloomingdale's, 1000 Third Ave, 212/705-2318)

Ettia Holistic Day Spa (239 W 72nd, 212/362-7109)

Frederic Fekkai Beauté de Provence (15 E 57th St, 212/753-9500): the ultimate

Haven (150 Mercer St, 212/343-3515): calm and refreshing

Helena Rubinstein Beauty Gallery & Spa (135 Spring St, 212/343-9963): facials, massages

Juvenex (26 W 32nd St, 646/733-1330): 24-hour Korean oasis

Lia Schor (686 Lexington Ave, 212/486-9670): efficient, reasonable

Metamorphosis (30 E 60th St, 212/751-6051): small but good, men and women

Mezzanine Spa at Soho Integrative Health (62 Crosby St, 212/431-1600): medical spa

Oasis Day Spa (108 E 16th St and 1 Park Ave, 212/254-7722)

Paul Labrecque Salon and Spa (Reebok Sports Center, 160 Columbus Ave, 212/595-0099): Thai massages, facials

Peninsula New York Spa (Peninsula New York Hotel, 700 Fifth Ave, 212/390-3910)

Plaza Spa (Plaza Hotel, 768 Fifth Ave, 212/546-5444): new and beautiful, couples massage

Prema Nolita (252 Elizabeth St, 212/226-3972): deluxe hand and foot treatments

Qiora (535 Madison Ave, 212/527-0400): holistic

Repéchage (115 E 57th St, 212/751-2500): European spa, men also

Salon de Tokyo (200 W 57th St, Room 1308, 212/757-2187): Shiatsu parlor

Sam C's Spa (166 Fifth Ave, 2nd floor, 212/675-9355): hydrotherapy treatments

Shija Day Spa (37 Union Sq W, 212/366-0706): packages for couples, friends, mother/daughter

SkinCareLab (568 Broadway, Suite 403, 212/334-3142): body treatments, facials

Soho Sanctuary (119 Mercer St, 212/334-5550)

Spa at Chelsea Piers (Sports Center, Chelsea Piers, 60 Twelfth Ave, 2nd floor, 212/336-6780)

Spa at Equinox (140 E 63rd St, 2nd level, 212/750-4671)

Spa 227 (227 E 56th St, 212/754-0227)

Susan Ciminelli Day Spa (Bergdorf Goodman, 754 Fifth Ave, 9th floor, 212/872-2650): highly recommended; try the ultra spa package for men (and if you have to ask the price . . .)

Tracie Martyn Salon (59 Fifth Ave, 212/206-9333): peaceful atmosphere for face and body treatments

Ula (8 Harrison St, 212/343-2376): chestcials

Warren Tricomi (Sports Club LA, 45 Rockefeller Plaza, 212/218-8650): chair massage

Yi Pak (10 W 32nd St, 2nd floor, 212/594-1025)

Eyebrow Styling

Eliza Petrescu at Avon Salon and Spa (725 Fifth Ave, 212/755-2866): very popular

Showha Threading (594 Broadway, Suite 403, 212/931-8363): shaping

Family Haircuts

Snip 'n Sip (204 Waverly Place, 212/242-3880)

Hair Blow Dry

A.K.S. Salon (694 Madison Ave, 212/888-0707): Mika Rummo

Jean Louis David (locations throughout the city): good work at reasonable prices

Pedro Sanchez & Dominick Pucciarello (Warren Tricomi, 16 W 57th St, 212/262-8899): for work that lasts

Hair Care

A.K.S. Salon (694 Madison Ave, 212/888-0707): former stylists from Frederic Fekkai; try Mondays for quick service

Antonio Prieto (25 W 19th St, 212/255-3741): popular styling

Astor Place Hair Stylists (2 Astor Pl, at Broadway, 212/475-9854): one of the world's largest barber shops; very inexpensive

Bumble & Bumble (146 E 56th St, 212/521-6500): no-nonsense establishment

Elizabeth Arden Red Door Salon (Saks Fifth Ave, 611 Fifth Ave, concourse level, 212/940-4000): top grade, full service

Frederic Fekkai (15 E 57th St, 212/753-9500): elegant, with a staff of 150

Garren New York (Henri Bendel, 712 Fifth Ave. 3rd floor atrium, 212/841-9400): personally customized services

John Barrett Salon (Bergdorf Goodman, 754 Fifth Ave, penthouse, 212/872-2700): top cut

John Frieda (797 Madison Ave, 212/879-1000): very "in"

John Masters (77 Sullivan St, 212/343-9590): all-organic

Julian Farel Salon (605 Madison Ave, 2nd floor, 212/888-8988): upscale, computers available, private hair parties

Kenneth's (Waldorf-Astoria Hotel, 301 Park Ave, lobby floor, 212/752-1800): full service with an able staff, but a long wait for Kenneth himself

La Beauté (142 E 49th St, 212/754-0048): reasonably priced

Lady Barber (Kathleen Giordano, 212/826-8616): will come to offices

Laicale Salon (129 Grand St, 212/219-2424): no attitude

Lemetric Hair Center (124 E 40th St, 212/986-5620): hair enhancement

Mark Garrison (820 Madison Ave, 2nd floor, 212/570-2455): popular

Nardi Salon (111 E 56th St, 212/421-4810): long hair specialists

Oribe (Elizabeth Arden Building, 691 Fifth Ave, 10th floor, 212/319-3910): world-renowned

Ouidad Hair Salon (846 Seventh Ave, 212/333-7577): curly- and frizzy-hair specialists

Peter Coppola (746 Madison Ave, 212/988-9404): reliable

Pierre Michel (131 E 57th St, 212/593-1460): all services
Privé (310 West Broadway, 212/274-8888): all hair services, shampoos a specialty, trendy, Sunday hours
Sacha and Oliver (6 W 18th St, 212/255-1100): very French
Salon Above (2641 Broadway, 212/665-7149): salon, spa, art show
Salon Ishi (70 E 55th St, 212/888-4744): scalp massages for men and women
Simon Salon (22 E 66th St, 212/517-4566): hair conditioning, neighborhood favorite
Stephen Knoll (625 Madison Ave, 212/421-0100): highly recommended
Vidal Sassoon (730 Fifth Ave, 212/535-9200): popular with men and women
Yves Durif (130 E 655th St, 212/452-0954): reliable

Hair Coloring
Alexis Antonellis at A.K.S. Salon (694 Madison Ave, 212/888-0707)
Borja Color Studio (118 E 57th St, 212/308-3232)
Linda Tam Beauty Salon (680 Fifth Ave, 7th floor, 212/757-2555)
Louis Licari Salon (693 Fifth Ave, 212/758-2090)
Oribe (691 Fifth Ave, 212/319-3910)
Warren Tricomi (16 W 57th St, 212/262-8899)

Hair Loss Treatment
Le Metric Hair Center for Women (124 E 40th St, Suite 601, 212/986-5620)

Hair Removal
J. Sisters Salon (35 W 57th St, 212/750-2485): waxing
Laser Medicine (216 E 50th St, 212/888-3003)

Home Services
Eastside Massage Therapy Center (212/249-2927)
John Sahag Workshop (212/750-7772): styling
Joseph Martin (212/838-3150): hair coloring, nails, pedicure, makeup
Lori Klein (212/996-9390): makeup
Matt Lesser (917/771-6438): hair
Trish McEvoy (212/758-7790): makeup

Liposuction
Taranow Plastic Surgery (169 E 69th St, 212/772-2100)

Makeup
John Guanlao (888/941-2391): will come anywhere
Kimara Ahnert Makeup Studio (1113 Madison Ave, 212/452-4252)
Makeup Center (150 W 55th St, 212/977-9494): good value
Makeup Shop (131 W 21st St, 212/807-0447)

Men's Grooming
A.K.S. Salon (694 Madison Ave, 212/888-0707): hair coloring
Greenhouse Spa (62 Crosby St, 212/431-1600): manicure, pedicure
Kiehl's (109 Third Ave, 212/677-3171): toiletries
Mezzanine Spa (62 Crosby St, 212/431-1600): pedicure
Oscar Bond Salon & Spa (42 Wooster St, 212/334-3777): comfortable shaves for men
Pierre Michel (131 E 57th St, 212/593-1460): manicure
SkinCareLab (568 Broadway, Suite 403, 212/334-3142): manicure
Vital Gate (225 E 64th St, 212/873-4244): acupuncture facial
Warren Tricomi (Sports Club LA, 45 Rockefeller Plaza, 212/218-8650): pedicure

Close shave? One of the few places left where a fellow can get a straight-edged razor shave is **Pole Mole** (1031 Lexington Ave, 212/535-8461). Cost? A whopping $28!

Men's Hairstylist
Chelsea Barber (465 W 23rd St, 212/741-2254): inexpensive
Claudio Barber Shop (116th St bet First and Second Ave, no phone listed): old-time, inexpensive
Soon (318 E 11th St, 212/260-4432): ask for Danielle

Nails
Angel Nails (151 E 71st St, 212/535-5333): nail-wrapping, massage, body-waxing
Bloomie Nails (various locations): great prices
Christine Valmy School (437 Fifth Ave, 2nd floor, 212/779-7800): inexpensive
Edith Mattsis (212/666-8087): will come to offices (men, too)
John Allan's Men's Club (95 Trinity Pl, at Thames St, 212/406-3000): for men, full-service
Pierre Michel (131 E 57th St, 212/593-1460): old-school
Rescue Nail Spa (21 Cleveland Pl, 212/431-3805)
Sirene (1377 Third Ave, 212/585-2044)
Sweet Lily (222 West Broadway, 212/925-5441): "natural" nail spa and boutique

Pedicures
Jin Soon Natural Hand & Foot Spa (56 E 4th St, 212/473-2047 and 23 Jones St, 212/229-1070): Jin Soon herself is at the 4th Street location
Paul Labrecque Salon & Spa (160 Columbus Ave, 212/595-0099)
Rescue Beauty Lounge (34 Gansevoort St, 2nd floor, 212/206-6409)
Sirene (1377 Third Ave, 212/585-2044)

Skin Care
Advanced Skin Care Day Spa (532 Madison Ave, 2nd floor, 212/758-8867)
Alla Katkov (Miano Viel, 16 E 52nd St, 2nd floor, 212/980-3222): great facials
Anushka (241 E 60th St, 212/355-6404)
Bloomingdale's (1000 Third Ave, 212/705-2318)
D. Esse Spa (350 Hudson St, 212/206-1655)
Georgette Klinger (501 Madison Ave, 212/838-3200)
Glow Skin Spa (41 E 57th St, Suite 1206, 212/319-6654): skin transformation
Joean Skin Care (163 Hester St, 212/966-3668): Chinese style
Lia Schorr (686 Lexington Ave, 212/486-9670)
Ling Skin Care Salons (105 W 77th St, 212/877-2883; 12 E 16th St, 212/989-8833; and 128 Thompson St, 212/982-8833): great skin care
Oasis on Park (1 Park Ave, 212/254-7722): facials a specialty
Paul Labrecque East (171 E 65th St, 212/595-0099): Regina Viotto is a great facialist.

Tanning
Spa at Equinox (205 E 85th St, 212/396-9611): body bronzing
Tattoos and Body Piercing
Tattoo Seen (162 W 4th St, 212/691-3852)
Toupees
Bob Kelly (151 W 46th St, 212/819-0030)
Ira Senz (13 E 47th St, 212/752-6800)

Some real values on grooming can be had if you are willing to try training schools. Here are some of the better ones:

Dentistry: **New York University College of Dentistry** (345 E 24th St, 212/998-9800): initial visit, X-rays and all, for $90!

Facials and manicures: **Christine Valmy International School** (437 Fifth Ave, 212/779-7800): facials at $25, manicures for $10!

Haircut: **Vidal Sassoon** (90 Fifth Ave, 212/929-9668 and 767 Fifth Ave, 212/535-9200): haircuts $20 to $30, perms $120 to $200

Haircut (blow dry): **Jean Louis David** (10 B 41st St, 212/779-3555): $30 cut with clippers

Haircut (color): **Mark Garrison Salon** (820 Madison Ave, 212/570-2455): retail $400, training price $155!

Haircuts and manicures: **LTBS** (22 W 34th St, 212/6954555): an old-fashioned learning institute; perms are $20 and a color rinse on Tuesday is just $8 to $10

Hairstyling: **Bumble & Bumble** (146 B 56th St, 212/521-6500): good deals

Massage: **Swedish Institute** (226W 26th St, 212/924-5900): six one-hour Swedish-shiatsu massages for $125

Men's (and women, too) haircuts: **Atlas Barber School** (32 Third Ave, 212/475-1360 and 80 E 10th St, 212/475-5699): haircuts for $5

Bookbinding

TALAS
568 Broadway (at Prince St), Suite 107   212/219-0770
Mon-Fri: 9-5:30   www.talasonline.com

Jake and Marjorie Salik preside over this outlet, which offers tools, supplies, and books for artists, restorers, collectors, bookbinders, museums, archives, libraries, calligraphers, and retail customers. Expanded inventories feature custom boxes and portfolios, a wide variety of photo-storage and display items, and archival papers. They are also distributors of conservation supplies.

WEITZ, WEITZ & COLEMAN
1377 Lexington Ave (bet 90th and 91st St)   212/831-2213
Mon-Thurs: 9-7; Fri: 9-5; Sat: 12-5 (Sun and evenings by appointment)
www.weitzcoleman.com

Weitz is a highly respected name in the rare-book field. Leo Weitz began a rare-book business in New York in 1909 and became so well known that he did work for the Rockefellers, DuPonts, Firestones, three presidents (Ford,

Reagan, and Bush), and other famous families. Today, Herbert Weitz (his son) and partner Elspeth Coleman continue the tradition of fine bookbinding. Weitz and Coleman restore and rebind books and family heirlooms. They also design and create leather photo albums, guest books, archival boxes, presentation folders, and special gift books. Coleman's specialty is custom-designing to clients' specifications. Weitz and Coleman buy and sell rare books, too!

Cabinetry

HARMONY WOODWORKING
153 W 27th St (bet Ave of the Americas and Seventh Ave), Room 902
Daily: by appointment   212/366-7221

Jerry Gerber ran a cabinetry business and woodworking school until the demolition of his old location forced him to move. Instead of merely relocating, Gerber reassessed the entire operation. When he went back into business, he stressed aspects of the craft that most appealed to him. Nowadays Gerber devotes his time to making custom cabinetry—particularly bookcases, wall units, tables, turnings, and carvings.

JIM NICKEL
call afternoons or evenings for appointments   718/963-2138

Nickel, who lives in Brooklyn, is an expert in projects that use wood: cabinets, bookcases, wall sculptures, and much more. He prefers small- to medium-sized jobs and will do the entire project—from consultation and design to installation—all by himself. He brings more than two decades of practical experience to his job and is very conscious of budgets.

Calligraphy

CALLIGRAPHY STUDIOS
100 Reade St (bet Church St and West Broadway)   212/964-6007
by appointment   www.lindastein.com

Nothing sets off a card or a letter like calligraphy. Many claim to be experts, but if you really want first-class work, let Linda Stein and her crew customize your order. They are able to work in any language you desire. Moreover, they create mood portraits, 3-D memory boxes, custom monograms and logos, leatherbound books, invitations, and party accessories. This studio is tops in protocol.

Camping Equipment

DOWN EAST ENTERPRISES
188 Mulberry St   212/925-2632
Mon-Fri: 11-6; Sat: 12-6   www.downeastny.com

This firm provides a phenomenal range of services to outdoors enthusiasts. Down East, in fact, began as a service center for biking, hiking, camping, and outdoor equipment. Outdoor gear can be repaired and customized here. They'll custom-make bags and silk-screen logos onto portage bags for individuals and companies.

> Here's an idea for an unusual party or some serious exercise: **Extra Vertical Climbing Center** (Harmony Atrium, 61 W 62nd St, 212/586-5718, www.extravertical.com). This indoor climbing gym features a 30-foot indoor wall and a 50-foot outdoor climbing wall. Lessons, lockers, and a changing room are available.

Carpentry

Finding a reliable carpenter is not easy. I have done a lot of research in this area and determined that the best outfit to call is **R&N Construction** (914/699-0292). These folks do quality work, prices are reasonable, and they are nice to deal with. Ask for Nick Alpino.

If you are interested in cabinetry, call Joe Lo Nigro at **European Woodworking** (914/969-5724). Their custom millwork is outstanding, and believe it or not, some claim that he "tends to undercharge"!

Carriages

CHATEAU STABLES/CHATEAU THEATRICAL ANIMALS/ CHATEAU WEDDING CARRIAGES
call for reservations   212/246-0520
Mon-Fri: 8:30-6:30   www.chateaustables.com

If you would like to arrive at your next dinner party in a horse-drawn carriage, Chateau is the place to call. They have the largest working collection of horse-drawn vehicles in the United States. Although they prefer advance notice, requests for weddings, group rides, tours, movies, and overseas visitors can be handled at any time. There is nothing quite as romantic as a ride in an authentic hansom cab.

Cars for Hire

AAMCAR CAR RENTALS
315 W 96th St (bet West End Ave and Riverside Dr)
Mon-Fri: 7:30-7:30; Sat, Sun: 9-5   212/222-8500, 800/722-6923

506 W 181st St (at Amsterdam Ave)   212/927-7000
Mon-Fri: 9-7; Sat: 9-1   www.aamcar.com

This independent car rental company has a full line of cars, vans, and sport utility vehicles. AAMCAR has been around for several decades and offers over 200 cars.

CAREY LIMOUSINE NY
212/599-1122 (reservations), 718/898-1000 (office), 800/336-4646
24 hours   www.ecarey.com

Carey is the grandfather of car-for-hire services. They provide chauffeur-driven limousines and sedans at any time and will take clients anywhere in almost any kind of weather. Last-minute reservations are accepted on an as-available basis. Discuss rates before making a commitment.

CARMEL CAR SERVICE
2642 Broadway (at 100th St)   212/666-6666, 800/9CARMEL
24 hours   www.carmellimo.com

These people are highly commended for good service and fair prices. Full-size and luxury sedans, minivans, passenger vans, and limos are available. Prices for limos begin at $59 per hour.

COMPANY II LIMOUSINE SERVICE
24 hours   718/430-6482

Steve Betancourt provides a responsible and efficient service at reasonable prices. I can personally vouch that his reputation for reliability is well earned.

Stretch limos are big these days (in more ways than one!). If you want to make a big impression or take a carload of friends or kids out for a fun time, try **Dav-El Chauffered Transportation Network** (800/922-0343).

Casting

SCULPTURE HOUSE CASTING
155 W 26th St (bet Ave of the Americas and Seventh Ave)
Mon-Fri: 8-5:30; Sat: 10-3   212/645-9430, 888/374-8665
     www.sculptshop.com

Sculpture House has been a family-owned business since 1918, making it one of the city's oldest casting firms. A full-service casting foundry, it specializes in classical plaster reproductions, mold-making, and casting in all mediums and sizes. Sculpting tools and supplies and ornamental plastering are also available.

Chair Caning

VETERAN'S CHAIR CANING AND REPAIR SHOP
442 Tenth Ave (bet 34th and 35th St)   212/564-4560
Mon-Thurs: 7:30-4:30; Fri: 7:30-4; Sat: 8-2

John Bausert, a third-generation chair caner, has written a book about his craft. Certainly, his prices and craftsmanship are among the best in town. Bausert believes in passing along his knowledge, encouraging customers to repair their own chairs. The procedure is outlined in Bausert's book, and necessary materials are sold in the shop. If you don't want to try, Veteran's will repair the chair. For a charge, they'll even pick it up from your home. In addition to caning, Veteran's also stocks materials for chair and furniture repair, does wicker repair, and repairs and reglues wooden chairs.

WESTSIDE CHAIR CANING AND REPAIR
call for consultation or to schedule pick-up and delivery   212/724-4408

Though no longer a storefront, Jeffrey Weiss and his talented crew continue with their hand-and machine-caning, rush- and splint-seating, wicker restoration, and furniture regluing and repair. They will conveniently pick up and deliver your special furniture piece.

China and Glassware Repair

CENTER ART STUDIO
307 W 38th St (bet Eighth and Ninth Ave), Room 1315   212/247-3550
Mon-Thurs: 9-6; Fri: 9-5 (by appointment only)   www.centerart.com

"Fine art restoration and display since 1919" is the motto here. The word *fine* should be emphasized, for owners of really good crystal, porcelain, china, and bronze art should make Center Art Studio *the* place to go for repairs. The house specialty is antiques restoration. They will restore or repair scagliola, lacquer, porcelain, terra-cotta, shells, and precious stones. Their craftsmen will also restore antique furniture and decorative objects, using original materials whenever possible. They'll even design and install display bases and cases. They also stock packing materials and shipping crates. Among the oldest and most diverse art restoration studios in the city, Center Art offers a multitude of special services, like designs and sketches by fax and multilingual personnel for overseas shoppers. The owner, Lansing Moore, has a superbly talented staff that has worked on furniture designed by the likes of Frank Lloyd Wright.

GLASS RESTORATIONS
1597 York Ave (bet 84th and 85th St)   212/517-3287
Mon-Fri: 9:30-5

Chip your prize Lalique glass treasure? Glass Restorations restores all manner of crystal, including pieces by Steuben, Baccarat, Daum, and Waterford, as well as antique art glass. This place is a find, as too few quality restorers are left in the country. Ask for Gus!

HESS RESTORATIONS
200 Park Ave S (at 17th St)   212/260-2255, 212/979-1143
Mon-Fri: 11-4, and by appointment

Hess has been in business since 1945, providing a restoration service so professional that previous damage is usually unnoticeable. Repairing and restoration of silver and crystal are available. Their emphasis is on fine European porcelains, ivory, tortoise shell, sculptures, and objets d'art. They are recommended by leading museums, auction houses, and galleries in Manhattan. The replacement of blue glass liners for antique silver salt dishes is unique. Hess accepts insured shipments of items to be repaired and will send an estimate for restoration work.

Clock and Watch Repair

FANELLI ANTIQUE TIMEPIECES
790 Madison Ave (bet 66th and 67th St), Suite 202   212/517-2300
Mon-Fri: 10-6; Sat: 11-5

In a beautiful clock gallery, Cindy Fanelli specializes in the care of high-quality "investment-type" timepieces, especially carriage clocks. They have one of the nation's largest collections of rare and unusual Early American grandfather clocks and vintage wristwatches. They do sales and restoration, make house calls, give free estimates, rent timepieces, and purchase single pieces or entire collections.

J&P TIMEPIECES
1057 Second Ave (at 56th St) 212/980-1099
Mon-Fri: 10-5:30; Sat: 11-4 www.jptimepieces.com

In Europe, fine-watch repairing is a family tradition, but this craft is slowly being forgotten in our country. Fortunately for Manhattan, the Fossners have passed along this talent from father to son for four generations. Jeff Morris has now joined Peter Fossner as an owner. You can be confident in their work on any kind of mechanical watch. They guarantee repairs for six months and will generally turn around jobs within ten days.

SUTTON CLOCK SHOP
139 E 61st St (at Lexington Ave) 212/758-2260
Mon-Fri: 11-4; Sat: 1-2

Sutton's forte is selling and acquiring unusual timepieces, but they are equally interested in the maintenance and repair of antique clocks. Some of the timepieces they sell—even the contemporary ones—are truly outstanding, and a long list of satisfied customers endorses their repair work. They sell and repair barometers as well.

TIME PIECES REPAIRED
115 Greenwich Ave (at 13th St) 212/929-8011
Tues-Fri: 10:30-6:30; Sat: 9-5; Mon by appointment
www.timepiecesrepaired.com

Grace Szuwala services, restores, repairs, and sells antique timepieces. Her European training makes her an expert on antique watches and clocks. She has a strong sensitivity for pieces that have more sentimental than real value.

Clothing Repair

FRENCH-AMERICAN REWEAVING COMPANY
119 W 57th St (bet Ave of the Americas and Seventh Ave), Room 1406
Mon-Fri: 10:30-5:30; Sat: 11-2 212/765-4670

Has a tear, burn, or other catastrophe ruined your favorite outfit? These folks will work on most any garment for men or women in nearly every fabric. Often a damaged item will look just like new!

Need a quick repair? Go straight to **Ban Custom Tailor Shop** (1544 First Ave, 212/570-0444), and they will take care of you right away.

Computer Service and Instruction

ABC COMPUTER SERVICES
375 Fifth Ave (bet 35th and 36th St), 2nd floor 212/725-3511
Mon-Fri: 9-5 www.abccomputerservices.com

These folks provide sales, service, and supplies for desktop and notebook computers, as well as all kinds of printers. ABC will work on Apple, Microsoft, and Novell-based systems, and are an authorized Hewlett-Packard service center. They will come to your home or office for computer instruction. They have been around for over a decade, which in itself is a good recommendation.

COMPUTRS
Daily: 10-10   212/254-9000 (by phone only)

This business does exactly what their name indicates—computer repair and upgrades. They specialize in laptops, and their prices are competitive. Ask for Brian.

For computer rentals, try **Business Equipment Rental** (250 W 49th St, 212/582-2020). Prices are reasonable; pickup and delivery are available. These are the best shops in town for computer repair:
Data Vision (445 Fifth Ave, 212/689-1111)
Machattan (145 Ave of the Americas, 212/242-9393): Macintosh only
RCS Computer Experience (575 Madison Ave, 212/949-6935)

TEKSERVE CORPORATION
119 W 23rd St (bet Ave of the Americas and Seventh Ave)
Mon-Fri: 9-7; Sat: 10-5   212/929-3645

For Apple Computer sales and service, you can't do better than this outfit. Tekserve carries a huge inventory of computers and peripherals, and the firm is noted for their excellent customer care. A full range of services, including data recovery, is available.

If you find yourself in need of some special part for your computer, copier, fax machine, or printer, call **E.T. Computer Supplies & Services** (718/789-2973). Same-day service is available.

Craft Instruction

CRAFT STUDENTS LEAGUE
YWCA of the City of New York   212/735-9731
610 Lexington Ave (at 53rd St)   www.ywcanyc.org/csl

Since 1932, the Craft Students League has offered programs in crafts and fine arts. The wide-ranging curriculum includes bookbinding, jewelry, mixed media, pottery, woodworking, drawing, painting, beading, and wearable art. For anyone yearning for a creative outlet, this school—with its convenient midtown location and professional teaching staff—is a winner. It's easy on the pocketbook, too!

Delivery, Courier, Messenger Services

AIRLINE DELIVERY SERVICES
60 E 42nd St (bet Park and Madison Ave)   212/687-5145
Daily: 24 hours

Even before the big guys got in the business, this outfit was doing round-the-clock local and long-distance deliveries. If you have time-sensitive material, give them a call. They'll promptly pick up your item, even in the middle of the night or a snowstorm. There are several branches throughout the city.

KANGAROO COURIER
41 E 29th St (at Madison Ave)   212/684-2233
Mon-Fri: 8-6 (scheduled services all the time)

Kangaroo is set up to provide any and all courier services. They can handle everything from a crosstown rush letter (delivery completed within an hour) to delivering a box in the tri-state area, tracking the job all the way.

NOW VOYAGER
45 W 21st St (at Ave of the Americas), 5th floor   212/459-1616
Mon-Fri: 10-6

Now Voyager is a full-service, low-end travel consolidator with bargains in every travel sector for willing couriers. The firm has a schedule of flights to various areas— mostly Europe, South America, Mexico and the Far East. You can travel at a fraction of the regular fare if you're willing to take only carry-on luggage. They have great deals on domestic flights and cruises. Usually flights are booked some weeks ahead, so call as early as possible. Discounted domestic and international non-courier flights are also available. Who knows? You might take an exciting trip for next to nothing!

Detectives

DECISION STRATEGIES
33 E 33rd St (bet Fifth and Madison Ave), 4th floor   212/935-4040
Daily: 24 hours

Need a corporate investigation? Are you suspecting infidelity? Want assistance with fraud prevention? Bart Schwartz and his staff of more than a dozen top-notch investigators are the ones to call. Their experience in nearly every field can save you headaches—and maybe a lot of cash. They also do online forensics.

Doll Repair

NEW YORK DOLL HOSPITAL
787 Lexington Ave (bet 61st and 62nd St), 2nd floor   212/838-7527
Mon-Sat: 10-6

New York Doll Hospital has been fixing, mending, and restoring dolls to health since 1900. Owner Irving Chais has operated in this cramped two-room "hospital" since 1947. That was the year he took over from his father, who had begun fixing dolls for his clients' children in his hair salon. Chais has replaced antique fingers, reconstructed china heads and German rag dolls, and authentically restored antique dolls. Additional services include appraisals, made-to-order dolls, and buying and selling antique dolls and toys. He will also work on teddy bears and other stuffed animals, and he can fix talking dolls with computer chips.

Dry Cleaners, Laundries

CLEANTEX
2335 Twelfth Ave (at 133rd St)   212/283-1200
Mon-Fri: 8-4

In business since 1928, Cleantex specializes in cleaning draperies, furniture, balloon and Roman shades, vertical blinds, and Oriental and area rugs.

They provide free estimates, free pickup, and delivery service. Museums, churches, and rug dealers are among their satisfied clients.

HALLAK CLEANERS
1232 Second Ave (at 65th St)   212/879-4694
Mon-Fri: 7-6:30; Sat: 8-3   www.hallak.com

Hallak has been a family business for nearly 40 years. Joseph Hallak, Sr., a native of France, instilled his work ethic and dedication to detail into sons John-Claude and Joseph, Jr. This no doubt accounts for the pride and personal service they offer customers. Much of their work comes from referrals by such boutiques as Armani, Brioni, Turnbull and Asser, Celine, Hermes, Ferragamo, and St. John, to name a few. Hallak does all work in their state-of-the-art plant. They will clean shirts, linens, suede, leather, and draperies. Their specialty is museum-quality cleaning and preservation of wedding gowns. For those (like your author) who have trouble with stains on ties, Hallak is the place to go for help. Their skilled work takes time, though rush service is available at no additional cost.

If you need a really good cleaner, there is none better than **Chris French Cleaners** (57 Fourth Ave, 212/475-5444), in the East Village.

LEATHERCRAFT PROCESS OF AMERICA
call for locations   212/564-8980
Mon-Fri: 7:30-6:30

Leathercraft will clean, re-dye, re-line, repair, and lengthen or shorten any suede or leather garment. That includes boots, gloves, clothing, and handbags, as well as odd leather items. Because leather is extremely difficult to clean, the process can be painfully expensive. However, Leathercraft has a reputation dating back to 1938, and their prices remain competitive.

MADAME PAULETTE CUSTOM COUTURE CLEANERS
1255 Second Ave (bet 65th and 66th St)
Mon-Fri: 7:30-7; Sat: 8-5   212/838-6827, 877/COUTURE
                                                www.madamepaulette.com

What a clientele: Christian Dior, Vera Wang, Chanel, Givenchy, Saks, Burberry, and Henri Bendel. This full-service establishment has been in business for nearly 40 years. They do dry cleaning (including knits, suedes, and leathers), tailoring (including reweaving and alterations), laundry, and household and rug cleaning. They provide fur and box storage. Taking care of wedding dresses is a specialty. Their experts can repair water-, bleach- and fire-damaged garments, do wet cleaning, and clean upholstery and tapestry by hand. Madame Paulette offers free pickup and delivery throughout Manhattan, will set up charge accounts, and can do one-day service upon request.

MEURICE GARMENT CARE
31 University Pl (bet 8th and 9th St)   212/475-2778
Mon-Fri: 7:30-7; Sat: 7:30-5   wwwgarmentcare.com

245 E 57th St (bet Second and Third Ave)   212/759-9057
Mon-Fri: 8-6; Sat: 7:30-5

Meurice specializes in cleaning and restoring fine garments. They handle each piece individually, taking care of details like loose buttons and tears. Special services: exquisite hand-finishing, expert stain removal and dyeing, museum-quality preservation, cleaning and restoration of wedding gowns, special handling of ultra fragile and chemically sensitive garments, and on-site leather cleaning and repairs. They even do work for Christie's. Delivery and shipping are available.

MIDNIGHT EXPRESS CLEANERS
Mon-Fri: 9 a.m-11 p.m.; Sat: 9-3   212/921-0111, 800/7MIDNITE
www.midnightexpressny.com

What a handy place to know about! Midnight Express does dry cleaning, shirt laundering, leather and suede cleaning and repair, and bulk laundering. Best of all, they will pick up and deliver, day or night. Prompt return is assured. They specialize in dry-cleaning restoration of smoke, fire, and water-damaged goods. This is Manhattan's only OSHA-compliant laundry service. Be sure to keep their number near your phone!

Lucky New Yorkers get to listen to **Joan Hamburg** on radio station WOR (710 AM) from 10 a.m. to noon, Monday through Friday. Joan is the leading consumer expert in the area. This charming lady is so popular she could easily be elected mayor of New York!

NEW YORK'S FINEST FRENCH CLEANERS & TAILORS
154 Reade St (bet Hudson and Greenwich St)   212/431-4010
Mon-Fri: 7:30-6:30; Sat: 8:30-5

Three generations of the same family have operated this quality business, featuring pickup, delivery, and one-day service. Tailoring and storage are available, as is care for fine silks and leathers.

TIECRAFTERS
252 W 29th St (bet Seventh and Eighth Ave)   212/629-5800
Mon-Fri: 9-5   www.tiecrafters.com

Old ties never die or even fade away at Tiecrafters. Instead, they're dyed, widened, narrowed, straightened, and cleaned. They believe that a well-made tie can live forever, and they provide services to make longevity possible. In addition to converting tie widths, they restore soiled or stained ties and clean and repair all kinds of neckwear. Owner Andy Tarshis will give pointers on tie maintenance. (Hint: if you roll a tie at night, wrinkles will be gone by morning.) Tiecrafters offers several pamphlets on the subject, including one that tells how to take out spots at home. Their cleaning charge is reasonable, and they also make custom neckwear.

Electricians

ALTMAN ELECTRIC
283 W 11th St (at Bleecker St)   212/924-0400, 800/287-7774
Daily: 24 hours

The licensed crew of 18 at this reliable outfit is available day and night.
They will do small or large jobs at home or office, and rates are reasonable.
They have been in business for over half a century.

Embroidery

JONATHAN EMBROIDERY PLUS
256 W 38th St (bet Seventh and Eighth Ave)   212/398-3538
Mon-Fri: 9-6; at: 9-4

Any kind of custom embroidery work can be done at this classy workshop.
Bring a photo or sketch, or just give them an idea, and they will produce the
design, which you can then amend or approve.

Exterminators

ACME EXTERMINATING
460 Ninth Ave (bet 35th and 36th St)   212/594-9230
Mon-Fri: 8-5

Acme is expert at debugging private homes, offices, stores, museums,
and hospitals. They employ state-of-the-art integrated pest-management
technology.

Eyeglass Repair

E. B. MEYROWITZ AND DELL
19 W 44th St (at Fifth Ave)   212/575-1686
Mon-Fri: 9-6 (till 5:30 in July, Aug);
Sat: 9-3 (closed Sat in July, Aug)

If you desperately need E. B. Meyrowitz and Dell, you probably can't read
this. No need to worry, as they do on-the-spot emergency repair of glasses.
This is *the* place to go for eyeglass emergencies in the city. There is a large
frame selection, from 18-karat gold to buffalo horn. They also repair binoculars. You're welcome to stop by for regular optical needs, too.

Fashion Schools

FASHION INSTITUTE OF TECHNOLOGY
Seventh Ave at 27th St   www.fitnyc.suny.edu
     212/217-7675 (admissions), 212/217-7999 (general information)

The Fashion Institute of Technology (FIT), a branch of the State University
of New York, is the fashion industry's premier educational facility. The
school was founded almost 60 years ago. Its graduate roster reads like a
"who's who" of the fashion world, including Jhane Barnes, Calvin Klein, and
Norma Kamali. The school offers a multitude of majors: accessories; advertising; display and exhibit; toy; jewelry, interior, textile, and fashion design;
illustration; photography; fine arts; fashion buying and merchandising;

apparel production management; patternmaking; and marketing. FIT also maintains a student placement service. All students are top-caliber. The Museum at FIT is the world's largest repository of fashion, with over a million articles of clothing. Call 212/217-5800 for information about exhibits and shows.

Formal Wear Rental and Sales

A. T. HARRIS FORMALWEAR
11 E 44th St (bet Madison and Fifth Ave), 2nd floor   212/682-6325
Mon, Tues, Wed, Fri: 9-5:45; Thurs: 9-6:45
Sat: 10-3:45 (by appointment)

Ten U.S. presidents have been fitted for formal attire at this store! A. T. Harris has been in business since 1892, selling and renting formal wear of the highest quality. You will find cutaways, tails, tuxedos, shoes, top hats, stud and cuff-link sets, and kid and suede gloves.

BALDWIN FORMALS
1156 Ave of the Americas (at 45th St)   212/245-8190, 800/427-0072
Mon-Fri: 9-7; Sat: 10-5

If you are invited to some upscale function, Baldwin will take care of the dressing details. They rent and sell all types of formal attire: suits, overcoats, top hats, shoes, and more. They will pick up and deliver for free in midtown and for a slight charge to other addresses. Same-day service is guaranteed for rental orders received by early afternoon. Rapid alteration service (two or three days) is available on sale merchandise.

Funeral Service

FRANK E. CAMPBELL FUNERAL CHAPEL
1076 Madison Ave (at 81st St)   212/288-3500
Daily: 24 hours   www.frankecampbell.com

In time of need, it is good to know of a highly professional funeral home. These folks have been in business since 1898, providing superior service.

Furniture Rental

CHURCHILL CORPORATE SERVICES
6 E 32nd St (bet Fifth and Madison Ave), 2nd floor   212/686-0444
Mon-Fri: 9-5; Sun: 11-5   www.furnishedhousing.com

Mention Churchill, and you think of staid old England, right? Well, *this* Churchill is starkly contemporary, as well as traditional. They can fill any size order for a business or residence, and they offer free interior-decorating advice and a lease-purchase plan. A customer simply selects what is needed from stock or borrows from the loaner program until special orders are processed. Churchill also offers a comprehensive package, including housewares and appliances. They specialize in executive relocations and will rent out anything from a single chair to an entire home. Churchill offers corporate apartments and housing on a short- or long-term basis. Their clients include team-sports managers, executives on temporary assignment, and actors on short-term contracts.

CORT FURNITURE RENTAL
711 Third Ave (bet 44th and 45th St)   212/867-2800
Mon-Sat: 9-6   www.cort1.com

Cort rents furnishings for a single room, entire apartment, or office. They show accessories as well. All furnishings (including electronics and housewares) are available for rental with an option to purchase. An apartment location service is offered, free professional decorating is available, and a multilingual staff is at your service. Working with Japanese clients is a specialty. The stock is large, delivery and setup can often be done within 48 hours, and all styles of furniture and accessories are shown in their 12,000-square-foot showroom, conveniently located near Grand Central Station.

IFR FURNITURE RENTALS
345 Park Ave (at 51st St), Level C   212/421-0340
Mon-Thurs:9-6; Fri: 9-5:30; Sat: 10-2   www.rent-ifr.com

IFR is one of the largest home and office furniture-rental firms in the metropolitan area. A decorating and design specialist is available for free consultation. The company carries accessories to coordinate with furnishings. All items are executive quality, and quick delivery from their warehouse is a plus.

Gardening

COUNCIL ON THE ENVIRONMENT OF
NEW YORK CITY
51 Chambers St (bet Broadway and Centre St), Room 228
Mon-Fri: 9-5   212/788-7900
www.cenyc.org

It's a little-known fact that the city will loan tools to groups involved in community-sponsored open-space greening projects. Loans are limited to one week, but the waiting period is not long and the price (nothing!) is right. You can borrow the same tools several times a season. A group can be as few as four people. The council also runs Greenmarket—the city's weekly farmers markets in 27 locations, including Union Square. The council will design office-waste prevention and recycling programs for commercial and other large businesses. They carry a number of interesting free publications.

Where to get things fixed:

Ceramics: **Ceramic Restorations** (224 W 29th St. 12th floor, 212/564-8669)

Clocks: **Sid Shapiro** (212/925-1994)

Furniture: **Joseph Biunno** (129 W 29th St, 212/629-5630)

Glass and mirrors: **Glass Restorations** (1597 York Ave, 212/517-3287)

Jewelry: **Murrey's Jewelers** (1395 Third Ave, 212/879-3690)

Lamps and appliances: **AABCO A/C, TV, and Vacuum Repairs** (1594 York Ave, 212/585-2431)

Leather restoration: **Robert Falotico** (315 E 91st St, 212/369-1217)

Silver: **Thome Silversmiths** (49 W 37th St, 212/764-5426)

Gift Baskets

BASKETFULL
276 Fifth Ave (at 30th St), Room 201   212/686-2900, 800/645-GIFT
Mon-Fri: 9-5:30   www.basketfullinc.com

For a unique and innovative basket, Basketfull is the place to call. Basketfull has gift collections for everyday occasions, holidays and special events, corporate, private, and labeling programs. Included are "get well, feel better" baskets as well as fruit, sympathy and condolence baskets, specialty chocolate indulgence baskets, and New York baskets (with deli salamis, bagel chips, and rugelach pastries). You can choose from Basketfull's dozens of baby baskets, which include personalization with baby's name! Same-day delivery is available in Manhattan, and arrangements can be made for shipment anywhere in the world. They are great to deal with!

Haircuts

Children

COZY'S CUTS FOR KIDS
1125 Madison Ave (at 84th St)   212/744-1716
448 Amsterdam Ave (at 81st St)   212/579-2600
Mon-Sat: 10-6; Sun: 11-5 (Madison Ave)

www.cozyscutsforkids.com

Cozy's really takes care of kids of all ages, including the offspring of many famous personalities. What an experience here: videos and videogames, themed barber chairs, Polaroid pictures, balloons, candy, and free toys. They issue a "first-time" diploma with a keepsake lock of hair! Besides providing professional styling services, Cozy's is a toy boutique. There are "glamour parties" for girls on Sunday at the Amsterdam Avenue location. Adults are well taken care of, too!

Family

ASTOR PLACE HAIR STYLISTS
2 Astor Pl (at Broadway)   212/475-9854
Mon-Sat: 8-8; Sun: 9-6

The personnel inside of what was once a modest neighborhood barbershop give some of New York's trendiest and most far-out haircuts. It all started when the Vezza brothers inherited a barbershop from their father in the East Village at a time "when not even cops were getting haircuts." Enrico took note of the newly gentrified neighborhood's young trendies and their sleek haircuts and changed the name of the shop to "Astor Place Hair Stylists." Now, the shop is staffed with a resident manager, a doorman, and an ever-increasing number of barbers.

ATLAS BARBER SCHOOL
32 Third Ave (bet 9th and 10th St)   212/475-1360
Mon-Fri: 9-7:45; Sat: 9-4:45

This school teaches general barbering and shaving techniques. They've been at it for 55 years. High style it isn't; great value it is!

FEATURE TRIM
1108 Lexington Ave (bet 77th and 78th St)   212/650-9746
Tues-Sat: 11-6

This neighborhood establishment maintains its standard of basic hair care for men, women, and children. Low maintenance is the key to Feature Trim's haircuts. Easy care, reasonable prices, friendly faces, and more than 50 years of combined experience keep an impressive clientele asking for proprietors Victor and Joe. Appointments are encouraged, but walk-ins are welcome.

PAUL MOLE FAMILY BARBERSHOP
1031 Lexington Ave (at 74th St)   212/535-8461
Mon-Fri: 7:30-6:30; Sat: 7:30-5:30; Sun: 9-3:30

This shop is just what it says: a family business. They will trim the heads of both dad and the kids, with customer-friendly hours and pocket-book-friendly prices. The place is packed after school and on weekends, so appointments are suggested.

PEPPE AND BILL
Plaza Hotel
768 Fifth Ave (at Central Park S), mezzanine   212/751-8380
Mon-Fri: 9-6; Sat: 9-1 (closed Sat in July and Aug)

When you pay the kind of prices charged here, you expect the best. That is exactly what you get with highly professional hairstyling by Jacques and first-rate manicure work by his wife, Marie. You can be confident of the other personnel here, too.

Health and Fitness

With all the interest in fitness, health clubs keep springing up all over Manhattan. Some do not last long, so be careful about making long-term financial arrangements with any but the largest and most secure operations. Prices and facilities vary. For those who live in the city, watch newspaper and television ads for special introductory offers. For visitors, many clubs honor reciprocal memberships or allow you to purchase one- or two-day guest memberships. A number of hotels have excellent facilities, including the Peninsula New York, Crowne Plaza Manhattan, Four Seasons, Barclay Inter-Continental, Le Parker Meridien, Crowne Plaza at the U.N., the Plaza, Regal U.N. Plaza Hotel, the Regent Wall Street, Ritz-Carlton New York (Battery Park and Central Park), St. Regis, Trump International, and RIHGA Royal. New York Health and Racquet Club and New York Sports Club are recommended chains. Following are some of the better clubs, arranged by district.

Downtown
Battery Park Swim & Fitness (375 South End Ave, 212/321-1117)
Crunch Fitness (404 Lafayette St, 212/614-0120; 152 Christopher St, 212/366-3725; 623 Broadway, 212/420-0507; and 25 Broadway, 212/269-1067)
David Barton Gym (552 Ave of the Americas, 212/727-0004)
Dolphin Fitness (155 E 3rd St, 212/533-0090; 110 Greenwich St, 212/233-0700; 90 John St, 212/732-4445; 18 Ave B, 212/777-1001; and 94 E 4th St, 212/387-9500)
Eastern Athletic Club (80 Leonard St, 212/966-5432)

Equinox (97 Greenwich Ave, 212/620-0103; 54 Murray St, 212/566-6555; and 14 Wall St, 212/964-6688)
Hanson's Fitness (63 Greene St, 212/431-7682; 132 Perry St, 212/741-2000; and 826 Broadway, 212/982-2233)
Lucille Roberts Health Club (80 Fifth Ave, 212/255-3999)
New York Health and Racquet Club (24 E 13th St, 212/924-4600 and 39 Whitehall St, 212/269-9800)
New York Sports Club (30 Cliff St, 212/349-7700; 151 Reade St, 212/571-1000; 503 Broadway, 212/925-6600; 217 Broadway, 212/791-9555; 30 Wall St, 212/482-4800; Battery Park City, 102 North End Ave, 212/945-3535; 10 Irving Pl, 212/477-1800; 125 Seventh Ave S, 212/206-1500; and 160 Water St, 212/363-4600)
Plus One Fitness (106 Crosby St, 212/334-1116)
Printing House Fitness (421 Hudson St, 212/243-7600)
World Gym (232 Mercer St, 212/780-7407)

Special features at athletic complexes:

Asphalt Green (555 E 90th St, 212/369-8890): Astroturf field, Olympic-size pool, outdoor running track, belly-dancing classes, yoga, aerobics
Battery Park Swim and Fitness (375 South End Ave, 212/321-1117): great view and outdoor pool with retractable top, tanning beds
Chelsea Piers (Sports Center, Pier 60, West Side Highway, 212/336-6000): huge facility, indoor wall, boxing ring, indoor track, yoga
Clay (25 W 14th St, 212/206-9200): private saunas, coed lounge
Duomo Gym (11-13 E 26th St, 212/689-9121): inviting, classy equipment and staff, pool table
Equinox (250 E 54th St, 212/277-5400): good food, yoga classes
Manhattan Plaza Health Club (482 W 43rd St, 212/563-7001): climbing wall and cave, pool
New York Sports Club (128 Eighth Ave, 212/627-0065): caters to gay community
Printing House Fitness (421 Hudson St, 212/243-7600): squash courts, rooftop sundeck
Reebok Sports Club NY (160 Columbus Ave, 212/362-6800): pricy but beautiful spa
Sports Club/LA (45 Rockefeller Plaza, 212/218-8600 and 33 E 61st St, 212/355-5100): affiliated with Reebok Sports Clubs NY
24/7 (7 E 17th St, 212/366-4426): for serious workouts
World Gym (232 Mercer St, 212/780-7407): boxing instruction, cardiovascular workouts

---

Midtown
Bally Sports Club (335 Madison Ave, 212/983-5320; 139 W 32nd St, 212/465-1750; and 350 W 50th St, 212/265-9400)
Bally Total Fitness (641 Ave of the Americas, 212/645-4565 and 45 E 55th St, 212/688-6630)
Crunch Fitness (54 E 13th St, 212/475-2018; 144 W 38th St, 212/869-7788; 555 W 42nd St, 212/594-8050; 554 Second Ave, 212/545-9757; and 1109 Second Ave, 212/758-3434)
Dolphin Fitness (242 E 14th St, 212/615-0390; 50 E 42nd St, 212/286-0999; and 330 E 59th St, 212/486-6966)
Duomo Gym (11 E 26th St, 212/689-9121)

Equinox (1633 Broadway, 212/541-7000; 521 Fifth Ave, 212/972-8000; 897 Broadway, 212/780-9300; 250 E 54th St, 212/277-5400; and 420 Lexington Ave, 212/953-2499)

Gold's Gym (250 W 54th St, 212/307-7760)

Gravity (Le Parker Meridien Hotel, 119 W 56th St, 212/245-1144)

Manhattan Plaza Health Club (482 W 43rd St, 212/563-7001)

New York Health and Racquet Club (132 E 45th St, 212/986-3100; 20 E 50th St, 212/593-1500; 110 W 56th St, 212/541-7200; 115 E 57th St, 212/826-9650; and 60 W 23rd St, 212/989-2300)

New York Sports Club (50 W 34th St, 212/868-0820; 380 Madison Ave, 212/983-0303; Crowne Plaza Manhattan, 1601 Broadway, 212/977-8880; Crowne Plaza at the U.N., 502 Park Ave, 212/308-1010; 614 Second Ave, 212/213-5999; 575 Lexington Ave, 212/317-9400; 633 Third Ave, 212/661-8500; 200 Madison Ave, 212/686-1144; 131 E 31st St, 212/213-1408; 113 E 23rd St, 212/982-4400; 270 Eighth Ave, 212/243-3400; 34 W 14th St, 212/337-9900; 1372 Broadway, 212/575-4500; 128 Eighth Ave, 212/627-0065; 3 Park Ave, 212/686-1085; 1221 Ave of the Americas, 212/840-8240; 19 W 44th St, 212/768-3535; 230 W 41st St, 646/366-9400; and 200 Park Ave, 212/682-4440)

Plus One Fitness (Waldorf-Astoria Hotel, 301 Park Ave, 212/872-4970)

Sports Center at Chelsea Piers (Pier 60, West Side Hwy at 23rd St, 212/336-6000)

Synergy Fitness (201 E 23rd St, 212/679-7300)

24/7 Fitness Club (47 W 14th St, 212/206-1504 and 7 E 17th St, 212/366-4426)

YMCA (125 W 14th St, 212/741-9210)

YWCA (610 Lexington Ave, 212/755-4500)

Upper East Side

Asphalt Green (1750 York Ave, 212/369-8890)

Bally Total Fitness (144 E 86th St, 212/722-7371)

David Barton Gym (30 E 85th St, 212/517-7577)

Equinox Fitness Club (205 E 85th St, 212/430-8500 and Barbizon Hotel, 140 E 63rd St, 212/750-4900)

New York Health and Racquet Club (1433 York Ave, 212/737-6666)

New York Sports Club (151 E 86th St, 212/860-8630; 349 E 76th St, 212/288-5700; and 1637 Third Ave, 212/987-7200

92nd Street Y Health and Fitness Center (1395 Lexington Ave, 212/415-5700)

Synergy Fitness (1781 Second Ave, 212/426-0909)

Upper West Side

Crunch Fitness (162 W 83rd St, 212/875-1902)

Equinox (344 Amsterdam Ave, 212/721-4200 and 2465 Broadway, 212/799-1818)

Lucille Roberts Health Club (2700 Broadway, 212/961-0500)

New York Sports Club (248 W 80th St, 212/873-1500; 61 W 62nd St, 212/265-0995; 2162 Broadway, 212/496-2444; 23 W 73rd St, 212/496-6300; 1657 Broadway, 212/307-9400; and 2527 Broadway, 212/665-0009)

Paris Health Club (752 West End Ave, 212/749-3500)

Reebok Sports Club NY (160 Columbus Ave, 212/362-6800)

Synergy Fitness (700 Columbus Ave, 212/865-5454)

West Side YMCA (5 W 63rd St, 212/875-4100)
World Gym (1926 Broadway, 212/874-0942)

Uptown
Dolphin Fitness (209 W 125th St, 212/864-0200)
New York Sports Club (2311 Frederick Douglass Blvd, 212/316-2500)

Health and Fitness Specialists

Acupuncture
Vital Gate (212/873-4244)

Fitness Consultant
Edward Jackowski (Exude, 16 E 52nd St, 212/644-9559): best in the business

Hypnotist
Skyler Madison Wellness Center (515 Madison Ave, 212/994-1822)

Massage
Amber Hunt (917/507-4919)
Eastside Massage Therapy Center (351 E 78th St, 212/249-2927): 13 massage therapists; Swedish, sports, and deep-muscle therapy
John Wehr (Reebok Sports Club NY, 160 Columbus Ave, 212/362-6800)
Lewis Harrison (40 W 72nd St, 212/724-8782): hotel and house calls; stress management
Nickel (77 Eighth Ave, 212/242-3203); for men
OSAKA 46 (37 W 46th St, 212/575-1303): Oriental skin therapy
OSAKA 56 (50 W 56th St, 212/956-3422): Oriental skin therapy
Spa Sun (26 W 20th St, 212/337-0020): couples

Kevin Coulthard (917/515-8039) is a top experienced professional in the specialties of massage and personal training.

Specialized massage
Blissage: **Ivete Martins** (212/219-8970)
Chinese back rub: (212/334-3909)
Hot rocks: **Spa at Equinox** (212/439-8500)
Russian/Turkish: (212/674-9250)

Personal trainers
Bodysmith (212/249-1824): women only
Casa Specialized Private Fitness (212/717-1998)
Dorit Baxter (47 W 57th St, 212/371-4542): tummy tightener
Gina Allchin (Trump World, 646/312-7630)
Lotte Berk (212/288-6613)
Mike Creamer (Anatomically Correct, 212/353-8834)
Rich Barretta (Duomo Gym, 11 E 26th St, 212/689-9121)
Timothy Callaghan (212/585-4245)
Victoria Dell (646/698-9257)

Pilates
Jonathan Urla (212/996-7088)
re:AB (33 Bleecker St, 212/420-9111): novices welcome
Victoria Dell (646/698-9257)

Yoga
Integral Yoga Institute (227 W 13th St, 212/929-0585)
Integral Yoga Uptown Center (200 W 72nd St, 212/721-4000)
Jivamukti Yoga Center (404 Lafayette St, 212/353-0214)
Jonathan Urla (212/996-7088)
Victoria Dell (646/698-9257)

What's in a name? Plenty! One of the best is a spa called **Just Calm Down** (32 W 22nd St, 212/337-0032). They say their mission is to soothe the inner soul. With massages called "Venus on the Half Shell," body treatments like "Diamond in the Buff," and facials described as "Peelin' Groovy," you're bound to have fun and receive attentive care.

Hotels

The Manhattan hotel scene has changed a great deal in recent years. A number of new operations have arrived in both luxury and budget categories. Small boutique hotels have become very popular, especially for the single traveler. Some of the best names in the industry have opened multiple units in the city. Room rates have been adjusted because of the economic downturn facing the city and nation. A drop in international visitors has affected occupancy. Hotel dining has improved immeasurably in the past few years (see "Hotel Dining" in the Restaurants chapter). Practically every hotel now has some kind of athletic facility. The new ones have large, elaborate setups, while the old-time hotels have been converting space for this much asked-for amenity. Spas are increasingly popular. Kids programs are featured by a number of hotels that cater to families.

The best hotel rates can still be found by calling the hotel directly, many times at the last minute. Be careful, as always, of high charges for in-room bars, telephone calls, room service, and laundry service. New York has many fine hotels in every price category. Your choice should take into account the type of accommodations you desire and the area of the city that will be the most convenient.

Try a hotel consolidator like **Quikbook** (800/789-9887), **Hotels.com** (800/964-6835), or **Priceline** (www.priceline.com). They buy up excess rooms and pass along the savings.

Checklist

If any of these particularly matter to you, ask about them when making reservations. It might make the difference between a successful stay and a disastrous one.

- adjustable thermostat
- good reading lights
- good quality towels—and an adequate supply
- comfortable in-room sitting area
- on-site dining facilities
- free on-site parking
- conveniently located ice machine

- direct-dial phones
- nonsmoking rooms
- late checkout
- shuttle service to and from airports
- hotel drugstore or newsstand
- windows that open
- express checkout
- free morning paper
- evening turndown service
- concierge
- 24-hour room service
- health-club facilities
- removable closet hangers
- in-room safe
- reliable message service
- umbrella in room
- well-marked fire escapes

Special Hotel Classifications

Boutique hotels

Hotel Giraffe (365 Park Ave 5, 212(685-7700)
Iroquois NY (49 W 44th St, 212/840-3080)
Library Hotel (299 Madison Ave, 212/9834500)
Regent Wall Street (55 Wall St, 212/845-8600)
Tribeca Grand (2 Ave of the Americas, 212/519-6600)
W New York (541 Lexington Ave, 212/755-1200)
W New York—The Court (130 E 39th St, 212/685-1100)
W New York—Tuscany (120 E 39th St, 212/686-1600)
Wales Hotel (1295 Madison Ave, 212/876-6000)

Extended Stays

If you are planning to stay awhile in Manhattan, check out these extended-stay facilities. Some require a 30-day minimum stay. Washers and dryers are conveniently available.

Bristol Plaza (210 E 65th St, 212/753-7900): kitchens, daily maid service, health club, concierge
Phillips Club (155 W 66th St, 212/835-8800): kitchens, daily maid service, computer friendly, business center, concierge
Sutton Hotel (330 E 56th St, 212/752-8888): kitchens, daily maid service, health club, concierge
Worldwide Apartments (www.nothotels.com)

Hostels

Big Apple Hostel (119 W 45th St, 212/302-2603): midtown location, dorms and private rooms
Central Park Hostel (19 W 103rd St, 212/678-0491): dorm-style rooms with shared baths ($30 and up); lockers
Chelsea International Hostel (251 W 20th St, 212/647-0010): dormitory rooms start at $45 for singles and $108 for doubles
Chelsea Star Hostel (300 W 30th St, 212/244-7827): hotel ($60 and up) and hostel ($30 and up)

New York International American Youth Hostel (891 Amsterdam Ave, 212/932-2300): one of the world's largest; prices start at about $40
Times Square Roommates (356 W 40th St, 2nd floor, 212/216-0642): dorms and private rooms with shared baths and lockers

Inexpensive
Carlton Arms (160 E 25th St, 212/679-0680)
Edison (228 W 47th St, 212/840-5000)
Excelsior (45 W 81st St, 212/362-9200)
59th Street Bridge Apartments (351 E 60th St, 212/754-9388)
Habitat House (130 E 57th St, 212/753-8841)
Hostelling International (891 Amsterdam Ave, 212/932-2300)
Hotel 31 (120 E 31st St, 212/685-3060)
Hotel 41 (206 W 41st St, 877/847-4444)
Larchmont (27 W 11th St, 212/989-9333
Manhattan (273 W 38th St, 212/921-9791)
Milburn (242 W 76th St, 212/362-1006)
Murray Hill Inn (143 E 30th St, 212/683-6900)
Off-Soho Suites (11 Rivington St, 212/979-9808)
Portland Square Hotel (132 W 47th St, 212/382-0600)
Ramada Inn Eastside (161 Lexington Ave, 212/545-1800)
Stanford Hotel (43 W 32nd St, 212/563-1480)
Super 8 Times Square (59 W 46th St, 212/719-2300)
Union Square Inn (209 E 14th St, 212/614-0500)
Washington Square (103 Waverly Pl, 212/777-9515)
Webster (419 W 34th St, 212/967-9000): women only
Wellington (871 Seventh Ave, 212/247-3900)
Westside Inn (237 W 107th St, 212/866-0061)
Wolcott (4 W 31st St, 212/268-2900)

Small luxury hotels
Elysee (60 E 54th St, 212/753-1066)
Fitzpatrick Manhattan (687 Lexington Ave, 212/355-0100)
Inn at Irving Place (56 Irving Pl, 212/533-4600)
Le Marquis New York (12 E 31st St, 212/889-6363)
Lowell Hotel (28 E 63rd St, 212/838-1400)
The Mark Hotel (25 E 77th St, 212/7444300)
Regent Wall Street (55 Wall St, 212/845-8600)
Stanhope Park Hyatt New York (995 Fifth Ave, 212/774-1234)

Time Shares
Manhattan Club (200 W 56th St, 212/489-8488)

Kid-Friendly Hotels
Barclay InterContinental (111 E 48th St, 212/755-5900): backpack full of goodies
Doubletree Guest Suites Times Square (1568 Broadway, 212/719-1600): kids' playroom
Le Parker Meridien (118 W 57th St, 212/245-5000): in-elevator videos
Novotel New York (226 W 52nd St, 212/315-0100): kids' corner with entertainment
The Plaza (768 Fifth Ave, 212/759-3000): Young Ambassadors' Club activities—and don't forget Eloise lives here!

Ritz-Carlton New York, Battery Park (2 West St, 212/344-0800): "Ritz Kids" program, with exciting perks

Westin New York Times Square (270 W 43rd St, 212/921-9575): kids' club with amenities

Pet-Friendly Hotels

The Mark Hotel (25 E 77th St): headquarters for dog weddings!

Mayflower Hotel (15 Central Park W): They'll even provide room for your favorite kangaroo!

Regent Wall Street (55 Wall St, 212/845-8600)

Soho Grand Hotel (310 West Broadway): puppy bar in front

Swissotel New York—The Drake (440 Park Ave): in-room dog sitters

---

If you want to exercise your pet, try these parks: **DeWitt Clinton Park** (Eleventh Ave at 52nd St), **Madison Square Park** (Madison Ave at 25th St), **Margaret Meade Park** (Columbus Ave at 81st St), **Robert Moses Park** (First Ave at 41st St), and **Carl Schurz Park** (York Ave at 86th St).

Hotel Concierges

A concierge is the handiest person in a hotel if you want special services or advice. There is no charge for this help, but tipping is expected. Ten dollars is about right for the average service, more if a request takes an unusual amount of time or trouble. For requests above and beyond the call of duty, 15% of the value of the service is a good guideline. If you are a regular guest, it is wise to cultivate a good relationship with these helpful folks.

A few services a concierge can help with: babysitting, couriers, emergency medical services, escorts, flowers, gifts, health and beauty care, kennels, massage, notary public, party venues, pet services, photographers, rental cars, restaurants, secretarial services, tickets for events, shows, transportation, tours, translators, and videos. In other words, concierges can be almost as helpful as this book!

Hotel Lingo

All-suite hotels: multi-room suites, often with free breakfast and evening cocktails

American plan: room rate includes breakfast, lunch, and dinner

Corporate rate: room price for employees of corporations

Double occupancy rate: price per person, two to a room

Double room rate: full price of a room shared by two

Economy hotels: good beds, basic rooms, and often a free continental breakfast for about half the price of traditional hotel rooms

European plan: breakfast included

Extended-stay hotels: fully equipped apartments in townhouse-style developments for longer stays

Full-service hotels: top-of-the-line amenities for when you want to be pampered

Half-board/demi-pension: room rate includes breakfast and either lunch or dinner

Hostel: inexpensive dorm rooms available for rent

Hotel broker: a service provider that quotes prices and makes confirmed reservations; fee paid by hotels

Hotel consolidator: acts as a clearinghouse for unsold hotel accommodations

Limited-service hotels: oversized guest rooms with work spaces but no on-premises restaurant and few other amenities; prices are about one-third less than traditional hotel rates

Modified American Plan: room rate includes breakfast and dinner

Rack rate: full retail price of a room as listed on rate cards and brochures

Service charge: fixed percentage automatically added to room and meal bills

Hotels Near Airports

The following are conveniently located, provide airport transportation, have restaurants, and are reasonably priced (ask for corporate rates). Some have recreational facilities, such as fitness gyms and pools.

John F. Kennedy International: **Courtyard by Marriott** (166 rooms, Jamaica, Queens, 718/848-2121), **Hampton Inn** (216 Rooms, Jamaica, Queens, 718/322-7500), **Holiday Inn** (360 rooms, Jamaica Queens, 718/659-0200), **Radisson** (386 rooms, Jamaica, Queens, 718/322-2300), **Sheraton** (184 rooms, Jamaica, Queens, 718/489-1000)

LaGuardia: **Courtyard by Marriott** (238 rooms, East Elmhurst, Queens, 718/446-4800), **Crowne Plaza** (358 rooms, East Elmhurst, Queens, 718/457-6300), **Marriott** (437 rooms, East Elmhurst, Queens, 718/565-8900), **Sheraton** (173 rooms, Flushing, Queens, 718/460-6666), **Wyndham Garden Hotel** (229 rooms, East Elmhurst, Queens, 718/426-1500)

Newark International: **Hilton** (253 rooms, Newark, NJ, 973/622-5000), **Holiday Inn** (412 rooms, Newark, NJ, 973/589-1000), **Marriott** (596 rooms, Newark, NJ, 973/623-0006), **Sheraton** (260 rooms, Elizabeth, NJ, 980/528-1600)

Hotels That Are New

At press time, a new hotel that's scheduled to open soon is the **Mandarin Oriental** (Columbus Circle, 212/207-8880), with 249 deluxe rooms and suites and fabulous views of Central Park. It will be part of the AOL/Time Warner complex, with broadcasting studios, retail and residential complexes, and a world-class performance hall for jazz at Lincoln Center.

In the up-and-coming Meatpacking District, the **Hotel Gansevoort** (212/228-1500) will include 187 rooms and suites, a large roof-deck restaurant and event loft, full-service spa, and glassed-in pool with underwater music.

Several new budget hotels include **Hampton Inn** in Chelsea, the Financial District/South Street Seaport, and Herald Square in midtown. Marriott's newest will be a **Residence Inn** with a Times Square location.

Hotels with Swimming Pools

Crowne Plaza Manhattan (1605 Broadway): for exercise buffs
Le Parker Meridien (118 W 56th St): visibly exciting
Millenium Hilton (55 Church St): gorgeous
Peninsula New York (700 Fifth Ave): very classy
Sheraton Manhattan (790 Seventh Ave): kid-friendly
Trump International Hotel and Tower (1 Central Park W): magnificent

New York's Finest Hotels

Remembering that this *is* New York, I have categorized hotels by room tariff per night (without taxes) as follows:

* Inexpensive: $199 and under
* Moderate: $200 to $399
* Expensive: $400 and up

AFFINIA HOSPITALITY
Affinia Dumont, 150 E 34th St (bet Third and Lexington Ave)
212/320-8019

Beekman Tower, 3 Mitchell Pl (at 49th St)
212/320-8018

The Benjamin, 125 E 50th St (at Lexington Ave)
212/320-8002

Eastgate Tower, 222 E 39th St (bet Second and Third Ave)
212/320-8021

Lyden Gardens, 215 E 64th St (bet Second and Third Ave)
212/320-8022

Plaza Fifty, 155 E 50th St (at Third Ave)
212/320-8024

Shelburne Murray Hill, 303 Lexington Ave (at 37th St)
212/320-8025

Southgate Tower, 371 Seventh Ave (at 31st St)
212/320-8026

Surrey Hotel, 20 E 76th St (bet Madison And Fifth Ave)
212/320-8027

Moderate to moderately expensive   www.affinia.com

Looking for style and value? These all-suites hotels are among the most reasonably priced and conveniently located in New York. Each features 24-hour attendants and modern kitchens. Over 2,000 suites in all—studio, junior, and one- or two-bedroom suites—are available at very attractive daily, weekly, or monthly rates. These are particularly convenient for long-term corporate visitors and traveling families, who can economize by having the kids sleep on pull-out couches and by using the fully equipped kitchens. Fitness centers are available at most properties. Food facilities vary. The famous Cafe Boulud can be found at the Surrey. Women especially like these accommodations when they must travel and dine alone. A great buy!

ALGONQUIN HOTEL
59 W 44th St (bet Fifth Ave and Ave of the Americas)
Moderately expensive   212/840-6800, 888/304-2047
www.algonquinhotel@destinationhotels.com

The Algonquin is truly legendary; it was designated a historic landmark by the city of New York in 1987. This home of the famous Round Table—where Dorothy Parker, Harold Ross, Robert Benchley, and other literary wits sparred and dined regularly—now exudes the same charm and character as it did in the Roaring Twenties! There are 174 rooms, including 20 suites (some named after well-known personalities), and the atmosphere is intimate and friendly. The remodeled lobby is the best place in the city for people-watching, and the Oak Room is arguably the best cabaret venue in New York.

THE AVALON
16 E 32nd St (bet Madison and Fifth Ave)   212/299-7000
Moderate   www.theavalonny.com

The Avalon is a European-style boutique hotel, located in the heart of Manhattan's shopping and convention area. Features include continental breakfasts, library, club room, room service, and airport "meet and greet."

Many female readers will remember the legendary Barbizon Hotel in Manhattan. A $50 million renovation has transformed this property into the luxury **Melrose Hotel** (140 E 63rd St, 212/838-5700).

CASABLANCA
147 W 43rd St (bet Broadway and Ave of the Americas)
Moderate   212/869-1212
www.casablancahotel.com

Now that the Times Square area has been cleaned up, you might consider staying at Casablanca, an attractive, safe, and clean boutique hotel with a Moroccan flavor. It's small (48 rooms and suites), newly renovated, family-owned, and offers complimentary amenities, along with comfortable rates. Best of all, the atmosphere is friendly. Special attractions: complimentary continental breakfast, free beer, wine, and snacks on weekday evenings; passes to the New York Sports Club; free Internet browsing on the lounge computers; and free bottled water, iced tea, and chocolates in the rooms. Besides, you are right in the center of the action!

CITY CLUB HOTEL
55 W 44th St (bet Fifth Ave and Ave of the Americas)   212/921-5500
Moderate   www.cityclubhotel.com

City Club is a small luxury hotel that features Frette linens, feather beds, guest privileges at the nearby New York Sports Club, large marble bathrooms, and best of all, Daniel Boulud's DB Bistro Moderne restaurant on-premises. This excellent operation also provides room service for the hotel.

The best travel agents for New York (and other big-city) hotels:
Barbara Galley, Linden Travel Bureau, 212/421-3320
Jody Bear, Bear & Bear/VWT, 212/532-3400
Valerie Ann Wilson, Valerie Wilson Travel, 212/532-3400

ELYSEE
60 E 54th St (bet Park and Madison Ave)   212/753-1066
Moderate   www.elyseehotel.com

The Elysee is a private boutique hotel with newly renovated rooms and suites. Located within walking distance of Manhattan's best shopping, it is very popular with business travelers, has a multilingual staff, and offers kitchenettes in some rooms and suites. Rooms are filled with attractive antique pieces, marble baths invite the visitor to take a relaxing soak after a tough day, and rates include continental breakfast. Complimentary wine and cheese are offered on weeknights. The Steakhouse at Monkey Bar is one of New York's hottest sipping and dining spots.

ESSEX HOUSE, A WESTIN HOTEL
160 Central Park S (bet Ave of the Americas and Seventh Ave)
Moderately expensive to expensive   212/247-0300
                                                            www.essexhouse.com

A lady friend of mine who travels all over the world claims that this is the best hotel she has ever stayed at! The Essex House has been restored to its original art decor grandeur, and it is a beauty. The restaurants—Cafe Botanica on the Park and Alain Ducasse—offer top French cuisine. Guest rooms feature classic Louis XVI and Chippendale decor, and many have spectacular views of Central Park. All offer two-line speaker phones, voice mail and message retrieval, in-room fax, minibar, and a safe. The all-marble bathrooms come with robes, scale, hair dryer, and superb toiletries. A business center and health spa are added features. Great weekend getaway packages are available through the reservations department. You can't do better!

FOUR SEASONS HOTEL
57 E 57th St (bet Madison and Park Ave)   212/758-5700
Expensive   www.fourseasons.com

In the hotel world, fewer names elicit higher praise or win more awards than Four Seasons. They are considered one of the best in the business. Now upscale visitors to the Big Apple have an elegant, 52-story Four Seasons to call their home away from home. Designed by I. M. Pei and Frank Williams, the Four Seasons provides 364 oversized rooms and suites, some with terraces; several fine eating places, including the top-notch Fifty Seven Fifty Seven and a lobby lounge for light snacks and tea; a fully equipped business center, complete with freestanding computer terminals and modem hookups; a 5,000-square-foot fitness center and spa, with all the latest equipment; and numerous meeting rooms. The principal appeal, however, is the size of the guest rooms, which average 600 square feet, offer spectacular views of the city, and feature huge, luxurious marble bathrooms with separate dressing areas. A classy staff makes this another award-winning property.

HILTON NEW YORK
1335 Ave of the Americas (bet 53rd and 54th St)   212/586-7000
Moderate to moderately expensive   www.newyorktowers.hilton.com

This Hilton flagship at Rockefeller Center has just undergone a $100 million renovation and redesign. The Hilton New York features two restaurants: New York Marketplace, an all-day dining facility, and Etrusca, an intimate Italian room featuring Tuscan foods and wines. Special features include an outstanding art collection, upscale executive floors with private lounge and large luxury suites, dozens of rooms equipped for the disabled, a highly trained international staff, and an 8,000-square-foot state-of-the-art fitness club and spa. As a popular business and convention hotel, the Hilton equips its rooms with data ports and other modern communications equipment. For those leisure travelers interested in shopping, the theater, Radio City Music Hall, and other midtown attractions, this location is highly desirable.

HUDSON HOTEL
356 W 58th St (bet Eighth and Ninth Ave)   212/554-6000
Inexpensive to moderate   www.ianschragerhotels.com

Ian Schrager has done something special with this property. He has opened an affordable hotel in an often unaffordable area. A lushly landscaped courtyard garden is open to the sky. You will find abundant amenities plus a reasonably priced restaurant, busy bars, and a new spa and Olympic-sized pool. There are 1,000 guest rooms with minimal decor and furniture, but with prices as low as $145, you won't worry too much about that. There are, in fact, some nice decorative touches, such as the attractive wood paneling. But the scene is really the big thing here!

THE IROQUOIS NEW YORK
49 W 44th St (bet Fifth Ave and Ave of the Americas)   212/840-3080
Moderate   www.iroquoisny.com

A multimillion-dollar facelift has transformed this 1923 hotel into a comfortable, modern facility with 114 rooms (including 9 suites) furnished in elegant French decor. It has always been a favorite of tourists and overseas tour groups. Round-the-clock room service, a multilingual staff, marble bathrooms, and an on-premises restaurant are among the amenities.

KIMBERLY HOTEL
145 E 50th St (bet Lexington and Third Ave)   212/755-0400
Moderate   www.kimberlyhotel.com

If big hotels turn you off, then the Kimberly may be just what you are looking for. This charming and hospitable boutique suites hotel in the center of Manhattan offers guests the kind of personal attention that is a rarity in today's commercial world. There are 185 luxury guest rooms, marble bathrooms, one- and two-bedroom suites with fully equipped kitchens, and private terraces with most suites. There is fine French cuisine at Olica or enjoy the scene at VUE, a popular night club. Access to the New York Health and Racquet Club is complimentary and room service is available.

LIBRARY HOTEL
299 Madison Ave (at 41st St)   212/983-4500
Moderate   www.libraryhotel.com

For the avid reader, check out the Library! Each room has a collection of books. Guests can also enjoy the Poetry Terrace, which houses volumes of verse by assorted authors. A daily breakfast and wine-and-cheese reception are included in the rate. The 60 rooms are equipped for high-speed Internet access. A unique feature: room numbers are based on the Dewey decimal system of classifying books.

LOWELL HOTEL
28 E 63rd St (bet Park and Madison Ave)   212/838-1400
Moderately expensive

This classy, well-located hotel features 44 suites and 21 deluxe rooms. Amenities include a 24-hour multilingual concierge service, at least two phones per room, fax machine with a dedicated line, VCRs and outlets for personal computers, marble bathrooms, complimentary shoeshine service, fitness center, and all the rest that goes with a top operation. Thirty-three suites have wood-burning fireplaces, and ten have private terraces. One even has a separate gym, stereo, and seven telephones! The Hollywood suite has all the latest entertainment amenities, plus a fully equipped kitchen.

THE MARK HOTEL
25 E 77th St (bet Fifth and Madison Ave) 212/744-4300
Moderately expensive www.mandarinoriental.com

An older residency building (the Hyde Park, built in 1926) has been converted into one of the most charming hotels in New York. There are 125 guest rooms and 60 suites done in English-Italian style, all decorated in exquisite taste. Every room has cable TV and two-line phones, and most have pantries. I strongly recommend the suites, which have separate vanities and marble baths. Some even have libraries, wet bars, and terraces with views of Central Park. The location is terrific, and the personnel (including a multilingual concierge) are extremely accommodating. Mark's, an excellent restaurant just off the lobby, serves all meals, plus tea and brunch. Guests get Frette linens, heated towel racks, down pillows, umbrellas, and Molton Brown of London soaps. The bar is sensational!

From time to time an area of Manhattan will suddenly get hot. Currently it is the Meatpacking District. One of the newest attractions in this district is the **Maritime Hotel** (363 W 16th St, 212/242-4300). This boutique hotel is in the space that used to serve as the headquarters for the National Maritime Union of America. The 135 rooms are done in good taste. Features include two restaurants (Japanese and Mediterranean), a ballroom, and a large garden area. Penthouse suites and public areas are spectacular. Rates are moderate.

THE MARMARA-MANHATTAN
301 E 94th St (at Second Ave) 212/427-3100, 800/621-9029
www.marmaramanhattan.com

The conveniently located Marmara-Manhattan is a relatively new extended-stay hotel that provides turn-key living for folks who need temporary quarters for personal or professional reasons. They offer flexible lease terms for stays beyond 30 days. Suites with up to three bedrooms, as well as studio apartments, are available. Choose from sleek and sophisticated to more traditional, "comfy" rooms. Amenities include modern kitchens with cooking and serving utensils, daily housekeeping, 24-hour concierge and doorman services, spacious bathrooms, terraces, and an exercise room. There are over 100 custom-decorated suites, many with sensational views. You'll be greeted by a complimentary welcome basket.

MAYFLOWER HOTEL
15 Central Park W (at 61st St) 212/265-0060, 800/223-4164
Moderate

If you are coming to New York for cultural events at Lincoln Center or Carnegie Hall, the Mayflower is an ideal place to stay. Overlooking Central Park, it is a safe, comfortable hotel with 365 spacious rooms and suites of intimate European charm. Most have serving pantries—(i.e., a refrigerator and sink). There are a number of two- and three-bedroom suites and several terraced penthouses, all with pantries and refrigerators. A fitness center and restaurant are on the property. Room service is available until midnight.

THE MERCER
147 Mercer St (at Prince St)   212/966-6060
Expensive   www.mercerhotel.com

The Mercer has enjoyed fame mainly because it is the location of Jean-Georges Vongerichten's Mercer Kitchen restaurant, from which 24-hour room service is also offered. The rooms are relatively less spacious than the bathrooms, the decor is already showing signs of wear, and rooms can be quite noisy. A plus: good location in Soho. My bottom line: not worth the exorbitant prices.

MILFORD PLAZA
270 W 45th St (at Eighth Ave)   212/869-3600, 800/221-2690
Moderate   www.milfordplaza.com

Value is the key word here. The Milford Plaza, located at the edge of the Theater District, offers reasonable rates that are partially offset by its location. Rest assured the hotel has extremely tight security. Newly redecorated, the 1,300 guest rooms are small but clean, and late-night dining is available. There is now a state-of-the-art fitness center. Very attractive rates are available on weekends and for groups.

MILLENIUM HILTON
55 Church St (at Trinity Pl)   212/693-2001
Moderate   www.newyorkmillenium.hilton.com

Though the Millenium Hilton did not sustain structural damage in the September 11, 2001, terrorist attack, it has still been completely renovated. Conveniently situated in Lower Manhattan, this hotel offers over 500 rooms and suites, meeting space, business center, swimming pool, fitness center, and lobby bar and restaurant.

NEW YORK MARRIOTT FINANCIAL CENTER
85 West St (at Battery Park)   212/385-4900
Moderate   www.marriott.com

Though it was damaged by the September 11, 2001 terrorist attack, this 504-room hotel has since been completely renovated, from lobby to guest rooms. Features include Roy's restaurant (from Hawaii), 85 West bar and grill, a fitness center, and swimming pool.

NEW YORK MARRIOTT MARQUIS
1535 Broadway (bet 45th and 46th St)   212/398-1900
Moderate to moderately expensive   www.nymarriottmarquis.com

The New York Marriott Marquis has over 1,900 guest rooms and suites, sizable meeting and convention facilities, and one of the largest hotel atriums in the world. Guests can enjoy a 500-seat two-story revolving restaurant and lounge atop the building. In addition, a legitimate Broadway theater, a fully equipped health club, eight restaurants and lounges, and a special concierge level are on the property.

THE NEW YORK PALACE
455 Madison Ave (bet 50th and 51st St)   212/888-7000
Expensive   www.newyorkpalace.com

Located close to Saks Fifth Avenue, the 896-room New York Palace offers commanding views of the city skyline, which is particularly enchanting in the evening. The public rooms encompass the 120-year-old Villard Houses, a legendary New York landmark. A comprehensive renovation added such facilities as an expansive fitness center, an executive lounge, and the two-floor Villard Center (with its selection of meeting and function rooms). A casually elegant Mediterranean restaurant called Istana offers New American cuisine. The famous Manhattan restaurant Le Cirque 2000 has its quarters in the Villard Houses. Don't miss the Villard Bar and Lounge, whose Tiffany windows are worth a visit in themselves.

THE PENINSULA NEW YORK
700 Fifth Ave (at 55th St)   212/956-2888
Expensive

When the name Peninsula is mentioned, the words *quality* and *class* immediately come to mind. This is especially true in Manhattan, where a $45 million facelift has made the property even more luxurious than before. The building is a 1902 landmark with 185 rooms and 54 suites, including the palatial Peninsula Suite (more than 3,000 square feet at $8,500 per night!). Room features include oversized marble bathrooms, in-room fax machines, large work desks, audiovisual systems with cable, and numerous bathroom amenities. Amenities at the 21st floor Peninsula New York Spa and Health Club include an indoor pool, jacuzzi, sun decks, modern fitness equipment, and spa service (spa menu, too).

Given the astronomical rents charged for apartments in Manhattan, you might need a roommate to share costs. **Roommates NYC** (212/982-6265) may be of some help.

THE PIERRE HOTEL
2 E 61st St (at Fifth Ave)   212/838-8000
Expensive

Combine the Pierre's name with the Four Seasons' reputation and you're bound to get top quality. Overlooking Central Park, this property provides 201 elegant rooms and suites with 1930s detailing, a magnificent lobby, the Rotunda (famous for afternoon tea and light meals), and Cafe Pierre (a fine-dining spot offering continental cuisine for breakfast, lunch, and dinner). Function rooms are the site of many of Manhattan's glitziest events. A fitness center, outfitted with Italian marble, provides the latest in cardiovascular equipment. With a staff of over 650, you can be assured of highly personalized service.

THE PLAZA
768 Fifth Ave (at Central Park South)   212/759-3000
Expensive   www.fairmont.com

Every great city has a legendary hotel, and in New York it is the Plaza. With a fabulous location, this grande dame of Manhattan exudes the grace and physical charm that has made it the home of distinguished guests and New York visitors for decades. The public rooms host some of Manhattan's most chi-chi affairs. The lobby Palm Court, as romantic a setting as you will find in the city, offers afternoon tea and an outstanding Sunday brunch. The legendary Oak Room and Oak Bar offer historic surroundings. The Oyster Bar is a popular meeting place. Guest rooms and suites vary in size. Magnificent floral arrangements, priceless chandeliers, and gilded ceilings adorn the foyers. Exceptionally polite and efficient bellmen and doormen, some of whom have been at the hotel since I first visited as a child, provide friendly greetings. Horse-drawn carriages wait at the front door to take you on a never-to-be-forgotten Central Park experience. A health facility has replaced a theater and restaurant downstairs. The hotel offers a luxurious 8,000-square-foot spa. Perched on the corner of Fifth Avenue and Central Park South, the restaurant One C.P.S. offers a brasserie menu and legendary views of Central Park.

PLAZA ATHENEE HOTEL
37 E 64th St (bet Park and Madison Ave)   212/734-9100
Expensive   www.plaza-athenee.com

This European-style hotel ranks with New York's best in several categories, including service. Most of the rooms have been renovated, and all have marble bathrooms. Some of the suites on the higher floors feature solariums and roof terraces. Additional amenities include a workout facility, CD players in every room, high-speed Internet access, twice-daily maid service, 24-hour room service, and the outstanding Arabelle restaurant. Check out Bar Seine, their trendy lounge.

THE REGENCY
540 Park Ave (at 61st St)   212/759-4100
Moderately expensive to expensive   www.loewshotels.com

With an outstanding location on Park Avenue and a room renovation that created a more contemporary and relaxed feeling, this Loews hotel offers 351 spacious guest rooms and 86 outstanding suites, including 12 grand suites that have housed many of the entertainment world's greats. The one-bedroom suites feature two bathrooms. Rooms contain modern business conveniences such as fax machines, printers, two-line phones, and data ports. Use of the fitness center and overnight shoeshine service are complimentary amenities. Two excellent restaurants—the classy, renovated 540 Park and The Library, an intimate, residential-style lounge—offer daily meal service. Feinstein's at the Regency is a classy nightclub. Power breakfasts at the Regency are legendary. More than 70% of the hotel's guests are repeat visitors!

THE REGENT WALL STREET
55 Wall St (at William St)   212/845-8600
Expensive   www.regenthotels.com

This historic building was once headquarters for the U.S. Merchants Exchange and the Customs House. Jail cells in the basement were once used to house customs cheaters! Converted into one of the lodging jewels of Lower Manhattan, the Regent's spectacular features include an elegant lobby; large, luxurious, and beautifully appointed rooms and bathrooms; 55 Wall, an excellent restaurant overlooking bustling Wall Street; and a high-end spa and fitness center with five treatment rooms. The Regent also boasts one of the city's most dramatic ballrooms, which is a perfect venue for special events. (Liz Taylor had her last wedding reception here!) Christopher R.J. Knable, a star in the hotel world, oversees an operation with superbly trained personnel who exemplify the word *service*.

The best current rates for Manhattan hotel rooms can be obtained at **www.nycvisit.com** (click on Accommodations). Remember that prices can change day to day, hour to hour.

RIHGA ROYAL NEW YORK
151 W 54th St (bet Ave of the Americas and Seventh Ave)
Moderately expensive   212/307-5000
www.rihgaroyalny.com

The RIHGA Royal New York, a JW Marriott Hotel, is a luxury residential-style all-suites hotel that is great for international travelers. Between them, the staff speaks 54 languages! The conveniently located hotel offers a fully equipped 24-hour business center, fitness center, and complimentary newspapers. Guests of their "Pinnacle" suites receive complimentary Town Car service from New York area airports, personalized business cards, cell phones, and more. The on-site restaurant Halcyon is a casual, elegantly appointed room serving contemporary American cuisine.

RITZ-CARLTON NEW YORK, BATTERY PARK
2 West St (at Battery Park)   212/344-0800
Expensive
RITZ-CARLTON NEW YORK, CENTRAL PARK
50 Central Park S (at Ave of the Americas)   212/308-9100
www.ritzcarlton.com

These two relatively new hotels have added luster to the Manhattan hotel scene, providing all the usual amenities and outstanding service identified with this brand name. You'll find great views at each, top-grade lobby-level restaurants, gym and spa services, luxurious rooms and bathrooms, and business centers. Club-level guests get special treatment. The Battery Park location offers a 14th-floor bar.

THE ST. REGIS
2 E 55th St (at Fifth Ave)   212/753-4500
Expensive   www.stregis.com

The St. Regis, a historic landmark in the heart of Manhattan, is the crown jewel of Starwood Hotels, and for good reason. With 315 oversized and overpriced deluxe rooms and 91 suites, the hotel provides luxurious accommodations. Each room has marble baths. Round-the-clock butler service is provided (including free pressing of two garments upon arrival), and 24-hour room service is available. Outstanding restaurants are a feature here: Astor Court (breakfast, lunch, afternoon tea, and dinner) and the King Cole Bar (great Bloody Marys). The St. Regis' ballroom—the only hotel-roof ballroom in the city—is available for private functions.

SALISBURY HOTEL
123 W 57th St (bet Ave of the Americas and Seventh Ave)
Moderate   212/246-1300
                                                    www.nycsalisbury.com

I highly recommend this place to the price-savvy traveler. The Salisbury, capably run by Bill Alvarado, has about 300 rooms and suites, most of which have been redecorated. Many are outfitted with butler's pantries and refrigerators. Suites are large, comfortable, and reasonably priced. The thick walls are really soundproof! If you want to be near Carnegie Hall and other midtown attractions, the Salisbury is for you. If you've waited until the last minute for reservations, the Salisbury is a good place to call. Since it is not well-known among out-of-towners, rooms are usually available.

SHERATON MANHATTAN
790 Seventh Ave (at 52nd St)   212/581-3300, 800/325-3535
Moderate   www.starwood.com

With a convenient location and upgraded "Corporate Club" rooms available, this 650-room hotel is ideal for both families and business travelers. It is within easy walking distance of Manhattan's best stores, theaters, and restaurants. The Sheraton Manhattan features a 50-foot indoor swimming pool (a rarity in midtown), a first-rate health club, an excellent on-property restaurant (Russo's Steak & Pasta), and 24-hour room service.

SHERATON NEW YORK HOTEL AND TOWERS
811 Seventh Ave (at 52nd St)   212/581-1000, 800/325-3535
Moderate to moderately expensive   www.starwood.com

The outstanding location in central Manhattan and a wide selection of restaurants and lounges (Hudson's Grill & Sports Bar, Streeters New York Cafe, Lobby Court Lounge) make the Sheraton New York an excellent choice for tourists and business travelers. Sheraton Towers—the more luxurious upper floors—offers exclusive digs that include butler service. "Corporate Club" rooms come equipped with office amenities. A wide selection of package deals and seasonal specials are available.

SHERATON RUSSELL
45 Park Ave (at 37th St)   212/685-7676
Moderately expensive   www.starwood.com

This 146-room boutique hotel is designed in the traditional style of a 19th-century English club. All guest rooms offer in-room refreshment centers, coffeemakers, voice mail, hairdryer, iron, and 24-hour room service. Each of the "Corporate Club" rooms provides a virtual office with an oversized desk, ergonomic swivel chair, task lighting, in-room data port, dual phone lines, and a printer/fax/copier. A complimentary continental breakfast buffet and evening hors d'oeuvres are served to Corporate Club guests.

SOHO GRAND HOTEL
310 West Broadway (at Grand St)   212/965-3000
Moderately expensive   www.sohogrand.com

If business or pleasure takes you to Soho, this facility may be for you . . . but at a price. The custom-designed rooms will not appeal to traditionalists, though yuppies will love them. Four penthouse suites with outdoor terraces are special. A fitness center, business amenities, 24-hour room service, and valet parking are available. The on-premises Grand Bar & Lounge offers cocktail cuisine.

THE STANHOPE PARK HYATT NEW YORK
995 Fifth Ave (at 81st St) 212/774-1234
Moderately expensive www.stanhopepark.hyatt.com

The Stanhope is a quiet and refined hotel that's just right for those who are touring museums or wish to be away from the throngs. The hotel has 185 rooms (55 of which are spacious and attractive suites), a health club, and a wonderful park view from many rooms. The Terrace, an outside garden for tea and snacks, is pleasant. Melrose restaurant offers periodic entertainment.

A classy hotel on the Lower East Side? Yes, in the near future! The **Surface** (107 Rivington St) will open with 111 rooms, featuring soaking tubs or oversized showers. Rates will start at $250. A ground-floor restaurant is also planned. What a different look for a historic district!

SWISSOTEL NEW YORK—THE DRAKE
440 Park Ave (at 56th St) 212/421-0900
Moderate www.swissotel.com

Former guests will not recognize the refurbished Drake, with 495 rooms and 108 suites that are operated with typical Swiss efficiency. It's got a multilingual concierge staff, spa, valet parking, a good central location, limo service to Wall Street, fully equipped guest rooms, and 12 meeting rooms for receptions and events. A fashionable restaurant and a branch of Fauchon, the French patisserie, are on-premises.

TRUMP INTERNATIONAL HOTEL AND TOWER
1 Central Park W (at 60th St) 212/299-1000
Expensive www.trumpintl.com

This is everything you would expect from a place with the name Trump attached. There are special amenities (fresh flowers, umbrellas, telescopes, garment bags), 24-hour room service, complete office facilities, entertainment centers in every room, state-of-the-art fitness center, swimming pool, marble bathrooms, and complimentary cellular phones (on request). One of Manhattan's best (and most expensive) restaurants, Jean Georges, will pamper your taste buds.

W NEW YORK
541 Lexington Ave (bet 49th and 50th St) 212/755-1200
Moderately expensive www.whotels.com

The former Doral Inn has been reborn as a hotel with a single letter for a name. Located in midtown, this Starwood property has 713 rooms (61 spacious suites), a large ballroom, full-service spa and health club, 24-hour room service, and two-line telephones with data ports in every room. The look is strictly modern, right down to the black staff uniforms. Health-food addicts will love the place. There's a juice bar near the front entrance, Oasis Bar is right off the lobby, and Heartbeat, a Drew Nieporent restaurant, is also on-premises.

W NEW YORK TIMES SQUARE
1567 Broadway (at 47th St)   212/930-7400
Moderately expensive   www.whotels.com

With over 500 rooms in the heart of Times Square, this new 57-story W flagship offers the Blue Fin restaurant (seafood), a classy retail store, a fitness room and spa, 24-hour room service, and other quality Starwood amenities. Ask for rooms as high up as possible, as the views are dramatic. The Whiskey Bar is an underground watering hole and screening room (with a coed bathroom!).

If you need to find a short-term renter, try **Affordable New York City** (21 E 10th St, 212/533-4001, www.affordablenyc.com). Ask for Susan Freschel.

THE WALDORF-ASTORIA
301 Park Ave (at 50th St)   212/355-3000
Moderately expensive   www.waldorfastoria.com

Hilton invested more than $200 million restoring their flagship property. The work shows, and renovations are ongoing. The rich, impressive lobby is bedecked with magnificent mahogany wall panels, hand-woven carpets, and a 148,000-tile mosaic floor. Responding to complaints about the size of some guest rooms, the management created larger spaces by reducing the number of units. Oversize executive business rooms are available. All-marble bathrooms have been installed in some suites. There is a fitness center, several restaurants, and deluxe rooms and suites in the Waldorf Towers/A Conrad Hotel. An event at the Waldorf is sure to be something special. Junior League members have access to rooms at substantial savings. Sign up for a behind-the-scenes tour of the Waldorf on Friday and Sunday by calling 212/872-4790.

THE WESTIN NEW YORK AT TIMES SQUARE
270 W 43rd St (at Eighth Ave)   212/201-2700
Moderate to moderately expensive   www.westinnewyork.com

With an exciting multicolored exterior and much-talked-about atrium lobby, the Westin New York heralds a new look for midtown Manhattan. The lobby is actually on the second floor; the hotel is a 45-story, $300 million unit, with 863 rooms and suites, high-speed Internet access, heavenly beds, a Don Shula steakhouse, and all the amenities associated with Westin. It is the largest newly built hotel in Manhattan in 17 years.

THE WOLCOTT
4 W 31st St (bet Fifth Ave and Broadway)   212/268-2900
Inexpensive   www.wolcott.com

This is one of Manhattan's better-kept hotel-bargain secrets. Here you will find a good location (just south of midtown), refurbished rooms with private baths, good security, direct-dial phones, TVs with in-room movies and video games, and fitness and business centers. No wonder students, foreign travelers, and savvy business people are regular patrons! Free coffee and muffins are served in the morning.

WYNDHAM HOTEL
42 W 58th St (at Fifth Ave)   212/753-3500
Moderate

John Mados has created a winner! This charming hotel is more like a large home in which rooms are rented out. Many guests regularly make the Wyndham their Manhattan headquarters. Advantages are numerous: great location, uniquely decorated rooms and suites, complete privacy, individual attention, and no business conventions. On the other hand, the hotel is always busy, and reservations may be difficult for newcomers. There is a restaurant (no room service, however), and suites have pantries with refrigerators.

Here are general tipping guidelines for U.S. hotel stays.

Bellhop: $1 per bag minimum; more if bags are heavy

Chambermaid: $2 per person per night, in upscale hotel; $1 per person, per night, in less expensive hotel

Concierge: $2-$10 depending on the complexity of the service; 15% of the cost of scarce theater tickets

Doorman: $1 for hailing a taxi; $2-$3 if it's raining or difficult to find a taxi

Parking valet: $1-$2

Porter: $2-$3 for deliveries to your room

Room service: Check for service charge; if there is none, 15% or a minimum of $2 per delivery

---

Alternative Housing

ABINGDON GUEST HOUSE
13 Eighth Ave (bet 12th and Jane St)   212/243-5384
Moderate   www.abingdonguesthouse.com

This is a simply charming bed and breakfast located in Greenwich Village. The Brewbar Coffee Bar is available for continental breakfast and lunch. All rooms are smoke free, and each has a private bath and distinctive decor. Abingdon offers its guests many amenities, including daily maid service.

ABODE
P.O. Box 20022, New York, NY 10021   212/472-2000
Mon-Fri: 9-5   800/835-8880 (outside tri-state area)
Moderate to moderately expensive   www.abodenyc.com

Do you have your heart set on staying in a delightful old brownstone? How about a contemporary luxury apartment in the heart of Manhattan? Abode selects apartments with great care, and all homes are personally inspected to ensure the highest standards of cleanliness, attractiveness, and hospitality. All are nicely furnished. Nightly rates begin at $135 for a studio and rise to $400 for a two-bedroom apartment. Extended stays of a month or longer receive a discounted rate. There is a minimum stay of four nights.

BED AND BREAKFAST NETWORK OF N.Y.
130 Barrow St, Room 508   212/645-8134
Mon-Fri: 8-6   800/900-8134
Moderate   www.bedandbreakfastnetny.com

At Bed and Breakfast Network of N.Y. you have your choice of over

200 hosted and unhosted accommodations in Manhattan. The hosted rate runs from $80 to $150 a night, depending on single or double occupancy. The weekly rate varies from $500 to $1000. For unhosted apartments of up to three bedrooms, the fee ranges from $130 to $400 a night and from $900 to $2500 a week. Monthly rates are also available. Leslie Goldberg has been in business since 1986, and this is a very reliable outfit.

BROADWAY BED & BREAKFAST INN
264 W 46th St (at Eighth Ave)   212/997-9200
Moderate   800/826-6300

This is the only European country-style inn in New York City. The 41 rooms are immaculate, the atmosphere is homey, the location in the Theater District is safe, and the operation is family-owned and affordable. Additional features include continental breakfast and a library stocked with newspapers. The facility, built as a hotel in 1907, has been fully restored. Special amenities are offered!

HOSTELLING INTERNATIONAL NEW YORK
891 Amsterdam Ave (at 103rd St)   212/932-2300
Inexpensive   www.hinewyork.org

This facility is available to visitors of all ages (although those under 18 must be accompanied by an adult). The hostel provides over 624 beds in a newly renovated, century-old landmark. They offer meeting spaces, cafeteria, coffee bar, airport shuttle, catering, tours, self-service kitchens, and laundry facilities to individuals and groups. Best of all, the price is right!

Dirty windows? The folks to call are **Frank's Window Cleaning Company** (212/288-4631).

INN NEW YORK CITY
266 W 71st St (bet West End and Broadway)   212/580-1900
Moderately expensive   www.innnewyorkcity.com

A townhouse has been tastefully transformed into Inn New York City, a luxury four-suite hotel. A two-night minimum stay is mandated, and extended-stay facilities are available. Fully equipped kitchens are stocked with delicacies, washers and dryers are provided, and the livingrooms and bedrooms have cable TV and VCR. Daily newspapers, maid service, and a 24-hour concierge are also provided. Computer lines and on-site copy and fax machines are available, too.

INTERNATIONAL HOUSE
500 Riverside Dr (at 122nd St)   212/316-8436 (admissions)
Moderate   212/316-8473 (guest rooms and suites)
                                              www.ihouse-nyc.org

International House is a community of over 700 graduate students, interns, trainees, and visiting scholars from nearly 100 countries. Occupants spend anywhere from a day to a few years in New York City. It is located on the

Upper West Side near Columbia University and the Manhattan School of Music. Special features include a low-budget cafeteria, pub, gymnasium, and self-service laundry. Free programs for residents include ballroom dancing, lectures, films, recitals, and organized sports. During the summer, single-room occupancy (for periods of one to ten days) with shared bath runs $45 per night. The rate drops to $40 per night for stays of 10-20 days. Rates are less still by the semester. Reasonably priced guest suites ($105-$130 per night) with private bath, air conditioning, daily maid service, and cable television are also available.

METRO HOME
515 Madison Ave (at 53rd St), 25th floor   212/813-2244
Moderate   www.metro-home.com

If you are looking for a reasonably priced, full-service, short-term furnished apartment in Soho, midtown, the Upper West Side, Greenwich Village, Chelsea, or the Theater District, this is a good number to call. They have over 200 apartments in their inventory and feature discounts for extended stays.

92ND ST Y (DE HIRSCH RESIDENCE)
1395 Lexington Ave (at 92nd St)   212/415-5650
Mon-Thurs: 9-7; Fri: 9-5; Sun: 10-5   800-858-4692
Inexpensive   www.dehirsch.com

This facility offers convenient, inexpensive, and secure housing for men and women between the ages of 18 and 30. Special discounts for Y health-club memberships and single and double rooms are available. Lengths of stay can range from 30 days to one year. Admission is by application.

PHILLIPS CLUB
Lincoln Square
155 W 66th St (at Broadway)   212/835-8800
Moderate to moderately expensive   www.phillipsclub.com

This 180-unit residential hotel near Lincoln Center is designed for long-term visitors, but they will also take nightly customers. Suites come with fully equipped kitchens, individually assigned telephone numbers, and stereo systems. Other impressive features include a 24-hour business center and concierge, laundry and valet service, in-room safes, a handy conference room, and preferential membership at the nearby Reebok Sports Club NY.

SOLDIERS', SAILORS', MARINES', AND AIRMEN'S CLUB
283 Lexington Ave (bet 36th and 37th St)   212/683-4354
Inexpensive

Here is a great find in the Murray Hill area of Manhattan for American and allied servicemen and women—active, retired, veterans, reservists, military cadets, and Coast Guard personnel alike! Rates are extremely low (with no tax), and the hotel/club has 29 comfortable rooms and club-style facilities to enjoy. There are several lounges with fireplaces, TVs with VCRs, and a lobby canteen with refrigerator, microwave, and coffee.

WEBSTER APARTMENTS
419 W 34th St (at Ninth Ave)   212/967-9000
Inexpensive   www.websterapartments.org

This is one of the best deals in the city for working women with moderate incomes. It is not a transient hotel but operates on a policy developed by Charles B. Webster, a first cousin of Rowland Macy (of the department-store family). Webster left the bulk of his estate to found these apartments, which opened in 1923. Residents include college students, designers, actresses, secretaries, and other business and professional women. Facilities include diningrooms, recreation areas, a library, and lounges. The Webster also has private gardens for its guests, and meals can be taken outdoors in nice weather. Rates are $170-$218 per week, which includes two meals a day and maid service. Visitors must be sponsored by a current guest. The Webster is a secret find known mainly to residents and readers of this book.

Interior Designers

AERO STUDIOS
132 Spring St (bet Wooster and Greene St)   212/966-4700
Mon-Sat: 11-6   www.aerostudios.com

Whether it is a design project for a major commercial space or just a little one at home, the Aero Studios staff is well equipped to handle the task. Be sure to visit their store, and you'll no doubt come away with some special ideas.

ALEX CHANNING
250 W 19th St (bet Seventh and Eighth Ave), Suite 11C
By appointment   212/366-4800
                                    www.alexchanning.com

Licensed interior designer Alex Channing has built a reputation as one of Manhattan's young up-and-comers. He does furniture design and custom-made furnishings, and he'll help with site selection, move-ins, and installations. Channing does commercial and residential work.

DESIGNER PREVIEWS   212/777-2966
                                  www.designerpreviews.com

Having problems finding the right decorator? Designer Previews keeps tabs on over 300 of Manhattan's most trustworthy and talented designers, architects, and landscaping experts. They will help you select the best designer based on your style and personal requirements through consultation or online presentation. Karen Fisher, the genius behind this handy service, is the former design editor for *Woman's Wear Daily* and *Esquire*.

MARTIN ALBERT INTERIORS
9 E 19th St (bet Broadway and Fifth Ave)
Mon-Fri: 9-5   212/673-8000, 800/525-4637

Martin Albert specializes in window treatments. They measure and install their product line at prices that are considerably lower than most decorators. Martin Albert offers 250,000 fabric samples, ranging from $8 to $400 a yard. Custom upholstery and slipcovers, a furniture shop, and a large selection of drapery hardware are also available, and they'll deliver to all 50 states.

PARSONS SCHOOL OF DESIGN
66 Fifth Ave (at 13th St)   212/229-8940
Mon-Fri: 9-5   www.parsons.edu

Parsons, a division of the New School for Social Research, is one of the top two schools in the city for interior design. Those who call for design assistance will get their request posted on the school's board, and every effort is made to match clients with student decorators. Individual negotiations determine the price and length of a job, but it will be considerably less than what a practicing professional charges. Most of these students don't yet have a decorator's card, but one can always be borrowed. This is a good place to contact if you just want a consultation.

RICHARD'S INTERIOR DESIGN
1390 Lexington Ave (bet 91st and 92nd St)   212/831-9000
Mon-Fri: 10-6; Sat: 10-4   www.richardsinteriordesign.com

Here you will find over 10,000 decorator fabrics, including tapestries, damasks, stripes, plaids, silks, velvets, and floral chintzes. These are all first-quality goods at competitive prices. The fabrics are imported from the same European mills used by Kravet, Lee Jofa, Robert Allen, Brunswig & Fils, and Clarence House. Richard's does upholstery, furniture, reupholstery, slipcovers, draperies, top treatments, shades, bedroom ensembles, and wall coverings. Design services, in-home consultation, and installation are available.

Looking for an architect or decorator? The best of the best include:

Bilhuber (330 E 59th St, 6th floor, 212/308-4888): Jeffrey Bilhuber does contemporary things.

Glenn Gissler Design (36 E 22nd St, 8th floor, 212/228-9880): Glenn Gissler works well with art.

Miles Redd (300 Elizabeth St, 212/674-0902): a color expert

Mr. Architecture & Decor (150 W 28th St, Suite 1102, 212/989-9300): David Mann is very practical.

Ruby (41 Union Square W, Studio 1036, 212/741-3380): Alysa Weinstein and Bella Zakarian treat budgets like their own.

Specht Harpman (338 W 39th St, 10th floor, 212/239-1150): Scott Specht and Louise Harpman are pocketbook conscious.

Steven Holl Architects (450 W 31st St, 11th floor, 212/629-7262): Homes are a specialty.

Jewelry Services

GEM APPRAISERS & CONSULTANTS
608 Fifth Ave (at 49th St), Suite 602   212/333-3122
Mon-Fri: 9-5 by appointment

Robert C. Aretz, who owns Gem Appraisers & Consultants, is a graduate gemologist and director of the Appraisers Association of America. He is a past officer and director who currently sits on the admissions committee. He is entrusted with appraisals for major insurance companies, banks, and retail jewelry stores. His specialty is antique jewelry, precious colored stones, diamonds, and natural pearls. Aretz will do appraisals and/or consultations for estate, insurance, tax, equitable distribution, and other purposes.

RISSIN'S JEWELRY CLINIC
4 W 47th St (at Fifth Ave)   212/575-1098
Mon, Tues, Thurs: 9:30-5; closed first two weeks of July

This is indeed a clinic! The assortment of services is staggering: jewelry repair and design, antique repair, museum restorations, supplying diamonds and other stones, eyeglass repair, pearl and bead stringing, restringing of old necklaces, stone identification, and appraisals. The patent for his Earquilizer (an earring stabilizer), has been approved, and you can try it at the store. (Bring your own earrings.) Joe and Toby Rissin run the place. Joe's father was a master engraver, so the family tradition has been passed along. *Honesty* and *quality* are bywords here. Estimates are gladly given, and all work is guaranteed.

ZDK COMPANY
48 W 48th St (bet Fifth Ave and Ave of the Americas), Suite 1410
By appointment only   212/575-1262

Zohrab David Krikonian has created rare and original pieces for neighbors in the Diamond District, and he will do professional work for you, too, in his free time. In addition to making jewelry, ZDK mends and fixes broken jewelry as only a professional craftsman and artist can. He makes complicated repairs look easy and has yet to encounter a job he can't handle. If he can't exactly match the stones in an antique earring or other piece of jewelry, he'll redo the whole item so that it looks even better than before. He loves creating the latest designs from traditional materials, and his prices are reasonable.

Can a New York guide be complete without mentioning pawn shops? Here are several to consider. Good luck!
Century Pawnbrokers (725 Eighth Ave, 212/245-7977)
New York Pawnbrokers (177 Rivington St, 212/228-7177)

Lamp Repair

THE LAMP DOC
Mon-Sat: 8 a.m.-10 p.m.   917/414-0426

Roy and Lois Schneit do lamp repairs and rewiring at customers' homes, offices, and apartments. Services include work on table and floor lamps, chandeliers, and wall sconces. Roy has had over 30 years experience in this business.

Leather Repair

CARNEGIE LUGGAGE
1392 Ave of the Americas (bet 56th and 57th St)   212/586-8210
Mon-Sat: 9-6; Sun: 11-6

It's a pleasure to do business with these people. Carnegie Luggage is handy to most major midtown and Central Park hotels. Rush service is possible if you let them know you're in a hurry. Expert repair is done on-premises. They offer reliable work at competitive prices. A complete line of luggage and travel accessories includes Delsey and Samsonite.

MODERN LEATHER GOODS
2 W 32nd St (bet Fifth Ave and Broadway), 4th floor   212/279-3263
Mon-Fri: 8:30-5; Sat: 8-1:30

Is your briefcase, suitcase, or handbag looking a bit tacky of late? Some people think that signs of wear on leather are a mark of class, but I like to see things looking good. Modern Leather Goods, a family business for over 60 years, is the place to go for repairs. Ask for owner Tony Pecorella. They also do needlepoint mounting, reglaze alligator bags, and clean leather and suede clothing. Free pickup and delivery in Manhattan are offered.

SUPERIOR REPAIR CENTER
7 W 30th St (at Fifth Ave), 9th floor   212/967-0554
Mon-Fri: 10-6; Sat: 10-3   www.superiorleathernyc.com

Do you own a fine leather garment that's been damaged? Leather repair is the highlight of the service at Superior. Many major stores in the city use them for luggage and handbag work. They are experts at cleaning leather (suede and shearling are their specialties), and repairing or replacing zippers on leather items. They specialize in Tumi luggage repair. They will also work on sporting equipment, such as tents and backpacks. If there is a leather problem, Superior has the answer. Just ask Gucci, Calvin Klein, Chanel, Escada, St. John, Bergdorf-Goodman, and Prada!

Locksmiths

AAA LOCKSMITHS
44 W 46th St (at Ave of the Americas)   212/840-3939
Mon-Thurs: 8-5:30; Fri: 8:30-5   www.aaahardware.com

You can learn a lot from trying to find a locksmith in New York. For one thing, as a profession it probably has the most full-page ads in the Manhattan Yellow Pages. For another, this particular "AAA" is *not* the place to call about an automobile emergency. However, in an industry that does not often inspire loyalty or recommendations, AAA Locksmiths has been in the business for over a half-century, and that says a lot right there.

LOCKWORKS LOCKSMITHS
By appointment   212/736-3740

Lock problems? Give Joel at Lockworks a call. He has been in the locksmith trade for over two decades, and there isn't anything he can't do. This gentleman does not advertise, but he is highly regarded by some of the top businesses in Manhattan.

NIGHT AND DAY LOCKSMITH
1335 Lexington Ave (at 89th St)   212/722-1017
Mon-Thurs: 8-6:30; Fri: 8-6; Sat: 9-6 (24 hours for emergencies)

Carry Night and Day's number in case you're ever locked out! Locksmiths must stay ahead of the burglar's latest expertise and offer fast, on-the-spot service for a variety of devices designed to keep criminals out. (After all, no apartment has just *one* lock.) Mena Safer, Night and Day's owner, fulfills these rigid requirements. The company answers its phone 24 hours a day; posted hours are for the sale and installation of locks, window gates, intercoms, car alarms, safes, and keys. Inside and outside welding is a specialty.

Marble Works

PUCCIO MARBLE AND ONYX
661 Driggs Ave, Brooklyn (warehouse showroom)
212/688-1351, 800/7-PUCCIO
www.puccio.info

Work of the highest quality is a tradition with Puccio. The sculpture and furniture designs range from traditional to sleekly modern. John and Paul Puccio show dining and cocktail tables, chairs, chests of drawers, buffets, desks, consoles, and pedestals. Custom-designed installations include foyer floors, bathrooms, kitchens, bars, staircases, fountains, and fireplaces. Retail orders are accepted. They are the largest distributor and fabricator of onyx in the country.

Matchmaking

FIELD'S EXCLUSIVE SERVICE
317 Madison Ave (at 42nd St), Suite 1600
Daily   212/391-2233, 800/264-7539

The motto "New York lives by this book!" is a big challenge. In an attempt to be comprehensive, I've even included a matchmaking service. Dan Field's company has been playing Cupid for three quarters of a century. If Dan is successful for you, how about a testimonial for *Where to Find It, Buy It, Eat It in New York*—the Romance Edition, of course!

Medical Services

LEAGUE FOR THE HARD OF HEARING
71 W 23rd St (bet Fifth Ave and Ave of Americas)   917/305-7700
Mon-Fri: by appointment

This not-for-profit organization works with people of all ages who have hearing disabilities. They dispense hearing aids, sponsor classes, and work with patients and families to find alternatives to help the hearing impaired. They come highly recommended, and their services are a real value.

Medical Tip

If you experience chest pains that start to radiate into the arms and/or jaw, you might be in the early stages of a heart attack. If you are alone, with no possible source of care nearby, you can greatly improve your chances of survival by doing the following:

Without help, the person whose heart stops beating properly and begins to feel faint has only about 10 seconds left before losing consciousness. You can help yourself by coughing repeatedly and vigorously. A deep breath should be taken before each cough, and the cough must be repeated about every two seconds until help arrives or until the heart is again beating normally. Experts tell us that deep breaths get oxygen into the lungs, and coughing movements squeeze the heart to help keep blood circulating. This could save your life. Bottom line: get yourself to a hospital, even if the symptoms subside.

(adapted from *Health Cares,* Rochester
General Hospital newsletter)

N.Y. HOTEL URGENT MEDICAL SERVICES
212/737-1212   www.travelmd.com

Here is one of the most valuable contacts in Manhattan! Dr. Ronald Primas, the CEO and medical director of this outfit, is tops in his field. This service is locally based and has been in operation for over a decade. All manner of health care is available on a 24-hour, seven-day-a-week basis: internists, pediatricians, obstetricians, surgeons, dentists, chiropractors, and more. Doctors will come to your hotel or apartment, arrange for tests, prescribe medications, admit patients to hospitals, and even provide nurses. The urgent-care center is also available around the clock by appointment for patients not requiring a house call. Payment is expected at the time of service; credit cards may be used. All physicians are board-certified and have exemplary bedside manners.

STATSCRIPT PHARMACY
197 Eighth Ave (at 20th St)   212/691-9050
Mon-Fri: 9-9; Sat: 9-6   www.chronimed.com

This pharmacy provides home delivery of prescription medications, comprehensive claims management, and links to community resources and national support networks. Their specialties include prescriptions for patients with HIV or transplants. All pharmaceuticals are available, as is an extensive line of vitamins and homeopathic and holistic products. Many rare items can be provided with one-day service. They will bill insurance companies directly so that customers need not pay up front. Nationwide shipping is available.

When it becomes necessary to look into long-term home health care, call **Priority Home Care** (212/401-1700). They check out well.

Metal Work

ATLANTIC RETINNING AND METAL REFINISHING
549 W 26th St (at Tenth Ave)   212/244-4896, 973/848-0700
Mon-Fri: 9-6   www.retinning.com

Jamie Gibbons has taken over a long-established Manhattan business whose specialty is retinning (which is basically tin plating). Drawing upon many years of experience in the field, Gibbons restores brass and copper antiques; designs and creates new copperware; restores lamps, chandeliers, and brass beds; and sells restored copper pieces.

Movers

BIG APPLE MOVING & STORAGE
83 Third Ave (bet Bergen and Dean St), Brooklyn
Mon-Fri: 9-5; Sat: 9-12   212/505-1861, 718/625-1424

This is a handy number to have. Even though Big Apple is not located in Manhattan, they do 80% of their local moving business there. They handle antiques, art, and high-end moves, yet manage to keep rates reasonable. They stock every size box, container, and crate needed for moving or storage, as well as bubble pack, plate dividers, custom paper, and "French wraps" for crystal and delicate breakables. Many expert packers have been with Big

Apple since they opened in 1979. Save money on moving supplies by shopping at their "do-it-yourself" moving store in the same building. For those who need overnight or short-term storage, Big Apple will bring your entire truckload of furniture *inside* their high-security heated warehouse. Interstate and international moving is also provided, and every item is fully wrapped and padded before leaving your residence. These folks receive high marks from satisfied customers.

BROWNSTONE BROS. MOVING
321 Rider Ave, Bronx   718/665-5000
Mon-Fri: 8:30-5   www.brownstonebros.com

Brownstone Bros. has been offering moving and storage services since 1977, with a very personal touch by head man Bill Gross. They are highly rated by customers.

MOVING STORE
644 Amsterdam Ave (bet 91st and 92nd St)   212/874-3800
Mon-Fri: 8-6; Sat: 9-4; Sun: 9-3

Steve Fiore started West Side Movers in the kitchen of his studio apartment more than three decades ago. Business got so good he soon moved into a storefront. He was happy there until he realized the magnitude of requests he was getting from people who wanted dollies and boxes of all sizes. Fiore then moved into a brownstone storefront on Amsterdam Avenue, where he sells nothing but moving aids and paraphernalia. The main stock-in-trade is boxes. They come in a multitude of sizes, including three different ones just for mirrors. He rents and sells dollies and moving pads. Since all items have been built to the specifications of professional movers, they are durable.

WEST SIDE MOVERS
644 Amsterdam Ave (bet 91st and 92nd St)   212/874-3800
Mon-Fri: 8-6; Sat: 9-4; Sun: 9-3

West Side Movers—sister operation of the Moving Store (see preceding entry)—pays close attention to efficiency, promptness, care, and courtesy. Customer after customer has called their staff the most courteous they've dealt with—and they don't nick the furniture, either!

Office Services

KINKO'S
60 W 40th St (across from Bryant Park)	212/921-1060
500 Seventh Ave (at 37th St)	646/366-9166
1211 Ave of the Americas (at 47th St)	212/391-2679
191 Madison Ave (at 34th St)	212/685-3449
16 E 52nd St (at Madison Ave)	212/308-2679
Daily: 24 hours	www.kinkos.com

Got a late night project? Kinko's is open 24 hours, and all locations offer photocopying services, custom printing (documents, signs, banners), digital photo service, on-site computer rental (IBM or Macintosh), document scanning, and office supplies. Some sites also offer video conferencing. A customer service hotline (800/254-6567) is helpful in identifying a specific service or location.

PURGATORY PIE PRESS
19 Hudson St (bet Duane and Reade St), Room 403   212/274-8228
Mon-Fri: by appointment only   www.purgatorypiepress.com

Purgatory Pie Press is ideal for small printing jobs. They do typography designs, hand letterpress printing, die cutting, and hand bookbinding. They'll also craft handmade envelopes, do logos and other identity designs, and provide handmade paper with uniquely designed watermarks. Specialties include printing and calligraphy for weddings and parties. They also carry limited-edition postcards and artists' books.

WORLD-WIDE BUSINESS CENTRES
575 Madison Ave (at 57th St)   212/605-0200, 800/296-9922
Mon-Fri: 9-5:30   www.wwbcn.com

Alan Bain, a transplanted English lawyer, has created a business that caters to executives who need more than a hotel room and companies that need a fully equipped, furnished, and staffed office in New York on short notice. The operation grew out of Bain's own frustrations in trying to put together a makeshift office. On-premises administrative, word-processing, clerical, and mail-room services are available. So are high-quality voice and data communications capabilities, including high-speed Internet access and video conferencing. Desk space, private offices, and conference rooms may be rented on a daily, weekly, monthly, or quarterly basis. The daily rate includes a private office, telephone answering, and receptionists

Painting

BERNARD GARVEY PAINTING   718/894-8272

I am constantly asked to recommend an outstanding and reliable painter who can also do plastering and decorative finishes. Well, I have found a top outfit for you with Bernard Garvey Painting. He provides services for residential clients, and his customers say he charges reasonable prices and does terrific work.

Other reliable painters include:
Robert Star Painting (212/737-8855)
Roth Painting (212/758-2170)

Parenting Resources

PARENTING CENTER AT THE 92ND STREET Y
1395 Lexington Ave (at 92nd St)   212/415-5609
Mon-Fri: 9-5 (office hours)   www.92y.org

Just about everything the 92nd Street Y does is impressive, and its Parenting Center is no exception. It offers every kind of class you can imagine: a newborn-care class for expectant parents, a baby massage class for new parents and their infants, a cooking class for preschoolers, and so on. As this Y is a Jewish institution, Shabbat get-togethers and a Jewish heritage class for preschoolers are offered, along with workshops and seminars on a wide range of topics, from potty training to raising an only child. They provide babysitting for various parenting classes (as well as unrelated Y classes) and host new-parent get-togethers. Perhaps most important, they act as a resource and support center for members. Membership costs $175 a year, and benefits include discounts and priority sign-up. Non-members are welcome to take classes, too.

PARENTS LEAGUE

115 E 82nd St (bet Lexington and Park Ave)   212/737-7385
Mon-Thurs: 9-4; Tues: 9-6; Fri: 9-12   www.parentsleague.com

This nonprofit organization is a goldmine for parents in New York. In addition to putting together a calendar of events for children of all ages, the Parents League maintains extensive files on babysitters, birthday party places, tutors, summer camps, early childhood programs, and independent schools throughout the city. For a membership fee of $85 per academic year, you can access those files and attend workshops and other events. If you are the parent of a small child, you also get a copy of *The Toddler Book,* an invaluable list of more than 275 activities in New York for little ones.

SOHO PARENTING CENTER

568 Broadway (at Prince St)   212/334-3744
www.sohoparenting.com

This terrific place is dedicated to the notion that parenting ought to be talked about and shared. It conducts workshops and group discussions for parents of newborns, toddlers, and even older children. It offers play groups where children can be dropped off and picked up while parents talk about their experiences and challenges. Individual parent counseling is available.

Party Services

AMERICAN FOLIAGE & DESIGN GROUP

171 W 71st St (bet Ave of the Americas and Seventh Ave)
Mon-Fri: 8-5   212/741-5555

For events of all kinds, American Foliage & Design can be a great help. They provide items for television, movie, and commercial production design, plus silk lanterns, terrace designs, and anything to do with gardens and exteriors. Full service is provided, including trucking and installation. Both sales and rentals are offered.

If you're in need of party items, I have two suggestions: **Service Party Rentals/Just Linens** (770 Lexington Ave, 212/688-8808; by appointment) stocks top-quality tables, chairs, platters, china place settings, linens, and more. **AAA Best Chair Rentals** (212/929-8888), offers excellent prices on non-fancy chair rentals, plus china and silverware; they

---

BALOOMS

147 Sullivan St (bet Prince and Houston St)   212/673-4007
Mon-Fri: 10-6; Sat: 12-6; Sun: available for parties

Balooms is a small balloon store that encourages browsing. In addition to balloon bouquets, they offer party decorating and custom-designed bouquets with names and logos. Balooms will deliver in Manhattan and the boroughs and can ship anywhere. The store also rents helium tanks. As befits this lighthearted business, owners Marlyne Berger and Raymond Baglietto are delightful.

BLAIR McMILLEN
917/334-6488   www.blairmcmillen.com

If you are seeking top-notch piano entertainment, look no further. Blair McMillen is an extremely talented and personable concert pianist, having performed for President Clinton, Mikhail Gorbachev, and the Japanese Royal family. McMillen, a Julliard School graduate, will work with other musicians in the area. Flexible in style, he is adept at Broadway, pop, New Age, Latin, and jazz standards, although classical piano is his first love.

BUBBY GRAM
60 E 8th St (at Broadway)   212/353-3886
Daily (by phone): 10-9   www.bubbygram.com

If creating fun and laughter is on your mind, call this number. These folks have outrageous and humorous acts that run from a simple singing telegram to a complete show for a party or business meeting.

ECLECTIC ENCORE
620 W 26th St (at Eleventh Ave)   212/645-8880
Mon-Fri: 9-5   www.eclecticprops.com

This outfit specializes in extremely hard-to-find props for a party at home, a set for motion pictures or television, or some novel product announcement. They have been in business since 1986 and are known for an extensive collection of 18th-, 19th- and 20th-century furniture and accessories. You can find everything from an armoire to a zebra—even one of those cakes from which a scantily clad lady pops out.

EXPRESSWAY MUSIC & EVENTS
104 E 40th St (bet Park and Lexington Ave), Suite 208   212/953-9367
By appointment   www.expresswaymusic.com

If you are interested in entertainment for any kind of personal or business event, give these folks a call. Their artists include the Expressway Music Jazz Trio (modern jazz), and the Professionals (a six-piece band that plays 70s disco, rock, dance music, swing, jazz, and more). Other ensembles include chamber music, duets, trios, and quartets (for weddings, cocktail hours, etc.) and a steel drum band of up to seven pieces. David Swirsky is the director.

HIGHLY EVENTFUL
11 Fifth Ave (at 8th St), Suite 7C   212/777-3565
Daily: 10-6   www.highlyeventful.com

Since 1994, Highly Eventful has been arranging events in New York and throughout the world. These folks take charge of everything, including food, liquor, equipment rentals, tents, flowers, lighting, music, and trained personnel. They offer prime locations, such as grand ballrooms, churches (like the Cathedral Church of St. John the Divine), museums (like the Metropolitan), and yachts.

LINDA KAYE'S BIRTHDAYBAKERS, PARTYMAKERS
195 E 76th St (bet Lexington and Third Ave)   212/288-7112
Mon-Fri: 9-6; parties can be scheduled for any day
                                                          www.partymakers.com

Linda Kaye offers children's birthday parties at two of Manhattan's most desirable locations: the Central Park Wildlife Center and the American

Museum of Natural History. The Wildlife Center parties are for children up to ten years old. Themes include Breakfast at the Zoo, Animal Alphabet Party, Safari Treasure Hunt, and Mystery Movie Making. The Natural History parties are for children five and up, with such themes as Dinosaur Discovery, Cosmic Blast-Off, Underwater Treasure, Safari Adventure, and Global Mysteries. Linda Kaye's website serves as a resource and shopping site for birthday party needs, providing listings of entertainers and party locations. She carries paper goods in over 60 themes. Corporate events and creative custom cakes, including pop-out cakes, are other specialties.

MARCY L. BLUM ASSOCIATES
259 W 11th St (bet 4th and Bleecker St)   212/929-9814
By appointment only

What a great lady! Marcy is so well organized that no matter what the event—wedding, reception, birthday party, bar mitzvah, dinner for the boss —she will execute it to perfection. As anyone knows, it's the details that count, and Marcy is superb at the nitty-gritty.

Are you tired of cooking at home, or are you planning a party? Here are some of the best personal chefs in New York:

Belinda Clarke (212/253-6408)
Bill Feldman (212/983-2952)
Jayson Grossberg (917/414-1947)
Michael Yang (718/380-1149)

The **United States Personal Chef Association** (212/946-1640, 800/ 747-2433, www.newyorkpersonalchefs.com) can provide more names.

PARTY POOPERS
104 Reade St (bet West Broadway and Church St)   212/587-9030
Call ahead   www.partypoopers.com

Party Poopers is really a group of entertainers who never throw the same party twice. Offering some of the best private party rooms in New York, they handle setup, clean-up, and entertainment, allowing parents to sit back and relax. Themes include fairytales, superheroes, game shows, dance parties, murder mysteries, or anything you can dream up. They also have costume characters, magicians, and other party entertainers. There's even an online store, the Pooper Cavern, which carries favors, theme paper goods, balloons, and gift items.

PROPS FOR TODAY
330 W 34th St (bet Eighth and Ninth Ave)   212/244-9600
Mon-Fri: 8:30-5   www.propsfortoday.com

This is the handiest place in town when you are planning a party. Props for Today has the largest rental inventory of home decorations in New York. Whether you want everyday china and silver or unique antiques going back a hundred years, they've got the goods. There are platters, vases, tablecloths, and more. They have a Christmas section, children's items, books, fireplace equipment, artwork, garden furniture, foreign items, and ordinary kitchenware. Over a million items are available! Phone orders are taken, but it is a good idea to check out the inventory for yourself at the storefront or online.

Pen and Lighter Repair

AUTHORIZED REPAIR SERVICE
30 W 57th St (bet Fifth Ave and Ave of the Americas), 2nd floor
Mon, Tues, Thurs, Fri: 9-5; Wed: 9-6; Sat: 10-3:30 212/586-0947
www.shavers.com, www.vintagelighters.com

After more than four decades, this outfit remains incredibly busy, perhaps because it is almost without competition. Those who use fountain pens or are interested in vintage pens or lighters are devoted customers. Authorized Repair sells and services nearly every brand, and the shop can refill all kinds of ballpoint, cartridge, and fountain pens and lighters. Authorized also sells at a discount and services electric shavers. Tourists headed overseas can pick up 220-volt appliances and adapter plugs. The polite and helpful staff is well versed in the fine points of each brand.

FOUNTAIN PEN HOSPITAL
10 Warren St (bet Broadway and Church St)
Mon-Fri: 8-6   212/964-0580, 800/253-7367
www.fountainpenhospital.com

This experienced establishment, located across from City Hall, sells and repairs fountain pens of all types. It also carries one of the world's largest selections of modern and vintage writing tools.

Personal Services

A. E. JOHNSON EMPLOYMENT AGENCY
380 Lexington Ave (at 42nd St)   212/644-0990
Mon-Fri: 8:30-4:30   www.aejohnsonagency.com

Dating from 1890, Johnson is the oldest licensed employment agency in the U.S. dealing exclusively with household help. They specialize in providing affluent clients with highly qualified butlers, cooks, housekeepers, chauffeurs, valets, maids, and couples. Both temporary and permanent workers are available, many on a moment's notice. Employment references, criminal records, and drivers' licenses are checked.

BIG APPLE GREETER
1 Centre St (at Chambers St)   212/669-8198
Office: Mon-Fri: 9-5:30
By appointment (available daily)   www.bigapplegreeter.org

More than 400 volunteers from all five boroughs will meet families or individuals traveling together and show them around various New York City neighborhoods. Three weeks advance notice is requested for those who need greeters in languages other than English. Greeters will come to a visiting group's hotel and arrange a special itinerary of sights of interest. This is a wonderful way to get an insider's view of the city. Tipping, home visits, and use of private transportation are considered inappropriate. Visitors are provided with transportation maps. It is like having a new friend show you the wonders of the city!

CELEBRITIES & EXECUTIVES DOMESTIC SERVICES
198 Broadway (bet John and Fulton St), Suite 706   212/227-3877
Mon-Fri: 9-5   www.celebrities-staffing.com

This is a handy firm to know about! If you are in the market for baby nurses, nannies, housekeepers, chefs, butlers, executive assistants, personal shoppers, chauffeurs, caregivers, or other types of personnel, these people have a good track record. Not surprisingly, bodyguards are one of the more popular service categories.

COLUMBIA BARTENDING AGENCY
Mon-Fri: 10-5   212/854-4537
                                  www.columbia.edu/cu/ccs/bartending

Columbia Bartending Agency (part of the Columbia University School of Mixology) uses students who are so expert at bartending that one wonders what profession they could possibly do as well after college. The service has been around a long time, and there is none better. Columbia also supplies waiters, waitresses, and coat checkers.

DIAL-A-SECRETARY
208 E 85th St (bet Second and Third Ave)   212/348-8982
521 Fifth Ave (bet 43rd and 44th St)   212/348-9575
Open daily   www.dial-a-pro.com

If you need a resume written or reproduced, a book or screenplay processed, or an audiotape transcribed, the folks at Dial-a-Secretary will do it in a hurry. Their list of clients includes several movie stars. The business started in owner Natalie Parnass' apartment over 30 years ago with one electric typewriter. Now they have a staff of super-talented people, some of whom can type 160 words a minute. They also offer Dial-a-Resume and Dial-an-Editor services.

DOMESTICITY
307 Sixth Ave (at 2nd St), Room 2R, Brooklyn   718/768-3040
Daily: 9-9

You will want to become friends with partners Katherine Hammond and Kathejo Bohlman. Technically, they are a design and organizing team (both have art and design backgrounds) who will help improve your home environment. In reality, they will do just about anything associated with in-home styling and decorating, including such chores as putting up a Christmas tree, wrapping gifts, and baking cookies. They can shop and locate anything you desire.

EMILY CHO
By appointment   212/289-7807, 201/816-8530

Emily Cho's job is to make her clients "look and feel terrific!" She has been a clothing psychologist for nearly three decades. The process begins with an in-depth interview at your home or hotel, where your wardrobe is reviewed. She will organize your existing wardrobe, do extensive research for ideal new additions, and then escort you on a fun personal shopping spree. Emily finds new resources every year, and she promises to stay within a client's budget. Corporate services and an intensive two-day course in personal image consulting are also available. This talented professional has written four books and appeared on *Oprah* several times.

ETIQUETTE PROFESSIONNELLE
337 E 54th St (bet Second and First Ave)   212/751-1653
Call for appointment

Did you know that showing the sole of your shoe while crossing your legs is an insult in the Middle East? You'll learn this and much more from Jacqueline Baertschi, who teaches the fine points of manners and comportment in the international business community. Classes are available also for children and members of the hospitality industry.

FASHION UPDATE
Mon-Fri: 9-5   718/377-8873, 888/447-2846
www.fashionupdate.com

Sarah Gardner is a mother of three who wants the most value for every clothing dollar spent. Gardner found she could buy apparel for her family at wholesale prices from some manufacturers, so she decided to share her discoveries. She started *Fashion Update,* a quarterly publication that uncovers over 250 bargains per season in women's, men's, and children's designer clothing and accessories, plus furniture and home accessories. She conducts shopping expeditions to designer showrooms at $175 per person for 2½ hours.

FLATIRON CLEANING COMPANY
230 E 93rd St (at Second Ave)   212/876-1000
Mon-Fri: 7:30-4:30   www.flatironcleaning.com

Can you imagine how many homes and apartments these people have cleaned since opening for business in 1893? Expert services include residential house and window cleaning, installing and refinishing wood floors, and maid service. You might call the Rockefellers for references!

Reorganizing that closet? **California Closets** (1625 York Ave, 212/517-7877) will organize that dreary space and also will paint it!

FLOOD'S CLOSET
By appointment   212/348-7257

Want to be pampered? Barbara Flood will shop for or with you. She can even bring items to consider in your own home. She will help with clothes, jewelry, and decor; organizing closets; and other time-consuming chores.

INTREPID NEW YORKER
220 E 57th St (bet Second and Third Ave)   212/750-0400
Mon-Fri: 9-5   www.intrepidny.com

Like your author, Tory Masters delights in helping folks unravel the hassles and confusion of this great city. She provides one of the most complete businesses in the area and is available at any time. A corporate relocation service for people moving within a 75-mile radius of Central Park is available.

LET MILLIE DO IT!
By appointment   212/535-1539

Millie Emory is a real problem solver! She has worked for over two decades as a professional organizer, saving people time, money, and stress. She especially likes working for theatrical folks but can help anyone with a broad variety of tasks. She will organize and unclutter apartments, desks, files, closets, libraries, attics, basements, garages, and storage rooms. She will also pay bills, balance checkbooks, and get papers in order for a tax accountant or IRS audit. She can help with paper flow, time management, and space problems. Millie is also good at finding antiques and out-of-print books and records. She assists seniors in dismantling their homes before entering nursing facilities. When a loved one dies, Millie will handle estate liquidations, sales, and donations, and leave the space "broom clean."

LIGHTEN UP! FREE YOURSELF FROM CLUTTER!
254 W 98th St (bet Seventh and Eighth Ave), Suite 3F
By appointment   212/222-2488
                                          www.freefromclutter.com

Michelle Passoff, the genius behind this operation, calls New York City "the clutter capital of the world." Lighten Up is a service for people who want to free themselves from all the clutter in their lives and develop new habits. Being very much an "unclutterer" myself, I think Michelle offers a useful service in handling trash flow and all that goes with it. She offers private consultations, classes, workshops, training, lectures for organizations and corporations, and an audiotape instructional program. A new program called "Estate Organization and Resolution Service" provides assistance to heirs, executors, and attorneys in organizing the estate of the deceased. Right on, Michelle!

Make room in your Palm Pilot or Rolodex for Linda Siegal at **New York Concierge** (212/751-8591). Dinner reservations, theater tickets, events for groups from 50 to 500 people—Linda can get it done!

NEW YORK CELEBRITY ASSISTANTS (NYCA)
459 Columbus Ave, Room 216   212/803-5444
New York, NY 10024 (mailing address only)
                                          www.nycelebrityassistants.org

Are you in need of a professional assistant? This outfit is staffed with current and former assistants to top celebrities in film, TV, theater, music, sports, philanthropy, fashion, business, and politics. NYCA provides educational forums, networking opportunities, and employment referrals.

NEW YORK LITTLE ELVES
151 First Ave, Suite 204   212/673-5507
Daily: 7:30-5

Just finish a construction or remodeling job? Is the place a mess? If you need some elves to clean up, this is the outfit to call. They provide estimates, employ screened personnel, carry liability insurance, are fully bonded, and have an outstanding reputation. The "elves" will also help set up for a party and return afterwards to put your home or apartment back in shape.

PAVILLION AGENCY
15 E 40th St (bet Fifth and Madison Ave), Suite 400   212/889-6609
Daily: 9-5   www.pavillionagency.com

Pavillion has been a family-owned and -operated business for nearly 40 years. If you are in need of nannies, housekeepers, laundresses, couples, butlers, housemen, major-domos, chefs, chauffeurs, security personnel, caretakers, gardeners, property managers, or personal assistants, call and ask for Keith or Clifford Greenhouse. All staff are thoroughly screened.

RED BALL, INC.
221 E 85th St (bet Second and Third Ave)   212/861-7686
Mon-Fri: 8-5:30

These people have cleaned a lot of windows since opening in 1928! Still a family business, they specialize in residential and commercial window cleaning. The higher the windows, the happier they are. And after 75 years, they know what they're doing!

SAVED BY THE BELL
11 Riverside Dr (bet 73rd and 74th St)   212/874-5457
Mon-Fri: 9-7 (or by appointment)

Susan Bell's goal is to take the worry out of planning virtually any type of job for people who are too busy or disorganized to do it themselves. Bell says "doing the impossible is our specialty," and you can believe her. Specialties include weddings, fundraising and charity benefits, party planning, tag sales, relocations, shopping, delivery arrangements, and service referrals.

If you are interested in astrology, the lady to contact is **Susan Miller** (917/833-2480). Business consulting and strategizing are her specialties.

SMARTSTART
334 W 86th St (bet West End Ave and Riverside Dr)   212/580-7365
By appointment only

There is always someone in New York alert enough to fill a special niche or need. Such a person is Susan Weinberg. She learned from experience that many expectant mothers and fathers are too busy to plan for the arrival of their little bundle of joy. So she started Smartstart, a consulting service to aid folks in pulling everything together. Her service helps provide the basic things a newborn will need, as well as interior design, birth announcements, thank-you cards, gifts, and personal shopping. In addition, Susan sells hand-painted children's furniture—everything from table and chair sets to coat hooks and toy chests. Custom cabinet work is a specialty. She is truly the stork's number one assistant!

TALKPOWER
333 E 23rd St (bet First and Second Ave)   212/684-1711
Mon-Fri: 9-5   www.talkpowerinc.com

Do you know that speaking in front of a group is the single most feared experience? If you suffer from this phobia, give these folks a call. They are true professionals who train clients to make public appearances. Personal or group sessions are available for intensive weekends. They now offer a "Golf Power" program to enhance golfers' concentration (212/684-1711).

U NAME IT ORGANIZERS
226 E 10th St (bet First and Second Ave)   212/598-9868
Daily: 24 hours   www.masterorganizers.com

Eleni Marudis claims, "As long as it is legal, we will do it!" They perform more than 200 personal services, from uncluttering your home or office to finding a soulmate. They locate apartments and can even track down a plumber on Christmas Eve. In the crowded field of organizers, U Name It has been in business for over 16 years, which means they must be doing something right.

WHITE GLOVE ELITE
1265 Broadway (bet 31st and 32nd St), Room 801   212/684-4460
Mon-Fri: 8-6; Sat: 10-4 (cleaners available anytime)
www.whitegloveelite.com

Actors Sarah and Jim Ireland started this business as an adjunct to their stage careers. They provide trained cleaners for apartments in Manhattan, Bronx, Brooklyn, and Queens. About half of their cleaners are also actors between jobs.

Photographic Services

DEMETRIAD CREATIVE MEDIA
1674 Broadway (at 52nd St), 4th floor   212/315-3400
Mon-Fri: 9-7   www.demetriad.com

These folks were trained as commercial photographers and have parlayed their expertise into digital and document system imaging and restoration of old and damaged photographs. They are pros at retouching, making a copy negative when the original is missing, and doing quantity work at special prices. Developing and processing are hand-done.

HAND HELD FILMS
315 W 36th St (bet Eighth and Ninth Ave), Room 2E   212/502-0900
Mon-Fri: 9-6   www.handheldfilms.com

Hand Held Films rents motion-picture equipment for feature films, commercials, music videos, and documentaries. Avid media composers and digital video cameras are also available. You can be assured of finding the latest equipment and "toys," including lighting and digital editing.

PHOTOGRAPHICS UNLIMITED / DIAL-A-DARKROOM
17W 17th St (bet Fifth Ave and Ave of the Americas), 4th floor
Mon-Thurs: 9 a.m.-l0 p.m.; Fri: 9-7; Sat: 10-7;   212/255-9678
Sun: noon-7

Here's another only-in-New York idea. Photographics Unlimited offers photographers a full range of darkroom equipment and rental workspace. The shop has everything from the simplest equipment to an 8x10 Saltzman enlarger, as well as a lab for developing black-and-white and color photographs. They carry all kinds of printing paper and film supplies, and they also do custom processing and printing. Ed Lee claims his center is equipped to meet the needs of amateurs and advanced professional photographers alike. A hotline is available to answer technical questions.

STUYVESANT TOWN CAMERA SHOP
284 First Ave (bet 16th and 17th St)   212/674-0130
Mon-Fri: 9-7; Sat: 10-6

Finding a reliable place for camera and electronic repairs is not easy. Stuyvesant has been in business at the same location for over 50 years. In addition to repairs, they sell all types of electronics (including top brands such as Sony, Panasonic, JVC, and Toshiba), offer video rentals, and do high-quality film developing.

VISKO HATFIELD
Mon-Fri: 9-5   212/979-9322, 917/544-9300
                                           www.visko.cc

Here is an opportunity to have a truly one-of-a-kind portrait done by a talented young photographer. He has captured images of dozens of celebrities from the literary, fashion, art, and sports scenes. You could be next!

Plumbing and Heating

KAPNAG HEATING AND PLUMBING
150 W 28th St (at Seventh Ave), Suite 501   212/929-7111

When a reliable plumber and/or heating expert is needed, you can't do better than this outfit. They handle plumbing renovations for kitchens and bathrooms, replace toilets, repair pipes and heating equipment, and much more. Two dozen highly qualified workers have kept Kapnag at the top of the list since 1935.

Scissors and Knife Sharpening

HENRY WESTPFAL AND COMPANY
107 W 30th St (bet Ave of the Americas and Seventh Ave)
Mon-Fri: 9:30-6:30   212/563-5990

The same family has been running Henry Westpfal since 1874. They do all kinds of sharpening and repair, from barber scissors and pruning shears to cuticle scissors. They'll also work on light tools. Tools for leather workers, cutlery, shears, and scissors are all sold here. They also sell those often hard-to-find lefthanded scissors!

Shipping and Packaging

MAIL BOXES ETC. —THE UPS STORE
212/642-5000 (for information and nearest location)
                                           www.mbenyc.com

Mail Boxes Etc. has over 40 locations in New York. They represent all major carriers and can handle professional packaging and shipping jobs. Handy services (not all of them available at every location) include faxing, private mail boxes, mail forwarding, business cards, office stationery, notary and secretarial work, passport photos, laminating, key duplication, and computer-generated letters. They also sell stamps, envelopes, boxes, and packing supplies.

THE PADDED WAGON
1569 Second Ave (bet 81st and 82nd St)   212/570-5500
Mon-Fri: 9-7; Sat: 9-4; Sun: 12-5

For gift-wrapping help, this is the place to visit. The Padded Wagon carries all sizes of boxes and paper, and they can provide UPS and FedEx service.

UNITED SHIPPING & PACKAGING
200 E 10th St (at Second Ave)   212/475-2214
Mon-Fri: 9-8; Sat: 11-6

United Shipping will send anything anywhere in the world! They also sell packaging supplies and boxes. Additional services include faxing, mailboxes, office supplies, messenger services, and small moves within the city.

Shoe Repair

B. NELSON SHOE CORPORATION
1221 Ave of the Americas (at 49th St), Level C-2
Mon-Fri: 7:30-5:15   212/869-3552
                            www.bnelsonshoes.com

B. Nelson is very good at repairing dress, leisure, and athletic shoes. They have performed factory-method resoling for over a century. Prices are excellent (over-the-counter prices are cheaper than online), the service is terrific, and the client list is A-1.

JIM'S SHOE REPAIR
50 E 59th St (bet Madison and Park Ave)   212/355-8259
Mon-Fri: 8-5:45; Sat: 9-3:45; closed Sat in summer

This operation offers first-rate shoe repair, shoeshine, and shoe supplies. The shoe-repair field is rapidly losing its craftsmen, and this is one of the few shops that upholds the tradition. Owner Joseph A. Rocco specializes in orthopedic shoe and boot alterations.

TOP SERVICE
845 Seventh Ave (bet 54th and 55th St)   212/765-3190
Mon-Fri: 8-6; Sat: 9-3

Shoe repair is the main business at Top Service, but there is much more. Dance shoes are a specialty, and this source is used by many Broadway theater groups. In addition, they will cut keys, engrave anything, do luggage and handbag repair, and dye and clean shoes. This is a great place to know about in case of last-minute emergencies.

Silver Repair

BRANDT & OPIS
46 W 46th St (bet Fifth Ave and Ave of the Americas), 5th floor
Mon-Thurs: 8-5; Fri: 8-2   212/302-0294

If it has to do with silver, Roland Markowitz can handle it. This includes silver repair and polishing, buying and selling estate silver, repairing and replating silver-plated items, and fixing silver tea and coffee services. They restore combs and brushes (dresser sets), and replace old knife blades. Gold-plating, lamp restoration, and plating antique bath and door hardware are other services. In short, Brandt & Opis are complete specialists in metal restoration.

THOME SILVERSMITHS
49 W 37th St (bet Fifth Ave and Ave of the Americas), 4th floor
Wed, Thurs: 10-5   212/764-5426

Thome cleans, repairs, and replates silver. They also buy and sell some magnificent pieces. They have a real appreciation for the material, and it shows in everything they do. They will restore antique silver and objets d'art, repair and polish brass and copper, and repair and clean pewter. Thome can do silver- and gold-plating. They'll even restore the velvet backs of picture frames and velvet box linings.

Stained-Glass Restoration

VICTOR ROTHMAN FOR STAINED GLASS
212/255-2551, 914/969-0919

With over 30 years experience, this studio specializes in museum-quality stained-glass restoration, from residences to churches and public buildings. Consultation is provided, and specification reports are prepared for professional and private use. Stained-glass windows can be designed and fabricated.

If you are looking for a place to store art, furniture, records, or whatever, try family-owned (since 1910) **Sofia Storage Centers** (475 Amsterdam Ave, 139 Franklin St, and 4396 Broadway; 212/873-0700).

Tailors

BHAMBI'S CUSTOM TAILORS
14 E 60th St (bet Fifth and Madison Ave), Room 610   212/935-5379
Mon-Sat: 9-7   www.bhambis.com

With notice, this firm can cut suits in as little as two weeks. They have been in business for 35 years and have developed an excellent reputation. Next-day alterations and hand-stitching on suits are specialties. Choose from hundreds of bolts of cloth by such makers as Ermenegilo Zenga, Cerruit, Dormevil, Holland & Sherry, Toro Piana, and more.

Here are several outstanding tailors:
Leonard Logsdail (9 E 53rd St, 212/752-5030)
Tony Maurizio (18 E 53rd St, 5th floor, 212/759-3230)
William Fioravanti (45 W 57th St, 212/355-1540)

PEPPINO TAILORS
780 Lexington Ave (at 60th St)   212/832-3844
Mon-Fri: 8:30-6:30; Sat: 9-4

Joseph Peppino is a fine craftsman who has been in the tailoring field for over a quarter of a century. All types of garments, including evening wear, receive his expert attention for alterations. Delivery is offered.

SEBASTIAN TAILORS
767 Lexington Ave (at 60th St), Room 404   212/688-1244
Mon-Fri: 8:30-5:30; Sat 9-4:30

Tailors are a vanishing breed in New York. In a city that is the home of the garment industry, most professionals who repair garments call themselves "custom alteration and design specialists," or else they're dry cleaners who mend bedraggled outfits that have been brought in for cleaning. Sebastian Tailors is one of the few true tailor shops left in the city. Custom alterations for men and women are quick, neat, and reasonable. Sebastian also does reweaving. Best of all, everything is accomplished without the usual bally-hoo most such establishments seem to regard as their due.

If you have seen some sensational garment modeled on a fashion run-way but cannot afford designer prices, here are some suggestions on where to go for copies. These houses will usually quote prices from 20% to 60% less than the originals!

Atelier Eva Devecsery (201 E 61st St, 212/751-6091): alterations and custom work

Dynasty Custom Tailor (6 E 38th St, 212/679-1075)

Euroco (247 W 30th St, 212/629-9665): much of work is for Broadway shows

Felicia Farrar (25 Thompson St, 212/560-9128): create their own designs

Ghost Tailor (853 Broadway, 4th floor, 212/253-9727; by appointment)

Translation Services

BOWNE GLOBAL SOLUTIONS
132 W 31st St (bet Ave of the Americas and Seventh Ave), 12th floor
Mon-Fri: 9-5   917/339-4700
                                              www.bowneglobal.com

For translating (both verbal and written) this is *the* place. Bowne Global can be of major help with foreign languages.

Travel Services

MOMENT'S NOTICE
718/234-6295, 718/621-4548 (hotline)
Mon-Thurs: 9-9; Fri: 9-7; Sat: 10-4   www.momentsnotice.travel.com

Moment's Notice is the place to call for last-minute travel arrangements. A reputable operation that has been in the travel business for over 30 years, they are a clearinghouse for leading tour operators, airlines, and cruise lines that are often faced with undersold or canceled bookings. This outfit provides sizable discounts on all types of vacation destinations, including Caribbean packages and international cruises. Discounts are offered for travel 30 days or less prior to departure. Membership is required. A hotline announces last-minute travel bargains.

PASSPORT PLUS
20 E 49th St (bet Fifth and Madison Ave), 3rd floor
Mon-Fri: 9:30-5   212/759-5540, 800/367-1818
                                                              www.passportplus.net

Sometimes getting a passport and the proper visas can be a real pain in the neck. Passport Plus takes care of these tedious chores by securing business and tourist travel documents; renewing and amending U.S. passports; obtaining duplicate birth, death, and marriage certificates; and obtaining international driver's licenses. They work closely with the U.S. Passport Agency and Foreign Consulates and Embassies. Passport Plus can even offer aid in the case of lost or stolen passports. These folks serve customers all over the country.

To save time and money, log onto these useful travel websites:

Expedia (800/397-3342; www.expedia.com): lowest fares
Hotwire (www.hotwire.com)
Orbitz (www.orbitz.com)
Priceline (www.priceline.com): hotel consolidator
Travelocity (888/709-5983; www.travelocity.com): best flights

---

TRAVEL COMPANION EXCHANGE
P.O. Box 833, Amityville, NY 11701   631/454-0880
Mon-Fri: 8:30-4:30   www.travelcompanions.com

Tired of traveling alone? These folks can help find a compatible travel companion or partner. This nationwide outfit has been serving individuals from 20 to 80 years of age for two decades. A newsletter gives tips for solos, allowing you to make contacts in other cities. The service will find dining partners in New York. Although a number of good solo dining places are listed in the "Manhattan a la Carte" section at the front of this book, having someone to share the dining experience is a lot more fun. But do plan ahead. Call for ideas on how to find cut-rate hotel, travel, and rental car prices.

Uniform and Costume Rentals

I. BUSS & ALLAN UNIFORM RENTAL SERVICE
121 E 24th St (bet Lexington and Park Ave), 7th floor   212/529-4655
Mon-Fri: 9-5

Because most costumes are used only once, it is far less expensive to rent than buy. At this establishment you can rent any number of costumes: contemporary, period, animal, Santa, and more. They also provide a uniform rental service.

Upholstering

RAY MURRAY, INC.
143 W 29th St (bet Ave of Americas and Seventh Ave)   212/838-3752
Mon-Fri: 8:30-5

Ray Murray is an Old World shop that does things the old-fashioned way. It is a very fine and expensive drapery workroom that also does upholstery. Their specialty is creating classic custom-made furniture, and they can copy any design you want, including heirloom pieces.

VI. Where to Buy It: New York's Best Stores

Gerry's Tips for Saving When Shopping

The retail business is highly competitive these days. You'll find some good money-saving hints here:

- **Price-check**: Know prices, if possible, before going to a store.
- **Comparison shop**: There can be wide price differences.
- **Read ads carefully**: Sometimes the fine print is misleading.
- **Look beyond brand names**: Many items without fancy labels are just as good.
- **Color-coordinate**: Buy outfits that can be mixed and matched.
- **Budget your dollars**: Know exactly what you can afford to spend.
- **Frequent thrift shops**: Some excellent values can be found at secondhand stores.
- **Beware of garage sales**: Be very selective, as there can be lots of junk.
- **Shop alone**: Don't let peer pressure influence you.
- **Approach price tags warily**: Be leery of a series of markdown prices, as the merchandise might be undesirable.
- **Keep receipts**: Returns are much easier.
- **Avoid seasonal buying**: Buy in the off-season, when items are less expensive.
- **Avoid impulse buying**: You may regret it later.
- **Use coupons**: They can save you big bucks.
- **Look into store shopping programs**: Good discounts for regular customers can be had.
- **Barter**: Believe it or not, haggling is still possible in many stores!

The Best Places to Shop for Specific Items in New York: An Exclusive List

Things for the Person (Men, Women, Children)

Accessories, fashion (vintage): **Eye Candy** (329 Lafayette St)
Backpacks: **Bag House** (797 Broadway)
Bags, antique: **Sylvia Pines Uniquities** (1102-B Lexington Ave)
Boots, Western: **Lord John's Bootery** (428 Third Ave)
Boots and shoes, men's handmade: **E. Vogel Boots and Shoes** (19 Howard St)

Bridal gowns and accessories (expensive): **Vera Wang** (991 Madison Ave; by appointment)

Bridal gowns, used: **Michael's** (1041 Madison Ave)

Bridal wear, nontraditional: **Jane Wilson-Marquis** (130 E 82nd St, 212/452-5335 and 155 Prince St, 212/477-4408; appointments preferred)

Briefcases: **Per Tutti** (37 Greenwich Ave) and **Jobson's Luggage** (666 Lexington Ave)

Buttons: **Tender Buttons** (143 E 62nd St)

Clothing, antique: **Antique Boutique** (712-714 Broadway) and **Alice Underground** (481 Broadway)

Clothing, cancer survivors': **Underneath It All** (444 E 75th St)

Clothing, children's (basics): **Lester's** (1534 Second Ave), **Marsha D. D.** (1574 Third Ave), and **Morris Bros.** (2322 Broadway)

Clothing, children's French: **Jacadi** (787 Madison Ave and 1281 Madison Ave)

Clothing, children's (funky and fun): **Space Kiddets** (46 E 21st St) and **Peanutbutter & Jane** (617 Hudson St)

Clothing, children's party dresses and suits: **Prince and Princess** (33 E 68th St)

Clothing, children's resale: **Jane's Exchange** (207 Ave A)

Clothing, custom-made men's shirts and ties: **Ascot Chang** (7 W 57th St)

Clothing, designer, men's and women's: **Showroom Seven** (498 Seventh Ave, 24th floor)

Clothing, designer resale: **Ina** (101 Thompson St)

Clothing, hip-hop: **Mr. Joe** (500 Eighth Ave)

Clothing, imported designer: **India Cottage Emporium** (1150 Broadway)

Clothing, infants' (traditional): **Wicker Garden's Baby** (1327 Madison Ave)

Clothing, maternity (stylish): **Liz Lange Maternity** (958 Madison Ave) and **Pumpkin Maternity** (407 Broome St)

Clothing, men's & women's (vintage fabrics): **D.L. Cerney** (13 E 7th St)

Clothing, men's brand-name (discounted): **L.S. Men's Clothing** (49 W 45th St, 3rd floor) and **Century 21** (22 Cortlandt St)

Clothing, men's classic: **Peter Elliot** (1070 Madison Ave)

Clothing, men's custom-made: **Alan Flusser** (3 E 48th St)

Clothing, men's (good value): **Saint Laurie** (22 W 32nd St, 5th floor)

Clothing, party and wedding dresses: **Mary Adams** (138 Ludlow St)

Clothing, preppie: **Jay Kos** (986 Lexington Ave)

Clothing, "tween" girls': **Betwixt** (245 W 10th St) and **Space Kiddets** (46 E 21st St)

Clothing, unusual: **Gallery of Wearable Art** (34 E 67th St)

Clothing, urban: **Noho Transit N.Y.C.** (665 Broadway)

Clothing, vintage: **Ellen Christine** (255 W 18th St), **Reminiscence** (50 W 23rd St), and **Resurrection Vintage Clothing** (217 Mott St)

Clothing, women's (be careful of pricing): **S&W** (165 W 26th St)

Clothing, women's designer sportswear (discounted): **Giselle** (143 Orchard St)

Clothing, women's (good prices): **Miriam Rigler** (14 W 55th St)

Clothing, women's trendy: **Betsey Johnson** (248 Columbus Ave, 251 E 60th St, 1060 Madison Ave, and 138 Wooster St)

Clothing, youth: **TG-170** (170 Ludlow St)

Condoms: **Condomania** (351 Bleecker St)

Cuff links: **J. Mavec** (946 Madison Ave)

Cuff links, vintage: **Deco Jewels** (131 Thompson St)

Diamonds: **Rennie Ellen** (15 W 47th St, Room 503, 212/869-5525; by appointment)

Dresses, evening and wedding (made-to-order): **Jane Wilson-Marquis** (155 Prince St and 130 E 82nd St)

Dresses, knit sets and suits: **Sam's Knitwear** (93 Orchard St)

Earrings: **Ted Muehling** (27 Howard St)

Eyewear (discounted): **Quality Optical** (Conway Store, 1333 Broadway, lower level)

Eyewear, elegant: **Vision Fashion Eyewear** (34 W 46th St) and **Morgenthal-Frederics Opticians** (944 Madison Ave, 399 West Broadway, and 699 Madison Ave)

Fabrics, couture and designer: **Beckenstein Home Fabrics** (4 W 20th St)

Fabrics, decorator (discounted): **Harry Zarin** (72 Allen St)

Fabrics, designer (discounted): **B&J Fabrics** (263 W 40th St)

Fabrics, men's: **Beckenstein Men's Fabrics** (257 W 39th St)

Fabrics, Oriental: **New Age Design** (38 Mott St)

Footwear, women's small sizes: **Giordano's** (1150 Second Ave)

Fragrances, custom-blended: **Creed** (9 Bond St, 68 Madison Ave, and 897 Madison Ave)

Furs: **G. Michael Hennessy Furs** (345 Seventh Ave, 5th floor)

Furs, fashion: **Zamir Furs** (90 W Houston St)

Gloves, fabric and leather: **LaCrasia Gloves** (304 Fifth Ave)

Handbags (good value): **Fine and Klein** (119 Orchard St) and **RAFE New York** (1 Bleecker St)

Handbags, chic: **Lancel** (135 Prince St)

Handbags, custom: **Roberto Vascon** (140 W 72nd St)

Handbags (magnificent and very expensive): **Judith Leiber on Madison** (987 Madison Ave)

Handbags, vintage: **Chelsea Girl** (63 Thompson St)

Hats: **Dae Sung** (65 W 8th St)

Hats, custom fur: **Lenore Marshall** (235 W 29th St)

Hats, high-end: **Eugenia Kim** (203 E 4th St)

Hats, men's: **Arnold Hatter** (620 Eighth Ave), **J.J. Hat Center** (310 Fifth Ave), **P. Chanin Loft** (89 Christopher St), **Rod Keenan** (202 W 122nd St), and **Young's Hat Store** (139 Nassau St)

Hats, men's (discounted): **Makin's Hats** (212 W 35th St, 212/594-6666; call ahead)

Jackets, casual: **P.J. Huntsman** (36 W 44th St)

Jackets, leather: **Arizona** (91 Spring St)

Jackets, leather bomber: **Avirex** (652 Broadway)

Jeans, discounted: **O.M.G. Inc** (546 Broadway, 476 Broadway, 428 Broadway, 1523 Third Ave, 55 Third Ave, and 850 Second Ave)

Jewelry: **Fortunoff** (681 Fifth Ave)

Jewelry, American Indian: **David Saity** (450 Park Ave)

Jewelry, costume and travel: **Lanciani** (992 Madison Ave, 510 Madison Ave, and 826 Lexington Ave)

Jewelry, custom-designed: **Sheri Miller** (578 Fifth Ave)

Jewelry, fine: **Stuart Moore** (128 Prince St)

Jewelry, handmade: **Ten Thousand Things** (137 W 19th St)

Jewelry, victorian: **Antique Source** (212/681-9142; by appointment)

Jewelry, vintage: **Antique Addiction** (436 West Broadway)

Jewelry, vintage costume: **Deco Jewels** (131 Thompson St)
Jewels, rare and historic: **Edith Weber & Associates** (994 Madison Ave)
Kimonos: **Kimono House** (131 Thompson St)
Knit suits, sportswear: **Sam's Knitwear** (93 Orchard St)
Leather, jackets & wallets, men's & women's: **Rugby North America** (115 Mercer St)
Leather goods: **Dooney & Bourke** (20 E 60th St), **Il Bisonte** (120 Sullivan St), and **René** (1007 Madison Ave)
Lingerie (discounted): **Orchard Corset** (157 Orchard St) and **Howard Sportswear** (85 Orchard St)
Lingerie, fine: **The Bra Smyth** (905 Madison Ave)
Lingerie, sexy: **Victoria's Secret** (34 E 57th St, 1240 Third Ave, 115 Fifth Ave, 565 Broadway, and other locations)
Massage oils: **Fragrance Shoppe** (21 E 7th St)
Millinery, one-of-a-kind: **Kelly Christy** (235 Elizabeth St)
Outdoor wear: **Eastern Mountain Sports** (20 W 61st St)
Pashmina: **ABH Design** (160 E 56th St)
Pearls: **Sanko Cultured Pearls & J. Haas, Inc** (45 W 47th St, 212/819-0585; by appointment: Mon-Fri: 9-5)
Perfume: **Helmut Lang Parfumerie** (81 Greene St), **Warwick Chemists** (826 Seventh Ave), and a cluster of stores on lower Broadway between 25th and 31st streets
Perfume copies: **Essential Products** (90 Water St)
Perfume (discounted): **R.S.V. Trading** (49 W 27th St)
Prescriptions: **J. Leon Lascoff & Sons** (1209 Lexington Ave)
Resale, women's designer: **Kavanagh's** (146 E 49th St) and **New & Almost New** (65 Mercer St)
Sandals: **Barbara Shaum** (60 E 4th St)
Sandals, handmade: **Jutta Neumann** (317 E 9th St)
Secondhand items, unusual: **Out of the Closet Thrift Shop** (220 E 81st St)
Sewing patterns: **P&S Fabrics** (355 Broadway)
Shaving products: **The Art of Shaving** (141 E 62nd St and 373 Madison Ave)
Shirts, custom-made: **Arthur Gluck Shirtmaker** (47 W 57th St)
Shirts, men's Italian (great prices): **Acorn Shirts** (54 W 21st St, 4th floor, 212/366-1185; call ahead)
Shoes, adult comfort: **David Z** (655 Ave of the Americas, 556 Broadway, 384 Fifth Ave, and other locations)
Shoes, big sizes: **Tall Size Shoes** (3 W 35th St)
Shoes, bridal: **Peter Fox** (105 Thompson St)
Shoes, children's party (discounted): **Trevi Shoes** (141 Orchard St)
Shoes, children's upscale: **East Side Kids** (1298 Madison Ave), **Harry's Shoes** (2299 Broadway), and **Shoofly** (465 Amsterdam Ave)
Shoes (discounted): **Stapleton Shoe Company** (68 Trinity Pl)
Shoes, men's and women's (good value): **Co-Pilot** (645 Broadway)
Shoes, men's and women's custom-made: **Oberle Custom Shoes/Mathias Bootmaker** (56 W 45th St, Room 704, 212/391-9660; by appointment: 12-4)
Shoes, Mephisto: **Footlight Shoes** (1062 Third Ave)
Shoes, non-leather: **MooShoes** (207 E 26th St)
Shoes, walking: **Footlight Shoes** (1062 Third Ave)
Sneakers, limited edition: **Alife Rivington Club** (158 Rivington St)
Sneakers, men's and women's (discounted): **Shoe City** (120 Nassau St)

Soaps: **Fresh** (57 Spring St)
Sportswear, name-brand (discounted): **Atrium** (644 Broadway)
Sportswear, women's (good prices): **Giselle** (143 Orchard St)
Suits and dresses: **Blue** (137 Avenue A)
Suits, men's European: **Jodamo International** (321 Grand St)
Sweaters, men's and women's cashmere: **Best of Scotland** (581 Fifth Ave)
    and **David Berk** (781 Madison Ave)
Swimwear, men's: **Vilebrequin** (436 West Broadway)
Swimwear, women's: **Eres** (621 Madison Ave and 98 Wooster St), **Malia**
    Mills Swimwear (199 Mulberry St), and **Wolford** (122 Greene St)
T-shirts, baby-doll: **Eisner Bros.** (75 Essex St)
Ties, custom-made and limited edition: **Seigo** (1248 Madison Ave)
Ties (discounted): **Goidel** (138 Allen St)
Tuxedo shirts and accessories (discounted): **Ted's** (83 Orchard St)
Uniforms: **Ja-Mil Uniforms** (92 Orchard St)
Watchbands: **George Paul Jewelers** (1023 Third Ave)
Watches: **G. Wrublin Co.** (134 W 25th St), **Mostly Watches** (200 W 57th
    St), **Movado** (138 Spring St), and **Swatch** (640 Broadway)
Watches (discounted): **Yaeger Watch** (578 Fifth Ave) and **Foto Electric**
    Supply Co. (31 Essex St)
Wedding rings: **Wedding Ring Originals** (674 Lexington Ave)
Wigs: **Theresa's Wigs** (217 E 60th St) and **Jacques Darcel International**
    (1034 Third Ave)
Yachting wear, men and women's: **Paul & Shark** (772 Madison Ave)
Yardage: **P&S Fabrics** (355 Broadway)
Zippers: **A. Feibusch** (27 Allen St)

Things for the Home

Accents, bath and home: **Collectania** (1194 Lexington Ave)
Accessories (high end): **Etro** (720 Madison Ave)
Air conditioners: **Elgot Sales** (937 Lexington Ave)
Appliances (discounted): **Bloom and Krup** (504 E 14th St), **Kaufman Elec-**
    trical Appliances (365 Grand St), **Price Watchers** (800/336-6694), and
    LVT Price Quote Hotline (888/225-5588)
Appliances, kitchen: **Gringer & Sons** (29 First Ave) and **Zabar's** (2245
    Broadway)
Appliances for overseas: **Appliances & Video Overseas** (870 Ave of the
    Americas)
Art, American Indian: **Common Ground** (113 W 10th St and 55 W 16th St)
Art, ancient Greek, Roman, and Near Eastern: **Royal Athenia Galleries** (153
    E 57th St)
Art, antique Oriental: **Imperial Fine Oriental Art** (790 Madison Ave)
Art deco, French: **Maison Gerard** (53 E 10th St)
Art, decorative: **Susan Meisel Decorative Arts** (141 Prince St)
Art, erotic: **Erotics Gallery** (41 Union Sq W, Suite 1011, 212/633-2241; by
    appointment)
Art, great prices: **Miriam Rigler** (14 W 55th St)
Art, 19th- and 20th-century Western: **J.N. Bartfield Galleries** (30 W 57th St)
Art, pop: **Pop Shop** (292 Lafayette St)
Art, primitive: **Lands Beyond** (1218 Lexington Ave) and **Eastern Arts** (365
    Bleecker St)
Art, 20th century, American and European: **Timothy Baum** (212/879-4512)

Artifacts: **Jacques Carcanagues** (106 Spring St)

Bakeware (discounted): **Broadway Panhandler** (477 Broome St)

Baking supplies: **N.Y. Cake & Baking Distributor** (56 W 22nd St)

Baskets: **Bill's Flower Market** (816 Ave of the Americas)

Baskets, custom-scented: **Bath Island** (469 Amsterdam Ave)

Baskets, fruit: **Macres** (41 W 58th St and 30 E 30th St)

Bath and bed items: **Bed Bath & Beyond** (620 Ave of the Americas and 410 E 61st St)

Bath fixtures (expensive): **Boffi** (31½ Greene St, 212/431-8282)

Beds: **Charles Rogers Beds** (55 W 17th St)

Beds, Murphy: **Murphy Bed Center** (20 W 23rd St, 2nd floor)

Beds, sofa: **Avery-Boardman** (979 Third Ave)

Bird cages: **Lexington Gardens** (1011 Lexington Ave; in-store catalog orders)

Boxes, wooden: **An American Craftsman Galleries** (317 Bleecker St and other locations)

Candles: **Candleshtick** (181 Seventh Ave and 2444 Broadway), **Candle Shop** (118 Christopher St), and **Enchanted Candle** (22 Greenwich Ave)

Candles (discounted): **Empire Restaurant Supply** (114 Bowery)

Carpets, antique: **Ghiordian Knot** (212/722-1235; by appointment)

Chairs, folding (quality): **Coconut Company** (131 Greene St)

Chandeliers, vintage Italian: **The Lively Set** (33 Bedford St)

China, Amari: **Bardith** (901 Madison Ave)

China and glass (discounted): **Lanac Sales** (500 Driggs Ave, Brooklyn)

China, bargain pieces: **Fishs Eddy** (889 Broadway and 2176 Broadway)

Christmas decor: **Christmas Cottage** (871 Seventh Ave)

Christmas decorations (discounted): **Kurt Adler's Santa World** (1107 Broadway; mid-November through Christmas)

Christmas ornaments: **Matt McGhee** (22 Christopher St)

Clocks, cuckoo: **Alfry** (48 W 46th St, 5th floor) and **Time Pieces** (115 Greenwich Ave)

Closet fixtures: **Hold Everything** (1311 Second Ave and 104 Seventh Ave)

Closet items (bargain): **Creative Closets** (364 Amsterdam Ave)

Cookbooks, used: **Joanne Hendricks Cookbooks** (488 Greenwich St)

Cookware and dinnerware: **Bed Bath & Beyond** (620 Ave of the Americas and 410 E 61st St)

Dinnerware, Fiesta (individual pieces): **Mood Indigo** (181 Prince St)

Dinnerware, porcelain: **Bernardaud** (499 Park Ave)

Displays, jewelry: **Premier** (33 W 46th St)

Domestics: **Harris Levy** (278 Grand St)

Doorknobs: **Simon's Hardware** (421 Third Ave)

Electronics (good values): **The Wiz** (726 Broadway and other locations)

Electronics, vintage: **Waves** (251 W 30th St)

Fire-related merchandise: **Fire Zone** (34 W 51st St)

Fixtures, hard-to-find vintage: **Carpe Diem Antiques** (187 Ave of the Americas)

Floor coverings: **ABC Carpet & Home** (888 Broadway)

Floral arrangements, imported dried-flower: **Melonie de France** (41 E 60th St)

Floral designs: **Spring Street Garden** (36 N Moore St)

Flower bulbs: **Van Bourgondian's** (800/622-9997)

Flowers, silk: **Pany Silk Flowers** (146 W 28th St)

Foliage, live and artificial: **American Foliage & Design** (122 W 22nd St)
Frames, picture: **A.I. Friedman** (44 W 18th St) and **Framed on Madison** (740 Madison Ave)
Furnishings, traditional hand-carved: **Devon Shops** (111 E 27th St)
Furniture: **Design Within Reach** (142 Wooster St and 408 W 14th St)
Furniture, antique: **H.M. Luther Antiques** (35 E 76th St and 61 E 11th St)
Furniture, Asian: **Jacques Carcanagues** (106 Spring St)
Furniture, baby accessories: **Albee Baby Carriage** (715 Amsterdam Ave) and **Schneider's Juvenile Furniture** (20 Ave A)
Furniture, children's (basic): **Chelsea Kids Quarters** (33 W 17th St) and **Kids' Supply Company** (1343 Madison Ave)
Furniture, contemporary: **Totem Design Group** (71 Franklin St)
Furniture, custom-made: **Navedo Woodcraft** (179 E 119th St)
Furniture (discounted): **Knoll** (105 Wooster St)
Furniture, foam and mattresses: **Dixie Foam** (104 W 17th St)
Furniture, French country: **Pierre Deux Antiques** (625 Madison Ave)
Furniture, handcrafted, 18th-century American reproductions: **Barton-Sharpe** (200 Lexington Ave)
Furniture, hardwood: **Pompanoosuc** (124 Hudson St)
Furniture, leather: **Sofa So Good** (27 Mercer St)
Furniture (one-of-a-kind): **Props for Today** (330 W 34th St, 12th floor)
Furniture, pine: **Better Times Antiques** (201 W 84th St) and **Evergreen Antiques** (1249 Third Ave)
Furniture reproductions: **Foremost Furniture** (8 W 30th St, 5th floor)
Furniture, summer: **Smith & Hawken** (394 West Broadway)
Furniture, Swedish antique: **Eileen Lane** (150 Thompson St)
Furniture, wrought iron: **Morgik Metal Designs** (20 W 22nd St)
Gadgets: **Brookstone** (18 Fulton St)
Garden items: **Lexington Gardens** (1011 Lexington Ave)
Glass: **Simon Pearce** (120 Wooster St and 500 Park Ave)
Glass, Venetian: **Gardner & Barr** (213 E 60th St)
Glass and tableware: **Avventura** (463 Amsterdam Ave) and **67th Street Wines & Spirits** (179 Columbus Ave)
Glassware, Steuben (used): **Lillian Nassau** (220 E 57th St)
Glassware, vintage: **Mood Indigo** (181 Prince St)
Hardware: **Gracious Home** (35 W 44th St)
Home accessories: **Carole Stupell** (29 E 22nd St)
Housewares: **Dinosaur Designs** (250 Mott St)
Housewares, upscale: **Lancelotti** (66 Ave A)
Ice buckets, vintage: **Mood Indigo** (181 Prince St)
Kitchen gadgets: **Bed Bath & Beyond** (620 Ave of the Americas and 410 E 61st St)
Kitchenware, professional: **Hung Chong Imports** (14 Bowery) and **J.B. Prince** (36 E 31st St)
Knives: **Roger & Sons** (268 Bowery)
Lampshades: **Just Shades** (21 Spring St)
Lampshades, custom-made: **Oriental Lamp Shade** (223 W 79th St and 816 Lexington Ave) and **Unique Custom Lamp Shades** (247 E 77th St)
Lightbulbs: **Just Bulbs** (936 Broadway)
Lightbulbs (discounted): **Wiedenbach-Brown** (800/243-0030; mail order only)
Lighting, custom and antique: **Lampworks** (231 E 58th St)

Lighting fixtures: **City Knickerbocker** (781 Eighth Ave) and **Lighting by Gregory** (158 Bowery)

Linens: **Bed Bath & Beyond** (620 Ave of the Americas and 410 E 61st St) and **Nancy Koltes at Home** (31 Spring St)

Linens, antique: **Jana Starr** (236 E 80th St)

Linens, Indian: **Pondicherri** (454 Columbus Ave)

Linoleum, vintage: **Secondhand Rose** (138 Duane St)

Locks: **Lacka Lock** (253 W 46th St)

Mattresses (good value): **Town Bedding & Upholstery** (205 Eighth Ave)

Movie-star photos: **Movie Star News** (134 W 18th St)

Perfume bottles, vintage: **Gallery 47** (1050 Second Ave)

Pianos, decorative grand: **Maximiliaan's House of Grand Pianos** (305 Second Ave, Suite 322, 212/689-2177; by appointment)

Plumbing parts: **George Taylor Specialties** (76 Franklin St)

Posters, 1880 to present: **Philip Williams** (85 West Broadway)

Posters (best selection): **Carraudi Gallery** (138 W 18th St) and **Paris Images** (170 Bleecker St, Room N15)

Posters, international movie: **Jerry Ohlinger Movie Material Store** (242 W 14th St)

Posters, theater: **Triton Gallery** (323 W 45th St)

Posters, vintage: **La Belle Epoque Vintage Posters** (280 Columbus Ave)

Pottery, handmade: **Our Name Is Mud** (1566 Second Ave)

Prints, botanical: **W. Graham Arader** (29 E 72nd St and 1016 Madison Ave)

Prints, classic wildlife and sporting: **Holland & Holland** (50 E 57th St)

Quilt fabric: **City Quilter** (157 W 24th St)

Quilts: **Down and Quilt Shop** (518 Columbus Ave and 1225 Madison Ave) and **J. Schachter's** (5 Cook St, Brooklyn)

Quilts, antique: **Susan Parrish** (390 Bleecker St)

Rugs, vintage: **Doris Leslie Blau** (724 Fifth Ave, 6th floor, 212/586-5511; by appointment)

Safes: **Empire Safe** (6 E 39th St)

Screens, shoji: **Miya Shoji** (109 W 17th St)

Shelves: **Shelf Shop II** (1295 First Ave)

Silver, unusual: **Jean's Silversmiths** (16 W 45th St)

Silverware and holloware (good values): **Eastern Silver** (4901 16th Ave, Brooklyn and 67 Lee Ave, Brooklyn)

Sofas, vintage: **Regeneration Modern Furniture** (38 Renwick St)

Software: **Electronics Boutique** (1217 Third Ave, 901 Ave of the Americas, and 687 Broadway)

Stairs and rails, replacement: **Stairbuilders by B&A** (516/432-1201)

Stationery, personalized: **Jamie Ostrow** (876 Madison Ave)

Stone pieces: **Modern Stone Age** (54 Greene St)

Storage equipment: **Creative Closets** (364 Amsterdam Ave)

Strollers and other baby equipment: **Schneider's** (20 Ave A)

Tabletop merchandise: **April Cornell** (487 Columbus Ave)

Tableware: **Fishs Eddy** (889 Broadway and 2176 Broadway)

Tapestries: **Lovelia Enterprises** (356 E 41st St, 212/490-0930; by appointment) and **Saint-Remy** (818 Lexington Ave)

Textiles: **Designs in Textiles by Mary Jaeger** (51 Spring St)

Tiles: **Mosaic House** (62 W 22nd St)

Tiles, ceramic and marble: **Quarry Tiles, Marble & Granite** (132 Lexington Ave) and **Tiles** (42 W 15th St)

Trays: **Extraordinary** (251 E 57th St)
Vacuum cleaners: **Desco** (1236 Lexington Ave and 131 W 14th St)
Venetian glass: **End of History** (548½ Hudson St)
Wallpaper, antique: **Secondhand Rose** (138 Duane St)
Wallpaper (discounted): **Janovic** (136 Church St and other locations)
Wrought-iron items: **Morgik Company** (20 W 22nd St)

Things for Leisure Time

Accordions: **Main Squeeze** (19 Essex St)
Art supplies: **Pearl Paint Company** (308 Canal St)
Athletic gear: **Modell's** (many locations)
Athletic gear, team: **Yankee Clubhouse** (110 E 59th St and 393 Fifth Ave)
    and **New York Mets' Clubhouse** (143 E 54th St)
Beads: **Beads of Paradise** (16 E 17th St) and **Beads World** (1384 Broad-
    way)
Bicycles: **Bicycle Habitat** (244 Lafayette St)
Binoculars: **Clairmont-Nichols** (1016 First Ave)
Books, academic: **Labyrinth Books** (536 W 112th St)
Books, African-American history: **Liberation Bookstore** (421 Lenox Ave)
Books, art: **Hacker-Strand Art Books** (45 W 57th St, 5th floor)
Books, astrology: **New York Astrology Center** (370 Lexington Ave, Suite
    416)
Books (bargain): **Bargain Books** (34 Carmine St)
Books, children's and parents': **Bank Street Book Store** (610 W 112th St)
Books, coffee table and decorative arts: **Archivia** (1063 Madison Ave)
Books, exam-study and science-fiction: **Civil Service Book Shop** (89 Worth
    St)
Books, fashion design: **Fashion Design Bookstore** (234 W 27th St)
Books, Japanese: **Zakka** (147 Grand St)
Books, military: **Military Bookman** (29 E 93rd St)
Books, mystery: **Black Orchid Bookshop** (303 E 81st St), **Murder Ink**
    (2486 Broadway), and **Partners & Crime** (44 Greenwich Ave)
Books, mystical and religious: **Quest Bookshop** (240 E 53rd St)
Books, plate (lithographs): **George D. Glazer** (28 E 72nd St, Room 3A)
Books, rare: **Imperial Fine Books** (790 Madison Ave, 2nd floor), **J.N. Bart-
    field Galleries** (30 W 57th St), **Martayan Lan** (48 E 57th St), and **Strand
    Book Store** (828 Broadway)
Books, revolution: **Revolution Books** (9 W 19th St)
Books, tribal art: **Oan-Oceanie-Afrique Noire** (15 W 39th St, 2nd floor)
Books, used and review copies: **Strand Book Store** (828 Broadway)
Cameras: **Cine 60** (630 Ninth Ave)
Chess sets: **Chess Forum** (219 Thompson St)
Cigarettes, luxury: **Nat Sherman** (500 Fifth Ave)
Cigars: **Arnold's Tobacco Shop** (323 Madison Ave), **Davidoff** (535 Madi-
    son Ave), and **J.R. Cigars** (562 Fifth Ave)
Cigars, hand-rolled: **PB Cuban Cigars** (137 W 22nd St)
Comic books: **Village Comics** (214 Sullivan St)
Comic books, vintage: **Metropolis Collectibles** (873 Broadway)
Compact discs, records, tapes, DVDs (discounted): **Disc-O-Rama** (40 Union
    Sq E, 146 W 4th St, and 186 W 4th St; records only at 4th St location)
Compact discs, rock: **Smash Compact Discs** (33 St. Marks Pl)

Compact discs, used: **NYCD** (426 Amsterdam Ave) and **St. Mark's Sounds** (20 St. Marks Pl)

Computers: **Apple Store Soho** (103 Prince St)

Computers, hand-held: **RCS Computer Experience** (575 Madison Ave)

Costumes, makeup, and accoutrements: **Halloween Adventure** (104 Fourth Ave)

Dance-related items: **World Tone Dance** (230 Seventh Ave)

Diving equipment: **Pan Aqua Diving** (460 W 43rd St) and **Sea Horse Divers** (1416 Second Ave)

Dogs, exotic breeds: **International Kennel Club** (1032 Second Ave)

Dolls, vintage: **Manhattan Dollhouse Shop** (236A Third Ave)

Dollhouses: **Tiny Doll House** (1179 Lexington Ave)

Drums: **Drummer's World** (151 W 46th St, 3rd floor)

Embroidery, custom-designed: **Jonathan Embroidery Plus** (256 W 38th St)

Films, videotape (classics and foreign): **Evergreen Video** (37 Carmine St)

Filofax (discounted): **Altman Luggage** (135 Orchard St)

Fishing tackle: **Orvis** (525 Fifth Ave)

Games, tabletop: **Games Workshop** (54 E 8th St)

Games, war: **Compleat Strategist** (11 E 33rd St)

Gifts: **Mxyplyzyk** (125 Greenwich Ave)

Globes, antique world and celestial: **George Glazer Gallery** (28 E 72nd St, Room 3A)

Golf equipment (best selection): **New York Golf Center** (131 W 35th St)

Guitars: **Carmine Street Guitars** (42 Carmine St), **Guitar Salon** (45 Grove St, 212/675-3236; by appointment), **Ludlow Guitars** (164 Ludlow St), **Matt Umanov Guitars** (273 Bleecker St), and **Rogue Music** (251 W 30th St, 10th floor)

Guns: **Beretta Gallery** (718 Madison Ave)

Handicrafts and art, imported: **Sam's Souk** (979 Lexington Ave)

Harley-Davidson merchandise: **Harley-Davidson of New York** (686 Lexington Ave)

Holographs: **Holographic Studio** (240 E 26th St)

Home Entertainment: **J&R Music & Computer World** (23 Park Row)

Horseback-riding equipment: **Copperfield's New York** (117 E 24th St)

Kaleidoscopes: **Enchanted Forest** (85 Mercer St)

Kites: **Big City Kite Company** (1210 Lexington Ave)

Knitting supplies: **Yarn Company** (2274 Broadway)

Luggage, soft: **Bag House** (797 Broadway)

Magazines: **DINA Magazines** (72nd St and Broadway), **Eastern Newsstand** (many locations), **Union Square Magazine Shop** (200 Park Ave S), and **Universal News** (977 Eighth Ave and 676 Lexington Ave)

Magazines, back issues: **Jay Bee Magazine** (150 W 28th St)

Magic tricks: **Tannen's** (24 W 25th St)

Maps: **Hagstrom Map and Travel Store** (57 W 43rd St)

Maps, prints, and books of "Old New York": **Pageant Books & Print Shop** (212/674-5296; by appointment)

Maps, rare, vintage: **Richard B. Arkway** (59 E 54th St, 6th floor)

Maps and prints, antiquarian: **Argosy Book Store** (116 E 59th St)

Marine supplies: **E&B Goldberg's Discount Marine** (12 W 37th St)

Movie-star photos: **Movie Star News** (134 W 18th St)

Musical gifts and souvenirs: **Backstage Memories** (1638 Broadway)

Musical instruments: **Manny's Music** (156 W 48th St), **Music Inn** (169 W 4th St), and **Sam Ash Music Store** (160 W 48th St)

Needlecraft: **Yarn Company** (2274 Broadway)

Newspapers, out-of-town: **Hotalings News Agency** (212/974-9419)

New York history: **Museum of the City of New York** (1220 Fifth Ave)

Novelties (5,000 choices!): **Gordon Novelty** (52 W 29th St)

Outdoor gear: **Tent & Trails** (21 Park Pl)

Paper items (huge selection): **Paper Access** (23 W 18th St)

Papers, elegant: **Il Papiro** (1021 Lexington Ave)

Pens, antique: **Arthur Brown & Brother** (2 W 46th St)

Pet supplies (discounted): **Petland Discounts** (numerous locations)

Photographic supplies: **Ben Ness Camera & Studio** (111 University Pl) and **Calumet** (16 W 19th St)

Pipes: **Connoisseur Pipe Shop** (PaineWebber Bldg, 1285 Ave of the Americas, concourse level)

Pool tables: **Blatt Billiards** (809 Broadway)

Quilting supplies: **City Quilter** (157 W 24th St)

Records: **Tower Records and Video** (692 Broadway, 1961 Broadway, and 725 Fifth Ave)

Records, Broadway shows: **Footlight Records** (113 E 12th St)

Records, 45s and LPs (out-of-print): **House of Oldies** (35 Carmine St)

Records, vintage rock and roll: **Strider Records** (22 Jones St)

Science fiction: **Forbidden Planet** (840 Broadway)

Science fiction and New Age gifts: **Star Magic** (1256 Lexington Ave)

Scuba-diving equipment: **Pan Aqua Diving** (460 W 43rd St)

Skateboards, offbeat: **Supreme** (274 Lafayette St)

Skating equipment: **Blades Board & Skate** (120 W 72nd St, 160 E 86th St, 659 Broadway, and other locations)

Snorkeling equipment: **Scuba Network** (124 E 57th St and 655 Ave of the Americas)

Soccer supplies: **Soccer Sport Supply** (1745 First Ave)

Software, computer: **J&R Music & Computer World** (15 Park Row)

Soldiers, lead: **Second Childhood** (283 Bleecker St)

Soldiers, toy: **Classic Toys** (218 Sullivan St)

Sports cards: **Alex's MVP Cards** (256 E 89th St)

Sports video: **Famous Sports Video** (32 W 39th St)

Stationery: **Kate's Paperie** (561 Broadway, 1282 Third Ave, and 8 W 13th St)

Theater items: **One Shubert Alley** (1 Shubert Alley)

Tobacco: **J.R. Tobacco** (562 Fifth Ave)

Totes, canvas: **Tribeca Luggage & Leather** (90 Hudson St)

Toys, general selection: **Kidding Around** (60 W 15th St)

Toys, high-quality imports: **Geppetto's Toy Box** (10 Christopher St)

Toys, Japanese imports: **Image Anime** (103 W 30th St)

Toys, museum-quality (1900-1950): **Bizarre Bazaar** (130¼ E 65th St, 212/517-2100; appointment suggested)

Toys, novelties and party supplies: **E.A.T. Gifts** (1062 Madison Ave)

Toys, sex: **Toys in Babeland** (94 Rivington St)

Toys, video games: **Gamequest** (1596 Third Ave)

Toys, vintage: **Alphaville** (226 W Houston St), **Classic Toys** (218 Sullivan St), and **Darrow's Fun Antiques** (212/838-0730; by appointment)

VCRs (discounted): **Sound City** (58 W 45th St)

Videos, rare and foreign-film: **Evergreen Video** (37 Carmine St)

Videotapes, hard-to-find (for sale or rent): **Evergreen Video** (37 Carmine St)
Violins: **Universal Music** (732 Broadway)
Woodwinds: **Roberto's Woodwind** (146 W 46th St)
Writing instruments (great selection): **Rebecca Moss** (510 Madison Ave)
Yarns, luxury: **Gotta Knit** (498 Ave of the Americas)

Things from Far Away

African art: **Boca Grande Arts & Crafts** (66 Greene St) and **York's** (319 Bleecker St and 99 Spring St)
African handicrafts: **Craft Caravan** (63 Greene St)
African merchandise: **Bangally African Expo** (30 Greenwich Ave)
British imports: **99X** (84 E 10th St)
Buddhas: **Leekan Design** (93 Mercer St)
Chinese dinnerware: **Wing On Wo & Co.** (26 Mott St)
Chinese goods: **Pearl River Emporium** (277 Canal St) and **Chinese American Trading Company** (91 Mulberry St)
Chinese sandals: **Phoenix Import Corporation** (96 Bayard St)
Egyptian and Near-Eastern antiquities: **Royal-Athena Galleries** (153 E 57th St)
European pottery: **La Terrine** (1024 Lexington Ave)
Himalayan craft items: **Himalayan Crafts** (2007 Broadway)
Indian imports: **Sarajo** (130 Greene St)
Indian rugs, shawls, and more: **Kashmir** (157 E 64th St)
Indonesian art: **Eastern Arts** (365 Bleecker St)
Italian clothing and shoes: **Cellini Uomo** (59 Orchard St)
Japanese gift items: **Katagiri** (224 E 59th St)
Japanese kimonos: **Old Japan** (382 Bleecker St)
Japanese prints: **Japan Gallery** (1210 Lexington Ave)
Korean imports: **Opane of Manhattan** (6 W 32nd St)
Lampshades, Oriental: **Oriental Lamp Shade Co.** (223 W 79th St)
Leather items, imported: **Il Bisonte** (120 Sullivan St)
Mexican imports: **Pan American Phoenix** (857 Lexington Ave) and **Quinto Sol** (937 Madison Ave)
Middle East caftans: **Paracelso** (414 West Broadway)
Moroccan gifts: **Gates of Morocco** (8 Prince St)
Oriental lampshades: **Oriental Lamp Shade Co.** (223 W 79th St)
Scandinavian imports: **Antik** (104 Franklin St)
Scottish kilts and tartans: **Scottish Products** (172 Madison Ave, Room 206)
Tibetan rugs, handicrafts: **Potala** (9 E 36th St)
Tibetan treasures: **Do Kham** (51 Prince St and 304 E 5th St), **Tibet Bazaar** (473 Amsterdam Ave), **Tibetan Handicrafts** (144 Sullivan St), and **Vision of Tibet** (167 Thompson St)
Turkish carpets: **Beyond the Bosphorus** (79 Sullivan St)
Ukrainian items: **Arka** (26 First Ave)

Miscellaneous Other Things

Bottles, perfume: **Gallery 47** (1050 Second Ave)
Butterflies: **Mariposa, the Butterfly Gallery** (South Street Seaport, Pier 17, 2nd floor)
Calendars: **Calendar Club** (888/422-5637, www.calendars.com)

Cat memorabilia: **Just Cats** (244 E 60th St)
Firefighting memorabilia: **New York Firefighters' Friend** (263 Lafayette St)
Fish, tropical: **New World** (204 E 38th St)
Flags and banners: **Art Flag Co.** (8 Jay St)
Holographs: **Holographic Studio** (240 E 26th St)
Office furniture (discounted): **Frank Eastern Company** (599 Broadway, 6th
   floor) and **Discount Office Furniture** (132 W 24th St)
Office supplies: **MoMA Design Store** (44 W 53rd St and 81 Spring St) and
   Seventh Avenue Stationers (470 Seventh Ave)
Optical instruments: **Clairmont-Nichols** (1016 First Ave)
Pharmaceutical items: **Windsor Pharmacy** (1419 Ave of the Americas)
Plexiglas & Lucite: **Plexi-Craft Quality Products** (514 W 24th St)
Portfolios: **House of Portfolios** (52 W 21st St)
Stone items: **Modern Stone Age** (54 Greene St)
Store fixtures: **Liberty Display & Supply** (138 W 25th St)
Surveillance equipment, covert: **Counter Spy Shop** (444 Madison Ave)
Travel items: **Flight 001** (96 Greenwich St)
Typewriter ribbons: **Abalon Office Equipment** (60 E 42nd St)

Factory Outlet Centers in the Tri-State Area

Connecticut

Clinton Crossing Premium Outlets (20 Killingsworth Turnpike, Clinton,
   CT; 860/664-0700): 70 outlets, including Anne Klein, Barney's New York,
   Brooks Brothers, The Gap, Liz Claiborne, Nautica, Off 5th (Saks Fifth
   Avenue Outlet), Polo/Ralph Lauren, Waterford/Wedgewood, and more.

New Jersey

Flemington Area

Circle Outlet Center (Route 202 at Route 31, Flemington, NJ; 908/782-
   4100): presently under construction; no information on stores
Flemington Cut Glass (156 Main St, Flemington, NJ; 908/782-3017): Bill
   Healy Crystal, Cookware & More, Flemington Cut Glass, Framing
   Gallery, Main Street Antiques, and more.
Heritage Place (Route 31 at Church St, Flemington, NJ): Jockey, Levi's,
   Reebok, Rockport, and Springmaid/Wamsutta
Liberty Village Premium Outlets (1 Church St, Flemington, NJ; 908/782-
   8550): Over 60 outlets, including Anne Klein, Brooks Brothers, Geoffrey
   Beene, Izod, Liz Claiborne, L.L. Bean, Polo/Ralph Lauren, Sunglass
   World, Totes, Villeroy & Boch, and more.

A money-saving guide to outlet malls:
- Beware of items that were never sold in retail stores.
- Look carefully at the quality of garments.
- Be sure to save merchandise tags for possible return.
- Don't assume that all outlet stores have bargain prices.
- Ask for a volume discount from store managers.
- Sign up for your favorite store's mailing list.
- Request coupon books from your favorite outlet store.
- Visit www.outletbound.com before you shop, and request a free
  VIP voucher.

Secaucus Area

Designer Outlet Gallery (55 Hartz Way, Secaucus, NJ; 201/392-9756): Donna Karan, DKNY Jeans, Jones NY, Jones NY Country, OshKosh B'gosh, Tahari, and more.

Harmon Cove Outlet Center (20 Enterprise Ave N, Secaucus, NJ; 877/OUTLET2): Carter's Childrenswear, Decor Home Furnishings, Geoffrey Beene, Bass Shoes, London Fog, Perry Ellis, and more.

Other New Jersey Areas

Circle Factory Outlets (Route 35 at Manasquan Circle, Wall Township, NJ; 732/223-2300): Bass Shoes, Carter's Childrenswear, Harry and David, Izod, Jones NY, Mikasa, Samsonite, and more.

Jackson Village Outlet (537 Monmouth Rd, Jackson, NJ; 732/833-0680): Brooks Brothers, Banana Republic, Casual Corner Woman, Claire's Accessories, Conair, Donna Karan, Dress Barn, Sunglass Hut, Timberland, and more.

Jersey Gardens (651 Kapkowski Rd, Elizabeth, NJ; 877/SAY-VALU): 200 outlets including Banana Republic, Brooks Brothers, Gap Outlet, Kenneth Cole, Nautica Jeans, Pacific Sunwear, Perry Ellis, Vans Shoes, Wilson Leather Outlet, and more.

Marketplace I (Route 34, Matawan, NJ; 732/583-8700): Dress Barn, Nine West, Calico Corners, Bernina Sewing Center, Cinderella Bridal, Lighting for Less, Van Heusen, Wholesale for Kids, and more.

Marketplace II (Route 34, Matawan, NJ; 732/583-8700): Bon Worth, Carter's Childrenswear, L'eggs/Hanes/Bali, and more.

Old Lafayette Village (Route 15 at Route 94, Lafayette, NJ; 973/383-8323): Bass, Geoffrey Beene, Izod, Marty's Shoes, Van Heusen, and more.

Princeton Forrestal Village Factory Outlet Stores (Route 1 at College Rd W, Princeton, NJ; 609/799-7400): Bass Shoes, Casual Corner, Dansk, Izod, Van Heusen, and more.

New York

Manufacturers Outlet Center (195 N Bedford Rd, Mt. Kisco, NY; 914/241-8503): undergoing renovation; no information on stores

Outlets at Bellport (10 Farber Dr, Bellport, NY; 631/286-3872): Bass, Dress Barn, Gap Outlet, Liz Claiborne, Pfaltzgraff, Springmaid/Wamsutta, and more.

Woodbury Common Premium Outlets (Route 32, Central Valley, NY; 845/928-4000): 220 outlet stores, including Adidas, Banana Republic, Coach, Donna Karan, Gap, Geoffrey Beene, Neiman Marcus Last Call, Off 5th (Saks Fifth Avenue outlet), Polo/Ralph Lauren, Reebok, Rockport, and more.

Pennsylvania

Franklin Mills (1455 Franklin Mills Circle, Philadelphia, PA: 800/336-MALL): Close to 200 stores, including BCBG, Nautica, Guess, Off 5th (Saks Fifth Avenue outlet), Neiman Marcus Last Call, and more.

Big Names

Here's where to find them in Manhattan:

A La Vielle Russie (781 Fifth Ave, 212/752-1727): antiques

Asprey (725 Fifth Ave, 212/688-1811): royal gifts

A. Testoni (665 Fifth Ave, 212/223-0909): luxury leather goods

Baccarat (625 Madison Ave, 212/826-4100): crystal

Bang & Olufsen (927 Broadway, 212/585-2081; 330 Columbus Ave, 212/501-0926; and 952 Madison Ave, 212879-6161): home entertainment gadgets

Bernardaud (499 Park Ave, 212/371-4300): elegant tableware and furniture

Bottega Veneta (635 Madison Ave, 212/371-5511): fashions

Botticelli (666 Fifth Ave, 212/586-7421; 620 Fifth Ave, 212/582-6313; and 522 Fifth Ave, 212/221-9075): leather goods

Brioni (55 E 52nd St, 212/355-1940 and 57 E 57th St, 212/376-5777): apparel

Buccellati (46 E 57th St, 212/308-2900): silver flatware and jewelry

Burberry (131 Spring St, 212/925-9300 and 9 E 57th St, 212/407-7100): plaid everything

Calvin Klein (654 Madison Ave, 212/292-2000): fashions for the body and home

Carolina Herrara (954 Madison Ave, 212/249-6552): wedding gowns and fine attire

Cartier (653 Fifth Ave, 212/308-0843): jewelry

Chanel (15 E 57th St, 212/355-5050 and 139 Spring St, 212/334-0055): classic apparel and accessories

Chopard (725 Madison Ave, 212/218-7222): jewelry, watches

Christian Dior (21 E 57th St, 212/223-0144): clothing, accessories, and cosmetics

Christofle (680 Madison Ave, 212/308-9390): silver, crystal, porcelain, and table linens

Daum (694 Madison Ave, 212/355-2060): crystal gifts and lamps

Dolce & Gabbana (825 Madison Ave, 212/249-4100): clothing, sunglasses

Donna Karan (819 Madison Ave, 212/861-1001): clothing, home furnishings

Emanuel Ungaro (792 Madison Ave, 212/308-3653): clothing

Emilio Pucci (24 E 64th St, 212/752-8957): retro clothing

Ermenegildo Zegna (743 Fifth Ave, 212/421-4488): haberdashery

Escada (715 Fifth Ave, 212/755-2200): women's fashions

Etro (720 Madison Ave, 212/317-9096)

Ferragamo, Salvatore (661 Fifth Ave, 212/754-5200 and 124 Spring St, 212/226-4330): shoes, clothing

Frette (799 Madison Ave, 212/988-5221): bedding and accessories

Georg Jensen (683 Madison Ave, 212/759-6457): silver gifts

Givenchy (710 Madison Ave,212/688-4338): classic clothes

Gucci (685 Fifth Ave, 212/826-2600 and 840 Madison Ave, 212/717-2619): sportswear, leather goods, accessories

Harry Winston (718 Fifth Ave, 212/245-2000): serious jewels

Hermés (691 Madison Ave, 212/751-3181): scarves, ties, fragrances

Hickey Freeman (666 Fifth Ave, 212/586-6481): menswear

Hugo Boss (717 Fifth Ave, 212/485-1800): men's and women's clothing

Issey Miyake (119 Hudson St, 212/226-0100 and 992 Madison Ave, 212/439-7822): innovative apparel

Jaeger (818 Madison Ave, 212/628-3350): clothing, accessories, leather goods

Jean Paul Gaultier (759 Madison Ave, 212/249-0235): fashions for men and women

Judith Leiber (987 Madison Ave, 212/327-4003): luxury handbags and accessories

Lalique (712 Madison Ave, 212/355-6550): crystal, jewelry, leather goods

Leron (750 Madison Ave, 212/753-6700): linens for the home, lingerie

Louis Vuitton (703 Fifth Ave, 212/758-8877 and 116 Greene St, 212/274-9090): leather goods, fashions, accessories

Manolo Blahnik (31 W 54th St, 212/582-3007): sexy shoes for women

Michael Kors (974 Madison Ave, 212/452-4685): his and her sportswear

Missoni (1009 Madison Ave, 212/517-9339): men's and women's knit items

Porthault (18 E 69th St, 212/688-1660): luxurious linens, gifts

Prada (575 Broadway, 212/334-8888; 724 Fifth Ave, 212/664-0010; and 841 Madison Ave, 212/327-4200): clothing, shoes, accessories

Pratesi (829 Madison Ave, 212/288-2315): linens, towels, bathrobes

Steuben (667 Madison Ave, 212/752-1441): fine glassware

Thomas Pink (520 Madison Ave, 212/838-1928 and 1155 Ave of the Americas, 212/840-9663): shirts and accessories

Tiffany & Co. (727 Fifth Ave, 212/755-8000): luxurious jewelry and gifts

Turnbull & Asser (42 E 57th St, 212/752-5700): custom- and ready-made classic shirts and clothes for men and women

Valentino (747 Madison Ave, 212/772-6969): formalwear and accessories

Van Cleef & Arpels (744 Fifth Ave, 212/644-9500): jewelry

Yves St. Laurent Rive Gauche (855 Madison Ave, 212/472-5299): clothing and accessories

New York Stores: The Best of the Lot

Anatomical Supplies

EVOLUTION
120 Spring St (bet Greene and Mercer St)   212/343-1114
Daily: 11-7   www.evolutionnyc.com

Evolution is one of the most unique stores in Manhattan. This Soho emporium offers mounted butterflies and beetles, seashells, fossils, skulls and skeletons, horns, feathers, jewelry, books, and more. You've got to see it to believe it!

MAXILLA & MANDIBLE, LTD.
451 Columbus Ave (bet 81st and 82nd 51)   212/724-6173
Mon-Sat: 11-7; Sun: 1-5 (call ahead; closed Tues
and some days seasonally)   www.maxillamandible.com

Henry Galiano grew up in Spanish Harlem. On the days his parents weren't running their beauty parlor, the family often went to the American Museum of Natural History. His interest in things skeletal increased when he got a job at the museum as a curator's assistant. He soon started his own collection of skeletons and bones. That, in turn, led to his opening Maxilla & Mandible (the scientific names for upper and lower jaw, respectively), which is the first and only such store in the world. How many people need complete skeletons—or even a single maxilla? More than you might think! The shop started by supplying museum-quality preparations of skulls, skeletons, bones, teeth, horns, skins, butterflies, beetles, seashells, fossils, taxidermy mounts, and anatomical charts and models to artists, sculptors, painters, interior decorators, jewelry manufacturers, propmasters, medical personnel, scientists, and educators. They also carry African art, Papua New Guinea art, bronze skeletal models, and scientific equipment.

One big difference between "uptown" and "downtown" stores is their hours. While those in midtown, the East Side, and the West Side often open at 9 or 10 in the morning, many stores in Greenwich Village, Soho, and Tribeca don't open until 11 or even noon. The same is often true of museums as well.

Animals, Fish, and Accessories

PACIFIC AQUARIUM & PET
46 Delancey St (bet Forsyth and Eldridge St)   212/995-5895
Daily: 10-7:30

Goldfish are the specialty of the house, but Pacific Aquarium & Pet also carries all types of freshwater and saltwater fish, parakeets and finches, and every kind of aquarium and supply you could imagine. They will even come to your home and maintain an aquarium while you're away.

PETCO
147-149 E 86th St (at Lexington Ave)   212/831-8001
560 Second Ave (at 30th St)   212/779-4550
860 Broadway (at Union Square W)   212/358-0692
Mon-Sat: 9-9; Sun: 10-6   www.petco.com

With a selection of over 10,000 items, including food, toys, treats, and pet-care products, this store is a pet owner's treasure trove. There are sections for cats, dogs, birds, fish, and even reptiles!

PETLAND DISCOUNTS
85 Delancey St (at Orchard St)   212/477-6293
132 Nassau St (bet Beekman and John St)   212/964-1821
7 E 14th St (bet Fifth Ave and University Pl)   212/675-4102
530 E 14th St (at Ave B)   212/228-1363
312 W 23rd St (bet Eighth and Ninth Ave)   212/366-0512
137 W 72nd St (bet Columbus and Amsterdam Ave)   212/875-9785
404 Third Ave (bet 28th and 29th St)   212/447-0739
976 Second Ave (bet 51st and 52nd St)   212/755-7228
389 Ave of the Americas (bet 8th St and Waverly Pl)   212/741-1913
734 Ninth Ave (at 50th St)   212/459-9562
2708 Broadway (at 104th St)   212/222-8851
304 E 86th St (bet First and Second Ave)   212/472-1655

1954 Third Ave
Hours vary from store to store

212/987-6714
www.petlanddiscounts.com

The folks at the New York Aquarium recommend this chain for fish and aquarium accessories. Petland also carries birds and discount food and accessories for dogs, cats, and other pets.

Animation

ANIMAZING GALLERY—SOHO

461 Broome St (bet Greene and Wooster St)
Mon-Sat: 10-7; Sun: 11-6

212/226-7374
www.animazing.com

No one is better at showing animation than Animazing Gallery. They are New York City's largest authorized Disney art gallery. They also showcase the *Peanuts* pop art of Tom Everhart, friend of the late Charles Schultz. Vintage and contemporary cels and drawings from all major studios are featured. Specialties include appraisals, consignments, searches, and autographed books; there are also monthly gala events, shows, and sales. Their expanded location now includes 3D work by master American craftspeople, new sculpture glass art, Wild Home furnishings, and Art to Wear jewelry.

Antiques

Bleecker Street area
Les Pierre Antiques (369 Bleecker St, 212/243-7740): French Country
Susan Parrish (390 Bleecker St, 212/645-5020: quilts

Chelsea
Ares Rare (40 W 25th St, 212/352-2344): jewelry and more
Chelsea Antiques Building (40 W 25th St, 212/989-3414): 150 dealers
Showplace (40 W 25th St, 212/741-8520): 100 dealers
Upstairs Downtown Antiques (12 W 19th St, 212/989-8715): eclectic

East 60th Street area
Darrow's Fun Antiques (1101 First Ave, 212/838-0730): lighthearted pieces
Paris to Province (207 E 60th St, 212/750-0037): French and English furniture

Greenwich Village area
Agostino Antiques, Ltd. (808 Broadway, 212/533-3355): English and French 17th- to 19th-century furniture
Donzella (17 White St, 212/965-8919): 1930s, 1940s, and 1950s furnishings
End of History (548½ Hudson St, 212/647-7598): vintage hand-blown glass
George N. Antiques (67 E 11th St, 212/505-5599): mirrors
Howard Kaplan Antiques (827 Broadway, 212/674-1000): *belle époque*
Hyde Park Antiques (836 Broadway, 212/477-0033): English antique furniture
Karl Kemp & Associates (34 E 10th St, 212/254-1877): furniture
Kensington Place Antiques (80 E 11th St, 212/533-6378): furniture
Kentshire Galleries (37 E 12th St, 212/673-6644): English antiques
L'Epoque (30 E 10th St, 212/353-0972): armoires
Little Antique Shop (44 E 11th St, 212/673-5173): formal antiques
Maison Gerard (53 E 10th St, 212/674-7611): French art deco
Proctor Galleries (824 Broadway, 212/388-1539): European antiques
Ritter-Antik (35 E 10th St, 212/673-2213): Beidermeier (early first period)

Lexington Avenue area
Bob Pryor Antiques (1023 Lexington Ave, 212/861-1601): English brass and crystal paperweights
Evergreen Antiques (1249 Third Ave, 212/744-5664): furniture
Hayko (857 Lexington Ave, 212/717-5400): kilims
L'Art de Viere (978 Lexington Ave, 212/734-3510): early 20th century
Nancy Brous Antiques (1008 Lexington Ave, 212/772-7515): furniture
S. Wyler (941 Lexington Ave, 212/879-9848): silver, china
Sam's Souk (979 Lexington Ave, 212/535-7210): chests and accessories
Sara (952 Lexington Ave, 212/772-3243): Japanese pottery and porcelain
Sylvia Pines Uniquities (1102 Lexington Ave, 212/744-5141): diverse

Madison Avenue area
Alice McAdams (942 Madison Ave, 212/517-4400): English 18th- and 19th-century furniture
Antiquarium (948 Madison Ave, 212/734-9776): jewelry, antiquities
Art of the Past (1242 Madison Ave, 212/860-7070): south and southeast Asia
Barry Friedman (32 E 67th St, 212/794-8950): art deco
Bernard & S. Dean Levy (24 E 84th St, 212/628-7088): American furniture and silver
Cora Ginsburg (19 E 74th St, 212/744-1352): antique textiles
DeLorenzo (956 Madison Ave, 212/249-7575): art deco
Didier Aaron (32 E 67th St, 212/988-5248): 17th-, 18th- and 19th-century pieces
Eagles Antiques (1097 Madison Ave, 212/772-3266): Georgian formal furniture
Edith Weber & Associates (994 Madison Ave, 212/570-9668): rare and historic jewels
Fanelli Antique Timepieces (790 Madison Ave, Suite 202, 212/517-2300): antique timepieces
Florian Papp (962 Madison Ave, 212/288-6770): furniture
Guild Antiques II (1089 Madison Ave, 212/717-1810): English formal
J. J. Lally (41 E 57th St, 503/371-3380): Chinese art
L'Antiquaire & the Connoisseur (36 E 73rd St, 212/517-9176): French and Italian furniture
Leigh Keno American Antiques (980 Madison Ave, 2nd floor, 212/734-2381): 18th-century American furniture
Leo Kaplan, Ltd. (967 Madison Ave, 212/249-6766): ceramics and glass
Linda Horn Antiques (1015 Madison Ave, 212/772-1122): eclectic
Macklowe Gallery & Modernism (667 Madison Ave, 212/644-6400): Tiffany
Navin Kumar Gallery (212/734-4075; by appointment): Asian art
Orientations Gallery (212/772-7705): antique Japanese masterpieces
Time Will Tell (962 Madison Ave, 212/861-2663): watches
Ursus Books and Prints (981 Madison Ave, 212/772-8787): books
W. Graham Arader (29 E 72nd St, 212/628-3668): rare prints

Midtown Area
A La Vielle Russie (781 Fifth Ave, 212/752-1727): Russian art
Dalva Brothers (44 E 57th St, 212/758-2297): French furniture
Doris Leslie Blau (724 Fifth Ave, 6th floor, 212/586-5511): rugs
Gorevic & Sons (118 E 57th St, 212/753-9319): jewelry

Gotta Have It! (153 E 57th St, 212/750-7900): celebrity memorabilia
James Robinson (480 Park Ave, 212/752-6166): silver flatware
Manhattan Art & Antiques Center (1050 Second Ave, 212/355-4400): 100
  galleries
Martayan Lan (48 E 57th St, 4th floor, 212/308-0018): 16th- and 17th-
  century maps and prints
Nesle (151 E 57th St, 212/755-0515): lighting only
Newel Art Galleries (425 E 53rd St, 212/758-1970): antique gallery; all
  styles and periods
Philip Colleck (311 E 58th St, 212/505-2500): 18th- and early 19th-century
  English furniture
Ralph M. Chait Galleries (12 E 56th St, 212/758-0937): Chinese art
S.J. Shrubsole (104 E 57th St, 212/753-8920): English silver

Soho

Alan Moss (436 Lafayette St, 212/473-1310): furniture
Alice's of Soho (72 Greene St, 212/966-6867): iron beds
Antique Addiction (436 West Broadway, 212/925-6342): eclectic, personal
  items
Art & Industrial Design Shop (399 Lafayette St, 212/477-0116): 1940s,
  1950s, and 1960s items
Back Pages Antiques (125 Greene St, 212/460-5998): classic Americana
Beyond the Bosphorus (79 Sullivan St, 212/219-8257): Turkish kilims and
  pillows
Chameleon (231 Lafayette St, 212/343-9197): lighting
City Barn Antiques (269 Lafayette St, 212/941-5757): Heyword-Wakefield
Cobweb (440 Lafayette St, 212/505-1558): imported furniture
Cranberry Hole Road (252 Lafayette St, 212/334-0034): furniture
Crosby Street Studio Decorative Arts (117 Crosby St, 212/941-5045):
  Venetian glass
David Stypmann (190 Ave of the Americas, 212/226-5717): eclectic
Eileen Lane Antiques (150 Thompson St, 212/475-2988): Swedish art deco
Form and Function (95 Vandam St, 212/414-1800): furniture
Greene Street Antiques (65 Greene St, 212/274-1076): Scandinavian, Bei-
  dermeier
Historical Materialism (125 Crosby St, 212/431-3424): 19th-century col-
  lectibles
Lost City Arts (18 Cooper Square, 212/375-0500): furniture, fixtures
Rhubarb Home (26 Bond St, 212/533-1817): furniture
T&K French Antiques (200 Lexington Ave, Room 615, 212/213-2470):
  French furniture
WaterMoon Gallery (211 W Broadway, 212/925-5556): Chinese softwood
  furniture

Tribeca

Gill & Lagodich Fine Period Frames (108 Reade St, 212/619-0631; by
  appointment): frames
J.H. Antiques and Design (174 Duane St, 212/965-1443): furnishings
Oser (148 Duane St, 212/571-6737): Hawaiian, vintage rattan, surfboards
Secondhand Rose (138 Duane St, 212/393-9002): 19th-century Moorish
  antiques
Urban Archaeology (143 Franklin St, 212/431-4646): architectural antiques
Wyeth (315 Spring St, 212/925-5278; by appointment): furniture

Upper East Side
Bizarre Bazaar (130½ E 65th St, 212/517-2100): antique toys
Gardner & Barr (213 E 60th St, 212/752-0555): Murano glass
George D. Glazer (28 E 72nd St, 212/535-5706): maps, globes
Hugo, Ltd. (233 E 59th St, 212/750-6877): 19th-century lighting and decorative arts
Jean Hoffman Antiques (207 E 66th St, 212/535-6930): vintage wedding gowns, veils, bags, shoes, linen
Naga Antiques (145 E 61st St, 212/593-2788): antique Japanese screens

Upper West Side
La Belle Epoque Vintage Posters (280 Columbus Ave, 212/362-1770): advertising posters

Uptown
John Koch Antiques (157 W 124th St, 212/243-8625): furniture

Shopping in Tribeca
Beauty products: **Lafco New York** (200 Hudson St, 212/925-0001)
Bikes: **Gotham Bikes** (112 West Broadway, 212/732-2453)
Clothing: **Sorelle Firenze** (139½ Reade St, 212/528-7816) and **Tribeca Issey Miyake** (119 Hudson St, 212/226-0100)
Furniture: **Dane** (88 Franklin St, 212/925-6171)
Hats: **Hattitude** (93 Reade St, 212/571-4558)
Home furnishings: **Baker Tribeca** (129 Hudson St, 212/343-2956)

Art Supplies

LEE'S ART SHOP
220 W 57th St (at Broadway)   212/247-0110
Mon-Fri: 9-7; Sat: 9:30-6:30; Sun: 11:30-5:30

Ricky, the very able boss, offers an expanded stock of materials for amateur and professional artists and kids. There are architectural and drafting supplies, lamps, silk screens, art brushes, paper goods, stationery, pens, cards, gifts, and much more. Same-day on-premises framing is available, along with catalog ordering. Designer lighting equipment and good-looking furniture are available at Lee's other stores (1755 Broadway and 1069 Third Ave). This place is a must-visit!

NEW YORK CENTRAL ART SUPPLY
62 Third Ave (at 11th St)   212/473-7705
Mon-Sat: 8:30-6:30; Sun: 11-5   www.nycentral.com

Since 1905 artists have looked to this firm for fine-art materials, especially unique and custom-made items. There are two floors of fine-art papers, including one-of-a-kind decorative papers and over a thousand Oriental papers from Bhutan, China, India, Japan, Thailand, Taiwan, and Nepal. Amateur and skilled artisans will find a full range of decorative paints and painting materials. This firm specializes in custom priming and stretching of artists' canvas. The canvas collection includes Belgian linens and cottons in widths from 54" to 197". Their collection of brushes is outstanding.

PEARL PAINT COMPANY
308 Canal St (bet Broadway and Church St)   212/431-7932
Mon-Fri: 9-7; Sat: 10-6:30; Sun: 10-6   800/221-6845
www.pearlpaint.com

Thirteen retail selling floors contain a vast selection of arts, graphics, and crafts merchandise. Selections and services include fabric paint, silk-screening and gold-leaf items, drafting and architectural goods, a fine-writing department, and custom framing. They provide fine-art supplies at some of the best prices in town and can ship overseas. The furniture and lighting sections have been expanded, and their **Custom Frame Factory** (56 Lispenard St, 212/431-7932, x6966) sells custom frames at discount prices.

SAM FLAX
425 Park Ave (at 55th St)   212/935-5353
12 W 20th St (bet Fifth Ave and Ave of the Americas)
Mon-Fri: 9-7; Sat: 10-7; Sun: 12-5   212/620-3000
www.samflax.com

Sam Flax is one of the biggest and best art supply houses in the business. The stock is enormous, the service special, and the prices competitive. They carry a full range of art and drafting supplies, gifts, pens, furniture and home decor items, and photographic products. Framing services are offered at both stores, and one-day framing is available.

UTRECHT ART AND DRAFTING SUPPLIES
111 Fourth Ave (at 11th St)   212/777-5353
Mon-Sat: 9-7; Sun: 11-5   www.utrecht.com

Utrecht is a major manufacturer of paint, art, and drafting supplies with a large factory in Brooklyn. At this retail store, factory-fresh supplies are sold at discount, and both quality and prices are superb. Utrecht also carries other manufacturers' lines at impressive discounts.

Autographs

JAMES LOWE AUTOGRAPHS
30 E 60th St (bet Madison and Park Ave), Suite 304   212/759-0775
Mon-Fri: 9-4; appointment preferred

James Lowe is one of the nation's most established autograph houses. Regularly updated catalogs make visiting the gallery unnecessary, but in-person inspections are fascinating and invariably whet the appetite of autograph collectors. The gallery shows whatever superior items are in stock, including historic, literary, and musical autographs, manuscripts, documents, and 19th-century photographs. The offerings range from autographed pictures of Buffalo Bill to three bars of an operatic score by Puccini.

KENNETH W. RENDELL GALLERY
989 Madison Ave (at 77th St)   212/717-1776
Mon-Sat: 10-6 or by appointment   www.kwrendell.com

Kenneth Rendell has been in the business for over 40 years. He offers a fine collection of pieces from famous figures in literature, arts, politics, and science. Rendell shows autographed letters, manuscripts, documents, books, and photographs. All are authenticated, attractively presented, and priced according to rarity. Rendell evaluates collections for possible purchase.

Bathroom Accessories

A.F. SUPPLY CORPORATION
22 W 21st St (bet Fifth Ave and Ave of the Americas)   212/243-5400
Mon-Fri: 8-5 and by appointment   www.afsupply.com

A.F. Supply offers a great selection of luxury bath fixtures, whirlpools, faucets, bath accessories, door and cabinet hardware, saunas, steam showers, shower doors, medicine cabinets, and spas from top suppliers.

HOWARD KAPLAN BATH SHOP
827 Broadway (bet 12th and 13th St)   212/674-1000
Mon-Fri: 9-5   www.howardkaplanantiques.com

Howard Kaplan presents the largest assortment of top-quality antique bath items (1890–1920) in the country. Even the setting—an 1870 Napoleon III building—is special. You will definitely want to inspect the unusual French, English, and American merchandise.

SHERLE WAGNER INTERNATIONAL
60 E 57th St (at Park Ave)   212/758-3300
Mon-Fri: 9:30-5:30   www.sherlewagner.com

Sherle Wagner takes the often-skirted topic of the bathroom and places it in the most elegant location in the city, where it rubs elbows with silversmiths, art galleries, and exclusive antique shops. The luxurious bathroom fixtures, bed and bath items, and general home furniture are deserving of their 57th Street location. Fixtures come in a variety of materials, some so striking that they warrant being exhibited in a glass display case. Prices are high, as might be expected. The displays are on the lower level, and what seems like the world's slowest elevator may leave you feeling claustrophobic.

For bathroom and kitchen fix-ups, several firms stand out. **Krup's Kitchen & Bath** (11 W 18th St, 212/243-5787) is a good spot to go for appliances. For tiles, try **Get Real Surfaces** (37 W 20th St, 212/414-1620). Interesting furnishings are shown at **Wyeth** (315 Spring St, 212/243-3661). The best selection of specialty glass can be found at **Bendheim** (122 Hudson St, 212/226-6370). You can't do better than **George Taylor Specialties** (76 Franklin St, 212/226-5369) for all manner of plumbing supplies. **Simon's Hardware & Bath** (421 Third Ave, 212/532-9220) carries practically everything you could possibly want for your bathroom.

Beads

BRUCE FRANK BEADS & FINE ETHNOGRAPHIC ART
215 W 83rd St (bet Broadway and Amsterdam)   212/595-3746
Daily: 11-7:30   www.brucefrankbeads.com

You'll find one of the area's best selections of beads at this store, including semiprecious stones, sterling silver, gold-plated Czech and Japanese seed beads, brass beads, contemporary glass beads, and much more. Besides the selection of beads from all over the world (vintage and antique), the store carries a large stock of supplies and findings. There's more: weekly beading classes, re-stringing, and repair. Volume discounts are available.

GAMPEL SUPPLY
11 W 37th St (bet Fifth Ave and Ave of the Americas)
Mon-Fri: 9-5 212/575-0767
www.elveerosenberg.com

This is the kind of esoteric business New York does best. Request a particular kind of bead, and Gampel will invariably have it—at a cheap price, too. While single beads go for a dollar each at a department store one block away, Gampel sells them in bulk for a fraction of that price. Though they prefer to deal with wholesalers, individual customers are treated as courteously as institutions, and wholesale prices are offered to all. As for the stock—well, a visit to Gampel is an education. Pearlized beads alone come in over 20 different guises and are used for everything from bathroom curtains to earrings and flowers. Since many of its customers are craftspeople, Gampel also sells supplies for bead-related crafts. They stock needles, cartwheels, cord (in colors to match each bead), threads, glues, jewelry tools, jewelry findings, and costume-jewelry parts and pieces.

Bed and Bath

BED BATH & BEYOND
620 Ave of the Americas (bet 18th and 19th St) 212/255-3550
Daily: 8 a.m.-9 p.m.

410 E 61st St (at First Ave) 646/215-4702
Daily: 9-9 www.bedbathandbeyond.com

As a former retail merchant, I am always impressed with a store that does things in a big way while still making every customer feel that he or she is the most important person around. Bed Bath & Beyond is just that kind of place. The selections are huge. The quality is unquestioned. The service is prompt and informed. The store on the Avenue of the Americas has over 103,000 square feet of sheets, blankets, rugs, kitchen gadgets, hangers, towels, dinnerware, hampers, furniture, cookware, kiddie items, pillows, paper goods, appliances, and much more. The store on 61st Street has three levels jam-packed with great merchandise in 92,000 square feet. Prices are discounted, a cafe is ready to give you a lift after a great shopping experience, and goods can be shipped.

Books

The book business has changed drastically over the past decade. Superstores are now the name of the game. Unless a small dealer has a special location or niche in book marketing, times are not easy.

Antiquarian

COMPLETE TRAVELLER ANTIQUARIAN BOOKSTORE
199 Madison Ave (at 35th St) 212/685-9007
Mon-Fri: 10-7; Sat: 10-6; Sun: 11-5
www.completetravellerbooks.com

The largest collection of Baedeker Handbooks is but one feature of this store, which deals exclusively in rare, antiquarian, and out-of-print books pertaining to travel. The 8,000-book collection includes volumes on polar expeditions, adventure travel, and 18th- and 19th-century maps. Books on New York are also available.

Architecture

URBAN CENTER BOOKS
457 Madison Ave (bet 50th and 51st St)   212/935-3595
Mon-Thurs: 10-7; Fri: 10-6; Sat: 10-5:30
                                        www.urbancenterbooks.com

The Municipal Art Society is a nonprofit organization dedicated to urban planning and historic preservation. Although best known for exceptionally diverse and well-conceived walking tours, the organization also runs a gallery and bookstore at its headquarters in the north end of the elegant Villard Houses. The bookstore is among the best sources in the country for books, magazines, and journals on such topics as urban and land-use planning, architecture, and interior design. It also carries a wide selection of guidebooks to New York City.

Art

HACKER-STRAND ART BOOKS
45 W 57th St (bet 5th and 6th St), 5th floor   212/688-7600
Mon-Sat: 9:30-6

There can only be one "largest" in any field, and Hacker is it in art books. With the Strand's acquisition of this bookstore, great prices are now offered with an even larger selection. You'll find books on fine arts, decorative arts, architecture, and much more. They have been in business for 57 years. If Hacker doesn't have it, it probably doesn't exist!

PRINTED MATTER
535 W 22nd St (bet Tenth and Eleventh Ave)   212/925-0325
Tues-Fri: 10-6; Sat: 11-7   www.printedmatter.org

The name Printed Matter is a misnomer, since this store is one of a few in the world devoted exclusively to artists' books—a trade term for a portfolio of artwork in book form. They stock 24,000 titles by over 3,500 artists. The result is inexpensive, accessible art that can span an entire artist's career or focus on a particular period or theme. The idea is carried further with a selection of periodicals and audiotapes in a similar vein. Nearly all featured artists are contemporary (from 1960), so just browsing through the store will bring you up-to-date on what is happening in the art world. They sell wholesale and retail; a catalog is available.

Biography

BIOGRAPHY BOOKSHOP
400 Bleecker St (at 11th St)   212/807-8655
Mon-Thurs: 11-10; Fri, Sat: 11-11; Sun: 11-7

This shop specializes in books of a biographical nature. If you are researching a particular person or have an interest in someone's life story, this is the place to find it. There are biographies, books of letters, autobiographies, diaries, journals, current fiction and nonfiction, and biographies for children.

Children's

BANK STREET BOOKSTORE
2879 Broadway (at 112th St)   212/678-1654
                              800/439-1486 (outside New York State)
Mon-Thurs: 11-7; Fri-Sat: 10-6; Sun: 12-5
                                            www.bankstreetbooks.com

Adjacent to the Bank Street College of Education—a progressive graduate school for teachers and lab school for children—this store is a marvelous source of books for children, as well as books about children, education, and parenting. It also has a great selection of tapes, videos, and CDs, plus a small section of educational toys. While the store is a little cramped even when it isn't crowded and not conducive to snuggling up with a good book, the sales staff really knows its stock and cares enormously about quality children's literature. Make sure to ask about readings and other special events for children. A free monthly newsletter is available.

BOOKS OF WONDER
16 W 18th St (bet Fifth Ave and Ave of the Americas)   212/989-3270
Mon-Sat: 11-7; Sun: 12-6   www.booksofwonder.com

Owner Peter Glassman has moved his wonderful children's bookstore several times over the years, most recently to this good-sized space in this bustling part of lower Manhattan. In addition to the largest selection of Oz (as in *The Wizard of*) books in the world, the store is known for frequent "Meet the Author" events, beautiful used and often signed children's classics, a newsletter, and a story hour for young children on Sunday mornings. Books of Wonder remains an enchanting place. Look for gift-wrapping in the back of the store.

THE SCHOLASTIC STORE
557 West Broadway (bet Prince and Spring St)
Mon-Sat: 10-7; Sun: noon-6   212/343-6166, 877/286-0137
                                       www.scholastic.com/sohostore

The Scholastic Store is the world's only retail store of this educational publishing giant. It's a bright, cheerful space full of familiar titles and characters. In addition to children's books, the store stocks a range of toys, puzzles, software, videos, and Klutz products, as well as a tremendous selection of parent/teacher resource books on the second floor. Ask for a calendar of events, which lists readings, workshops, and performances.

Comics

ACTION COMICS
337 E 81st St (bet First and Second Ave)   212/639-1976
Mon-Fri: 12:30-8; Sat: 12-7; Sun: 12-6

Here you will find the best selection of comic books and more in the city. There are new comics from all publishers, collectors' comics from the 1930s to the present, new and collector's sports (and non-sports) cards, new and collectors' action figures, magic cards, T-shirts, and collecting supplies.

METROPOLIS COLLECTIBLES
873 Broadway (at 18th St), Suite 201   212/260-4147
Mon-Fri: 10-6   www.metropoliscomics.com

Metropolis specializes in vintage comic books from the turn of the century through the 1960s, with over 100,000 vintage titles in stock. It is the largest dealer of vintage comic books in the world, with a private showroom where fabulous one-of-a-kind books and horror movie posters are displayed. Ask to see the Boris Karloff poster from the 1931 movie *Frankenstein*.

ST. MARK'S COMICS
11 St. Mark's Pl (bet Second and Third Ave)   212/598-9439
Mon: 10 a.m.-11 p.m.; Tues-Sat: 10 a.m.-1 a.m.; Sun: 11-11

This unique store carries mainstream and licensed products, as well as hard-to-find small-press and underground comics. They have a large selection of back issues and claim, "If it's published, we carry it." The folks here are very service-oriented and will hold selections for you. Comic-related toys, T-shirts, posters, and cards are also stocked.

VILLAGE COMICS & COLLECTIBLES
214 Sullivan St (bet Bleecker and 3rd St)   212/777-2770
Mon, Tues: 10:30-7:30; Wed-Sat: 10-8:30; Sun: 11-7
                                             www.villagecomics.com

You will find just about everything for all tastes and age groups at Village Comics & Collectibles. There are collectors' items, a large selection of videos, old and new books, limited editions, collectors' cards, a large and varied adult section, a large selection of videos, hard-to-find items, and model kits of comic and horror figures in resin, vinyl, and plastic.

Can't find something? Here is a very useful service! **Anything on Earth** (800/928-7179) is one of the oldest and most experienced full-service custom acquisition firms in the country. They will help locate and acquire any item, product, or service in a professional and cost-effective manner. A free consultation is followed by a free preliminary investigation to estimate the cost and time required to locate what you want. The final fee is based on time spent, a percentage of the purchase price, or a combination of both, plus applicable expenses.

Cookbooks

CHARLOTTE F. SAFIR
1349 Lexington Ave, Apt 9B (mailing address)   212/534-7933
Phone anytime

If you want to add to a book collection or find out more about a particular author, Charlotte Safir can save you a lot of time and effort. This lady provides a search service for out-of-print books by mail or phone only. She has a fantastic network of contacts and can locate any kind of book, although she specializes in cookbooks and children's books. There is no charge for the search. Charlotte is efficient, persistent, and a pleasure to deal with.

KITCHEN ARTS & LETTERS
1435 Lexington Ave (at 94th St)   212/876-5550
Mon: 1-6; Tues-Fri: 10-6:30; Sat: 11-6; closed Sat in July and Aug

Cookbooks traditionally are strong sellers, and with all the renewed interest in health, fitness, and natural foods, they are selling better than ever. It should come as no surprise that Nachum Waxman's Kitchen Arts & Letters found immediate success as a store specializing in food- and wine-related books and literature. Imported books are a specialty. Waxman claims his store is the only one like it in the city and that there are fewer than ten in the entire country. He is a former editor at Harper & Row and Crown publishers, where he supervised cookbook projects. Bitten with the urge to start a specialty bookshop, he identified a huge demand for out-of-print cookbooks. So while the tiny shop stocks more than 10,000 current titles, much of the business consists of finding deleted and want-listed books.

Foreign

LIBRAIRE DE FRANCE/LIBRERIA HISPANICA
Dictionary Store/Learn-a-Language Store
Rockefeller Center Promenade
610 Fifth Ave (bet 49th and 50th St)   212/581-8810
Mon-Sat: 10-6 (call to see if open on Sun)

www.frencheuropean.com

A short stroll through Rockefeller Center Promenade takes you to this unique foreign-language bookstore, which has occupied the same location since 1934. Inside you will find an interesting collection of French magazines and newspapers, children's books, cookbooks, best sellers, greeting cards, and recorded French music. It is on the lower level, however, where most of the treasures are found. French books are available on almost every topic. There is a Spanish bookstore, as well as French and Spanish films on video, books on cassette, a multimedia section, books and recordings for learning more than a hundred foreign languages, and a specialized foreign-language dictionary section covering engineering, medicine, business, law, and dozens of other fields. You can even arrange to rent a car for your next European trip!

NEW YORK KINOKUNIYA BOOKSTORE
10 W 49th St (at Fifth Ave)   212/765-7766
Daily: 10-7:30   www.kinokuniya.com

Kinokuniya is Japan's largest and most esteemed bookstore chain. An American branch, located in Rockefeller Plaza, has two floors of books about Japan. It is the largest collection of Japanese books in the city. The atmosphere is the closest thing to Tokyo in New York. On the firstfloor are 20,000 English-language books on all aspects of Japanese culture: art, cooking, travel, language, literature, history, business, economics, martial arts, and more. The rest of the floor is rounded out with books on the same subjects written in Japanese. Comic books and Japanese stationery are sold on the second floor. Kinokuniya has the largest collection of Japanese books in the city.

If you're looking for new ideas in tabletop items, stop at **Clio** (92 Thompson St, 212/966-8991). You'll find attractive items from England, Czech Republic (great crystal), Finland, Hungary, and Italy.

General

BARNES & NOBLE
Branches throughout Manhattan   212/807-0099
Hours vary by store   www.bnnewyork.com

For value and selection, you can't beat Barnes & Noble. Their stores are beloved by book buyers and browsers in virtually every area of the city. Generations of New York students have bought textbooks at the main store (105 Fifth Avenue). Barnes & Noble has opened a number of magnificent superstores with enormous stocks of books (including bargain-priced remainders), comfortable shopping conveniences (including cafes), and a large selection of magazines. Best of all, they continue to offer discounts on best sellers and other popular titles. Barnes and Noble, Jr. stores target children with stocks that are similarly exciting and complete.

BORDERS BOOKS AND MUSIC
461 Park Ave (at 57th St)   212/980-6785
Mon-Fri: 9 a.m.-10 p.m.; Sat: 10-8; Sun: 11-8
576 Second Ave (at 32nd St)   212/685-3938
Mon-Sat: 9 a.m.-11 p.m.; Sun: 10-10
100 Broadway (bet Pine and Wall St)   212/964-1988
Mon-Fri: 7:30 a.m.-8 p.m.; Sat: 10-8; Sun: 11-8
                                                    www.borders.com

Borders is one of the major national bookstore chains, offering books, CDs, periodicals, places to read, and a coffee bar. The stock at Borders is wide and deep. There is plenty of well-informed help, and in-person author events draw crowds. Borders has customer kiosks allowing access to their extensive inventory via computerized searches by author, title, and keyword.

GOTHAM BOOK MART
41 W 47th St (bet Fifth Ave and Ave of the Americas)   212/719-4448
Mon-Fri: 9:30-6:30; Sat: 9:30-6

The Gotham is a New York institution founded in 1920 by the late Frances Steloff. In the early days, as is true today, there was a heavy emphasis on poetry, arts, and the theater, because those were her passions. Steloff, who could never understand how a book could be banned, once smuggled 25 first editions of Henry Miller's *Tropic of Cancer* into the country from Paris via Mexico. She developed a deep personal interest in authors and clients alike. Even as she grew older, Steloff would always make a daily visit downstairs to the shop around 2 p.m. Steloff lived to reach the century mark; her influence on this charming store will probably live on for another century.

RIZZOLI
31 W 57th St (bet Fifth Ave and Ave of the Americas)   212/759-2424
Mon-Sat: 10-7:30; Sun: 11-7   www.rizzoliusa.com

When you talk about class in the book business, Rizzoli tops the list. They have maintained an elegant atmosphere that makes a patron feel as if he or she is browsing a European library rather than a midtown Manhattan bookstore. The emphasis is on art, architecture, literature, photography, fashion, and interior design. There is a good selection of paperbacks. Upstairs you will find Italian books, a music department, and children's books.

STRAND BOOK STORE
828 Broadway (at 12th St)   212/473-1452
Mon-Sat: 9:30-10:30; Sun: 11-10:30   www.strandbooks.com
Strand Book Annex
95 Fulton St (at Gold St)   212/732-6070
Mon-Fri: 9:30-9; Sat, Sun: 11-8

For book lovers, no trip to New York is complete without a visit to the Strand. Family-owned for 75 years, this fabulous institution is the largest used bookstore (over 2.5 million volumes) in the world. For New Yorkers, the Strand is the place to start looking for that volume you must have. Outside are carts full of bargains. Inside, according to George Will, "the only eight miles worth saving in New York are the shelves at the Strand Book Store." These miles of books are tagged at up to 85% off list price. This enormous bookstore houses secondhand, out-of-print, and rare books at heavily discounted prices. In addition, the Strand offers thousands of new books at 50% off publisher's list price, plus a huge stock of quality remainders. In the rare-book department, located on the third floor, individual titles are priced up to $125,000. There is also a fine selection of more moderately priced collectibles, including 20th-century first editions, limited signed editions, fine bindings, and art books. The store imports English remainders, sells to libraries, sells books by the foot (supplying decorators, TV networks, and hotels), and does a booming mail-order business. Strand Book Annex, located three blocks east of Broadway, has 15,000 square feet of books and is surprisingly sunny and organized. There's even a children's reading room. Owner Fred Bass is one of the nicest and brightest individuals in the book business.

THREE LIVES & CO.
154 W 10th St (at Waverly Pl)   212/741-2069
Mon-Tues: 12-8; Wed-Sat: 11-8:30; Sun: 12-7

Unfortunately, we are seeing fewer independent bookstores, which have added so much to the pleasure of book lovers. Three Lives is one of the best of the remaining few. Founded in 1978, they specialize in literary fiction and nonfiction, with good sections on poetry, art, New York, cooking, and gardening. Best of all, the staff is super friendly and knowledgeable.

Music

JUILLIARD BOOKSTORE
60 Lincoln Center Plaza (65th St at Broadway, plaza level)
Mon-Thurs: 9:30-7:30; Fri, Sat: 10-6   212/799-5000, ext 237
www.bookstore.juilliard.edu

With over 20,000 sheet-music titles and scores in stock, this bookstore claims to carry every classical music book in print! But there is more: imprinted stationery and apparel, conductor's batons, metronomes, historic recordings, and music software.

Mystery

BLACK ORCHID BOOKSHOP
303 E 81st St (bet First and Second Ave)   212/734-5980
Mon-Fri: 12-7; Sat: 11-6:30; Sun: 12-5 (closed Sun in July and Aug)
www.ageneralstore.com

The Black Orchid caters to all kinds of mystery readers, stocking current titles and out-of-print books. A number of signed titles are available.

MURDER INK®
2486 Broadway (bet 92nd and 93rd St)   212/362-8905
Mon-Sat: 10-9; Sun: 11-7   www.murderink.com

For the diehard Sherlock Holmes fan, this is the place! They have a great selection of rare mystery books, as well as signed first editions of current mysteries. Also, sister store **Ivy's Books** (2488 Broadway, 212/362-8905) carries new and used literature, rare and collectible titles, kids' books, and volumes on New York.

MYSTERIOUS BOOKSHOP
129 W 56th St (bet Ave of the Americas and Seventh Ave)
Mon-Sat: 11-7   212/765-0900
                                         www.mysteriousbookshop.com

Otto Penzler is a Baker Street Irregular, a Sherlock Holmes fan extraordinaire (an elementary deduction!), and the Mysterious Bookshop's owner. As you might expect, the shop is friendly, and spontaneous conversation among customers is the norm. Mysterious stocks new hardcover and paperback books that deal with all types of mystery. Upstairs, via a winding circular staircase, the store branches out to the width of two buildings and is stocked floor-to-ceiling with out-of-print, used, and rare books. Amazingly, they seem to know exactly what is in stock. If it is not on the shelves, they will order it. There is as much talk as business conducted here, and you can continue the conversation with authors who sign their works from time to time in the back room. Mysterious carries thousands of autographed books, and several store-sponsored book clubs provide autographed first editions to members.

New York

CITYSTORE
1 Centre St (Municipal Bldg at Chambers St), north plaza
Mon-Fri: 9-4:30   212/669-8246
                                  www.nyc.gov/html/citybook/home.html

This city government bookstore has access to more than 120 official publications, all of which are dedicated to helping New Yorkers cope with their complex lives. *The Green Book* is the official directory of the city of New York, listing phone numbers and addresses of more than 900 government agencies and 6,000 officials. It includes state, federal, and international listings, as well as courts and a section on licenses. There is also a unique collection of New York memorabilia: city-seal ties, pins, and more.

Out-of-Print

ARGOSY BOOK STORE
116 E 59th St (bet Park and Lexington Ave)   212/753-4455
Mon-Fri: 10-6; Sat: 10-5 (closed May-Sept)   www.argosybooks.com

Argosy is the largest out-of-print, secondhand, and rare-volume bookstore in New York. The six-story building houses a stock of books from the 16th through the 20th centuries, including modern first editions and regional American-history volumes, as well as others on art, science, and medicine. A separate autograph section includes items from a number of well-known personalities. Their print department is famous for its large collection of antique maps from all over the world, prints of every conceivable subject, and vintage posters.

Rare

ALABASTER BOOKSHOP
122 Fourth Ave (bet 12th and 13th St)   212/982-3550
Mon-Sat: 10-8; Sun: 11-8

There was a time when Fourth Avenue was known as "Bookshop Row." Back then, it was *the* place for used books in Manhattan. All that has changed with the advent of superstores and the demise of smaller entrepreneurs. Well, Steve Crowley has bucked the trend, offering a great selection of used and rare books in all categories, ranging from $2 paperbacks to a $1,000 first edition. Specialities include New York City, photography, and modern first editions.

BAUMAN RARE BOOKS
Waldorf-Astoria Hotel
301 Park Ave (at 50th St), lobby level   212/759-8300
535 Madison Ave (bet 54th and 55th St)   212/751-0011
Mon-Sat: 10-6   www.baumanrarebooks.com

Bauman offers a fine collection of books and autographs dating from the 15th through the 20th centuries. Included are works of literature, history, economics, law, science, medicine, nature, travel, and exploration. They also provide services from designing and furnishing libraries to locating books for customers.

IMPERIAL FINE BOOKS
790 Madison Ave (bet 66th and 67th St), 2nd floor   212/861-6620
Mon-Sat: 10:30-6   www.imperialfinebooks.com

If you are in the market for books that look as great as they read, Imperial is the place to visit. You will find fine leather bindings, illustrated books, vintage children's books, unique first editions, and magnificent sets of prized volumes. Their inventory includes literary giants like Twain, Dickens, Brontë, and Shakespeare. There is also an outstanding Oriental art gallery, featuring Chinese, Japanese, and Korean ceramics and antiques. (They will purchase fine pieces.) Services include complete restoration and binding of damaged or aged books. A search office will locate titles and make appraisals.

J.N. BARTFIELD GALLERIES AND FINE BOOKS
30 W 57th St (bet Fifth Ave and Ave of the Americas), 3rd floor
Mon-Fri: 10-5; Sat: 10-3 (closed Sat in summer)   212/245-8890

This shop is a spectacular hunting ground for lovers of fine paintings and rare books. Since 1937 they have specialized in masters of the American West and 19th-and 20th-century American paintings and sculptures. I have purchased outstanding collections of leatherbound books from them and can vouch for their expertise. First editions, sporting books, and high-quality antiquarian books are featured. Who wouldn't be excited to browse elegantly bound volumes that once graced the shelves of old family libraries?

PAGEANT BOOKS AND PRINT SHOP
By appointment only   212/674-5296
                                                    www.pageantbooks.com

Give these folks a call for a great selection of antiquarian books, maps, prints, etchings, rare volumes, and first editions from the 15th to the 20th centuries. Pageant is one of the last outfits in Manhattan to carry a really wonderful inventory in all of these categories.

Religious

CHRISTIAN PUBLICATIONS BOOK STORE
315 W 43rd St (bet Eighth and Ninth Ave)   212/5824311
Mon-Fri: 9:30-7:45; Sat: 9:30-6:45   www.christianpub.com

This is the largest Christian bookstore in the metropolitan area. It has over 20,000 titles in stock, along with religious CDs, tapes, videos, and church and school supplies. A large number of these items are available in Spanish, as befits the Latino neighborhood.

J. LEVINE BOOKS & JUDAICA
5 W 30th St (bet Fifth Ave and Broadway)   212/695-6888
800/5-JEWISH (outside New York City)
Mon-Wed: 9-6; Thurs: 9-7; Fri: 9-2; Sun: 10-5 (closed Sun in July)
www.levinejudaica.com

The history of the Lower East Side is reflected in this store. Started back in 1902 on Eldridge Street, it was a fixture in the area for many years. Now J. Levine operates out of uptown, just off Fifth Avenue. Being one of the oldest Jewish bookstores in the city, Levine is a leader in the Jewish-book marketplace. Though the emphasis is still on the written word, they have expanded the store with many gift items, tapes, coffee-table books, and thousands of items of Judaica. A 100-page catalog is available.

ST. PATRICK'S CATHEDRAL GIFT STORE
15 E 51st St (bet Fifth and Madison Ave)   212/355-2749, ext 400
Daily: 10-6

This store is an oasis of calm in midtown. Lovely music plays in the background as you browse displays of rosary beads, books on Catholicism, statues of saints, and related items. Proceeds of every sale benefit the cathedral.

Theater

APPLAUSE THEATER & CINEMA BOOKS
211 W 71st St (at Broadway)   212/496-7511
Mon-Sat: 10-9; Sun: 12-6

Quite simply, this store offers the best selection of theater and cinema books in the world. There is great interest in theater literature, and these folks are on the cutting edge. They specialize in new and out-of-print plays, film scripts, and videos.

DRAMA BOOK SHOP
250 W 40th St (bet Seventh and Eighth Ave)
Mon-Sat: 10-8; Sun: 12-6   212/944-0595, 800/322-0595
ww.dramabookshop.com

This shop has been providing a valuable service to the performing arts community since 1923. Its stock includes publications dealing with theater, film, dance, music, puppetry, magic, design, and more. The Drama Book Shop is known for courteous and knowledgeable service, both in-store and by mail.

RICHARD STODDARD—PERFORMING ARTS BOOKS

By appointment   212/598-9421
www.richardstoddard.com

Richard Stoddard runs a one-man operation dedicated to rare, out-of-print, and used books, and to memorabilia relating to the performing arts. Equipped with a Ph.D. from Yale in theater history and more than 25 years of experience as a dealer and appraiser of performing arts materials, Stoddard offers a broad range of items. He has the largest collection of New York playbills (about 20,000) for sale in the U.S., as well as books, autographs, souvenir programs, and original stage designs. He is the sole agent for the estate of Jo Mielziner, an esteemed Broadway designer, and he also offers designs by a half-dozen other set designers.

Butterflies

MARIPOSA, THE BUTTERFLY GALLERY

South Street Seaport (at Fulton St), Pier 17   212/233-3221
Daily: 10-9

At Mariposa, butterflies are regarded as art. Marshall Hill is a renowned designer in this unusual medium. Butterflies are unique, and Mariposa (the Spanish word for butterfly) displays them separately, in panels, and in groups. Butterfly farms breed and raise butterflies, which live their full one-month life spans under ideal conditions for creating this art.

Buttons

TENDER BUTTONS

143 E 62nd St (bet Lexington and Third Ave)   212/758-7004
Mon-Fri: 10:30-6; Sat: 10:30-5:30

Owner Millicent Safro has assembled a retail button store that is complete in variety as well as size. One antique wooden display cabinet shows off Tender Buttons' selection of original buttons, many imported or made exclusively for the store. There are buttons of pearl, wood, horn, Navajo silver, leather, ceramics, bone, ivory, pewter, and semiprecious stones. Many are antiques. Some are as highly valued as artwork; a French enamel button, for instance, can cost almost as much as a painting! Unique pieces can be made into special cuff links—real conversation pieces for the lucky owner. They also have a fine collection of antique and period cuff links and men's stud sets. I am a cuff-links buff and have purchased some of my best pieces from this shop. They also have wonderful small antiques.

Candles

CANDLE SHOP

118 Christopher St (bet Bleecker and Hudson St)   212/989-0148
Mon-Thurs: 11-8; Fri, Sat: 11-9; Sun: 12-7   888/823-4823
www.candlexpress.com

Thomas Alva Edison's inventions haven't made a flicker of an imprint on the folks at the Candle Shop, the oldest specialty candle store in New York. They have assembled a collection of beeswax, paraffin, and stearin candles in an assortment of sizes and colors. It's positively illuminating to learn that candles are available in so many configurations! They will fulfill custom requests. The shop also carries candle holders and accessories, oil lamps, and incense.

OTHER WORLDLY WAXES
131 E 7th St (bet Ave A and First Ave)   212/260-9188
Daily: 2-10   www.candletherapy.com

In this interesting store you'll find scented candles, aromatherapy products, hand-blended oils, and incense. They also offer spiritual advice, promising that their candles "merge psychological goals with whatever spiritual framework you have," Here's a sampling of the properties associated with their oils and incense: "Cleopatra" (balm of Gilead) is a secret weapon of seduction, while "Vavoom" (coconut) promises big-time sex appeal and flair. Who knows? A visit here might change your life! Ask for Catherine Riggs-Bergesen, who is a practicing clinical psychologist. Private consultations are by appointment.

China, Glassware

CRATE & BARREL
650 Madison Ave (at 59th St)   212/308-0011
Mon-Fri: 10-8; Sat: 10-7; Sun: 12-6

611 Broadway (at Houston St)   212/780-0004
Mon-Sat: 10-9; Sun: 12-7   www.crateandbarrel.com

Even if you aren't in the market for china, glassware, bedroom furnishings, or casual furniture, the displays will make shopping hard to resist. First, the place is loaded with attractive, quality merchandise at sensible prices. Second, it is fixtured magnificently, with every item shown to best advantage. Third, the lighting and signing are masterfully done. Finally, the store layout and number of checkout stands make for quick work in completing a sale. These folks are professional merchants in the best sense of the word.

FISHS EDDY
889 Broadway (at 19th St)   212/420-9020
2176 Broadway (at 77th St)   212/873-8819
Mon-Sat: 10-9; Sun: 11-8   www.fishseddy.com

Besides being treasure troves for bargain hunters, these shops are fun to browse for some of the most unusual industrial-strength china and glassware items available anywhere. Everything is made in America, and the stock changes on a regular basis. For young people setting up a new residence or a business looking for unique pieces, try Fishs Eddy first.

Clothing and Accessories

Antique and Vintage

THE FAMILY JEWELS
130 W 23rd St (bet Ave of the Americas and Seventh Ave)
                                                 212/633-6020
Sun-Wed: 11-7; Thurs, Fri, Sat: 11-8   www.familyjewels_nyc.com

This is *the* place for vintage clothing and accessories. The stock is well-organized, the selections are huge, the service is excellent, and shopping is fun! Even the decor is 1940s, and appropriately, retro music plays. Prices are reasonable. A costume and styling service is available.

FROM AROUND THE WORLD
209 W 38th St (bet Seventh and Eighth Ave), Suite 1207
Mon-Fri: 9:30-5:30, by appointment   212/354-6536

This place is a vintage-design resource showroom, wardrobe lending library, and retail outlet specializing in quality one-of-a-kind vintage apparel and accessories from all over the world. The constantly changing selection covers the 1920s through the 1980s. You'll find children's clothes, work wear, military items, Hawaiian, Western, peasant, ethnic, mod, athletic, and even evening wear.

HARRIET LOVE
126 Prince St (at Wooster St)   212/966-2280
Daily: 11-7

Harriet Love is on the front line in the field of "new with retro-feel" apparel and accessories. Her shop overflows with beautiful purses, sweaters, jackets, and jewelry. Harriet also buys from vendors who interpret vintage pieces to create new treasures that have a classic feeling.

REMINISCENCE
50 W 23rd St (bet Fifth Ave and Ave of the Americas)   212/243-2292
Mon-Sat: 11-7:30; Sun: 12-7

It's fun to revisit the 1960s and 1970s at this hip emporium, created by Stewart Richer on lower Fifth Avenue. Although he is a child of this era, most of Richer's customers are between the ages of 13 and 30. The finds here are unusual and wearable, with large selections of colorful vintage clothing and attractive displays of jewelry, hats, gifts, and accessories. Richer's goods, although vintage in style, are mostly new, and the company has become a manufacturer that sells to outlets all over the world. Because of its vast distribution, Richer is able to produce large quantities and sell at low prices.

SCREAMING MIMI'S
382 Lafayette St (bet 4th and Great Jones St)   212/677-6464
Mon-Fri: 12-8; Sat: 12-8; Sun: 1-7

Laura Wills presides over this shop, which features accessories for men and women from the 1940s through the 1980s, as well as contemporary merchandise. There is an excellent showing of handbags, shoes, jewelry, sunglasses, and lingerie, plus a good selection of sportswear. A new department has opened featuring designer and vintage couture. Everyone agrees this is a fun place to shop!

TRASH & VAUDEVILLE
4 St. Mark's Pl (bet Second and Third Ave)   212/982-3590
Mon-Thurs: 12-8; Fri: 11:30-8:30; Sat: 11:30-9; Sun: 1-7:30

This place is hard to pin down, since the stock changes constantly and seems to have no boundaries. Trash & Vaudeville describes its stock as punk clothing, accessories, and original designs. "Punk clothing" means rock and roll styles from the 1950s to the present, including outrageous footwear. They also carry new clothing from Europe.

VINTAGE DESIGNS/WHAT COMES AROUND GOES AROUND

351 West Broadway (bet Broome and Grand St)   212/343-9303
Mon-Sat: 11-8; Sun: 12-7   www.nyvintage.com

If vintage clothing is your thing, then don't miss this place, which claims to be one of the largest vintage outlets in the world, with over 60,000 items in stock. Many of the labels are familiar, and the prices are right. Denim and military wear are especially well represented.

> One of my hobbies is collecting cuff links, though finding a good selection of French-cuff shirts can be a problem. **Thomas Pink** (520 Madison Ave, 212/838-1928 and 1155 Ave of the Americas, 212/840-9663) has a good selection. Some great links can also be found at **Links of London** (535 Madison Ave, 212/588-1177).

Bridal

HERE COMES THE BRIDESMAID . . .

238 W 14th St (bet Seventh and Eighth Ave)   212/647-9686
Tues-Thurs:11-8; Fri, Sat: 11-5   www.bridesmaids.com

After walking down the aisle as a bridesmaid in 13 weddings, Stephanie Harper decided it was time that bridesmaids had a store of their own. Her establishment carries gowns from Siri, Lazzaro, Nicole Miller, Jim Hjelm, and others. She also features gowns that can be hemmed and worn again to occasions other than weddings. Weekend hours make Here Comes the Bridesmaid especially convenient for working women, but be sure to call ahead for an appointment.

KLEINFELD

8202 Fifth Ave (at 82nd St), Brooklyn   718/765-8500
Tues, Thurs: 12:30-9:30; Fri: 10-6; Sat: 9:30-6; Sun: 10-6
(call for an appointment or Sun hours)   www.kleinfeldbridal.com

The bridal business has changed a great deal. Today there are very limited collections at some specialty stores, but there is only one true bridal complex. Kleinfeld stocks up to 1,000 styles of bridal gowns. Yes, I know this is a book about Manhattan, but no store can match Kleinfeld. The mother of the bride will find a special section called Kleinfeld's P.M., which specializes in evening wear. Kleinfeld carries every major name in bridal wear and accessories, including Amsale, Caroline Herara, and Scassi. One-fifth of the collection is of international origin. The store operates by appointment and can handle over a hundred customers a day with their specialized personnel. This is the place to come when wedding bells will soon be ringing.

VERA WANG

991 Madison Ave (at 77th St)   212/628-3400
Mon, Fri: 9:30-6; Tues-Thurs: 11-7; Sat: 9-6   www.verawang.com

Vera Wang is one of the top bridal designers in the nation, and this is her only salon. Be prepared for beautiful styles that are priced accordingly. Wedding gowns are in the $3,000 to $20,000 range. Exclusive evening-wear designs may be purchased off the rack. A special store for bridesmaids is located across the street at 980 Madison Avenue (212/628-9898).

Children's—General

Before describing what I consider to be the best selection of children's clothing stores in New York, let me be clear about what I'm *not* including: big chains and the haughty "just so" boutiques that line Madison Avenue. That is not to say some of the chains don't have great stores here. **Baby Gap** and **Gap Kids**, **The Children's Place**, **Gymboree, OshKosh B'Gosh**, and even Europe's **Oilily** all have good selections, as does the cavernous "big-box" **buybuy Baby**. But unlike the stores listed below, they sell very little that you can't buy in any other city in America. As for the haughty boutiques, I see no reason to patronize these wildly overpriced and unwelcoming places.

BETWIXT
245 W 10th St (at Hudson St)   212/243-8590
Mon-Fri: 11:30-6:30; Sat: 11-6; Sun: noon-5

The latest rage among marketers are so-called "tweens," that group of children who aren't really little anymore but aren't quite teenagers either. This airy, well-designed clothing store in the West Village—complete with a logo that will remind Baby Boomer parents of the old *Bewitched* television show—caters to "tween" girls. Cool, sophisticated clothing, shoes, and accessories line the shelves, while cool, sophisticated girls and petite women fill the store.

BU AND THE DUCK
106 Franklin St (bet Church St and West Broadway)   212/431-9226
Mon-Sat: 10-7; Sun: 12-6

Ask owner-designer Susan Lane-Camacho about the unusual store name and what it means. Quality is the byword here. Come to Bu and the Duck for outstanding handmade sweaters and clothing for infants to eight-year-olds. All designs are original.

G.C. WILLIAM
1137 Madison Ave (near 84th St)   212/396-3400
Mon-Sat: 10-6:30; Sun: 12-5   www.gcwilliam.com

If your preteen or teenager wants to dress hip, but you want him or her to look more classic and conservative, this is the perfect compromise. The clothes—from size 6 to 16 for girls (preteen) and 6 to 22 (husky sizes) for boys—are partly European, the fabrics are beautiful, and the designs are stylish but not over-the-top. Another plus: unlike other popular stores for kids this age, G.C. William is well organized, spacious, and inviting to parents.

LESTER'S
1522 Second Ave (at 79th St)   212/734-9292
Mon-Fri: 10-7; Sat: 10-6; Sun: 12-5

If you're looking for basic clothes, shoes, campwear, and/or accessories for children and don't want to leave the East Side, Lester's is your best bet. A recent renovation has created a much larger and more inviting space, including a downstairs section dedicated entirely to boys. In fact, you can clothe everyone from infants to teenagers here. While nothing carried here is going to win any fashion awards, Lester's is just stylish enough to keep East Side moms and kids coming back.

LILLIPUT

265 Lafayette St (bet Spring and Prince St)   212/965-9567
Tues-Sat: 11-7; Sun-Mon: 12-6   www.lilliputsoho.com

Children's clothing stores in New York's hot shopping neighborhoods have multiplied in recent years, and a lot of them start to look alike after awhile. Sometimes a good buyer with a sharp eye can set a store apart, however. In certain respects Lilliput resembles a lot of other relatively upscale children's stores, and some of what you'll find here is neither unusual nor well-priced. But look a little closer and you'll see certain items, including a wide selection from Lili Gaufreete, that make a trip here worthwhile. In addition to a wide and varied selection of infant clothes, Lilliput has a great shoe selection, unusual accessories, a few toys, and a diverse range of clothes for young children to size 8. A sister store, **Lilliput Soho Kids** (240 Lafayette St, 212/965-9201), is across the street and down the block. It offers clothes for girls to size 16; hours are the same.

MARSHA D.D.

1324 Lexington Ave (bet 88th and 89th St)   212/831-2422
Mon-Sat: 10-6 (Thurs to 7); Sun: 12-5:30

With backpacks, stylish clothing, and accessories galore, this friendly East Side institution is a hot spot for "tweens" and their younger siblings. Owner Marsha Drogin Dayan has a really good feel for what's "in," and she makes everyone feel welcome. Unlike the separate girls' and boys' stores she maintained for years, this spot is comfortable and spacious.

MORRIS BROS.

2322 Broadway (at 84th St)   212/724-9000
Mon-Sat: 9:30-6:30; Sun: 12-5:30

You can't be a parent or kid on the Upper West Side and not know about Morris Bros. Whether you're looking for a backpack, hat, tights, pajamas, jeans, underwear, or clothes for gym class and camp, this is the place to go for basic kids' clothing and accessories at decent prices. One negative: the selection for girls is significantly smaller than that for boys. In fact, while Morris Bros. carries sizes 4 through 20 for boys, it carries only sizes 7 through 14 for girls.

PEANUTBUTTER & JANE

617 Hudson St (at 12th St)   212/620-7952
Mon-Sat: 10:30-7; Sun: 11-6

A friend describes this store as "very Village." In addition to a varied and fun selection of clothing, it carries funky things like ruby slippers for children, leather jackets for toddlers, and wonderfully imaginative dress-up clothes. Indeed, almost everything is unique to the store. Unlike a lot of children's clothing stores in which older children wouldn't be caught dead, Peanutbutter & Jane appeals both to teenagers and their younger siblings. You'll find a few select toys as well.

SPACE KIDDETS

46 E 21st St (bet Fifth and Madison Ave)   212/420-9878
Mon-Tues, Fri: 10-6; Wed, Thurs: 10-7; Sat: 10-5:30

This cheerful store is overflowing with funky children's clothes, shoes, and accessories. It has been around for a long time but somehow always feels fresh and fun. The prices may seems a bit high if you're from out-of-town, but they're downright reasonable compared to some of the boutiques in trendier neighborhoods. Moreover, the sales staff is welcoming and helpful. Clothing for little boys and girls can be found on street level in the main store, while clothing for preteens is located upstairs through a separate entrance.

Z'BABY
996 Lexington Ave (at 72nd St)   212/472-2229
100 W 72nd St (at Columbus Ave)   212/579-2229
Mon-Sat: 10-7; Sun: 12-5

I am not a fan of the haughty, mostly French boutiques on the Upper East Side, but this one—with stores on both the East Side and West Side—is different. The clothes and shoes, culled from lines in Italy, France, and the U.S., are overpriced, and the staff, particularly at the East Side location, can be disinterested in customers who don't look like they have big bucks to spend. But the clothes are great, the selection is wide and varied, and the stores are well designed. For these reasons, I've made an exception and included Z'Baby. Clothes for girls run from newborn to size 16, while boys' sizes go up to 10. If your teenage girl has outgrown Z'Baby, try **Z'Girl** (976 Lexington Ave, 212/879-4990).

Children's — Used

CHILDREN'S RESALE
303 E 81st St (bet First and Second Ave)   212/734-8897
Mon-Fri: 11-7; Sat: 10-6; Sun: 12-5

This newcomer to the children's consignment-store scene is brimming with good-quality used clothing, toys, games, strollers, and the like. Things for babies and toddlers are upstairs, while children's clothes from size 7 to 12 are down the steep back steps. If you don't have kids in tow, you might want to step across the street to the store's big sister, **Designer Resale** (324 E 81st St, 212/734-3639).

GOOD-BYES
230 E 78th St (bet Second and Third Ave)   212/794-2301
Mon-Fri: 11:30-5:15; Sat: 12-5

This comfortable, inviting and friendly little place on a largely residential street is a great relief from the upscale snobbery of nearby boutiques. In addition to clothing (up to size 8, although the focus is on younger ones), Good-Byes carries strollers, car seats, bassinets, toys, and the range of items that go along with having a baby or small children. Everything is high quality and in good condition, the service is very personal and attentive, and prices are a fraction of those at retail stores. If you're interested in selling clothing or equipment, call first for an appointment.

JANE'S EXCHANGE
207 Ave A (bet 12th and 13th St)   212/674-6268
Mon-Fri: 10-6; Sat, Sun: 12-6

Hands down, this is the best (and most friendly) children's consignment store around. In a spacious spot just south of Stuyvesant Town, Jane's carries a wide selection of baby's, toddler's, and children's clothing and shoes, as well as maternity clothes, strollers, cribs, and other such equipment. The prices are good, the store is wonderfully well organized, and the welcoming atmosphere makes you want to pause and have a cup of tea. Consignments are by appointment only.

Costumes

ABRACADABRA
19 W 21st St (bet Fifth Ave and Ave of the Americas) 212/627-5194
Mon-Sat: 11-7   www.abracadabrasuperstore.com

Abracadabra can transform you into almost anything! They rent and sell costumes, provide theme-oriented needs, offer costume accessories, magician's supplies, theatrical makeup, and stock props for magic tricks. It is a gagster's heaven! Free magic shows are given on Saturday afternoon.

HALLOWEEN ADVENTURE
104 Fourth Ave (bet 11th and 12th St)   212/673-4546
Mon-Sat: 11-8; Sun: 12-7 (extended hours at Halloween time)
www.halloweenadventure.com

Your kids will be the talk of the neighborhood after a visit here. You'll find wigs, costumes for adults and kids, hats, gags, magic items, props, and all manner of games and novelties. In addition, a professional makeup artist is on hand most of the time.

PARAMOUNT
52 W 29th St (bet Broadway and Ave of the Americas) 212/696-9664
Mon-Fri: 9-5

Crowns, tiaras, headpieces, false teeth, wigs, beards, eyepatches, eyelashes, swords, fake blood—name the prop or theatrical accessory, and chances are good this fading old store sells it either singly or by the dozen. The collection of masks is extensive.

Furs

FURS BY DIMITRIOS
130 W 30th St (bet Ave of the Americas and Seventh Ave)
Mon-Fri: 9-6; Sat: 9-4 (Sun: 10-4, winter only)   212/695-8469

This store is the best source for men's fur coats at wholesale prices. The racks are shaggy with furs of all descriptions and sizes for both genders. Prices are wholesale but go up slightly if the garment has to be specially ordered. This shouldn't be necessary, though, since the high-quality off-the-rack selection is the most extensive in the city.

G. MICHAEL HENNESSY FURS
345 Seventh Ave (bet 29th and 30th St), 5th floor   212/695-7991
Mon-Fri: 9:30-5; Sat: by appointment

Fur lovers should get to know Michael Hennessy and his wife, Rubye, a former fashion editor. Like Hennessy cognac, Hennessy furs are famous worldwide. The label assures you of superior pelts, great designs, and the lowest possible prices. Their showroom in the wholesale fur district stocks hundreds of furs ranging from highly coveted minks and sables to sporty boutique furs and shearlings. You'll find all the newest fashion looks, colors, shapes, and techniques. A spectacular Italian fur collection is exclusive to Hennessy. Today's fur technology is evident in skillfully executed sheared and grooved minks, "double-face" reversible styles, and furs that weigh next to nothing but still keep you warm. No wonder the Hennessys command such a large international following. While this is a sizable company, Michael, Rubye, or one of the Hennessy sons is always on hand to assist you.

GUS GOODMAN
345 Seventh Ave (bet 29th and 30th St), 16th floor   212/244-7422
Mon-Fri: 10-5; Sat: 10-2 (Sat by appointment in summer)

Since 1918, the Goodmans have been creating fine fur styles. Father Gus and sons David and Mark are continuing the family tradition, offering a quality collection of fur-lined and reversible fur coats and jackets for men and women. You may choose from an array of furs, including mink, sheared mink, and fine sables. Your out-of-date or unused fur coats can be brought back to life with a new all-weather design. The Goodmans have introduced a custom cashmere knit collection under the label Buonuomo ("good man"), made in an Italian cashmere factory and trimmed with luxurious furs. Additionally, they have developed an innovative line of fur accessories, including scarves, collars, and handbags. Goodman has a full-time staff designer specializing in custom designs.

HARRY KIRSHNER AND SON
307 Seventh Ave (bet 27th and 28th St)   212/243-4847
Mon-Fri: 9-6; Sat: 10-5

Kirshner should be one of your first stops for any kind of fur product, from throw pillows to full-length mink coats. They re-line, clean, alter, and store any fur at rock-bottom prices. They are neither pushy nor snobbish. Harry Kirshner offers tours of the factory. If nothing appeals to a customer, a staff member will design a coat to specifications. Often, however, the factory offers a collection of restored secondhand furs in perfect and fashionable condition. Many customers come in for a new fur and walk out with a slightly worn one for a fraction of what they expected to spend.

LIBRA LEATHER
259 W 30th St (bet Seventh and Eighth Ave)   212/695-3114
Daily: 8:30-6:30

For over a half century this family-owned business has been the ultimate source for fashion fur and leather skins. You'll find leather, suede, and shearling skins for home furnishings, women's and men's better clothing, and accessory items such as bags, belts, and shoes. The inventory is enormous, with quality skins from Italy, France, and Spain, and the staff is multilingual.

RITZ FURS
107 W 57th St (bet Ave of the Americas and Seventh Ave)
Mon-Sat: 9-6 (closed Sat in July);   212/265-4559
Sun: 11-5 (Nov-Jan)   www.ritzfurs.com

For luxurious furs at affordable prices, no one beats the Ritz! Famous for great prices for over half a century, the Ritz is New York's department store for fur. Styles run from contemporary to classic, fun to funky, and include mink, sable, fox, lynx, and more. They offer an ever-changing variety of one-of-a-kind designer furs, luxurious shearlings, and fur-lined and fur-trimmed outerwear. In addition, the Ritz has one of New York's largest selections of previously owned luxury furs at good savings. The Ritz takes gently used furs on consignment and occasionally buys them outright. The experienced, multilingual staff offers personal service.

Hosiery

FOGAL
510 Madison Ave (at 53rd St)   212/355-3254
Mon-Sat: 10-6:30   www.fogal.com

Before Fogal came to New York from Switzerland, the thought of a Madison Avenue boutique devoted to hosiery was, well, foreign. But since opening in 1982, it's hard to imagine Manhattan without it. If it's fashionable and different leg wear you're after, Fogal has it. Plain hosiery comes in nearly 100 hues, at last count; the designs and patterns make the number of choices almost incalculable. You might say that Fogal has a leg up on the competition! Also carried at Fogal are lingerie, bodywear, and men's socks.

LOUIS CHOCK
74 Orchard St (bet Broome and Grand St)   212/473-1929
Sun-Thurs: 9-5; Fri: 9-1   www.chockcatalog.com

It's hard to find a classification for this store. It seems to stock a little of everything, but perhaps the old-fashioned term "dry goods" best sums it up. Louis Chock sells dry goods for the home, school, and entire family from some of the nation's best: Berkshire, Burlington, Carter's, Calvin Klein, Hanes, Duofold, and Munsingwear. They specialize in hosiery and underwear. Children's nightwear is available in a large choice of colors and sizes, and the hosiery section stocks something for every member of the family. Furthermore, everything in the store is sold at a discount that begins at 25%. An even larger discount is given on quantity purchases. Louis Chock also has a mail-order department, offering a 25% to 30% discount on everything in stock. A catalog can be obtained for $2 (refundable with first order).

Leather

BARBARA SHAUM
60 E 4th St (bet Bowery and Second Ave)   212/254-4250
Wed-Sat: 1-6

Barbara Shaum does magical things with leather. She's a wonder with sandals, bags, sterling-silver buckles, belts (with handmade brass, nickel-silver, inlaid wood, and copper buckles), jewelry, attaché cases, and briefcases. Everything is designed in the shop, and Shaum meticulously crafts each item using only the finest materials. She is regularly featured in leading fashion magazines.

Men's and Women's—General

AVIREX
652 Broadway (bet Bleecker and Bond St)   212/254-4000
Mon-Sat: 11-7; Sun: 12-6   www.avirex.com

This is a fascinating store for folks who travel. A fabulous collection of flight jackets, varsity leather jackets, motorcycle jackets, T-shirts, coveralls, sweaters, insignias, watches, bags, flight suits, and gift items is available.

BALLANTYNE CASHMERE
965 Madison Ave (bet 75th and 76th St)   212/988-5252
Mon-Sat: 10-6

At this shop, every possible type of cashmere clothing from all over the world is available. Weights vary, making it possible to wear cashmere year-round. The styles vary as well, reflecting different lifestyles. There's clothing for men and women, as well as cashmere throws for the home. A visit here will make cashmere a necessity in one's life!

CO-OP BARNEY'S NEW YORK
236 W 18th St (bet Seventh and Eighth Ave)   212/593-7800
Mon-Fri: 11-8; Sat: 11-7; Sun: 12-6   www.barneys.com

You will find the same merchandise at the co-op that is sold on the upper two floors of Barney's Uptown. There are T-shirts and jeans, shoes, men's and women's clothes, and the usual Barney's look in sportswear. For those who can't miss a Barney's warehouse sale, this space will be used for those twice-yearly events.

DAFFY'S
111 Fifth Ave (at 18th St)   212/529-4477
Mon-Sat: 10-9; Sun: 12-7

335 Madison Ave (at 44th St)   212/557-4422
Mon-Fri: 8-8; Sat, Sun: 10-6:30

1311 Broadway (at 34th St)   212/736-4477
Mon-Fri: 10-9; Sat: 10-8; Sun: 11-6

462 Broadway (at Grand St)   212/334-7444
Mon-Fri: 11-8; Sat: 11-9; Sun: 12-6

125 E 57th St (bet Lexington and Park Ave)   212/376-4477
Mon-Fri: 10-8; Sat: 10-7; Sun: 12-6

1775 Broadway (at 57th St)   212/294-4477
Mon-Fri: 9-8:30; Sat: 10-7; Sun: 11-6

Daffy's describes itself as a bargain clothing outlet for millionaires. Since a lot of folks got to be millionaires by saving money, perhaps Daffy's has something going for them! Great bargains can be found in better clothing (including unusual European imports) for men, women, and children. Fine leather items are a specialty. This is not your usual "off-price" store, as they have done things with a bit of flair.

FILENE'S BASEMENT
2222 Broadway (at 79th St)   212/873-8000
Mon-Sat: 9:30-9; Sun: 11-7

620 Ave of the Americas (at 18th St)   212/620-3100
Mon-Sat: 9:30-9; Sun: 11-7   www.filenesbasement.com

Anyone who has shopped in Boston knows the name Filene's Basement, recognized for outstanding bargains. Well, Filene's is also in New York, offering great bargains in brand-name goods for misses and men. The store claims 30% to 60% savings. Sometimes it's more and sometimes less, but you can always depend on the quality. The store is easy to shop in, and there are huge stocks of merchandise in every category.

H&M

640 Fifth Ave (at 51st St)	212/489-0390
Mon-Sat: 10-9; Sun: 11-7	
1328 Broadway (at 34th St)	646/473-1164
Mon-Sat: 10-9; Sun: 11-8	
558 Broadway (bet Prince and Spring St)	212/343-2722
Mon-Sat: 10-9; Sun: 11-8	
435 Seventh Ave (at 34th St)	212/643-6955
Mon-Sat: 10-9; Sun: 11-7	www.hm.com

From the day it opened, H&M has been packing them in, and it's no secret why! In a convivial atmosphere, up-to-date clothing and accessories for the young (and those who want to remember their carefree days) can be found at very reasonable prices. Don't come here for pricey labels; what you will find are knockoffs of merchandise that sells for much more at boutiques and department stores. The Swedes have a winner, and they have learned quickly that American yuppies like nothing better than to fill their closets with clothing that doesn't cost very much. This is the place to get it!

HARLEM UNDERGROUND

2027 Fifth Ave (at 125th St)	212/987-9385
Mon-Thurs: 10-7; Fri, Sat: 10-8	www.harlemunderground.com

This is a good stop for comfortable, reasonably priced, and "cool" urban wear. The merchandise has the feel of the historic area it represents. Personal or corporate embroidery is available for denim shirts and jackets, T-shirts, sweats, and caps.

HOUSE OF MAURIZIO

18 E 53rd St (bet Fifth and Madison Ave), 5th floor	212/759-3230
Mon-Fri: 9-5	

Tony Maurizio caters to men and women who like the functional and fashionable tailored look of suits. Although almost any kind of garment can be copied, this house is known for coats, two- to four-piece suits, and mix-and-match combinations. This look is favored by busy executives, artists, and journalists who have to look well-dressed but don't have hours to spend dressing. House of Maurizio's tailors create blazers or suits in a range of 2,000 fabrics, and those in silk, linen, cotton, and solid virgin wool are sensational. In addition to women's garments, they can design and create coats and suits for men in the same broad range of fabrics. Tony promises fast service, expert tailoring, and moderate prices.

JEFFREY—NEW YORK

449 W 14th St (bet Ninth and Tenth Ave)	212/206-1272
Mon-Wed, Fri: 10-8; Thurs: 10-9; Sat: 10:30-7; Sun: 12:30-6	

Jeffrey Kalinsky's store is a breath of fresh air in the Meatpacking District. It offers men's and women's clothing and accessories (with a big emphasis on shoes). His Atlanta operation has been very successful, and now he's brought such fashion names as Prada, Gucci, Manolo Blahnik, Yves St. Laurent, and Burberry to downtown Manhattan. It's worth checking out!

LANGUAGE
238 Mulberry St (bet Spring and Prince St)   212/431-5566
Mon-Wed, Fri, Sat: 11-7; Thurs: 11-8; Sun: 12-6

www.language-nyc.com

For those who want to be first among their friends with merchandise from the hottest new designers, this is *the* spot to visit! International up-and-comers with the latest fashions, furniture, and fashion accessories are showcased here.

POLO—RALPH LAUREN
867 Madison Ave (at 72nd St)   212/606-2100
379 West Broadway (bet Spring and Broome St)   212/625-1660
Mon-Sat: 10-7; Thurs: 10-7; Sun: 12-5   www.polo.com

Ralph Lauren has captured the mood of the times, and I admit to being a fan. He has probably done as much as anyone to bring a classic look to American fashion and furnishings. His showcase store in Manhattan, housed in the magnificent remodeled Rhinelander mansion, is fabulous. Four floors of merchandise for men, women, and the home are beautifully displayed and expertly accessorized. You will see a much larger selection here than in the many specialty Polo boutiques in department stores. There are several things to be aware of, however. One is the above-it-all way some of the staff greet customers who don't look like they have big bucks to spend. Moreover, although the clothes and furnishings are stylish and classy, one can find items of equal or better quality elsewhere at considerably lower prices. But shopping elsewhere is not nearly as stylish as carrying out your item in one of those popular green bags. That little monogrammed horse says something about your taste and lifestyle! **Polo Sport** (888 Madison Ave, 212/606-2100), also done with class and flair, is across the street. There is also a Soho outlet.

REPLAY STORE
109 Prince St (at Greene St)   212/673-6300
Mon-Sat: 11-7; Sun: 11-6

This very attractive Soho store carries 25 different washings and fits in jeans and more than 45 shirt styles. Outdoor clothing is featured. Downstairs, a cafe will take care of hunger pangs. This is one of the better-stocked stores in the area, and prices are as comfortable as the merchandise.

SMAAK
219 Mulberry St (bet Prince and Spring St)   212/219-0504
Mon-Wed, Sun: 11-7; Thurs-Sat: 11-8   www.smaak.com

Owner Susannah Gaterud-Mack tells me that SMAAK means "taste" in Swedish and Dutch. The word is appropriate, for her shop offers an eclectic mixture of international designer clothing for men and women, sportswear, and separates. One thing is certain: you won't see similar merchandise elsewhere in Manhattan.

Men's Formal Wear

JACK AND COMPANY FORMAL WEAR
128 E 86th St (bet Lexington and Park Ave)   212/722-4609
Mon-Fri: 10-7; Sat: 10-4   www.jacktuxedos.com

Jack and Company rents and sells men's ready-to-wear formal wear. They carry an excellent selection of sizes and names (After Six and Lord West), and they've had a good reputation for service since 1925. In sales or rentals, Jack's can supply head-to-toe formal wear. The staff is excellent at matching outfits to customers, as well as knowing exactly what is socially required for any occasion. Same-day service is available, and the full rental price will be applied toward purchase!

ZELLER TUXEDOS
201 E 23rd St (at Third Ave), 2nd floor
459 Lexington Ave (at 45th St), 3rd floor
1010 Third Ave (at 60th St)
421 Seventh Ave (at 33rd St), 2nd floor
212/355-0707 (for store hours and information)

Zeller does an excellent job of providing sales and rentals of ladies' and gentlemen's formal wear. You'll find tuxedos, formal shirts, and accessories for all occasions. The brand names are worthy of an Academy Awards night: Kenneth Cole, Valentino, Calvin Klein, Joseph Aboud, Bill Blass, Hugo Boss, Mani by Giorgio Armani, and more. They also provide courier service to hotels for guests and emergency rentals.

Men's—General

CAMOUFLAGE
141 Eighth Ave (at 17th St)   212/741-9118
Mon-Fri: 12-7; Sat: 11:30-6:30; Sun: 12-6

At Camouflage you'll find men's branded clothing, plus private-label trousers, shirts, ties, and accessories. Prices range from reasonable (their chinos are one of the best buys in the city) to good, considering some of the pricey designer names. Camouflage has the ability to dress customers with a dignified but unique look. Clothing from Camouflage definitely won't blend into the wallpaper!

EISENBERG AND EISENBERG
16 W 17th St (bet Fifth Ave and Ave of the Americas)   212/627-1290
Mon-Wed, Fri: 9-6; Thurs: 9-7; Sat: 9-5; Sun: 10-4
www.eisenbergandeisenberg.com

The Eisenberg and Eisenberg style is a classic one that dates from 1898. E&E consistently offers top quality and good prices on suits, tuxedos, coats, and sportswear. They also stock outerwear, slacks, name-brand raincoats, cashmere sport jackets, and 100% silk jackets. All are sold at considerable discounts, and alterations are available. London Fog coats are featured, and no label is better known for wet-weather needs.

FACONNABLE OF NEW YORK
689 Fifth Ave (at 54th St)   212/319-0111
Mon-Wed, Fri, Sat: 10-7; Thurs: 10-8; Sun: 12-6
www.faconnable.com

Facconable (a French outfit) has made a name for itself in the fashion world with clothes that appeal to conservative dressers. Their New York store—which admittedly does not match the class or selection of the Beverly Hills shop—carries a good showing of men's sportswear, tailored clothing, watches, and suits.

J. PRESS
7 E 44th St (bet Fifth and Madison Ave)   212/687-7642
Mon-Sat: 9-6   www.jpressonline.com

As one of New York's classic conservative men's stores, J. Press takes pride in its sense of timelessness. Its salespeople, customers, and attitude have changed little from the time of the founder. Styles are impeccable and distinguished. Blazers are blue, and shirts are button-down and straight. Even in the days when button-down collars were out, they never went away at J. Press.

L.S. MEN'S CLOTHING
49 W 45th St (bet Fifth Ave and Ave of the Americas), 3rd floor
Mon-Thurs: 9-7; Fri: 9-3; Sun: 10-4   212/575-0933
                                                      www.lsmensclothing.com

L.S. Men's Clothing bills itself as "the executive discount shop," but I would go further and call them a must for fashion-minded businessmen. For one thing, the expanded midtown location means one needn't trek down to Fifth Avenue in the teens, which is the main area for men's discount clothing. Better still, as owner Israel Zuber puts it, "There are many stores selling $400 suits at discount, but we are one of the few in mid-Manhattan that discount the $550 to $1,500 range of suits." The main attraction, though, is the tremendous selection of executive-class styles. Within that category, a man could outfit himself almost entirely at L.S. Natural, soft-shoulder suits by name designers are available in all sizes. A custom-order department is available, with over 2,500 bolts of Italian and English goods in stock. Custom-made suits take four to six weeks and sell for around $595; sport coats are priced at $445. This is one of the very best spots for top-drawer names. I would make it number one on my midtown shopping itinerary.

NAPOLEON
Trump Plaza
1048 Third Ave (at 62nd St)   212/308-3000
Mon-Fri: 10-6:30; Sat: 10-6

Plaza Hotel
768 Fifth Ave (at 59th St), lobby   212/759-8000
Mon-Sat: 10-6   www.napoleonfashions.com

Napoleon carries clothes fit for a king—at kingly prices, too! You will find an extensive selection of handmade suits and jackets with high-fashion Italian tailoring in luxurious fabrics of cashmere and wool. Many are exclusive to this house. Great-looking shirts (they should be at those prices!) are cut from the finest Egyptian cottons. Leather goods by Zilli, handmade shoes of exotic skins and leathers, and a good showing of evening wear and accessories round out the appeal of this shop, where informed, professional service is the norm.

PAUL STUART
Madison Ave at 45th St   212/682-0320
Mon, Tues, Wed, Fri: 8-6:30; Thurs: 8-7; Sat: 9-6; Sun: 12-5
                                                      www.paulstuart.com

This is the store for shoppers who don't really know what they want, have trouble putting things together to make a "look," and worry about quality. You would be hard-pressed to find a better selection of men's and women's fine apparel and accessories. One drawback: there is little excitement here, either in the presentation or merchandise. Nonetheless, the men's suits, ties, and sport jackets are first-class, as is the collection of handmade English shoes.

ROTHMAN'S
200 Park Ave S (at 17th St)   212/777-7400
Mon-Wed, Fri: 10-7; Thurs: 10-8; Sat: 9:30-6; Sun: 12-5:30
www.rothmansny.com

Forget your image of the old Harry Rothman operation. Harry's grandson, Ken Giddon, runs this classy men's store, which offers a huge selection of quality clothes at discounts of up to 40% in a contemporary and comfortable atmosphere. He carries top names like Canali, Hickey-Freeman, Corneliani, Joseph Aboud, Calvin Klein, and Valentino. Sizes at Rothman's range from 36 to 50 in regular, short, long, and extra long. Raincoats, slacks, sport jackets, and accessories are stocked at the same attractive prices.

SAINT LAURIE MERCHANT TAILORS
22 W 32nd St (bet Fifth Ave and Ave of the Americas), 5th floor
Mon-Fri: 9-6; Sat: 9-5:30   212/643-1916
www.saintlaurie.com

Saint Laurie has been in business since 1913—that's four generations!—offering good-looking, made-to-measure clothing for men and women at rack prices. A laser body scanner insures accurate measurements. The firm buys directly from the weavers, resulting in some price savings. In addition, the showroom is located where the clothing is made, shortening delivery time to two weeks.

For gentlemen who don't want to pay uptown prices or don't like the haughty airs of uptown salesmen, here are some suggestions for shopping downtown:

Alife (178 Orchard St, 646/654-0628): shoes, T-shirts, sweatshirts
Memes (3 Great Jones St, 212/420-9955): cool and casual clothes
Seize Sur Vingt (243 Elizabeth St, 212/343-0476): ritzy, custom-made suits, shirts, and sweaters in beautiful fabrics from Scotland and Italy
Stussy (140 Wooster St, 212/995-8787): for the hip set
Urns (226 Elizabeth St, 212/431-5533): colorful sweaters
Vice (252 Lafayette St, 212/219-7788): shoes and shirts in an intimate, attitude-free setting

---

Men's Hats

J.J. HAT CENTER
310 Fifth Ave (at 32nd St)   212/239-4368, 800/622-1911
Mon-Fri: 9-6; Tues, Wed, Fri, Sat: 9:30-5:30   www.jjhatcenter.com

This outfit stocks over 15,000 pieces of major-brand hat and caps (to size 8) from all over the world. Founded in 1911, it is New York's oldest hat shop. Special services include free brush-up, hat stretching or tightening, custom orders, and a free catalog.

Men's Shirts

MARK CHRISTOPHER
55 W 26th St (bet Broadway and Ave of the Americas), 35th floor
Mon-Fri: 11-8; Sat: 12-7; Sun: 12-6 (by appointment)   212/686-9190
www.markchristophercustomshirts.com

When it comes to custom shirts for well-dressed executives or upwardly mobile types aspiring to the big time, manager Mark Lingley is the guy to see. The classy shirts at Mark Christopher are made of fine cotton and hand-cut with superb tailoring. You pay for such special merchandise, but the service (they will make office calls) and care (the typical shirt requires about 20 measurements for a fitting) are worth the extra bucks. Shirts are the foundation of the operation, but suits and ties are also available.

SHIRT STORE
51 E 44th St (bet Vanderbilt and Madison Ave)   212/557-8040
Mon-Fri: 8-6:30; Sat: 10-5   www.shirtstore.com

The attraction here is that you buy directly from the manufacturer, so there's no middle man to increase the price. The Shirt Store offers all-cotton shirts for men, from the smallest (14x32) to the largest (18½x37). Although the ready-made stock is great, they will also do custom work and even come to your office with swatches. Additional services include mail-order, alterations, and monogramming.

STATS
331 W 57th St (bet Eighth and Ninth Ave), Suite 280   22/262-5844
Mon-Fri: 8-7; weekends by appointment

What does STATS stand for? Shirts, ties and terrific service, of course! Julie Mains sells custom dress and casual shirts, neckwear, braces, and accessories in the private convenience of one's office or home. She carries tailoring tools and fabrics, and can do special orders for fabrics not in stock. Appointments can be made at any time to suit your busy schedule. She also takes the extra step of a sample shirt fitting.

Men's Ties

GOIDEL NECKWEAR
138 Allen St (bet Rivington and Delancey St)   212/475-7332
Sun-Fri: 9:30-3

Since 1935 this has been the place for bargains on ties, cummerbunds, men's jewelry, and accessories. They triple as manufacturers, wholesalers, and retailers, so savings are passed on to customers. Special note to groups: these folks will match most items brought in, usually within a week or two.

Men's Underwear

UNDER WARES
210 E 58th St (bet Second and Third Ave)   212/838-1200
Mon-Fri: 10-7; Sat: 10-6; Sun: 12-5   800/237-8641
www.underwaresforhim.com

It used to be the average fellow couldn't tell you what kind of underwear he wore and probably didn't buy it himself. All that changed when ads began featuring celebrity jocks. These days men's underwear makes a fashion statement. Under Wares sells over a hundred styles of briefs and boxer shorts. They stock the largest selection of men's undergarments in the world, carrying many top labels. There are also T-shirts, hosiery, robes, pajamas, workout wear, swimwear, and gift items. You can browse and order from their website, too.

Men's Western Wear

BILLY MARTIN'S
220 E 60th St (bet Second and Third Ave)   212/861-3100
Mon-Fri: 10-7; Sat: 10-6; Sun: 12-5 (Oct-Dec)   www.billymartin.com

If Western wear is on your shopping list, Billy Martin's has a great selection of deerskin jackets, shirts, riding pants, skirts, hats, and parkas. They also boast one of the best collections of cowboy boots in the city for men and women. Great accessory items like bandannas, jewelry, sterling-silver buckles, and belt straps complete the outfit. The items are well-tooled, well-designed, and priced accordingly.

Resale Clothing

ALLAN & SUZI
416 Amsterdam Ave (at 80th St)   212/724-7445
Mon-Sun: 12-7   www.allanandsuzi.net

This "retro clothing store" is quite an operation! Under one roof you'll find current designer and vintage clothing for men and women, old and new shoes, and accessories. There are big names (like Galliano, Lacroix, Ungaro, and Versace) and new ones you haven't heard of. Some outfits are discounted. They are proud of the fact that they dress a number of Hollywood and TV personalities. Ask for Allan Pollack or Suzi Kandel.

DESIGNER RESALE
324 E 81st St (bet First and Second Ave)   212/734-3639
Mon-Wed, Fri: 11-7; Thurs: 11-8; Sat: 10-6; Sun: 12-5
www.resaleclothing.org

"Gently worn" is the byword here! Designer Resale offers previously owned ladies' designer clothing and accessories at moderate prices. Most major fashion names are represented. You might find Chanel, Armani, Hermes, or Valentino garments on the racks. If items do not sell, prices are marked down further. Call to ask about the latest bargains. Two related operations close by offer quality resale clothing, **Gentleman's Resale** (322 E 81st St, 212/734-2739) and **Children's Resale** (303 E 81st St, 212/ 734-8897).

ENCORE
1132 Madison Ave (bet 84th and 85th St), upstairs   212/879-2850
Mon-Wed, Fri: 10:30-6:30; Thurs: 10:30-7:30; Sat: 10:30-6;
Sun: 12-6 (closed Sun in July and Aug)   www.encoreresale.com

Because it is so chic and select, Encore can honestly be billed as a "resale shop of gently worn clothing of designer/couture quality." When one sees the merchandise and clientele at this shop, you'll see why. For one thing, it is a consignment boutique, not a charity thrift shop. Its donors receive a portion of the sales price, and according to owner Carole Selig, many of the donors are socialites and other luminaries who don't want to be seen in the same outfit twice. Selig can afford to be picky, and so can you. The fashions are up-to-date and are sold at 50% to 70% off original retail prices. There are over 6,000 items in stock. Prices range from reasonable to astronomical—but just think how much they sold for originally!

Thrift Shops

Chelsea
Housing Works Thrift Shop (143 W 17th St, 212/366-0820)

East 20s
City Opera Thrift Shop (222 E 23rd St, 212/684-5344)
Goodwill Superstore (220 E 23rd St, 212/447-7270)
Marble Thrift Shop (382 Third Ave, 212/532-5136)
Housing Works Thrift Shop (157 E 23rd St, 212/529-5955)
Salvation Army Thrift Store (212 E 23rd St, 212/532-8115)
St. George's Thrift Shop (61 Gramercy Park N; 212/475-2674)

Upper East Side
Arthritis Foundation Thrift Shop (121 E 77th St, 212/772-8816)
Bis Designer Resale (1134 Madison Ave, 2nd floor, 212/396-2760)
Cancer Care Thrift Shop (1480 Third Ave, 212/879-9868)
Council Thrift Shop (246 E 84th St, 212/439-8373)
Housing Works Thrift Shop (202 E 77th St, 212/772-8461)
Kavanagh's (146 E 49th St, 212/702-0152)
Memorial Sloan-Kettering Thrift Shop (1440 Third Ave, 212/535-1250)
Michael's (1041 Madison Ave, 212/737-7273)
Out of the Closet Thrift Shop (220 E 81st St, 212/472-3573)
Spence-Chapin Thrift Shop (1473 Third Ave, 212/737-8448)
Stuyvesant Square Thrift Shop (1704 Second Ave, 212/831-1830)

West Side
Housing Works Thrift Shop (306 Columbus Ave, 212/579-7566)

GENTLEMEN'S RESALE
322 E 81st St (bet First and Second Ave)   212/734-2739
Mon-Fri: 11-7; Sat: 10-6; Sun: 12-5   www.resaleclothing.org

Gentlemen interested in top-quality designer suits, jackets, and sportswear now have a place where they can save a bundle. Shopping here is like a treasure hunt, and that is half the fun. Imagine picking up a $1,000 Armani suit for $200! You might also earn a few extra bucks by consigning some of your own wardrobe.

KAVANAGH'S
146 E 49th St (bet Third and Lexington Ave)   212/702-0152
Tues-Fri: 11-6; Sat: 11-4

I can vouch highly for this designer resale shop! It is owned by Mary Kavanagh, whom I had the pleasure of knowing and working with at Bergdorf Goodman. She has superb taste! As former director of personal shopping, she had access to the finest labels in the world. At Kavanagh's she carries many of those same labels: Chanel, Versace, Valentino, Ungaro, Armani, Galanos, Beene, Bill Blass, Oscar de la Renta, and many more. Chanel clothes and accessories are a specialty. Mary describes her store as a "sunny, happy spot filled with attractive antiques." It is a classy shopping haven where customers come first. Moreover, she will open early, stay late, or open on Sunday for special groups.

MICHAEL'S, THE CONSIGNMENT SHOP FOR WOMEN
1041 Madison Ave (at 79th St)　　　　　　　　212/737-7273
Mon-Wed, Fri, Sat: 9:30-6; Thurs: 9:30-8
　　　　　　　　　　　　　　　　www.michaelsconsignment.com

Is your mouth watering for one of those gowns you have seen in the papers or on TV? Do you think you could look like one of the stars? Here's the place to come for pieces from top designers like Chanel, Prada, Gucci, Hermes, YSL, Dolce and Gabanna, Armani, and others. Personal attention is assured, and prices are right.

TATIANA
111 St Mark's Pl (bet First Ave and Ave A)　　　212/755-7744
Mon-Fri: 11-7; Sat: 11-6　　　　　　　　　　　www.tatianas.com

This is a unique designer consignment boutique outlet. For consigners, Tatiana offers free estimates and pickup service. For retail customers, she will try to find whatever ouffit they may want. The stock is top-grade, with clothing, jewelry, bags, shoes, hats, and furs bearing some of the best names: Chanel, Gucci, Valentino, Armani, YSL, Versace, and Bill Blass.

Shoes—Children's

EAST SIDE KIDS
1298 Madison Ave (bet 92nd and 93rd St)　　　　212/360-5000
Mon-Fri: 9:30-6; Sat: 9-6

East Side Kids stocks footwear items up to a woman's size 10 and a man's size 9. They can accommodate older children and juniors, plus adults with small to more or less average-sized feet. Of course, there is also a great selection of children's shoes in both domestic and imported styles. Frequent-buyer cards are kept on file for special discounts. The store is known for helpful service.

LITTLE ERIC SHOES
1331 Third Ave (at 76th St)　　　　　　　　　　212/288-8987
Mon-Sat: 10-6; Sun: 12-5
1118 Madison Ave (at 83rd St)　　　　　　　　　212/717-1513
Mon-Sat: 10-6; Sun: 12-5

This is the place to find shoes for your small fry. They are comfy, with many lined in soft leather. You'll note that most of the "in" styles are made in Italy. The staff are just as colorful as the shoes they sell!

SHOOFLY
465 Amsterdam Ave (bet 82nd and 83rd St)　　　212/580-4390
42 Hudson St (bet Duane and Thomas St)　　　　212/406-3270
Mon-Sat: 11-7; Sun: 12-6　　　　　　　　　　　www.shooflynyc.com

Shoofly carries attractive and reasonably priced imported shoes for infants to 14-year-olds. Lots of women with tiny feet will appreciate Shoofly's chic selection of footwear as well. Shoofly will take care of your shoewear needs with styles both funky and classic.

Shoes—Family

BUFFALO CHIPS USA
355 West Broadway (bet Broome and Grand St) 212/625-8400
Mon-Sat: 11-7; Sun: 12-6

The best of the West comes East! You'll enjoy the Western ambience of the wall art, Indian and contemporary Western jewelry, leather items, artifacts, pottery, rugs, and blankets from this attractive outlet. Best of all are the unique Western boots, all designed by store personnel. Buffalo Chips can produce custom-made boots in 8 to 12 weeks.

E. VOGEL BOOTS AND SHOES
19 Howard St (one block north of Canal St, bet Broadway and
   Lafayette St) 212/925-2460
Mon-Fri: 8-4; Sat: 8-1:30 (closed Sat in summer and first two weeks
   of July) www.vogelboots.com, www.vogelshoes.com

Hank and Dean Vogel and Jack Lynch are the third and fourth generation family members to join this business since 1879. They will happily fit and supply made-to-measure boots and shoes for any adult who can find the store. Howard is one of those streets that even native New Yorkers don't know exists. Many beat a path to Vogel for top-quality shoes and boots, equestrian boots, personal advice, excellent fittings, and prices that, while not inexpensive, are reasonable for the service involved. Made-to-measure shoes do not always fit properly, but they do at Vogel. Moreover, once your pattern is on record, they can make new shoes without a personal visit. For craftsmanship, this spot is top-drawer. There are more than 500 Vogel dealers throughout the world, but this is the original store, and the people here are super.

KENNETH COLE
597 Broadway (at Houston St) 212/965-0283
353 Columbus Ave (bet 76th and 77th St) 212/873-2061
95 Fifth Ave (at 17th St) 212/675-2550
107 E 42nd St (bet Vanderbilt and Park Ave) 212/949-8079
Mon-Sat: 10-8; Sun: 12-7 www.kennethcole.com

In addition to signs that induce hearty laughter at the expense of some well-known personalities, Kenneth Cole offers quality shoes, belts, scarves, watches, outerwear, and accessories at sensible prices. **Kenneth Cole Reaction** (130 East 57th St, 212/688-1670), a branch location on the East Side, specializes in more casual merchandise.

LORD JOHN'S BOOTERY
428 Third Ave (bet 29th and 30th St) 12/532-2579
Mon-Fri: 10-8; Sat: 10-7 www.lordjohnshootery.com

Lord John's Bootery has been family-owned and operated for three generations, spanning almost 50 years. The store has been renovated and expanded and now carries one of the largest selection of dress, casual, and comfort shoes in the area. They offer footwear for men and women from such manufacturers as Ecco, Mephisto, Paul Green, Rockport, Sebago, Birkenstock, Merrell, Camper, Kenneth Cole, Santana, and Dansko.

T.O. DEY CUSTOM SHOE MAKERS
9 E 38th St (bet Fifth and Madison Ave), 7th floor   212/683-6300
Mon-Fri: 9-5; Sat: 9-12:30   www.todeyshoes.com

T.O. Dey is a solid jack-of-all-trades operation. Though their specialty is custom-made shoes, they also repair any kind of shoe. These folks will create men's or women's shoes based on a plaster mold of a customer's feet. Their styles are limited only by a client's imagination. They make arch supports, cover shoes to match a garment, and sell athletic shoes for football, basketball, cross-country, hockey, boxing, and running.

Shoes—Men's

CHURCH ENGLISH SHOES
689 Madison Ave (at 62nd St)   212/758-5200
Mon-Sat: 10-6   www.churchshoes.com

Anglophiles have a ball here, not only because of the *veddy* English atmosphere but also for the pure artistry and "Englishness" of the shoes. Church has been selling English shoes for men since 1873 and is known for classic styles, superior workmanship, and fine leathers. The styles basically remain unchanged year after year, although new designs are occasionally added as a concession to fashion. All shoes are custom-fitted, and if a style or size does not feel right, they will special-order a pair that does.

McCREEDY AND SCHREIBER
213 E 59th St (bet Second and Third Ave)   212/759-9241
Mon-Sat: 9:30-7; Sun: 12:30-5:30

How about a department store for shoes and boots? McCreedy and Schreiber features Lucchese, Tony Lama, Frye, Justin, and Timberland boots, as well as Bass and Alden shoes. Boots come in sizes up to 15, and prices are competitive.

STAPLETON SHOE COMPANY
68 Trinity Pl (at Rector St)   212/964-6329
Mon-Thurs: 8-6; Fri: 8-5

Their motto is "better shoes for less," but that doesn't begin to cover the superlatives Stapleton deserves. Gentlemen, this is the place to get Bally, Alden, Allen-Edmonds, Cole-Haan, Timberland, Rockport, Johnston & Murphy, and a slew of other top names at discount. Stapleton is located on the same block as the American Stock Exchange, near Ground Zero. There isn't a better source for quality shoes. They are size specialists, carrying men's sizes 5-18 in widths A-EEE.

Shoes—Women's

ANBAR SHOES
60 Reade St (bet Church St and Broadway)   212/227-0253
Mon-Fri: 9-6:30; Sat: 11-6

Bargain hunters, rejoice! Anbar customers can find great deals on brand-name styles at discounts up to 80%. This is a good place to save money.

GIORDANO'S PETITE SHOES
1150 Second Ave (at 60th St)   212/688-7195
Mon-Fri: 11-6:30; Sat: 11-5:30   www.petiteshoes.com

Susan Giordano has a very special clientele. Her store stocks a fine selection of women's designer shoes in small sizes (a range that is nonexistent in regular shoe stores). If you're a woman who wears shoes in the 4 to 5½ medium range, you are probably used to shopping in children's shoe departments or having shoes custom-made, either of which can cramp your style. For these women, Giordano's is a godsend. Brands carried include Anne Klein, Charles Jourdan, Stuart Weitzman, Donald Pliner, and Nickels.

PETER FOX SHOES
105 Thompson St (bet Prince and Spring St)   212/431-7426
Mon-Sat: 11-7; Sun: 12-6

Peter Fox has been the downtown trailblazer for women's shoes. His shop carries only exclusive, limited-edition designer footwear. Perhaps because of the Soho location, Fox's designs seem more adventurous than those of its competitors; the look is younger and more casual. If you're looking for shoes to be seen in, this is the place to go. Bridal and everyday shoes are available.

TALL SIZE SHOES
3 W 35th St (at Fifth Ave)   212/736-2060
Mon-Wed, Fri, Sat: 9:30-6; Thurs: 9:30-7

Finding comfortable shoes if you are a "tall size" is not easy. This store can solve the problem, as they carry a broad selection of shoes to size 14 in widths from AAAA to extra-wide. There are custom-made shoes and designer names to choose from: Nickels, Via Spiga Vanelli, Sesto Meucci, Moda Spana, Costa Blanca, Proxy, and many more. They also have a Cinderella department with a wide selection of shoes from size 4 on up. They will take phone orders and ship anywhere.

If you have large feet, these outfits have shoes that will fit them.
Johnston & Murphy: men's to size 15 (345 Madison Ave and 520 Madison Ave)
Stapleton Shoe Company: men's to size 18 (68 Trinity Pl)
Tall Size Shoes: women's to size 14 (3 W 35th St)

Sportswear

GERRY COSBY AND COMPANY
2 Pennsylvania Plaza (32nd St at Seventh Ave)   212/563-6464
Mon-Fri: 9:30-7:30; Sat: 9:30-6; Sun: 12-5   877/563-6464
www.cosbysports.com

There's a lot to like about this company. Located in the famous Madison Square Garden lobby, they are a professional business in an appropriate venue for "team sportswear"—that is, what athletes wear. Gerry Cosby designs and markets protective equipment and is a top supplier of professionally licensed products. The protective equipment and bags are designed for pros, but are available to the general public as well. They accept mail and phone orders for all, including personalized jerseys and jackets.

HOWARD SPORTSWEAR
85 Orchard St (at Grand St)   212/226-4307
Sun-Fri: 9-5:30

Howard transformed itself from a typical Lower East Side shop into a fashionable boutique without sacrificing the bargain prices. They carry an excellent selection of women's wear, including top names like Hanes, Bali, Vanity Fair, Warners, Maidenform, Wacoal, Olga, Lilyette, and Jockey.

NBA STORE
666 Fifth Ave (at 52nd St)   212/515-6270
Mon-Sat: 10-7; Sun: 11-6

The National Basketball Association does a tremendous job of marketing itself and its teams. This two-story store in a prime tourist location on Fifth Avenue is always busy with people buying team jerseys, watching NBA videos, and eating at the Hang Time Cafe on the lower level.

NIKETOWN NEW YORK
6 E 57th St (bet Fifth and Madison Ave)   212/891-6453
Mon-Sat: 10-8; Sun: 11-7   www.niketown.com

Product innovation and Nike's sports heritage are the foundations of Niketown New York. They offer a huge selection of Nike products, including footwear, apparel, carry gear, items for timing and vision, and hot new tech-lab products. If you don't see your favorite athletes on the giant 36' by 22' video screen, you might find them shopping next to you.

Surplus

KAUFMAN'S ARMY & NAVY
319 W 42nd St (bet Eighth and Ninth Ave)   212/757-5670
Mon-Wed, Fri: 11-6; Thurs: 11-7; Sat: 12-6
                              www.kaufmansarmynavy.com

Kaufman's has long been a favorite among New Yorkers and visitors alike for its extensive selection of genuine military surplus from around the globe. Over the last half-century, Kaufman's has outfitted dozens of Broadway and TV shows and supplied a number of major motion pictures with military garb. The store is a treasure trove of military collectibles, hats, helmets, uniforms, and insignias. Over a thousand military pins, patches, and medals from armies the world over are on display.

Sweaters

BEST OF SCOTLAND
581 Fifth Ave (bet 47th and 48th St), penthouse   212/644-0403
Mon-Sat: 10-6   www.bestofscotlandnyc.com

Two real pluses here: one of the largest collections of cashmere sweaters in the world and competitive prices. There is a big difference between cashmere from Scotland and the Far East. Best of Scotland carries only the best Scottish sweaters, coats and jackets, baby blankets, ladies' capes, scarves, mufflers, and blankets for both men and women. Ladies will find sizes up to 48. Large gentlemen (i.e., those in the 6'6", 300-pound range) will find sweaters up to size 62! A variety of cableknit sweaters is an added attraction. Best of Scotland now offers all 250 colors produced by Todd & Duncan and Z. Hinchliffe & Sons on a custom-order basis.

GRANNY-MADE
381 Amsterdam Ave (bet 78th and 79th St)   212/496-1222
Mon-Fri: 11-7; Sat: 10-6; Sun: 12-5   www.granny-made.com

Michael Rosenberg (grandson of Bert Levy, the namesake "Granny") has assembled an extensive collection of sweaters for infants, young people, and adults. These include handmade sweaters from all over the world, as well as ones hand-loomed right here at home. The selection of women's sweaters, knitwear, suits, dresses, skirts, slacks, soft items, and accessories is unique, as are the men's sweaters and T-shirts. Granny-Made has an extremely service-oriented, knowledgeable staff. They also sell "moon and star" cookies, made from a recipe passed down three generations!

T-Shirts

EISNER BROS.
75 Essex St (bet Grand and Delancey St)   212/475-6868
Mon-Thurs: 8:30-6:30; Fri: 8:30-3; Sun: 8:30-4:30   800/426-7700
www.eisnerbros.com

Eisner Bros. carries a full line of licensed NBA, NFL, NHL, MLB, collegiate, and other character and novelty products in T-shirts and sweat shirts. Major quantity discounts are offered. You will also find police, fire, emergency department logos, as well as Disney and Harley-Davidson. Personalizing is featured on all items. They are the largest source in the area for blank, printable corporate sportswear T-shirts, sweat shirts, caps, jackets, work clothing, uniforms, tote bags, towels, aprons, umbrellas, gym and exercise equipment, team sports outfitting, cheerleading, and much more.

Uniforms

JA-MIL UNIFORMS
92 Orchard St (at Delancey St)   212/677-8190
Mon-Thurs, Sun: 10-5

This is *the* bargain spot for those who wear uniforms and do not want to spend a fortune on work clothes. There are outfits for doctors, nurses, and technicians, as well as the finest domestic uniforms and chef's apparel. Dansks clogs and SAS shoes are available in white and colors. Mail orders are accepted.

Women's Accessories

EURO SPORTS
39 W 29th St (bet Broadway and Ave of the Americas) 212/685-5226
Mon-Thurs: 8-6; Fri: 8-5; Sat: 8-1

Kim Hyuk, Jr., runs an importing company exclusively devoted to handbags. Importing and wholesaling companies are common in this area. What is uncommon is the courtesy and selection Kim gives individual retail customers. She has a knack for making everyone feel like a valued customer and does not take offense when a finicky lady picks through the entire stock in search of the perfect handbag. Besides, it shouldn't be too hard to find, within certain guidelines. "Imported" here usually refers to origins from points west rather than east. Hyuk imports vinyl, canvas, and nylon handbags. Most of this is average, serviceable stuff, but there are a few stars in the line. Prices border on magnificent. Minimum purchase is 12 pieces.

FINE AND KLEIN
119 Orchard St (at Delancey St)   212/674-6720
Sun-Fri: 9-4:30

The finest handbag store for value and selection is not in Rome, Paris, or London. It is not even on Fifth Avenue in New York. It is on the Lower East Side, and the name is Fine and Klein. What a selection! There is a bag for every purpose, any time of day, in every fabric. Top labels are sold for a fraction of what you would pay uptown. In addition, shopping at Fine and Klein is fun. The crowds, especially on Sundays and holidays, are so large that the number allowed to enter must be controlled! My good friends Julius Fine and Murray Klein are the epitome of old-time merchants, and you will be delighted with their service. Tell them I sent you!

SUAREZ
450 Park Ave (bet 56th and 57th St)   212/753-3758
Mon-Fri: 10-6; Sat: 10-5

Suarez has been in business for more than a half-century (three genera-tions). In that time, they have cultivated a reputation for quality merchandise, good service, excellent selection, and reasonable prices. For years the Suarez name has been whispered by women-in-the-know as a resource for fine leather goods. They offer a great selection of exotic skin bags in a wide vari-ety of colors.

Women's—General

BETSEY JOHNSON
248 Columbus Ave (bet 71st and 72nd St)	212/362-3364
138 Wooster St (bet Prince and Houston St)	212/995-5048
251 E 60th St (at Second Ave)	212/319-7699
1060 Madison Ave (at 80th St)	212/734-1257
Hours vary by store	www.betseyjohnson.com

In the 1960s and 1970s, Betsey Johnson was *the* fashion designer. Her designs appeared everywhere, as did Betsey herself. As an outlet for those designs not sold to exclusive boutiques, Betsey cofounded Betsey Bunky Nini, but her own pursuits led to more designing and ultimately a store in Soho. The Soho store proved so successful that Betsey moved to larger quar-ters and then up and across town, as well as into such department stores as Bloomingdale's. While her style has always managed to be avant-garde, it has never been too far out. Johnson believes in making her own statement, and each store seems unique, despite the fact that she has over 40 of them across the country and internationally. Prices, particularly at the Soho store (which started as an outlet), are bearable. Incidentally, it's hard to overlook the shops: pink with neon accents, yellow floral with gold accents, great win-dows, and funky, personable staff.

BEVERLY M. LTD.
By appointment only   212/744-3726

Beverly Madden will design and make skirts, blouses, and jackets in a selection of unusual fabrics just for you. Sizing adjustment is done at no extra cost. Delivery takes two to three weeks, depending on fabric availability.

EILEEN FISHER

314 E 9th St (bet First and Second Ave)	212/529-5715
521 Madison Ave (bet 53rd and 54th St)	212/759-9888
341 Columbus Ave (bet 76th and 77th St)	212/362-3000
166 Fifth Ave (bet 21st and 22nd St)	212/924-4777
1039 Madison Ave (at 79th St)	212/879-7799
395 West Broadway (bet Spring and Broome St)	212/431-4567
Open every day; hours vary by store	www.eileenfisher.com

For the lady who likes her clothes cool, loose, and casual, look no further than Eileen Fisher. This talented designer has put together a collection of easy-care, mostly washable natural-fiber outfits that travel well and will be admired for their simple and attractive lines. The colors are earthy. From a small start in the East Village to six units all over Manhattan and space in some of the top stores, Eileen has produced a winner. The East Village store features discounted merchandise and first-quality goods.

Most New York shopping districts long ago began to dissipate or have faded away altogether, but a few odd remnants remain:

- For handbags, try 30th Street between Avenue of the Americas and Seventh avenues.
- If you need a part for that old sewing machine, go down to 25th Street between Avenue of the Americas and Seventh avenues.

ELENY

7 W 56th St (at Fifth Ave)	212/245-0001
Mon-Sat: 10-6, by appointment	www.eleny.com

Have you dreamed about designing a dress for yourself? Well, at Eleny, this is possible. The customer-oriented personnel here enjoy receiving input from their clients, and you can rest assured your gown will not be seen anywhere else. Some extras: they will send sketches and finished gowns anywhere, and Eleny (who has been designing clothes for over two decades) gives each client her undivided attention. All fabrics are imported from Europe.

FORMAN'S

82 Orchard St (bet Broome and Grand St)	212/228-2500
Sun-Wed: 9-6; Thurs: 9-7; Fri: 9-2	
59 John St (bet Dutch and William St)	212/791-4100
Mon-Wed: 7:30-7; Thurs: 7:30 a.m.-8 p.m.; Fri: 7:30-3	
560 Fifth Ave (bet 45th and 46th St)	212/719-1000
Mon-Thurs: 8 a.m.-9 p.m.; Fri: 8-2; Sun: 10-6	
145 E 42nd St (bet Lexington and Third Ave)	
Mon-Thurs: 8-9; Fri: 8-2; Sun: 10-6	212/681-9800

Forman's has a well-deserved reputation for being the "fashion oasis of the Lower East Side." You'll find trendy discounted sportswear, separates, and outerwear from such famous houses as Evan Piccone, Jones NY, Kasper, and Liz Claiborne in sizes that will satisfy petites, normal figures, and plus-size women alike. The stock changes rapidly, so periodic visits are in order.

GALLERY OF WEARABLE ART
34 E 67th St (bet Madison and Park Ave)   212/425-5379
Tues-Sat: 10-6   www.galleryofwearableart.com

The best phrase to describe this innovative business is "anti-trendy." The Gallery of Wearable Art carries New York's largest collection of unusual clothing, jewelry, and accessories from all over the world. It is primarily a cottage industry with a specialty in creating and designing special-occasion and bridal wear. Make this your destination if you are looking for unusual evening gowns, cocktail suits, bridal alternatives for nontraditional weddings, attractive jewelry, one-of-a-kind art jackets in antique textiles, and lace collage ensembles. You can even create your own gown. One thing is guaranteed: you won't see similar apparel on a friend or relative!

GISELLE SPORTSWEAR
143 Orchard St (bet Delancey and Rivington St)   212/673-1900
Sun-Thurs: 9-6; Fri: 9-3   www.gisellenewyork.com

Women's designer sportswear, current-season goods, a large selection (sizes 4 to 20), and discount prices are among the reasons Giselle is one of the more popular shopping spots on the Lower East Side. All merchandise is first quality. Factor in excellent service, and it's certainly worth the trip.

JANET RUSSO
262 Mott St (bet Prince and Houston St)   212/625-3297
Mon-Sat: 11:30-7; Sun: 12-6:30   www.janetrusso.com

Looking for a very daring and stylish dress? This is the place to start! Janet travels a great deal, and she brings back good ideas and interesting merchandise. If you have a big evening coming up, drop by and take a look.

LAURA ASHLEY
398 Columbus Ave (at 79th St)   212/496-5110
Mon-Sat: 11:30-7; Sun: 12-6:30   www.lauraashley.com

Laura Ashley mixes a contemporary new look with the classic theme that has been so popular over the years. In targeting a younger audience, she's designed some exciting new fashions. Dresses for children are sure to please discriminating gift-buyers. There are also women's dresses, home furnishings, wallpaper, fabric for curtains, and bolt fabrics.

LEA'S DESIGNER FASHION
119 Orchard St (near Delancey St), mezzanine level   212/677-2043
Mon-Fri: 9:30-5; Sun: 9-5

You don't have to pay full price for your Louis Feraud, Valentino, or various European designer clothes. Lea's, a popular Lower East Side outlet, discounts her merchandise up to 30% and sells the previous season's styles for 50% to 60% off. Don't expect much in the way of amenities, but you'll save enough here to afford a special dinner to show off your new outfit!

MIRIAM RIGLER
14 W 55th St (at Fifth Ave)
Mon-Sat: 10-6 (Thurs: 10-7)   212/581-5519

Miriam Rigler is the quintessential ladies' dress shop. They have it all: personal attention, expert alterations, wardrobe coordination, custom designing (including bridal), and a large selection of sportswear, knits, and evening gowns in sizes 4 to 20. Also featured: custom headpieces, traditional and nontraditional bridal gowns, mother-of-the-bride ensembles, and debutante dresses. Despite the location, all items are discounted, including special orders. Don't miss the costume jewelry!

1 ON G
55 Great Jones St (bet Bowery and Lafayette St)   212/505-6610
Mon-Thurs: 1-8; Fri, Sat: 12:30-9:30; Sun: 12:30-7

1 on G is both a store and showroom space. Well-known clothing and jewelry by Japanese and other international designers are showcased. Most items are one-of-a-kind.

PALMA
521 Broome St (at Thompson St)   212/966-1722
Tues-Sat: 11-7; Sun: 12-6

To have remained in business in Soho for over two decades is a tribute to sound retailing—and that is exactly what you get at Palma. This store carries designs for men and women from American, Canadian, French, and Spanish designers.

Large-Size Fashions
Plus-size clothing lines are now offered by some of the top names in the fashion world, including Ellen Tracy, Carole Little, Jones NY, Liz Claiborne, and Eileen Fisher. Special departments for large-size fashions can be found at Macy's, Bloomingdale's, and Saks Fifth Avenue.

S&W
165 W 26th St (at Seventh Ave)   718/431-2800
Mon-Thurs: 10-6:30; Fri: 10-3; Sun: 10-6

S&W is one of the best places in the city for ladies' designer clothing —coats, shoes, and bags. Unlike so many other discount boutiques, S&W maintains a consistent level of quality. On the down side, they would hardly win any "service with a smile" awards.

SAN FRANCISCO CLOTHING
975 Lexington Ave (at 71st St)   212/472-8740
Mon-Sat: 11-6   www.sanfrancisco.com

The women and children's clothing at San Francisco Clothing are just right for a casual weekend. Their merchandise is comfortable, colorful, and classy. The mature woman will find an especially good selection. Separates to go with your evening clothes are also a specialty.

SPITZER'S
101 Rivington St (at Ludlow St)   212/477-4088
Sun-Thurs: 9:30-5; Fri: 9:30-2:30   www.spitzersclothing.com

Spitzer's on Rivington is a Lower East Side landmark. There are two good reasons for shopping here: an excellent selection of marked-down designer clothing and terrific prices. On the down side, you have to put up with less than helpful salespeople, unmarked merchandise, and three rooms jammed with goods. A bit of haggling may be necessary, but you should be able to get some great bargains and have a memorable shopping experience to boot.

TG-170
170 Ludlow St (bet Houston and Stanton St)   212/995-8660
Mon-Sun: 12-8   www.tg170.com

You won't see the clothes carried here in any other store. That is because most of the merchandise is made in small quantities especially for this store. TG-170 started as a studio where baseball hats and T-shirts were made but has graduated into a retail showroom that displays unique items from young, emerging designers, like Martin and Freitag bags.

Women's—Maternity

Readers interested in maternity clothes ought to visit such national chains as **Mimi Maternity** and **Pea in the Pod**, both of which have several well-stocked Manhattan locations. The stores I list here are unique to New York.

LIZ LANGE MATERNITY
958 Madison Ave (bet 75th and 76th St)   212/879-2191
Mon-Fri: 10-7; Sat: 10-6; Sun: 12-5

Having moved to a spacious new Madison Avenue storefront from a second-floor walk-up—no doubt encouraged by the warm reception expectant New York moms have given Liz Lange Maternity in recent years—this boutique carries its own line of very stylish maternity clothes. The prices are about what you would expect, given the location and high-end clothes Liz Lange sells, but the sales people are friendly and the clothes are well-made.

MATERNITY WORKS
16 W 57th St (bet Fifth Ave and Ave of the Americas), 3rd floor
                                                     212/399-9840
Mon-Wed: 10-7; Thurs: 10-8; Fri, Sat: 10-6; Sun: 12-6

The building is grubby and the elevator to the third floor is incredibly cramped, but the bargains on maternity basics are well worth the trip. This is an outlet of sorts, selling both Mimi Maternity (which has branches throughout Manhattan and across the U.S.) and Motherwork clothes and related items at sometimes quite significant discounts.

PUMPKIN MATERNITY
407 Broome St (near Lafayette St)   212/334-1809
Mon-Sat: 12-7; Sun: 12-5   www.pumpkinmaternity.com

Pumpkin Wentzel has made it easier for fashionable downtown women to get through their pregnancy. The buzz around her stylish line of maternity basics has been hot since she first began producing them out of her apartment almost a decade ago. Now there's a big and welcoming retail outlet where you can browse her collection. Call for a free catalog (800/460-0337) or shop online. This is a great find!

Women's Millinery

BARBARA FEINMAN MILLINERY
66 E 7th St (bet First and Second Ave) 212/358-7092
Mon-Sat: 12:30-8; Sun: 1-7 (open later on weekends in summer)
                                                 www.feinmanhats.com

Although accessories are carried here, the big draw is the hats, made on-premises from original designs. If you are looking for something really funky . . . or very classy . . . try this spot first.

THE HAT SHOP
120 Thompson St (at Prince St)   212/219-1445
Mon-Sat: 12-7; Sun: 1-6 (closed Mon in summer)

Owner Linda Pagan has quite a background. Formerly a Wall Street broker, then a bartender and world traveler, she's now the boss at the Hat Shop. The stock reflects that diverse history, with showings from some 20 local designers. For those who cannot visit the shop, Linda will send photos so that customers may choose the right look!

MANNY'S MILLINERY SUPPLY COMPANY
26 W 38th St (bet Fifth Ave and Ave of the Americas)   212/840-2235
Mon-Fri: 9:30-5:30; Sat: 10-4

To say that Manny's carries millinery supplies is an understatement. Row after row of drawers are dedicated to particular aspects of head adornment. The section for ladies' hatbands alone takes up almost a hundred boxes and runs the gamut from thin pearl lines to wide Western-style leather belts. They have rhinestone banding and an enormous selection of artificial flowers and feathers. The center of the store is lined with tables displaying odds and ends, as well as several bins bulging with larger items that don't fit in the wall drawers. At the front, hat forms adorn hat-tree stands, and sample hats are displayed in no particular order. Manny's will help accessorize any hat with interchangeable decorations. They also sell completed hats, close-outs, and samples. They will even re-create an old hat!

PAUL'S VEIL AND NET
28 W 38th St (bet Fifth Ave and Ave of the Americas)
Mon-Fri: 8:30-4; Sat: 8:30-2   212/391-3822

The mob scene at this bridal headpiece outlet is repeated at stores up and down the block, reflecting the dimensions of the bridal business. Despite the competition from its neighbors (or perhaps because of it), Paul's gets my top recommendation for any bride-to-be searching for a bridal headpiece. Although they deal in illusion (lace, that is), they are one of the few stores on the block that does not maintain the illusion that they are a wholesale-only outfit, doing the lowly retail customer a big favor by unbarring the doors. The staff at Paul's seems genuinely glad to share your joy and help create a truly unique bridal veil or crown. The store stocks all that's needed for the rest of the bridal party, as well as unusual accessories and bridal supplies. The lucky bride-to-be will find both the selection and savings extraordinary.

Women's Undergarments

A. W. KAUFMAN
73 Orchard St (bet Broome and Grand St)
Sun-Thurs: 10:30-5; Fri: 10:30-2   212/226-1629, 212/226-1788

Trying to find a gift for that special someone? A.W. Kaufman offers imported underwear, socks, robes, pajamas (even nightshirts for men). For three generations, Kaufman has combined excellent merchandise with quality customer service. Among the many outstanding labels found here are Hanro, Diamond Tea, Chantelle, Pluto, Zimmerli, and Oscar De La Renta.

IMKAR COMPANY (M. KARFIOL AND SON)
294 Grand St (bet Allen and Eldridge St)   212/925-2459
Sun-Thurs: 10-5; Fri: 9:30-2; Sun (summer): 10-3

Imkar carries pajamas, underwear, and shifts for women at about a third off retail prices. A full line of Carter's infants' and children's wear is also available at good prices. The store has a fine line of women's lingerie, including dusters and gowns. Featured names include Model's Coat, Vanity Fair, Arrow, Jockey, Lollipop, and Munsingwear. Gold Toe Hosiery and Arrow and Van Heusen shirts for men are also stocked.

LA PETITE COQUETTE
51 University Pl (bet 9th and 10th St)   212/473-2478
Mon-Wed, Fri, Sat: 11-7; Thurs: 11-8; Sun: 12-6

Interested in a male-friendly lingerie store that will take care of your gift needs? La Petite Coquette offers a large, eclectic mix of lingerie from around the world. I like their description of the atmosphere: "Flirtatious!" You'll find everything from classic La Perla, Chantelle Thomas, and Wolford hosiery to edgy designers like Damaris and Buttress & Snatch. There are also old standbys like Cosabella, Hanky Panky, Mary Green, On Gossamer, Only Hearts, Eberjey, La Cosa, and more.

SCHACHNER FASHIONS
95 Delancey St (bet Orchard and Ludlow St)   212/677-0700
Sun-Fri: 9-5:30

Schachner is a Lower East Side institution, selling brand-name robes, sleepwear, underwear, and loungewear at discount prices for more than 40 years. They'll special-order any style.

UNDERNEATH IT ALL
444 E 75th St (at York Ave)   212/717-1976
Mon-Thurs: 10-6

Underneath It All is a one-stop shopping service for women who have had breast cancer or are undergoing chemotherapy. You can be assured of attentive, informed, and personal service, as some of the staff are breast-cancer survivors. The store carries a large selection of breast forms in light and dark skin tones and in a variety of shapes, sizes, and contours. There is also a complete line of mastectomy bras and name-brand bras; mastectomy and designer swimwear; sleepwear, loungewear, and body suits; and wigs and fashionable head accessories. They will accept insurance coverage with Medicare, Medicaid, Empire Blue Cross Blue Shield, and Aetna.

VICTORIA'S SECRET
34 E 57th St (bet Park and Madison Ave)   212/758-5592
1240 Third Ave (at 72nd St)   212/717-7035
163-165 E 86th St (bet Lexington and Third Ave)   646/672-9183
Mon-Sat: 10-8; Sun: 12-7   www.victoriassecret.com

These have to be some of the sexiest stores in the world. The beautiful lingerie and bedroom garb, bridal peignoirs, exclusive silks, and accessories are displayed against the most alluring backdrops. The personnel are absolutely charming as well. There are numerous additional locations for Victoria's Secret besides those listed above.

Coins, Stamps

H.R. HARMER
3 E 28th St (bet Madison and Fifth Ave), 7th floor   212/532-3700
Mon-Fri: 9:30-5:30   www.hrharmer.com

If you think you have a stamp that will make you a millionaire, these are the people to talk to. The same family has run this business since 1918. They will appraise your rare stamps and autographs. You can stay informed about their stamp auctions via catalogs and brochures.

STACK'S RARE COINS
123 W 57th St (at Ave of the Americas)   212/582-2580
Mon-Fri: 10-5   www.stacks.com

Established in 1858, Stack's is the country's oldest and largest rare-coin dealer. Moreover, it is still a family operation. Specializing in coins, medals, and paper money of interest to collectors, Stack's has a solid reputation for individual service, integrity, and knowledge of the field. In addition to walk-in business, Stack's conducts 11 public auctions a year. Both neophytes and experienced numismatists will do well at Stack's.

Computers
(See also "Electronics")

COMPUSA
420 Fifth Ave (bet 37th and 38th St)   212/764-6224
Mon-Fri: 8:30-8; Sat: 10-7; Sun: 11-6
1775 Broadway (at 57th St)   212/262-9711
Mon-Fri: 9-8; Sat: 10-7; Sun: 11-6   www.compusa.com

There are over 5,000 computer products in stock at these computer super-stores, from modern desktop models to sophisticated software. The best part of the operation, besides the selection and competitive pricing, is the service. Even though these CompUSA franchises are incredibly big and busy, the courteous sales staff will take time to answer even the simplest questions.

GAMESTOP
Locations throughout Manhattan
Hours vary by store   www.gamestop.com

Gamestop is the largest resource in the area for computer accessories and games, with highly competitive prices and informed service.

You will find a very good stock of all kinds of computers and hand-held devices at **RCS Computer Experience** (575 Madison Ave, 212/572-9888). Informed service is a plus.

Cosmetics, Drugs, Perfumes

BATH ISLAND
469 Amsterdam Ave (bet 82nd and 83rd St)   212/787-9415
Sun-Fri: noon-8; Sat: 10-8   www.bathisland.com

The customer is queen here. Custom scenting of products and custom gift packages are offered at this shop, which provides highly personal service. Over a hundred essential perfume oils are available, plus a great variety of creams, cleansers, lotions, and hair and shaving products.

BOYD'S MADISON AVENUE DEPARTMENT STORE
655 Madison Ave (at 60th St)   212/838-6558
Mon-Fri: 8:30-7:30; Sat: 9:30-7; Sun: 12-6   www.boydsnyc.com

Boyd's is a drugstore in a city full of drugstores, so it has to have something special to be worthy of mention. In addition to a drug and prescription service, Boyd's carries a complete line of cosmetics, magnifying mirrors, soaps, jewelry, and brushes. The latter range from the common to the esoteric: i.e., nail brushes and mustache combs in a variety of sizes and shapes. Boyd's has one of the city's most complete selections of drugs, cosmetics, and sundries. A boutique department carries handbags, lingerie, hats, scarves, gloves, jackets, and hair accessories. However, service by unfriendly salespeople can be very frustrating.

One of the best places to find a large selection of perfumes and fragrances at really good discounts is **Columbus Perfumery** (274 Columbus Ave, 212/496-4160).

ESSENTIAL PRODUCTS
90 Water St (bet Wall St and Hanover Sq)   212/344-4288
Mon-Fri: 9-5

Essential Products has been manufacturing flavors and fragrances for over a century. They know that advertising and packaging drive up the price of name-brand colognes and perfumes, so they set out to see how closely they could duplicate expensive scents at cheap prices. They describe their fragrances as "elegant interpretations" of designer names, sold at a fraction of the original price. Essential features 50 perfumes and 23 men's colognes, and they offer a money-back guarantee. If you send a self-addressed stamped envelope, they will return scented cards and ordering information.

KIEHL'S
109 Third Ave (bet 13th and 14th St)   212/677-3171, 800/543-4571
Mon-Sat: 10-7; Sun: 12-6   www.kiehls.com

Kiehl's has been a New York institution since 1851. Their special treatments and preparations are made by hand and distributed internationally. Natural ingredients are used in their full lines of cleansers, scrubs, toners, moisturizers, eye-area preparations, men's creams, masks, body moisturizers, bath and shower products, sports items, ladies' leg-grooming formulations, shampoos, conditioners, and treatments. Customers will also enjoy the unusual collection of memorabilia related to aviation and motorcycles.

Crafts

ALLCRAFT JEWELRY & ENAMELING CENTER
135 W 29th St (bet Ave of the Americas and Seventh Ave), Room 205
Mon-Fri: 9-4:45   212/279-7077, 800/645-7124
                                                      www.allcraft.peachost.com

Allcraft is the definitive jewelry-making supply store. Their catalog includes a complete line of tools and supplies for jewelry making, silver- and metal-smithing, lost-wax casting, and much more. Out-of-towners usually order from their catalog, but New Yorkers shouldn't miss an opportunity to visit this gleaming cornucopia. Call for a catalog or browse it online.

CITY QUILTER
157 W 24th St (at Seventh Ave)   212/807-0390
Tues-Fri: 11-7; Sat: 10-6; Sun: 11-5   www.cityquilter.com

This is the only shop in Manhattan that's completely devoted to quilting. They serve beginners to professionals with classes, books, notions, thread, gifts, and all-cotton fabrics.

CLAYWORKS POTTERY
332 E 9th St (bet First and Second Ave)   212/677-8311
Tues-Thurs:3-7; Fri: 3-8:30; Sat: 1-8:30; Sun: 3-8:30
(call ahead, as hours can vary)

For three decades, talented Helaine Sorgen has been at work here! If you are interested in stoneware and porcelain, Clayworks is the place to go. All of Clayworks' pottery is lead-free and dishwasher- and microwave-safe. Small classes in wheel-throwing are given for adults. Everything here is individually produced, from teapots to casseroles, mugs, and sake sets. One-of-a-kind decorative pieces include vases, goblets, platters, and bowls.

ERICA WILSON
717 Madison Ave (at 63rd St), 2nd floor   212/832-7290
Mon-Sat: 10-6

Erica Wilson is a lady of many talents. This British émigré not only writes books and newspaper columns about needlework, but she also finds time to design needlepoint kits for the Metropolitan Museum of Art. You'll find the city's finest selection of hand-painted needlepoint patterns from London and elsewhere. You can select finished pillows, hand-painted canvases, gifts, needlepoint and velvet shoes or slippers, and beautiful accessories from Erica's stock. Her chintz bags are very special. Blocking, padding, mounting, and finishing—as well as classes in these skills—are available.

GOTTA KNIT!
498 Ave of the Americas (bet 12th and 13th St), 2nd floor
Mon-Fri: 11-6 (Thurs till 8); Sat, Sun: 11-4   212/989-3030

Here you will find luxury yarns for hand-knitting, crocheting, and custom pattern-writing for unique garments, as well as a selection of accessories, books, and buttons. Individual instructions and classes are offered.

LOVELIA ENTERPRISES
356 E 41st St (in Tudor City Place)   212/490-0930, 800/843-8438
Mon-Fri: 9:30-5 (by appointment only)

Lovelia F. Albright's establishment is one of New York's great finds. From a shop overlooking the United Nations from Tudor City Place, she dispenses the finest European Gobelin, Aubusson, and Beauvais machine-woven tapes-tries at prices that are often one-third that of other places. The tapestries are exquisite. Some depict the ubiquitous unicorns cavorting in a medieval scene; others are more modern. They come in all sizes. The latest additions include tapestries for upholstery, wool-pile miniature rugs for use as mats under objets d'art, and an extensive line of tapestry-woven borders. They're designed by Albright and made exclusively for her in Austria and France.

WOOLGATHERING
318-B 84th St (bet First and Second Ave)   212/734-4747
Tues-Fri: 10:30-6; Sat: 10:30-5

Woolgathering is a unique oasis dedicated to the fine art of knitting! A big selection of quality European woolen, cotton, and novelty yarns are featured. There's free instruction for all skill levels. They carry many exclusive classic and contemporary designs, a complete library of knitting magazines and books, and European-made knitting implements and gadgets. They also provide very professional finishing services.

Dance Items

CAPEZIO DANCE THEATRE SHOP
1650 Broadway (at 51st St)   212/245-2130
                                                 www.capeziodance.com
CAPEZIO 57TH STREET
1776 Broadway (at 57th St)   212/586-5140
CAPEZIO EAST
136 E 61st St (at Lexington Ave)   212/758-8833
CAPEZIO EAST UPTOWN (children's)
1651 Third Ave (bet 92nd and 93rd St), third floor   212/348-7210
ON STAGE WITH CAPEZIO (premier dancewear)
197 Madison Ave (bet 34th and 35th St)   212/725-1174
                                                 www.onstagedancewear.com

Known for their service and selection, Capezio stores offer one-stop shopping for all your dance, theater, and fitness needs. Capezio Dance Theatre Shop is the largest dance and theater retail store in the world, with specialized sections for men, Flamenco, Skatewear, and a wide variety of shoes. Capezio East reflects the fashion-conscious East Side neighborhood. On Stage serves professional ballet and theater companies across the world, including the New York City Ballet, but individuals are welcome.

Department Stores

BARNEY'S NEW YORK
660 Madison Ave (bet 60th and 61st St)   212/826-8900
Mon-Fri: 10-8; Sat: 10-7; Sun: 11-6   www.barneys.com

Barney's once was *the* place to buy clothing and accessories for men and boys. Third-generation family members borrowed money to expand rapidly throughout this country and overseas, and the results spelled financial and merchandising disaster. The flagship store on Madison Avenue is a combination women's and men's operation, and it is difficult to shop here. Merchandise is, in many cases, on the cutting edge of fashion; however, prices are high and service can be less than accommodating. There is a good food operation (Fred's) on the ninth floor. Still, with so many fine department stores in New York, seasoned shoppers no longer make this their first choice. Be sure to attend their twice-yearly warehouse sales, which are worth the effort.

BERGDORF GOODMAN
754 Fifth Ave (at 58th St)   212/753-7300
BERGDORF MEN'S
745 Fifth Ave (at 58th St)   212/753-7300
Mon-Wed, Fri, Sat: 10-7; Thurs: 10-8

Occupying a prime location on Fifth Avenue, just off the southwest corner of Central Park, Bergdorf Goodman is the epitome of style. The store has broadened its appeal, reaching out to young and affluent customers. Lines have been expanded, and practically every major fashion name in the world is represented here. Dollar sales per square foot are among the highest in the nation. Bergdorf Goodman emphasizes top fashion names in all departments, and many of the styles are found exclusively in this store. Their windows usually display a fine selection of this apparel. The seventh floor presents an exciting array of home-accessory merchandise, carefully selected and beautifully displayed. Downstairs, an impressive cosmetics department is one of the busiest in the store. Personnel are great if they know you; if not, don't appear in your grubbies. A very high-class men's store is located across the street, and you'll find top names and prices to match. If you're looking for a special men's gift or are intent on attiring yourself in the best-of-the-best, Bergdorf Goodman Men is the place to go.

BLOOMINGDALE'S
1000 Third Ave (at 59th St)   212/705-2000
Mon-Wed, Fri: 10-8:30; Thurs: 10-10; Sat: 10-7; Sun: 11-7
                                                   www.bloomingdales.com

Bloomingdale's is no longer the grand dame of America's department stores. Although the store is still the destination for thousands of local and visiting shoppers, one will not find the unique merchandise that once was the operation's hallmark. However, several standouts remain. The first floor cosmetics department is like no other in the world, and the "Main Course" home furnishings area is superb. The fashion departments appeal particularly to the working woman. Chocolates at Martine's on the sixth floor are some of the best in the city. What was once an outstanding furniture department, with great model rooms, is now very mundane. The men's departments can't hold a candle to New York stores like Saks and Macy's (although the latter is under the same ownership). Service can be very frustrating, as part-timers often have little knowledge of the merchandise.

CENTURY 21 DEPARTMENT STORE
22 Cortlandt St (bet Broadway and Church St)   212/227-9092
Mon-Wed, Fri: 7:45-8; Thurs: 7:45-8:30; Sat: 10-8; Sun: 11-7
                                                      www.c21stores.com

Century 21, always great because of its genuine bargains, has been modernized and expanded since the September 11, 2001, terrorist attacks. Ask anyone who works in the Wall Street area where they most like to shop, and most will say Century 21. Why? Because the 16 departments in this bargain palace carry an amazing selection of quality merchandise for men, women, children, and the home at discounts that run from 25% to 75%. Outstanding departments include housewares, women's shoes, and children's apparel, where brand names are tops and prices comfortable. Don't expect fancy fitting rooms and special amenities. However, service is informed and courteous, and you will not be disappointed.

HENRI BENDEL
712 Fifth Ave (bet 55th and 56th St)   212/247-1100
Mon-Sat: 10-7 (Thurs: 10-8); Sun: 12-6   www.henribendel.com

Founded in 1896 as a millinery store, Bendel's was a fixture on 57th Street for years. In a boutique setting, the store catered to high-fashion women's apparel for the upwardly mobile New Yorker. The present store, in the former Coty Building, keeps the same boutique atmosphere. Wood is used prominently throughout, and the magnificent original windows by Rene Lalique have been incorporated into the store design. Bendel's "stylists" can take you from boutique to boutique via oval staircases. Unfortunately, the store does not have the class it once did, though the restrooms are nice.

Some good values can be had at these department-store clearance centers:

Lord & Taylor (3601 Hempstead Turnpike, Levittown, Long Island, NY; 516/731-5031): clothing for the family

Macy's (155 Glencove Rd, Carleplace, Long Island, NY; 516/742-8500): furniture, mattresses

---

LORD & TAYLOR
424 Fifth Ave (at 39th St)   212/391-3344
Mon-Fri: 10-8:30; Sat: 10-8; Sun: 11-7   www.lordandtaylor.com

America's oldest specialty store, Lord & Taylor is a retailing institution on New York's fashion front. The late Dorothy Shaver made it that way. The "L" and "T" could easily stand for Luxury and Tradition, because the store has been recognized for quality, service, and value since 1826. Now owned by the May Company, Lord & Taylor on Fifth Avenue is the flagship of stores nationwide that display their allegiance to American designers. Merchandise and advertising tout "the Signature of American Style," especially in dresses. Shoppers will find ten floors of famous-name options for everyone—from fashions to gifts for the home, plus special-size shops for petites and larger women. The traditional Soup Bar on the sixth floor is popular. During December, Lord & Taylor becomes one of New York's most popular attractions because of its award-winning Christmas windows. On the down side, service is uneven, the men's sections leave much to be desired, and the store's phone system is abysmal.

MACY'S
151 W 34th St (at Herald Square, bet Broadway and Seventh Ave)
Mon-Sat: 10-8:30; Sun: 11-7   212/695-4400
www.macys.com

Macy's is billed as "the world's largest department store," and I doubt anyone would dispute that! Changes in the retail field have had a profound impact on this store. The retail giant is now owned by Federated. (Who would ever have thought that Bloomingdale's and Macy's would be brothers?) The store has renewed sparkle, more inventory, better service, and an increased showing of top names in clothing and accessories. The downstairs housewares-filled "Cellar" is a highlight. The food market place in The Cellar is colorful and busy. In the rest of the store, you'll find a great selection of items for kids, an outstanding home furnishings section, and several fun places to rest and grab a snack. At Easter time, Macy's flower show is magnificent.

SAKS FIFTH AVENUE
611 Fifth Ave (at 50th St)   212/7534000
Mon-Sat: 10-7 (Thurs till 8); Sun: 12-6   www.saksfifthavenue.com

Saks Fifth Avenue is a retail institution that demonstrates an ongoing commitment to quality and excellence in fashion merchandising and service. In a prime location on Fifth Avenue at Rockefeller Center, this store continues to be a favorite shopping place for overseas visitors, tourists, and local residents. The Evening Boutique on the third floor is *the* shopping place for women who want to dress with flair for a special occasion. The men's sections offer the top names in the country. The professional woman will find timeless fashions in clothing and accessories. Cafe SFA, with gourmet lunches and light fare, is a delightful eighth-floor resting place with a great view. There is much more: outstanding departments for infants and young people, a beauty salon, complimentary "One to One" shopping service, and multilingual sales help for foreign visitors. Saks' premium credit-card program, "SaksFirst," rewards loyal shoppers for their yearly spending with a bevy of bonuses and perks.

TAKASHIMAYA
693 Fifth Ave (bet 54th and 55th St)   212/350-0100
Mon-Sat: 10-7; Sun: 12-5   www.takashimaya.com

Located on prestigious Fifth Avenue, right in the middle of the Tiffanys and Guccis, this store is as much a museum and gallery as it is a retail establishment. It certainly is different from most American department stores. Upstairs you'll find beautiful Japanese-made clothing and accessory items, home furnishings, and gifts. The top floor is also an urban oasis for beauty addicts, with fragrances, hair-care products, makeup—all top-end merchandise. Gorgeous flower arrangements are featured on the first floor. The downstairs Tea Box is a restful Japanese cafe where teas and related accessories are sold.

Instead of having to make a long journey to Southeast Asia, you can pick up some Vietnamese treasures at **Saigoniste** (239 Mulberry St, 212/925-4610, www.saigoniste.com). The store is in the Nolita area.

Domestics

D. PORTHAULT
18 E 69th St (bet Madison and Fifth Ave)   212/688-1660
Mon-Sat: 10-5:30   www.porthault.com

Porthault, the French queen of linens, needs no introduction. Custom-made linens are available in a range of 600 designs, scores of colors, and weaves of luxurious density. Wherever the name Porthault appears—e.g., some fancy hotels—you know you're at a top-notch operation. Their printed sheets seem to last forever and are handed down from one generation to another. Porthault can handle custom work of an intricate nature for odd-sized beds, baths, and showers. Specialties include signature prints, printed terry towels, unusual gift items, and decorative accessories like trays, wastebaskets, tissue-box covers, and room sprays.

HARRIS LEVY

278 Grand St (at Forsyth St)   212/226-3102
Sun-Fri: 9-5   www.harrislevy.com

Harris Levy, one of New York's legendary linen resources since 1894, has long been known for its vast selection, service, and prices. Many of their high-fashion linens are exclusive imports from around the world. From fine bed, bath, and table linens to down comforters, pillows, mattress pads, and closet accessories, they offer good value. They are experts in custom work, embroidery, and monogramming. The best-kept secret of the well-heeled for many generations, this Lower East Side linen source is currently operated by the fourth generation of its founders.

Daily Bargains

Bed Bath & Beyond (410 E 61st St, 646/215-4702 and 620 Ave of the Americas, 212/255-3550): one-stop home furnishings

B&H Photo-Video Pro Audio (420 Ninth Ave, 212/444-6600): camera, audio, video superstore

Bis Designer Resale (1134 Madison Ave, 212/396-2760): upscale clothing, shoes, accessories

Broadway Panhandler (477 Broome St, 212/966-3454): kitchenware

Century 21 (22 Cortlandt St, 212/227-9092): discount department store

Crate & Barrel (611 Broadway, 212/780-0004 and 650 Madison Ave, 212/308-0011): housewares and furniture

H&M (1328 Broadway, 646/473-1164; 558 Broadway, 212/343-2722; 640 Fifth Ave, 212/489-0390; 435 Seventh Ave, 212/643-6955; and 125 W 125th St, 212/665-8300): family clothing

Jam Paper & Envelope (111 Third Ave, 212/473-6666 and 611 Ave of the Americas, 212/255-4593): specialty stationery and office products

M&J Trimming Co. (1000-1008 Ave of the Americas, 212/391-9072): fine sewing and upholstering notions

Old Navy (150 W 34th St, 212/594-0115; 610 Ave of the Americas, 212/645-0663; and 503-511 Broadway, 212/226-0838): clothing

Pearl River Mart (477 Broadway, 212/431-4770 and 200 Grand St, 212/966-1010): Asian emporium

Pier 1 Imports (461 Fifth Ave, 212/447-1610; 71 Fifth Ave, 212/206-1911; and 1550 Third Ave, 212/987-1746): imports, gifts

Super Runners Shop (360 Amsterdam Ave, 212/787-7665; Grand Central Station, 646/487-1120; 1337 Lexington Ave, 212/369-6010; and 1246 Third Ave, 212/249-2133): shoes, apparel, and accessories

SYMS (400 Park Ave, 212/317-8200 and 42 Trinity Pl, 212/797-1199): family fashions

Zara (580 Broadway, 212/343-1725; 101 Fifth Ave, 212/741-0555; 750 Lexington Ave, 212/754-1120; and 39 W 34th St, 212/868-6551): men's and women's clothing from Spain

---

J. SCHACHTER'S

5 Cook St (at Manhattan St), Brooklyn   718/384-2732, 800/INTOBED
Mon-Thurs: 10-5; Fri: 10-1:30

J. Schachter's is the foremost purveyor of quilts in the New York area and perhaps on the entire continent. Schachter's is the oldest quilting firm in New York. They make them in white goose down, polyester, lamb's wool, and cotton. The talented staff can make a quilt in any size and in 20 different quilting patterns from any fabric given to them. They can also do outline quilting for bedspreads. Baby ensembles are a specialty. Schachter's has a complete line of linens as well. Some of their bed linens come from Europe and are offered at guaranteed lowest prices. Custom pillows can be made while you wait. Entire bedrooms and bathrooms—from rugs to ceiling and wall coverings—can be coordinated. The experts at Schachter's refurbish down pillows, comforters, and sofa cushions, as well as window treatments and balloon, Venetian, or Roman shades.

JAN DE LUZ
345 West Broadway (bet Broome and Grand St) 212/343-9911
Daily: 11-7

This shop specializes in French linens and antiques. Their linens are woven exclusively for them in the Basque country. You'll find some very attractive unbleached Egyptian cotton bath towels, robes, and slippers. They carry French personal-care products as well as olive oils and vinegars from Italy and Greece, too! Custom monogramming and embroidery are also available.

NANCY KOLTES AT HOME
31 Spring St (bet Mott and Mulberry St) 212/219-2271
Mon-Sat: 11-7; Sun: 12-6 (Mon-Sat: 12-8 in summer)
www.nancykoltes.com

Visit Nancy Koltes if you are interested in quality luxury home products, including beautiful bed and table linens made of the finest Italian yarns.

PONDICHERRI
454 Columbus Ave (at 82nd St) 212/875-1609
Daily: 11-8 www.pondicherrionline.com

The beautiful window displays might make you think you could never afford anything inside Pondicherri. However, if you like exotic cotton prints and are looking for pillows, pillowcases, bags, trays (from Hong Kong), handicrafts and furniture (from Indonesia), tablecloths, quilts, clothing, and the like, by all means go in. Both selection and prices are excellent! You'll find items from Tibet, India, Africa, and other exotic spots, including Moroccan ceramics. Keep an eye out for unusual pottery and interesting knick-knacks, too. Because the selection is large and most items are folded on shelves, you might want to ask for help.

PORTICO BED & BATH
903 Broadway (at 21st St) 212/473-6662
72 Spring St (bet Crosby and Lafayette St) 212/941-7800
450 Columbus Ave (at 81st St) 212/579-9500
Mon-Sat: 10-7; Sun: 12-6 www.porticohome.com

PORTICO BED & BATH OUTLET STORE
Chelsea Market
75 Ninth Ave (bet 15th and 16th St) 212/243-8515
Mon-Sat: 10-7; Sun: 12-6

Portico is known for its highly unusual collection of bath and body-care products, cast- and wrought-iron beds, and fine domestic and imported linens. This is not a store for bargain hunters; rather, Portico is for discerning shoppers who take pride in making their home a very special place.

PRATESI LINENS
829 Madison Ave (at 69th St)   212/288-2315
Mon-Sat: 10-6

Pratesi says it carries the best linens the world has to offer, and they're right. Families hand them down for generations. Customers who don't have affluent ancestors will wish to avail themselves of the new collections that come out in spring and fall. The Pratesi staff is unsurpassed in coordinating linens to decor or creating a custom look. This three-story store has a garden that sets the mood for perusing the luxurious linens. Towels are made exclusively for Pratesi in Italy and are of a quality and thickness that must be felt to be believed. Bathrobes are magnificent, plush, and quietly understated. (So are the price tags.) Cashmere pillows, throws, and blankets are available, and there is also a baby boutique.

Electronics and Appliances

DALE ELECTRONICS
7 E 20th St (bet Broadway and Fifth Ave)   212/475-1124
Mon-Fri: 9:30-5:30   www.daleproaudio.com

A family business for nearly half a century, this professional audio dealership carries a large inventory of Sony and Panasonic replacement parts, as well as merchandise for the recording, broadcast, DJ, and sound-contracting community. They know their stuff and have earned great respect from repeat customers.

GRINGER & SONS
29 First Ave (at 2nd St)   212/475-0600
Mon-Fri: 8-5:30; Sat: 8-4:30 (summer: Wed until 7:30)

Come to Gringer & Sons for major brand-name appliances at good prices. Gringer's informed personnel sell dishwashers, washers, dryers, and sinks to residential and commercial customers.

HARVEY ELECTRONICS
2 W 45th St (at Fifth Ave)   212/575-5000
Mon-Fri: 10-7 (Thurs: 10-8); Sat: 10-6; Sun: 12-5
                                          www.harveyonline.com

Not everyone understands the fine points of all the new technologies flooding the market. For those who need professional advice and individual attention, Harvey's is the place to shop. They offer state-of-the-art audio/video components, with home theater and high-definition television being their specialty. Harvey has an in-home design and installation division that will integrate audio and video systems into new and existing residences.

J&R MUSIC & COMPUTER WORLD
23 Park Row (across from City Hall)   212/238-9000, 800/221-8180
Mon-Sat: 9-7:30; Sun: 10:30-6:30   www.jandr.com

These folks pride themselves on being one of the nation's most complete computer, electronics, and home-entertaimnent department stores. They carry cameras, radios, televisions, speaker systems, VCRs, DVDs, cassette and CD players, personal electronics, records, tapes, compact discs, computer systems, telephones and answering machines, typewriters, microwave ovens, and breadmakers. The place is well organized, though it can get rather hectic at times. Prices are competitive and merchandise is guaranteed.

LYRIC HIGH FIDELITY
1221 Lexington Ave (bet 82nd and 83rd St) 212/439-1900
Mon, Wed, Fri, Sat: 10-6; Tues, Thurs: 10-7

Lyric is a favorite among audiophiles, catering to those with a passion for recorded music and the cash to indulge their wildest audio fantasies. You can buy a basic music system at Lyric for under $1,000, but you can also part with a six-figure sum for an exotic component ensemble. Michael Kay has owned Lyric since 1959, selling audio equipment to people who want the best, and he's very particular about the lines he carries.

P.C. RICHARD & SON
120 E 14th St (bet Third and Fourth Ave) 212/979-2600
205 E 86th St (bet Second and Third Ave) 212/289-1700
Mon-Fri: 9 a.m.-9:30 p.m.; Sat: 9-9; Sun: 10-7 www.pcrichard.com

For nearly a century, this family-owned and -operated appliance, electronics, and computer store has been providing superior service to customers. They offer a large inventory, good prices, delivery seven days a week, and an in-house service center. The store started as a hardware outfit, and unlike so many other family operations, the genius of personalized service has been successfully passed from one generation to the next.

SHARPER IMAGE
4 W 57th St (at Fifth Ave) 212/265-2550
900 Madison Ave (at 73rd St) 212/794-4974
Mon-Fri: 10-7; Sat: 10-6; Sun: 12-6

50 Rockefeller Plaza (bet Fifth Ave and Ave of the Americas)
Mon-Sat: 10-8; Sun: 10-7 646/557-0861
Pier 17, South Street Seaport 212/693-0477
Daily: 10-9 www.sharperimage.com

If you are a gadget freak like me, you'll go wild at this fascinating emporium. This is truly a grown-up's toy store! The latest electronic gadgets, household helpers, sports items, games, novelties, and clothing make browsing the Sharper Image a unique experience.

SONY STYLE
550 Madison Ave (bet 55th and 56th St) 212/833-8800
Mon-Sat: 10-7; Sun: 11-6 www.sonystyle.com

You'll delight at this mixture of two Sony retail stores and a consumer-friendly atrium. Sony is often at the cutting-edge of new developments in consumer electronics, so periodic visits here will keep you up to date with the latest in radios, televisions, audio equipment, home-theater systems, cameras, clocks, and more. When you can find them, Sony's sales personnel are patient and knowledgeable, despite a somewhat overbearing security atmosphere. Their phone service is unbelievably bad.

STEREO EXCHANGE
627 Broadway (at Houston St)   212/505-1111
Mon-Fri: 11-7:30; Sat: 10:30-7; Sun: 11-6   www.stereoexchange.com

For high-end audio-video products, you can't do better than this outfit! They carry top names and can handle customer installation. The personnel really seem to care about their products.

> If you are browsing the numerous electronics, camera, and office-supply stores along Fifth Avenue and in the 50s along Avenue of the Americas, don't be misled by discounts quoted off the marked retail figure. In many cases, those list prices are grossly inflated and the discounts are no bargain. It is wise to shop around at reputable stores before deciding on a purchase.

WAVES
251 W 30th St (bet Seventh and Eighth Ave)   212/273-9616
Mon-Sat: 11-6   www.rubylane.com/shops/wavesradios

Bruce and Charlotte Mager are trying to make the past last forever with their collection of vintage record players, radios, receivers, and televisions. They have scorned the electronics age in favor of the age of radio. Their shop is a virtual shrine to the 1930s and before. At Waves you'll find the earliest radios (still operative!) and artifacts. There are promotion pieces, such as a radio-shaped cigarette lighter. Gramophones and anything dealing with the radio age are available. Waves also rents phonographs, telephones, and neon clocks. They make appraisals and will answer questions about repairs, sales, or rentals.

Eyewear and Accessories

THE EYE MAN
2264 Broadway (bet 81st and 82nd St)   212/873-4114
Mon, Wed: 10-7; Tues, Thurs: 10-7:30; Fri, Sat: 10-6;
Sun: 12-5 (closed Sun in summer)

Dozens of stores in Manhattan carry eyeglasses, but few take special care with children. The Eye Man carries a great selection of frames for young people, as well as specialty eyewear for grownups.

GRUEN OPTIKA
1225 Lexington Ave (bet 82nd and 83rd St)	212/628-2493
599 Lexington Ave (bet 52nd and 53rd St)	212/688-3580
1076 Third Ave (bet 63rd and 64th St)	212/751-6177
740 Madison Ave (at 64th St)	212/988-5832
2382 Broadway (at 87th St)	212/724-0850
2009 Broadway (at 69th St)	212/874-8749

Mon-Fri: 10-7; Sat: 10-5:30

The same faces and quality care can be found at Gruen Optika year after year. The firm enjoys a reputation for excellent service, be it emergency fittings or one-day turnaround, and they carry a superb selection of specialty eyewear. Their sunglasses, theater glasses, sport spectacles, and party eyewear are noteworthy.

JOEL NAME OPTIQUE DE PARIS
65 W Houston St (at Wooster St)
Mon-Fri: 11-7; Sat: 11-6   212/777-5888

Service is the name of the game here. Owner Joel Nommick and his crew of professionals stock some of the most fashionable specs in town.

LIGHTHOUSE INTERNATIONAL
111 E 59th St (bet Park and Lexington St)   212/821-9384
Mon-Fri: 10-6; Sat: 10-5   www.lighthouse.com

This is a wonderful place for the visually impaired and the blind. They also carry items for seniors who have mobility problems. Over 200 articles are displayed, including reading and writing supplies, large print books, canes, talking appliances, and vision-enhancing electronic devices.

MORGENTHAL-FREDERICS OPTICIANS
699 Madison Ave (bet 62nd and 63rd St)   212/838-3090
Mon-Fri: 9-7; Sat: 10-6; Sun: 12-6

944 Madison Ave (bet 74th and 75th St)   212/744-9444
Mon-Fri: 10-7; Sat: 10-6; Sun: 12-6

399 West Broadway (at Spring St)   212/966-0099
Mon-Fri: 11-8; Sat: 11-7; Sun: 12-6

Bergdorf Goodman, 754 Fifth Ave (at 58th St)   212/872-2526
Mon-Sat: 10-7

10 Columbus Circle (opening Fall 2003)
                                    www.morganthalfredericks.com

If you're looking for unique eyewear and accessories, Morgenthal-Frederics is one of the places of choice. Owner Richard Morgenthal displays a well-conceived collection of innovative styles, including exclusive designs. With Morgenthal-Frederics' various locations and attentive staff, clients are truly well serviced. They'll even make appointments with some of New York's best ophthalmologists.

20/20
150 E 86th St (bet Third and Lexington Ave)   212/876-7676
57 E 8th St (bet Broadway and University St)   212/228-2192
Mon-Fri: 10-7:30; Sat: 10-6; Sun: hours vary
                                    www.twenty-twentyeyewear.com

Whether you see glasses as a simple necessity, a statement of style, or both, the large selection at 20/20 will suit your needs. For over two decades they have offered trendsetting eyewear in a casual, appealing atmosphere. They also offer convenient services like overnight delivery, eye exams, and prescription fulfillment.

Fabrics, Trimmings

A.A. FEATHER COMPANY
(GETTINGER FEATHER CORPORATION)
16 W 36th St (bet Fifth Ave and Ave of the Americas), 8th floor
Mon-Thurs: 9-6; Fri: 9-3   212/695-9470
                                    www.gettingerfeather.com

Do you need an ostrich plume, feather fan, or feather boa for your latest ensemble, or have you made a quilt that you'd like to stuff with feathers? Well, you're in luck with A.A. Feather (a.k.a. Gettinger Feather Corporation). The Gettingers have been in the business since 1915, and first grandson Dan Gettinger runs it today. There aren't many family businesses left, and there are almost no other sources for fine-quality feathers. This is a find!

A. FEIBUSCH—ZIPPERS & THREADS
27 Allen St (bet Canal and Hester St)   212/226-3964
Mon-Fri: 9-5; Sun: 9:30-1 (closed Sun in summer)

www.zipperstop.com

A. Feibusch boasts of having "one of the biggest selections of zippers in the U.S.A," as if they really believe there are zipper stores throughout the country! They stock zippers in every size, style, and color (hundreds of them), and can make zippers to order. I saw one woman purchasing tiny zippers for doll clothes! Feibusch carries matching threads to sew in a zipper as well. Eddie Feibusch assured me that no purchase is too small or large, and he gives each customer prompt, personal service.

ALMAR FABRICS/BARON TEXTILES
227 W 40th St (bet Seventh and Eighth Ave)   212/398-3370 (Almar)
Mon-Fri: 9-5:30; Sat: 10-4   212/869-9616 (Baron)

Almar Fabrics specializes in bridal, mother-of-the bride, bridesmaids, and other special-occasion fabrics at reasonable prices. Baron, a sister company under the same roof, is known for imported high-end woolens (super 80s, super 160s) at discount.

B&J FABRICS
525 Seventh Ave (at 38th St), 2nd floor   212/354-8150
Mon-Fri: 8-5:45; Sat: 9-4:45   www.bandjfabrics.com

B&J started in the fabric business in 1940 and is now run by the second and third generations of the Cohen family. They carry fashion fabrics, many imported directly from Europe. Specialties of the house: natural fibers, designer fabrics, bridal fabrics, ultra-suede, Liberty of London, and silk prints (over a thousand in stock)! Swatches are sent free of charge. You will also find a wonderful selection of hand-dyed batiks.

BECKENSTEIN MEN'S FABRICS—FABRIC CZAR USA, INC.
257 W 39th St (bet Seventh and Eighth Ave)
Mon-Sat: 9-6   212/475-6666, 800/221-2727

Beckenstein is the finest men's fabric store in the nation. Proprietor Neal Boyarsky and his son Jonathan have been called "the fabric czars of the U.S." These folks sell to a majority of custom tailors in the country and to many top manufacturers of men's clothing, so you know the goods are best quality. Their customer list reads like a who's who: Warren Beatty, Al Pacino, Robert DeNiro, diplomats and politicians like the Kennedys and Rockefellers, Magic Johnson, Wayne Gretsky, and all three *Godfather* movies. You will find every kind of fabric, from goods selling for $10 a yard to fabulous pieces at $1,000 a yard. There are pure cashmeres, fine English suitings, silks, camel hair, and more.

HANDLOOM BATIK
214 Mulberry St (at Spring St)   212/925-9542
Thurs-Sat: 12-8; Sun: 1-6   www.handloombatik.com

At Handloom you'll find one of the largest and best collections of batik outside of a crafts museum. Carol Berlin runs Handloom Batik with near reverence for her merchandise. All of the fabrics are handmade, and she is quick to show how each can be set off to best advantage. Imported hand-woven and hand-batiked fabrics (primarily from India and Indonesia) are sold by the yard as fabric or are made up as clothing, napkins, tablecloths, and handiwork. Handloom Batik will also use its own fabrics for custom-made shirts and other garments. In addition, a gift selection features handicrafts of wood, stone, brass, and paper from the aforementioned countries. Pillows, bed covers, curtains, and napkins can be custom-made from the store's cotton ikat and batik.

HARRY ZARIN CO.
318 Grand St (at Allen and Orchard St)   212/925-6112
Sun-Thurs: 9-6; Fri: 9-5; Sat: 10-6   www.harryzarin.com

Founded in 1936, Harry Zarin is the largest and oldest warehouse in Manhattan (or so the folks here claim). This "fabric heaven" occupies an entire city block stocked with thousands of designer fabrics and trim at below wholesale prices. With one of the largest selections of designer fabrics in the country, Harry Zarin is a favorite inside source for decorators, set designers, and celebrity clientele. Remodeled in early 2003, Harry Zarin now carries some of the finest ready-made collections of window panels and other home furnishings. Another worthy Zarin operation is BZI Distributors (318 Grand St, 212/966-6690), which sells trimmings, fringe, and drapery and upholstery hardware.

HYMAN HENDLER AND SONS
67 W 38th St (bet Fifth Ave and Ave of the Americas)   212/840-8393
Mon-Fri: 9-6; Sat: 10-2:30 (closed Sat in July and Aug)
                                            www.hymanhendler.com

Although Hyman Hendler has passed away, the store that proudly bears his name is in the capable hands of his sons and niece. In the middle of the trimmings center of the world, it is one of the oldest businesses (established in 1900) and the crown head of the ribbon field. This organization manufactures, wholesales, imports, and acts as a jobber for every kind of ribbon. It's hard to believe as many variations exist as are jammed into this store.

LONG ISLAND FABRIC WAREHOUSE
406 Broadway (bet Canal and Walker St)   212/431-9510
Daily: 9-7

Long Island Fabric Warehouse has one huge floor of every imaginable kind of fabric and trimming. Since all are sold at discount, it's one of the best places to buy fabrics. Some of the attractions include an extensive wool collection and such dressy fabrics as chiffon, crepe, silk, and satin. Most amazing are the bargain spots, where remnants and odd pieces go for so little it's laughable. They sell an excellent selection of patterns, notions, trimmings, and dollar-a-yard fabrics.

M&J TRIMMING CO.
1000 and 1008 Ave of the Americas (bet 37th and 38th St)
Mon-Fri: 9-6; Sat: 10-5   212/391-9072
                                                          www.mjtrim.com

These folks claim to have the largest selection of trims at one location, and
I'm inclined to believe them! You will find imported trims, buttons, decorator trims, and various fashion accessories. One store specializes in clothing
and fashion trims, and the other features interior decor trim. They have over
a half century of experience in this business.

MARGOLA CORP. (Cinderella Division)
48 W 37th St (bet Fifth Ave and Ave of the Americas)
Mon-Fri: 8:30-6; Sat: 10-4   212/564-2929
                                                          www.margola.com

In the midst of a particularly cold and dreary winter not so long ago,
Seventh Avenue fashions began to blossom with artificial flowers as the "in"
look for spring. The department stores quickly got the message, and in a few
weeks people were removing their fur-lined gloves to hand over $30 for a sin-
gle flower for their lapel. Many such transactions were made along 34th
Street or Fifth Avenue, and only a few wise New Yorkers walked an extra two
blocks to the "trimmings district," where they could buy an identical flower
for $5. There were even buyers of the $30 variety who knew of the district
and wrongly assumed they couldn't get in! Margola's Cinderella stocks the
country's largest selection of feather trimmings, decorations, craft supplies,
and conversation pieces. You'll also find silk and other artificial flowers, veil-
ing, netting, and feather boas in many colors.

PARON FABRICS/PARON II
56 W 57th St (bet Fifth Ave and Ave of the Americas), 2nd floor
Mon-Sat: 9-5:45   212/247-6451

PARON EAST
855 Lexington Ave (bet 64th and 65th St)   212/772-7353
Mon-Sat: 9-5:45 (Thurs till 7)

PARON WEST
206 W 40th St (at Seventh Ave)   212/768-3266
Mon-Sat: 9-5:45 (Thurs till 7)   www.paronfabrics.com

Paron carries an excellent selection of contemporary designer fabrics at
discount prices. Many of the goods are available only in their stores. This is
a family operation, so personal attention is assured. Paron East now offers a
personal couture service with professional dressmakers. Paron Annex, their
half-price outlet, adjoins Paron West.

PIERRE DEUX FRENCH COUNTRY
65 Madison Ave (bet 58th and 59th St)   212/570-9343
Mon-Sat: 10-6 (Thurs till 7); Sun: 12-5   www.pierredeux.com

Pierre Deux, the French Country home-furnishings company, specializes
in authentic handcrafted products from the provinces of France. Everything
from 18th-century antique and reproduction furniture to fabrics, brightly
colored pillows, handbags, faience, pewter, lighting, wallpaper, table linens,
and glassware can be found here. Services include a personalized bridal
registry and custom orders.

SILK SURPLUS/BARANZELLI HOME
942 Third Ave (bet 56th and 57th St)   212/753-6511
Mon-Fri: 10-6; Sat: 10-5

Silk Surplus is the exclusive outlet for Scalamandre close-outs of fine fabrics, trimmings, and wallpaper, as well as Baranzelli's own line of imported and domestic informal fabrics and trimmings. Scalamandre sells for half of retail, and a choice selection of other luxurious fabrics is offered at similar savings. There are periodic sales, even on already discounted fabrics, at this elegant fabric store. They have added custom workrooms for making upholstery slipcovers and custom furniture.

TINSEL TRADING
47 W 38th St (bet Fifth Ave and Ave of the Americas)   212/730-1030
Mon-Fri: 10-5:30; Sat: hours vary   www.tinseltrading.com

Tinsel Trading claims to be the only firm in the United States specializing in antique gold and silver metallics from the 1900s. They have everything from gold thread to lamé fabrics. Tinsel Trading offers an amazing array of tinsel threads, braids, fringes, cords, tassels, gimps, medallions, edging, banding, gauze lamés, bullions, tinsel, fabrics, ribbons, soutache, trims, and galloons. All are genuine antiques, and many customers buy them for accenting modern clothing. The collection of military gold braids, sword knots, and epaulets is unsurpassed.

TOHO SHOJI (NEW YORK)
990 Ave of the Americas (at 36th St)   212/868-7466
Mon-Fri: 9-7; Sat: 10-6; Sun: 10-5

Ever hear of a bead and trimmings supermarket? Only in New York will you find an establishment like Toho Shoji, which stocks all manner of items that allow customers to design and make custom jewelry: earring parts, metal findings, chains, and every kind of jewelry component. Items are well displayed for easy selection.

THE YARN COMPANY
2274 Broadway (bet 81st and 82nd St), Room 1C   212/787-7878
Tues-Sat: 12-6; Wed: 12-8   www.theyarnco.com

The largest selection of unique high-end knitting yarns in the city can be found here. You'll find cashmeres, merino wools, silk, linen, rayon, and more. The best part of this second-floor operation is the personal interest shown customers by the owners. There are many samples to look at, and these folks are up to date on new yarns and designs. Workshops and classes are available.

Fans

SUPERIOR LIGHT & FAN
936 Broadway (at 22nd St)   212/677-9191
Mon-Fri: 8-6; Thurs: 8-7; Sat: 10-6; Sun: 12-6

Superior is the spot to go for a large selection of top names in ceiling and portable fans. They offer informed help, installation, and repair. Contemporary residential lighting is also a specialty.

Fireplace Accessories

DANNY ALESSANDRO
308 E 59th St (bet First and Second Ave)   212/421-1928
Mon-Fri: 9-5 (open weekends seasonally)

New Yorkers have a thing for fireplaces, and Danny Alessandro caters to that infatuation. Alessandro has been in business for more than four decades. Just as New York fireplaces run the gamut from antique brownstone to ultra-modern blackstone, Danny Alessandro's fireplaces and accessories range from antique pieces to a shiny new set of chrome tools. The shop also stocks antique marble and sandstone mantelpieces, andirons, and an incredible display of screens and tool kits. In the Victorian era, paper fans and screens were popular for blocking fireplaces when not in use. The surviving pieces stocked at Alessandro are great for modern decorating. Danny Alessandro will also custom-order mantels, mantelpieces, and accessories. Bear in mind that this is a fireplace accessory source and doesn't repair or clean fireplaces.

WILLIAM H. JACKSON COMPANY
210 E 58th St (bet Second and Third Ave)   212/753-9400
Mon-Fri: 9:30-5 (Fri till 4 in summer)   www.wmhj.com

"WBFP" in the real-estate ads stands for "wood-burning fireplace," and they are the rage in New York. In business since 1827, William H. Jackson is familiar with the various types of fireplaces in the city. In fact, they orginally installed many of those fireplaces. Jackson has hundreds of mantels on display in its showroom. They range from antiques and reproductions (in wood or marble combinations) to starkly modern pieces. There are also andirons, fire sets, screens, and excellent advice on enjoying your fireplace. Jackson does repair work (removing and installing mantels is a specialty), but they're better known for selling fireplace paraphernalia. Handy item: a reversible sign that reads "Damper Is Open"/"Damper Is Closed."

Lower East Side Shopping
Alife (178 Orchard St, 646/654-0628): shoes, clothing, art
Alife Rivington Club (158 Rivington St, 212/375-8128): sneakers (some vintage)
Nort235 (235 Eldridge St, 212/777-6102): shoes
Recon (237 Eldridge St, 212/614-8502): clothing
Studio 101 (101 Stanton St, 646/602-0570): clothing

Flags

ACE BANNER FLAG AND GRAPHICS
107 W 27th St (at Ave of the Americas)   212/620-9111
Mon-Fri: 7:30-4   www.acebanner.com

If you need a flag, Ace is the place. Established in 1916, Ace prides itself on carrying the flags of every nation in the world. Other kinds of flags can be made to order. They range in size from 4" by 6" desk flags to bridge-spanning banners. Ace also manufacturers custom banners, from podium to building size. If you're running for any kind of office, campaign paraphernalia can be ordered with a promise of quick delivery. Outfitting grand openings and personalizing equipment with such items as boat flags accounts for much of Ace's business. Ask for owner Carl Calo!

Floor Coverings

BEYOND THE BOSPHORUS
79 Sullivan St (bet Spring and Broome St)   212/219-8257
Tues-Sun: 11-7

Ismail Basbag, the owner of this establishment, was a kilim dealer for 12 years in Istanbul's grand bazaar before opening his shop in Soho in 1985. Anyone who can survive at that colorful, crowded, and noisy marketplace can certainly do business in Manhattan! Here you will find hand-woven Turkish kilim rugs and pillows in a variety of sizes, patterns, and colors. A new line of Turkish bolsters is available. Basbag travels to Turkey several times a year and will try to unearth customers' special requests. Rug cleaning and repair are available.

CENTRAL CARPET
81 Eighth Ave (at 14th St)   212/741-3700
Mon-Fri: 10-7 (Thurs: 10-8); Sat: 10-6; Sun: 11-6
www.centralcarpet.com

Imagine over 20,000 rugs in stock! Central Carpet carries handsome, new, antique, and semi-antique Oriental rugs from Persia, China, India, and Tibet; machine-made rugs from Belgium and Egypt; and hand-hooked rugs from China. Also featured are needlepoints, kilims, area rugs, and items suitable for children's rooms. A large selection of broadloom, as well as sisal carpeting and rug padding, is shown. Everything is sold at discount prices, and all rugs are displayed on racks for easy viewing.

COUNTRY FLOORS
15 E 16th St (bet Fifth Ave and Union Square W)   212/627-8300
Mon-Fri: 9-6; Sat: 9-5 (closed Sat in summer)
www.countryfloors.com

Country Floors is one of New York's biggest retail success stories, no doubt because they offer a magnificent product. Begun in 1964 in the tiny, cramped basement under the owner's photography studio, Country Floors has grown to include huge stores in New York and Los Angeles, with nearly 60 affiliates nationwide in Canada and Australia. Customers from across the country have learned that Country Floors carries the finest in floor and wall tiles and stone. Their sources include artisans from all over the world. A visit—or at least a look at their catalog—is necessary to appreciate the quality and intricacy of each design. Even the simplest solid-color tiles are beautiful.

ELIZABETH EAKINS
21 E 65th St (bet Fifth and Madison Ave)   212/628-1950
Mon-Fri: 10-5:30

Elizabeth Eakins is a first-class source for hand-woven wool and cotton rugs. She custom designs and makes hand-woven and hand-hooked rugs in standard and hand-dyed colors.

I.J. PEISER'S SONS
475 Tenth Ave (bet 36th and 37th St), 9th floor   212/279-6900
Mon-Fri: 9-5 (by appointment)

In business for nearly a century, these folks specialize in furnishing and installing new hardwood flooring. They work with top-end architects, designers, and general contractors. A large showroom displays various types of wood that can be installed in residential and commercial spaces.

MOMENI INTERNATIONAL
36 E 31st St (bet Park and Madison Ave), 2nd floor   212/532-9577
Mon-Fri: 9-5   www.momeni.com

The people here will tell you they are wholesale only, but don't let that scare you away. Those who visit their expanded showroom will be rewarded by one of the best sources for Oriental rugs in the city. Since they don't officially suffer individual retail customers, their prices reflect wholesale rather than retail business. That doesn't make them cheap (good Oriental rugs never are), but it does assure top quality at a fair price.

NEMATI COLLECTION
Art and Design Building
1059 Third Ave (bet 62nd and 63rd St), 3rd floor
Mon-Fri: 9-6; Sat: 10-4 (or by appointment)   212/486-6900
                                     www.nematicollection.com

The Nemati Collection was founded by Parviz Nemati, author of *The Splendor of Antique Rugs and Tapestries*. He has been dealing in antique Oriental rugs and tapestries for four decades. The tradition is now carried on by his son, Darius Nemati. In addition to an extensive collection of antique Oriental rugs and period tapestries, the gallery also features modernist and contemporary rugs, as well as an exclusive collection of custom carpeting and natural-fiber flooring. Services includes a full restoration and conservation department, consulting, insurance appraisals, and professional cleaning.

PASARGAD CARPETS
180 Madison Ave (bet 33rd and 34th St)   212/684-4477
Mon-Fri: 9-6; Sat: 10-6; Sun: 11-5   www.pasargadcarpets.com

Pasargad is a fifth-generation family business established in 1904. They know everything about antique, semi-antique, and new Persian and Oriental rugs. They have one of the largest collections in the country, and they provide decorating advice, repair and cleaning, and pickup and delivery service. Pasargad will also buy or trade quality antique rugs.

THE PILLOWRY
P.O. Box 6902, New York, NY 10128-0016   212/308-1630
By appointment

Although she has given up her store, Marjorie Lawrence still maintains a superior collection of antique and semi-antique pillows, which she has been creating since 1971. In a shop-size room at a warehouse, she gives personal attention to those interested in individually created pillows from over a thousand fragments in her possession: tapestry, needlepoint, silk, knotted rug, Aubusson, and more. There are also antique and semi-antique rugs, plus textiles that lend themselves to wallhanging, framing, and other exotic uses.

RUG WAREHOUSE
1 E 28th St (bet Fifth and Madison Ave), 5th floor   212/779-7373
Mon-Fri: 10-5 (by appointment)

The Rug Warehouse stocks one of the largest collections of antique and semi-antique Oriental rugs in the city. The current owners come from a family tradition of five decades in the rug business. A huge inventory of over 2,000 antique and semi-antique rugs in all sizes is available. Modern premises provide an attractive setting for rugs offered at good discounts.

SAFAVIEH CARPETS
153 Madison Ave (at 32nd St)   212/683-8399
238 E 59th St (at Second Ave)   212/888-0626
Mon-Fri: 9-6; Sat: 10-5
902 Broadway   212/477-1234
Mon-Sat, 10-7; Sun: 11-6   www.safavieh.com

There was a time when it was possible to visit the teeming markets of Tehran and find some real bargains in rugs. At Safavieh one is still able to see a vast selection of these beautiful works of art, even if the setting is a little less glamorous. Safavieh has one of the finest collections of Persian, Indian, Pakistani, and Chinese rugs in this country. They're displayed in a showroom spacious enough for customers to visualize how the prized pieces would look in their home or place of business. These rugs are truly heirlooms, and you will want to spend time hearing about their exotic origins. Prices, although certainly not inexpensive, are competitive for the superior quality represented. It doesn't hurt to do a little haggling.

Shopping in Harlem

Books: **Hue-Man Bookstore** (2319 Frederick Douglass Blvd, 212/665-7400) and **Liberation Bookstore** (421 Malcolm X Blvd, 212/281-4615)

Clothing and accessories: **Grandview** (2531 Frederick Douglass Blvd, 212/694-7324)

Housewares: **Xukuma** (183 Malcolm X Blvd, 212/222-0490)

Shoes: **Sole Kitchen** (236 W 135th St, 212/862-3757)

Flowers, Plants, and Gardening Items

CHELSEA GARDEN CENTER HOME
435 Hudson St (at Morton St)   212/727-7100
Mon-Fri: 11-8; Sat, Sun: 10-7   www.chelseagardencenter.com

This is a lifestyle store for the urban gardener, carrying a wide selection of plants and flowers, soil, fertilizer, containers, fountains, tabletop items, lighting, candles, bath products, holiday decor, tools, stationery, indoor and outdoor furniture, garden books, and much more. The selection at Chelsea

Garden Center Home—located in a former warehouse between Greenwich Village and Tribeca—is as broad as you will find in Manhattan. They also have a nursery (455 W 16th St, 212/929-2477) that's open daily from 9 to 7.

COUNTRY GARDEN
186½ Spring St (bet Thompson and Sullivan St)   212/966-2015
Mon-Fri: 9:30-6; Sat: hours vary seasonally

The service at Country Garden is highly personalized, and they show a great selection of cut flowers and plants. They arrange everything to order and will deliver all over Manhattan. You'll enjoy the picturesque 19th-century building.

SIMPSON & COMPANY FLORISTS
852 Tenth Ave (at 56th St)   212/772-6670
Mon-Sat: 9-6   www.newyorkflorist.com

Simpson specializes in unusual baskets, cut flowers, plants, and orchids. These folks can decorate for gatherings of all sizes, and their prices are very competitive.

TREILLAGE
418 E 75th St (at York Ave)   212/535-2288
Mon-Fri: 10-6; Sat: 10-5 (closed weekends in July and Aug)
                                        www.treillageonline.com

People forget that New Yorkers have gardens, too, although they are small. Many times they are just patios, but still they add a special dimension of charm to city living. Treillage can help make an ordinary plot of outside living into something special. There are all sorts of garden items, including furniture and accessories for indoors and outdoors, with a great selection of unusual pieces that will set your place apart. They sell everything except plants and flowers! Prices are not inexpensive, but why not splurge to enhance your little corner of the great outdoors?

VSF
204 W 10th St (bet 4th and Bleecker St)   212/206-7236
Mon-Fri: 10-5; Sat: by appointment

Those who want a special look when it comes to fresh-cut flowers or dried creations know you can't do better than this outfit. They have a top-drawer list of clients who take advantage of their talents for weddings and other special events. Ask for owners Jack Follmer or Todd Rigby.

ZEZÉ FLOWERS
398 E 52nd St (bet First Ave and East River)   212/753-7767
Mon-Fri: 8-6 (also open holiday weekends)

Zezé came to New York several decades ago from Rio de Janeiro, a city known for its dramatic setting, and he brought a bit of that drama to the flower business in Manhattan. Zezé's windows reflect his unique talent. The exotic orchid selection is outstanding. Here you will find the ultimate in personalized service, including same-day deliveries and special requests.

Frames

HOUSE OF HEYDENRYK
417 E 76th St (bet First and York Ave)   212/249-4903
Mon-Fri: 9:30-5; Sat: 9:30-3

The folks at House of Heydenryk have been doing frame reproductions of the highest caliber since 1935. They stock over 3,000 antique and reproduction frames. Specialties include Georgian-era English and American folk-art frames.

Furniture, Mattresses

General

CHARLES P. ROGERS & CO.
55 W 17th St (bet Fifth Ave and Ave of the Americas)   800/561-0467
Mon-Fri: 9-8; Sat: 10-7; Sun: 12-6   www.charlesprogers.com

Rogers has been allowing folks to sleep comfortably since 1885! Their brass beds are made from heavy-gauge brass tubing with solid brass castings. Iron beds are hand-forged, making them exceptionally heavy and sturdy. Wooden beds are available, too. Rogers stocks bed linens made from the finest materials, including European linen and Egyptian and Supima cotton. All are machine washable.

Hell's Kitchen is not just for eating! Some interesting shops in the area:

Domus Unaffected Living (413 W 44th St, 212/581-8099): household items

Mansa Mussa (628 Tenth Ave, 212/707-8736, by appointment): furniture, apartment size

Terrastacio (664 Tenth Ave, 212/245-0070): floral

FOREMOST FURNITURE SHOWROOMS
8 W 30th St (at Fifth Ave), 5th floor   212/889-6347
Mon-Fri: 10-6 (Thurs until 7); Sat: 10-5; Sun: 11-5
www.foremostfurniture.com

Decorators recommend Foremost to friends who want to get quality furniture while avoiding decorator commissions. Foremost has five full floors of furniture with about 250 furniture lines represented. The personnel are friendly and helpful, making this an excellent source. The values are indeed very good, so shop around and then make this one of your last stops.

GRANGE
200 Lexington Ave (at 32nd St), 2nd floor   212/685-9057
Mon-Fri: 9-6   www.grange.fr

Superb French furniture and accessories dominate the selling floor of this very attractive showroom. The goods are all French-inspired, and the furniture is clean-lined, functional, and in great taste. Note, however, that this is not a place for bargain hunters.

KENTSHIRE GALLERIES
37 E 12th St (bet University Pl and Broadway)   212/673-6644
Mon-Fri: 9-5   www.kentshire.com

Kentshire presents eight floors of English furniture and accessories, circa 1690-1870, with a particular emphasis on the Georgian and Regency periods. This gallery has an excellent international reputation, and the displays are a delight to see, even if the price tags are a bit high. There is also a collection of 18th- and 19th-century English jewelry. A Kentshire boutique at Bergdorf Goodman features antique jewelry.

KLEINSLEEP
962 Third Ave (at 58th St)   212/755-8210
Mon-Fri: 10-9; Sat: 10-8; Sun: 11-7

Kleinsleep is a chain specializing in bedding sold below department-store prices. The byword is *discount*, and at their New York location, prices are reduced even further. Kleinsleep features mattresses from Stearns & Foster, Sealy, Simmons, Serta, Kingsdown, and their own handcrafted line of Aireloom products. The Aireloom models feature an eight-way hand-tied box spring at prices you'd normally pay for a regular mattress. At Kleinsleep, customers get expertise and discounts up to 65%.

LOST CITY ARTS
18 Cooper Square (Bowery at 5th St)   212/375-0500
Mon-Fri: 10-6; Sat, Sun: 12-6   www.lostcityarts.com

Lost City Arts shows mid-20th-century (1950s and 1960s) modern classic furniture and lighting fixtures, plus many more vintage items.

NORTH CAROLINA FURNITURE SHOWROOM
12 W 21st St (at Fifth Ave), 5th floor   212/645-2524
Mon-Sat: 10-6 (Thurs till 8); Sun: 12-5   www.ncarolinafurniture.com

You'll find over 400 famous name brands here, and most everything is discounted. There are items for livingrooms and bedrooms, diningroom tables and chairs, sofa beds, recliners, platform beds and bedding, and furniture for children's rooms. For New Yorkers, who must make every square inch of apartment space count, this place is a must-visit.

OAK-SMITH & JONES
1510 Second Ave (bet 78th and 79th St)   212/327-3462
Mon-Sat: 10-8; Sun: 11-7   www.oaksmithandjones.com

A distinct foreign accent can be detected in the furniture and accessories carried here. Unique original and reproduction antiques and accessories from all over the world are shown next to an outstanding collection of antique pine items, brass and iron beds, vintage jewelry, and unusual gift items. Upholstery and decorating services are available.

OFFICE FURNITURE HEAVEN
22 W 19th St (bet Fifth Ave and Ave of the Amercas), 7th floor
Mon-Fri: 9-6   212/989-8600
                                                  www.officefurnitureheaven.com

Have you nearly exhausted your budget opening a new office? Relax. This place has bargains in first-quality contemporary pieces. Some are manufacturer's close-outs, while others are discontinued items. You'll find such names as Knoll, Herman Miller, and Steelcase here. There are conference tables, chairs, bookcases, file cabinets, accessories, and much more.

OSBORNE & OSBORNE
508 Canal St (1 block from Hudson River)   212/431-7075
By appointment

Since 1975, Kipp and Margot Osborne have been building custom-made hardwood furniture for private and corporate clients. Each of their pieces is signed, dated, and numbered, marking the continuing evolution of their work and the unique nature of each piece. Their work is shown in a landmark 1872 rowhouse in Tribeca. Traditional, time-proven cabinetmaking techniques and joinery provide the quality basis for Osborne furniture. Using these methods in conjunction with a careful process of wood selection and matching of wood grain, the Osbornes have created more than 2,000 pieces to date.

PHILIP ENGEL
205 Lexington Ave (at 32nd St)   212/684-7555
Mon-Fri: 10-7; Sat: 10-6; Sun: 12-5

They like to call themselves the "world's greatest leather store." Indeed, Philip Engel features outstanding pieces of furniture in leather and microfiber: sofas, diningroom tables and chairs, sectionals, sofa beds, and reclining chairs from all over the world. The company has been in business since 1967. Prices are reasonable, delivery is quick, pieces may be custom-ordered, and a free in-store design service is available.

Infants and Children

ALBEE BABY CARRIAGE
715 Amsterdam Ave (at 95th St)   212/662-5740
Mon-Sat: 9-5:30 (Thurs till 7)

This place makes me crazy. It's got one of the city's best selections of basics for infants and toddlers—everything from strollers and car seats to cribs and rocking chairs—and the staff can be very helpful. But it's a disaster area, and it's sometimes hard to get anyone's attention in the chaos, particularly on weekends. That said, Albee Baby Carriage is very popular with Manhattan parents (and grandparents), and it's worth a visit if you're expecting. Prices aren't the best in town, but they are the best north of 23rd Street.

Burlington Coat Factory (707 Ave of the Americas, 212/229-2247) is the sort of place that has many New Yorkers bemoaning the "mailing" of their city. But if you need basic baby furniture and equipment and know what you want, the prices at the Baby Depot on the third floor are often the best in town—that is, if you can find someone to help you. Another one-stop option for new parents is **buybuy Baby** (270 Seventh Ave, 917/344-1555), a cavernous Bed Bath & Beyond relative. The sales help and selection are better than at Burlington Coat Factory, but most prices aren't nearly as good.

CHELSEA KIDS QUARTERS
33 W 17th St (bet Fifth Ave and Ave of the Americas)
Mon-Sat: 10-6:30; Sun: 11-5:30   212/627-5524

There is nothing fancy about this relative newcomer to the children's furniture scene, but the selection of beds (including lots of bunk beds), desks, dressers, and other children's room basics is good, prices are reasonable, and the salespeople are friendly. If you're turning a nursery into a child's room and don't want to break the bank, Chelsea Kids Quarters is definitely worth a look.

GRANNY'S RENTALS
By appointment only   212/876-4310

Whether you're a new parent wanting to try out a particular item or a visitor who needs a stroller for a week, this is a great spot to know about! Granny's Rentals has all sorts of equipment and furniture for babies and children, including strollers, cribs, breast pumps, and car seats. They also rent tables and chairs for children's parties. The minimum rental is for one week, and they'll deliver directly to you from their warehouse in the Bronx.

LAURA BETH'S BABY COLLECTION
By appointment   212/717-2559
                                    www.laurabethsbabycollection.com

Laura Beth, who spent nearly a decade as the senior buyer for Barney's fashionable baby department, offers one-stop shopping for moms-to-be to create the perfect nursery, right down to crib linens, gliders, and decorative accessories. Shopping here is like perusing a private boutique, with Laura Beth on hand to provide expert guidance. Once the room is complete, Laura Beth can help choose your birth announcement from a wide selection of the finest stationery at prices that are better than retail.

PLAIN JANE
525 Amsterdam Ave (bet 85th and 86th St)   212/595-6916
Mon-Sat: 11-6   www.plainjanekids.com

What a pleasure it is to discover a store brimming with quality merchandise and a friendly, knowledgeable staff! This welcome addition to the baby and small child home-furnishing scene offers unique furniture, bedding, and accessories. Prices are higher than you'd pay straight off the shelf, but you're receiving excellent personal service and terrific style at Plain Jane. If you're having a baby or know somebody who is, stop in and look around.

SCHNEIDER'S JUVENILE FURNITURE
20 Ave A (at 2nd St)   212/228-3540
Mon-Sat: 10-6

If you are in the market for baby furniture and accessories, this little-known store (at least to "uptown" people) often has the best prices in Manhattan. On top of that, the friendly staff knows its stock, and there's enough space in the store to take a stroller for a test drive. Whether you're looking for cribs, car seats, strollers, diaper bags, backpacks, or other items for little ones, Schneider's is well worth a visit. They carry juvenile furniture as well.

WICKER GARDEN'S BABY
1327 Madison Avenue (at 93rd St)   212/348-1166
Mon-Sat: 10-6

There are no two ways about it: Pamela Scurry has a great sense of style. If you like wicker furniture, handpainted detail, and unusual, often whimsical designs, you'll love the baby and juvenile furniture on the second floor of this East Side institution. Moms-to-be will want to note that their selection of nice-looking (and comfortable) gliders is the best in the city. You'll also no doubt be quite taken with the extensive selection of almost quaintly formal infant's and children's clothing on the first floor.

Games—Adult

COMPLEAT STRATEGIST
11 E 33rd St (at Fifth Ave)   212/685-3880, 800/225-4344
Mon-Wed, Fri, Sat: 10:30-6; Thurs: 10:30-9
www.thecompleatstrategist.com

The Compleat Strategist was established over a quarter of a century ago as an armory of sorts for military games and equipment. As the only such place in the city, it was soon overrun with military strategists. As time went on, the store branched into science fiction, fantasy, and murder-mystery games, as well as adventure games and books. Today people who are fighting the Civil War all over again can browse alongside Dragon Masters. The stock is more than ample, and the personnel are knowledgeable and friendly. For more cerebral sorts, they have chess and backgammon sets—even good old Monopoly! Free shipping is offered on mail orders.

GAME SHOW
474 Ave of the Americas (bet 11th and 12th St)   212/633-6328
Mon-Sat: 12-7 (Thurs till 8); Sun: 12-5

1240 Lexington Ave (bet 83rd and 84th St)   212/472-8011
Mon-Sat: 11-6 (Thurs till 7); Sun: 12-5

If you can't find a kid's or adult's game or puzzle at Game Show, it probably doesn't exist. This store is crammed with the best of the lot, and the folks here love to talk to customers about their stock.

MINNESOTA FATS' "ALL FUN & GAMES"
160 W 26th St (bet Ave of the Americas and Seventh Ave)
Mon-Wed, Fri: 10-6:30; Thurs: 10-8; Sat, Sun: 11-5   212/366-6981
(closed Sun in summer)   www.mnfats.com

If you are looking for games and game equipment, this is the place. You'll find pool and ping-pong tables, plus equipment for shuffleboard, blackjack, roulette, chess, darts, backgammon, cribbage, bingo, Foosball, air hockey, craps, and much more. Rentals are available, too.

VILLAGE CHESS SHOP
230 Thompson St (bet Bleecker and 3rd St)   212/475-9580
Daily: noon-midnight   www.chess-shop.com

People who enjoy chess can play at the Village Chess Shop for a small price. Those searching for unique chess pieces should patronize this shop as well. Chess sets are available in pewter, brass, ebony, onyx, and more.

Village Chess has outstanding backgammon sets, too. In short, this should be your first stop if you're planning on moving chess pieces—either from one square to another or from their store to your home!

Gifts, Accessories

ADRIEN LINFORD
927 Madison Ave (bet 73rd and 74th St)   212/628-4500
1339 Madison Ave (at 93rd St)   212/426-1500
Daily: 11-7

At Adrien Linford you will find an eclectic mixture of gifts, decorative accessories for the home, occasional furniture, lighting, jewelry, and whatever else Gary Yee finds interesting and exciting. The atmosphere and price tags are definitely upscale; you'll be suitably impressed with the tasteful stock.

À LA MAISON
1078 Madison Ave (bet 81st and 82nd St)   212/396-1020
Mon-Sat: 10-6:30; Sun: 11-6

This place is a wonderful shop for those who want to present a really spectacular table! There are tabletop items, gifts for the home, some Parisian furniture items, and a bridal registry. All of the merchandise is of European origin.

BE-SPECKLED TROUT
422 Hudson St (at St. Luke's Pl)   212/255-1421
Mon-Sat: 10-8; Sun: 10-7

This turn-of-the-century general store features unique items for fishermen and anyone else with good taste. There is folk art, tea-related antiques, and handmade chocolates, plus the owner's collection of angling antiquities and eccentricities. An old-fashioned soda fountain of early 20th-century vintage serves egg creams, cherry-lime Rickeys, malts, lemonade, and more. Craig and Charlotte Hero's grandfather owned the shop's original fixtures. You can try homemade American pies on what used to be a real fishing ground. Yes, Be-Speckled Trout occupies the former site of Minetta Creek, which still flows under the Village.

BIZARRE BAZAAR
130¼ E 65th St (bet Lexington and Park Ave)   212/517-2100
Mon-Sat: 12-6

Some people collect baseball cards while others find political buttons fascinating. I collect "Do Not Disturb" signs from hotels I have stayed at! For the discerning and serious collector, Bizarre Bazaar offers antique toys, aviation and automotive memorabilia, vintage Louis Vuitton luggage, enamel glassware, French perfume bottles, Lalique pieces, artists' mannequins, architectural miniatures, and much more of good quality.

CAROLE STUPELL
29 E 22nd St (bet Park Ave and Broadway)   212/260-3100
Mon-Sat: 12-6   www.carolestupell.com

In my opinion, Carole Stupell is the finest home-accessories store in the country. The taste and thought that has gone into the selection of merchandise is simply unmatched. Keith Stupell, a second-generation chip-off-the-old-block, has assembled a fabulous array of china, glassware, silver, table-top and imported gift treasures designed solely for this store, and he displays them in spectacular settings. In addition, there is a large selection of china and glassware replacement patterns that date back over 30 years. Prices are not in the bargain range, but the quality is unequaled.

EXTRAORDINARY
251 E 57th St (bet Second and Third Ave)   212/223-9151
Daily: 11:30-10

An international gift selection is the draw here. Owner J. R. Sanders has a background as a museum exhibition designer, and it shows. You'll find boxes, bowls, trays, candleholders, lamps, jewelry, and other items for the home. The round-the-world theme includes merchandise from the Philippines, Japan, Thailand, China, Vietnam, India, Morocco, Ghana, Peru, and other stops. Quite a unique jewel!

FELISSIMO DESIGN HOUSE
10 W 56th St (bet Fifth Ave and Ave of the Americas)
Mon-Sat: 11-6 (Fri till 8)   212/247-5656

Constructed with the senses in mind, Felissimo Design House is a venue for "design experiences in everyday life." They sell not only products but also "space, inspiration, experience, and opportunity." The first four floors showcase the latest in everyday product design, while the fifth floor is an ever-changing exhibition space.

FLIGHTS OF FANCY
1502 First Ave (bet 78th and 79th St)   212/772-1302
Mon-Fri: 11-7 (Wed till 8); Sat: 10-7; Sun: 12-6
www.flightsoffancynyc.com

Flights of Fancy exudes charm, presenting soft music and an array of American treasures in a Victorian parlor setting beckoning passers-by. Many of the gifts are handmade and exclusive to the shop. Certain items are so unusual and special that orders pour in from around the country. Prices range from $2 to $2,000, so there is something for every gift-giving budget. A handmade American theme runs through the ever-changing stock.

IT'S A MOD, MOD WORLD
85 First Ave (bet 5th and 6th St)   212/460-8004
Mon-Thurs: noon-10; Fri, Sat: noon-11; Sun: noon-8
www.citysearch.com/nyc/modworld

Weird is the operative concept here. In a highly unique atmosphere, you will find all manner of whimsical and unusual items, like appliquéd clocks and altered Barbie dolls. If you feel inventive, they will even design special items (clocks, candles, votives, etc.) per your specifications. Don't miss the amazing floor lamps.

KIRNA ZABETE
96 Greene St (bet Prince and Spring St)   212/941-9656
Mon-Sat: 11-7; Sun: 12-6

Eclectic is the proper word for this store. What a collection! You'll find some high-end, top-name designer clothing, as well as candy, dog accessories, baby items, and a selection of unusual gifts. They also do home closet consultations. I get the feeling that co-owners Beth and Sarah have as much fun as their customers!

MAYA SCHAPER CHEESE & ANTIQUES
106 W 69th St (at Columbus Ave)   212/873-2100
Mon-Sat: 10-8; Sun: 12-7

Maya Schaper is one of those special personalities who knows what she likes and wants to share her interest in cheese and food-related antiques. Granted, this is an unusual combination. But Maya is an unusual person. You'll find interesting gifts, gift baskets, imported dried flower arrangements from France, country antiques, and painted furniture. Schaper will locate special items for customers. An interesting note: Scenes from the movie *You've Got Mail* were filmed in this shop.

MICHAEL C. FINA
545 Fifth Ave (at 45th St)   212/557-2500, 800/BUY-FINA
Mon-Fri: 10-7 (Thurs till 8); Sat: 10-6; Sun: 12-6
                                              www.michaelcfina.com

A New York tradition for over 60 years, Michael C. Fina is a popular bridal-registry firm with an extensive selection of sterling silver, china, crystal, jewelry and brand-name watches, and housewares. Prices are attractive, quality is top-notch, and the store is well organized.

ONLY HEARTS
386 Columbus Ave (at 79th St)   212/724-5608
230 Mott St (bet Prince and Spring St)   212/431-3694
Mon-Sat: 11-8; Sun: 11-6   www.only hearts.com

Helena Stuart offers romantics a fascinating array of intimate apparel and lingerie (including her own brand), heart-shaped or printed jewelry, balloons, boudoir pillows, soaps, and tissues. Heart-shaped candles and pasta, too!

PEPPER JONES
146 Beekman St (bet Front and South St)   212/964-9164
Daily: 8 a.m.-9 p.m.   www.pepperjones.com

An unusual combination here! On one hand, Pepper Jones is a neighborhood cafe in the South Street Seaport area that serves wonderful sandwiches, pastries, and the like. On the other, it is a tabletop gift store with an excellent selection at comfortable prices. If you have time, stick around and read the paper or play some games!

STAR MAGIC
1256 Lexington Ave (bet 84th and 85th St)   212/988-0300
Daily: 11-7   www.starmagic.com

Stepping through Star Magic's door is like visiting the future. From its midnight-black ceiling with suspended galactic spheres to its spacecraft-like walls, Star Magic is designed to make a visitor forget contemporary New York and enter a timeless universe. The motto "Yesterday's Magic Is Today's Science" describes the eclectic selection of what owner Shlomo Ayal calls "space-age gifts." There are toys and items for anyone with a scientific bent. Books have been chosen for their ability to make a reader "ponder the cosmos." Star Magic offers minerals and prisms, scientific instruments to explore the universe, high-tech toys, and new-age music that is positively futuristic.

SUSAN P. MEISEL DECORATIVE ARTS
141 Prince St (bet West Broadway and Wooster St)   212/254-0137
Tues-Sat: 10-6   www.meiselgallery.com

Meisel is really a toy store for nostalgic men. You will find the area's largest selection in certain specialized categories: pond sailboats, pinup originals, cigar paraphernalia, and airplanes of all sorts. It's a rather unusual combination, but if the mentioned items are on your want list, this is the place to visit!

WORKS GALLERY
1250 Madison Ave (bet 89th and 90th St)   212/996-0300
Mon-Thurs: 10-6:30; Fri, Sat: 10-6; Sun: 12-5
                                                www.worksgallery.com

Sometimes we all need a unique gift for a special person or occasion. At Works Gallery you will find one-of-a-kind jewelry and art-glass items hand-made by talented artists. You can even have a personal piece made from your own stones. They have been in business for two decades.

YELLOW DOOR
1308 Avenue M (bet 13th and 14th St), Brooklyn   718/998-7382
Mon-Fri: 10-5:45; Sun: 11-5   www.theyellowdoor.com

One of the best things about Brooklyn is a discount gift store on Avenue M in Flatbush, off the promenade of Ocean Parkway. It is run by native-born entrepreneur Sallee Bijou. For over 30 years the Yellow Door has been providing "Madison Avenue style at Brooklyn prices." The store carries an unparalleled selection of the finest name brands (Lalique, MacKenzie-Childs, Waterford, Baccarat, Lenox, Orrefors, Alessi, Towle) in 14- and 18-carat gold jewelry, gifts, china, table accessories, and bath items. Many items are priced at least 20% to 30% below suggested retail. Services include free local delivery, a bridal registry, and phone orders.

Greeting Cards

UNICEF CARD & GIFT SHOP
3 United Nations Plaza (44th St bet First and Second Ave)
Mon-Fri: 10-6   212/326-7054
                                            www.usfund@unicef.org

For half a century the United Nations Children's Emergency Fund (UNICEF) has been improving the lives of the world's children. One way this tremendous organization raises money for its life-saving projects and programs is through the sale of cards and gifts. If you've never seen UNICEF products before, then you're in for a treat at this well-planned and friendly store, which carries greeting cards, stationery, books and games for children, apparel, and a fascinating assortment of Nepalese paper products. It also sells cards chosen for sale in Asia, Africa, Europe, and South America. In fact, it's the only store in the U.S. that sells these exotic cards!

UNTITLED
159 Prince St (at West Broadway)   212/982-2088
Daily: 10-8 (Fri, Sat till 9)

The Metropolitan Museum of Art and the Louvre each have approximately 1,500 art cards for sale. Untitled, by contrast, has 4,000-plus cards in stock at any given moment. Those cards include modem-art postcards, greeting cards, and note cards. The postcards are filed either as pre- or post-1945, and they're further ordered within those classifications by artist. There are also postcards featuring famous photos and depictions of every possible type of art. Some of these items are good for gags, while others are suitable for framing. Untitled also sells design magazines, boxed cards, and books on art, design, typography, architecture, and photography.

Hearing Aids

EMPIRE STATE HEARING AID BUREAU
31 W 43rd St (bet Fifth Ave and Ave of the Americas)   212/921-1666
Mon, Tues, Thurs: 8:30-5:30; Wed: 8:30-6; Fri: 8:30-5

If President Reagan left no other legacy, he set a shining example by not being ashamed to wear a hearing aid. The latest hearing aids are so small that most people cannot even tell they're being used. Empire State has been in the business for over 50 years and carries the top names in the field: Siemens, Starkey, Bosch, Danavox, and the lastest in digital hearing aids by Widex. Skilled personnel will test and fit quality hearing aids in a quiet, unhurried atmosphere.

Hobbies

AMERICA'S HOBBY CENTER
263 W 30th St (bet Seventh and Eighth Ave)   212/675-8922
Mon-Fri: 9-5:30; Sat: 9-3:30   www.ahc1931.com

While hobbies and models are serious business here, there's also a light-hearted touch evident in the shop. Marshall Winston introduces himself as the "known authority on vehicular hobbies," which include model airplanes, boats, ships, trains, cars, radio-controlled objects, model books, helicopters, model rocketry, tools, and everything for model builders. They also sell wholesale to dealers and by mail order to retail customers, as well as conducting an export business. Ask for a catalog to see what they have in your field of interest.

JAN'S HOBBY SHOP
1435 Lexington Ave (bet 93rd and 94th St)   212/987-4765
Daily: call for hours

Jan's is one of my favorite examples of New York retailing! When Fred Hutchins was young, he was obsessed with building models and dioramas, particularly on historical themes. Eventually, his parents bought his favorite source of supply. Now he runs the shop, keeping Jan's stocked with everything a serious model builder could possibly want. The store has a superb stock of plastic scale models, model war games, paints, books, brushes and all kinds of model cars, trains, planes, ships, and tanks. It also carries remote-controlled planes, sailboats, ships, and tanks. Fred himself creates models and dioramas to order for television, advertising, and private customers. He is noted for accurate historical detail and can provide information from his vast library of military subjects. There is yet a third business: showcase building. Because any hobbyist likes to show his wares, Fred builds custom-made wood, plexiglass, glass, and mahogany showcases.

Home Furnishings—General

It used to be that only those with designer's cards were admitted to some trade buildings. Now, however, a number of design outfits will take care of individual customers, even if the signs on their doors say "Trade Only." Listed below are some of the buildings in New York to check out; each has a multitude of shops where you can find just about anything you want to fix up an apartment or home.

Architects & Designers Building: 150 E 58th St; Mon-Fri: 9-5
Decoration & Design Building: 979 Third Ave; Mon-Fri: 9-5 (It's a good idea to bring a decorator along with you.)
Fine Arts Building: 232 E 59th St; Mon-Fri: 9-5
Interior Design Building: 306 E 61st St; Mon-Fri: 9-5
Manhattan Art & Antiques Center: 1050 Second Ave; Mon-Fri: 10:30-6; Sun: 12-6

ABC CARPET & HOME
888 Broadway (at 19th St) 212/473-3000
Mon-Fri: 10-8; Sat: 10-7; Sun: 11-6:30 www.abchome.com

If you can visit only one home-furnishings store in Manhattan, this should be it! What started in 1897 as a pushcart business has grown and expanded into one of the city's most unique, exciting, and well-merchandised emporiums. (It's actually two buildings located across the street from each other.) ABC is the Bergdorf Goodman of home furnishings. There are floors of great-looking furniture, dinnerware, linens, gifts, accessories, antiques and more. You will see many one-of-a-kind pieces as you explore corner after corner. There is an entire floor of fabrics by the yard and an extensive carpet and rug selection at great prices. An outlet store is located in the Bronx (1055 Bronx River Avenue, at Bruckner Blvd; 718/842-8772).

AUTO
805 Washington St (bet Gansevoort and Horatio St) 212/229-2292
Tues-Sat: 12-7; Sun: 12-6 (closed Sun in Aug) www.thisisauto.com

Stock at Auto includes specially designed and sometimes hard-to-find home furnishings such as pillows, ceramics, glassware, and throws, plus some accessories. Most are handmade and one-of-kind. It's worth a visit!

BEDFORD & CO.
995 Lexington Ave (bet 71st and 72nd St) 212/772-7000
Mon-Fri: 10:30-6; Sat: 11-5 (closed Sat in July and Aug)

Donna D'Urso has assembled a fascinating collection of home furnishings and accessories, all selected with good taste and priced reasonably. For unusual vases, trays, pillows, and framed artwork, this is a good place to start.

KARKULA
68 Gansevoort St (bet Greenwich and Washington St)   212/645-2216
Tues-Sat: 11-7; Sun: 12-6   www.karkula.com

"Sexy" urban contemporary furniture and home furnishings with an American and European flair are shown to advantage at this hip outfit. A lot of new and up-and-coming designers get their start here. Designs feature such materials as bronze, solid wood, leather, and felt.

SURPRISE! SURPRISE!
91 Third Ave (bet 12th and 13th St)   212/777-0990
Mon-Fri: 10-7; Sat: 10-6; Sun: 11-5   www.surprisesurprise.com

Surprise! Surprise! offers a complete line of reasonably priced items for the home. They claim to possess the stock and knowhow to make your new apartment look like a home the same day you move in! You'll find a large selection of kitchenware, furnishings, and patio furniture.

Housewares, Hardware

BRIDGE KITCHENWARE
214 E 52nd St (bet Second and Third Ave)   212/688-4220
Mon-Fri: 9-5:30; Sat: 10-4:30   www.bridgekitchenware.com

Bridge Kitchenware is a unique-to-New York store that supplies almost every restaurant within 500 miles. Named for founder Fred Bridge, the store carries bar equipment, cutlery, pastry equipment, molds, copperware, cast-ironware, woodenware, stoneware, and kitchen gadgets. All goods are professional quality and excellent for home gourmets. Be sure to see the lines of imported French copperware, professional knives, and baking pans. After cooking with them, people use no other. Call for a catalog.

BROADWAY PANHANDLER
477 Broome St (at Wooster St)   212/966-3434, 866/266-5927
Mon-Fri: 10:30-7; Sat: 11-7; Sun: 11-6

www.broadwaypanhandler.com

Thousands of cutlery, bakeware, tabletop items, and cookware pieces are available at sizable savings. Guest chefs make periodic appearances, and a fine selection of professional items is offered to both walk-in customers and restaurant and hotel buyers.

CK&L HARDWARE
307 Canal St (at Broadway)   212/966-1745
Mon-Sat: 8:30-5:45; Sun: 9:30-5:30

In New York, a shopping trip for hardware isn't complete without a trip to Canal Street. CK&L is the oldest and best hardware store down here. Years ago, these stores dealt in industrial and war surplus. With the passing demand for such goods and an influx of electronics, the Canal Street surplus stores turned to what is best described as "hardware and whatever." All of the stores do business the same way. Sawed-off cardboard boxes containing an assortment of junk are "displayed" in front. The real merchandise is inside. There are hand tools, power tools, plumbing and electrical goods, accessories, and supplies. Prices are much lower than at retail stores uptown. When you see the place, you'll understand why the overhead is so low.

GARBER HARDWARE
49 Eighth Ave (bet Horatio and Jane St)   212/929-3030
Mon-Fri: 8-5; Sat: 8-2:30

This is another unique family business that has become a New York institution. The Garbers have been operating since 1884 at the same location with the appealing motto "Either we have it or we can get it for you." You will find a complete inventory of paints, hardware, plumbing and electrical supplies, housewares, locks, tools, and building materials. Same-day or next-day local delivery, custom window shades, lamp repair, key-cutting, and pipe-cutting to size are among the many handy services offered.

GARRETT WADE
161 Ave of the Americas (at Spring St)   212/807-1155, 800/221-2942
Mon-Fri: 9-5:30; Sat: 10-3   www.garrettwade.com

The Garrett Wade customer appreciates fine woodworking tools, as the store prides itself on offering the highest-quality tools from all over the world. The main business is mail-order, and the catalog is all-encompassing. It lists every imaginable woodworking aid, explaining each piece's function. It reads like a how-to guide! Garrett Wade assumes that anyone can put together a rocker or, at the very least, appreciate the function of a lightweight spokeshave. After a visit here, you may become a believer, too!

GEORGE TAYLOR SPECIALTIES
76 Franklin St (bet Church and Broadway)   212/226-5369
Mon-Thurs: 7:30-5; Fri: 7:30-4

Taylor stocks plumbing replacement parts to fit all faucets, and custom faucets can be fabricated via special order. They also offer reproduction faucets and custom designs of fittings for unique installations. Antique-style towel bars, bath accessories, and pedestal sinks are a specialty. Founded in 1869, Taylor remains a family-run operation. Ask for father Chris, daughter Valerie, or son John.

GRACIOUS HOME
1217 and 1220 Third Ave (bet 70th and 71st St)   212/517-6300
Mon-Fri: 8-7; Sat: 9-7; Sun: 10-6

1992 Broadway (at 67th St)   212/231-7800
Mon-Thurs: 8-8; Fri, Sat: 8-9; Sun: 9-7   www.gracioushome.com

For over four decades Gracious Home has been a popular shopping spot for savvy New Yorkers. It is a must-visit for anyone interested in fixing up their home, establishing a new one, looking for gifts, or just browsing a store that typifies the New York lifestyle. The style, expertise, and service are outstanding. You'll find appliances, wall coverings, gifts, hardware, decorative bath accessories, lighting, china, casual furniture, bedding, shelving, pots and pans, and heaven knows what else! They install window coverings, large appliances, and countertops; offer tool rental and repair services; provide a special-order department; and deliver in Manhattan.

LEESAM KITCHEN AND BATH CENTER
124 Seventh Ave (at 17th St)   212/243-6482
Tues-Fri: 10-5:45; Sat: 11-5   www.leesamkitchens.com

For over a half-century these folks have been fixing up kitchens and bathrooms. Whether you're shopping for medicine cabinets, kitchen cabinets, faucets, shower enclosures, or counters, you will see one of the largest selections of top brands from domestic suppliers. There's no excuse not to remodel your cluttered, dysfunctional old kitchen using one of their computer-designed plans.

Remodelers and builders, take note! For lumber, plywood, masonite, bricks, cork, paint, and much more, **Metropolitan Lumber and Hardware** (175 Spring St, 212/966-3466 and 617 Eleventh Ave, 212/246-9090) is a good name to remember.

P.E. GUERIN
23 Jane St (bet Greenwich and Eighth Ave)   212/243-5270
Mon-Fri: 9-5:30 (by appointment)   www.peguerin.com

Andrew Ward, P.E. Guerin's current president, is the fourth generation to run the oldest (1857) decorative hardware firm in the country and the only foundry in the city. What's more, they've been on Jane Street since 1892. In that time, the firm has grown into an impressive worldwide operation. The main foundry is now in Valencia, Spain (although work is still done at the Village location), and there are branches and showrooms across the country and in Puerto Rico. The Jane Street location is still headquarters for manufacturing and importing decorative hardware and bath accessories. Much of it is done in brass or bronze, and the foundry can make virtually anything in those materials, including copies and reproductions. The Gueridon table has garnered design and production awards and enjoys a worldwide reputation. No job is too small for this firm, which operates like the hometown industry it thinks it is. They offer free estimates and help with any hardware problems.

SIMON GREENSPAN HARDWARE
261 W 35th St (bet Seventh and Eighth Ave)   212/244-3496
Mon-Fri: 9-5; Sat: 9-3

This store has been in the same location since the early 1930s, and the collection of merchandise reflects that time period. They specialize in supplies for the garment industry, but there is much more—like kerosene lamps, duct tape, and sewing dummies. It's worth coming in to take a look around and visit with proprietor Bernie Wittie.

SIMON'S HARDWARE & BATH
421 Third Ave (bet 29th and 30th St)   212/532-9220
Mon-Fri: 8-5:30 (Thurs till 7); Sat: 10-6 www.simons-hardware.com

This is really a hardware supermarket. Simon's offers one of the city's finest selections of quality decorative hardware items, and bath and kitchen fixtures and accessories. The personnel are patient, even if you just need something to fix a broken handle on a chest of drawers.

WILLIAMS-SONOMA
1175 Madison Ave (at 86th St)   212/289-6832
110 Seventh Ave (at 17th St)   212/633-2203
121 E 59 St (bet Park and Lexington Ave)   917/369-1131
Hours vary by store   www.williams-sonoma.com

From humble beginnings in the wine country of Sonoma County, California, these stores have expanded over the nation and now are referred to as the "Tiffany of cookware stores." The serious cook will find a vast display of quality cookware, bakeware, cutlery, kitchen linens, specialty foods, cookbooks, small appliances, kitchen furniture, glassware, and tableware. The stores also offer a gift- and bridal-registry service, cooking demonstrations, free recipes, gift baskets, and shopping assistance for corporations or individuals. Ask for their attractive catalog, which includes a number of excellent recipes.

Imports
Afghan

NUSRATY AFGHAN IMPORTS
215 W 10th St (at Bleecker St)   212/691-1012
Sun-Thurs: 1-9; Fri-Sat: 1-11

Abdul Nusraty has transformed a corner of the Village into a vision of Afghanistan that is fascinating (and thankfully free of political strife). Nusraty is one of the best sources of Afghan goods on the continent. There are magnificently embroidered native dresses and shirts displayed alongside semiprecious stones mounted in jewelry or shown individually. One area of the store features carpets and rugs, while another displays antique silver and jewelry. Nusraty has an unerring eye; all of his stock is of the highest quality and is often unique as well. The business operates on both a wholesale and retail level.

Highlights in British goods, from our good friends across the water.
British sweets: **Carry On Tea & Sympathy** (110 Greenwich St, 212/807-8329)
Clothes and housewares: **Eskandar** (Bergdorf Goodman, 754 Fifth Ave, 3rd floor, 212/872-8659)
Fashion designer: **Alexander McQueen** (417 W 14th St, 212/645-1797)
Paper goods: **Smythson of Bond Street** (4 W 57th St, 212/265-4573)
Purses, shoes, umbrellas, socks: **Lulu Guinness** (394 Bleecker St, 212/367-2120)
Soccer gear: **Onion Bag Soccer Shop** (299 E 11th St, 212/982-2095)

Chinese

CHINESE PORCELAIN COMPANY
475 Park Ave (at 58th St)   212/838-7744
Mon-Fri: 10-6; Sat: 11-5   www.chineseporcelainco.com

Look here for Chinese ceramics and works of art. There is Chinese, Tibetan, Indian, Khymer, and Vietnamese sculpture, as well as English, French, and continental furniture.

WING-ON TRADING
145 Essex St (bet Delancey and Houston St)   212/477-1450
Mon-Sat: 9-6

No need to go to Hong Kong to get your Chinese porcelain or earthenware.

Even though it is located on the disorganized Lower East Side, Wing-On has a complete and well-organized stock of household goods. One of their specialties is Chinese teas, sold at low prices.

Eskimo/Native American

ALASKA ON MADISON
937 Madison Ave (bet 74th and 75th St)   212/879-1782
Tues-Sat: 11:30-6 (or by appointment)   www.alaskaonmadison.com

This gallery is New York's most complete source for Eskimo art. Rare antiquities and artifacts of centuries-old Arctic cultures are displayed next to sculptures of Indians of the Northwest. Periodic shows highlight aspects of these cultures. A number of contemporary artists whose works have been shown here have gained international acclaim.

General

JACQUES CARCANAGUES
21 Greene St (bet Grand and Canal St)   212/925-8110
Daily: 11:30-7

After a stint in the diplomatic service, Frenchman Jacques Carcanagues decided to assemble and sell the finest artifacts he had encountered in his world travels. So while the store is mostly Southeast Asian, it is, in Jacques own words, "a complete ethnic department store, not a museum." Yet the stock is all of museum quality. Textiles and tansus (dressers) are everywhere, as are jewelry and lacquerware. It is also very appealing to Soho shoppers, who can choose among Indian, Burmese, and Thai sculptures of many periods and unusual household objects not likely seen elsewhere in New York. The overall effect is that of an Eastern marketplace, lacking only water pipes and music.

KATINKA
303 E 9th St (at Second Ave)   212/677-7897
Tues-Sat: 4-7 (call ahead, as hours vary)

This is an import paradise, with jewelry, natural-fiber clothing, shoes, scarves, belts, hats, musical instruments, incense, and artifacts from India, Thailand, Pakistan, Afghanistan, and South America. The most popular items are colorful shoes and embroidered silk skirts from India. The place is small, and prices are reasonable. Jane Williams and Billy Lyles make customers feel like they have embarked on a worldwide shopping expedition!

PIER 1 IMPORTS
461 Fifth Ave (at 40th St)   212/447-1610
Mon-Sat: 9-8; Sun: 11-7

71 Fifth Ave (at 15th St)   212/206-1911
Mon-Fri: 10-9; Sat: 10-9; Sun: 11-7

1550 Third Ave (at 87th St)   212/987-1746
Mon-Sat: 10-9; Sun: 11-7   www.pier1.com

Pier 1 is one of my very favorite stores! No need to spend your time or money running off to distant places; just come to Pier 1. Here you will find imported diningroom sets, occasional furniture, bathroom accessories, picture frames, brassware, china and glassware, floor coverings, bedding, pillows, and much more. The goods come from exotic lands throughout Asia and the rest of the world. The selections are inviting, the prices are right, and the stores are fun to visit. Besides, the chain's head honcho, Marvin Girouard, is one of the best merchants in the business!

SHEHERAZADE IMPORTS
121 Orchard St (bet Delancey and Rivington St)   212/539-1771
Daily: 11-7   www.scheherazadenyc.com

Sheherazade features handcrafted merchandise from a number of countries, all imported directly. You'll find home furnishings from North Africa, the Middle East, and Asia, including antique and contemporary furniture, carpets, tapestries, chandeliers, lanterns, jewelry, and gifts. Custom-made furniture can be ordered.

Indian

INDIA COTTAGE EMPORIUM
1150 Broadway (at 27th St)   212/685-6943
Mon-Fri: 9:30-6:30; Sat: 10-5

India Cottage features clothing, jewelry, handicrafts, and gifts imported directly from India. Moti R. Chani has a sharp eye for the finest details; the Indian clothing he sells reflects his taste and expertise. The clothing is prized by Indian nationals and neighborhood residents for its sheer beauty. The garments are made of cotton and feature unique madras patterns. Pay particular attention to the leather bags.

When you are out shopping, take a stroll down Mott Street in Nolita (North of Little Italy, next to Soho). You'll find several interesting boutiques worthy of shopping for gifts.
Dinosaur Designs (250 Mott St, 212/680-3523): housewares
Polux Fleuriste (248 Mott St, 212/219-9646): flowers
Room One (229 Mott St, 212/625-9444): sheets and towels

Italian

CAROSELLO PENTAGRAMMA ITALIANO
119 Mulberry St (at Canal St)   212/925-7253
Mon-Sun: 10-11

Every section of New York with a concentrated ethnic population has a grouping of stores that serve its specific needs. Usually it will include a bakery, coffee shop, bookstore, and import shop featuring various items from the homeland. Often one shop is devoted to a distinctive characteristic of that nationality. What could be more natural than a shop in Little Italy dedicated to recordings and music? Carosello is primarily a music shop specializing in Italian recordings and operas, but it is also a bookstore, import store, and gift shop. One can find perfumes, Italian newspapers and magazines, and gifts, as well as Caruso recordings. The atmosphere is informal, and customers can often be heard humming arias while perusing record jackets.

FORZANO ITALIAN IMPORTS
128 Mulberry St (at Hester St)   212/925-2525
Daily: 10 a.m.-midnight   www.forzanoitalianimports.com

If you are looking for something Italian, Forzano is the place. You will find imported Italian CDs and cassettes; espresso, cappuccino, and pasta machines; soccer-team shirts; and all kinds of novelties. Forzano is a landmark in Little Italy, run by the same family since 1958.

Japanese

SARA
952 Lexington Ave (bet 69th and 70th St)   212/772-3243
Mon-Fri: 11-7; Sat: 12-6   www.saranyc.com

Looking for something with a Japanese flair? Sara is the place to go for modern Japanese ceramics, glassware, tableware, and gifts.

THINGS JAPANESE
127 E 60th St (bet Lexington and Park Ave), 2nd floor
Mon-Sat: 11-5 (Tues: 11-6)   212/371-4661
                                                  www.thingsjapanese.com

Things Japanese believes that the Japanese "things" most in demand are prints. So while there are all sorts of Japanese artworks and crafts, prints highlight the selection. They know the field well and will help would-be collectors establish a grouping or assist decorators in finding pieces to round out decor. There are also original 18th- to 20th-century Japanese woodblock prints, porcelains, baskets, chests, lacquers, and books. Prices range from $10 to several thousand dollars, and every piece is accompanied by a certificate of authenticity. Things Japanese claims that you need to appreciate both the subject matter and the artistry in the works it sells, and that's not a difficult or unpleasant task at all.

Middle Eastern

PERSIAN SHOP
534 Madison Ave (bet 54th and 55th St)   212/355-4643
Mon-Sat: 10-6

This outfit has been in business since 1940, featuring unusual Middle Eastern items: end tables, chairs, frames, mirrors, and brocades sold by the yard or made into magnificent neckties for men. The jewelry selection is especially noteworthy. You'll find precious and semiprecious items, silver and gold cuff links, rings, earrings, bracelets, necklaces, and heirloom pieces. There are also Chinese vases, garden stools, Russian and Greek icons, and planters that will add a special air of interest to any setting.

Ukrainian

SURMA (THE UKRAINIAN SHOP)
11 E 7th St (at Third Ave)   212/477-0729
Mon-Sat: 11-6   www.surmastore.com

Since 1918, Surma has conducted business as the "general store of the Slavic community in New York City." Quite honestly, it seems capable of serving the entire hemisphere. Surma is a bastion of Ukrainianism. Once inside, it is difficult to believe you're still in New York. The clothing here is ethnic opulence. There are dresses, vests, shirts, blouses, hand-tooled and soft-soled leather dancing shoes, and accessories. All are hand-embroidered with authentic detailing. For the home, there are accent pieces (including an entire section devoted to Ukrainian Easter-egg decorating), brocaded linens, and Surma's own Ukrainian-style honey (different and very good). Above all, Surma is known for its educational tapes, and books. Pay particular attention to the paintings and stationery, which feature modern-day depictions of ancient Ukrainian glass paintings.

Jewelry

BILL SCHIFRIN & HERMAN ROTENBERG
National Jewelers Exchange
4 W 47th St (at Fifth Ave), Booth 86   212/221-1873, 800/877-3874
Mon-Fri: 10-5:30   www.unusualweddingrings.com

From a booth in the National Jewelers Exchange—better known for its collection of gold, platinum, and diamond wedding and engagement rings —Bill Schifrin and son-in-law Herman Rotenberg preside over a collection of over 2,000 unusual wedding rings. Prices range from under $100 to several thousand dollars, depending upon the work's complexity, metal, and stones used. Bill has been doing this for over 50 years and knows the story behind each ring.

CHROME HEARTS
159 E 64th St (bet Lexington and Third Ave)   212/327-0707
Mon-Sat: 11-7   www.chromehearts.com

Chrome Hearts shows a broad selection of handmade jewelry, clothing in leather and fabric, gadgets for people who think they have everything, handcrafted furniture in exotic woods, great-looking eyewear, and much more. All merchandise is of a nontraditional nature. If you're looking for unique accessories, this is a good place to start.

DAVID SAITY/SAITY JEWELRY
450 Park Ave (bet 56th and 57th St)   212/223-8125
Mon-Sat: 11-6   www.davidsaityny.com

David Saity's magnificent store showcases his renowned collection of authentic Native American jewelry. There are numerous rare and breathtaking turn-of-the-century collector's items, such as watchbands, belt buckles, bow ties, squash-blossom necklaces, chokers, bracelets, rings, hair accessories, cuff links, earrings, and concha belts. Over 10,000 original masterpieces—handcrafted by artisans of the Zuni, Navajo, Hopi, and Santa Domingo tribes—are shown here. They have received a large quantity of rare and antique jewelry from isolated reservations. The collection spans more than a half a century, featuring sterling silver, turquoise, coral, jet, and mother-of-pearl gemstones.

DIAMONDS BY RENNIE ELLEN
15 W 47th St (bet Fifth Ave and Ave of the Americas), Room 401
Mon-Fri: 10-4:30 (by appointment)   212/869-5525
                                      www.rennieellen.com

Rennie Ellen is a wholesaler offering the sort of discounts the city's wholesale businesses are famous for. She was the first female diamond dealer in the male-dominated Diamond District. Ellen personally spent so much time and effort keeping the district straight and honest that she earned the title

"Mayor of 47th Street." Ellen's reputation is impeccable. Her diamond-cutting factory deals exclusively in diamond jewelry. There are pendants, wedding bands, engagement rings, and diamonds to fit all sizes, shapes, and budgets. All sales are made under Ellen's personal supervision and are strictly confidential. Call for the $3 mail-order catalog.

FORTUNOFF
681 Fifth Ave (at 54th St)   212/758-6660
Mon-Sat: 10-6 (Thurs till 7); Sun: 12-5   www.fortunoff.com

This is one of the best stores in Manhattan devoted to quality merchandise. Prices on all items are competitive. There is a crystal and clock department, but it is in the jewelry area (especially antique silver) that the store really shines. A jeweler is on duty at all times. Fortunoff shows one of the largest and finest collections of 14- and 18-karat gold jewelry in the city, as well as a fine selection of precious and semiprecious stones, brand-name watches, and flatware.

JEWELS BY JEN
1277 Third Ave (bet 73rd and 74th St), Suite 1A   212/826-3892
Mon-Fri: 10-5 (by appointment)   www.jewelsbyjen.com

Jennifer Miller specializes in slightly altered versions of classic and estate jewelry, ranging from the looks of Harry Winston and Cartier to contemporary artisans like Bulgari. The assortments change from time to time. No one will even know that you aren't wearing an original! Prices are reasonable, and clients can leave a wish list for thoughtful spouses (or whoever) looking for a special gift.

MAX NASS
118 E 28th St (bet Park Ave S and Lexington Ave)   212/679-8154
Mon-Fri: 9:30-6; Sat: 9:30-4

The Shah family members are jewelry artisans. Arati and Araceli are the designers and Parimal ("Perry") is the company president. Together they make and sell handmade jewelry; service, repair clocks and watches; and restore antique jewelry. At Max Nass, they deal in virtually every type of jewelry: antique (or merely old), silver and gold, as well as semiprecious stones. Two special sales each year bring their already low prices down even further. One is held the last three weeks in January (33% discount), and the other runs for two weeks in July (25% discount). In between, Arati will design pieces on a whim or commission. His one-of-a-kind necklaces are particularly impressive. The store also restores, restrings, and redesigns necklaces.

MURREY'S JEWELERS
1395 Third Ave (bet 79th and 80th St)   212/879-3690
Mon-Sat: 9:30-6

I heartily recommend this shop! Family jewelers since 1936, Murrey's sells fine jewelry, watches, and giftware. In the service area, they do fine-jewelry repair, expert special-order design and manufacturing, European clock repair, engraving, pearl stringing, and watch repair. The talented staff includes three goldsmiths, two watchmaker/clockmakers, one stringer, and one of the world's top European watchmakers.

MYRON TOBACK
25 W 47th St (bet Fifth Ave and Ave of the Americas)   212/398-8300
Mon-Fri: 8-4   www.myrontoback.com

Myron Toback is ostensibly a refiner of precious metals with a specialty in findings, plate, and wire. Not very useful to the average customer, you might think. But note the address. Toback is not only in the heart of the Diamond District but is also the landlord of an arcade crammed full of wholesale artisans of the jewelry trade. Taking their cue from Toback, they are open and friendly to individual retail customers. So bookmark Toback as a source of gold, gold-filled, and silver chains sold by the foot at wholesale prices. And don't overlook the gold and silver earrings, beads, and other jewelry items sold at prices that are laughably less than those at establishments around the corner on Fifth Avenue. Tools and other materials for stringing beads and pearls are also carried here. Though most customers are professional jewelers or wholesale organizations, Toback is simply charming to do-it-yourselfers, schools, and hobbyists. Now his son and daughter have joined him.

PEDRO BOREGAARD
18 E 53rd St (bet Fifth and Madison Ave), 15th floor   212/826-3660
Mon-Fri: 10-6 (by appointment)   www.boregaard.com

Unusual rings, earrings, brooches, chains, and bracelets—all handmade and each a true work of art—are hallmarks of this very talented designer, who features items for men and women. Pieces may combine rubies, saphires, and diamonds shaded in colors from champagne to cognac, and pink, white or yellow gold. Boregaard's credentials are impressive: apprenticeship and professional work in Germany, a jewelry workshop in England, and work with Tiffany for designers such as Angela Cummings, Elsa Peretti, and Paloma Picasso.

Ladders

PUTNAM ROLLING LADDER COMPANY
32 Howard St (bet Lafayette St and Broadway)   212/226-5147
Mon-Fri: 8:30-4:30   www.putnamrollingladder.com

Putnam is an esoteric shop on an esoteric street! Why, you might ask, would anyone in New York need those magnificent rolling ladders used in traditional formal libraries? Could there possibly be enough business to keep a place like this going since 1905? The answer is that clever New Yorkers turn to Putnam to improve access to their lofts (especially sleeping lofts). Recent customers include President and Mrs. George W. Bush for their Crawford, Texas home. Here's a partial list of ladders, which come in many hardwoods: rolling ladders (custom-made, if necessary), rolling work platforms, telephone ladders, portable automatic ladders, scaffold ladders, pulpit ladders, folding library ladders, library stools, aerial platforms, library carts with steps, steel warehouse ladders, safety ladders, electric stepladders for industrial use, and mechanics' stepladders.

Leather Goods, Luggage

JOBSON'S LUGGAGE
666 Lexington Ave (bet 55th and 56th St)
Mon-Sat: 9-6; Sun: 11-5   212/355-6846, 800/221-5238
                                               www.luggageisus.com

The key to a successful luggage store in New York is to offer a vast selection at discount prices. With the exception of a store such as T. Anthony, which depends on quality and service to offset its high prices, most of the stores I've listed offer good variety and discounts. At Jobson's, they stock the largest selection of brand-name luggage, attaché cases, and small leather goods in the metropolitan area. Their sales volume enables them to sell at prices that are close to wholesale. While other stores make similar claims, Jobson's sales staff and personal attention set it apart. They also offer free monogramming, a complete repair department, and free delivery in Manhattan.

ORIGINAL LEATHER STORE
176 Spring St (bet Thompson St and West Broadway)   212/219-8210
Mon-Fri: 11-8; Sat: 10-8; Sun: 12-8
256 Columbus Ave (at 72nd St)   212/595-7051
Mon-Sat: 11-8; Sun: 11-7
1100 Madison Ave (at 82nd St)   212/585-4200
Mon-Sat: 10-7; Sun: 12-6
171 W 4th St (bet Ave of the Americas and Seventh Ave)
Mon-Wed: 11-8; Thurs-Sat: 11 a.m.-12 a.m.; Sun: 12-9 212/675-2303
1124 Third Ave (at 66th St)   212/472-2120
Mon-Sat: 10-7; Sun: 11-6   www.originalleather.com

This store is a must for leather lovers, trendsetters, and the fashion elite. Original Leather offers just what the name says: one-of-a-kind coats, leather pants, stylish shearlings, and jackets in every leather, length, and size. They also carry handbags, classy briefcases, and travel bags. Most garments are designed and made in-house from imported leather, suede, and exotic skins of France, Italy, and Spain. There is a stylish selection of modern classics, boasting funky and functional designs at competitive prices.

T. ANTHONY
445 Park Ave (at 56th St)   212/750-9797, 800/722-2406
Mon-Fri: 9:30-6; Sat: 10-6   www.tanthony.com

T. Anthony handles luxurious luggage of distinction. Anything purchased here will stand out in a crowd. Luggage ranges in size from small overnight bags to massive pieces like steamer trunks. Their briefcases, jewelry boxes, desk sets, albums, key cases, and billfolds make terrific gifts, individually or in matched sets. Don't come looking for discount prices; however, their high quality and courteous service are well-established New York traditions. Exclusive T. Anthony products are also available through the store's catalog.

Lighting Fixtures and Accessories

CITY KNICKERBOCKER
781 Eighth Ave (bet 47th and 48th St)   212/586-3939
Mon-Fri: 8:30-5   www.cityknickerbocker.com

The fourth generation of the Liroff family operates this outfit, which has been in business since 1906. If it has anything to do with lighting—including quality antique reproductions, glassware, and first-rate repair—these folks are completely reliable. In addition to a large sales inventory, rentals are available. Not all of the inventory is vintage; their art-glass lamps, for instance, are new.

JUST BULBS
936 Broadway (bet 21st and 22nd St)   212/228-7820
Mon-Fri: 9-6 (Thurs till 7); Sat: 10-6; Sun: 12-6 www.justbulbs.com

This store stocks almost 25,000 types of bulbs, including some that can be found nowhere else. In addition to all the standard sizes, Just Bulbs has lightbulbs for use in old fixtures. The shop looks like an oversized backstage dressing-room mirror. Everywhere you turn there are bulbs connected to switches that customers are invited to flick on and off.

JUST SHADES
21 Spring St (at Elizabeth St)   212/966-2757
Tues-Sat: 9:30-4

Just Shades specializes in lampshades. They are experts at matching shades to lamps and willingly share their knowledge with retail customers. They have lampshades of silk, hide, parchment, and just about any other material imaginable. Interestingly, they say their biggest peeve is customers who neglect to remove the protective cellophane from their shades and fully enjoy their lamp. When left on, the cellophane actually collects ruinous dust.

LAMPWORKS
231 E 58th St (bet Second and Third Ave)   212/750-1500
Mon-Fri: 9-6 (Tues evening by appointment)

You will find an extensive selection of table lamps, antiques, imports, custom lampshades, and exterior lighting fixtures at Lampworks. Over 45 different lines are available to individual customers and commercial designers.

LIGHTING BY GREGORY
158 Bowery (bet Delancey and Broome St)   212/226-1276
Mon-Fri: 8:30-5:30; Sat, Sun: 9-5:30   www.lightingbygregory.com

No false modesty here! This full-service discount lighting store claims to be the most technically knowledgeable such outfit in the country. They are major dealers of Lightolier, Tech Lighting, and Casablanca ceiling fans, and are also experts in track lighting.

LIGHTING PLUS
676 Broadway (bet 2nd and 3rd St)   212/979-2000
Mon-Sat: 10-7; Sun: 11-7

Do you need an electrical gadget or replacement part to fix a lamp, ceiling fan, or whatever? Save yourself a lot of running around and go straight to Lighting Plus. In this well-organized store, you can find just about anything connected with ceiling fixtures, and the personnel are eager to help.

TUDOR ELECTRICAL SUPPLY
222-226 E 46th St (bet Second and Third Ave)   212/867-7550
Mon-Thurs: 8:30-5; Fri: 8:30-4:30

Although at first glance you may feel like you need an engineering degree to patronize Tudor Electrical, the staff is trained to explain everything in stock. Lightbulbs are the store's forte. They are cataloged by wattage, color, and application by a staff who can quickly locate the right bulb for your needs. For your information quartz, tungsten, and halogen bulbs offer undistorted light, while incandescent and fluorescent lamps are best for desk work. Tudor discounts by at least 20%.

UPLIFT
506 Hudson St (bet Christopher and 10th St)   212/929-3632
Daily: 12:30-8   www.americandeco.com

This uplifting store mainly sells art-deco and Victorian lighting fixtures. Uplift has one of the largest collections of original American art-deco chandeliers in the country. They also carry less expensive reproductions and a full line of fantasy figures, including wizards and dragons made of pewter.

Magic

LOUIS TANNEN/ TANNEN MAGICAL DEVELOPMENT COMPANY
24 W 25th St (bet Broadway and Ave of the Americas), 2nd floor
Mon-Fri: 10-5:30; Sat: 10-4   212/929-4500
www.tannens.com

Tannen is the world's largest supplier of magician's items, stocking more than 8,000 magic tricks, books, and DVDs. They have all that a magician of any level could possibly need. Tannen's showroom is patronized by the finest magicians in the country buying the greatest magic products on the market. The floor demonstrators are some of the best in the business—always friendly, helpful, and eager to share their knowledge with those willing to really study the art of magic. Tannen also runs a "Magic Summer Camp," for boys and girls ages 12 to 18, that has spawned some of today's greatest working magicians.

Maps

HAGSTROM MAP AND TRAVEL CENTER
57 W 43rd St (at Ave of the Americas)   212/398-1222
Mon-Wed, Fri: 8:30-6; Thurs: 8:30-7; Sat: 10:30-4:30
125 Maiden Ln (at Water St)   212/785-5343
Mon-Fri: 8:30-6   www.hagstrom.com

Hagstrom is the only complete map and chart dealer in the city, highlighting the maps of major manufacturers and three branches of government. There are also nautical, hiking, global, and travel guides, plus globes, atlases, and foreign-language phrase books. The staff are experts when it comes to maps and travel information.

Memorabilia

CBS STORE
1691 Broadway (at 53rd St)   212/975-8600
Mon-Sat:10-8; Sun: 12-5   www.cbs.com

Just down the street from the Ed Sullivan Theater (where David Letterman's Late Show is filmed), this store stocks T-shirts, mugs, and all sorts of other merchandise with the CBS company logo or images from the network's shows.

GOTTA HAVE IT! COLLECTIBLES
153 E 57th St (bet Lexington and Third Ave)   212/750-7900
Mon-Fri: 10-6; Sat: 11-5   www.gottahaveit.com

Do you have a favorite sports star, Hollywood personality, musical entertainer, or political figure? If you are a collector or are looking for a gift for someone who is, Gotta Have It features original and unique products in these categories. There are signed photos, musical instruments, baseball bats, used sports uniforms, documents, and movie props. All items are fully authenticated and guaranteed for life.

MOTION PICTURE ARTS GALLERY
133 E 58th St (at Lexington Ave), Suite 1001   212/223-1009
Tues-Fri: 12-5   www.mpagallery.com

The Motion Picture Arts Gallery displays and sells original posters and lobby cards from motion pictures. Ira Resnick's customers include film buffs and vintage poster collectors and investors. A *Casablanca* poster that could be had for a couple of dollars in the early 1960s fetches upward of $20,000 today! Over 15,000 items are stocked here.

MOVIE STAR NEWS
134 W 18th St (bet Ave of the Americas and Seventh Ave)
Tues-Fri: 10-5; Sat: 11-5   212/620-8160

Movie Star News may be the closest thing to Hollywood on the East Coast! It claims to have the world's largest collection of movie photos. Stars past and present shine brightly in this shop, which offers posters and other movie memorabilia. The store is laid out like a library. Ira Kramer, who runs the shop, does a lot of research for magazines, newspapers, and the media.

NBC EXPERIENCE STORE
30 Rockefeller Plaza (49th St bet Fifth Ave and Ave of the Americas)
Mon-Sat: 8-7; Sun: 9-6   212/664-3770
                                                    www.shopnbc.com/nbcstore

The NBC Experience Store offers walking tours that take visitors behind the scenes of NBC's studios and around one of New York's most recognizable landmarks, Rockefeller Center. The 20,000-square-foot facility is located directly across from Studio 1A, home of the *Today Show*. It stocks T-shirts, mugs, keychains, and other merchandise with the NBC logo or images from its television shows.

NEW YORK FIREFIGHTERS' FRIEND
263 Lafayette St (bet Prince and Spring St)   212/226-3142
Mon-Sat: 10-6; Sun: 12-5   www.nyfirestore.com

Firemen, kids and firefighting buffs from all over the world will no doubt find this the most fascinating store in Manhattan! New York Firefighter's Friend carries patches, T-shirts, toys, turnout coats, work shirts, FDNY memorial shirts, and related items. Firefighter jackets for kids are a big hit!

NEW YORK 911
263½ Lafayette St (bet Prince and Spring St)   212/219-3907
Mon-Sat: 10-6; Sun: 12-5   www.ny911.com

For police buffs, this place is heaven! Cops and just plain folks can find police T-shirts, caps, pins, shirts, kids' clothes, gifts, and toys. New York 911 is truly a one-stop cop shop!

ONE SHUBERT ALLEY
1 Shubert Alley (45th St bet Broadway and Eighth Ave)
          212/944-4133, 800/223-1320 (mail order only)
Mon-Sat: 12-8; Sun: 12-6:30   www.broadwaynewyork.com

Shubert Alley is often used as a shortcut between Broadway theaters. One Shubert Alley is the only retail establishment in the alley. It's a fascinating place to browse for T-shirts, posters, recordings, buttons, and other paraphernalia from current shows on and off-Broadway. They have a mail-order catalog and a special number for phone orders.

NYSALE
P.O. Box 527
Church St Station   212/2-NYSALE
New York, NY 10008   www.nysale.com

NYSALE is an Internet-based company that informs consumers about sample, warehouse, outlet, clearance, and promotional sales. Categories include apparel, housewares, and accessories. Information can be accessed by company name, product type, and date. The service is free. In addition, an NYSALE brochure listing weekly sales events is available at many Manhattan hotels.

Mirrors

SUNDIAL-SCHWARTZ
159 E 118th St (bet Lexington and Third Ave)
Mon-Fri: 8-4   800/876-4776, 212/828-8972
          www.antiquemirror.net

The people at Sundial supply "decorative treatments of distinction." Anyone who has ever seen a cramped New York apartment suddenly appear to expand with the strategic placement of mirrors will understand that claim. Sundial deals with professional decorators and do-it-yourselfers, and both benefit from the staff's years of experience. They carry windows, tabletop glass, shower doors, and mirrors for the home, office, and showroom. In addition, Sundial will remodel, re-silver, and antique mirrors. Sundial also custom designs window treatments, blinds, shades, and draperies.

Museum and Library Shops

As anybody on a mailing list knows, scores of museums across the country produce catalogs that allow people to browse their gift shops from a great distance. In New York, however, you can browse in person at more than four dozen museums. Even at museums that charge an admission fee, you need not pay if you're there to shop. Rather than simply list all the museum gift shops in New York, I've chosen particularly large or unique ones. Indeed, whether you're looking for a one-of-a-kind gift or unusual books and posters, I highly recommend shopping in the following places. Instead of Empire State Building salt-and-pepper shakers, expect to find classy, well-made items. In most cases, at least some of the wares relate directly to current and past exhibits or the museum's permanent collection. You might save money by becoming a member and taking advantage of discounts.

AMERICAN FOLK ART MUSEUM
45 W 53rd St (bet Fifth Ave and Ave of the Americas)
Daily: 10-6 (Fri till 8)   212/265-1040, ext. 113
1 Lincoln Square (Columbus Ave bet 65th and 66th St)
Tues-Sun: 11-7:30   212/977-7170

Both at its beautiful new home on 53rd Street and its homey branch location across from Lincoln Center, the American Folk Art Museum runs great gift shops stocked with lots of unusual handcrafted items in various price ranges. Although the Lincoln Square location has a particularly good selection of books about quilting, both stores are excellent sources for books on folk and decorative arts. Children's toys and books are also available at both locations.

AMERICAN MUSEUM OF NATURAL HISTORY
Central Park West bet 77th and 81st St   212/769-5100
Sat-Thurs: 10-5:45; Fri: 10-7:45

The museum's triplex shop features a wide selection of unusual merchandise related to the natural world, diverse cultures, and exploration and discovery. Jewelry, books, videos, toys, ceramics, gifts, posters, and some great T-shirts are among the many offerings. The main shop is accessible through the rotunda inside the museum's Central Park West entrance. Five smaller satellite shops throughout the museum offer children's toys, space-themed merchandise, and dinosaur-related items. Temporary shops are also set up to accompany some of the museum's special exhibits.

ASIASTORE
725 Park Ave (at 70th St)   212/327-9276
Tues-Sat: 10-6 (Fri till 9); Sun: 12-5

The AsiaStore is a little-known treat for anyone interested in Asiana. Housed inside the Asia Society's recently renovated headquarters, their collection of books on Asian religions, philosophy, art, culture, history, and other topics is among the largest in the nation. The store also carries a wide range of children's, language, and coffee-table books, as well as games, dolls, prints, jewelry, scarves, wrapping paper, stationery, and other Asian imports.

CATHEDRAL CHURCH OF ST. JOHN THE DIVINE
1047 Amsterdam Ave (at 112th St)   212/222-7200
Mon-Fri: 9-6; Sat, Sun: 9-5

Known as the Cathedral Shop, this pleasant gift shop is tucked off the left side of the main sanctuary. It specializes in stained glass and antique crosses. They also carry Christian books, creches, and Christmas tree ornaments from all over the world. Pressed flowers in glass, wrapping paper, wind chimes, mobiles, jewelry, Ghanaian kente cloth, note cards and stationery, jams, spices, and children's books are just a sampling of the eclectic selection. Ask about "adopting" an organ pipe if you want a unique gift for a music lover.

THE CLOISTERS
Fort Tryon Park   212/650-2277
Tues-Sun: 9:30-5 (till 4:15 in winter)

The Cloisters gift shop is stocked with items related to the museum's medieval collection. The shop closes a bit earlier than the museum.

COOPER-HEWITT NATIONAL DESIGN MUSEUM
2 E 91st St (bet Fifth and Madison Ave)   212/849-8400
Tues: 10-8:45; Wed-Fri: 10-4:45; Sat: 10-5:45; Sun: noon-5:45

Housed in the enchanting library of Andrew Carnegie's incredible mansion, this terrific store offers an eclectic mix of items that relate to the museum's extensive collection or reflect its dedication to design excellence and innovation. Whether you're looking for pens or other office items, tea cups, jewelry, clocks, vases, lamps, plates, or an unusual wedding present, this is a good place to start. The store also has a pretty good collection of books and toys for children, as well as an extensive offering of books relating to the museum's collection. Be sure to look around at the room (and the ceiling!) as you browse. The shop closes 15 minutes earlier than the museum.

DIA BOOK SHOP
548 W 22nd St (near Eleventh Ave)   212/989-5566
Wed-Sun: 11-6

This bookshop is adjacent to the Dia Center for the Arts in the heart of Chelsea's burgeoning gallery district. The sleek store, complete with lots of glass and unusual, colorful tiles, is a piece of art itself. You'll find an enormous collection of exhibition catalogs, books on photography and various other art forms, and a good selection of art magazines.

EL MUSEO DEL BARRIO
1230 Fifth Ave (at 105th St)   212/831-7272
Wed-Sun: 11-5

This unique museum gift shop was added to the museum during its 1994 renovation. In addition to housing a small collection of Latin American art books and books about such topics as Caribbean culture and the Puerto Rican experience in New York, the shop sells children's books in English and Spanish. It also sells carnival masks made in Puerto Rico and a variety of crafts from throughout the Caribbean and Latin America.

FRICK COLLECTION
1 E 70th St (bet Fifth and Madison Ave)   212/288-0700
Tues-Sat: 10-5:45 (Fri till 8:45); Sun: 1-5:45   www.frick.org

The Frick's gift shop makes the most of its small space by concentrating on exquisite cards, stationery, maps, guidebooks, and art books. The shop closes 15 minutes earlier than the museum.

GUGGENHEIM MUSEUM STORE
1071 Fifth Ave (bet 88th and 89th St)   212/423-3615
Sat-Thurs: 10-6; Fri: 10-8   www.guggenheimstore.org

Although much that's for sale in this store is ordinary—including scarves, T-shirts, prints and posters, tote bags, umbrellas, note cards and stationery, jewelry, and children's toys—the design and craftsmanship are anything but. If you're looking for an unusual clock, a great wedding present, or the right pair of earrings to set you apart from the crowd, look here. Just be aware that prices are often through the roof. Of course the store also carries books on modern art and exhibition catalogs. Note that the store is open on Thursday, but the museum itself is not.

INTERNATIONAL CENTER OF PHOTOGRAPHY
1133 Ave of the Americas (at 43rd St)   212/857-0000
Tues-Thurs: 10-5; Fri: 10-8; Sat, Sun: 10-6

Just inside the entrance to the ICP's midtown gallery, this store is definitely worth a look if you're shopping for a photography buff with high-quality gifts in mind. It has an excellent collection of books about the history and technology of photography and photojournalism. You can also find coffee-table books of collected works by photographers, as well as prints, picture frames, and unusual postcards.

INTREPID SEA-AIR-SPACE MUSEUM
Pier 86 (46th St at Hudson River)   212/245-0072
Daily: 10-5; (weekends till 7 in summer)

This museum's two-floor gift shop has huge volumes of touristy junk for youngsters, but it's also a great source for books on military history, space exploration, and aircraft and weapon systems for adults and children alike. It is a good place to look for model airplanes, ships and action figures, too.

JEWISH MUSEUM
1109 Fifth Ave (at 92nd St)   212/423-3200
Sun-Wed: 11-5:45; Thurs: 11-8; Fri: 11-3

This relatively large store is an excellent source for Jewish literature, decorative art, and Judaica. Its selection of menorahs is among the classiest in the city. The store also sells cards, coffee-table books, and a wide selection of children's books with Jewish themes and characters. **Celebrations**, the Jewish Museum's Design Shop, is housed in a brownstone next to the museum. It is worth a look if you're interested in very high-quality ceremonial objects, jewelry, and things for the home. A branch of the museum's gift shop recently opened at the **Jewish Community Center** (Amsterdam Avenue at 67th Street) as well. Note the abbreviated Friday hours.

METROPOLITAN MUSEUM OF ART
1000 Fifth Ave (bet 80th and 84th St)   212/570-3894
Tues-Sun: 9:30-5:15 (Fri, Sat till 8:45)
Macy's Herald Square (34th St at Ave of the Americas), mezzanine
212/268-7266

Rockefeller Center (15 W 49th St, bet Fifth Ave and Ave of the Americas)
212/332-1360
Soho (113 Prince St, bet Wooster and Greene St)   212/614-3000
The Cloisters (Fort Tryon Park)   212/923-3700
www.metmuseum.org

The two-floor store inside the Metropolitan Museum of Art is the grand-father of all museum gift shops. It specializes in reproductions of paintings and other pieces in the Met's incredible collection, as well as museum collections around the world. You can find jewelry, statues, vases, scarves, ties, porcelains, prints, rugs, napkins, silver serving dishes, and scores of other beautiful gift ideas. They also carry books relating to special exhibits and the museum's extensive holdings, as well as umbrellas, tote bags, and other items with the Metropolitan's name emblazoned on them. There's even a bridal-registry department! Prices range from reasonable to wildly expensive, and the salespeople are usually patient and helpful. Satellite gift shops are located inside the museum itself (a beautiful one across the main entrance hall specializes in jewelry) and throughout Manhattan. Hours at the satellite shops vary. The second floor of the main store in the Met and the satellite shop in Rockefeller Center have particularly good children's sections.

METROPOLITAN OPERA SHOP
Metropolitan Opera House   212/580-4090
Lincoln Center (Columbus Ave at 65th St)
Mon-Sat: 10 to end of second intermission; Sun: noon-6

This is an opera lover's heaven. In addition to operas on video, compact discs, and other media, you'll find books, mugs, umbrellas, stationery, T-shirts, and pillows for the opera buff. Be sure to check out the **Performing Arts Shop** on the lower concourse, too. And if you're looking for posters and prints from various seasons, visit **The Gallery**, also on the lower concourse.

MUSEUM OF AMERICAN FINANCIAL HISTORY
28 Broadway (bet Morris St and Battery Pl)   212/908-4613
Tues-Sat: 10-4

A small but unusual find in the basement of John D. Rockefeller's old Standard Oil headquarters, this may be the only museum shop in the country dedicated to financial memorabilia and art. Wonderful bronze bull and bear bookends, unique "nest egg" sculptures, and even some antique stock certificates are among the eclectic items.

MUSEUM OF THE CITY OF NEW YORK
1220 Fifth Ave (bet 103rd and 104th St)   212/534-1672, ext 227
Wed-Sat: 10-5; Sun: 12-5

This is an exciting place to shop, thanks to the efforts of a store manager who really cares about New York and this museum. You will find black-and-white prints from the museum's extensive archives, videos on such subjects as the construction of the subway system, books on the outer boroughs, imaginative children's toys and books, and selections relating to the museum's exhibitions.

MUSEUM OF JEWISH HERITAGE
18 First Pl (adjacent to Battery Park)   212/968-1800
Sun-Wed: 10-6; Thurs: 10-8; Fri: 10-3

Tucked off to the right of the museum's main entrance, this store is a fitting companion to the museum in its celebration of Jewish art, crafts, and culture. The selection of items, many of which are related to the museum's collection, is diverse. Everything here is high-quality and much of it is quite unusual. A small but carefully chosen section includes books and gifts for children of various ages. The prices are remarkably good. Note that the store and the museum are closed on all major Jewish holidays.

MUSEUM OF MODERN ART DESIGN STORE
44W 53rd St (bet Fifth Ave and Ave of the Americas)   212/767-1050
Sat-Thurs: 10-6:30; Fri: 10-8

SOHO DESIGN TOO
81 Spring St (at Crosby St)   646/613-1367
Mon-Sat: 11-8; Sun: 11-6

Across the street from the Museum of Modern Art's once and future home—and now with a satellite shop in Soho, too—these magnificent stores are dedicated to what the curators consider the very best in modern design. Furniture, textiles, vases, ties, kitchen gadgets, silverware, frames, watches, lamps, and toys and books for children are just a few things you'll find. These items are not cheap, and I've found some of the salespeople at the midtown location to be disinterested, but the selection is really exceptional. You'll find books and furniture on the lower level of the Soho store.

NATIONAL MUSEUM OF THE AMERICAN INDIAN
1 Bowling Green (at the foot of Broadway)
Museum Shop   212/514-3766
The Gallery   212/514-3767
Daily: 10-4:45

Like everything else about the National Museum of the American Indian, its two gift shops are classy operations. The Gallery, on the main floor to the right of the entrance, has a wide selection of books and high-quality Native American weavings, jewelry, and other handicrafts. The Museum Shop, down the grand marble staircase from the main entrance, is more focused on kids and families. Children's books, videos, toys, craft kits, and the obligatory arrowheads are for sale, along with T-shirts and some moderately priced jewelry. Both stores close 15 minutes before the museum. Because the museum is part of the Smithsonian Institution, both stores offer discounts to Smithsonian Associates.

THE NEUE GALERIE BOOKSTORE AND DESIGN SHOP
1048 Fifth Ave (at 86th St)   212/628-6200
Mon, Wed-Sun: 11-6 (Fri till 9)

The Neue Galerie Bookstore is clearly *the* source for books on the art, architecture, and cultural life in Germany, Austria, and even Central Europe in the 19th and 20th centuries. The Design Shop has a small but well-chosen selection of beautiful high-end jewelry, tableware, textiles, and other decorative arts by modern German and Austrian designers. Both stores are immediately to the left of the museum's entrance.

NEW YORK PUBLIC LIBRARY SHOP
Fifth Ave bet 41st and 42nd St   212/930-0641
Mon, Thurs-Sat: 10-6; Tues, Wed: 10-7

If ever there was a perfect gift shop for intellectuals, this is it. Located just off the main lobby of the New York Public Library's main branch, it features everything from magnets with sayings like "I Think, Therefore I'm Dangerous" and "Think for Yourself, Not for Me" to books about the library's history. In addition to stocking a high-quality selection of unusual merchandise, the staff is particularly pleasant and helpful.

NEW YORK TRANSIT MUSEUM
Grand Central Station   212/878-0106
Mon-Fri: 8-8; Sat, Sun: 10-4   www.nta.info

Run by the Metropolitan Transportation Authority, this little shop makes train and subway buffs downright giddy. Items for sale include books, conductor's caps, clever T-shirts, replicas of old station signs, banks for children in the shape of city buses, giant chocolate subway tokens, jewelry made from old tokens, and very classy mirrors made by one of the artists restoring the subway system's mosaics. Bus and subway maps, as well as other MTA information, are also available. Note that this shop is only a branch of the much larger main store at the New York Transit Museum in Brooklyn (Boerum Place at Schermerhorn Street, 718/694-5100).

PERFORMING ARTS SHOP
Metropolitan Opera House
Lincoln Center (Columbus Ave at 65th St), lower concourse
Mon-Sat: 10 a.m. until second intermission; Sun: noon-6
                    917/441-1195

This store is lots of fun for anyone interested in opera, classical music, and ballet. Much like the Metropolitan Opera Shop on the floor above, the Performing Arts Shop also has a wide selection of music, books, instruments, and toys for children, plus an even wider selection of recordings and various ballet-related items. It stays open weekdays and Saturdays until the end of the second intermission. If you're interested in prints and posters from past seasons, walk a little farther down the hall and visit The Gallery.

THE SHOP AT SCANDINAVIA HOUSE
58 Park Ave (bet 37th and 38th St)   212/879-9779
Tues-Sat: 12-5:45

Tucked into the back of the first floor behind Cafe AQ, this little gem is a tribute to Scandinavian design and good taste. Household items—including vases, tableware, and glasses—are featured, as are beautiful pieces of jewelry and a small selection of children's items.

THE STORE AT THE MUSEUM OF ARTS AND DESIGN
40 W 53rd St (bet Fifth Ave and Ave of the Americas)
Daily: 10-6 (Thurs till 8)   212/956-3535, ext. 157

Though the name is a mouthful—thanks in part to the renaming of the American Craft Museum—this well-conceived gem of a shop is a great complement to the other museum shops on West 53rd Street. Showcasing the work of exceptional craftspeople from around the United States, the store offers jewelry, textiles, housewares, and other items.

STUDIO MUSEUM
144 W 125th St (bet Malcolm X and Adam Clayton Powell, Jr Blvd)
212/864-4500, ext 237
Wed-Fri: 12-5:45; Sat, Sun: 10-5:45

Located just inside the museum's entrance on the right, this store sells a wide and generally high-quality selection of jewelry, textiles, crafts, note-cards, and calendars created by African and African-American artists. It also sells an unusually broad selection of cookbooks, fiction, biographies, and children's books by and about Africans and African-Americans. The store closes 15 minutes before the museum.

UKRAINIAN MUSEUM
203 Second Ave (bet 12th and 13th St), 5th floor 212/228-0110
Wed-Sun: 1-5

This unique little place is not exactly on any tourist routes and you may actually need to ask to have it opened. It's a real goldmine for anyone interested in Ukrainian Easter eggs (already made and kits for do-it-your-selfers), embroidery, and other handicrafts. Be sure to ask about holiday baking, embroidery, beading, and Easter egg classes.

UNITED NATIONS
First Ave bet 45th and 46th St 212/963-4475
Daily: 9-5 (March-Dec); Mon-Fri: 9-5 (Jan, Feb)

On the lower level of the main UN building is a bookstore, post office (a real treat for stamp collectors), small UNICEF shop, and an even smaller shop run by the UN Women's Guild. That's in addition to the main gift shop, also on the lower level. The bookstore features calendars, postcards with the flags of member nations, holiday cards in dozens of languages, and a wide variety of books about the UN and related subjects. The main gift shop (212/425-1157) features a wonderful array of carvings, jewelry, scarves, dolls, and other items from all over the world. The better imports can get pricey, but it's definitely going to a good cause! One final thought: if you are interested in UNICEF cards and gifts but find the selection at the UN itself rather thin, then visit the store in the lobby of the nearby **UNICEF House** (331 East 38th Street, 212/326-7000). Note that the UN stores are closed on weekends in January and February.

Music

ACADEMY RECORDS & CDs
12 W 18th St (at Fifth Ave) 212/242-3000
Mon-Sat: 11:30-8; Sun: 11-7 www.academy-records.com

Academy Records & CDs has Manhattan's largest stock of used, out-of-print, and rare classical LPs and CDs. Emphasizing opera, contemporary classical, and early music (the Baroque period and earlier), Academy boasts an international reputation. Prices are fair, and a catalog of rarer records (popular and classical) is issued occasionally. The rock and jazz holdings, while less extensive, continue to grow.

AT THE GRYPHON
233 W 72nd St (at Broadway)   212/874-1588
Mon-Fri: 9:30-8:30; Sat: 11-9; Sun: 12-6

Gryphon remains one of the few stores specializing in rare-and out-of-print LPs. Compact discs have been added to the stock of 80,000 LPs. You'll also find printed music and books on the performing arts, fine arts, photography, fiction, and poetry. Merlin Chapman-Webb and Raymond Donnell will lead customers through their classical, jazz, rock, pop, and spoken-word holdings.

BLEECKER BOB'S GOLDEN OLDIES RECORD SHOP
118 W 3rd St (bet MacDougal St and Ave of the Americas)
Sun-Thurs: 11 a.m.-1 a.m.; Fri, Sat: 11 a.m.-3 a.m.   212/475-9617
www.bleeckerbobs.com

Let us sing the praises of Bleecker Bob, who is nothing if not perverse. (Name another store that's open till 3 a.m. on Christmas Day!) For one thing, although there is a real Bob (Plotnik, the owner), the store isn't on Bleecker Street. For another, Bleecker Bob is an institution to generations of New Yorkers who have sifted through his vast selection of rock, punk, and heavy-metal recordings. They stock vintage rock and soul records (plus some rare jazz), hold autograph parties for rock stars, and boast that they can fill any wish list. Bleecker Bob's is also the gathering place in the wee hours of the morning in the Village. Above all, it's a great source for out-of-print, obscure, and imported compact discs.

FOOTLIGHT RECORDS
113 E 12th St (bet Third and Fourth Ave)   212/533-1572
Tues-Fri: 11-7; Sat: 10-6; Sun: 12-5   www.footlight.com

In keeping with this outfit's passion for rare and unusual records and compact discs, the emphasis is on show tunes, film soundtracks, and jazz. Their prices are among the best around, and many of their records just aren't available anywhere else. If there's an original cast album of a Broadway show, you can bet Footlight has it. They stock one of the most comprehensive collections of film scores in the country. They also carry whole collections of artists from the 1920s through the 1960s; an impressive showing of European and Japanese imports in related fields, and a large selection of big-band and early-jazz recordings.

FRANK MUSIC
244 W 54th St (bet Broadway and Eighth Ave), 10th floor
Mon-Fri: 10-6   212/582-1999
www.frankmusiccompany.com

Founded in 1938, this professional business has never advertised, relying instead on word of mouth. They sell classical sheet music from European and American publishers. There is an aisle for voice and violin, another for piano, and so on. Frank Music gladly fills mail orders. Ask for Heidi Rogers, the helpful owner, or Dean Streit, her assistant.

JAZZ RECORD CENTER
236 W 26th St (bet Seventh and Eighth Ave), Room 804　212/675-4480
Tues-Sat: 10-6 (Sept-May); Mon-Fri: 10-6 (June-Aug)
www.jazzrecordcenter.com

This is the only jazz specialty store in the city. They deal primarily in out-of-print jazz records but also carry CDs, videos, books, posters, photos, periodicals, postcards, and T-shirts on the topic. The store buys collections, runs a search service, fills mail orders, and offers appraisals. Every two years a jazz rarities auction is held. The operation is run by Frederick Cohen, a charming guy who really knows his business.

JOSEPH PATELSON MUSIC HOUSE
160 W 56th St (at Seventh Ave)　　　　　　　212/582-5840
Mon-Sat: 9-6 (Thurs till 7; closed Sat in summer)

www.patelson.com

Located behind Carnegie Hall, Joseph Patelson is known to every student of music in the city. From little first graders to artists from Carnegie Hall, everyone stops here first because of the fabulous selection and excellent prices. The stock includes music scores, sheet music, music books, and orchestral and opera scores. All are neatly cataloged and displayed in open cabinets. One can easily browse a given section of interest—be it piano music, chamber music, orchestral scores, opera scores, concerts, ethnic scores, or instrumental solos Sheet music is filed in bins the way records are elsewhere. There are also musical accessories, like metronomes and pitch pipes. Patelson is an unofficial meeting place for the city's young musicians. Word goes out that "we're looking for a violinist," and meetings are often arranged in the store. Mail and phone orders are accepted.

NOSTALGIA . . . AND ALL THAT JAZZ
217 Thompson St (bet Bleecker and 3rd St)　　　　212/420-1940
Mon-Thurs: 1-8; Fri: 1-9; Sat: 1-10; Sun: 1-7:30

Recorded nostalgia—especially jazz, original cast, and soundtrack recordings—is the main focus of this business. Items are very reasonably priced. The shop has a sideline in photography, with Kim Deuel and Mort Alavi doing a healthy business producing, cataloging, and reproducing photos. Nostalgia will reproduce any photograph, in any size or quantity, up to 30" x 40". They also have a good collection of posters, sports photos, movie and jazz stills, and large (16" x 20") showbiz photos in black-and-white and color.

TOWER RECORDS AND VIDEO
692 Broadway (at 4th St)	212/505-1500
Trump Tower, 725 Fifth Ave (bet 56th and 57th St)	212/838-8110
1961 Broadway (at 66th St)	212/799-2500
383 Lafayette St (at 4th St)	212/505-1166
Hours vary by store	www.towerrecords.com

These stores feature different categories by location. Stock includes records tapes, CDs, videos, and DVDs. The Lafayette Street location focuses on video sales and rentals, and it also has an upstairs outlet with discounted merchandise. The Lincoln Center location on Broadway even has a Ticketmaster outlet.

VINYL MANIA RECORDS
60 Carmine St (at Bedord St)   212/924-7223
Mon-Thurs: 11-8; Fri, Sat: 11-9   www.vinylmania.com

Vinyl Mania Records is New York's specialty shop for DJs. Its business is 80% vinyl, as they cater to the dance, hip-hop, disco classics, and rap audiences. They also carry a choice selection of imported and domestic CDs.

Musical Instruments

DRUMMERS WORLD
151 W 46th St (bet Ave of the Americas and Seventh Ave), 3rd floor
Mon-Fri: 10-6; Sat: 10-4   212/840-3057
                                                www.drummersworld.com

This is a great place unless the patron is your teenager or an upstairs neighbor! Barry Greenspon and his staff take pride in guiding students and professionals through one of the best percussion stores in the country. Inside this drummer's paradise is everything from commonplace equipment to one-of-a-kind antiques and imports. All of the instruments are high-quality symphonic percussion items, and customers receive the same attention whether they are members of an orchestra, rock band, or rap act. The store also offers instructors and how-to books. There are esoteric ethnic instruments for virtuosos who want to experiment. Drummers World has a catalog and will ship anywhere in the country.

GUITAR SALON NY
45 Grove St (at Sheridan So)   212/675-3236
By appointment only

Beverly Maher's Guitar Salon NY is a unique one-person operation located in a historic brownstone in Greenwich Village. You will find handmade classical and flamenco guitars for students, professionals, and collectors. Outstanding personal service is provided by Maher, whose salon specializes in 19th- and 20th-century vintage instruments. Appraisals are available, and lessons are given on all styles of guitars. Even the Rolling Stones shop here!

MANNY'S MUSIC
156 W 48th St (bet Ave of the Americas and Seventh Ave)
Mon-Sat: 10-7; Sun: 12-6   212/819-0576
                                                www.mannysmusic.com

Manny's is a huge discount department store for musical instruments. "Everything for the Musician" is their motto, and it is borne out by a collection of musical equipment so extensive that each department has its own salespeople. The emphasis is on modern music, as evidenced by the hundreds of autographed pictures of contemporary musicians on the walls and the huge collection of electronic instruments. All of the instruments, equipment, accessories, and supplies are sold at discount. They also have a large computer department for musical software needs.

RITA FORD MUSIC BOXES
19 E 65th St (at Madison Ave)   212/535-6717
Mon-Sat: 9-5   www.ritaford.com

Gerry and Nancy Wright and Joseph and Diane Tenore collect antique music boxes and have become experts in all aspects of the business. Stock consists of valuable antique and new music boxes. The main stock-in-trade is expertise; having been in business for half a century, these folks know all there is to know about music boxes. They are acknowledged experts on music box scores, workings, and outer casings. Some pieces are rare antiques that are priced accordingly. Contemporary reproductions are more modestly priced. The store also does repairs.

Photographic Equipment and Supplies

ADORAMA CAMERA
42W 18th St (bet Fifth Ave and Ave of the Americas)   212/741-0052
Mon-Thurs: 9-6:15; Fri: 9-1:30; Sun: 9:30-5:30

                         www.adoramacamera.com

These people operate one of the largest photographic mail-order houses in the country. They carry a huge stock of photographic equipment and supplies, telescopes, video paraphernalia, and digital equipment, all sold at discount.

ALKIT PRO CAMERAS
820 Third Ave (at 50th St)   212/832-2101
222 Park Ave S (at 18th St)   212/674-1515
830 Seventh Ave (at 53rd St)   212/262-2424
Hours vary by location

If you want to shop where photographers of the Elite and Ford modeling agencies go, Alkit is the place. You don't have to be a professional to come here, however. While most establishments that deal with the pros have little time for amateurs, nothing gives store president Edward Buchbinder more pleasure than introducing the world of photography to neophytes. Alkit maintains a full line of digital and film cameras, film, and equipment. They have a one-hour professional processing lab on-premises. The shop repairs and rents photographic equipment, and it also publishes an informative catalog full of praise and gripes about particular models.

B&H PHOTO-VIDEO-PRO AUDIO
420 Ninth Ave (bet 33rd and 34th St)   212/444-6600
Mon-Thurs: 9-7; Fri: 9-2; Sun: 10-5   www.bhphotovideo.com

This is quite a store! You'll find professional and nonprofessional departments for video, pro audio, pro lighting, darkroom, film and film processing, books, used equipment, and more. Trade-ins are welcome, and used equipment is sold. The store has been in operation since 1974 and is staffed by knowledgeable personnel. Inventory levels are high, prices are reasonable, and hands-on demo areas make browsing easy. A catalog is available.

CALUMET PHOTOGRAPHIC
16 W 19th St (bet Fifth Ave and Ave of the Americas)   212/989-8500
Mon-Fri: 8-6   www.calumetphoto.com

In business for over 60 years, this firm provides start-to-finish photographic service. Professional camera equipment, film, digital cameras and accessories, printers, and scanners are all available at good prices.

KEN HANSEN PHOTOGRAPHIC
509 Madison Ave (at 53rd St), 18th floor   212/317-0923
Mon-Fri: 9-5; Sat: 9-2   www.kenhansenphotographic.com

This is a classy, upscale outlet for photographic equipment. There is a vast selection of merchandise and a great showing of cameras not found elsewhere. Equipment is available for rent. You will find Ken Hansen and his crew to be professional and well-informed.

LAUMONT DIGITAL
333 W 52nd St (bet Eighth and Ninth Ave)   212/245-2113
Mon-Fri: 9-5:30 (evenings and weekends by appointment)

Whether you're a professional or amateur, Laumont can take care of your photographic needs. They do excellent work producing exhibition-quality Cibachrome, Fuji, Lambda, Iris, and pigment prints. They are patient and understanding with those who need advice. Laumont's staff are also experienced digital retouchers and duplicators, and they can repair damaged originals or create brand-new images on state-of-the-art computers. Lamination and print-mounting are done on-premises.

NEW YORK FILM WORKS
928 Broadway (at 21st St)   212/475-5700
Mon-Fri: 8-8:30; Sat: 10-4   www.nyfilmworks.com

Specialties include digital and conventional imaging and printing, video application, and photo processing. These folks can produce a color photograph in one hour at extremely competitive prices.

WILLOUGHBY'S KONICA IMAGING CENTER
136 W 32nd St (bet Ave of the Americas and Seventh Ave)
212/564-1600, 800/378-1898
Mon-Thurs: 8:30-7; Fri: 8:30-4; Sun: 10-7   www.willoughbys.com

Established in 1898, this is New York's oldest camera store. Willoughby's has a huge stock, an extensive clientele, and a solid reputation. They can handle almost any kind of camera order, either in person or by mail order. They service cameras, supply photographic equipment, and recycle used cameras. Moreover, they sell computers, video cameras, cellular phones, and other high-tech equipment.

Pictures, Posters, and Prints

CARRANDI GALLERY
138 W 18th St (bet Ave of the Americas and Seventh Ave)
Tues-Sat: 12-6   212/242-0710
www.carrandigallery.com

You've never seen a poster gallery like this one! Carrandi Gallery (formerly Poster America) features original posters from 1880 to 1970, nearly all of which are lithographs. One of the oldest galleries in the country devoted to vintage poster art, it is set in a former stable and carriage house that used to serve the department stores on Ladies' Mile in the 1880s. The magnificent mahogany-and-glass storefront still catches the eyes of passers-by, luring them into a huge, well-appointed gallery. The shop is known for brilliant graphics and the magnitude of its rare and unusual posters, including vintage circus and magic posters.

JERRY OHLINGER'S MOVIE MATERIAL STORE
242 W 14th St (bet Seventh and Eighth Ave)   212/989-0869
Daily: 1-7:45   www.moviematerials.com

Jerry Ohlinger has a huge selection of movie posters and photographs from film and TV. He also does research for these kinds of items and will gladly provide a catalog.

OLD PRINT SHOP
150 Lexington Ave (bet 29th and 30th St)   212/683-3950
Tues-Thurs: 9-5; Fri, Sat: 9-4 (closed Sat in summer)
                                                 www.oldprintshop.com

Established in 1898, the Old Print Shop exudes an old-fashioned charm, and its stock only reinforces the impression of timelessness. Kenneth M. Newman specializes in Americana, including original prints, town views, Currier and Ives prints, and original maps that reflect America as it used to be. Most of the nostalgic bicentennial pictures that adorned calendars and stationery were copies of prints found here. Amateur and professional historians have a field day in this shop. Newman also does "correct period framing," and prints housed in his custom frames are striking. Everything bought and sold here is original, and Newman will purchase estates and single items.

TRITON GALLERY
323 W 45th St (bet Eighth and Ninth Ave)   212/765-2472
Mon-Sat: 10-6; Sun: 1-6   www.tritongallery.com

Theater posters are presented at Triton like nowhere else. The posters of current Broadway shows are but a small part of what's available. There's also a broad range of older show posters from here and abroad. Show cards, the most readily available items, are the standard 14" x 22" size. Posters range in size from 23" x 46" to 42" x 84" and are priced according to rarity, age, and demand. The collection is not limited to Broadway or even American plays, and some of the more interesting pieces are from other times. Triton also does custom framing. Much of the business is conducted via mail and phone orders.

Plastics

INDUSTRIAL PLASTICS
309 Canal St (bet Mercer St and Broadway)   212/226-2010
Mon-Fri: 9-5:30; Sat: 10-4:30   www.yourplasticsupermarket.com

Industrial Plastics is dedicated to hard and soft plastics. Their line includes waterproofing material, Lucite cubes, and plastic sheets. They are particularly accommodating to do-it-yourselfers.

PLEXI-CRAFT QUALITY PRODUCTS
514 W 24rd St (bet Tenth and Eleventh Ave)   212/924-3244
Mon-Fri: 9:30-5   www.plexi-craft.com

Plexi-Craft offers anything made of Lucite and Plexiglas at wholesale prices. If you can't find what you want among the pedestals, tables, chairs, shelves, computer tables, and cubes shown here, they will make it for you. The helpful personnel will point out various styles of cocktail tables, shelves, magazine racks, television stands, and chairs. A catalog is available for $2.

Religious Arts

GRAND STERLING SILVER COMPANY
345 Grand St (bet Essex and Ludlow St)   212/674-6450
Sun-Thurs: 10:30-5:30   www.grandsterlingusa.com

Ring the bell and you will be admitted to a stunning collection of silver religious art pieces. You'll also find almost anything from silver toothpick holders to baroque candelabras over six feet tall. Grand Sterling will repair or polish any item, religious or secular. They are manufacturers and importers of fine sterling holloware. Silver is revered with unmatched dedication here!

Rubber Goods

CANAL RUBBER SUPPLY COMPANY
329 Canal St (at Greene St)   212/226-7339
Mon-Fri: 9-5; Sat: 9-4   wwwcanalrubber.com

"If It's Made of Rubber, We Have It" is the motto at this wholesale-retail operation. There are foam mattresses, bolsters, cushions, pillow foam, pads cut to size, hydraulic hoses, rubber tubing, vacuum hoses, floor matting, tiles, stair treads, sheet-rubber products, and much more.

Security and Surveillance Devices

CCS COUNTER SPY SHOP
444 Madison Ave (at 49th St)   212/688-8500
Mon, Fri: 9-6; Tues-Thurs: 9-7; Sat: 10-4   www.spyzone.com

With security and surveillance high on many people's minds these days, CCS Counter Spy Shop can provide do-it-yourself investigation and security equipment for business and private use. They carry bulletproof clothing—every thing from T-shirts to safari outfits. Other items include covert video systems, night-vision equipment, debugging devices, phone or fax scramblers, voice-stress analyzers, and lie detectors. There are even bulletproof cars! It's all here, and confidential consultations can be arranged.

EMPIRE SAFE COMPANY
6 E 39th St (bet Fifth and Madison Ave)   212/6842255, 800/543-5412
Mon-Fri: 9-5   www.empiresafe.com

Empire shows one of the largest and most complete selections of safes. Their products are used in residences and businesses, with delivery and installation offered. Also on display are rare antique and art-deco safes, memorabilia, old photos, and historical documents. Whether you want to protect documents in a small apartment or huge office building, these folks are able to help.

QÜARK SPY CENTRE
537 Third Ave (at 36th St)   212/889-1808, 800/345-6443
Mon-Fri: 10-6:30; Sat: 12-5 (by appointment)   www.quarkfiles.com

Qüark is Manhattan's most extensive countersurveillance showroom. With more than 400 items on display, Qüark is able to service all personal, professional, and government security needs, no matter how unique. Products include night-vision equipment, bug detection and telephone security items, body armor, voice scramblers, long-play recording devices, and alarm briefcases.

Sexual Paraphernalia

COME AGAIN
353 E 53rd St (at First Ave)   212/308-9394
Mon-Fri: 11-7; Sat: 11-6

Come Again is a large shopping center for sexual paraphernalia. There's exotic lingerie for men and women to size 4XL, adult books and magazines, oils and lotions, gift baskets, party gifts, and toys and equipment of a decidedly prurient nature. They offer a 20% discount for readers of this book!

CONDOMANIA
351 Bleecker St (bet 10th and Charles St)   212/691-9442
Sun-Thurs: 11-11; Fri, Sat: 11 a.m.-midnight www.condomania.com

Yes, this store specializes in condoms: all shapes, sizes, and colors. Mixed in are bachelor and bachelorette gift items, mood enhancers, and the like. Reflecting the liberated times, Condomania is as popular with ladies as gentlemen.

EVE'S GARDEN INTERNATIONAL
119 W 57th St (bet Ave of the Americas and Seventh Ave), Suite 1201
Mon-Sat: 11-7   212/757-8651
www.evesgarden.com

Eve's Garden is a pleasure chest of games, books, and videos to seduce the mind and a vast array of sensuous massage oils, candles, and incense to help realize your wildest fantasies.

Signs

LET THERE BE NEON
38 White St (bet Broadway and Church St)   212/226-4883
Mon-Fri: 9-5   www.lettherebeneon.com

Though the image of neon is modern, it harks back to 1915, when Georges Claudes captured it from oxygen. While the flashing neon sign has perhaps become the ultimate urban cliché, here it is rendered as artistic fine art. Let There Be Neon operates as a gallery with an assemblage of sizes, shapes, functions, and designs to entice the browser. Almost all of their sales are custom pieces. Even a rough sketch is enough for them to create a literal or abstract neon sculpture. Some vintage pieces are available.

Silver

JEAN'S SILVERSMITHS

16 W 45th St (at Fifth Ave)   212/575-0723
Mon-Fri: 9-4:45   www.jeanssilversmiths.com

Having a problem replacing a fork that went down the garbage disposal?
Proceed directly to Jean's, where you will find over a thousand discontinued,
obsolete, and current flatware patterns. They specialize in antique and
secondhand silver, gold, and diamond jewelry, and they also sell watches.

ROGERS AND ROSENTHAL

Mailing address: 2337 Lemoine Ave, #101
Ft. Lee, NJ 07024
Mon-Fri: 10-4   201/346-1862 (mail order)

Rogers and Rosenthal is one of the very best sources for silver, china, and
crystal. Nearly all of their business is done by mail. They feature major brand
names and offer a 25% or more discount on every piece by mail. They will
send price lists upon request, and what isn't in stock can be ordered.

TIFFANY AND COMPANY

727 Fifth Ave (at 57th St)   212/755-8000
Mon-Fri: 10-7; Sat: 10-6; Sun: 12-5   www.tiffany.com

Despite the fact that Tiffany has appeared in plays, movies, books, and
songs, this legendary store really isn't that formidable or forbidding, and it
can be an exciting place to shop. Yes, there really is a Tiffany diamond, and
it can be viewed on the first floor. That floor also houses the watch and
jewelry departments. While browsing is welcome, salespeople are quick to
approach loiterers. The store carries clocks, silver jewelry, sterling silver, bar
accessories, centerpieces, leather accessories, scarves, knickknacks, china,
crystal, glassware, flatware, and engraved stationery. The real surprise is that
Tiffany carries an excellent selection of reasonably priced items, many
emblazoned with the Tiffany name and wrapped in the famed blue box.

Sporting Goods

Bicycles and Accessories

BICYCLE RENAISSANCE

430 Columbus Ave (at 81st St)   212/724-2350
Mon-Fri: 10-7:30; Sat, Sun: 10-5 (till 7:30 in summer)

Biking is a way of life at Bicycle Renaissance. Services include custom-
building bikes and bicycle repair, and the mechanics aim for same-day
service on all makes and models. They carry racing and mountain bikes by
Trek, Cannondale, and Specialized, as well as custom frames for Seven,
Shimano, and others. Prices are on par with so-called discount shops.

LARRY & JEFF'S SECOND AVENUE BICYCLES PLUS

1690 Second Ave (at 87th St)   212/722-2201
Daily: 10-7 (till 8:30 in summer)

Larry started fixing bicycles at age 15, so you can bet he knows all about
them. He then taught the art to Jeff, and together they have been operating
this unique shop since 1977. Bikes range in price from $200 to $5,000, and
plenty of parts and accessories are stocked, too. Special services include a
lifetime of free tune-ups with the purchase of a new bicycle, bike rentals for
rides through Central Park, and free delivery.

Billiards

BLATT BILLIARDS
809 Broadway (bet 11th and 12th St)   212/674-8855
Mon-Fri: 9-6; Sat: 10-4 (closed Sat in summer)

www.blattbilliards.com

Blatt's six floors are outfitted from top to bottom with everything for billiards. You can also get friendly pointers from a staff that seems, at first glance, to be all business.

Exercise Equipment

GYM SOURCE
40 E 52nd St (bet Park and Madison Ave)   212/688-4222
Mon-Fri: 9-7; Sat: 10-6   www.gymsource.com

This is the largest exercise-equipment dealer in the Northeast. They carry treadmills, bikes, stair-steppers, weight machines, rowers, and more. Over 300 top brands at good prices are available, and Gym Source's skilled technicians provide competent service. They also rent equipment and can even provide items for use in a Manhattan hotel room.

Fishing

CAPITOL FISHING TACKLE COMPANY
218 W 23rd St (at Seventh Ave)   212/929-6132
Mon-Fri: 9-6 (Thurs till 7:30); Sat: 9:30-5

Where else but in New York could you find a fishing store so totally land-locked that a subway roars beneath it, yet it offers bargains unmatched at seaport fishing stores? Set amid the hustle and bustle of Chelsea, where it shares an address with the Chelsea Hotel, Capitol features a complete range of fishing tackle. They carry such brand names as Penn, Shimano, Garcia, and Daiwa at low prices. There is a constantly changing selection of specials and close-outs. Capitol buys up surplus inventories, bankrupt dealers, and liquidations, and the savings are passed onto customers.

URBAN ANGLER
206 Fifth Ave (bet 25th and 26th St), 3rd floor
Mon-Fri: 10-6; Wed: 10-7; Sat: 10-5   212/979-7600

www.urbanangler.com

Urban Angler is the only pro fly-fishing shop in Manhattan. You'll find fly-fishing tackle, high-end spin and surf tackle, and travel clothing in an expanded atmosphere. They offer casting and fly-tying lessons, and are able to plan fishing trips locally and around the world. Urban Angler is the only pro fly-fishing shop in Manhattan.

General

EASTERN MOUNTAIN SPORTS (EMS)
20 W 61st St (bet Broadway and Columbus Ave)   212/397-4860
Mon-Fri: 10-9; Sat: 10-8; Sun: 12-6   www.ems.com

This is the place for outdoor clothing and gear. Although prices can be bettered elsewhere, it's an excellent source for one-stop shopping and the merchandise is of better quality than that carried in department stores. EMS covers virtually all outdoor sports, including mountain climbing, backpacking, skiing, hiking, tenting, kayaking, and camping.

G&S SPORTING GOODS
43 Essex St (at Grand St)   212/777-7590
Mon-Fri, Sun: 9-6   www.gandsboxinggear.com

If you are looking for a place to buy a birthday or Christmas gift for a sports buff, I'd recommend G&S. They have a large selection of brand-name sneakers, inline skates, boxing equipment, balls, gloves, toys, games, sports clothing, and accessory items. Prices reflect a 20% to 25% discount.

MODELL'S
51 E 42nd St (bet Madison and Vanderbilt Ave)   212/661-4242
606 W 181st St (at Saint Nicholas Ave)   212/568-3000
300 W 125th St (at Eighth Ave)   212/280-9100
55 Chambers St (at Broadway)   212/732-8484
1293 Broadway (at 34th St)   212/244-4544
234 W 42nd St (bet Seventh and Eighth Ave)   212/764-7030
Hours vary by store   www.modells.com

You can't beat this outfit for quality and value! Founded in 1889, Modell's is America's oldest family-owned and -operated sporting-goods chain. The stores specialize in sporting goods, footwear, and a large selection of apparel for men, women, and children. Make note of Modell's low-price guarantee.

NBA STORE
666 Fifth Ave (at 52nd St)   212/515-NBA1
Mon-Sat: 10-7; Sun: 11-6   www.nba.com/nycstore

You'll find the largest assortment of NBA and WNBA merchandise in the nation in this attractive and well-laid-out store. A winding ramp allows full exposure to areas featuring apparel and accessories, jewelry, watches, photographs, collectibles, headwear, practice gear, basketballs, and more. The store also features multimedia presentations of game action and highlights of historic moments. A basketball half-court surrounded by bleachers is a popular spot for the store's more athletic shoppers. Hang Time Cafe, on the lower level, is a great place to catch a quick bite to eat.

PARAGON SPORTS
867 Broadway (at 18th St)   212/255-8036
Mon-Sat: 10-8; Sun: 11-6:30   www.paragonsports.com

This is truly a sporting-goods department store, with over 100,000 square feet of specialty shops devoted to all kinds of sports and fitness equipment and apparel. There are separate departments for team equipment, athletic footwear, skateboards, ice skates, inline skates, racquet sports, aerobics, swimming, golf, skiing and snowboarding, hiking, camping, diving, biking, sailing, and anything else done in the great outdoors. There are also gift items, and the stock is arranged for easy shopping.

Golf

NEW YORK GOLF CENTER
131 W 35th St (bet Seventh Ave and Broadway)   212/564-2255
Mon-Fri: 10-8; Sat: 10-7; Sun: 11-6   888/465-7890
                                           www.nygolfcenter.com

This shop is the ultimate hole-in-one for golfers! New York Golf Center, the Big Apple's only golf superstore, offers goods at prices that average 20% below list. There are clubs, bags, clothing, shoes, accessories, and novelties . . . everything except one's own hard-won expertise. They carry pro-line equipment such as Callaway, Taylor Made, Cleveland, Titleist, Ping, and Nike. The folks here couldn't be nicer or more helpful. Mention this book and receive a free sleeve of golf balls with any $20 purchase.

Guns

JOHN JOVINO GUN SHOP
5 Centre Market Pl (at Grand St)   212/925-4881
Mon-Fri: 9:30-5:30; Sat: 9:30-3:30   www.johnjovinogunshop.com

These folks have been in business since 1911 and are recognized leaders in the field. They carry all major brands of handguns, rifles, shotguns, and accessories, including ammunition, holsters, bulletproof vests, knives, and scopes. Major brands include Smith & Wesson, Colt, Ruger, Beretta, Browning, Remington, Walther, Glock, Winchester, and Sig Sauer. Jovino is an authorized warranty repair station for gun manufacturers, with a licensed gunsmith on the premises.

Marine

WEST MARINE
12 W 37th St (at Fifth Ave)   212/594-6065
Mon-Fri: 10-6 (Thurs till 6:30); Sat, Sun: 10-3
www.westmarine.com

West sells marine supplies as if it were situated in the middle of a New England seaport rather than the heart of Manhattan. The staff sometimes looks like a ship's crew on leave in the Big Apple, and they actually are that knowledgeable. They carry marine electronics, sailboat fittings, big-game fishing tackle, lifesaving gear, ropes, anchors, compasses, clothing, clocks, barometers, and books. Foul-weather suits are a star attraction, and there is also a line of clothes for yacht owners.

Outdoor Equipment

TENT AND TRAILS
21 Park Pl (bet Broadway and Church St) 212/227-1760, 800/237-1760
Mon-Wed, Sat: 9:30-6; Thurs, Fri: 9:30-7; Sun: 12-6
www.tenttrails.com

Whether you are outfitting yourself for a weekend camping trip or an ascent of Mt. Everest, Tent and Trails is the place to go! In the urban canyons near City Hall, this 6,000-square-foot store is devoted to camping. The staff is experienced and knowledgeable. There are boots from Asolo, Merrell, Vasque, Hi Tee, Scarpa Footwear, and Nike. They carry camping gear from Patagonia, Camp Trails, Moonstone, JanSport, Gregory Packs, Mountainsmith Packs, Eureka Tent, Mountain Hardwear, Coleman, Moss Tent, Timberland, and NorthFace. You'll find backpacks, sleeping bags, tents, down clothing, and much more. Tent and Trails also rents camping equipment.

Running

ATHLETIC STYLE

118 E 59th St (bet Park and Lexington Ave) 212/838-2564
Mon-Fri: 10-5 www.athleticstyle.com

Athletic Style is one of the top outlets in the city in terms of quality, value, and service. The 59th Street store has evolved into a custom outlet offering personalization in print, embroidery, and laser engraving. Owners Vic and Dave are always on the job. Footwear includes many famous names. They also carry a good stock of clothing, including logo merchandise and personalized T-shirts, caps, and sweats

SUPER RUNNERS SHOP

1337 Lexington Ave (at 89th St) 212/369-6010
360 Amsterdam Ave (at 77th St) 212/787-7665
1246 Third Ave (bet 71st and 72nd St) 212/249-2133
Grand Central Station (42nd St at Lexington Ave) 646/487-1120
Hours vary by location www.superrunnersshop.com

Co-owner Gary Muhrcke was the winner of the first New York City Marathon in 1970 and continues his passion through his livelihood. Entry blanks for local races are available in the stores. The stock includes a superb selection of men's and women's running and racing shoes, as well as performance running clothes. The informed staff, who are themselves runners, believe that each person should be fitted individually in terms of sizing and need.

Skating

BLADES BOARD & SKATE

120 W 72nd St (bet Broadway and Columbus Ave) 212/787-3911
160 E 86th St (bet Lexington and Third Ave) 212/996-1644
659 Broadway (at Bleecker St) 212/477-7350
Chelsea Piers (Pier 62, 23rd St at Hudson River) 212/336-6299
Sky Rink (Pier 61, 23rd St at Hudson River) 212/336-6199
Manhattan Mall, 901 Ave of the Americas (at 32nd St) 212/563-2448
Mon-Sat: 11-9; Sun: 11-7 (varies somewhat by location)

www.blades.com

Founded in 1990 by Jeff Kabat, Blades Board & Skate has become the largest action sports retail company in the nation. There are a number of reasons for this: a great selection of equipment for snowboarding, skateboarding, and in-line skating; a good stock of lifestyle apparel; informed service; and a guarantee that they'll match any competitor's price for 30 days.

PECK AND GOODIE

917 Eighth Ave (bet 54th and 55th St) 212/246-6123
Mon-Fri: 11-8; Sat: 10-8; Sun: 10-7

Peck and Goodie, owned by Blades Board & Skate, offer equipment and apparel to skaters who need the best with minimum fuss. The store carries a complete stock of roller skates, ice skates, in-line skates, skateboards, and accessories. With skates costing at least a hundred dollars a pair, it's wise to patronize an expert.

Skiing

SCANDINAVIAN SKI AND SPORT SHOP
40 W 57th St (bet Fifth Ave and Ave of the Americas)   212/757-8524
Mon, Tues, Fri, Sat: 10-6; Wed: 10-6:30; Thurs: 10-7; Sun: 11-5
www.skishop.com

Despite its name, this shop is really an all-around sporting goods store. They stock a full range of goods, from skis and skiwear to bikes and skates. They offer repairs and advice, and can also outfit for ski and bike trips.

Soccer

SOCCER SPORT SUPPLY COMPANY
1745 First Ave (bet 90th and 91st St)   212/427-6050, 800/223-1010
Mon-Fri: 10-6; Sat: 10-3   www.homeofsoccer.com

Hermann and Jeff Doss, the proprietors of this 70-year-old soccer and rugby supply company, claim that half their business involves importing and exporting equipment around the world. Visitors to the store have the advantage of seeing the selection in person, as well as receiving guidance from a staff that knows the field (excuse the pun) completely

Tennis

MASON'S TENNIS MART
56 E 53rd St (bet Park and Madison Ave)   212/755-5805
Mon-Fri: 9-7; Sat: 10-5

Mason's is the only tennis specialty store left in Manhattan. Mark Mason offers a superb collection of clothing with all the best brand names: Fila, Polo, Tail, LBH, Nike, Wimbledon, Lacoste, Ralph Lauren, and more. U.S. Open products are carried from May to December. You will also find ball machines, bags, and other tennis paraphernalia. They will match any authorized dealer on racquet prices and special-order any tennis product a customer may want. Same-day stringing is offered. A yearly half-price clothing (except children's) sale takes place in mid-January.

Stationery

JAM PAPER AND ENVELOPE/HUDSON ENVELOPE
111 Third Ave (bet 13th and 14th St)   212/473-6666
611 Ave of the Americas (at 18th St)   212/255-4593, 800/8010-JAM
Mon-Fri: 8:30-7; Sat, Sun: 10-6   www.jampaper.com

This outfit has become the largest paper and envelope store in the city and perhaps the world! They stock over 150 kinds of paper, with matching card stock and envelopes. They also have a vast selection of presentation folders. Close-outs and discounted items provide excellent bargains. Ask for their free catalog!

JAMIE OSTROW
876 Madison Ave (bet 71st and 72nd St)   212/734-8890
Mon-Sat: 10-6

For contemporary personalized stationery and invitations, you can't do better than Jamie Ostrow. Items are designed and manufactured to customers' specifications, and Crane stationery and wedding invitations are carried. A good selection of boxed Christmas and holiday cards is shown, and personalized Christmas cards are a specialty.

KATE'S PAPERIE
561 Broadway (bet Prince and Spring St)   212/941-9816
Mon-Fri: 10-7:30; Sat: 10-7; Sun: 11-7

8 W 13th St (at Fifth Ave)   212/633-0570
Mon-Fri: 10-7:30; Sat: 10-6; Sun: 12-6

140 W 57th St (bet Ave of the Americas and Seventh Ave)
Mon-Fri: 9-8; Sat: 10-7; Sun: 10-6   212/459-0700

1282 Third Ave (bet 73rd and 74th St)   212/396-3670
Mon-Fri: 10-7; Sat, Sun: 11-6   www.katespaperie.com

Here you will find one of the largest selections of decorative and exotic papers in the country. Kate's has thousands of kinds of papers, including papyrus, hand-marbled Italian, Japanese lace, and recycled papers from Zimbabwe, and just about anything else you can think of. But that isn't all. There are leatherbound photo albums and journals, classic and exotic stationery, boxes, wax seals, rubber stamps, pens, and desk accessories. They will do custom printing and engraving, personal and business embossing, and custom and corporate gift selection and gift-wrapping.

MRS. JOHN L. STRONG
699 Madison Ave (bet 62nd and 63rd St), 5th floor   212/838-3848
Mon-Fri: 10-5 and by appointment

Several barriers must be crossed to reach this high-end stationery establishment in a fifth-floor room. First, a claustrophobic elevator. Then a locked door. When you are buzzed in, the atmosphere is strictly high-altitude, as are the noses of some of the salesladies. Strong sells very high-quality papers, invitations, and announcements—with very high prices to match. If you are looking for the best, this is the place to splurge.

PAPER ACCESS
2030 Broadway (at 70th St)   212/799-4900
Mon-Fri: 10-8; Sat: 11-8; Sun: 11-6

23 W 18th St (bet Fifth Ave and Ave of the Americas)   212/463-7035
Mon-Fri: 9-7; Sat: 11-6; Sun: 12-6   www.paperaccess.com

If it is made of paper, this is the place to go for huge selections and quality merchandise. Business cards, writing paper, invitations, brochures, postcards, envelopes, folders, Oriental laser paper, bags, labels, and more are shown in quantity. Certificate plaques are also available.

PAPIVORE
233 Elizabeth St (bet Prince and Houston St)   212/334-4330
Mon-Sat: 11-7; Sun: 12-6

Unusual notepads, writing papers, notebooks, photo albums, and correspondence cards from Europe and Americas are featured at Papivore. They also specialize in custom printing.

PURGATORY PIE PRESS
19 Hudson St (bet Duane and Reade St), Room 403   212/274-8228
Mon-Fri: by appointment   www.purgatorypiepress.com

The name may be strange, but the people at Purgatory Pie know what they are doing. They do letterpress printing from hand-set metal and wood type. In addition, they do book production, albums, custom hand bookbinding, yearly date books, invitations, coasters, artists' books, and handmade paper with uniquely designed watermarks. Classes are taught in making handmade books and typography.

REBECCA MOSS
510 Madison Ave (at 53rd St)   212/832-7671
Mon-Sat: 10-6   www.rebeccamoss.com

If you are in the market for pens, this is the place! Moss carries the largest selection and the latest items from Montblanc, Parker, Waterman, Aurora, Pelikan, Omas, and all the other big names. Moreover, the personnel are informed and friendly. It is a family-owned business, and customers are treated as part of the clan. The late Rebecca Moss would be pleased at the job her grandson is doing!

Tiles

IDEAL TILE
405 E 51st St (at First Ave)   212/759-2339
Mon-Fri: 9-5; Sat: 10-3

Ideal Tile imports ceramics, porcelain, marble, granite, and terra cotta from Italy, Spain, and Brazil. They have absolutely magnificent hand-painted Italian ceramic pottery as well. This outfit guarantees installation of tiles by skilled craftsmen. They also offer marble and granite fabrication for fireplaces, countertops, windowsills, and tables.

TILES—A REFINED SELECTION
42 W 15th St (bet Fifth Ave and Ave of the Americas)   212/255-4450
227 E 59th St (bet Second and Third Ave)   212/813-9391
Mon-Fri: 9:30-5:30 (Thurs till 8); Sat: 10:30-5
(closed Sat in summer)

If you are in the market for quality tiles, try Tiles' "refined selection." There are American art tiles, glass, ceramic, slate, granite, molded tiles, marble and limestone mosaics, glass tiles, and a large assortment of handmade tiles. Design services are available, and the selection is tops.

Tobacco and Accessories

BARCLAY-REX
75 Broad St (bet Beaver and William St)   212/962-3355
Mon-Fri: 8-6:30
70 E 42nd St (bet Madison and Park Ave)   212/692-9680
Mon-Fri: 8-6:30; Sat: 9:30-5:30

570 Lexington Ave (at 51st St)   212/888-1015
Mon-Fri: 8-7:30; Sat: 9:30-5:30
3 World Financial Center (at Winter Garden)   212/385-4632
Mon-Fri: 8-7; Sat: 11-5; Sun: 12-5   www.barclayrex.com

Established in 1910, Barclay-Rex is the product of three generations of the
Nastri family. The shop caters to devotees of fine cigars, pipes tobaccos, and
smoking-related gifts and accessories. They have one of the city's best selections of pipes. Their shops are stocked with more than 200 brands of
imported and domestic tobaccos. The finest tobaccos from all over the world
are hand-blended and packaged under the Barclay-Rex label, and custom
blending is one of their specialties. Cigars are housed in "walk-in" humidors
at controlled temperatures.

CONNOISSEUR PIPE SHOP
1285 Ave of the Americas (bet 51st and 52nd St), concourse level
Mon-Fri: 10:15-5:30   212/247-6054

Edward Burak has assembled a beautiful collection of hand-carved pipes
that range in price from $47 to over $6,000. His store features natural unvar-
nished pipes, custom-made pipes, custom-blended tobacco, and expert repair.
Burak will also do appraisals for insurance purposes. If your pipe came from
Connoisseur, you'll get admiring glances from those who know quality.

J.R. CIGARS
562 Fifth Ave (at 46th St)   212/997-2227
Mon-Fri: 8-7; Sat: 10-5; Sun: 11-4   www.jrcigars.com

For years Lew Rothman has claimed to offer the world's largest selection
of cigars and pipe tobacco at the world's lowest prices. Over 3,000 styles and
300 brands of cigars are stocked. Prices are 20% to 70% off retail.

OK CIGARS
383 West Broadway (bet Spring and Broome St)   212/965-9065
Sun-Wed: 12-8; Thurs-Sat: 12-10   www.ok-cigars.com

Looking for a really good cigar? Len Brunson promises some of the best
in a pleasant atmosphere. Unique accessories are available, including some
of the finest and most peculiar antique tobacciana to be found.

Toys and Children's Items
General
CHILDREN'S GENERAL STORE
Grand Central Station (Lexington Ave at 42nd St)   212-682-0004
Mon-Fri: 8-7:30; Sat: 10-5:30; Sun: 11-4:30

Along the Lexington Avenue Passage to Grand Central Station, this is a
terrific all-purpose toy store. The emphasis is less on space-age wizardry and
battery-operated gizmos than on basic, well-made toys designed to encourage creative and imaginative play. The diverse stock is chosen by people who
clearly know and love children. Sadly, the original location on Broadway is
no longer open, although an East Side location is planned.

CLASSIC TOYS

218 Sullivan St (bet Bleecker and 3rd St)   212/674-4434
Daily: noon-6:30   www.classictoysnyc.com

Classic carries old and new toys that have proven popular with generations of youngsters. It is also a haven for collectors and those (like your author) who just like to browse toy shops. Here you will find the largest selection of die-cast vehicles in New York, with pieces of old Matchbox, Dinky, and Corgi that go back to the 1930s. Over a hundred years of toy soldiers are on display, as well as other miniatures, stuffed animals, and a great selection of antiques that will charm parents and children. They thoughtfully maintain a list of stores for shoppers who can't find what they want here!

DINOSAUR HILL

306 E 9th St (bet First and Second Ave)   212/473-5850
Mon-Sat: 11-7; Sun: 11-6

At Dinosaur Hill you can travel the world through toys! There are marbles from England, tin windups from China, papier-maché masks from Venice, wooden pull toys from Greece, and solid wooden blocks made right here in the U.S.A. In addition, there is handmade clothing in natural-fiber fabrics for infants through four years and a wonderful assortment of hats, music boxes, monkeys, moons, and mermaids! They also keep a birthday book.

ENCHANTED FOREST

85 Mercer St (bet Spring and Broome St)   212/925-6677
Mon-Sat: 11-7; Sun: 12-6

The Enchanted Forest physically and philosophically lives up to its name. Owners David Wallace and Peggy Sloane hired theatrical set designer Matthew Jacobs to create an enchanted-forest backdrop for a collection of toys, whimsies, and artwork. The shop purports to be a "gallery of beasts, books, and handmade toys celebrating the spirit of the animals, the old stories, and the child within." The emphasis is on the gallery aspect, so it really isn't a suitable place for energetic small children. Featured items include a fine selection of fairy tales and myths, puppets, kaleidoscopes, baskets brimming with unusual little treasures, and various eclectic gems. This place truly is enchanted!

EXOTICAR MODEL CO.

280 Park Ave (at 48th St)   212/573-9537
Mon-Sat: 10-6; Sun: 11-5   www.exoticar.com

For the automobile buff, Exoticar is surely the place! You'll find all manner of collectibles, apparel, books, magazines, and accessories. Ask to see the Munster Koach; this model is worth a visit in itself!

F.A.O. SCHWARZ

767 Fifth Ave (at 59th St)   212/644-9400
Mon-Wed: 10-6; Thurs-Sat: 10-7; Sun: 11-6   www.faoschwarz.com

Ask any kid where he on she wants to go in New York, and the answer will likely be F.A.O. Schwarz! Long the first name in toy stores, it is actually much more than a retail establishment. Youngsters grow wide-eyed at the enormous selection and exciting demonstrations. The store has three levels arranged into small shops that specialize in stuffed animals, bears, games, electronics, dolls, soldiers, Star Wars, Barbie, and all that you'd expect from a first-rate toy emporium. Look for **F.A.O. Baby** on the store's Madison Avenue side. There is even a counter by the door where those in a hurry can pick up a last-minute gift to take home. Just don't expect bargains. We're talking top-of-the-line!

GEPPETTO'S TOY BOX
10 Christopher St (bet Ave of the Americas and Seventh Ave)
Mon-Sat: 11-8; Sun: 1-7 (shorter hours in winter)   212/620-7511

This West Village toy store moved to larger quarters with more stock available. Although the owners clearly have become more consumer-savvy, stocking trendy favorites, the heart of this store is its exceptionally high-quality teddy bears, jack-in-the-boxes, snow globes, marionettes, and other whimsical toys and games. Moreover, it's obviously run with great passion and care. You'll also find a variety of interesting items made by local artists and a small but carefully chosen selection of books. If you're a toy collector, have a child in your life, or simply like a store with class and grace, make a visit to Geppetto's a top priority. If you're visiting in the winter, be sure to call ahead, as hours are shortened.

KIDDING AROUND
60 W 15th St (bet Fifth Ave and Ave of the Americas)
Mon-Sat: 10-7; Sun: 11-6   212/645-6337

This bright, spacious emporium in the heart of Greenwich Village is arguably the city's best toy store. Books, toys, puzzles, balls, games, craft supplies, birthday-party favors—you name it, they've got it. In addition to a wide selection of Playmobil, Brio, and Corrole dolls, Kidding Around stocks an amazing assortment of quality wooden toys for riding, building, and just having fun. The store's collection of clothing is small but well chosen, and the dress-up clothes are great, too. A new location in Montclair, New Jersey, features a more extensive clothing selection.

MARY ARNOLD TOYS
1010 Lexington Ave (at 72nd St)   212/744-8510
Mon-Fri: 9-6; Sat: 10-5

You won't find any great bargains and likely won't see anything you haven't seen before, but Mary Arnold Toys is a spacious, well-organized, and well-stocked source for the basics. There are separate sections for games, puzzles, books, stuffed animals, craft kits and supplies, Playmobil, videos, and Madame Alexander dolls. The dress-up collection deserves a special look.

RAIN OR SHINE GENERAL STORE
202 E 29th St (bet Second and Third Ave), 3rd floor   212/685-8556
Mon-Sat: 10-5

This children's toy and clothing emporium is a real find. Unfortunately, it's a bit *hard to find* as well. The building itself is more than a little grubby, and the elevator to the third floor does not inspire confidence, but persevere and you'll be rewarded with great baby gifts, lots of fun dress-up clothes, imaginative toys, a wide selection of nursery furniture (including New York's only line of Maine Cottage), and Zutano clothes for babies and toddlers. Take time to look around; they've squeezed in a lot of terrific stuff.

TOYS 'R' US
1514 Broadway (at 44th St)   800/869-7787
Mon-Sat: 10-10; Sun: 11-8   www.toysrus.com

No visit to Manhattan is complete for the young ones in the family (and the young at heart) without a visit to Toys 'R' Us—the toy store of all toy stores! Set in the heart of the city, this $32 million store features a huge stage set with a giant animatronic dinosaur and a 60-foot tall ferris wheel in the atrium, with each car modeled after a different toy. Seemingly every square inch of this busy store is devoted to showing merchandise. You have to see it to believe it!

ZITTLES
969 Madison Ave (at 76th St), 3rd floor   212/737-2040
Mon-Fri: 9-8; Sat: 9-7; Sun: 10-6

Housed on the third floor of Zitomer, Madison Avenue's often amusingly snobby drugstore-cum-department-store, Zittles has one of the most extensive selections of toys, games, stuffed animals, dolls, books, software, and videos for children in the city. There are neither bargains nor much imagination here, but there is a lot of space, and every inch of it is filled with all the basics and more. On your way up the elevator, which is back by the 76th Street entrance, look on the second floor for an extensive selection of children's clothing and accessories.

Gifts and Accessories

ART & TAPISSERIE
1242 Madison Ave (bet 89th and 90th St)   212/722-3222
Mon-Fri: 10:30-6:30; Sat: 10-6; Sun: noon-5

In the very heart of classy Madison Avenue comes this little gem of a store where French is indeed often the language spoken and everything is chosen with thought and care. I'm very down on the scores of Madison Avenue boutiques where the staff sneers at casual customers, but this charming place almost makes up for the lot of them. If you're looking for the right gift for a baby or young child, come here and ask for help. Games, furniture, dress-up clothes, and books are all available.

LITTLE EXTRAS
676 Amsterdam Ave (at 93rd St)   212/721-6161
Mon-Fri: 10:30-6:30 (Thurs till 7); Sat: 10:30-6; Sun: 11-5
(closed Sun in summer)

Whether you're looking for a personalized bathrobe, the perfect picture frame, a baby present, or hand-painted furniture, this cheerful store is teeming with gifts and accessories for infants and children. Owner Terry Siegel's great taste shows in everything. Make sure to look up at the mobiles and other things hanging from the ceiling! An added bonus: Little Extras offers a wide selection of birth announcements, thank-you's, and party invitations at a discount.

Specialty and Novelty

ALPHABETS

115 Ave A (bet 7th and 8th St)	212/475-7250
Daily: 12-8	
47 Greenwich Ave (bet Charles and Perry St)	212/229-2966
Daily: 12-8	
2284 Broadway (near 82nd St)	212/579-5702
Mon: 12-8; Tues-Fri: 11-9; Sat: 10-9; Sun: 11-7	

www.alphabetsnyc.com

These crowded little spaces are part toy store, part novelty shop, and part stroll down memory lane for baby boomers. If you're looking for a Desi Arnaz wristwatch, a Gumby and Pokey piggy bank, some kitschy ceramics, or a T-shirt with the Velveeta logo on it, this is the place to come. They also carry offbeat New York souvenirs. The Upper West Side location is a somewhat tamer version of the other two.

BALLOON CENTER OF NEW YORK

5 Tudor City Pl (bet First and Second Ave)	212/682-3803
Mon-Fri: 9:30-5	

Balloon Center of New York sells balloons individually or in multitudes of up to 50,000. There are graduations in diameter, thickness, style, and type (including Mylar balloons). Sizes range from peewees to blimps and extra-long shapes. Helium, ribbon, balloon clips, and balloon imprinting are also available. Most of this whimsical business is done for advertising campaigns and corporate and special events.

BIG CITY KITE COMPANY

1210 Lexington Ave (at 82nd St)	212/472-2623, 888/476-5483
Mon-Fri: 11-6:30 (Thurs till 7:30); Sat: 10-6	www.bigcitykites.com

Big City's David Klein sells kites for people's houses: i.e., mobiles and wall hangings. There are custom-made specialty kites and brilliantly colored fighter kites made of tissue paper. Prices run from $2 to $300. The staff's devotion is evident in the community programs it sponsors: kite festivals, exhibitions, and even "kite-ins." They also offer a kite-repair service and carry a full line of darts, dartboards, and accessories for recreational and competitive use.

DISNEY STORE

218 W 42nd St (at Times Square)	212/302-0595
Mon-Tues: 10-8; Wed-Sat: 10-11; Sun: 11-9:30	
711 Fifth Ave (at 55th St)	212/702-0702
Mon-Sat: 10-8; Sun: 11-6	
141 Columbus Ave (at 66th St)	212/362-2386
Mon-Sat: 10-8; Sun: 12-6	
300 W 125th St (at Eighth Ave)	212/749-8390
Mon-Sat: 10-8; Sun: 11-6	www.disneystore.com

If the "malling" of New York hasn't gotten you down, these stores—particularly the one on 42nd Street—can be fun places to shop. Unlike the staff at a lot of the huge stores that have popped up all over New York, these folks really know their stock and are personable to boot. If you don't have a Disney Store back home and are looking for kids' luggage with Mickey Mouse on it, backpacks in the shape of Winnie the Pooh, or any other Disney-related item, visit one of these locations.

E.A.T. GIFTS
1062 Madison Ave (bet 80th and 81st St)   212/861-2544
Mon-Sat: 10-6; Sun: 12-5   www.elizabar.com

It's impossible to sum up what this store offers in a few sentences. E.A.T. Gifts is a wonderland of imaginative party favors and stocking stuffers that must be seen to be believed. From tiny tea sets, party supplies, and invitations to the pinatas on the ceiling and seasonal holiday items, you'll want to inspect every square foot of this store. Indeed, it's the kind of place where you inevitably spot just one more thing as the salesperson is totaling up your purchases! The focus is mostly on kids and items you'll remember from childhood, but there is something for just about everyone at this wonderful store. As the Madison Avenue address suggests, there's nothing inexpensive about what you'll find here, and sometimes the whines of overprivileged young children can be a bit tiresome. But if you want to put together a special party bag, seasonal stocking, or gift basket, this is the place to go.

FORBIDDEN PLANET
840 Broadway (at 13th St)   212/473-1576
Mon-Sat: 10-10; Sun: 11-8

Mike Luckman's unique shop is a shrine of science-fiction artifacts. Forbidden Planet stocks sci-fi comic books and publications, videos, posters, T-shirts, cards, toys, and games.

GAMEQUEST
1596 Third Ave (bet 89th and 90th St)   212/423-0697
Mon-Sat: 11-7; Sun: noon-6

I can't tell a Playstation from a Game Boy, but I do know that a generation of kids—and some adults, too—are crazy about videogames. Kids in the know crowd this long, narrow store for a wide range of systems. Give these folks your system specs and an idea of what you're looking for, and chances are you'll walk away happy (poorer, too—this is not a cheap hobby!).

IMAGE ANIME
103 W 30th St (at Ave of the Americas)   212/631-0966
Mon-Fri: 11-7; Sat: noon-6   www.imageanime.com

Image Anime specializes in imported Japanese toys and collectibles. If that category is of interest to you—and there are a great many children and adults who are almost fanatically devoted to it—then this packed little store will thrill you. Lines include Gundam, Pokémon, Transformers, Robotech, Anime, and just about any other popular Japanese line you might want.

LOVE SAVES THE DAY
119 Second Ave (at 7th St)   212/228-3802
Daily: 1-9

As Starbucks and The Gap slowly take over the East Village, stores like

Love Saves the Day are a welcome relief. The floor-to-ceiling merchandise ranges from vintage clothing and accessories (including some really great go-go boots) to Star Wars action figures to more Pez dispensers than I've ever seen. If you're nostalgic for the 60s and 70s or just want to hang out with some funky folk, you're really going to groove on this place. Oddly enough, there's a branch in New Hope, Pennsylvania, as well.

MANHATTAN DOLL HOUSE
236A Third Ave (bet 19th and 20th St)   212/253-9549
Mon-Fri: 11-6:30 (Thurs till 7:30); Sat: 11-5:30; Sun: 12-5
                              www.manhattandollhouseshop.com

Edwin Jacobowitz operates the Manhattan Doll House, which boasts the city's largest collection of dolls (including Madame Alexander), dollhouses, and related furniture and paraphernalia. The store is also a hospital, where most injured dolls can be made well again.

POKÉMON
10 Rockefeller Plaza (bet Fifth Ave and Ave of the Americas)
Sun-Thurs: 10-8; Fri, Sat: 9-9   212/307-0900

Young ones and their elders will love Pokémon, where the latest Pokémon toys—some exclusive to this shop—are available along with many unusual experiences. For the novice, Pokémon is a fantasy universe of characters who possess a diverse array of strengths, weaknesses, and special powers. There are Pokémons hanging from the ceiling, fabulous sound and light shows, computer-controlled figures, and a training gym where kids can try out the newest Pokémon games. Don't miss it!

Once one of the most famous areas of Manhattan, "Ladies' Mile" is again on the itineraries of wise shoppers. And there is good reason! There are some great stores, all conveniently grouped together on Avenue of the Americas between 18th and 19th streets:

Bed Bath & Beyond: wonderful store, with huge selection of bed, bath, and home furnishings at good prices
Filene's Basement: famous for clothing bargains
Old Navy: very "in," especially with the young and not-quite-so-yuppie set; clothing is fashionable and priced right
T.J. Maxx: values in clothing and accessories for the family

RED CABOOSE
23 W 45th St (bet Fifth Ave and Ave of the Americas), basement
Mon-Fri: 11-7; Sat: 11-5:30   212/575-0155
                              www.theredcaboose.com

Owner-operator Allan J. Spitz will tell you that 99% of his customers are not wide-eyed children but sharp-eyed adults who are dead serious about model railroads.Unfortunately, there aren't huge numbers of model-train enthusiasts anymore, and this store—in an area that 50 years ago had five such stores—struggles to survive. If you happen to be a train buff, however, you've found your spot. The Red Caboose claims to have 100,000 items on hand, including a line of 300 hand-finished, imported brass locomotives.

Spitz claims that the five basic sizes—1:22, 1:48, 1:87, 1:161, and 1:220, in a ratio of scale to life size—will allow a model railroader to build layouts sized to fit into a desk drawer or a basement. They also carry an extensive line of plastic kits, paints, tools, and model supplies.

STUYVESANT TRAINS & HOBBIES
345 W 14th St (bet Eighth and Ninth Ave), 2nd floor
Tues-Fri: 12-6; Sat: 11-4   212/254-5200

Bigger isn't always better, and Stuyvesant proves it. They claim to be the smallest store with the largest inventory around! This place is for the young and young at heart. The stock of train and hobby supplies is superb. If you don't see something, they will special-order it for you.

Travel Items

CIVILIZED TRAVELLER
864 Lexington Ave (at 65th St)   212/288-9190
2003 Broadway (bet 68th and 69th St)   212/875-0306
Mon-Sat: 10-7   www.civilizedtraveller.com

For the person on the go, these stores are the most helpful places around! Books, maps, and videos are specialties, but you will also find unique and handy travel items like personal grooming pieces, pocket tailors, shoe kits, water purifiers, packable rainwear, slippers, travel-size games, travel alarm clocks, luggage on wheels, world-time calculators and clocks, translators, travel clothing, and organizational packing systems.

FLIGHT 001
96 Greenwich Ave (bet Jane and 12th St)   212/691-1001
Mon-Sat: 11-8; Sun: 12-6   877/FLIGHT1
                                                      www.flight001.com

Traveling these days isn't always that much fun, but a trip to Flight 001 will make it more bearable. You will find novel and useful travel aids, including cosmetics, bags, guidebooks, stationery, electronics, and more.

Variety, Novelty

ODD JOB TRADING
390 Fifth Ave (bet 35th and 36th St)   212/239-3336
299 Broadway (at Duane St)   212/964-6574
66 W 48th St (bet Fifth Ave and Ave of the Americas) 212/575-0477
149 W 32nd St (bet Ave of the Americas and Seventh Ave)
                                                      212/564-7370
465 Lexington Ave (bet 45th and 46th St)   212/949-7401
601 Eighth Ave (at 39th St)   212/714-0106
169 E 60th St (at Third Ave)   212/893-8447
36 E 14th St (at University Pl)   212/741-9944
Mon-Fri: 8-8; Sat, Sun: 10-7   www.oddjobstores.com

Odd Job has a well-deserved reputation as the best of the close-out stores. It consistently comes up with good buys on quality merchandise. What differentiates this chain from others is that its stock is more current. Anything from book racks to perfume may turn up, but it's always interesting.

Videotapes

EVERGREEN VIDEO
37 Carmine St (at Bleecker St)   212/691-7362
Mon-Thurs:10-10; Fri: 10-11; Sat: noon-11; Sun: noon-10

Here you will find more than 10,000 titles, including New York's largest rental collection of silent films; films of the 1930s, 1940s, and 1950s; foreign-language titles and documentaries; and 2,000 DVDs for sale or rent. Evergreen is particularly popular with folks in the arts and media.

VIDEO ROOM
1487 Third Ave (at 84th St)   212/879-5333
300 Rector Pl (South End Ave at W Thames St)   212/962-6400
Mon-Thurs:10-10; Fri, Sat: 10-11; Sun: 12-10   www.videoroom.net

Video Room stocks a large selection of foreign films and classics, and a highly competent staff of film students is motivated to help inquiring customers. There is also an in-depth selection of new releases, home pickup and delivery service ($89 per year), and a special-order department for hard-to-find films.

Watches

TEMPUS FUGIT AT THE SHOWPLACE
40 W 25th St (bet Ave of the Americas and Broadway) 212/633-6063
Sat, Sun: 8:30-5

If you're looking for a vintage Rolex, this is the place. They carry other top brands and watchbands, all at considerable savings. Watch repair is also available.

YAEGER WATCH CORPORATION
578 Fifth Ave (at 47th St)   212/819-0088
Mon-Fri: 10-5; Sat: 10-3 (closed Sat in summer)
                                              www.yaegerwatch.com

Over 2,000 discounted watches are carried at Yaegar Watch. Choose from name brands retailing from $100 to $150,000 in a store that has been owned by the same family since 1970. Watch repair and warranties are offered, and prices are quoted over the phone.

New York's best watch stores include **Cellini Fine Jewelry** (509 Madison Ave, 212/888-0505), **Kenjo** (40 W 57th St, 212/333-7220), **Tourneau** (500 Madison Ave, 212/758-6098; 12 E 57th St, 212/758-7300; and 200 W 34th St, 212/563-6880), and **Wempe** (700 Fifth Ave, 212/397-9000).

VII. Where to "Extras"

As I research each new edition of this book, I'm always struck by how much information doesn't fit neatly into any of the other chapters. That's why I came up with this chapter of "Extras": where to go dancing, take kids, spend a romantic evening, and host a special event. Those are just several of the subjects this chapter addresses.

WHEN TO GO
Annual Events

While stores, museums, restaurants, and the like are open all year, some special events are held only during certain seasons or once a year. The "For More Resources" section at the end of this chapter offers suggestions about how to find out what's happening in New York at any given time. *Time Out New York* is a tremendous source of up-to-date information, as are *New York* magazine and *The New Yorker*.

JANUARY
Polar Bear Club New Year's dip (Coney Island)
Ice skating (Rockefeller Center and Central Park)
Winter Antiques Show (Seventh Regiment Armory)
Kids' Night on Broadway
Chinese New Year (January or February)

FEBRUARY
Westminster Kennel Club Dog Show (Madison Square Garden)
Empire State Run-up (Empire State Building)
National Antiques Show (Madison Square Garden)
Valentine's Day wedding ceremony (Empire State Building)
Winter Festival (Great Lawn of Central Park)
Art Dealers Association exhibition (Seventh Regiment Armory)

MARCH
St. Patrick's Day Parade (Fifth Avenue)
International Cat Show (Madison Square Garden)
Spring Armory Antiques Show (Seventh Regiment Armory)

Big East and NIT college basketball tournaments (Madison Square
   Garden)
New York Flower Show (Pier 92)
Macy's Spring Flower Show
Radio City Easter Show (Radio City Music Hall)

APRIL
International Auto Show (Jacob K. Javits Convention Center)
Baseball season opens (Yankee Stadium and Shea Stadium)
New York Antiquarian Book Fair (Seventh Regiment Armory)

MAY
International Food Festival (Ninth Avenue)
Ukrainian Festival (East Seventh Street)
Fleet Week (week before Memorial Day)
Brooklyn Bridge birthday walk (Adventures on a Shoestring)
Lower East Side Jewish Festival
Washington Square Outdoor Art Exhibit

JUNE
Salute to Israel Parade (Fifth Avenue)
Free concerts and performances (Central Park and other parks throughout
   the city)
Museum Mile Festival (Fifth Avenue)
Feast of St. Anthony of Padua (Little Italy)
Summer restaurant "sale" (throughout the city)
Lower Manhattan Cultural Council's Buskers Fair
Jazz festivals (Bryant Park, Carnegie Hall and other locations)

JULY
Free concerts and performances (Central Park and other parks throughout
   the city)
Free movies (Bryant Park and other locations)
Fourth of July fireworks (East River and other locations)
American Crafts Festival (Lincoln Center)
Mostly Mozart (Avery Fisher Hall)
Midsummer's Night Swing (Lincoln Center)

AUGUST
Free concerts and performances (Central Park and other parks throughout
   the city)
Free movies (Bryant Park and other locations)
New York City Triathlon
Lincoln Center Out-of-Doors Festival (Lincoln Center)
Festival Latino (Public Theater and other locations)
U.S. Open begins (National Tennis Center)

SEPTEMBER
Autumn Crafts Festival (Lincoln Center)
New York Is Book Country (Fifth Avenue from 40th to 57th streets)
Third Avenue Festival
Feast of San Gennaro (Little Italy)
New York Film Festival (Lincoln Center)
Broadway Cares/Equity Fights AIDS flea market and auction (Shubert
   Alley)

OCTOBER
Columbus Day Parade (Fifth Avenue)
Basketball and hockey seasons open (Madison Square Garden)
Soho Arts Festival
Fall Antiques Show (Pier 92)
Halloween Parade (Greenwich Village)
New York Marathon (October or November)

NOVEMBER
Home Show (Jacob K. Javits Convention Center)
Corel/WTA Women's Tennis Tournament (Madison Square Garden)
Margaret Meade Film Festival (American Museum of Natural History)
Macy's Thanksgiving Day Parade (Central Park West and Broadway)
Thanksgiving dinner and vintage movies (Screening Room)
Christmas tree lighting (Rockefeller Plaza)

DECEMBER
Christmas windows (Saks Fifth Avenue, Macy's Herald Square, and other
     locations)
Messiah Singalong (Avery Fisher Hall)
Radio City Christmas Show (Radio City Music Hall)
Holiday bazaar (Grand Central Station)
Menorah lighting (Grand Army Plaza)
Christmas Day walking tour (Big Onion Walking Tours)
New Year's Eve celebrations (Times Square and other locations)
First Night celebrations (Grand Central Station, Central Park, and other
     locations)

Holidays
2004 (Leap Year)

January 1	New Year's Day
January 19	Martin Luther King, Jr. Day
February 14	Valentine's Day
February 16	Presidents' Day
March 17	St. Patrick's Day
April 4	Palm Sunday
	Daylight Savings Time begins
April 6	Passover begins (eight days)
April 9	Good Friday
April 11	Easter Sunday
May 9	Mother's Day
May 31	Memorial Day
June 20	Father's Day
July 4	Independence Day
July 5	Independence Day (observed)
September 6	Labor Day
September 16	Rosh Hashana (two days)
September 25	Yom Kippur
October 11	Columbus Day
October 31	Daylight Savings Time ends
	Halloween
November 11	Veterans' Day

November 25   Thanksgiving Day
December 9   Hanukkah begins (eight days)
December 25   Christmas

2005

January 1   New Year's Day
January 17   Martin Luther King, Jr. Day
February 14   Valentine's Day
February 21   Presidents' Day
March 17   St. Patrick's Day
March 20   Palm Sunday
March 25   Good Friday
March 27   Easter Sunday
April 3   Daylight Savings Time begins
April 24   Passover begins (eight days)
May 8   Mother's Day
May 30   Memorial Day
June 19   Father's Day
July 4   Independence Day
September 5   Labor Day
October 4   Rosh Hashana begins (two days)
October 10   Columbus Day
October 13   Yom Kippur
October 30   Daylight Savings Time ends
October 31   Halloween
November 11   Veterans' Day
November 24   Thanksgiving Day
December 25   Christmas
December 26   Hanukkah begins (eight days)

WHERE TO SIT
Parks

As hard as it may be to believe when you're standing amid the sky-scrapers of midtown, Manhattan has almost 2,600 acres of parkland. That means 17% of the city is grass, trees, rocks, lakes, playgrounds, and walking trails. Spanning 843 acres in the middle of the island, Central Park is the biggest and certainly the most famous. Smaller ones like Carl Schurz Park and Lighthouse Park on Roosevelt Island can be more peaceful, however, because fewer people know about them. Inwood Hill Park and Fort Tryon Park on Manhattan's northern tip are so wooded and hilly that you won't believe you're in New York.

Unless you are going to a scheduled event such as a play or concert, you probably don't want to walk around in any park late at night. (It is worth noting, however, that the Central Park police precinct is the safest in all of Manhattan.) If you are by yourself, stay away from isolated and densely veg-etated areas even during the day. That said, the parks are real treasures to explore and enjoy. They offer a wonderful respite from the concrete and chaos, and thanks to a concerted effort to clean and refurbish them, the city's parks are looking better than they have in the 20 years I've been writing various editions of this book.

The following is an annotated listing of some of the city's biggest parks, as well as some personal favorites among the lesser known ones.

BATTERY PARK
southern tip of Manhattan (below State St and Battery Pl)

This 23-acre park was named for the gun battery built along its old shoreline during the War of 1812. Castle Clinton, a National Monument originally built as a fort during the War of 1812 and now the place to buy tickets for the Statue of Liberty and Ellis Island, is located here. One of the last remaining kiosks for the original subway system is in Battery Park, too. The Staten Island Ferry Terminal is adjacent to the park's eastern edge. The marvelous National Museum of the American Indian is directly north of the park, and the Museum of Jewish Heritage is on the park's northwest edge. You'll find lots of benches and pathways here, as well as an excellent view of New York Harbor.

Artwork valued at more than $100 million, including public pieces as well as pieces in private collections, was destroyed in the September 11, 2001 attack on the World Trade Center. The Sphere, a sculpture that once stood in the World Trade Center plaza, survived, battered but intact, and now sits in Battery Park.

BRYANT PARK
Ave of the Americas (bet 40th and 42nd St)

Behind the New York Public Library, this was the site of the 1853 World's Fair, where Isaac Singer unveiled the sewing machine and Elisha Otis introduced the elevator. After years of neglect, the park underwent a multimillion-dollar renovation in the early 1990s and is now a real gem. The benches are great resting spots, and you'll find lots of vendors and a fine garden in the spring and summer. You'll also find games like checkers and Scrabble for rent, toy boats to rent and sail in the fountain, a wonderful new carousel in warmer months, and free movies on Monday nights in summer. Imagine 10,000 people watching *The Wizard of Oz* and singing "Somewhere Over the Rainbow"! Bryant Park even has clean and safe public restrooms (just off 42nd Street, behind the library), complete with security guards, attendants, and fresh flowers in the ladies' room.

CENTRAL PARK
Fifth Ave to Central Park W (bet 59th and 110th St)

Designed in 1858 by Frederick Law Olmsted, the same landscape architect who designed the U.S. Capitol Grounds in Washington, D.C., this is the ultimate urban park. The 843-acre park has two ice-skating rinks (in winter), lakes, ponds, a marvelous wildlife conservation center, theaters, jogging tracks, a reservoir, baseball diamonds and other playing fields, playgrounds, tennis courts, a miniature golf course (in summer), and a castle. You can even find a wonderful restaurant (Park View at the Boathouse, near 72nd Street on the east side), a more downscale cafe (near 65th Street on the west side), and two warm-weather Italian sidewalk cafes (inside the Columbus Circle entrance). There's lots of open space and 58 miles of paths. Thanks to the Central Park Conservancy, the park has had a major facelift with updates and renovations of everything from the Great Lawn to the pond near the park's southwest entrance. In summer, Central Park is home to a wide variety of cultural events, including Shakespeare in the Park, various concerts on the "Summer Stage," and free concerts by the New York Philharmonic and the Metropolitan Opera.

For maps and a current schedule of events, stop by the Visitor Information Center at The Dairy, just behind Wollman Rink at what would be 65th Street and Avenue of the Americas (if those roads went into the park); the Henry Luce Nature Observatory, in Belvedere Castle at mid-park near 79th Street; or at the Charles A. Dana Discovery Center, in the park's northeast corner, near 110th Street and Fifth Avenue. If you ever get lost in the park, remember that the first digits of the number plate on the lampposts correspond to the nearest cross street.

Official signs posted in city parks: "If you're not responsible enough to clean up after your dog, you don't deserve to have one."

FORT TRYON PARK
Riverside Dr to Broadway (bet 192nd and Dyckman St)

This 66-acre gift from John D. Rockefeller, Jr., is a hilly and wooded treasure with magnificent views of the Hudson River and the Palisades. Make sure to visit the beautiful but little known Heather Garden, the largest public garden in Manhattan, as well as The Cloisters. Take a friend along, however, if you plan on exploring off the beaten path.

INWOOD HILL PARK
northwest tip of Manhattan

The second largest park in Manhattan, Inwood Hill Park is bordered by the Harlem River to the north and the Hudson River on the west. These rugged 200 acres are home to a marsh, caves once used by Algonquin Indians, and the island's last remaining stands of virgin timber. (Most of the original forests were cut down by British troops during the Revolutionary War.) Hiking and climbing enthusiasts will love its relatively unspoiled wilderness, but travel in groups for safety's sake. Drop by the Urban Ecology Center (inside the park at 218th St) for information on nature walks and other scheduled events.

LIGHTHOUSE PARK
northern tip of Roosevelt Island

If you really want to get away but only have a little time, take a short ride out to this magical place on the northern tip of Roosevelt Island in the middle of the East River. The view of the Manhattan skyline from the west side of the park is among the best in the city. A tram to Roosevelt Island leaves frequently from its own station on Second Avenue between 59th and 60th streets. It costs $2 each way, and the bus that takes you from the tram station to the northern end of the island costs one thin dime.

MADISON PARK
Madison Ave to Fifth Ave (bet 23rd and 26th St)

Thanks to a tremendous recent restoration, you can transport yourself back to 19th century New York in this swath of greenspace in Lower Manhattan. Yes, this was the site of the original Madison Square Garden, as well as P. T. Barnum's Hippodrome. But no, that's not James Madison—or even Abraham Lincoln, whom it really resembles—in the park's southeast corner. It's actually U.S. Senator and Secretary of State William Seward. The fountains at the park's south end are particularly impressive.

What Are Those Flags Flying All Over New York?

The presence of the United Nations means that flags of many countries fly in New York. However, there are two flags flown over the city that you won't find in any atlas. The white one with the green maple leaf is the New York City Parks and Recreation Department's flag, while the blue, white and orange one is the official flag of New York City.

ROBERT WAGNER, JR. PARK, BATTERY PARK ESPLANADE, and NELSON A. ROCKEFELLER PARK
southwest edge of Manhattan

These are a series of relatively new and expanding parks marching their way up the west side of the island. As you head north through Battery Park City and up toward TriBeCa, you'll find open spaces, walkways, benches, playgrounds, and lots of New Yorkers reveling in the reclaimed waterfront. For a real treat, start your walk at Chambers Street and head south along the river for some of the most sweeping views in the city. The views of Ellis Island and the Statue of Liberty are particularly spectacular from Robert Wagner, Jr. Park, just above Battery Park at the south end of Battery Park City.

RIVERSIDE PARK
Riverside Dr to Hudson River (bet 72nd and 159th St)

Like Central Park, this is another of Frederick Law Olmsted's creations. In addition to playgrounds, great paths for walking, jogging, and bicycling, popular clay tennis courts at 92nd Street, and a terrific view of the Hudson River, the park is home to the Eleanor Roosevelt statue (at 72nd Street), the 79th Street Boat Basin, the Soldiers and Sailors Monument (at 89th Street), and Grant's Tomb (at 122nd Street). People used to complain about erosion and vandalism in the park, but those who live around it now have adopted it and take responsibility for its upkeep.

UNION SQUARE PARK
Broadway to Park Ave S (bet 14th and 17th St)

Once known for its drug scene, this old park has really come back to life. It stretches between Broadway (called Union Square West here) and Park Avenue South (Union Square East) and is home to the city's most popular Greenmarket. You'll also find playgrounds, picnic benches, and, in warmer months, an outdoor bar and cafe near the Abraham Lincoln statue at the park's north end. The George Washington statue at the south end was erected in 1856 to commemorate the 80th anniversary of the signing of the Declaration of Independence, while a statue of nonviolence leader Mohatma Ghandi graces the park's southwest corner.

WASHINGTON SQUARE PARK
foot of Fifth Ave below 8th St

Long considered the emotional if not the geographic center of Greenwich Village, this park sits at the foot of Fifth Avenue and is best known for the Washington Memorial Arch. The park was constructed in 1827, but the marble arch was not dedicated until 1895. (It replaced a wooden one.) The park is near New York University, and its chess tables, playgrounds, and other amenities are much used by students and neighborhood residents.

For recorded information on what's happening in the parks around Manhattan and the other boroughs, call 212/360-3456 or 888/NY-PARKS.

WHERE TO PLAY
Nightlife

Whether you want an evening of elegant dining and dancing, rocking and rolling till the wee hours, dropping in on a set of jazz, or catching some stand-up comedy, New York's club scene offers endless choices. For descriptions of places to go and information about who is playing, look under "Night Life" in the front of *The New Yorker* or under specific listings in the back of *New York* magazine and throughout *Time Out New York*. I've listed several popular places in each category to get you started. Most levy a cover charge, many offer at least a light menu, and a few require reservations and jackets for men. As with so many other things, it is wise to call in advance.

Cabaret Rooms
Bemelmans Bar, Carlyle Hotel (35 E 76th St, 212/744-1600)
Danny's Skylight Room (346 W 46th St, 212/265-8133)
Don't Tell Mama (343 W 46th St, 212/757-0788)
Feinstein's at the Regency, Regency Hotel (540 Park Ave, 212/339-4095)
Firebird Supper Club and Cafe (363 W 46th St, 212/586-0244)
Oak Room, Algonquin Hotel (59 W 44th St, 212/840-6800)
Torch (137 Ludlow St, 212/228-5151)

Do you want to hear Woody Allen (yes, *that* Woody Allen) tooting the clarinet? He plays most Monday nights at **Cafe Carlyle**, in the Carlyle Hotel (35 E 76th St, 212/570-7189), but call ahead to be sure.

Comedy Clubs
Caroline's Comedy Cellar (1626 Broadway, 212/757-4100)
Comedy Cellar (117 Macdougal St, 212/254-3480)
Dangerfield's (1118 First Ave, 212/593-1650)

Gotham Comedy Club (34 W 22nd St, 212/367-9000)
Stand-up New York (236 W 78th St, 212/595-0850)

Dancing

China Club (268W 47th St, 212/398-3800): live music and DJs on the week-
end
Culture Club (179 Varick St, 212/243-999): 1980s retro
Limelight (660 Ave of the Americas, 212/807-7850): a church turned disco
Polly Esther's (186 W 4th St, 212/924-5707): retro, disco
SOB (204 Varick St, 212/243-4940): Latin and Caribbean beats
Supper Club (240 W 47th St, 212/921-1940): weekend ballroom dinner
dances

Gay and Lesbian Clubs

Boiler Room (86 E 4th St, 212/254-7536): gay
G Lounge (223 W 19th St, 212/929-1085): gay
Monster (80 Grove St, 212/924-3557): gay
Meow Mix (269 E Houston St, 212/254-0688): lesbian
Rubyfruit Bar and Grill (531 Hudson St, 212/929-3343): lesbian

Jazz Clubs

Birdland (315 W 44th St, 212/581-3080)
Blue Note (131 W 3rd St, 212/475-0049)
Cotton Club (656 W 125th St, 212/663-7980)
Iridium (1650 Broadway, 212/582-2121)
Jazz Standard (116 E 27th St, 212/576-2232)
Smoke (2751 Broadway, 212/864-6662)
Village Vanguard (178 Seventh Ave S, 212/255-4037)

You'll find nightly piano entertainment at the **Lobby Court Lounge** in
the Sheraton New York Hotel & Towers (811 Seventh Ave, 212/581-1000).

Rock and Folk Clubs

Bitter End (147 Bleecker St, 212/673-7030): one of the original Greenwich
Village folk clubs
Bottom Line (15 W 4th St, 212/228-6300): long-lived industry showcase
club for rock, folk, and blues
CBGB (315 Bowery, 212/982-4052): the home of punk-rock

"Let's Have a Drink"

Aquavit (13 W 54th St, 212/307-7311)
Campbell Apartment (Grand Central Station, 42nd St at Vanderbilt Ave,
212/953-0409)
Fifty Seven Fifty Seven, Four Seasons Hotel (57 E 57th St, 212/758-5757)
Grand Bar, Soho Grand Hotel (310 West Broadway, 212/965-3000)
Mark's Bar, The Mark Hotel (25 E 77th St, 212/879-1314)
21 Club (21 W 52nd St, 212/582-7200)

Villard Bar and Lounge, New York Palace Hotel (24 E 51st St, 212/888-7000)

Some theater productions close almost as soon as they open and others run for only a couple months. But one has been going on almost since I began writing this book: **Tina 'n' Tony's Wedding.** It's theater with a twist: you follow the couple from their wedding (St. Luke's Church, 308 W 48th St) to the reception (Edison Hotel, 221 W 46th St), complete with a pasta dinner, champagne, and wedding cake. Intrigued? Call 212/239-6200 for more information.

Music in the Museums

Brooklyn Museum (200 Eastern Parkway, 718/638-5000): music and dancing on the first Saturday of every month

Frick Collection (1 E 70th St, 212/288-8700): chamber music every other Sunday at 5 p.m.

Guggenheim Museum (1071 Fifth Ave, 212/423-3500): live jazz on Friday and Saturday evening in warmer months only

Metropolitan Museum of Art (Fifth Ave bet 80th and 84th St, 212/535-7710): classical music on Friday and Saturday evening

Rose Center for Earth and Space (81st bet Columbus Ave and Central Park West, 212/769-5100): jazz on Friday night

Theodore Roosevelt Birthplace (28 E 20th St, 212/260-1616): concerts at 2 p.m. on many Sundays

Medieval music concerts are sometimes performed in the dramatic 12th-century Fuentiduena Chapel at **The Cloisters** (Fort Tryon Park, 212/923-3700). Call for a schedule. Advance tickets are strongly recommended.

Recreation

Visitors sometimes see Manhattan as nothing but concrete and can't imagine what those who live here do for exercise other than walking. The people who live here, however, know that you can do just about anything in New York that can be done anywhere else—and then some! Whether it's a batting cage, golf, horseback riding, or a driving range, chances are that New York has it if you just know where to look. Unless otherwise noted, call the New York City Department of Parks and Recreation (212/360-8133) for information.

Baseball—There are seven public baseball diamonds in Central Park and at least a dozen more in other parts of Manhattan. There are also batting cages in the Field House at Chelsea Piers (212/336-6500) and at the Baseball Center NYC at 202 West 74th Street (212/362-0344).

Basketball—Between schoolyards and city parks, you'll find more than a thousand public basketball courts in Manhattan. The most famous of many city courts is the one at 4th Street and Avenue of the Americas. The Field House at Chelsea Piers (212/336-6666), Basketball City (212/924-4040), and most of the city's Ys also have good courts and lots of action.

Bicycling—You can ride bikes on the 6.2-mile loop in Central Park, in Riverside Park, or on the 5.5-mile route that runs along the Hudson River down to Battery Park. You can even pedal the city's streets, if you have the nerve! One caveat: off-road mountain biking in New York is illegal and punishable with a fine. Bicycles are rented during warmer months at Loeb Boathouse (212/517-2233) in Central Park and most bicycle shops in the city.

Billiards—Manhattan has several dozen pool and billiards halls. Chelsea Billiards (212/989-0096), at 54 West 21st Street, is thought to be the best. You can also try the Billiard Club, at 344 Amsterdam Avenue (212/496-8180) and 210 East 86th Street (212/570-4545).

Birdwatching—Believe it or not, nearly half of the more than 600 bird species in the United States can be spotted here sometime during the year. There's even a hotline for reporting rare and interesting sightings (212/979-3070). Call the New York Audubon Society (212/691-7483) for information about outings, or check in at the Charles A. Dana Discovery Center (212/860-1370) in Central Park.

Bowling—Try Bowlmor Lanes (212/255-8188), at 110 University Place (between 12th and 13th streets), or Leisure Time Bowling (212/268-6909), on the second floor of Port Authority Bus Terminal. There's also a state-of-the-art facility in the Chelsea Piers complex (212/835-2695).

Chess, Checkers, and Backgammon—You can often find a game of chess in the afternoon and evening (it's open until midnight) at the Chess Shop (212/475-9580), at 230 Thompson Street. In warm weather, games are usually going at Washington Square Park, at the Chess and Checkers House in Central Park, at Bryant Park, or in Nelson Rockefeller Park, just north of the World Financial Center.

Climbing—The city maintains an indoor climbing wall at the North Meadow Recreation Center (212/348-4867). The Sports Center at Chelsea Piers has a 10,000-square-foot rock-climbing wall (212/336-6000). You can also try the Extra Vertical Climbing Center (212/586-5718).

Fencing—Private and group fencing lessons for skill levels from beginners to Olympians are available at Metropolis Fencing (114 W 26th Street, 212/463-8044) daily from noon until 10 p.m. These people have been operating in New York for nearly eight decades!

Fishing—If you want to borrow poles and fish with the kids in the well-stocked Harlem Meer in Central Park in spring, summer, and fall, bring your picture ID to the Charles A. Dana Discovery Center (212/860-1370), near Fifth Avenue at 110th Street. More serious anglers can check in at Urban Angler (118 East 25th Street, 800/255-5488).

Golf—Given the value of land in New York, it's no wonder Manhattan doesn't have a single golf course. However, duffers can play at some of the nation's great courses, thanks to video technology, or go down to the Golf Academy at Chelsea Piers (212/336-6400) and hit a bucket of balls at the four-tiered driving range on Pier 59. The best public course in the outer boroughs is Split Rock, in the Bronx (718/885-1258).

Ice Skating—The most famous rink in New York and possibly the world is the one in front of Rockefeller Plaza (212/332-7654), just off Fifth Avenue between 49th and 50th streets. Central Park also has rinks at its north and south ends: Lasker Rink (212/396-0388), near 110th Street and Lenox Avenue, and Wollman Rink (212/396-1010), near what would be 62nd Street and Avenue of the Americas. You can also try the clean, spacious rink in Riverbank State Park (212/694-3642), at 145th Street and Riverside Drive, or the Ice Studio (212/535-0304), on Lexington Avenue between 73rd and 74th streets. Sky Rink (212/336-6100) used to be on the 16th floor of a building (hence, the name) but has moved to Chelsea Piers. Sky Rink is open all year, but the others have limited seasons, so call ahead to make sure they're open. All of these rinks rent skates.

If you have your heart set on ice skating at Rockefeller Plaza, I suggest going on a weekday morning. There's no wait and relatively few people will be watching in case you hit the ice!

Rollerblading—The proper name for this sport is "in-line skating," as Rollerblade is actually a brand name. Whatever you call it, it's a great way to get around in Manhattan. You can rent skates by the hour or day from Blades Board & Skate (eight locations in Manhattan; check Chapter VI under "Sporting Goods") and Manhattan Sports (212/580-4753), at 2188 Broadway. A variety of other sporting goods stores also rent them.

Roller Skating—Try the Chelsea Piers Roller Rinks (212/336-6100).

Running—Two of Manhattan's most popular places to run are along the Hudson River in Riverside Park and the 1.5-mile trail that circles the reservoir in Central Park. If you want some other jogging routes or company (the latter is always a good idea), call the New York Road Runners Club (212/860-4455). The Road Runners can also tell you about upcoming races.

Soccer—Central Park has four public soccer fields. One is on the Great Lawn, behind the Metropolitan Museum of Art, and three are in the North Meadow near the park's north end. The Field House at Chelsea Piers (212/336-6500) has two excellent indoor soccer fields.

Swimming—You can find public beaches in the other boroughs out on Long Island, but swimming in Manhattan is almost entirely limited to pools. Believe it or not, endurance swimmers circumnavigate the island for the annual Manhattan Island Marathon, and a 400-yard strip of imported sand off the Gansevoort Pier on the Hudson River is due to open soon. Until then, inexpensive, relatively uncrowded swimming options include the Carmine Street Recreation Center (212/242-5418), at 1 Clarkson Street; the Vanderbilt YMCA (212/756-9600), at 224 East 47th Street; All-Star Fitness Center (212/265-8200), at 75 West End Avenue; Asphalt Green (212/369-8890), at 90th Street and York Avenue; and the pool in Riverbank State Park (212/694-3665), on Riverside Drive at 145th Street.

Tennis—Manhattan has more than a hundred public tennis courts. Seasonal permits cost $50 and can be purchased at The Arsenal (Central Park, Fifth Avenue at 64th Street). For more information, call 212/360-8133. To find out about lessons at the Central Park Tennis Center during warmer months, call 212/280-0201. Private facilities include Manhattan Plaza Racquet Club (212/594-0554), Sutton East Tennis (212/751-3452), Roosevelt Island Racquet Club (212/935-0250), and Columbus Tennis Club (212/662-8367). Believe it or not, two indoor courts are tucked into the third floor of Grand Central Station. Call the Tennis Club at Grand Central (212/687-3841) for details. And if you want to feel like a pro, call the USTA National Tennis Center in Queens (718/760-6200) to reserve a court.

Video games—The city is awash in video arcades, and many of the hipper stores have at least a couple games tucked in a back corner. The greatest concentration is in Times Square, including Broadway City (241 W 42nd Street, 212/997-9797), XS New York (1457 Broadway, 888/972-7529), and the ESPN Zone (1472 Broadway, 212/921-3376).

The Ys in Manhattan include the **92nd Street YMHA** (212/427-6000), at 1395 Lexington Avenue; the **West Side YMCA** (212/875-4100), at 5 West 63rd Street; the **Vanderbilt YMCA** (212/756-9600), at 224 East 47th Street; the **YWCA** (212/735-9753), at 610 Lexington Avenue; and the **McBurney YMCA** (212/741-9210), at 215 West 23rd Street.

For $25 a year ($10 for senior citizens over 55 and children 12 to 17), facilities and classes are offered at 13 recreation centers run by the Department of Parks and Recreation. Among the better ones are **Asser Levy Recreation Center** (212/447-2020), at Avenue A and 23rd Street; the **59th Street Recreation Center** (212/397-3166), at 533 West 59th Street; and **Carmine Street Recreation Center** (212/242-5418), at 1 Clarkson Street. Seasonal passes to **Riverbank State Park**, on Riverside Drive at 145th Street (212/694-3600), are inexpensive, and facilities are excellent.

For information about gyms and fitness centers, see the "Health and Fitness" section of Chapter IV.

Spectator Sports

Some people associate New York with fine food and expensive stores, while others link the city with the Yankees, the Mets, the Knicks, the Rangers, and other professional sports teams. The New York area is home to more than half a dozen professional sports teams—although only basketball's Knicks and hockey's Rangers actually play in Manhattan. (Home field for the city's two pro football teams, the Jets and the Giants, is across the river in New Jersey, although there's been a lot of talk about a future stadium for the Jets in Manhattan.) Diagrams of all area stadiums appear near the front of the Manhattan Yellow Pages.

Tickets for regular-season baseball games can often be purchased as late as game day. Tickets for football's Giants and Jets, however, are almost impossible to find unless you have a generous friend with season tickets. Even Knicks tickets are hard to come by. If you're planning a trip to New York, it's worth finding out which team is in town and who they're playing.

A word of warning: New York sports fans are like no others. They are loud, rude, and typically very knowledgeable about their teams and the sport they're watching. If you're cheering against the home team, keep your voice down —and your head, too!

BASEBALL

NEW YORK METS
Shea Stadium (Queens)   718/507-8499

The easiest ways to get to Shea stadium from Manhattan are by subway (take the 7 line from Times Square or Grand Central Station to the Willets Point/Shea Stadium stop) or boat (call New York Waterway at 800/533-3779 for game-day sailings and fare information). Tickets are easy to get and relatively inexpensive. The season runs between April and September.

NEW YORK YANKEES
Yankee Stadium (The Bronx)   212/307-1212

Although the Yankees may eventually move to a new stadium in Manhattan, the so-called House that Ruth Built (because Babe Ruth played here for many years) is a great place to watch a baseball game. It's also an easy subway ride (take the C or D line from Manhattan's West Side or the 4 line on the East Side to the 161st Street/Yankee Stadium stop) or boat trip (call New York Waterway at 800/533-3779 for game-day sailings and fare information). Despite the Yankees' consistently winning ways, tickets remain plentiful until the playoffs. The season runs between April and September.

Baseball Has Returned to Brooklyn!
Almost a half century after the Brooklyn Dodgers moved west, baseball is again being played in Brooklyn. The Cyclones, a minor league team of the New York Mets, play on Coney Island. For information and tickets, call 718/449-8497.

BASKETBALL

NEW YORK KNICKS
Madison Square Garden   212/465-6741

The Knicks play at Madison Square Garden, directly above Penn Station in the heart of Manhattan. The better the Knicks are doing, the harder tickets are to come by. And be forewarned: tickets are expensive. The season runs from late October through April.

NEW YORK LIBERTY
Madison Square Garden   212/564-9622

The Liberty are a perennial powerhouse in the Women's National Basketball Association. These tickets are a great deal: they are easy to get, not very expensive, and buy a terrific evening of basketball. Their season runs from late May through August.

FOOTBALL

NEW YORK GIANTS
The Meadowlands (New Jersey)   201/935-8111

Getting tickets to a game is virtually impossible. In case you do land tickets, buses run between Port Authority Bus Terminal and Giants Stadium in the Meadowlands. The season runs from September through December.

NEW YORK JETS
The Meadowlands (New Jersey)   516/560-8200

Tickets for Jets games are almost as hard to get as Giants tickets, but you can always try. Buses run between Port Authority Bus Terminal and Giants Stadium in the Meadowlands. The season runs from September through December.

HOCKEY

NEW YORK RANGERS
Madison Square Garden   212/465-6741

Everything I said at the outset about New York sports fans goes double for the Rangers. These games are loud and tough. Getting tickets is tough, too. The season runs from October through April.

TENNIS

U.S. OPEN
National Tennis Center (Queens)   718/760-6200

One of four Grand Slam tournaments in professional tennis, the U.S. Open is held at summer's end. Finals are played over Labor Day weekend. Tickets to the finals and semifinals sell out as soon as they go on sale, but tickets for earlier rounds can usually be purchased in the weeks leading up to the tournament.

WHAT TO EXPECT

Safety

There are more crimes committed in New York than any other American city because more people live here. But New York is not nearly as dangerous as people think. In fact, per capita crime in New York is lower than in any other major U.S. city. The violent crime rate has plummeted here and continues to fall, and security is probably tighter here than in any U.S. city other than Washington, D.C.

The percentages are definitely with you, especially if you observe a few commonsense "don'ts":

- Don't display big wads of money or flashy watches and jewelry. In fact, avoid taking them with you. Leave most of your cash and all of your valuables at home or in the hotel safe.
- Don't open your wallet in public.

- Don't use ATMs when no one else is around.
- Don't leave ATMs until you've put your money in a wallet and then put the wallet in your pocket or purse.
- Don't keep your wallet in your back pocket unless it's buttoned. Better yet, carry your wallet in a front pocket, along with keys and other important items.
- Don't wear your purse slung over one shoulder. Instead, put the strap over your head and keep your purse in front of you or to the side.
- Don't doze off on the subway or bus.
- Don't take the subway late at night or very early in the morning.
- Don't walk down empty streets or enter empty subway stations.
- Don't jog in Central Park or anywhere else after dark.
- Don't let yourself believe that staying in "good" neighborhoods protects you from crime. The only time I was ever mugged was on Park Avenue at 62nd Street, and you can't find a better neighborhood than that!
- Don't let anybody in your hotel room, even if they claim to work for the hotel, unless you've specifically asked them to come or have checked with the front desk to verify their authenticity.
- Don't talk to strangers who try to strike up a conversation unless you're sure of their motivations.
- Don't ever leave bags unattended. If you're going to put a bag or backpack on the floor at a restaurant or bathroom stall, put your foot or a leg of your chair through the strap.
- Don't hang your purse or anything else on the back of the door in a public bathroom stall.
- Don't walk around with your mouth open, camera slung over your shoulder, and map out while saying things like, "Gee, honey, we sure don't have buildings this tall back home!"
- Don't be afraid to cross the street if a situation doesn't feel right or shout for help if somebody is bothering you.
- Of course, it goes without saying these days that you should move away from any unattended packages and immediately report any suspicious items or behavior to authorities.

A final word of warning that has nothing to do with crime per se: watch where you walk. Manhattan has an incredible amount of traffic, and the struggle among cars, taxis, trucks, buses, and pedestrians is constant. The city has tried with limited success to erect pedestrian barriers at some of the most dangerously crowded intersections, like Fifth Avenue and 50th Street. Other particularly dangerous spots include Park Avenue at 33rd Street, Avenue of the Americas and Broadway at 33rd and 34th streets by Herald Square, and 34th Street and Eighth Avenue at Port Authority Bus Terminal. It may sound silly to repeat a warning from childhood, but look both ways before stepping into the street, wherever you are.

Of course, it's always a good idea to plan a meeting place if you're traveling with a group or family. If there's an emergency, don't hesitate to call 911. If you need more general assistance, try the **Travelers' Aid Society** (212/944-0013). These kind folks will help with medical referrals, emergency flight changes, and anything else you might need in a pinch.

Tipping and Other Expenses

Be forewarned: New York is expensive. Really expensive. The city's hotels are by far the most expensive in the country, often costing upwards of $300 per night for a basic double room. The average dinner at a decent restaurant can easily run upwards of $50 per person, most theater and opera tickets are just plain outrageous, and even a quick lunch under $10 is increasingly hard to find. Everybody expects a tip, too. It's up to you, of course, but $1 per bag to the bellman, between 15% and 20% of your fare to the cab driver, and between 15% and 20% of your pre-tax restaurant bill (just double the tax—it's 8.25% on just about everything) to your waiter is typical. Most people also tip wine stewards (10% of the wine bill), parking valets ($2), private tour guides (at least $5 a day), and doormen who hail cabs ($1), among others.

The good news is that prices have not risen much in recent years. With a little effort, you can find cheaper hotels, less expensive restaurants, good deals, and even some free events and activities. You can also make an effort to make wise choices. The difference between buying a single bagel through room service at one midtown hotel and a deli a block away, for instance, is more than $10! However, in general my advice is be prepared to spend money—and lots of it—if you're here for a special visit. Don't nickel-and-dime yourself out of enjoying a priceless experience!

Checklists

If you're planning a trip to New York, think ahead about what you want to do and read the relevant sections of this book carefully. Pay special attention to things that require advance planning, like tickets to certain events, Broadway shows, television show tapings, and tours. Special sales or events require that you visit at certain times of year. Weather is always a consideration. Average temperatures range from highs in the 30s and 40s in December, January, and February (and snow is always a possibility) to highs in the 80s and 90s in June, July, and August (when the humidity can wilt even the sturdiest among us). Whenever you come and whatever you plan to do, however, I recommend packing these key items:

- comfortable walking shoes
- umbrella and raincoat (or warm coat, scarf, and boots)
- jacket and tie (still required in some places) or nice dress
- opera glasses
- address book and postcard stamps
- prescriptions and an extra pair of glasses
- fanny pack or money belt
- tickets (airplane and others)
- AARP and/or Medicare card
- student ID card
- a picture ID card

All the little items that you may want in your hotel room or when you're out and about cost a lot less at home than in New York. Most hotels will supply small sewing kits, many now have in-room coffeemakers, and some will let you borrow an umbrella or hair dryer for free. But consider packing film, aspirin, snacks, and gum. Plan what you're going to need for the day before leaving the hotel room. Put a couple of credit cards, driver's license, and some money in a secure pocket, fanny pack, or money belt and then stash everything else in a shoulder bag so there's no worrying about a stolen purse or wallet. Leave your room key at the front desk for the same reason. Depending on the time of year, here's a list of things I might take with me for a day of exploring:

- addresses and phone numbers of places you plan to visit and details about how to get there
- address and phone number of your hotel
- bus and subway maps
- tissues
- list of public bathrooms in the areas you'll be going
- umbrella
- coat or sweater
- unlimited-use MetroCard (for subways and buses)
- loose change and small bills
- finally, don't forget this book!

WHERE TO GO WITH CHILDREN

When I first began writing this book, I did so from the perspective of an adult who comes to New York without children. I quickly learned, however, that many people bring kids to New York, whether they're coming for business or pleasure. New York can be overwhelming for kids (the same is true for adults!), but it can also be a wonderland if you know where to go.

The "Kids" pages in the back of *New York* magazine and *Time Out New York,* and the "Family Fare" column in the Friday *New York Times* Weekend section are great places to look for children's events and activities in and around New York City. Look in toy shops and bookstores for seasonal calendars, *Big Apple Parent*, or one of the other free parenting magazines published in New York.

I've listed the best places for kids in several categories: entertainment, museums and sights, restaurants, and toy and bookstores. When a specific place is described in another part of the book, in many cases I've included only the address and phone number and marked the entry with an asterisk (*). When the place isn't described elsewhere, I've provided a bit more information. Of course, children's interests can vary, so I've inevitably included places that one child will love and another might find boring. I'll let you be the judge of that!

Entertainment

ARTime—Run by art historians, this organization offers tours of Soho and Chelsea art galleries geared for elementary school children and their families. Call 718/797-1573 for more information.

Arts Connection Center—Various kid-friendly performances and reasonable ticket prices can be found at this location (120 W 46th Street, 212/302-7433) near Times Square.

*Bryant Park—Kids (and adults) can rent such games as Scrabble and checkers for $4 an hour. That assumes you can pry them away from the wonderful new carousel. You can rent toy boats to sail in the fountain for $2 an hour.

*Central Park—Particularly during the spring and summer months, Central Park is full of events and activities for children. In addition to the marvelous Wildlife Conservation Center, there are activities for children on Saturday and Sunday afternoon at Belvedere Castle (212/772-0210), near 79th Street on the West Side; a puppet theater on weekday mornings near the 62nd Street playground (call The Dairy at 212/794-6565 to make reservations); a marionette theater near 81st Street and Central Park West (212/988-9093); and story readings at the Hans Christian Anderson Statue, by the Conservatory Water Pond, near 74th Street and Fifth Avenue, on Saturday morning. Make sure to call ahead, as some events require reservations and/or a small fee, and hours and locations may vary. You might also stop by the **Charles A. Dana Discovery Center** (212/860-1370), in the northeast corner near Fifth Avenue and 110th Street, to borrow fishing poles or attend a family workshop. At **Belvedere Castle** you can borrow a "discovery kit" complete with binoculars, guidebook, maps, and sketch pad. Every day from 10 to 7 (except Saturday) in warmer months, you can rent a small boat to sail in the **Conservatory Water Pond** (near 74th Street and Fifth Avenue). If you're looking for an unusual way to see the park, try a bicycle tour (call Bite of the Apple Tours at 212/541-8759 for more information). You can find out what is happening on any given day in Central Park and other parks throughout Manhattan by calling 212/360-3456.

Children's Museum of the Arts—This friendly Soho spot is a big favorite with children who like to create and explore with their hands. Designed for children between 18 months and ten years, this low-key, child-centered museum has various spaces where children can explore different media, play, and even snuggle up with a good book. Workshops for children of different ages are held throughout the day. The museum is open Wednesday from 10 to 7 and Thursday through Sunday from 10 to 5. Just look for the friendly zebra in Soho (182 Lafayette Street). Admission is $6 per person. Call 212/941-9198 for more information.

*Children's Museum of Manhattan—This museum (212 W 83rd St, 212/721-1234) has great play spaces for toddlers, preschoolers, and kids in early elementary school. Look for daily readings and arts and crafts workshops.

*Circle Line Sightseeing Yachts—Pier 83, Twelfth Avenue at 43rd Street (212/563-3200). For more information, see the "Tours" section in Chapter III.

Circuses—**Ringling Brothers** and **Barnum & Bailey** (800/755-4000) comes to Madison Square Garden in the spring. Look for Barnum's smaller **Kaleidoscope** in Bryant Park and the **Big Apple Circus** (800/922-3772) in Damrosch Park at Lincoln Center in the fall.

Donnell Library Children's Center—This branch of the New York Public Library (20 W 53rd St, 212/621-0636) houses a special room for children with more than 100,000 books, magazines, and recordings. Also look in a display case on the second floor for the original stuffed animals upon which

Winnie the Pooh and his friends were based. The library is open from noon to 6 on Monday, Wednesday, and Friday; 10 to 6 on Tuesday; noon to 8 on Thursday; and noon to 5 on Saturday.

*Dyckman Farmhouse Museum—This little gem in northern Manhattan offers free Early American craft classes most Saturday afternoons (4881 Broadway, 212/304-9422).

Field House at Chelsea Piers—You name it and Chelsea Piers teaches it to kids. There's even a toddler gym complete with ball pit for free play. The field house is near the entrance of the Chelsea Piers complex, at the west end of 23rd Street. Call 212/336-6500 for more information.

Helmbold Family Children's Learning Center—Occupying the fourth floor of Scandinavia House (58 Park Ave), this enchanting place is full of great dress-up clothes, books, and tables full of Legos and Brios. Unfortunately, it's only open to the public on Friday and Saturday. Call 212/879-9779 for more information.

Hi Art!—Founder (and mother) Cyndie Bellen-Berthezene offers children and their families innovative exposure to art, dance and music through museum and gallery visits, as well as studio workshops and classes. Call 212/362-8190 for more information.

IMAX Theater—Located inside the American Museum of Natural History, on Central Park West between 77th and 81st streets, this theater shows films on such diverse topics as African animals and tornados. The screen is enormous and the films well conceived. Call 212/769-5034 for more information.

Kaye Playhouse—Started by Danny Kaye and his wife, Sylvia, this wonderful theater always has something fun going on. It's located at Hunter College on 68th Street at Lexington Avenue; call 212/772-4448 for more information.

Kids at Art—What fun! Kids can roll up their sleeves and experiment with various art media at this Upper East Side storefront (1349 Lexington Ave). Classes are available for children from 2 to 11 (those under 4 must be accompanied by an adult). The best part is the gallery outside, where the youngsters' work is displayed. Call 212/410-9780 for more information.

*New Amsterdam Theater—Part of the revitalization of 42nd Street, this renovated theater once housed the Ziegfeld Follies and is now home to the wildly popular Disney production of *The Lion King*. It's located at 214 West 42nd Street; call 212/282-2900 for more information.

New Victory Theater—This theater is entirely devoted to productions for children and families. It's located at 209 West 42nd Street; call 212/564-4222 for more information.

92nd Street Y—This amazing institution (1395 Lexington Ave, 212/415-5611) offers classes for infants (two months and older) and children through its Parenting Center. Prices are a bit high, but the quality and new-mom networking opportunities are great.

Our Name Is Mud—A fun place for painting pottery on the East Side (1566 Second Ave, 212/570-6868), West Side (506 Amsterdam Ave, 212/579-5575), and Greenwich Village (59 Greenwich Ave, 212/647-7899).

Outdoor playgrounds—Manhattan has lots of safe, imaginative, and relatively clean public playgrounds. Look in Central Park along Central Park West or Fifth Avenue and on the promenade outside the World Financial Center, or call the Manhattan Department of Parks and Recreation (212/360-8111) for the location of a playground near you.

Museums and Sights

*American Museum of Natural History, Hayden Planetarium, and **Rose Center for Earth and Space**—Check out the museum's wonderful Discovery Room (Central Park West between 77th and 81st streets, 212/769-5100).

*Central Park Zoo—Central Park behind The Arsenal, on Fifth Avenue at 64th Street, 212/861-6030

*Children's Museum of Manhattan—212 West 83rd Street, 212/721-1234

*Dyckman Farmhouse Museum—4881 Broadway, 212/304-9422

*Ellis Island—In New York Harbor, off Battery Park, 212/363-7620

*Empire State Building Observation Deck—Fifth Avenue between 33rd and 34th Streets, 212/736-3100

*Fraunces Tavern Museum—54 Pearl Street, 212/425-1778

*Intrepid Sea-Air-Space Museum—Pier 86, Twelfth Avenue at 46th Street, 212/245-0072

*Madame Toussaud's—234 West 46th Street, 212/512-9600

*Metropolitan Museum of Art—Not everything at the Met (Fifth Ave between 80th and 84th streets, 212/535-7710) is for children, and strollers are not permitted on Sunday. Still, the Egyptian mummy exhibit and the gallery full of arms and armor will be big hits with kids. Call the Education Department (212/570-3756) for information about films and other special events for children.

*Museum of the City of New York—1220 Fifth Avenue, 212/534-1672

*Museum of Television and Radio—25 West 52nd Street, 212/621-6600

*National Museum of the American Indian—1 Bowling Green, at the foot of Broadway, 212/668-6624

*NBC Experience Studio Tour—Located at 50th Street between Fifth Avenue and Avenue of the Americas, this tour is not for children under six but is a big hit with older kids. Call 212/664-7174 for more information.

*New York City Fire Museum—278 Spring Street, 212/691-1303

*New-York Historical Society—170 Central Park West between 76th and 77th streets, 212/873-3400

New York Transit Museum—Boerum Place at Schermerhorn Street, Brooklyn, 718/243-3060

*Roosevelt Island Tram—The tram leaves from a station on Second Avenue between 59th and 60th streets.

*Sony Wonder Technology Lab—550 Madison Avenue, 212/833-8100

*South Street Seaport—Located at the east end of Fulton Street (212/732-7678), the seaport has a seasonal schedule of activities for children and families, plus a special interactive museum for children.

*Statue of Liberty—On Liberty Island in New York Harbor, off Battery Park

*United Nations—The visitors' entrance is on First Avenue, between 45th and 46th streets (212/963-7713). Strollers are not allowed on the grounds and children under five cannot go on the tour.

Restaurants

*America—A big restaurant (9 E 18th St, 212/505-2110) with large portions and heaps of French fries.

Avenue—This Upper West Side favorite (520 Columbus Ave, 212/579-3194) even has a baby-food menu!

Barking Dog Luncheonette—Good food and lots of canine knick-knacks to look at in these popular Upper East Side spots (1678 Third Ave, 212/831-1800 and 1453 York Ave, 212/861-3600).

*Brooklyn Diner USA—One of many theme restaurants in Manhattan, Brooklyn Diner USA (212 W 57th St, 212/977-1957) has basic diner foods that will make kids happy and parents nostalgic.

Bubby's—This kid-friendly bastion of southern cooking in Tribeca (120 Hudson St, 212/219-0666) has great ambience and food. Be sure to save room for dessert.

*Carnegie Delicatessen and Restaurant—Expect huge portions, rude waiters, and bench seats at this bustling New York institution (854 Seventh Ave, 212/757-2245).

Cowgirl—Small children can be entertained for hours looking at the walls of this low-key spot at 519 Hudson Street in the West Village. Call 212/633-1133 for more information.

EJ's Luncheonette—Friendly neighborhood places with basic food at good prices (447 Amsterdam Ave, 212/873-3444; 1271 Third Ave, 212/472-0600; and 432 Ave of the Americas, 212/473-5555).

Ellen's Stardust Diner—There isn't great dining in Times Square, but this Broadway diner is a fun spot (150 Broadway, 212/956-5151).

ESPN Zone—Sports, sports, sports! This Times Square play space (1472 Broadway, 212/921-3776) gets a little rowdy at night.

Gray's Papaya—Cheap, tasty hot dogs and more are served at this hurried, downscale spot at the corner of Broadway and 72nd Street (212/799-0243).

*Jackson Hole Burgers—You'll get great, juicy hamburgers and lots of thick fries and onion rings at this restaurant, which has several locations, including 232 East 64th Street (212/371-7187).

Jekyll & Hyde Club—There's usually a long line, but that's because kids love to dine at this not-too-scary haunted house (the food is not so great), complete with talking heads (1409 Ave of the Americas, 212/541-9505).

*John's Pizzeria—Many New Yorkers swear this is the best pizza around. The original John's is in the West Village at 278 Bleecker Street (212/243-1680), but new locations have popped up all over the city.

Lombardi's—The first licensed pizza place in New York is located at 32 Spring Street (212/941-7994).

Mars 2112—For aspiring astronauts and science-fiction buffs, this theme restaurant on 51st Street at Broadway (212/582-2112) has "crater masters" instead of waiters.

McDonald's—Kids love McDonald's, and the one at 160 Broadway has a store inside selling Ronald McDonald dolls and items with the McDonald's logo. They also offer table service on the second floor in the back. The McDonald's in Times Square is fun too—and it's hard to miss, thanks to 7,500 lights in its sign!

Nick & Toni's Cafe—A relative newcomer on the Upper West Side (100 W 67th St, 212/496-4000), this pleasant place does all the basics well.

Peanut Butter & Company—The name says it all! Try the do-it-yourself S'mores for dessert (240 Sullivan St, 212/677-3995).

Piece of Cake—This sweet Upper East Side spot (1370 Lexington Ave, 212/987-1700) is open for breakfast, lunch, and dinner, or you can just pop in for a cookie. Ask about their monthly cupcake decorating parties.

Planet Hollywood—When business started to drop at the former location on 57th Street, this pop culture icon simply moved to the next hot neighborhood, the "new" Times Square. Look for the lines at 1540 Broadway (212/333-7827).

*Serendipity 3—The East Side's favorite ice cream parlor is Serendipity 3 (225 E 60th St, 212/838-3531). It is the home of Frozen Hot Chocolate and other wondrous desserts, as well as good but overpriced meals.

*Tavern on the Green—The chef at this beautiful spot in Central Park (Central Park West at 67th St, 212/873-3200) has put together a terrific children's menu. After 5 p.m. on holidays, children eat free. Reservations are usually necessary.

Two Boots—This favorite pizza place loves kids (and vice versa). The original is at 37 Avenue A (212/505-2276), but locations are popping up all over the city, including the great food court at Grand Central Station.

Toy Stores and Bookstores

*Bank Street Bookstore—A tremendous source for children's books, as well as resources for parents and teachers, up near Columbia University (2875 Broadway, 212/678-1654).

*Books of Wonder—A legend among children's bookstores, known especially for its Wizard of Oz collection and Sunday morning story hours (16 W 18th St, 212/989-3270).

*Classic Toys—For people who believe that good toys don't need to change every season or even every generation (218 Sullivan St, 212/674-4434).

*Disney Store—The one on the corner of 42nd Street and Seventh Avenue (212/221 0430) is the best of several in town.

*F.A.O. Schwarz—The grandfather of all toy stores is on Fifth Avenue at 58th Street (212/644-9400). Crowded and overpriced, it's nonetheless a fantasyland.

*Geppetto's Toy Box—This special place is run by people who really care about toys and children, young and old (10 Christopher St, 212/620-7511).

*Kidding Around—Arguably the best toy store in the city (60 W 15th St, 212/645-6337).

*Scholastic Store—The world's only retail store for the giant educational publisher (557 Broadway, 212/343-6166).

*Toys 'R' Us—The chain's 110,000-square foot flagship store has taken up residence at Broadway and 44th Street in Times Square (201/225-8392).

*West Side Kids—It's about as kid-friendly as a toy store gets (498 Amsterdam Ave, 212/496-7282).

Just as some things are fun to do with kids, there are others that you shouldn't do with them. Museums like the Frick Collection, the Neue Galerie, and the Grolier Club's gallery, for example, are not places to bring small children. Indeed, children under 16 are not allowed on the tour of the Federal Reserve Bank, children under 12 are not welcome at the Neue Galerie, children under 10 are not allowed in the Frick, children under 6 can't go on the NBC Studio Tour, children under 5 are not welcome on the tour of the United Nations, and children under 4 are not allowed in most Broadway theaters. If you're going shopping at a perpetually crowded place like Zabar's or Fairway, don't take kids along or keep a firm grip on their hands if you do. The latter holds true just about everywhere in New York—it's easy for a young one to get lost in a crowd! And remember that kids tire more quickly than adults. Chances are you'll be doing a lot of walking, and they're taking two or three steps for every one of yours! As the *New York Times* once put it, "Baby miles are like dog years."

Finally, a word of warning: it's a real challenge to tote an infant or toddler in New York. While hundreds of thousands of children are born and raised in the city, visitors who are accustomed to carting their children through malls in strollers and around town in car seats may have trouble here. Many places, including the subway system, are not exactly stroller-accessible, and the United Nations, the Forbes Magazine Galleries, the Metropolitan Museum of Art (on Sundays), and the Museum of Jewish Heritage ban them altogether. (However, the Museum of Jewish Heritage offers free backpacks and Snugglies during your visit.) Taxis with functioning seatbelts have become much easier to find in recent years, but ones with car seats are a rarity. Only a few public restrooms have changing tables, and I've yet to hear of a store that has followed the Nordstrom chain's example and set aside space for nursing mothers. The good news is that up to three children under 44 inches tall ride free with a fare-paying adult on buses and subways.

New York has several dozen radio stations. *Time Out New York* lists radio highlights in each weekly edition. Some of the best stations:

89.1 FM (WNYU)	College radio
90.7 FM (WFUV)	Adult alternative
93.9 FM (WNYC)	National Public Radio
96.3 FM (WQXR)	*New York Times* and classical music
100.3 FM (WHTZ)	Top 40 hits
101.1 FM (WCBS)	oldies
101.9 FM (WQCD)	jazz
660 AM (WFAN)	Don Imus and sports talk
710 AM (WOR)	talk, information, and Joan Hamburg
770 AM (WCBS)	National Public Radio
820 AM (WNYC)	news, traffic updates, and weekend entertainment reports
1010 AM (WINS)	Radio Disney
1560 AM (WQEW)	

WHERE TO GO

In the Middle of the Night

New York bills itself as "the city that never sleeps," and many who live here are night people. They include not only actors and artists but also those who clean and maintain the huge office buildings, work for answering services, put together morning newspapers and newscasts, work the night shift at hospitals and other businesses that never close, and secretaries, transcribers, and editors who must make sure paperwork is ready overnight.

In general, stores and restaurants in Soho, Tribeca, and Greenwich Village stay open later than those in the rest of the city. The restaurants and mom-and-pop operations along Broadway on the Upper West Side and on Lexington and Third avenues on the Upper East Side also tend to keep late hours. As with everything else, call before setting out to make sure that they are still keeping the same hours.

If you're up late and looking for something to do, try:

B. Dalton Booksellers (396 Ave of the Americas, 212/674-8780, and other locations)
Barnes & Noble (2289 Broadway, 212/362-8835, and other locations)
Bowlmor Lanes (110 University Pl, 212/255-8188)
Chelsea Billiards (54 W 21st St, 212/989-0096)
Chess Shop (230 Thompson St, 212/475-9580)
Crunch Fitness (404 Lafayette St, 212/614-0120)
Johnny Lat's Gym (7 E 17th St, 212/366-4426)
Tower Records (Broadway at 4th St, 212/505-1500 and Broadway at 66th St, 212/799-2500)
Tower Video (383 Lafayette St, 212/505-1166)
Virgin Records Megastore (1540 Broadway, 212/921-1020)

Ten years ago, The Gap arrived in Manhattan seemingly overnight, and suddenly there were stores on every corner. Five years ago, it was Starbucks. Now it's **Duane Reade**, the 24-hour drug store. If you need to pick up some toiletries or have a prescription filled in the middle of the night, just look down the street: once just a small chain among many, there are Duane Reade stores on practically every corner!

If you need help in the middle of the night:
Altman Electric (212/744-7372)
Animal Medical Center (212/838-8100)
Doctors on Call (212/737-2333)
Emergency Dental Service (referral line, 212/679-3966)
Kapnag Heating and Plumbing (212/289-8847)
Manhattan Locksmiths (212/877-7787)
Midnight Express Cleaners (pickup service, 212/921-0111)
Moonlight Courier (212/473-2246)

For Free

There's no way to get around it: New York is expensive. Even the most frugal and resourceful visitors often feel as if they're bleeding money. ("Didn't we just get $200 out of the cash machine yesterday!?") Still, you can find some good deals and do a lot of sightseeing for free. Look in *Time Out New York*'s tremendous weekly listings of events for boxes noting free ones. You can also try some of the following:

Concerts and Other Performances—On Monday nights in summer, Bryant Park hosts (and HBO sponsors) free movies. This idea is catching on in other parks and neighborhoods, so keep an eye out. Also in the summer, Central Park comes alive with free concerts by the New York Philharmonic (212/875-5700), operas by the Metropolitan Opera (212/362-6000), Shakespeare in the Park (212/598-7100), and all sorts of performances on the Summer-Stage (212/360-2777). Call 212/360-3456 for recorded information about events in Central Park and other parks throughout the city. There's also the Midsummer Night Swing concerts at Lincoln Center Plaza (212/875-5400), concerts on Thursday and Friday evening at South Street Seaport (212/669-9400), and chamber music in Washington Square Park every Tuesday night. On the first Saturday of each month (except in September), revelers dress up and dance the night away at the Brooklyn Museum of Art (718/638-5000). It's not in Manhattan, but it's a great evening and a tremendous deal, given that you pay only the museum's suggested $4 admission. For information about concerts and other performances at the Winter Garden, in the World Financial Center, call 212/945-0505.

If you're interested in discount tickets for concerts, theater, and other performances, make sure to look in the "Tickets" section of Chapter III as well.

Museums and Sights—In alphabetical order, the free museums and sights in Manhattan include the American Bible Society's gallery, the Americas Society gallery, the Cathedral Church of St. John the Divine, the Equitable Center Gallery, Federal Hall National Memorial, the Forbes Magazine Galleries, the Ford Foundation Gardens, Grant's Tomb, the Grolier Club's gallery, the Hispanic Society of America, the Municipal Art Society's Urban Center Gallery, the Museum of American Illustration, the National Museum of the American Indian, New York Public Library, the New York Public Library for the Performing Arts, New York Unearthed, the Nicholas Roerich Museum, the PaineWebber Gallery, the Rose Museum at Carnegie Hall, the Schomburg Center for Research in Black Culture, the Sony Wonder Technology Lab, the Transit Museum Gallery in Grand Central Station, Trinity Church's small museum, and the Whitney Gallery and Sculpture Garden at Altria. Some of these places accept donations, but none pressures visitors for them.

NYC & Company, the city's savvy tourism and marketing arm, has been organizing lots of seasonal promotions, particularly in the wake of the September 11, 2001, terrorist attack and the subsequent decline in tourism. Promotions such as **Paint the Town** offer significant discounts on hotels, restaurants, theaters, museums and other venues. Information is available at www.nycvisit.com or at the tourist information center at 810 Seventh Avenue (near 53rd Street).

It used to be that the museums along Museum Mile offered free admission one night a week. Unfortunately, that tradition lives on only one night a year, in late June. Still, some museums in the city do offer pay-as-you-wish admission on different evenings throughout the year. They include the American Folk Art Museum (Friday from 6 to 8), the Cooper-Hewitt (Tuesday between 5 and 9), the International Center of Photography (Friday between 5 and 8), the Jewish Museum (Tuesday between 5 and 8), the Museum of Arts and Design (Thursday between 6 and 8), the New Museum of Contemporary Art (Thursday between 6 and 8), and the Whitney Museum of American Art (Friday between 6 and 9). The Studio Museum in Harlem is free on the first Saturday of every month. Active-duty military personnel are admitted free to the Intrepid Sea-Air-Space Museum.

Children under 12 are admitted to a lot of places for free. Smithsonian Associates are admitted without charge to the Cooper-Hewitt. Although it isn't free, you can go to both The Cloisters and the Metropolitan Museum of Art on the same day for one admission price.

CityPass gives discount admissions to several popular tourist spots, including the Empire State Building, the Whitney Museum, the Guggenheim, the Intrepid Sea-Air-Space Museum, the American Museum of Natural History, and the Circle Line harbor tour. Call 707/256-0490 for more information.

Tours—The very best bargain in this category is the free personalized tour offered by the city through its Big Apple Greeter program. A close runner-up is the marvelous free tour of Grand Central Station offered every Wednesday at 12:30 p.m. by the Municipal Art Society. Other free tours include the neighborhood around Grand Central Station, the Federal Reserve Bank, the New York Public Library, Penn Station, the Schomburg Center for Research in Black Culture, Times Square, the area on and around 34th Street, the Lower East Side, and Trinity Church. The Urban Park Rangers also conduct a variety of free tours in the city's parks. For more detailed information about tours, see the "Tours" section of Chapter III.

Transportation—Perhaps the best deal in all of New York is the unlimited-ride MetroCard. Whether you spend $7 for a one-day "Fun Pass" or $21 for a week's worth of rides, these tremendous cards are your key to the city's vast network of subways and buses.

Views—The best deal on a view of the New York skyline is a trip on the Staten Island Ferry. The trip is free and the ferry leaves every 30 minutes on week-days (less frequently at night and on weekends) from the end of Whitehall Street, in Battery Park. Another bargain view of the city can be had on the west side of Roosevelt Island. A trip on the tram (Second Avenue between 59th and 60th streets) costs $2 each way. And for nothing at all, you can go down to the elevated observation deck in Robert Wagner, Jr. Park, just north of Battery Park, or walk out on the Brooklyn Bridge for some stunning views of New York Harbor. A walk along the Hudson River on Battery Park Esplanade from Chambers Street down to Battery Park is a treat as well.

Walking—It doesn't cost a dime to walk around. Some of the more pleasant walking areas include Fifth Avenue in midtown, Soho (on Saturday afternoon and early evening), South Street Seaport and Central Park (particularly on weekends), Fifth and Madison avenues on the Upper East Side, the Lower East Side (on Sunday), the Lincoln Center area, and Greenwich Village (particularly on weekends). Take a look at the "Flea Markets" section of Chapter III; most cost nothing to browse and can be lots of fun!

New York has scores of 24-hour food shops where you can get a decent meal for relatively cheap. My favorite in midtown is **Longwood Gourmet**, on the corner of Lexington Avenue and 48th Street (212/980-3644). It has hot and cold salad bars, a deli, and sushi. Open daily 24 hours, 7 days a week, Longwood Gourmet is always clean and bright. Tables for eat-in are available.

For a Romantic Interlude

Whether you're falling in love for the first time or celebrating your golden anniversary, New York can be one of the most romantic places in the world. If you're in the mood for love or want to create a mood that's just right for romance, try the following:

- A getaway weekend swaddled in the first-class hotel luxury of the **Regent Wall Street** (55 Wall St).
- An intimate dinner amid the flowers in the French elegance of **La Grenouille** (3 E 52nd St).
- Drinks by the fireplace followed by dinner at **One If By Land, Two If By Sea** (17 Barrow St).
- A summertime dinner in the garden at **Barbetta** (321 W 46th St).
- Dinner in the discreet and classy **Le Périgord** (405 E 52nd St).
- Dinner at **Tavern on the Green's** sparkling Crystal Room (in Central Park off 67th St).
- Drinks in the **Campbell Apartment**, an elegant tucked-away spot in Grand Central Station (just east of Vanderbilt Avenue).

- A late-night visit to the **Empire State Building Observation Deck** (Fifth Ave between 33rd and 34th St).
- A night at the always-elegant **Plaza Hotel**, overlooking Central Park from its southeast corner at 59th Street and Fifth Avenue.
- Watching the sun rise from the **Brooklyn Bridge**, the **Battery Park Esplanade**, **Lighthouse Park** on Roosevelt Island, or the deck of the **Staten Island Ferry**.
- A visit to the restored **Winter Garden** (World Financial Center).
- A teatime interlude at **Payard Bistro** (1032 Lexington Ave).
- A picnic lunch looking out over the Hudson River from **The Cloisters**.
- A stroll through the splendid lobby of the **Waldorf-Astoria Hotel**.
- A weekend evening spent listening to classical music from the balcony of the **Metropolitan Museum of Art's Great Hall** or jazz at the **Guggenheim Museum**.
- A wintertime visit to the warmth and lush greenery of the **Ford Foundation Gardens** (320 E 43rd St).
- Cozying up in a love seat to watch a movie at the **Screening Room** (54 Varick St).
- A rowboat or gondola ride on **Central Park Lake** or a nightime sail around Manhattan.
- An evening carriage ride through **Central Park** in winter, after a fresh snow has fallen, or a springtime stroll on some of the park's less traveled paths.

For Parties and Special Events

If you're looking for the perfect spot to hold a wedding reception, bar mitzvah, or gala event for thousands, New York inevitably has the right place . . . and the people to put it together for you. The trick, of course, is finding them. The other trick is paying for them!

Note that you will not find museums, restaurants, or hotels in the following list. Many museum spaces, including the **Mount Vernon Hotel Museum and Gardens**, the new **American Folk Art Museum**, and the **Roosevelt Rotunda** at the **American Museum of Natural History** (complete with its dinosaur display), can be rented for parties and other events. Many restaurants have spaces for private parties, as do most hotels. Some of my favorite private party rooms in New York are at **Barbetta** (321 W 46th St), **Firebird** (365 W 46th St), the **Four Seasons** (99 E 52nd St), **Gramercy Tavern** (42 E 20th St), **Hard Rock Cafe** (221 W 57th St), the **Hudson River Club** (World Financial Center), **Le Cirque 2000** (New York Palace Hotel, 455 Madison Ave), **Le Périgord** (405 E 52nd St), **Lutèce** (249 E 50th St), **Montrachet** (239 Broadway), **One If By Land, Two If By Sea** (17 Barrow St), **Primavera** (1578 First Ave), **Serendipity 3** (225 E 60th St), **Tavern on the Green** (Central Park W at 67th St), **The Terrace** (400 W 119th St), **The Tonic** (108 W 18th St), and **Tribeca Grill** (375 Greenwich St). If you want to throw a party at your favorite museum, restaurant, hotel, or bar, by all means ask.

Some venues available for special events take care of all the catering, while others simply provide the space. Among the former are the **Art Club** (100 Reade St), the **Burden Mansion** (7 E 91st St), **New York Public Library** (Fifth Ave at 41st St), the **Puck Building** (Lafayette St at Houston St), and **Studio 450** (450 W 31st St). Among the latter are **Astra** (979 Third Ave),

The **Boathouse** in Central Park, **Glorious Foods** (522 B 74th St), **Museum Club at Bridgewaters** (South Street Seaport), **Pier 60** (at Chelsea Piers), and **Upper Crust 91** (91 Horatio St). Catering is optional at the **New York Botanical Garden** (in the Bronx) and the **Pratt Mansion** (1026 Fifth Ave). I mention these places simply to give you an idea of the breadth of spaces available rather than a complete list.

Before you forge ahead with planning a party in New York, be forewarned: it's going to cost a great deal of money. I'm talking *really* big bucks. You can save money by avoiding Saturday evening, holding your numbers down, and throwing your party in the off months of July and August or between January and early April. Some places and services will negotiate on price. But don't expect any great or even particularly good deals. And make your reservations at least a couple months (and as far as two years) in advance. The **Landmarks Conservancy** has a website with details about more than two dozen potential gathering spots and the cost of renting them. If you're interested, go to www.nylandmarks.org.

Talk about spectacular! The **Regent Wall Street Ballroom** (55 Wall St, 212/699-5695) is one of the most beautiful rooms in New York. Whether you are planning an event or just like to look at something that will take your breath away, you'll be most impressed. The history of Wall Street's only luxury hotel goes back to an 1842 building, now carefully crafted into a superb place to stay. The historic 12,000-square-foot ballroom, with a majestic balcony, boasts a 70-foot ceiling featuring a gold-leaf dome surrounded by Wedgewood panels. Wow! What a place for a wedding or reception.

Restrooms

Nothing can ruin a trek around New York more quickly than not being able to find a bathroom when one is needed. By law, public buildings are required to have public restrooms. They are not, however, required to be clean and safe.

Following is a list of bathrooms that meet at least a minimum standard of safety and cleanliness. You may need to ask for directions or a key at some of them, but all are free to the public. As a general rule, try hotel lobbies, department stores, schools, theaters, churches, libraries, and even hospitals. **Barnes & Noble** and **Starbucks** locations throughout the city are also good bets. Of course, if you have small children in tow, the manager of just about any store or restaurant will likely take pity.

Wherever you end up, be sure to follow a few safety tips. Leaving anything on the floor in a public restroom is a mistake, as purses, packages, and everything else have a bad habit of disappearing while you're occupied! The same is true of items left hanging on the back of a stall door. It's also a good idea to stay away from deserted bathrooms. No matter how badly you need to go, avoid bathrooms in parks (except the ones listed below) and most subway stations.

Below 14th Street

- **National Museum of the American Indian** (1 Bowling Green)
- **World Financial Center**
- **McDonald's** (160 Broadway)

- **Federal Hall National Memorial** (Wall St at Nassau St)
- **South Street Seaport** (Fulton at Water St)
- **City Hall** (Broadway at Chambers St)
- **Strand Bookstore** (Broadway at 12th St)

Gentlemen! If you are in the neighborhood when nature calls, by all means stop at the **21 Club** (21 W 52nd St) for a classy interlude! "The Reverend" (the attendant) will be there with a towel. Charles Baskerville murals will entertain you, and the company is usually quite interesting.

Between 14th and 42nd streets
- **Loehmann's** (Seventh Ave and 17th St)
- **ABC Carpet & Home** (Broadway at 19th St)
- **Supreme Court of the State of New York** (25th St bet Madison and Park Ave)
- **Macy's Herald Square** (Broadway at 34th St)
- **Science, Industry, and Business Library** (Madison Ave at 34th St)
- **Sheraton Park Avenue Hotel** (Park Ave and 37th St)
- **Grand Hyatt Hotel** (42nd St bet Park and Lexington Ave)
- **New York Public Library** (Fifth Ave bet 40th and 42nd St)
- **Bryant Park** (42nd St bet Fifth Ave and Ave of the Americas)

Midtown
- **United Nations** (First Ave bet 45th and 46th St)
- **Embassy Theater Tourist Information Center** (Seventh Ave bet 46th and 47th St)
- **Waldorf-Astoria Hotel** (Park Ave at 50th St)
- **Rockefeller Center** (bet Fifth Ave and Ave of the Americas from 49th to 51st St)
- **Olympic Tower** (bet Fifth and Madison Ave from 51st to 52nd St)
- **Park Avenue Plaza** (55 E 52nd St)
- **Trump Tower** (Fifth Ave bet 55th and 56th St)
- **Henri Bendel** (712 Fifth Ave)
- **Omni Park Central** (870 Seventh Ave)
- **Sony Wonder Technology Lab** (56th St at Madison Ave)

Upper East Side
- **McDonald's** (Third Ave bet 57th and 58th St)
- **Bloomingdale's** (1000 Third Ave)
- **Hunter College Student Center** (Lexington Ave at 68th St)
- **Asia Society** (725 Park Ave)
- **92nd Street Y** (1395 Lexington Ave)
- **Museum of the City of New York** (Fifth Ave bet 103rd and 104th St)
- **Charles A. Dana Discovery Center** (Central Park, Fifth Ave at 110th St)

Upper West Side
- **Avery Fisher Hall** (Lincoln Center, 64th St at Broadway)
- **New York Public Library for the Performing Arts** (Lincoln Center, 65th St at Broadway)
- **Barnes & Noble** (Broadway at 82nd St)

- **Cathedral Church of St. John the Divine** (Amsterdam Ave at 112th St)
- **Hispanic Society of America** (Audubon Terrace, off Broadway bet 155th and 156th St)

For More Information

I'd suggest doing a few things before packing your bags for New York. First call **NYC & Company** (800/692-8474), the city's marketing arm, to request a free copy of the official **NYC Guide**. (For a $5.95 shipping and handling fee, you can get the guide, a map, and a lot of brochures sent to you, but the guide is sufficient for most people.) Second, look through both the "Tours" and "Tickets" sections of Chapter III to find out which things you want to do that require advance reservations. Third, write the **New York City Transit Authority** (Attention: Customer Services, 370 John Jay Street, Brooklyn, NY 11201) for maps and brochures about the public transportation system so you can hit the ground (or subway) running.

Whether you're planning in advance or already sitting in your hotel room, get copies of *The New Yorker*, *New York* magazine, *Time Out New York*, and the *New York Times*. All but *Time Out New York* are generally available throughout the country (although the various out-of-town editions of the *New York Times* are abridged). The *New Yorker* (in the front), *New York* magazine (in the back), and *Time Out New York* (throughout) carry detailed information about current theater productions, movies, gallery and museum exhibitions, concerts, dance, and New York nightlife. Be forewarned that the free magazines in hotel rooms are paid for by advertisers and are not particularly useful (although maps and information about current museum exhibitions can be helpful).

If you don't have everything planned when you arrive, drop by one of several visitor information centers in Manhattan. **NYC & Company** runs a state-of-the-art tourist information center at 810 Seventh Avenue (at 53rd Street). Open from 8:30 to 6 on weekdays and from 9 to 5 on weekends, it has a multilingual staff and information about everything from current Broadway shows to ice-skating rinks in Manhattan. Another good tourist information center can be found just north of Times Square in the restored Embassy Theater (Seventh Ave between 46th and 47th streets). An information kiosk is staffed at the southern tip of City Hall Park in spring, summer, and fall. It's open on weekdays from 9 to 8 and on weekends from 10 to 8.

The front section of the Manhattan Yellow Pages is a good place to look for information and ideas. In addition to useful telephone numbers, it includes diagrams of major concert halls and sports stadiums. It also includes a short calendar of major annual events and maps of the subway and bus systems.

Finally, the World Wide Web has made accessing tourist information about New York as easy as clicking a mouse. Typing "New York City" into a search engine will generate several million hits, so here are some of the most useful sites:

- **www.ci.nyc.ny.us**: good links to hotels, outer borough tourism councils, transportation resources, even the New York Yellow Pages
- **www.cityguidemagazine.com**: updated information about current events and shows
- **www.GoCityKids.com**: Helpful ideas for parents about parks, restaurants, play spaces, stores, and babysitting services

- **www.mta.nyc.ny.us**: the official site of the Metropolitan Transportation Authority, with helpful information about the bus and subway systems
- **www.newyork.citysearch.com**: current schedules for plays, concerts, and movies, good descriptions of clubs, and a weekly calendar
- **www.newyorkmetro.com**: all the information from *New York* magazine
- **www.nyc.gov**: the city's official site, with links to attractions and events, as well as useful information for people who live in New York
- **www.nycvisit.com**: the NYC & Company site, where you can request publications, maps, and event calendars
- **www.nyctourist.com**: practical information, including a tip chart, maps, and directions to all sorts of places, plus links to hotel discounters and other potentially useful sites
- **www.nytoday.com**: produced by the *New York Times,* with access to its reviews, calendars, and classified ads

I have not included websites for museums and other tourist sites in New York because things change so frequently in this digital age. Still, most places have their own websites with information about hours, special events, and the like. An Internet search by name should turn up the home page for a given museum or tourist site without much difficulty.

Finally, if you're coming to New York in a wheelchair, you ought to know about a couple of additional resources. First, make sure to get a copy of "Access for All," an exceptional guide to the city's cultural institutions that describes in detail what sorts of facilities those institutions have for people in wheelchairs (as well as the blind and deaf). This invaluable guide is available from **Hospital Audiences** (220 West 42nd Street, New York, NY 10036) for $5 a copy. This organization also runs a hotline (888/424-4685) on weekdays. Second, the **Metropolitan Transit Authority** has a special phone number (718/596-8585) for information about routes accessible to people in wheelchairs and offers postage-paid fare envelopes to disabled riders. The **City of New York's Office for People with Disabilities** publishes an access guide. Call 212/788-2830 to request a copy or for general information. Finally, many Broadway theaters offer deeply discounted tickets for people in wheelchairs and their companions. Call individual theaters for more information.

A New York Philharmonic marketing tag line sums it up perfectly: "Expect the Extraordinary. This Is New York."

Index

(Note: Bolded page numbers signify listing's main entry.)

NOTES